PREFACE

This dictionary has been compiled as a manual to assist translators who are not familiar with legal terminology and others who have no time to consult more authoritative sources. It has no pretensions to completeness and many of the renderings are tentative or apply only in certain contexts. The English terms are those currently or formerly used in English law; French terms refer to the French legal system unless otherwise indicated – as Belgian ("Belg"), Canadian ("Can"), Luxembourg ("Lux") or Swiss ("Sw").

I should like to thank those colleagues who have come to discuss points of interest and in particular Martin Weston, who has not only supplied me with lists of suggested renderings, most of which I have adopted, but has also revised, copy-edited and proof-read the entire text for publication. I am also indebted to my son Steven, without whose encouragement and assistance the computer typescript would never have seen the light of day.

Frank Bridge

April 1994

F.H.S. Bridge

The Council of Europe
French–English
Legal Dictionary

Council of Europe Press, 1994

A companion dictionary has been published by the Council of Europe Press:

Lexique anglais-français (principalement juridique)

ISBN 92-871-2313-6

Publishing and Documentation Service
Council of Europe
F-67075 Strasbourg Cedex

ISBN 92-871-2496-5
© Council of Europe, 1994
Printed in Germany

A

ABANDON – desertion; waiver.

- **DÉCLARATION** judiciaire d'abandon – court declaration that a child has been abandoned.
- **DOMICILE** – abandon du domicile conjugal – desertion (of the matrimonial home).
- **ENFANT** – abandon d'enfant – abandonment (exposure) of a child.
- **ENFANT** – abandon d'enfants – deserting one's children.
- **FAMILLE** – abandon de famille – wilful neglect to maintain; wilful neglect or desertion.
- **FOYER** – abandon de foyer – desertion and failure to maintain.
- **MALICIEUX** – abandon malicieux – wilful desertion.

ABATTEMENT – downward adjustment; reduction; (tax) allowance.

AB INTESTAT – intestate.

AB IRATO – in anger.

ABONDEMENT – employer's contribution to a collective savings scheme.

ABORNEMENT – fixing the boundary.

ABROGATION – repeal (Act); revocation (regulations etc).

ABROGER – repeal (Act); revoke (regulations etc); cancel; abolish.

ABSENCE – situation of a person who is missing.

- **FAUTE** – absence de faute – absence of fault; absence of intention or negligence.

ABSENT – missing.

ABSOLU – (of a right) unqualified; unconditional; applying to everyone (and not only to certain persons) as opposed to **relatif**.

- **AUTORITÉ** absolue de la chose jugée – fact that a judgment is binding on the whole world (erga omnes), ie in rem.
- **MANIÈRE** – d'une manière absolue – in an unqualified manner; unconditionally.

ABSOLUTION – conviction without punishment; discharge (after conviction).

ABSOLUTOIRE

- **CIRCONSTANCES** absolutoires – circumstances exempting from punishment (in spite of a finding of guilt), eg superior orders or turning state's evidence.
- **EXCUSE** absolutoire – statutory ground for exemption from punishment.

ABSTENTION – judge's withdrawal from a case owing to the existence of grounds on which he could be challenged or for conscientious reasons.

- **DÉLICTUEUX** – abstention délictueuse – offence or tort of failing to comply with a legal duty to act to prevent an offence or damage to others; breach of duty; (of treason) misprision.

ABSTRACTO – see IN ABSTRACTO.

ABSTRAIT – notional; objective; effective without the requirement of an underlying "**cause**" or consideration.

- **GARANTIE** abstraite – security without possession.
- **OPINION** abstraite – the general view; the opinion of the reasonable man.
- **QUOTE-PART** abstraite – notional share.
- **TITRE** – un titre nouveau abstrait, c'est-à-dire indépendant de son titre d'acquisition – a new abstract title independent of the legal ground on which it was acquired.

ABUS

- **AUTORITÉ** – abus d'autorité – abuse (misuse) of official authority to induce a person to enter into a legal transaction.
- **BIEN SOCIAL** – abus des biens sociaux – misuse of a company's property or credit for personal advantage.
- **BLANC-SEING** – abus de blanc-seing – fraudulent misuse of a document signed in blank.
- **CONFIANCE** – abus de confiance – misappropriation; embezzlement (which can only be committed by a clerk or servant); fraudulent conversion; fraudulent breach of trust.
- **DROIT** – abus de droit – abuse of right.

- **JOUISSANCE** – abus de jouissance – excessive exploitation of a usufruct; waste; misuse.
- **POUVOIR** – abus de pouvoir – abuse (misuse) of (official) authority; acting in excess of one's authority or discretion.
- **PUISSANCE** – abus de puissance – misuse of economic power.

ABUSIF – unfair; unreasonable; wrongful; unjustified; improper; abusive.
- **CLAUSES** abusives – unfair clauses (in contracts).
- **DÉTENTION** abusive – wrongful detention.
- **LICENCIEMENT abusif** – unjustified dismissal.
- **RUPTURE** abusive – unjustified termination of a contract of employment.

ABUSIVEMENT – unreasonably.
- **ATTEINTE** – qui porte abusivement atteinte à l'intérêt qu'a une autre personne – which unreasonably interferes with another person's interest.

ACADÉMIE – educational district comprising several départements.

ACCÉLÉRER
- **PROCÉDURE** – accélérer la procédure – expedite the proceedings.

ACCEPTATION – acceptance; consent (by a party to the other party's discontinuing the proceedings).
- **RISQUE** – (théorie de l')acceptation des risques – volenti non fit injuria.

ACCESSION
- **DROIT** d'accession – right of the owner of property to all it produces and everything which becomes united to it, ie (1) all produce (periodical or other), (2) in the case of ownership of the surface, all that lies above or below it, (3) everything that becomes incorporated in it, (4) water springing from or flowing over the soil; right of accession or accretion.

ACCESSOIRE (adj) – consequential.
- **PEINE** – peine accessoire – ancillary (accessory) penalty (measure).
- **DE** – accessoire de – appurtenant to.
- **TITRE** – à titre accessoire – incidentally.

ACCESSOIRE (noun) – appurtenance; (in plural) ancillary matters.

ACCESSOIREMENT – alternately.

ACCIDENT
- **TRAVAIL** – accident du travail – industrial accident (injury).
- **TRAJET** – accident de trajet – accident occurring between work and home (or certain other specified destinations).

ACCIDENTEL
- **DÉLINQUANT** accidentel – casual offender.
- **DÉLIT** accidentel – casual offence.

ACCIPIENS – person who receives the performance of an obligation.

ACCISE – excise.

ACCLAMATION – acclamation.

ACCOMPLISSEMENT – compliance (with a formality).
- **CONDITION** – accomplissement d'une condition – satisfaction (fulfilment, occurrence) of a condition.

ACCORD – agreement; arrangement.
- **COLLECTIF** – accord collectif du travail – collective agreement.
- **COMMUN** – d'un commun accord – by consent.
- **COMPLÉMENTAIRE** – accord complémentaire – supplementary agreement.
- **FUSION** – accord de fusion – merger agreement.
- **GARANTIE** – accord de garantie – guarantee agreement.
- **ORDONNANCE** rendue sur la base d'un accord – consent order.
- **SIÈGE** – accord de siège – headquarters agreement.
- **SIMPLIFIÉ** – accord en forme simplifiée – agreement not requiring ratification or approval; executive agreement.
- **VOLONTÉ** – accord de volonté – being in agreement; ad idem.

ACCORDER – grant.
- **S'accorder avec** – be in conformity with.

ACCOSTAGE
- **VOITURE** – accostage en voiture – soliciting from a motor vehicle; kerb crawling.

ACCRÉDITIF – letter of credit.

ACCROISSEMENT

- **CLAUSE d'accroissement** – clause under which the surviving co-owner(s) etc succeed(s) to the interest(s) of the other(s) (ius accrescendi).

ACCUEILLIR – allow; grant (an application, objection, action, claim, appeal, petition); accept.

- **INJONCTION – accueillir la demande d'injonction** – grant an injunction.
- **MOYEN – les moyens ne peuvent être accueillis** – these arguments cannot be accepted.
- **RECOURS – accueillir un recours** – allow an appeal.

ACCUSATEUR – prosecutor.

ACCUSATION – accusation; charge; the prosecution (**c'est à l'accusation qu'il appartient de** – it is for the prosecution to).

- **CHAMBRE d'accusation** – Indictments Chamber.
- **PÉNAL – accusation en matière pénale** – criminal charge.

ACCUSATOIRE – adversarial; accusatorial.

ACCUSÉ – accused (in Assize Court).

- **RÉCEPTION – accusé de réception** – acknowledgement of receipt; advice of delivery; delivery note.

ACHALANDAGE – goodwill depending on the situation of the premises; "cat" goodwill.

ACOMPTE – (partial) advance; payment on account.

- **LOYER – acompte sur loyer** – advance payment of rent.

A CONTRARIO – arguing from the converse; by converse implication; conversely; principle that a rule of law shall not be extended to cover similar situations; principle of non-extensive interpretation; expressio unius est exclusio alterius (opposite of extension by analogy); restrictive interpretation.

ACQUÉREUR – purchaser.

ACQUÉRIR.

- **JOUR – être acquis jour par jour** – accrue from day to day; be apportionable from day to day.
- **PRESCRIPTION – la prescription est acquise** – limitation becomes effective; the claim, offence, etc is statute-barred.

ACQUÊTS

- **COMMUNAUTÉ d'acquêts (réduite (limitée) aux acquêts)** – community of after-acquired property.
- **PARTICIPATION aux acquêts** – sharing of after-acquired property.
- **SOCIÉTÉ d'acquêts** – community of after-acquired property.

Note. The above three entries refer to the system of marital property under which each spouse keeps his own property and at the end of the marriage each takes half the other's after-acquired property.

ACQUIESCEMENT

- **DEMANDE – acquiescement à la demande** – admission of the opponent's case and discontinuance of the action; acceptance of the plaintiff's claim.
- **JUGEMENT – acquiescement au jugement** – acceptance of the judgment and waiver of one's right of appeal.

ACQUIT – paid.

- **DOUANE – acquit de douane** – customs receipt; customs release.
- **LIBÉRATOIRE – acquit libératoire** – discharge.

ACQUIT-A-CAUTION – document issued by the revenue against security permitting the holder to move wines and spirits (or other property).

ACQUITTEMENT – acquittal (by the Assize Court).

ACQUITTER

- **OBLIGATION – s'acquitter d'une obligation** – discharge (perform) an obligation.

ACTE – legal instrument or transaction; act; decision; measure; step; process; document; certificate; entry; official copy.

- **ABSTRAIT – acte abstrait** – contract whose validity does not depend on the existence of consideration (**cause**).
- **ACCUSATION – acte d'accusation** – indictment.
- **ACQUISITION – acte d'acquisition** – conveyance.

- **ADMINISTRATIF** – **acte administratif** – administrative decision; exercise of an administrative discretion; administrative act; administrative measure.
- **ADMINISTRATION** – **acte d'administration** – act for the administration of property. In a narrower sense it does not include acts disposing of the property.
- **APPARENT** – **acte apparent** – ostensible (as opposed to the real) transaction.
- **APPEL** – **acte d'appel** – (former term for) notice of appeal.
  - •• **INCIDENT** – **acte d'appel incident** – notice of cross-appeal.
- **ARBITRAIRE** – **acte arbitraire** – arbitrary action.
- **AUTEUR** de l'acte – person making the document.
- **AUTHENTIQUE** – **acte authentique** – officially or notarially recorded instrument (cf an English deed).
- **AVOCAT** – **acte d'avocat à avocat** – document notified by one barrister to another through a court bailiff.
- **CAUSE DE MORT** – see MORT below.
- **COMMERCE** – **acte de commerce** – legal transaction governed by commercial law.
- **CONDITION** – **acte-condition** – legal transaction rendering a legal rule or rules applicable to an individual.
- **CONSENSUEL** – **acte consensuel** – legal transaction requiring no particular formalities.
- **CONSERVATOIRE** – **acte conservatoire** – legal step or transaction for the purpose of protecting a right.
- **CONSTITUTIF** – **acte constitutif** – instrument or legal transaction creating or altering rights.
  - •• **GAGE** – **acte constitutif de gage** – contract of pledge.
  - •• **HYPOTHÈQUE** – **acte constitutif d'hypothèque** – mortgage (referring to the instrument).
  - •• **INFRACTION** – **acte constitutif de l'infraction** – actus reus.
- **DÉCÈS** – **acte de décès** – death certificate; record of death.
- **DÉCLARATIF** – **acte déclaratif** – declaratory instrument.
- **DISPOSITION** – **acte de disposition** – instrument or legal transaction disposing of rights or property; disposal; conveyance; deed of gift.

- **DONNER** acte de – (officially, formally) confirm; take formal note of; note a declaration on the record.
- **ÉTAT CIVIL** – **acte de l'état civil** – civil-status record (entry) or certificate.
- **ÉTATIQUE** – **acte étatique** – official document; state paper.
- **EXÉCUTION** d'un acte – execution of an instrument.
- **EXÉCUTION** – **acte d'exécution** – execution (enforcement) measure; measure of execution.
- **EXTRAJUDICIAIRE** – **acte extrajudiciaire** – extrajudicial process or formality (eg formal demand for payment, protest).
- **FACULTÉ** – **acte de pure faculté** – act tolerated on his premises by a property owner which cannot be relied on for the purposes of prescription.
- **FAUTIF** – **acte fautif** – offending act.
- **FICTIF** – **acte fictif** – simulated transaction.
- **FRANCISATION** – **acte de francisation** – French ship's registration certificate.
- **FRUSTRATOIRE** – **acte frustratoire** – invalid or defective process, document, formality or step in the proceedings.
- **GÉNÉRAL** – **acte général** – decision, act, measure of general application.
- **GOUVERNEMENT** – **acte de gouvernement** – certain acts falling within the government's prerogative which cannot be questioned by legal proceedings; prerogative act; exercise of the government's prerogative; act of state.
- **HYPOTHÈQUE** – **acte d'hypothèque** – mortgage deed.
- **ILLICITE**
  - •• **CIVIL** – **acte illicite civil** – civil tort.
- **INDIVIDUEL** – **acte individuel** – administrative decision concerning a specific individual or individuals.
- **INSTRUCTION** – **acte d'instruction** – measure of investigation (investigative measure) taken or ordered by the investigating judge; procedural step in preparation for trial.
- **INSTRUMENTAIRE** – **acte instrumentaire** – document established to evidence a legal situation.
- **INTRODUCTIF** – **acte introductif d'instance** – writ; originating procedure.
- **JUDICIAIRE** – **acte judiciaire** – court process (writ, witness summons, drawing and serving pleadings, etc).

- **JURIDICTIONNEL** – acte juridictionnel – decision by which a court or other competent authority decides on the legality of an act or legal transaction.
- **JURIDIQUE** – acte juridique – legal transaction (expression of will intended to produce legal effect).
- **LÉGISLATIF** – acte législatif – legislative act.
- **MATÉRIEL** – acte matériel – physical act.
- **MINUTE** – (acte en) minute – the original instrument kept by the solicitor (**notaire**) in his archives. (The execution copy of a directly enforceable instrument is known as the **grosse** and other copies are called **expéditions**.)
- **MIXTE** – acte mixte – transaction which is commercial for one of the parties and civil for the other.
- **MORT** – acte à cause de mort – instrument not taking effect until death.
- **NAISSANCE** – acte de naissance – birth certificate; record of birth.
- **NOTAIRE** – acte devant notaire – see NOTARIÉ below.
- **NOTARIÉ** – acte notarié – officially (ie notarially) recorded instrument; notarial act; document drawn by a solicitor. (Cf an English deed.)
- **NOTORIÉTÉ** – acte de notoriété – officially recorded document containing statements by a number of persons as to matters of common knowledge.
- **OPPOSITION** – acte d'opposition – application to set aside.
- **PALAIS** – acte du Palais – in-court document notified by one barrister to another through the court bailiff; informal communication between lawyers.
- **POURSUITE** – acte de poursuite – step in criminal proceedings.
- **POURVOI** – acte de pourvoi – notice of appeal; grounds of appeal.
- **PRENDRE** acte de – take formal note of; take official notice of.
- **PRÉPARATOIRE** – acte préparatoire – (non-punishable) act in preparation of an offence.
- **PRINCE** – acte du prince – exercise of the (royal) prerogative; prerogative act; act of state.
- **PROCÉDURE** – acte de procédure – step in judicial proceedings (writ, pleading, application, etc); procedural formality; process; procedural document; procedural step; procedural measure.
  - **NOTIFICATION** des actes de procédure – service of process.
  - **SIGNIFICATION** des actes de procédure – service of judicial process (by a bailiff).
- **PROCURATION** – acte de procuration – power of attorney; authority.
- **PUISSANCE PUBLIQUE** – acte de puissance publique – act of public authority; act of state.
- **PURE FACULTÉ** – see FACULTÉ above.
- **RECOGNITIF** – acte recognitif – instrument recognising the existence of a situation, right or obligation created or evidenced by an earlier instrument.
- **RÉGLEMENTAIRE** – acte réglementaire – regulation(s).
- **SEING PRIVÉ** – acte sous seing privé – private document, ie one which has not been officially recorded; signed writing.
- **SIGNIFICATION** – acte de signification – record of service.
- **SOCIÉTÉ** – acte de société – articles of partnership; memorandum and articles of association of a company.
- **SOLENNEL** – acte solennel – instrument in solemn form.
- **SOUVERAINETÉ** – acte de souveraineté – sovereign act; act of state.
- **SUSCRIPTION** – acte de suscription – solicitor's endorsement on the sealed envelope of a secret will.
- **TOLÉRANCE** – acte de (simple) tolérance – act done with the express or tacit permission of the landowner which may be terminated at will.
- **TRANSLATIF** – acte translatif – legal transaction transferring rights.
- **TRANSMISSION** des actes de procédure – notification of process.
- **TYPE** – acte type – standard form of document imposed by a superior authority.
- **UNILATÉRAL** – acte unilatéral – unilateral transaction (undertaking).
- **VENTE** – acte de vente – contract of sale; conveyance; registered transfer. (NB in French law the contract can actually transfer ownership, in which case it is a contract and conveyance (transfer) in one instrument.)
- **VIOLENCE** – acte de violence – violent offence.

ACTE-CONDITION – legal transaction rendering a legal rule or rules applicable to an individual.

ACTIF – assets; positive balance.

- **CIRCULANT** – **actif circulant** – current assets.
- **ÉLÉMENT actif** – asset.
- **NET**
  - **UTILISÉ** – **actif net utilisé** – (balance sheet) net assets employed.
- **SUJET actif (d'un droit, d'une obligation)** – person entitled to the benefit of a right or obligation (obligee, promisee, creditor, victim of a tort).

ACTION – share; action; right (cause) of action.

- **ANNULATION** – **action en annulation** – action to set aside.
- **APPORT** – **action d'apport** – share issued in return for a contribution in kind.
- **ASSOCIATIONNEL** – **action associationnelle** – action brought by an interested association.
- **CIVIL** – **action civile** – civil action; claim for damages in civil proceedings.
- **COLLECTIF** – **action collective** – group (representative, class) action.
- **CONFESSOIRE** – **action confessoire** – action in rem to be put into possession of a usufruct or establish one's title to an easement, profit, etc as a right in rem.
- **CONTESTATION** – **action en contestation d'état** – action to disprove one's descent from one's ostensible parents; action to disprove a person's apparent status, descent or nationality.
- **DÉCLARATION**
  - **JUGEMENT COMMUN** – **action en déclaration de jugement commun** – third-party notice.
  - **SIMULATION** – **action en déclaration de simulation** – action to set aside a simulated transaction.
- **DÉCLARATOIRE** – **action déclaratoire** – action to obtain a declaration.
- **DIMINUTION** – **action en diminution** – action by the purchaser for a reduction in the price of goods.
- **DIRECT** – **action directe** – action by a creditor directly against a third party who has a contractual obligation to his debtor.
- **DOMMAGES-INTÉRÊTS** – **action en dommages-intérêts** – action for (in) damages.

- **ESTIMATOIRE** – **action estimatoire** – action for a reduction of price on account of defects.
- **ÉTAT** – **action d'état** – action to establish, contest or change one's personal status (descent, marriage, etc); status action.
- **ÉVACUATION** – **action en évacuation** – action for possession.
- **EXHIBENDUM** – **action ad exhibendum** – application for the production of a document.
- **EXPULSION** – **action en expulsion** – action for possession.
- **FIXATION** – **action en fixation** – action for a declaration (declaratory judgment).
- **GARANTIE** – **action en garantie** – action to enforce a guarantee or warranty; share certificate deposited as a security.
- **IMMOBILIER** – **action immobilière** – action to recover land; action to establish a right in rem or in personam over land.
- **INDEMNITÉ** – **action en indemnité** – action for damages.
- **IN REM VERSO** – **action de in rem verso** – action based on unjust enrichment.
- **INTERROGATOIRE** – **action interrogatoire** – action to force a person who has the right to choose between several alternatives to do so.
- **JACTANCE** – **action de jactance** – action to force someone who publicly claims a right to prove his title or remain silent.
- **JOUISSANCE** – **action de jouissance** – share whose capital has been repaid (on drawing of lots) but which is still entitled to dividends etc.
- **JUGEMENT** – see DÉCLARATION above.
- **JUSTICE** – **action en justice** – action; legal proceedings.
- **MIXTE** – **action mixte** – action to enforce a right in personam and a right in rem in the same proceedings.
- **MOBILIER** – **action mobilière** – action to recover movable property.
- **NAISSANCE** – **donne naissance à l'action en garantie dans la personne de l'acheteur** – gives the purchaser a right (cause) of action under the warranty.
- **NÉGATOIRE** – **action négatoire** – action to establish the non-existence of an easement, profit, servitude, etc.
- **NOMINATIF** – **action nominative** – registered share.

•• **LIÉ** – **action nominative liée** – registered share which can only be transferred with the company's consent.

• **NULLITÉ** – **action en nullité** – action to set aside (declare void).

• **OBLIQUE** – **action oblique** – action brought by a creditor in the name of his debtor.

• **PATERNITÉ** – **action en recherche de paternité** – affiliation proceedings; action to establish paternity.

• **PAULIEN** – **action paulienne** – action by which a creditor can have declared void certain transactions by a debtor with third parties prejudicial to his interests.

• **PERSONNE** – **action attachée (exclusivement) à la personne** – strictly (purely) personal action; non-pecuniary action.

• **PERSONNEL** – **action personnelle** – action to enforce a right in personam.

•• **DÉLIVRANCE** – **action personnelle en délivrance** – action in personam to be put in possession of a usufruct (life tenancy).

• **PÉTITION** – **(action en) pétition d'hérédité** – action to obtain possession of an estate from a person claiming to be the heir; action to claim (a share in) an estate.

• **PÉTITOIRE** – **action pétitoire** – action to establish ownership or another right in rem.

• **POPULAIRE** – **action populaire** – action which may be brought by any member of the public, whether or not he is in any way concerned with the case; actio popularis; sometimes used in the sense of an action by one of a class of persons affected on behalf of the others; group (representative, class) action.

• **PORTEUR** – **action au porteur** – bearer share; share warrant; bearer stock.

• **POSITIF** – **action positive** – (human rights) affirmative action.

• **POSSESSOIRE** – **action possessoire** – action to protect or recover possession; possessory action. There are three types: **complainte** – trespass, ie when possession is disturbed by some factual or legal action; **dénonciation de nouvel œuvre**, when works are commenced completion of which would interfere with possession; and **réintégrande**, where a person has been deprived of possession.

• **PRIORITÉ** – **action de priorité** – preference share.

• **PROVOCATOIRE** – **action provocatoire** – action to force a person to to establish the validity of a claim he asserts against the plaintiff.

• **PUBLIC** – **action publique** – (public) prosecution; criminal proceedings.

• **QUERELLEUR** – **action querelleuse** – vexatious proceedings.

• **RÉCLAMATION** – **(action en) réclamation d'état** – action to establish descent from a parent (legitimacy).

• **RECONVENTIONNEL** – **action reconventionnelle** – counterclaim; cross-action; cross-petition.

• **RÉCURSOIRE** – **action récursoire** – third-party proceedings; third-party notice.

•• **ÉTAT** – **action récursoire de l'État contre l'agent fautif** – state's action for indemnity against a public officer who has committed a fault for which the state is liable.

• **RÉDHIBITOIRE** – **action rédhibitoire** – action for rescission (against the seller of defective goods or animals).

• **RÉDUCTION** – **action en réduction** – action to reduce the price (of defective goods).

• **RÉEL** – **action réelle** – action to enforce a right in rem or a right of possession.

• **RÉPÉTITION** – **action en répétition de l'indu** – action for restitution of money paid without legal cause (for money had and received).

• **RESCISION** – **action en rescision (pour lésion)** – action for rescission for inadequate consideration.

• **RÉSILIATION** – **action en résiliation** – action to terminate a continuing contract (ex nunc).

• **RÉSOLUTION** – **action en résolution** – action to set aside a contract; action for rescission.

• **RESPONSABILITÉ** – **action en responsabilité** – action for damages.

• **RESTITUTION** – **action en restitution** – action for recovery of possession.

• **RETRANCHEMENT** – **action en retranchement** – action by the children of a former marriage to recover property from the marital community or a spouse.

• **REVENDICATION** – **action en revendication** – action to establish title (ownership); action in detinue.

•• **HÉRÉDITÉ** – **action en revendication d'hérédité** – action to obtain possession of an estate from a person not claiming as heir or under a will.

- **RÉVOCATION** – **action en révocation** – action to set aside for error, deceit, duress, etc.
  - •• **DONATION** – **action en révocation de (d'une) donation** – action to revoke a gift.
- **RÉVOCATOIRE** – **action révocatoire (Sw)** – action to set aside a debtor's suspected transactions.
- **SIMULATION** – see DÉCLARATION above.
- **SOCIAL** – **action sociale** – action brought by a company, (professional or other) association, trade union, etc.
- **SUBSIDE** – **action à fin de subsides** – action for maintenance (support payments) by an illegitimate child whose descent has not been established.

ACTIONNER
- **JUSTICE** – **actionner (en justice)** – sue; bring an action or (legal) proceedings against.

ACTIVITÉ
- **COMMISSION** – **l'activité de la Commission (des Droits de l'Homme)** – the Commission's practice.

ACTUALISER – adjust for inflation; discount.

ADHÉRER – accede.

ADHÉSION – accession.
- **CONTRAT** d'adhésion – standard-form contract (imposed by the stronger party).
- **TRAITÉ** d'adhésion – friendly agreement on the transfer of (or amount of compensation for) property with respect to which expropriation proceedings have commenced.

ADJOINDRE
- **CONSEIL** – **adjoindre un conseil juridique à** – provide with legal assistance.

ADJUDICATAIRE – highest bidder.

ADJUDICATION
- **ADMINISTRATIF** – **adjudication administrative** – contract by a government department for supplies, public works, etc; public-works contract.
- **METTRE en adjudication** – advertise (call) for (invite) tenders.

ADMETTRE – accept.

- **RECOURS** – **admettre un recours** – allow an appeal.

ADMINICULE – some evidence (or additional evidence) which though incomplete is of sufficient weight to allow witnesses to be heard in a civil case.

ADMINISTRATEUR – company director; administrative officer; administrator; assistant principal; manager (of an institution).
- **DÉLÉGUÉ** – **administrateur délégué** – managing director; acting chairman of the board of directors.
- **JUDICIAIRE** – **administrateur judiciaire** – administrator appointed by the court.
- **LÉGAL** – **administrateur légal** – statutory representative of a minor.

ADMINISTRATIF
- **ACTE administratif** – administrative decision; exercise of an administrative discretion; administrative act; administrative measure.

ADMINISTRATION – in French the term indicates not the government but those carrying out the government's policy: the public service, ie the civil service, local government officers and employees of public corporations (as required by the context); (government) department; administration; authority.
- **PREUVE** – **administration d'une (de la) preuve (des preuves)** – adducing evidence; bringing evidence to establish; (of procedure in court) taking evidence.

ADMINISTRER
- **PREUVE** – **administrer une (la) preuve (des preuves)** – adduce evidence; bring evidence to establish; (of procedure in court) take evidence.

ADMISSIBLE
- **LÉGALEMENT admissible** – which the law allows.

ADMISSION
- **FORCÉ** – **admission forcée** – compulsory admission.

ADMONESTATION – reprimand; warning.

ADOPTER – pass; enact; adopt (a child).

ADOPTION – passing; enactment; adoption (of a child).
- **PLÉNIER** – **adoption plénière** – full adoption (which terminates all legal connection with the family of origin).

- **SIMPLE** – **adoption simple** – simple adoption (which does not terminate the connection with the family of origin).

ADOUCISSEMENT

- **PEINE** – **adoucissement de peine** – mitigation of penalty.

ADRESSER

- **DIRECTIVE** – **adresser des directives** – issue directives.

ADVERSAIRE – opposing party; other side.

ADVERSE

- **PARTIE adverse** – other side; opposing party. (It may be preferable to specify "plaintiff", "respondent", etc.)

AFFACTURAGE – factoring.

AFFAIRE – case.

- **ÉTAT** – **affaire en état** – case ready for hearing (trial).
- **JUSTICE** – **affaire entre les mains de la justice** – case sub judice.
- **MATRIMONIAL** – **affaire matrimoniale** – matrimonial cause.

AFFECTATION – reservation for a special purpose; utilisation; type of use; use class; classification as; inclusion in the category of; being set aside (earmarked) for.

- **LOGEMENT** – **affectation de logement** – allocation of accommodation.
- **PATRIMOINE d'affectation** – collection of assets and liabilities allocated or reserved for a special purpose; special-purpose fund.
- **RÉSULTAT** – **affectation du résultat** – allocation of the (credit) balance.
- **SOUMIS à affectation spéciale** – set aside (earmarked) for a special purpose.
- **USAGE** – **affectation à usage public** – dedication (as a public right of way).

AFFECTER – earmark; set aside for.

- **CONDITION** – **affecté d'une condition** – subject to a condition.

AFFECTIO SOCIETATIS – intention to co-operate in a partnership and right to supervise its administration.

AFFÉRANT

- **A** – **afférant à** – appertaining to.

AFFERMER – lease (an agricultural holding).

AFFICHAGE

- **TRIBUNAL** – **affichage au tribunal** – posting on the court notice-board.

AFFIRMATION – solemn declaration.

AFFLICTIF – (of punishment) executed on the person, ie capital punishment or long-term or severe imprisonment; (more generally) harsh; punitive.

AFFRÉTEUR – charterer.

ÂGE

- **PÉNAL** – **âge pénal** – age at which a person becomes criminally liable.

AGENT – person committing an offence; offender.

- **AFFAIRE** – **agent d'affaires** – business agent.
- **CHANGE** – **agent de change** – stockbroker.
- **ÉTAT** – **agent d'État** – civil servant; state employee.
- **FORCE PUBLIQUE** – **agent de la force publique** – police officer; constable; member of the police force.
- **JUDICIAIRE** – **Agent judiciaire du Trésor** – Treasury Solicitor.
- **POLICE** – **agent de police** – police officer; constable; member of the police force.
- **PRINCIPAL** – **agent principal** – principal offender.
- **PROBATION** – **agent de probation** – probation officer.
- **PUBLIC** – **agent public** – public servant.

AGGRAVATION

- **PEINE** – **aggravation de peine** – aggravation of penalty.

AGIR

- **JUSTICE** – **agir en justice** – bring legal proceedings.
- **PRIX** – **agir en paiement de prix** – sue for the price.

AGISSEMENTS – unsatisfactory conduct; misconduct.

AGRÉATION – licence (eg to deal in firearms); acceptance.

AGRÉÉ – partially qualified legal practitioner permitted to appear before the commercial courts.

AGRÉMENT – consent to, approval of, a transaction by a third party (eg landlord's consent to a sublease).

- **CLAUSE** – **clause d'agrément** – approval clause (eg requiring a company's approval for the sale of its shares).

AGRESSION – attack; assault.
- **VERBAL** – **agression verbale** – (prisons) insult(ing the staff).

AIDE
- **ENFANCE** – **aide sociale à l'enfance** – child care.
- **JUDICIAIRE** – **aide judiciaire** – legal aid; legal advice and assistance.

AISANCE
- **VOIRIE** – **aisances de voirie** – rights of owners of property abutting on a highway.

AJOURNEMENT – writ; summons; adjournment.
- **EXPLOIT d'ajournement** – writ or summons (served on the defendant).
- **PEINE** – **ajournement (du prononcé) de (la) peine** – deferment of sentence.

ALERTE
- **PROCÉDURE d'alerte** – procedure enabling an auditor or works council to call for explanations from the managers when the economic position of a business appears precarious.

ALERTER
- **PARQUET** – **alerter le parquet** – inform the public prosecutor's office.

ALIÉNATION – transfer; disposal; assignment.
- **GRÉ À GRÉ** – **aliénation de gré à gré** – sale to a willing purchaser (at arm's length); sale by private treaty (as opposed to an auction); sale on the open market.

ALIÉNER – transfer; dispose of; alienate; assign.

ALIGNEMENT – building line; fixing by the authorities of the boundary between public and private property.

ALIMENTAIRE
- **PENSION alimentaire** – maintenance; alimony (judicial separation only).
- **PROVISION alimentaire** – maintenance during divorce proceedings.

ALIMENTS – maintenance.
- **CRÉANCE d'aliments contre la succession** – right to claim maintenance from the estate.

ALLÉGATION – contention; allegation.

ALLÉGUER – claim; allege.

ALLER
- **JUSTICE** – **aller en justice** – bring legal proceedings.

ALLIANCE – relationship by marriage.

ALLOCATION – benefit; allowance.
- **CHÔMAGE** – **allocation de chômage** – unemployment benefit.
- **DÉCÈS** – **allocation de (au) décès** – death grant.
- **DÉPENS** – **allocation des dépens** – order for costs.
- **FAMILIAL** – **allocations familiales** – family allowances.
- **FIN DE DROITS** – **allocation de fin de droits** – fixed-rate allowance granted when normal unemployment allowance ceases to be payable.
- **FRAIS** – **allocation pour frais funéraires** – death grant; death allowance.
- **GLOBAL** – **allocations globales** – block grants; lump-sum allowances.
- **LOGEMENT** – **allocation de logement** – rent allowance (mortgage interest allowance).
- **LOYER** – **allocation de loyer** – rent allowance.

ALLONGE – allonge; rider.

ALLOUER
- **DÉPENS** – **allouer des dépens** – award costs.
- **INDEMNITÉ** – **allouer une indemnité** – award damages; grant (award) compensation.

ALLUVION – land gradually deposited by a river along its banks, or by the sea along the shore; alluvion.

ALTÉRATION
- **ÉCRITURE** – **altération d'écritures** – forgery.
- **FACULTÉ MENTALE** – **altération des facultés mentales** – mental disorder.
  - •• **PERMANENT** – **altération permanente des facultés mentales** – permanent insanity.
- **LIEN CONJUGAL** – **altération profonde du lien conjugal** – irretrievable breakdown of the marriage.
- **PREUVE** – **altération des preuves** – tampering with evidence.

ALTÉRER – have an adverse effect on; falsify.

A MAXIMA
- **APPEL a maxima** – appeal by the prosecution to reduce a sentence.

AMBULANT
- **PROFESSION ambulante** – itinerant trade or occupation.

AMÉNAGEMENT – fixtures; installation; system of operation; application (des divergences apparaissent lorsqu'il s'agit de son aménagement); planning; arrangement.
- **COMMUNAL – plan d'aménagement communal** – local development plan.
- **CONCERTÉ – zone d'aménagement concerté** – special planning area.
- **DIFFÉRÉ – zone d'aménagement différé** – deferred-development area.
- **FONCIER – société d'aménagement foncier et d'établissement rural** – agrarian planning association.
- **SPÉCIAL – aménagement spécial** – special planning provision.
- **TERRITOIRE – aménagement du territoire** – physical planning; spatial planning; town and country planning; regional planning; regional development.

AMENDE
- **APPEL – amende de fol appel** – fine for lodging a frivolous appeal.
- **COMPOSITION – amende de composition** – (former term for) summary order imposing a fine which the defendant may have set aside if he wishes to have a full trial; sentence order.
- **FORFAITAIRE – amende forfaitaire** – fixed fine.
- **FRACTIONNÉ – amende fractionnée** – fine payable by instalments.
- **FOU – amende de fol appel** – fine for lodging a frivolous appeal.
- **JOUR-amende** – day-fine.
- **ORDRE – amende d'ordre (Sw)** – police or administrative fine.
- **POLICE – amende de simple police** – fine for a summary (petty) offence.
- **TRANSACTIONNEL – amende transactionnelle** – police fine; (Belg) payment (fine) in settlement of a regulatory offence (fine by way of settlement).

AMENDEMENT
- **DÉPOSER un amendement** – table an amendment.
- **NOTE d'amendement** – assessment of improvement (on a prisoner's personal file).
- **PROJET d'amendement** – draft amendment.
- **PROPOSER un amendement** – propose an amendment; (orally also) move an amendment.
- **PROPOSITION d'amendement** – motion to amend; proposed amendment.
- **SOUTENIR un amendement** – speak to an amendment; move an amendment.

AMEUBLISSEMENT – transfer to the community of land which under the applicable system of marital property is the separate property of one of the spouses.

AMIABLE
- **À l'amiable – n'accepte pas à l'amiable de voir supprimer la servitude de passage** – does not voluntarily accept the extinguishment of the right of way.
- **ACCORD amiable** – friendly settlement.
- **COMPOSITEUR – comme amiable compositeur** – as a mediator; ex aequo et bono; on equitable principles.
- **RÈGLEMENT amiable** – friendly settlement.
- **TRAITÉ amiable** – friendly agreement on the transfer of (or amount of compensation for) property with respect to which expropriation proceedings have commenced.
- **TRANSACTION amiable** – friendly settlement.
- **VENTE amiable** – sale by private treaty.

A MINIMA
- **APPEL a minima** – appeal by the prosecution to increase a sentence.

AMODIATION – lease in which the rent is calculated as a proportion of the produce of the land.

AMORTISSABLE – repayable; redeemable.

AMORTISSEMENT – depreciation; writing off; redemption; repayment in instalments.

AMPLIATIF
- **MÉMOIRE ampliatif** – further pleadings.

AMPLIATION – certified copy; office copy.

ANALYTIQUE
- IMPÔTS analytiques – specific taxes.

ANATOCISME – compound interest.

ANCIEN – see DROIT.

ANGARIE – requisition in its territorial waters of a neutral ship by a belligerent; angary.

ANNEXION – annexation.

ANNOTATION
- QUOTIDIEN – annotations quotidiennes (sur un registre) – daily records.

ANNUITÉ – annual payment comprising interest due and part repayment of capital; annual instalment.

ANNULABILITÉ – voidability.

ANNULABLE – voidable.

ANNULATION
- ACTION en annulation – action to set aside.
- FRAIS – annulation des frais – disallowance of costs.
- MARIAGE – annulation du mariage – granting a decree of nullity; annulment of (a) marriage.
- RECOURS en annulation – (civil procedure) application to set aside; (administrative procedure) (abbreviation of recours en annulation pour excès de pouvoir) – application to an administrative court to set aside an administrative decision on grounds such as lack of jurisdiction, error of procedure, misapplication of the law, misuse of a discretion or ultra vires (exceeding or misusing one's authority); application for judicial review.

ANNULER – set aside; declare void.

ANTÉCÉDENT
- JUDICIAIRE – antécédents judiciaires – criminal record; police record.

ANTÉRIORITÉ – prior right or state of affairs which renders void an industrial property right.

ANTICHRÈSE – mortgage in which the mortgagee takes possession, receiving the produce, rents and profits, which are set off against the interest and principal of the debt.

APAISER
- GRIEF – apaiser les griefs – satisfy the complaints.

APATRIDE – stateless person.

APÉRITEUR – member of a group of insurers who represents the group in dealings with the insured.

APORTIONNEMENT – advancement (settlement in advance of an adulterine child's inheritance rights).

A POSTERIORI – ex post facto; retrospective(ly); after the event; subsequent(ly).

APOSTILLE – marginal note; footnote.

APPARENCE
- GRIEF – apparence d'un grief justifié – prima facie case.
- THÉORIE de l'apparence – rule that in certain circumstances third-parties dealing in good faith with an apparent owner or agent are protected (cf holding out); theory protecting the position of a person acting in good faith in reliance on an apparently legal state of affairs.

APPARENT
- HÉRITIER apparent – ostensible heir.
- MANDAT apparent – allowing a person to hold himself out as one's agent.
- PROPRIÉTÉ apparente – ostensible ownership.

APPARTENIR
- JUGE – il appartiendra au juge d'ordonner des mesures provisoires – the court (judge) may order provisional or interim measures.

APPEL – appeal (to a superior court on fact and law).
- A MAXIMA – appel a maxima – appeal by the prosecution to reduce the sentence.
- A MINIMA – appel a minima – appeal by the prosecution to increase the sentence.
- CAUSE – audience d'appel des causes – hearing at which the presiding judge discusses the presentation of the case with counsel; hearing for directions.
- CHARGE – à charge d'appel – subject to appeal.
- CONCLUSIONS d'appel – notice and grounds of appeal.

- **CONCURRENCE** – appel à la concurrence – call for tenders.
- **CONTRIBUTION** – appel de contributions – call for contributions.
- **DÉCLARATION d'appel** – notice of appeal.
- **FAIRE appel** – appeal; lodge an appeal; give (enter) notice of appeal.
- **FONDS** – appel de fonds – call on not fully paid-up shares; call on shareholders etc.
- **FOU** – fol appel – frivolous or vexatious appeal.
  - •• **AMENDE de fol appel** – fine for lodging a frivolous appeal.
- **GARANTIE** – appel en garantie – proceedings against the guarantor which may take the form of giving third-party notice.
- **INCIDENT** – appel incident – cross-appeal.
- **INTERJETER appel** – appeal; lodge an appeal; give (enter) notice of appeal.
- **NOMINAL** – appel nominal – roll-call vote.
- **OFFRE** – appel d'offres – invitation to tender; advertisement (call) for tenders.
- **PROVOQUÉ** – appel provoqué – cross-appeal by a third party affected by the proceedings, eg a guarantor.
- **RETARDÉ** – appel retardé – postponed appeal (ie until after the decision in the main proceedings).
- **SANS appel** – not subject to appeal.

APPELANT – appellant.

APPELÉ – remainderman; person entitled in due course (eg on birth).
- **SUCCESSION** – appelé à la succession – entitled to inherit.

APPELER
- **CAUSE** – appeler en cause – join a party to the proceedings.
- **GARANTIE** – appeler en garantie – have recourse to (proceed against) the guarantor.
- **JUGEMENT** – appeler d'un jugement – appeal against a judgment.
- **PARTIE ADVERSE** – appeler la partie adverse – give the other side notice to appear.

APPELLATION
- **ORIGINE** – appellation d'origine – warranty (indication) of origin; name indicating origin.

APPLICABLE
- **À** – applicable à – applicable to; applying to; affecting.
- **DIRECTEMENT** – directement applicable – directly applicable; self-executing.

APPLICATION – application; implementation; enforcement.
- **ARTICLE** – en application de l'article 22 – pursuant to section (Article) 22.
- **CAS d'application** – case to which (a given provision) applies.
- **CHAMP d'application** – scope; ambit.
  - •• **MATÉRIEL** – champ d'application matérielle – (Sw) substantive scope; (social security) material (ie non-personal) scope.

APPLIQUER
- **LOIS appliquées** – relevant (applicable) legislation.
- **PEINE** – appliquer la peine – determine the sentence.
- **S'appliquer à** – relate to.

APPORT
- **ACTION d'apport** – share issued in return for a contribution in kind.
- **CAPITAL** – apport de capitaux – contribution of assets to a company or partnership.
- **COMMISSAIRE aux apports** – valuer of contributions in kind to the capital of a company.
- **DOTAL** – apport dotal – dowry; marriage settlement.
- **ESPÈCES** – apport en espèces – cash brought in; assets brought in in cash.
- **INDUSTRIE apport en industrie** – contribution in the form of (various) services.
- **SOCIÉTÉ** – apport en société – contribution to a partnership's assets.

APPRÉCIATION – discretion; assessment; consideration; finding; determination.
- **ACCUSATION** – appréciation de l'accusation – determination of the charge.
- **DISCRÉTIONNAIRE** – appréciation discrétionnaire – unfettered discretion.
- **ÉLÉMENTS d'appréciation** – evidence; factors to be taken into account.
- **ERREUR d'appréciation** – error (in assesing evidence or exercising a discretion).
- **LÉGALITÉ** – recours en appréciation de légalité – application to an administrative

court as a preliminary point to declare an administrative decision illegal.

- **LIBERTÉ d'appréciation du tribunal** – the court's discretion.
- **POUVOIR d'appréciation** – discretion; power (freely) to evaluate (assess) (evidence etc).
  - •• **SOUVERAIN – disposent d'un pouvoir souverain d'appréciation** – are completely unfettered in their assessment of evidence.
- **PREUVE – appréciation des preuves** – assessment of (the) evidence.
- **SOUVERAIN – appréciation souveraine de fait** – final (ie unappealable and discretionary) decision on the facts.
- **TRIBUNAL – appréciation du tribunal** – discretion of the court.

APPRÉCIER – judge; make a finding on; decide on; assess; determine.

- **SOUVERAINEMENT**
  - •• **JUGE DU FOND – apprécié souverainement par les juges du fond** – to be decided finally by the trial court; the trial court is free to form its assessment of; entirely within the competence of the trial court.
  - •• **MONTANT – apprécient souverainement le montant de** – have an unfettered discretion in assessing the amount of.

APPRÉHENDER – arrest.

- **ÊTRE appréhendé par le droit** – to be taken account of by the law.

APPRÉHENSION – taking physical possession.

APPROBATION – approval (of a treaty).

APPROPRIATION

- **OBJET – appropriation d'objet trouvé** – stealing by finding; conversion of property by a finder.

APPUYER

- **SUR – s'appuyer sur** – rely on.

APTITUDE

- **MARIAGE – aptitude au mariage** – capacity to marry.

APUREMENT – clearing; settlement.

AQUILIEN

- **RESPONSABILITÉ aquilienne** – liability in tort.

ARBITRAGE – arbitration; power to decide (decision of) policy differences within the government or administration.

- **CONVENTION d'arbitrage** – arbitration agreement. This covers both a **compromis**, ie an agreement to submit to arbitration when a dispute has already arisen, and a **clause compromissoire**, an agreement to submit future differences to arbitration.
- **COUR d'arbitrage** (Belg) – court deciding questions of administrative jurisdiction and legislative procedure; (Administrative) Jurisdiction and Procedure Court.

ARBITRAIRE – unreasonable.

- **INGÉRENCE arbitraire** – unjustified interference.
- **TRIBUNAL – l'arbitraire du tribunal** – arbitrary decisions by the court.

ARBITRE – arbitrator; mediator.

- **TIERS arbitre** – umpire.

ARGUER

- **DE – arguer de** – rely on.
  - •• **FAUX – arguer de faux** – allege that a document is forged; challenge the authenticity of a document.

ARGUMENT – submissions.

- **NOMBREUX – il existe de nombreux arguments** – there is a considerable case.
- **SOLIDE – argument solide** – substantial argument.
- **TIRER argument de** – rely on.

ARGUMENTATION – line of reasoning; submissions.

ARRACHÉ

- **VOL à l'arraché** – robbery; (informally) bagsnatching; snatch theft.

ARRANGEMENT – (technical or administrative) agreement; compromise.

- **FAMILLE – arrangement de famille** – transfer of land to a descendant in consideration of the latter's paying the transferor's debts.

ARRÉRAGE – instalment of an annuity or pension.

ARRÊT – judgment or decision of an appeal court or court of assize; (in plural) (Sw) short period of imprisonment for minor offences.

- **DÉFINITIF** – **arrêt définitif** – final judgment.
- **FORTERESSE** – **arrêts de forteresse** (mil) – detention in a fortress.
- **GRAND arrêt** – leading case.
- **MAISON d'arrêt** – remand prison; short-stay prison.
- **MANDAT d'arrêt** – arrest warrant; warrant to arrest and imprison a fugitive offender, suspect or accused.
- **OBLIGATOIRE** – **arrêt obligatoire** – binding judgment.
- **PILOTE** – **arrêt pilote** – leading case.
- **PRINCIPE** – **arrêt de principe** – leading case.
  - **RENDRE un arrêt de principe** – give an authoritative decision.
- **PRONONCÉ de l'arrêt** – delivery of the judgment.
- **RÉFÉRÉ** – **arrêt de référé** – judgment on an appeal from an order made on an urgent application.
- **RÈGLEMENT** – **arrêt de règlement** – legislative precedent formerly issued by a superior court.
- **SOI-MÊME** – **arrêts sur soi-même** (Sw) – garnishee order attaching a debt one owes to another as a security for a debt owed by him.

ARRÊTÉ – order; decree; regulation; decision; notice.

- **COMPTE** – **arrêté de compte** – acceptance of an account rendered.
- **CONFLIT** – **arrêté de conflit** – Prefect's order transferring a jurisdictional dispute (between the ordinary and the administrative courts) to the Jurisdiction Court (**Tribunal des conflits**); jurisdiction order.
- **EXPROPRIATION** – **arrêté d'expropriation** – expropriation order; compulsory-purchase order.
- **EXPULSION** – **arrêté d'expulsion** – expulsion warrant (order); deportation order.
- **EXTENSION** – **arrêté d'extension** – declaration that something is of general application.
- **MISE EN DEMEURE** – **arrêté de mise en demeure** – official order to put an end to a given state of affairs.

ARRHES – sum of money paid on the making of a contract to guarantee performance, as an advance or simply to mark the making of the contract; deposit; earnest (money).

ARRONDISSEMENT – (of a city) borough.

- **JUDICIAIRE** – **arrondissement judiciaire** – judicial district.

ARTICLE – (budget) subhead; (code, convention, treaty, decree, order) article; (Act or Law) section; (regulations) regulation; (rules) rule; (order, warrant, decree) paragraph; (Bill or contract) clause. The French, Belgian and Luxembourg Civil Codes are divided into **livres** (books), **titres** (parts), **chapitres** (chapters), **sections** (sections) and **articles** (articles). The Swiss Civil Code is divided into **livres** (books), **parties** (parts), **titres** (sections), **chapitres** (chapters) and **articles** (articles).

- **UNIQUE** – **article unique** – omit from translation.

ARTICULATION

- **FAIT** – **articulation des faits** – statement of the facts it is intended to prove.

ARTICULER – state (the facts one proposes to bring evidence to prove).

ARTIFICE

- **PROCÉDURE** – **artifice de procédure** – procedural device.

ARTISANAL

- **PROFESSION artisanale** – manual trade.

ARTISTE

- **EXÉCUTANT** – **artiste exécutant** – performing artist.

ASBL = association sans but lucratif.

ASCENDANT – ascendant.

ASPECT

- **PERTINENT** – **aspects pertinents de la situation** – relevant circumstances.

ASSAINIR – put on a sound basis; reorganise.

ASSAINISSEMENT – rehabilitation proceedings (alternative to bankruptcy).

- **FAILLITE** – **assainissement d'une faillite** – restabilising a bankruptcy.

ASSASSINAT – (premeditated) murder.

ASSEMBLÉE

- **CONTENTIEUX** – **assemblée du contentieux (du Conseil d'État)** – Combined Court (of the Conseil d'État).

- **CRÉANCIER** – **assemblée des créanciers** – creditors' meeting.
- **GÉNÉRAL** – **assemblée générale** – general meeting of a company etc; General Assembly (of the Court of Cassation).
  - •• **ORDINAIRE** – **assemblée générale ordinaire (du Conseil d'État)** – Ordinary General Assembly (of the Conseil d'État).
  - •• **PLÉNIER** – **assemblée générale plénière (du Conseil d'État)** – Full General Assembly (of the Conseil d'État).
- **PLÉNIER** – **assemblée plénière** – full (plenary) court (especially of the Court of Cassation).

ASSESSEUR – (non-presiding) judge.

ASSIETTE – (basis of) assessment; site; route.
- **IMPOSITION** – **assiette d'imposition** – basis of assessment.
- **PASSAGE** – **assiette du passage** – site of the right of way.

ASSIGNATION – writ (of summons); (divorce) petition; (originating) summons; notice of motion; notice to appear (eg to answer an appeal).
- **DOMICILE** – **assignation à domicile** – house arrest.
- **FAILLITE** – **assignation en déclaration de faillite** – presentation of a bankruptcy petition.
- **GARANTIE** – **assignation en garantie** – action to enforce a guarantee or warranty.
- **JOUR** – **assignation à jour fixe** – fixed-date proceedings.
- **JUSTICE** – **assignation en justice** – issuing a summons or writ against; bringing proceedings against.
- **RÉFÉRÉ** – **assignation en référé** – summons to attend urgent proceedings.
- **REPRISE** – **assignation en reprise d'instance** – notice (to the heirs) to continue the proceedings (on the death of a party).
- **RÉSIDENCE** – **assignation à résidence** – order requiring a person to reside in a particular place; compulsory residence order.

ASSIGNER – issue a summons or writ against; give notice of motion; summon to appear; sue.
- **JUSTICE** – **assigner en justice** – sue; issue a summons or writ against; bring proceedings against.
- **PERSONNE** – **assigner à personne** – serve personally with a writ (of summons).

- **RÉSIDENCE** – **assigné à résidence** – subject to a compulsory residence order.

ASSIMILER
- **À** – **assimiler à** – treat as; deem to be.
  - •• **COMPLÈTEMENT** assimilé à – treated in all respects as.

ASSISTANCE – representation in court (does not include power to bind one's client vis-à-vis the other party but is usually combined with **reprisentation**, which does).
- **ÉDUCATIF** – **assistance éducative** – educational measures which may be ordered by the court.
- **ENFANCE** – **assistance à l'enfance** – children's welfare department.
- **INFORMATISÉ** – **assistance informatisée au traitement des affaires** – litigation support.
- **JUDICIAIRE** – **régime d'assistance judiciaire** – legal-aid scheme.
- **MARITIME** – **assistance maritime** – salvage.
- **POSTPÉNITENTIAIRE** – **assistance postpénitentiaire** – after-care.

ASSISTER – represent in court.

ASSOCIATION – non-profit-making association.
- **BUT LUCRATIF** – **association sans but lucratif** – non-profit-making association.
- **MALFAITEUR** – **association de malfaiteurs** – criminal association; conspiracy; (informally) membership of a criminal gang.
- **PROFESSIONNEL** – **association professionnelle** – trade association.
- **SUBVERSIVE** – **association subversive** – treasonable conspiracy.
- **SYNDICAL** – **association syndicale** – landowners' association.
- **UTILITÉ PUBLIQUE** – **association reconnue d'utilité publique** – charity; recognised association.

ASSOCIÉ – partner; member (of a company, association, etc); (on a winding-up) contributory.

ASSUJETTISSEMENT
- **CONDITION** d'assujettissement – qualifying condition.
- **IMPÔT** – **assujettissement à l'impôt** – liability to taxation.

ASSUMER
- **ENGAGEMENT** – **assumer un engagement** – enter into an undertaking.

ASSURANCE
- **CHÔMAGE – assurance chômage** – unemployment insurance.
- **CRÉDIT – assurance crédit** – credit insurance.
- **DÉCÈS – assurance décès** – (whole) life insurance.
- **DÉFENSE – assurance défense et recours** – third-party insurance.
- **INDEMNITÉ d'assurance** – insurance money(s); insurance compensation.
- **INVALIDITÉ – assurance invalidité** – disablement insurance.
- **JUDICIAIRE – assurance judiciaire** – legal (-expenses) insurance, ie insurance to cover the cost of legal advice and litigation.
- **MALADIE – assurance maladie** – sickness insurance.
- **MATERNITÉ – assurance maternité** – maternity-benefits insurance.
- **PROTECTION – assurance protection juridique** – legal(-expenses) insurance.

ASSURANCE-RENTE – annuity insurance.

ASSURER
- **S'assurer de** – (of a court) be satisfied that.

ASTREINTE – (periodic pecuniary) penalty (for failure to comply with a court order or for non-performance of some other obligation); coercive fine (penalty).

ATERMOIEMENT – form of composition with creditors in which the debtor is given time to pay his debts in full; agreement for extension of time.

ATTACHE
- **POINT d'attache** – connecting factor.

ATTAQUE – assault.

ATTAQUER – challenge; complain of.
- **DÉCISION – attaquer une décision** – challenge a decision.
- **DÉCISION attaquée** – decision appealed against; decision of the court below (lower court or authority); impugned decision; decision being challenged.
- **JUGEMENT – attaquer un jugement** – appeal against a judgment.
- **JUSTICE – attaquer en justice** – sue; issue a summons or writ against; bring proceedings against.

ATTEINTE – infringement (violation, impairment) of or interference with (one's rights etc); trespass; restriction.

- **HONNEUR** – atteinte à l'honneur – insult; defamation; libel; slander.
- **INTÉGRITÉ**
  - **PERSONNE** – atteinte à l'intégrité de la personne – (assault causing) bodily harm.
  - **PHYSIQUE** – atteinte à l'intégrité physique – (assault causing) bodily harm.
  - **PHYSIQUE OU MORAL** – atteinte à l'intégrité physique ou morale – physical or psychological duress.
- **JUSTICE** – atteinte à l'autorité de la justice – contempt of court.
- **LIBERTÉ** – atteinte à la liberté – infringement of freedom.
- **LIEN CONJUGAL** – atteinte au lien conjugal – matrimonial offence.
- **PORTER atteinte à** – infringe; violate; interfere with; undermine; adversely affect.
- **PROPRIÉTÉ** – atteinte à la propriété privée – interference with private property.
- **PROPRIÉTÉ** – atteinte portée à la propriété du fonds enclavant – restriction on the ownership of the land surrounding the enclave.

ATTENDUS – recitals; reasons (in a judgment).

ATTENTAT – attack; outrage; killing; bombing.
- **MŒURS – attentat aux mœurs** – sexual offence.
- **PUDEUR – attentat à la pudeur** – indecent assault.

ATTENTATOIRE – violating.

ATTÉNUANT – mitigating (ie tending to reduce the penalty); extenuating (ie tending to render the offence excusable).

ATTÉNUATION
- **PEINE – atténuation de peine** – mitigation of penalty.
- **RECETTE qui vient en atténuation d'une dépense** – receipt to be set off against expenditure.

ATTESTATION – written deposition (of a witness); (unsworn) statement.
- **ÉCRIT – attestation écrite** – formal declaration as to the existence of facts; certificate.

ATTRIBUER – confer.

ATTRIBUTION

- **COMPÉTENCE d'attribution** – jurisdiction ratione materiae; jurisdiction based on the subject-matter; special jurisdiction.
- **CONDITIONS d'attribution** – eligibility.
- **CONFLIT d'attribution(s)** – dispute as to jurisdiction between the ordinary courts and the administrative authorities or courts, or between two administrative departments.
  - •• **NÉGATIF – conflit négatif d'attribution(s)** – situation where both courts (authorities) involved consider they have no jurisdiction to deal with the case; refusal of jurisdiction by both the ordinary and the administrative courts.
  - •• **POSITIF – conflit positif d'attribution(s)** – situation where both courts (authorities) involved claim jurisdiction; acceptance of jurisdiction by both the ordinary and the administrative courts.
- **CRÉDIT – attribution de crédits** – allocation of appropriations; attribution of expenditure to appropriations.
- **JURIDICTION d'attribution** – special administrative court.

ATTROUPEMENT – unlawful assembly; rout; riot.

AUDIENCE – hearing.

- **À l'audience** – in court.
  - •• **ORDINAIRE – à l'audience ordinaire du juge** – in the judge's ordinary court.
- **APPEL – audience d'appel des causes** – hearing at which the presiding judge discusses the presentation of the case with counsel; hearing for directions.
- **CONTRADICTOIRE – audience contradictoire** – hearing in the presence of the (both) parties.
- **JUGEMENT – audience de jugement** – reading of the judgment.
- **PLAIDOIRIE – audience des plaidoiries** – hearing; trial.
- **POLICE de l'audience** – (responsibility for) keeping order in court.
- **PUBLIC – audience publique** – public hearing; open court.
- **REGISTRE d'audience** – hearings register (kept by each chamber of a court); registrar's notes (record) of the hearing.
- **RENVOI à l'audience** – (immediate) entry (sending, committal, setting down) for trial (hearing).
- **RENVOYER – renvoyer à l'audience** – enter (send, commit, set down) for trial

(hearing).

AUDITEUR – junior officer at the Conseil d'État, the Court of Cassation and the Auditor-General's Department (**Cour des comptes**); (Belg, mil) judge advocate (ie military prosecutor or judge).

- **CHEF – auditeur en chef** – judge advocate general; chief military prosecutor.
- **CONSEIL D'ÉTAT – auditeur au Conseil d'État** – legal assistant (at the Conseil d'État).
- **COUR DE CASSATION – auditeur à la Cour de cassation** – administrative assistant (at the Court of Cassation).
- **COUR DES COMPTES – auditeur à la Cour des comptes** – assistant auditor (in the Auditor-General's Department).
- **GÉNÉRAL – auditeur général** (Belg, mil) – judge advocate general; chief military prosecutor.
- **JUSTICE – auditeur de justice** – legal service cadet; legal trainee.

AUDITION

- **PUBLIC – audition du public** – public hearing.
- **TÉMOIN – audition des témoins** – hearing (examination) of the witnesses.

AUDITORAT

- **MILITAIRE – auditorat militaire** – judge advocate's department.
- **TRAVAIL – auditorat de travail** (Belg) – Crown Counsel attached to the industrial tribunals (labour courts).

AUGMENT (AUGMENTATION is more usual)

- **CAPITAL – augment du capital** – increase of capital.

AUTEUR – previous owner; predecessor in title; person through whom one claims; person committing; perpetrator; principal; person responsible; parent (of an illegitimate child); draftsman.

- **ACTE – auteur de l'acte** – the person making the document.
- **DOMMAGE – auteur du dommage (du fait dommageable)** – tortfeasor; person causing the damage.
- **MATÉRIEL – lorsque l'instituteur est l'auteur matériel du préjudice** – where the teacher himself (personally, physically) causes the damage.

- **RECOURS** – auteur du recours – appellant.
- **VIOLENCE** – auteur de la violence – person using duress.

AUTHENTIFIER – certify the authenticity of; legalise.

AUTHENTIQUE – officially or notarially recorded.

AUTO-DÉFENSE – unlawful self-defence.

AUTONOMIE
- **VOLONTÉ** – autonomie de la volonté – freedom of the parties to arrange their own affairs; freedom of contract.

AUTORISATION
- **APPEL** – autorisation d'interjeter appel – leave to appeal.
- **JUSTICE** – autorisation de justice – permission of (authorisation by) the court; leave of the court.
- **PROSPECTION** – autorisation exclusive de prospection – exclusive prospecting licence.
- **RECHERCHE** – autorisation exclusive de recherche – exclusive prospecting licence.

AUTORITÉ
- **ABSOLU** – autorité absolue de la chose jugée – fact that a judgment is binding on the whole world (erga omnes), ie in rem.
- **CHOSE JUGÉE** – see CHOSE.
- **JUDICIAIRE** – autorité judiciaire – court; judicial authorities; judiciary; (occasionally) legal authorities.
- **JUGEMENT** – autorité de jugement – trial court.
- **JUSTICE** – par autorité de justice – by the court.
- **PARENTAL** – autorité parentale – parental authority.
- **PUBLIC** – autorité publique – the executive; the authorities; public authorities.
  - **EXERCICE de l'autorité publique** – exercise of official authority.
- **RELATIF** – autorité relative de la chose jugée – binding effect of a judgment on the parties (but not on strangers to the proceedings); res judicata.
- **TUTELLE** – autorité de tutelle – supervising authority; guardianship authority.
- **VOIE** – par voie d'autorité – by administrative order.

AUXILIAIRE
- **JUSTICE** – auxiliaires de (la) justice – barristers, public officers and other persons concerned in the administration of justice (registrars, bailiffs, attorneys, solicitors, valuers, liquidators); law officers; legal officials; lawyers and court officials; officers of the court.
- **SOCIAL** – auxiliaire social – welfare officer.

AVAL – signature guaranteeing a bill; backing a bill.

AVANCE
- **INTERÊT** – avance sans intérêt – interest-free loan.

AVANCEMENT
- **HOIRIE** – en avancement d'hoirie – by way of advancement.

AVANCER – maintain; argue.
- **GRIEF** – avancer un grief – make a complaint.

AVANT
- **DIRE** – avant dire (faire) droit – interlocutory.

AVANT-ACTE – pre-contract.

AVANTAGE
- **MATRIMONIAL** – avantage matrimonial – enrichment of a spouse by virtue of the rules governing matrimonial property. This is not subject to the rules on gifts.
- **NATURE** – avantage en nature – benefit in kind.

AVANT-CONTRAT – pre-contract (option agreement, pre-emption agreement).

AVENANT – supplementary agreement (modifying a previous contract or a standard-form contract).

AVÈNEMENT
- **CONDITION** – avènement d'une condition – occurrence, fulfilment, performance or satisfaction of a condition.

AVENIR – notice to appear (addressed to a solicitor (**avoué**)); notice to file pleadings.

AVENU
- **NON avenu** – non-existent.
  - **NUL et non avenu** – null and void.

AVERTISSEMENT – (prison sanction) caution (written warning).
- **COMPARUTION** – **avertissement suivi par la comparution volontaire de l'intéressé** – warning (information) issued by the public prosecutor followed by the voluntary appearance of the defendant.
- **TAXÉ** – **avertissement taxé** – warning coupled with a fee (financial penalty).

AVEU – admission; confession.

AVIS – notice; decision; opinion.
- **CONFORME** – **sur l'avis conforme de** – with the approval (consent) of.
- **CONSULTATIF** – **avis consultatif** – consultative opinion.
- **DÉFAVORABLE** – **émettre (rendre) un avis défavorable (à l'extradition etc)** – advise (rule) against.
- **EXPÉDITION** – **avis d'expédition** – notice (advice) of dispatch.
- **FAVORABLE** – **émettre (rendre) un avis favorable (à l'extradition etc)** – advise (rule) in favour of; authorise; approve.
- **IMPOSITION** – **avis d'imposition** – assessment.
- **JURIDIQUE** – **avis juridique** – legal opinion.
- **LICENCIEMENT** – **avis de licenciement** – notice of dismissal; letter of dismissal.
- **PASSAGE** – **avis de passage** – notice by the bailiff that he has called and left a copy of the document with a neighbour or at the town hall.
- **RÉCEPTION** – **avis de réception** – recorded delivery.
- **RECUEILLIR** – **après avoir recueilli l'avis de** – after consulting.
- **RÉFLÉCHI** – **avis mûrement réfléchi** – considered opinion.

AVISÉ – reasonable.
- **INSTITUTEUR** – **un instituteur avisé** – a reasonable schoolmaster.

AVOCAT – barrister; counsel; advocate; lawyer.
- **GÉNÉRAL** – **avocat général** – Solicitor-General (without political and advisory functions); (EU) Advocate-General; amicus curiae.
- **MINISTÈRE** – **dispensé de ministère d'avocat** – legal representation is not required.
- **OFFICE** – **avocat d'office** – official (officially assigned) defence counsel.
- **STAGIAIRE** – **avocat stagiaire** – pupil barrister.

AVOIR – (in plural) assets.
- **FISCAL** – **avoir fiscal** – tax credit.
- **NUMÉRAIRE** – **avoirs en numéraire** – cash in hand.

AVORTEMENT – abortion.

AVOUÉ – solicitor (for litigation only). ("Proctor" and "attorney" are old-fashioned terms which may be useful in some contexts.)

AVULSION – sudden detachment by a river of a considerable mass of land which becomes attached to that of another owner.

AYANT CAUSE – person claiming through.
- **PARTICULIER** – **ayant cause à titre particulier** – person deriving title from; assignee; assign; transferee; successor in title.
- **UNIVERSEL** – **ayant cause à titre universel** – person succeeding to a portion of another's legal position (assets and liabilities).
- **UNIVERSEL** – **ayant cause universel** – person succeeding to a person's whole legal position (assets and liabilities); universal successor; heir.

AYANT DROIT – person entitled to a right; beneficiary; licensee; registered holder; person entitled through or under another (may include a widow, whereas the expression **personne à charge** does not).

B

BAIL – lease; tenancy.
- **CHEPTEL** – **bail à cheptel** – lease of livestock.
- **COLONAT PARTIAIRE** – **bail à colonat partiaire** – lease on the basis of a division of produce and losses between tenant and landlord.
- **COMMERCIAL** – **bail commercial** – business tenancy.
- **CONSTRUCTION** – **bail à construction** – long building lease (18-70 years) conferring a right in rem on the lessee.
- **DOMAINE CONGÉABLE** – **bail à domaine congéable** – short-term agricultural tenancy in which the tenant retains ownership of (or is entitled to compensation for) his erections, plantations and crops and also has a right of pre-emption.
- **FERME** – **bail à ferme** – 9-year renewable agricultural tenancy.
- **HABITATION** – **bail à usage d'habitation** – residential tenancy.
- **NATURE** – **bail en nature** – tenancy in which the rent is paid in kind.
- **NOURRITURE** – **bail à nourriture** – contract to supply board and lodging for life.
- **RENTE** – **bail à rente** – rentcharge.
- **RURAL** – **bail rural** – agricultural tenancy.
- **TRIBUNAL paritaire de baux ruraux** – agricultural land tribunal.

BAILLEUR – landlord; lessor; hirer.
- **FONDS** – **bailleur de fonds** – person providing finance; money-lender.

BALANCE
- **COMPTE** – **balance des comptes en mouvement et en soldes** – turnover and balances of the accounts.

BALLOTTAGE – situation where none of the parties has obtained sufficient votes to be elected in the first round of an election.
- **SCRUTIN de ballottage** – second ballot.

BAN
- **RUPTURE de ban** – offence of returning to French territory (committed by a person who has been banished); also applies to persons under order not to live in a specific region.

BANDITISME – aggravated theft; aggravated larceny.

BANQUEROUTE – (negligent or fraudulent) bankruptcy.
- **FRAUDULEUX** – **banqueroute frauduleuse** – fraudulent bankruptcy
- **SIMPLE** – **banqueroute simple** – (negligent) bankruptcy

BANS – notice of an intended marriage posted on the notice-board of a mayor's office.

BARÈME
- **IMPÔT** – **barème de l'impôt sur les salaires** – salary-tax tables; (Schedule E) income-tax tables.

BARRE
- **PLAIDER à la barre** – address the court.

BARREAU – bar.

BARREMENT – crossing of a cheque.

BASE
- **IMPOSITION** – **base d'imposition** – taxable (rateable) value; value for tax purposes; basis of assessment.
- **LÉGAL** – **manque de base légale** – (judgment based on) faulty or insufficient reasons (ground for appeal to the Court of Cassation).
- **TEXTES de base** – relevant texts (documents); basic provisions.

BÂTONNIER – chairman of the bar.

BÉNÉFICE
- **DISCUSSION** – **bénéfice de discussion** – surety's right to require execution to be directed against the principal debtor before the creditor levies execution on the surety.
- **DISTRIBUÉ** – **bénéfice non distribué** – profit retained.
- **DIVISION** – **bénéfice de division** – surety's right to obtain a court order that the proceedings be directed against all the sureties.
- **DOUTE** – **au bénéfice du doute** – for lack of evidence.
- **ÉMOLUMENT** – **bénéfice d'émolument** – limitation of a spouse's liability for the community debts to his or her share of the community assets.

- **IMPÔT** – bénéfice avant impôts – profit before tax; pre-tax profit.
- **INVENTAIRE** – bénéfice d'inventaire – limitation of the heir's liability for the debts of the estate to the amount of the net assets he actually receives.

BÉNÉFICIAIRE – beneficiary.

- **PROMESSE** – bénéficiaire d'une promesse – promisee.

BÉNÉFICIER

- **DE** – bénéficier de – be entitled to.

BÉNÉVOLE

- **TRANSPORTÉ** bénévole – person given a free lift.
- **USAGER** bénévole – person using something free of charge.

BIEN – anything which may form the object of rights; property; goods; land; asset.
- **COMMUN** – bien commun – asset forming part of the community (of marital property).
- **COMMUNAL** – biens communaux – common land; common (belonging to all the inhabitants of a district).
- **CONSOMMABLE** – biens consommables – consumable articles or goods.
- **CONSOMPTIBLE** – biens consomptibles – consumable goods.
- **CORPOREL** – biens corporels – corporeal movables; goods; chattels.
- **DÉFAUT** – acte de défaut de biens (Sw) – bailiff's certificate that the execution debtor has no goods to seize; return of nulla bona.
- **DÉTERMINÉ** – biens déterminés – specific goods; specific property.
- **DOTAL** – biens dotaux – property settled on the wife by the marriage contract which is inalienable and cannot be taken in execution.
- **DROIT** des biens – law of property.
- **FAMILLE** – bien de famille – reserved family property (not liable to attachment or capable of being mortgaged); hereditary farm; long-standing family property; homestead.
- **IDENTIFIABLE** – biens identifiables – traceable property, ie which has not been converted into an unidentifiable form,
- **IMMOBILIER** – biens immobiliers – immovable property; real estate.
- **INCORPOREL** – biens incorporels – incorporeal (intangible) movables.
- **INDIVIS** – biens indivis – property held in common; co-property; property in undivided shares.

- **INSAISISSABLE** – biens insaisissables – property not subject to attachment.
- **JUGÉ** – le bien-jugé – the correctness (of a judgment etc).
- **JURIDIQUE** – biens juridiques – legally protected interests; interests.
- **MAÎTRE** – bien sans mantre – res nullius; ownerless (unclaimed) goods.
- **MÉNAGE** – biens du ménage – matrimonial property.
- **MOBILIER** – biens mobiliers – movable property; movables; personalty.
- **PARAPHERNAL** – biens paraphernaux – separate property of the wife under the dotal system of marital property (abolished in France with respect to future marriages as from 1965) which does not form part of her settled property (**biens dotaux**).
- **PRODUCTION** – biens de production – capital goods.
- **PROPRE** – biens propres – spouse's separate property.
- **RÉSERVÉ** – biens réservés – wife's property deriving from the exercise of a trade or profession: although part of the community, they are administered and may in principle be disposed of by the wife.
- **SUCCESSORAL** – biens successoraux – a deceased's assets, estate, etc.
- **VACANT** – biens vacants et sans mantre – ownerless realty which becomes property of the state.

BIENFAISANCE

- **CONTRAT** de bienfaisance – contract without consideration.

BIEN-FONDÉ – merits; substance; lawfulness.

- **ÉTABLIR** le bien-fondé de – make out (substantiate) (a claim); support (an appeal etc).
- **PRONONCER** – se prononcer sur le bien-fondé de ses allégations – give a decision on the merits of his allegations.
- **RECONNANTRE** le bien-fondé de la demande – allow the application.

BIEN-JUGÉ

- **PROCÈS** – le bien-jugé du procès – the correctness of the decision.

BILAN – balance sheet.

- **ÉTABLIR** – le bilan s'établit à – the balance sheet totalled.

BILLET
- **ORDRE** – **billet à ordre** – promissory note.
- **PORTEUR** – **billet au porteur** – bearer bill.

BIS – in numbering in French legislation leave untranslated and italicise; (otherwise) A.

BLÂME – reprimand.

BLANC
- **TRAITE des Blanches** – white slave trade.

BLANC-SEING – document signed in blank.

BLANCHISSAGE – laundering (of illegal profits, proceeds of crime, etc).

BLESSURE
- **IMPRUDENCE** – **blessures par imprudence** – negligent injury.
- **INVOLONTAIRE** – **blessures involontaires** – unintentional injuries.

BLOC
- **CONTRÔLE** – **bloc de contrôle** – controlling shareholding (interest).

BLOCAGE – freezing (provisional measure).
- **CRÉDIT** – **blocage de crédits** – blocking (freezing) of appropriations.

BLOQUER – freeze.
- **LISTE bloquée** – a list to be accepted or rejected in toto (in a vote).

BON
- **ACHAT** – **bon d'achat** – (pay in the form of a) voucher entitling the holder to purchase goods in his employer's shop.
- **CAISSE** – **bon de caisse** – fixed-deposit receipt (a negotiable instrument).
- **COMMANDE** – **bon de commande** – order form.
- **FOI** – **bonne foi** – good faith; honest dealing in legal transactions; erroneous but not negligent belief in the existence of a fact, right or rule of law.
- **IMPÔT** – **bon d'impôt** – tax-payment certificate; tax-reserve certificate.
- **JOUISSANCE** – **bon de jouissance** – certificate giving a right to share in profits or on liquidation or to subscribe for shares; participation certificate (not identical with a **bon de participation**).
- **MŒURS** – **bonnes mœurs** – accepted moral standards; morality.
- **PARTICIPATION** – **bon de participation** – participation certificate giving a right to share in profits or on liquidation or to subscribe for shares (not identical with a **bon de jouissance**).
- **PÈRE DE FAMILLE** – **bon père de famille** – reasonable, prudent man; careful, diligent owner.
  - **JOUIR en bon père de famille** – (obligation imposed on a tenant or hirer) to use rented etc property without damaging it, ie to keep the premises in good condition, fair wear and tear excepted.
- **RAISON** – **bonnes et sérieuses raisons** – well-founded reasons.
- **TRÉSOR** – **bon du Trésor** – Treasury bond.

BONI
- **LIQUIDATION** – **boni de liquidation** – surplus on a winding-up.

BONIFICATION
- **PRIME** – **bonification de la prime** – return of the premium.

BONUS-MALUS – motor-insurance clause varying the premium in accordance with the number of accidents.

BORDEREAU
- **IMPÔT** – **bordereau d'impôt** – tax assessment.

BORNAGE – fixing and marking boundaries.

BOULE DE NEIGE
- **VENTE à la boule de neige** – sale at a discount on condition that the purchaser introduces other purchasers; snowball selling.

BREF
- **DÉLAI** – **à bref délai** – speedily; promptly.

BREVET – patent; instrument drawn by solicitor (**notaire**) of which the original is handed to the parties.
- **ADDITION** – **brevet d'addition** - patent of addition.
- **AGENT** – **agent de brevets** – patent agent.
- **INVENTION** – **brevet d'invention** – patent.
- **PROCÉDÉ** – **brevet de procédé** – process patent.
- **VIOLATION de brevet** – infringement of a patent.

BRIGADIER – (police) constable.
- **CHEF** – **brigadier chef** – (police) sergeant.

BRIS

- **CLÔTURE** – bris de clôture – illegal breaking and entry of closed premises; breach of close; breaking a close.

BUDGET

- **ANNEXE** – budget annexe – subsidiary budget.
- **DÉPENSE** – budget des dépenses – expenditure budget.
- **PROJET** de budget – estimates.
- **RECETTE** – budget des recettes – revenue (income, receipts) budget.
- **RECTIFIÉ** – budget rectifié – amended budget.

BUDGET-PROGRAMME – programme-budget.

BULLETIN

- **EXPÉDITION** – bulletin d'expédition – dispatch note or slip.
- **PAIE** – bulletin de paie – pay slip.
- **VOTE** – bulletin de vote – ballot paper.

BUREAU

- **CASSATION** – bureau de la Cour de cassation – (Judges') Council of the Court of Cassation.
- **CONCILIATION** – bureau de conciliation – conciliation board.
- **HYPOTHÈQUE** – bureau des hypothèques – Mortgage Registry (Land (Charges) Registry).
- **JUGEMENT** – bureau de jugement – trial board.
- **VOTE** – bureau de vote – polling station.
  - •• **PRÉSIDENT** de bureau de vote – returning officer.

BUT

- **LUCRATIF** – à but lucratif – profit-making.
  - •• **NON** – à but non lucratif – non-profit-making.
- **SOCIAL** – but social – object of a company, association, etc.

—

C

CABINET – (Minister's) Private Office.
- **AVOCAT** – **cabinet d'avocat** – chambers.
- **JUSTICE de cabinet** – executive interference with the course of justice; Star Chamber justice.

CACHOT – cell.

CADASTRAL
- **PLAN cadastral** – index map (showing plots); official plan; registered plan; land survey.

CADASTRE – property register or registry; Land Registry; land survey (office).

CADRE
- **CONVENTION-cadre** – outline convention.
- **FAMILIAL** – **cadre familial rompu** – broken home.

CADUC
- **CITATION** – **déclarer la citation caduque** – strike the case off the list.
- **ÊTRE (devenir) caduc** – lapse.

CADUCITÉ – lapse.
- **DÉLAI de caducité** – period after which notice of appeal etc lapses if not followed up (eg by an application for listing).
- **ENTRAÎNER la caducité** – cause to lapse.
- **PEINE** – **sous peine de caducité** – if it is not to lapse; to be valid.

CAHIER
- **CHARGE** – **cahier des charges** – (terms and) conditions (of a building contract, sale, etc) (**aux conditions d'un cahier des charges annexé à l'acte constitutif de la concession** – on the conditions annexed to the instrument granting the concession); specifications.

CAÏDAT – intimidation (of prisoners, witnesses, etc by gangs or terrorist organisations).

CAISSE
- **CRÉDIT de caisse** – overdraft facility.
- **DÉPÔT** – **Caisse des dépôts et consignations** – Bank for Official Deposits.
- **FACILITÉ de caisse** – overdraft facility.
- **MALADIE** – **caisse de maladie** – sickness fund; health-insurance fund (association).

CALENDRIER – order of business.

CAMBIAIRE
- **ENGAGEMENT cambiaire** – liability under a bill of exchange.
- **RECOURS cambiaire** – recourse against the prior holders of a bill of exchange.

CAMBRIOLAGE – burglary; housebreaking.

CANTONNEMENT – restriction by the court of a mortgage etc to part only of the property by which it is guaranteed.

CAPABLE – possessing legal capacity.

CAPACITÉ
- **DILIGENCE et capacité** – care and skill.
- **ESTER** – **capacité d'ester en justice** – right to take part in court proceedings; standing (before the court); locus standi.
- **EXERCICE** – **capacité d'exercice** – independent capacity to exercise one's own rights without any form of representation, assistance or authorisation; legal capacity.
- **JOUISSANCE** – **capacité de jouissance** – capacity to possess rights and be bound by obligations; basic capacity; legal personality.
- **JURIDIQUE** – **capacité juridique** – capacity to possess rights and be bound by obligations; basic capacity; legal personality.
- **MATRIMONIAL** – **capacité matrimoniale** – capacity to marry.
- **TESTER** – **capacité de tester** – capacity to make a will.

CAPITAL – capital sum; (divorce) lump-sum provision.
- **EXPLOITATION** – **capital d'exploitation** – working capital.
- **PROPRE** – **capital propre et réserves et bénéfices non distribués** – shareholders' funds.
- **ROULEMENT** – **capital de roulement** – current assets; working capital.
- **SOCIAL** – **capital social** – (authorised) capital.
- **UTILISÉ** – **capital utilisé** – capital employed.

CAPITAL-ACTIONS – share capital.

CAPITALISATION

- **SYSTÈME de capitalisation** – (pension funds) funding system.

CAPTATION – obtaining a gift by deception.

- **HÉRITAGE** – **captation d'héritage** – attempting to obtain a succession by illegal or immoral means; legacy hunting.

CARACTÉRISÉ – established (le délit d'escroquerie est suffisament caractérisé lorsqu'il est constaté que... – the misdemeanour of obtaining by false pretences is sufficiently established when it is shown that...).

CARAMBOUILLAGE – resale of goods for which one has not paid (a form of obtaining by deceit).

CARENCE – failure to act; absence of seizable property.

- **DÉLAI de carence** – waiting time (period during which an insurer does not pay compensation); waiting period; qualifying period.
- **PROCÈS-VERBAL de carence** – official report (affidavit) of failure to attend or failure to perform some obligation or to do some specific thing; bailiff's return that there is no property to be seized (nulla bona).

CARRIÈRE – (in plural) minerals.

- **DE carrière** – permanent or career (civil servant, diplomat, etc); professional (judge).

CAS

- **APPLICATION** – **cas d'application** – case to which (a provision) applies.
- **CONCRET** – **cas concret** – specific case.
- **ÉCHÉANT** – **le cas échéant** – if necessary; where appropriate; in some cases; if the case (question) should arise.
- **ESPÈCE** – **cas d'espèce** – instant case; present case.
- **FORTUIT** – **cas fortuit** – unforeseen (unforeseeable) accident; (purely) accidental occurrence.
- **JURISPRUDENCE** – **cas de jurisprudence** – leading case; precedent; authority.
- **RÉSERVÉ** – **cas réservé** – case not covered by (excepted from) the general rule.

CASIER

- **CIVIL** – **casier civil** – register kept by the registrar of the regional court of all proceedings, orders, etc affecting the capacity of a person of full age.
- **JUDICIAIRE** – **casier judicaire** – criminal record; police record; criminal records office.

CASSATION – setting aside of a judgment (for error of law or procedure).

CASSER – set aside; annul; quash.

CASUEL

- **CONDITION casuelle** – condition whose occurrence depends entirely on chance.

CAUSAL

- **RESPONSABILITÉ causale** – liability for producing a given result irrespective of fault; strict liability.

CAUSE – typical, immediate reason for entering into a contract, eg in a gift the intention to give (animus donandi); in a contract involving mutual promises the **cause** is always the undertaking given by the other party, ie the existence of consideration; legal basis; legal ground; consideration; cause; proceedings; case.

- **CATÉGORIQUE** – **cause catégorique** – the **cause** regarded as a means of classifying contracts.
- **DÉFENDRE utilement sa propre cause** – present one's case effectively.
- **DEMANDE** – **cause de la demande** – facts and rule of law on which a party bases his case; cause of action.
- **EN cause** – **être en cause** – to be in issue.
- **ÉTAT** – **en tout état de cause** – at any stage in the proceedings.
- **ÉTRANGER** – **cause étrangère** – external (outside) cause; cause for which the promisor (defendant) is not liable; cause which cannot be imputed to the promisor (defendant) whose animal or thing caused the damage.
- **GÉNÉRATEUR** – **cause génératrice** – causa causans; effective cause.
- **HORS (de) cause** – not subject to (above, cleared of) suspicion; in the clear; cleared; exonerated.
- **INDÉPENDANT** – **causes indépendantes de sa volonté** – reasons beyond his control.
- **METTRE** – **être mis en cause** – have proceedings brought against one; be implicated.
- **MIS en cause** – against which the claim is directed; respondent.
- **MISE en cause** – third-party notice.
  - **DÉBITEUR** – **mise en cause du débiteur** – joinder of the debtor.
  - **RESPONSABILITÉ** – **mise en cause de la responsabilité de quelqu'un** – raising the question of someone's liability.

•• **RUINER** la mise en cause du requérant – destroy the case against the
applicant.

• **NULLITÉ** – **cause de nullité** – ground of
nullity.

• **PARTIE** en cause – party to proceedings.

• **PÉREMPTOIRE** – **cause péremptoire de
divorce** – absolute ground of divorce.

• **POURVOI** – **cause du pourvoi** – grounds of
appeal.

CAUTIO

• **JUDICATUM** – **cautio judicatum solvi** –
security for costs (and compliance with the
judgment).

CAUTION – surety; guarantor; security.

• **FOURNIR** une caution – offer (produce) a
surety.

• **JURATOIRE** – **caution juratoire** – promise
(by a life tenant) to conserve and restore
movable property; personal security of the
life tenant (usufructuary).

• **RÉEL** – **caution réelle** – person who, not
being himself liable for a debt, has mortgaged his land as a security for the debt of
another.

• **SOLIDAIRE** – **caution solidaire** – surety
jointly and severally liable with the principal
debtor.

CAUTIONNEMENT – contract of guaran-
tee (suretyship); bond; recognisance.

• **VERSER** un cautionnement comme
garantie de bonne conduite – give security
for good behaviour.

CÉDANT – assignor; transferor.

CÉDÉ – debtor or person liable to perform the
obligation assigned; person liable on the chose in
action assigned.

CÉDER – assign; transfer.

CÉDULE – acknowledgement.

• **CITATION** – **cédule de citation** – summons.

CÉLÉBRATION

• **MARIAGE** – **célébration du mariage** –
solemnisation of marriage.

CELLULAIRE

• **EMPRISONNEMENT** cellulaire – solitary
(cellular) confinement (detention).

• **ISOLEMENT** cellulaire – solitary (cellular)
confinement (detention).

• **RÉCLUSION** cellulaire – solitary (cellular)
confinement (detention).

• **RÉGIME** cellulaire – solitary (cellular) confinement (detention); prison with separate
cells.

• **SECTION** cellulaire – solitary-confinement
wing (division).

CELLULE

• **DISCIPLINAIRE** – **cellule disciplinaire** –
(prison sanction) punishment cell; solitary
confinement.

CENTIME

• **ADDITIONNEL** – **centimes additionnels**
– local tax on property and businesses, calculated in the form of a fictitious supplement
on certain defunct forms of direct state taxation – similar to UK rates.

CERTAIN

• **DOMICILE** certain – fixed abode.

CERTIFICAT

• **ADDITION** – **certificat d'addition** – patent
of addition.

• **CONFORMITÉ** – **certificat de conformité**
– certificate of compliance.

• **COUTUME** – **certificat de coutume** – certificate of foreign law.

• **DROIT DE VOTE** – see VOTE below.

• **INDIGENCE** – **certificat d'indigence** – certificate of lack of means (financial hardship).

• **INVESTISSEMENT** – **certificat d'investissement** – certificate of entitlement to the
pecuniary rights attaching to a share.

• **NOMINATIF** – **certificat nominatif** – registered certificate; certificate for registered
shares.

• **NON-APPEL** – **certificat de non-appel** –
certificate by the registrar that there has
been no appeal or application to set aside.

• **PORTEUR** – **certificat au porteur** – bearer
warrant; share warrant.

• **QUITUS** – **certificat de quitus** – certificate
of discharge given to an administrator, receiver, etc.

• **SCOLARITÉ** – **certificat de scolarité** –
(school) attendance certificate.

• **VIE** – **certificat de vie** – life certificate.

• **VOTE** – **certificat de droit de vote** – certificate of voting rights (belonging to a
share).

CERTITUDE

- **ÉTABLIR avec certitude** – prove beyond doubt.
- **PEINE – certitude de la peine** – fixed penalties; fixed sentences.

CESSATION – termination; suspension.

- **PAIEMENT – cessation de(s) paiement(s)** – cessation (suspension) of (a debtor's) payments (state preceding bankruptcy); inability to meet current liabilities; insolvency.

CESSIBLE – transferable; assignable.

CESSION – assignment.

- **ANTÉRIORITÉ – cession d'antériorité** – assignment of priority.
- **BAIL – cession à bail** – assignment by way of lease; grant of a lease.
- **BAIL – cession de bail** – assignment of a lease.
- **CRÉANCE – cession de créance** – assignment of a chose in action, ie of the right to receive payment of a debt or performance of some other obligation.
- **DÉCLARATION de cession** – notice of assignment.
- **DETTE – cession de dette** – transfer of the duty to pay a debt (or perform some other obligation).
- **ENCAISSEMENT – cession aux fins d'encaissement** – assignment (of debts) for collection.
- **FONDS – cession d'un fonds** – sale (transfer) of a business.
- **GARANTIE – cession à titre de garantie** – assignment by way of security.
- **LICENCE – cession de licence** – assignment of a licence.
- **MITOYENNETÉ – cession de mitoyenneté** – assignment of party rights in a wall, fence, ditch, etc.
- **SÛRETÉ – cession à titre de sûreté** – assignment by way of security.
- **USAGE – cession d'usage** – assignment (transfer) of a right of user (right to use).

CESSIONNAIRE – assignee.

- **FONDS – cessionnaire d'un fonds** – purchaser of a business.

CH = chiffre.

CHAMBRE – chamber; section; subdivision.
("Chamber" meaning a section of a court is not in general use in England though the word appears in the old Star Chamber and Exchequer Chamber. "Division" is usually a larger unit containing several **chambres**, but in courts (like the Court of Cassation) where a **chambre** itself contains several **sections** this is a suitable translation. The word "chamber" is used in the European Convention on Human Rights and in the Rules of the European Court of Human Rights but in other contexts the best translation is probably "court", "bench" or possibly "section" (where these expressions do not appear unnatural).)

- **ACCUSATION – chambre d'accusation (des mises en accusation)** – Indictments Chamber (of the Court of Appeal).
- **APPEL CORRECTIONNEL – chambre des appels correctionnels** – Criminal Appeals Chamber (Division); Criminal Chamber (Division) of the Court of Appeal.
- **COMMUNE – Chambre des communes** – (British) House of Commons.
- **COMPENSATION – chambre de compensation** – clearing-house.
- **CONSEIL – chambre du conseil** – judge's chambers; court in chambers.
    - **EN chambre du conseil** – in chambers; in private; the court in chambers.
- **CORRECTIONNEL – chambre correctionnelle** – Criminal Section (Chamber).
- **CRIMINEL – chambre criminelle** – Assize Chamber (Division); Criminal Division of the Court of Cassation.
- **DROIT PUBLIC – chambre de droit public** – public-law chamber (section, division).
- **ÉCONOMIQUE – chambre économique** – commercial section.
- **MÉTIER – chambre des métiers** – chamber (association) of (manual) trades; trades association; guild; corporation.
- **MIXTE – chambre mixte de la Cour de cassation** – court consisting of the judges of at least three divisions of the Court of Cassation (13–25 judges) which must hear a case if the division of the Court dealing with the case was equally divided or the Attorney-General applies for the case to be so heard and may hear certain other cases; enlarged court; mixed division.
- **NOTAIRE – chambre des notaires** – law society.
- **PAIR – Chambre des pairs** – (British) House of Lords; Upper House.
- **PARTIE – faire partie d'une chambre** – sit as a member of (belong to) a chamber.

- **PEUPLE** – **Chambre du peuple** – (British) House of Commons.
- **RESTREINT** – **chambre restreinte** – bench sitting with less than its full number of members; bench of two, three, etc judges.
- **RÉUNI** – **chambres réunies** – joint chambers; full court.
- **SÛRETÉ** – **chambre de sûreté** – temporary lock-up.
- **VACATION** – **chambre des vacations** – (formerly) vacation court.

CHAMP

- **APPLICATION** – **champ d'application** – scope; ambit.
  - **MATÉRIEL** – **champ d'application matérielle** – substantive scope; (social security) material (ie non-personal) scope.

CHANCELIER (Sw) – Secretary and Adviser to the Cabinet (with custody of the State Seal).

CHANCELLERIE – Ministry of Justice; (Sw) administrative section of the registry of a large court.

CHANGE

- **AUTORISATION de change** – exchange control permission.
- **BOURSE des changes** – foreign exchange market.
- **CONTRÔLE des changes** – exchange control.
- **DEUXIÈME de change** – second of exchange.
- **DROIT du change** – law of negotiable instruments (bills of exchange).
- **LETTRE de change** – bill of exchange.
- **MARCHÉ des changes** – foreign exchange market.
- **PREMIER** – **première de change** – first of exchange.
- **SECOND** – **seconde de change** – second of exchange.

CHANGEMENT

- **MAIN** – **changement de mains** – change of possession.

CHANTAGE – blackmail; extortion; demanding with menaces.

CHAPEAU – heading; headnote; short statement of principle or practice.

- **JURISPRUDENTIEL** – **chapeau jurisprudentiel** – headnote.

CHAPITRE – head (of budget or estimates); (code) chapter. The French, Belgian and Luxembourg Civil Codes are divided into **livres** (books), **titres** (parts), **chapitres** (chapters), **sections** (sections) and **articles** (articles). The Swiss Civil Code is divided into **livres** (books), **parties** (parts), **titres** (sections), **chapitres** (chapters) and **articles** (articles).

CHARGE – (of a notary) official appointment; encumbrance; accusation; incriminating evidence; (in plural) periodical expenditure connected with a residential building; service charges; liabilities; encumbrances; onerous conditions attached to a gift.

- **EXEMPT de charges** – unencumbered; free from encumbrances.
- **EXPLOITATION** – **charges d'exploitation** – operating expenses.
- **FAIT(S) à charge** – incriminating fact or evidence; evidence against the accused; evidence for the prosecution.
- **FONCIER** – **charges foncières** – encumbrances; taxation on land.
- **FRAIS** – **charge des frais** – burden of costs.
- **INALIÉNABILITÉ** – **charge d'inaliénabilité** – condition of inalienability.
- **LEGS avec charge** – legacy conditional on performing an obligation imposed by the testator.
- **METTRE à la charge de** – order (costs) against.
- **PÉRÉQUATION de charges** – equalisation of burdens.
- **PERSONNE à charge** – dependant; person for whose maintenance one is liable (the term does not usually include a widow).
- **PREUVE** – **charge de la preuve** – burden (onus) of proof.
- **PUBLIC** – **charges publiques** – public burdens.
- **RÉPARTITION des charges** – apportionment of charges; calculation of contributions.
- **TÉMOIN à charge** – prosecution witness.

CHARGÉ

- **MISSION** – **chargé de mission** – special adviser; special consultant.

CHARGER

- **FAIRE** – **charger quelqu'un de faire quelque chose** – instruct someone to do something.

CHARTE-PARTIE – charter-party.
- **PRENDRE en charte-partie** – charter.

CHEF – head; count; ground; point; part.
- **ACCUSATION** – chef d'accusation – count (in an indictment); charge.
- **BUREAU** – chef de bureau – principal.
- **DE** son chef – in one's own right.
- **DEMANDE** – chefs de demande – points of claim.
- **DISPOSITIF** – chef du dispositif – part of the formal order (operative words).
- **DIVISION** – chef de division – senior principal.
- **DU** chef de – on the ground of.
- **ÉTABLISSEMENT** – chef d'établissement – prison governor.
- **HIÉRARCHIQUE** – chef hiérarchique – official superior.
- **INCULPATION** – chef d'inculpation – count; charge.
- **IRRECEVABILITÉ** – chef d'irrecevabilité – ground of non-admissibility.
- **JUGEMENT** – chef de jugement – point for decision.
- **OPPOSITION** – chef de l'opposition – leader of the opposition.
- **PRÉJUDICE** – chef de préjudice – head of damage.
- **PRÉVENTION** – chef de prévention – charge; count.
- **SERVICE** – chef de service – (Assistant) Under-Secretary (of State).

CHEMIN
- **EXPLOITATION** – chemin d'exploitation – service road; farm road; track.

CHEPTEL
- **FER** – cheptel de fer – lease of livestock with an obligation to restore the equivalent in value.

CHÈQUE
- **BARRÉ** – chèque barré – crossed cheque.
- **BÉNÉFICIAIRE** du chèque – payee.
- **ENCAISSER** un chèque – collect a cheque.
- **OPPOSITION** – faire opposition sur un chèque – stop a cheque.
- **ORDRE** – chèque à ordre – order cheque.
- **PROVISION** – chèque sans provision – uncovered cheque, ie cheque issued without funds to meet it; bad (worthless) cheque.

CHICANE – misuse of procedure.

CHIFFRE – paragraph.
- **AFFAIRE** – chiffre d'affaires – turnover.
- **DEMANDE** – chiffre de la demande – amount involved (in the case); amount of the claim.

- **NOIR** – chiffre noir – undetected crime; dark figure.

CHIFFRER
- **PRÉTENTION** – chiffrer ses prétentions – quantify one's claims.

CHIROGRAPHAIRE
- **CRÉANCIER** chirographaire – unsecured creditor.

CHÔMÉ
- **JOUR** chômé – non-working day.

CHOSE – (item of) property (movable or immovable); material object; thing; chattel.
- **AUTRUI** – chose d'autrui – another's property; property of a third party.
- **COMMERCE** – choses hors (du) commerce – things whose sale is prohibited by law (not subject to legal transactions, not for sale); inalienable things.
- **COMMUN** – chose commune – thing whose use is common to all (eg air, water in a stream); res communis.
- **CORPOREL** – choses corporelles – physical goods; objects; chattels.
- **FAIT** des choses – damage caused by inanimate objects.
- **FONGIBLE** – choses fongibles – non-specific goods; generic (fungible) goods.
- **GENRE** – choses de genre – non-specific goods; generic, fungible goods.
- **JUGÉ** – chose jugée – res judicata; final court decision (si ceux-ci ne sont pas contraires à la chose jugée entre parties – provided that the latter are not incompatible with a final court decision between the parties).
  - **AUTORITÉ** – avoir l'autorité de la chose jugée – constitute res judicata (la décision d'une juridiction non répressive n'a pas l'autorité de la chose jugée à l'égard de l'action publique – the judgment of a non-criminal court does not constitute res judicata with respect to a prosecution); be (provisionally) binding on the parties. (A distinction is drawn between the **autorité de la chose jugée** acquired by a judgment as soon as it is given and the **force de chose jugée** which it acquires when its enforcement can no longer be suspended by an appeal.)

- **AUTORITÉ** – **décliner l'autorité de la chose jugée** – refuse to accept that one is bound by a judgment.
- **AUTORITÉ absolue de la chose jugée** – fact that a judgment is binding on the whole world (erga omnes), ie in rem.
- **AUTORITÉ relative de la chose jugée** – binding effect of a judgment on the parties (but not on strangers to the proceedings); res judicata.
- **EXCEPTION de chose jugée** – defence of res judicata.
- **EXÉCUTION tardive de la chose jugée** – late compliance with a court order.
- **FORCE** – **acquérir (couler en, passer en, prendre) force de chose jugée** – become final (of a judgment).
- **FORCE** – **ayant (coulé en, passé en, pris) force de chose jugée** – final (of a judgment).
- **FORCE** – **même dépourvu de la force de la chose jugée** – even if obiter.
- **RELATIVITÉ de la chose jugée** – rule that res judicata applies only between the parties and their privies, ie a judgment is binding on the parties to the proceedings and not on others.

CIRCONSCRIPTION
- **ÉLECTORAL** – **circonscription électorale** – constituency.
- **JUDICIAIRE** – **circonscription judiciaire** – judicial district.

CIRCONSTANCE – particular (specific) facts (of a case).
- **ABSOLUTOIRE** – **circonstances absolutoires** – circumstances exempting from punishment (in spite of a finding of guilt), eg superior orders or turning state's evidence.
- **AGGRAVANT** – **circonstances aggravantes** – aggravating circumstances.
- **ATTÉNUANT** – **circonstances atténuantes** – mitigating circumstances (ie tending to reduce the penalty); extenuating circumstances (ie tending to render the offence excusable).
- **CONTRAIGNANT** – **circonstances contraignantes** – compelling circumstances.
- **NOUVEAU** – **circonstances nouvelles** – fresh facts; fresh evidence; change of circumstances.

CIRCULATION
- **DÉCISION par voie de circulation** (Sw) – decision taken by circulating the file (among the judges).
- **DÉLAI de circulation** – currency (of a bill etc); period of validity.

CITATION – writ (of summons); (originating) summons; subpoena.
- **CADUC** – **déclarer la citation caduque** – strike the case out of the list.
- **COMPARAÎTRE** – **citation à comparaître en justice** – summons to appear in court.
- **DIRECT** – **citation directe** – direct summons; direct committal; summons bringing the accused directly before the court without a preliminary investigation; private prosecution.
- **JUSTICE** – **citation en justice** – writ; (originating) summons; subpoena; summons (to appear before the court).
- **REPRISE** – **citation en reprise d'instance** – summons to resume proceedings (which have been interrupted).

CITER
- **DÉFENDEUR cité** – defendant (who has been) served with a writ.
- **JUSTICE** – **citer en justice** – bring to court; take proceedings against.

CIVIL
- **DROIT civil** – civil law, ie non-commercial private law.
- **LITIGE civil** – civil action.
- **MATIÈRE** – **en matière civil** – in civil matters; when hearing civil cases.

CIVILISATION
- **JURIDIQUE** – **pays de civilisation juridique** – country with an advanced legal system.

CIVILISTE – expert in civil law.

CIVILEMENT
- **RESPONSABLE** – **civilement responsable** – person civilly liable (for the damage caused by an offence committed by another).

CLASSEMENT – decision to take no further action (not to prosecute); discontinuance (termination) of the proceedings; decision incorporating an item of property into the public property of a public authority.
- **SUITE** – **classement sans suite** – withdrawal or discontinuance of the proceedings.

CLASSER – terminate (discontinue, drop) (proceedings); refrain from (discontinue, drop) (prosecution); take no further action on; offer no evidence (in a case).

CLAUSE

- **ABUSIF – clause abusive** – unfair clause (in a contract etc).
- **ACCROISSEMENT – clause d'accroissement** – clause under which the surviving co-owner(s) etc succeed(s) to the interest(s) of the other(s) (ius accrescendi).
- **COMMERCIAL – clause commerciale** – clause in a marriage contract (marriage settlement) whereby a business belonging to one of the spouses is settled on the survivor or authorising him to purchase the business.
- **COMPÉTENCE – clause d'attribution de compétence** – jurisdiction clause.
- **COMPROMISSOIRE – clause compromissoire** – arbitration clause agreeing to submit future differences to arbitration.
- **DÉCHÉANCE – clause de déchéance** – forfeiture clause.
- **DURETÉ – clause de dureté** – hardship clause.
- **EXCLUSIVITÉ – clause d'exclusivité** – exclusive-rights clause.
- **EXORBITANT – clause exorbitante (du droit commun)** – (in a contract with a public authority) clause incompatible with the ordinary law which has the effect of causing the contract to be governed by administrative law.
- **FONDS DE COMMERCE – clause de fonds de commerce** – clause in a marriage contract (marriage settlement) whereby a business belonging to one of the spouses is settled on the survivor or the survivor authorised to purchase the business.
- **GARANTIE – clause de garantie** – guarantee clause; warranty.
- **HUMANITÉ – clause d'humanité** – hardship clause.
- **IRRESPONSABILITÉ – clause d'irresponsabilité** – exemption clause; clause excluding liability.
- **LÉONIN – clause léonine** – clause in articles of partnership depriving a partner of any share in the profits or some other similarly inequitable arrangement.
- **NATION – clause de la nation la plus favorisée** – most-favoured-nation clause.
- **NON-CONCURRENCE – clause de non-concurrence** – agreement not to compete.
- **NON-RÉEMBAUCHAGE – clause de non-réembauchage** – clause undertaking not to work for a competitor.
- **NON-RESPONSABILITÉ – clause de non-responsabilité** – exemption clause; clause excluding liability.
- **NON-RÉTABLISSEMENT – clause de non-rétablissement** – clause undertaking not to enter into competition with the purchaser of a business etc.
- **NORMATIF – clause normative** – rule-making clause; substantive clause.
- **ORDRE – clause à ordre** – order clause written on a cheque or bill (ie the words "or order"). (A bill of exchange is transferable by endorsement even without an express order clause unless it contains words expressly excluding such transfer.)
- **PÉNAL – clause pénale** – penalty clause.
- **PORTEUR – clause au porteur** – bearer clause.
- **RECONDUCTION – clause de reconduction** – renewal clause.
- **RÉSERVE – clause de réserve** – reservation (clause).
  - •• **PROPRIÉTÉ – clause de réserve de propriété** – reservation of title (ownership) clause.
  - •• **RÉFÉRÉ – clause de réserve de référé** – clause (in an order) reserving the defendant's right to apply to the urgent applications judge; liberty to apply.
- **RÉSOLUTOIRE – clause résolutoire** – clause providing that a contract shall be void in specified circumstances (eg non-performance within a certain time).
- **SAUVEGARDE – clause de sauvegarde** – saving clause.
- **SÉCURITE SYNDICALE – clause de sécurité syndicale** – closed shop or similar arrangement.
- **STYLE – clause de style** – standing clause.

CLERC

- **ASSERMENTÉ – clerc assermenté** – (bailiff's) sworn clerk (entitled to serve process).
- **NOTAIRE – clerc de notaire** – legal executive; solicitor's (notary's) clerk.

CLIENTÈLE – goodwill.

CLORE

- **DROIT de se clore** – right of enclosure.

CLOS

- **A huis clos** – in private; in camera.

CLÔTURE – enclosure.
- **BRIS de clôture** – illegal breaking and entry of closed premises; breach of close; breaking a close.
- **FORCÉ** – **clôture forcée** – right to require one's neighbour to contribute to the expenses of erecting and maintaining party walls and fences.
- **INSTANCE** – **clôture de l'instance** – conclusion of the proceedings.
- **ORDONNANCE de clôture** – order by which an investigating judge closes an investigation (ie discharge or committal for trial).
- **PRIVATIF** – **clôture privative** – enclosure (wall, fence, etc) in the exclusive ownership of one of the adjoining proprietors; non-party wall, fence, etc.
- **VIOLATION de clôture** – illegal breaking and entry of closed premises; breach of close; breaking a close.

CO-ACCUSÉ – co-accused; co-defendant.

CO-ACTIVITÉ – participation in an offence (as a principal).

CO-AUTEUR – joint principal; co-principal.
- **PRÉJUDICE** – **sont co-auteurs du préjudice** – both caused the damage.

COCONTRACTANT – the other contracting party; the other party to the contract.

CODE
- **ADMINISTRATION** – **Code d'administration locale** – local-government code.
- **INSTRUCTION** – **Code d'instruction criminelle** – Code of Criminal Procedure.
- **JUDICIAIRE** – **Code de l'organisation judiciaire** – Courts Act; Judicature Act; Administration of Justice Act; Judicial Code.
- **JUSTICE** – **Code de justice militaire** – Army Act; Military Criminal Code.
- **TRAVAIL** – **Code du travail** – Employment Code.
- **URBANISME** – **Code d'urbanisme** – town-planning code.

CODÉBITEUR
- **CONJOINT** – **codébiteurs conjoints** – persons severally liable (each for his share).

CODICILLE – codicil.

COFIDÉIJUSSEUR – co-guarantor; co-surety.

COGESTION – joint management; right to participate in management.

COGNITION
- **POUVOIR de cognition** – (extent of the) jurisdiction (of a court) to deal with (the various aspects of) a case.

COHABITATION – joint occupation; duty of spouses to have intimate relations.

COINDIVISAIRE – co-owner.

COLLATÉRAL – (person) of common descent but by a different line; collateral.

COLLATIONNEMENT – checking that a document is identical with the original; collating; checking that objects attached or forming part of an inventory have not been removed before sale.

COLLECTIF – Bill of Supply incorporating supplementary estimates.

COLLECTIVITÉ – community; body; authority; taxpayer.
- **LOCAL** – **collectivité locale** – local authority.
- **PUBLIC** – **collectivité publique** – public authority, public corporation.
- **TERRITORIAL** – **collectivité territoriale** – territorial authority.

COLLÈGE – bench; board.
- **MEMBRE d'un collège** – member of a bench.

COLLÉGIAL
- **FORMATION collégiale** – bench; chamber; court; full court (as opposed to the **juge unique**).
- **JURIDICTION collégiale** – a bench of judges; full court; court.
- **ORGANES collégiaux d'un fonds** – corporate bodies of a fund.

COLLÉGIALEMENT – acting as a bench; (members of a board, office, etc) acting together (as a body).
- **EN formation collégiale** – sitting as a bench.
- **SIÉGER collégialement** – sit as a bench.

COLLOCATION – classification of a debtor's creditors by the judge according to the order in which they should be paid; establishment of order of preference in bankruptcy.

COLLOQUER – settle the order of payment in bankruptcy.

- **ÊTRE** colloqué – les **créances sont colloquées dans l'ordre suivant sur le produit des biens de la masse** – the debts are satisfied from the proceeds of the bankruptcy in the following order.

COLONAT

- **PARTIAIRE** – **colonat partiaire** – agricultural tenancy in which the rent takes the form of a share of the produce or the loss.

COMITÉ

- **DIRECTEUR** – **comité directeur** – steering committee.
- **ENTREPRISE** – **comité d'entreprise** – works council.
- **RESTREINT** – **comité restreint** – select committee.

COMMAND

- **DÉCLARATION de command** – statement exercising the right of an ostensible purchaser to substitute the true purchaser for whom he was acting as an agent; naming one's principal at or after an auction.

COMMANDANT

- **POLICE** – **commandant de police** – (police) chief inspector.

COMMANDEMENT – formal notice (to pay a judgment debt etc) served by a bailiff holding an authority to levy execution; service of a peremptory order.

- **AUTORITÉ LÉGITIME** – **commandement de l'autorité légitime** – defence of lawful orders.
- **ITÉRATIF** – **commandement itératif** – final notice to pay before levying execution.
- **PAYER** – **commandement de payer** – order to pay.
- **POUVOIR de commandement** – factual power (not necessarily founded in law) to give orders relating to a thing.

COMMANDITAIRE – limited partner.

COMMANDITE – limited partnership.

- **ACTION** – **commandite par actions** – partnership limited by shares.
- **SIMPLE** – **commandite simple** – limited partnership.

COMMANDITÉ – general, active or managing partner in a limited partnership.

COMMENCEMENT

- **PREUVE** – **commencement de preuve par écrit** – signed writing rendering admissible

confirmatory oral evidence or presumptions which would otherwise be excluded; writing admitting oral evidence; some evidence in writing; prima facie case.

COMMENTATEUR – commentator; reporter; legal writer; authority.

COMMERÇANT – trader; merchant;

- **PETIT commerçant** – small trader.

COMMERCE

- **ACTE de commerce** – commercial transaction.
- **ENNEMI** – **commerce avec l'ennemi** – trading with the enemy.
- **FONDS de commerce** – business.
- **HORS (du) commerce** – whose sale is prohibited by law; not subject to legal transactions; inalienable; not for sale.
- **JURIDIQUE** – **commerce juridique** – legal transactions.
- **RAISON de commerce** – business name.
- **REGISTRE du commerce** – business-names register; commercial register.
- **TRIBUNAL de commerce** – Commercial Court.

COMMERCIALITÉ

- **SUBJECTIF** – **théorie de la commercialité subjective** – theory that certain acts or transactions fall within the jurisdiction of the commercial courts because they are performed by merchants or businessmen.

COMMETTANT – master; principal; person vicariously liable for the fault of his servant.

COMMINATOIRE – (of a penalty, fine or nullity) imposed to put pressure on one of the parties and revocable at the court's discretion according to the circumstances of the case.

- **JUGEMENT comminatoire** – order containing a revocable penalty for non-compliance with its terms.
- **MESURE comminatoire** – coercive measure (ie involving a threat of legal sanctions).

COMMISSAIRE – (police) superintendent.

- **APPORT** – **commissaire aux apports** – valuer of contributions in kind to the capital of a company.
- **CENTRAL** – **commissaire central** – chief superintendent.
- **COMPTE** – **commissaire aux comptes** – auditor.

- **DIVISIONNAIRE** – commissaire divisionnaire – chief superintendent.
- **ENQUÊTEUR** – commissaire enquêteur – commissioner appointed to hold an inquiry.
- **GOUVERNEMENT** – commissaire du gouvernement – prosecutor in a court martial; law officer whose task it is to present a completely impartial report on a case to an administrative court, especially the Conseil d'État, or to the Jurisdiction Court (**Tribunal des conflits**); officer representing the point of view of a ministry in an administrative division of the Conseil d'État.
- **POLICE** – commissaire (de police) – (police) superintendent.
- **PRINCIPAL** – commissaire principal – chief superintendent.
- **PRISEUR** – commissaire-priseur – valuer and auctioneer of movables.
- **RÉPUBLIQUE** – commissaire de la République (now again **préfet**) Département Commissioner, ie the government's representative in the département (county).
  - •• **RÉGION** – commissaire de la République de région (now again **préfet de région**) – Regional Commissioner (Government representative in the region).

COMMISSION – board; committee; commission; tribunal; instruction given by a court to a judge or other public officer.

- **ARBITRAL** – commission arbitrale – (arbitral) assessment board.
- **CONCURRENCE** – Commission de la concurrence – Fair Competition (Trading) Board.
- **CONTRAT** de commission – contract with a commission agent acting for an unnamed principal who is known to exist.
- **CONTENTIEUX** – commission contentieuse de la sécurité sociale – social-security tribunal.
- **DÉLIMITATION** – commission de délimitation – boundary commission; frontier commission.
- **DOMMAGE** – commission de dommages de guerre – war-damage board.
- **ENQUÊTE** – commission d'enquête – commission of inquiry; fact-finding committee; investigating committee.
- **EXAMEN** – commission d'examen – board of examiners.
- **MARCHÉ** – commission des marchés – tender board.

- **PARITAIRE** – commission paritaire – joint (equi-representational) committee.
  - •• **MIXTE** – Commission mixte paritaire – joint committee of the two chambers of the French parliament which prepares a compromise text when the two chambers disagree.
- **PARLEMENTAIRE** – commission parlementaire – parliamentary committee.
- **PERMANENT** – commission permanente – standing committee.
- **ROGATOIRE** – commission rogatoire – request for judicial assistance; request for evidence on commission; letters rogatory; delegation of powers by a judge; instruction(s) (eg by a judge to the police); warrant (eg to the police to seize evidence).
  - •• **REMETTRE** la commission rogatoire – report back (to the judge).
- **SÉCURITÉ SOCIALE** – commission de sécurité sociale – social-security board (tribunal).
- **TECHNIQUE** – commission technique – specialised committee; expert committee.
- **VÉRIFICATION DES COMPTES** – commission de vérification des comptes – board of auditors.

COMMISSIONNAIRE – commission agent; nominee; factor; agent of a principal whose existence is not disclosed.

- **DOUANE** – commissionnaire en douane – customs agent.
- **EXPÉDITEUR** – commissionnaire expéditeur – forwarding agent.
- **TRANSPORT** – commissionnaire de transport – forwarding agent.

COMMISSOIRE

- **PACTE** commissoire – foreclosure clause in a pledge or mortgage; clause permitting the pledgee or mortgagee to keep the object pledged or mortgaged in case of non-repayment; (more generally) rescission clause.

COMMODANT – lender.

COMMODAT – loan (for use of a non-consumable object).

COMMODATAIRE – borrower.

COMMUER

- **PEINE** – commuer une peine – commute a sentence.

COMMUN – in co-ownership; joint.

- **ACCORD** – d'un commun accord – by mutual consent.
- **DROIT** commun – the general law; ordinary or existing law.
- **ERREUR** commune – mistake common to to both parties; common mistake.
- **FRAIS** – **le bornage se fait à frais communs** – the cost of fixing and marking the boundary is borne jointly.
- **RENOMMÉE** – **commune renommée** – common repute.

COMMUNAUTÉ – community; co-owners.
- **ACQUÊT** – **communauté d'acquêts (réduite (limitée) aux acquêts)** – community of after-acquired property.
- **ACTION** – **communauté d'action** – action group.
- **BIEN** – **communauté de biens** – community of property (between spouses); marital community.
- **ÉPOUX** – **communauté entre époux** – community of property (between spouses); marital community.
- **HABITATION** – **communauté d'habitation** – cohabitation.
- **INTÉRÊT** – **communauté d'intérêt** – (as between parties to proceedings) common interest.
- **LÉGAL** – **communauté légale** – statutory community of marital property.
- **VIE** – **communauté de vie** – consortium and cohabitation; married (conjugal) life.

COMMUNE – local-government district; local authority; district council; borough; township; commune.

COMMUNICABLE
- **AFFAIRE** communicable – civil case in which the Attorney-General's Department is required by law to file pleadings.

COMMUNICATION – discovery (and inspection) or handing over (of documents).
- **DOCUMENT** – **obtenir communication des documents** – inspect the documents.
- **DOSSIER** – **communication du dossier** – making the file available for inspection; producing or handing over the file for inspection; right of civil servant etc to see his personal file.
- **PIÈCE**
  - •• **DEMANDE de communication de pièces** – application for production or handing over of documents for inspection (application for discovery).

- •• **EXCEPTION de communication de pièces** – objection which can be raised requesting the court to stay proceedings so long as the opposite party refuses to make his documents available.

COMMUNION
- **EXISTENCE** – **communion d'existence** – consortium.

COMMUNISTE – co-owner.

COMOURANTS – persons dying in the same incident.

COMPARAÎTRE – appear (before a court); enter an appearance (by appointing a solicitor or counsel).
- **CITER à comparaître en justice** – summon to appear in court.
- **INVITER à comparaître** – summon.
- **JURIDIQUEMENT** – **comparaître juridiquement** – appear in court.

COMPARUTION – appearance (in court), which implies appointment of counsel (**avocat**) and in the court of appeal a solicitor (**avoué**) as well.
- **DÉFAUT de comparution** – failure to appear; default of appearance.
- **IMMÉDIAT** – **comparution immédiate** – immediate summary trial in simple criminal cases (ie where no further investigations are required).
- **PERSONNEL** – **comparution personnelle** – examination of one or both parties (in civil proceedings).

COMPENSATION – set-off.
- **CHAMBRE de compensation** – clearing-house.
- **EXCEPTION de compensation** – set-off.

COMPENSATOIRE
- **PRESTATION compensatoire** – pecuniary provision on divorce (intended to equalise the position of the ex-spouses).

COMPENSER – set off; offset.
- **DÉPENS** – **compenser les dépens** – order each party to bear its own costs.

COMPÉTENCE – jurisdiction; power; authority; competence; function.
- **ABSOLU** – **compétence absolue** – jurisdiction ratione materiae; jurisdiction based on the subject-matter.

- **APPEL** – compétence à charge d'appel – jurisdiction subject to appeal.
- **ATTRIBUTION** – compétence d'attribution – special jurisdiction; jurisdiction ratione materiae (of a particular court); jurisdiction based on the subject-matter.
- **COMPÉTENCE de la compétence** – jurisdiction to decide questions of jurisdiction.
- **CONFLIT de compétence** – dispute as to jurisdiction.
- **CONSULTATIF** – compétence consultative – power to give advisory opinions; advisory jurisdiction.
- **DÉCLINATOIRE de compétence** – objection to jurisdiction.
- **DÉCLINER compétence** – refuse to assume or exercise jurisdiction.
- **DÉLÉGATION de la compétence** – delegation of authority; delegation of powers.
- **DÉVOLUTION de la compétence** – transfer of jurisdiction or powers.
- **ÉCHAPPER à la compétence de** – fall outside the jurisdiction of.
- **ÉLECTION** – compétence d'élection – jurisdiction of choice.
- **GRACIER** - compétence pour gracier – prerogative of mercy.
- **IMPLICITE** – compétence implicite – inherent jurisdiction.
- **JUDICIAIRE** – compétence judiciaire – jurisdiction of the ordinary courts.
- **JURIDICTION** – compétence de pleine juridiction – power to make any order required by the justice of a case (to deal with all aspects of a case).
- **LIÉ** – compétence liée – obligation to apply the law as it stands without exercising a discretion; official's duty to act strictly in accordance with the law with no margin for exercising his personal judgment.
  - •• **DE compétence liée** – limited or controlled in the exercise of a power or discretion.
- **LIEU** – compétence à raison du lieu – jurisdiction ratione loci.
- **MATÉRIEL** – compétence matérielle – jurisdiction of a criminal court to try felonies or misdemeanours or petty offences, as the case may be.
- **MATIÈRE** – compétence à raison de la matière – jurisdiction ratione materiae (based on the subject-matter).
- **OPTION de compétence** – choice of jurisdiction.

- **PERSONAE** – compétence ratione personae – juridiction rationae personae; personal jurisdiction; territorial jurisdiction
- **PERSONNALITÉ ACTIVE** – compétence de la personnalité active – jurisdiction based on the nationality (or domicile) of the offender or tortfeasor.
- **PERSONNEL** – compétence personnelle – personal jurisdiction of a criminal court to try certain classes of offender.
- **PLEINE JURIDICTION** – see JURIDICTION above.
- **PROROGATION de compétence** – extension of jurisdiction (of a court).
- **RATIONE LOCI** – compétence ratione loci – see LIEU above.
- **RATIONE MATERIAE** – compétence ratione materiae – see MATIÈRE above.
- **RATIONE TEMPORIS** – compétence ratione temporis – jurisdiction ratione temporis.
- **RÉEL** – compétence réelle – jurisdiction based on the subject-matter of the offence.
- **RELATIF** – compétence relative – territorial jurisdiction.
- **RESSORTIR à la compétence de** – fall within the jurisdiction of.
- **TAUX de compétence** – financial limit on the jurisdiction (of a lower court); sum up to which a court has jurisdiction.
- **TERRITORIAL** – compétence territoriale – territorial jurisdiction.
- **TRIBUNAL** – relevant de la compétence des tribunaux ordinaires – falling under the jurisdiction of the ordinary courts.

COMPLAINTE – action for interference with or denial of possession.

COMPLAISANCE
- **BILLET (EFFET, TRAITE) de complaisance** – accommodation bill.

COMPLÉMENT
- **ENQUÊTE** – complément d'enquête – further investigations; further inquiries (into the facts).
- **FAMILIAL** – complément familial – family supplement.
- **INSTRUCTION** – complément d'instruction – further investigations; further inquiries (into the facts).

COMPLÉMENTAIRE – supplementary; further.

- **ACCORD complémentaire** – supplementary agreement
- **OBSERVATIONS complémentaires** – further observations.
- **PEINE** – **peine complémentaire** – additional penalty (measure).

COMPLICE – accomplice; accessory; (divorce) co-respondent.

COMPLICITÉ – assistance in crime; aiding and abetting; instigating; complicity (in a crime).

COMPLOT – conspiracy.
- **SÛRETÉ** – **complot contre la sûreté de l'État** – treasonable conspiracy.

COMPOSANT
- **DROIT** – **composants du droit à un procès équitable** – ingredients of the right to a fair trial.

COMPOSER
- **TRIBUNAL** – **le tribunal n'était pas composé régulièrement** – the court was not properly constituted.

COMPOSITEUR
- **AMIABLE** – **comme amiable compositeur** – as mediator; ex aequo et bono; on equitable principles.

COMPROMETTRE
- **AFFAIRE** – **compromettre une affaire** – submit a case to arbitration.
- **CAPACITÉ de compromettre** – capacity to enter into an arbitration agreement.

COMPROMIS – arbitration agreement relating to a dispute which has already arisen; compromise; settlement; sale agreement; precontract.
- **EXTRAJUDICIAIRE** – **compromis extrajudiciaire** – settlement out of court.
- **JUDICIAIRE** – **compromis judiciaire** – judicial settlement.
- **SUCCESSORAL** – **compromis successoral** – family arrangement.

COMPROMISSOIRE
- **CLAUSE compromissoire** – arbitration clause agreeing to submit future differences to arbitration.

COMPTABILITÉ – accounting system; records; book-keeping.
- **PASSER en comptabilité** – enter in an account.
- **PIÈCE de comptabilité** – voucher.

COMPTABLE – accountant; bookkeeper.

COMPTANT
- **COURS au comptant** – spot price.

COMPTE
- **APURER un compte** – check and settle an account.
- **ARTICLE de compte** – entry.
- **BUDGÉTAIRE** – **compte budgétaire** – budget account.
- **DÉPENSE** – **compte de dépenses** – expenditure account.
- **DÉPÔT** – **compte de dépôt** – current account.
- **EXPLOITATION** – **compte d'exploitation** – production account; trading account.
- **GESTION** – **compte de gestion (budgétaire)** – (budgetary) management account.
- **JOINT** – **compte joint** – joint bank account.
- **RECETTE** – **compte de recettes** – revenue account.
- **RENDU**
  - **ANALYTIQUE** – **compte rendu analytique** – summary record.
  - **ANNUEL** – **compte rendu annuel** – annual report.
  - **DÉBAT** – **compte rendu des débats** – official record of debates.
- **RÉSULTAT** – **compte de résultat** – profit and loss account.
- **RETOUR** – **compte de retour** – amount of expenses added to a redraft; notarial charges on a dishonoured bill.
- **TENIR compte à quelqu'un des intérêts** – pay someone the interest on a sum.
- **TRÉSORERIE** – **compte de trésorerie** – treasury suspense account; (in plural) cash accounts.
- **VÉRIFICATION des comptes** – audit.

COMPULSOIRE – former procedure for compelling production of documents; discovery.

CONCÉDANT – authority granting a concession.

CONCENTRATION – limitation of an obligation to one of two alternative acts of performance; concentration of executive power at the seat of government.

CONCEPT
- **JURIDIQUE** – **concept juridique** – legal concept.
- **LÉGAL** – **concept légal** – statutory definition.

CONCERT
- **NATION** – **concert des nations** – the international community.

CONCERTATION
- **FRAUDULEUX** – **concertation frauduleuse** – collusion.

CONCESSION – concession; franchise.
- **IMMOBILIER** – **concession immobilière** – long lease of realty with certain statutory characteristics (eg no premium may be paid).
- **LICENCE** – **concession de licence** – granting (grant) of a licence.
- **VOIRIE** – **concession de voirie** – contractual grant by an administrative authority of the right to occupy part of the highway or some other public place.

CONCESSIONNAIRE
- **LICENCE** – **concessionnaire de licence** – licensee.
- **MINE** – **concessionnaire de mine** – person operating a mine under a concession.

CONCILIATEUR – Parliamentary Commissioner; Ombudsman; conciliator.

CONCILIATION – conciliation; (friendly) settlement.

CONCLUANT – cogent.

CONCLURE – enter into (a contract); file (written) pleadings; plead; make oral submissions; submit.
- **À** – **conclure à (l'absence de violation de la Convention)** – submit that (there has been no violation of the Convention).
- **FOND** – **conclure au fond** – plead on the merits.

CONCLUSION – submission; pleading; conclusion; finding.
- **AMPLIATIF** – **conclusions ampliatives** – supplementary pleadings.
- **APPEL** – **conclusions d'appel** – notice and grounds of appeal.
- **BÉNÉFICE** – **adjuger au demandeur le bénéfice de ses conclusions** – give judgment for the plaintiff (in accordance with his statement of claim).
- **DÉFENCE** – **conclusions en défence** – defence (pleadings).
- **DÉPOSER des conclusions** – make an application; file pleadings.
  - •• **BARRE** – **conclusions déposées à la barre** – pleadings filed in the registry.
- **DONNER** – **le ministère public a donné ses conclusions** – State Counsel presented his case.
- **EXCEPTIONNEL** – **conclusions exceptionnelles** – pleadings raising a preliminary objection.
- **FOND** – **conclusions au fond** – submissions on the merits.
- **PRENDRE des conclusions** – file pleadings; make an application (in court proceedings).
- **PRIS** – **conclusions prises en appel** – notice and grounds of appeal.
- **SUBSIDIAIRE** – **conclusions subsidiaires** – alternative submissions.
- **TRIBUNAL** – **conclusions du tribunal** – findings of the court.

CONCORDANCE
- **VOLONTÉ** – **concordance des volontés** – agreement of the parties, ie the fact that they are ad idem.

CONCORDANT
- **OPINION concordante** – concurring opinion.
- **TÉMOIGNAGES concordants** – corroborative evidence.

CONCORDAT – composition or arrangement with creditors (approved by the court); treaty between a state and the Holy See.

CONCOURS – concurrence.
- **CRÉANCIER** – **concours des créanciers** – rule that the creditors bear the loss (arising from insolvency) in proportion to the amount of their claims.
- **INFRACTION** – **concours d'infractions** – coincidence of several offences.
  - •• **IDÉAL** – **concours idéal d'infractions** – single act fulfilling the conditions required to constitute various offences; a complex action which, though fulfilling the conditions required to constitute various offences, is nevertheless treated as a single offence owing to the presence of some unifying factor; notional plurality of offences.
  - •• **RÉEL** – **concours réel d'infractions** – plurality of offences dealt with in the same proceedings.
- **LOI du concours** – equality of rights to payment on execution as between unsecured creditors.
- **VOLONTÉ** – **concours de volontés** – agreement; being ad idem; concordance of wills.

CONCRETO – see IN CONCRETO.

CONCUBIN – cohabitee; male partner; unmarried consort; reputed spouse.

CONCUBINAGE – unmarried cohabitation.

CONCURRENCE
- **APPEL à la concurrence** – call for tenders.
- **DÉLOYAL** – concurrence déloyale – unfair competition.
- **DÛ** – à due concurrence – pro tanto.
- **PLEIN** – principe de pleine concurrence – arm's-length principle.

CONCUSSION – extortion or dishonest receipt of money by a public officer.

CONDAMNATION – conviction (and sentence); sentence; judgment against.
- **ANTÉRIEUR** – condamnation antérieure – previous conviction.
- **CIVIL** – condamnation civile – judgment against the defendant in civil proceedings.
- **CONTUMACE** – condamnation par contumace – conviction in absentia.
- **DÉFAUT** – condamnation par défaut – (crim) conviction in absentia; (civ) judgment by default.
- **DÉPENS** – condamnation aux dépens – order for costs.
- **SURSIS** – condamnation avec sursis – conditional sentence; suspended sentence; probation.

CONDAMNÉ – convicted person.
- **PEINE** – condamné en cours de peine – prisoner serving his sentence; convicted prisoner.

CONDAMNER – find guilty (of); convict (of); order to pay; sentence (to).
- **AMENDE** – être condamné à une amende – sentenced to a fine; ordered to pay a fine.
- **VERSER** – condamner à verser une provision – order to make an advance payment (for maintenance etc).

CONDITION
- **ASSUJETTISSEMENT** – condition d'assujettissement – qualifying condition.
- **AVÈNEMENT d'une condition** – occurrence, fulfilment, performance or satisfaction of a condition.
- **CASUEL** – condition casuelle – condition whose occurrence depends entirely on chance.
- **ÉTRANGER** – condition des étrangers – status of aliens.

- **EXIGIBILITÉ** – condition d'exigibilité – condition on which payment may be demanded.
- **EXTINCTIF** – condition extinctive – condition subsequent (of (in) a contract etc, to a transaction etc).
- **FÉMININ** – condition féminine – status of women.
- **FOND** – condition de fond – essential condition (**la loi nationale régit les conditions de fond de leur mariage** – the law of the nationality governs the essential validity of their marriage).
- **FORME** – condition de forme – requirement as to form; formal requirement; formality.
- **GÉNÉRAL** – conditions générales – standard terms and conditions.
- **GESTION** – conditions de gestion d'un immeuble – rules for the management of a building.
- **IMPLICITE** – condition implicite – implied condition.
- **INDIVIDU** – la condition de l'individu – the rights, duties and liberties of the individual; status of the individual.
- **JURIDIQUE** – condition juridique – legal position; legal status.
- **MEILLEUR** – contracter dans les meilleures conditions – obtain the best terms.
- **MIXTE** – condition mixte – condition depending on the will of one of the parties and that of a third party.
- **NULLITÉ** – condition de nullité – ground of nullity.
- **PERSONNE** – condition des personnes – law of persons.
- **PRÉALABLE** – condition préalable – prior condition; prerequisite.
- **RÉSOLUTOIRE** – condition résolutoire – condition subsequent (of (in) a contract etc, to a transaction etc).
- **RESSOURCE** – condition de ressources – means test.
- **REQUIS** – condition requise – requirement.
- **RÉUNIR** – quand les conditions sont réunies – when the conditions are satisfied.
- **SURVENANCE d'une condition** – occurrence, fulfilment, performance or satisfaction of a condition.
- **SUSPENSIF** – condition suspensive – condition precedent (of (in) a contract etc, to a transaction etc).

CONDOMINIUM – condominion.

CONDUITE – behaviour.

CONFESSIONNEL – denominational.

CONFESSOIRE
- **ACTION confessoire** – action in rem to be put in possession of a usufruct (life tenancy) or to establish one's title to an easement, profit, etc as a right in rem.

CONFIANCE
- **ABUS de confiance** – misappropriation; embezzlement (which can only be committed by a clerk or servant); fraudulent conversion; fraudulent breach of trust.
- **HOMME de confiance** – confidential adviser or agent.
- **LÉGITIME** – **confiance légitime** – the reasonable (legitimate) expectations of the other party.

CONFINANT
- **À** – **confinant à** – abutting on.

CONFISCATION – confiscation; forfeiture.

CONFLIT
- **ARRÊTÉ de conflit** – Prefect's order transferring a jurisdictional dispute (between the ordinary and administrative courts) to the Jurisdiction Court (**Tribunal des conflits**); jurisdiction order.
- **ATTRIBUTION** – **conflit d'attribution(s)** – dispute as to jurisdiction between the ordinary courts and the administrative authorities or courts, or between two administrative departments.
  - •• **NÉGATIF** – **conflit négatif (d'attribution(s))** – situation where both courts (authorities) involved consider they have no jurisdiction to deal with the case; refusal of jurisdiction by both the ordinary and the administrative courts.
  - •• **POSITIF** – **conflit positif (d'attribution(s))** – situation where both courts (authorities) involved claim jurisdiction; acceptance of jurisdiction by both the ordinary and the administrative courts.
- **COLLECTIF** – **conflit collectif** – labour dispute; industrial dispute.
- **COMPÉTENCE** – **conflit de compétence** – dispute as to jurisdiction.
- **ÉLEVER le conflit** – (of the Prefect) raise the question of jurisdiction.
- **JUGEMENT** – **conflit de jugements** – procedure whereby a litigant can obtain a decision from the Jurisdiction Court (**Tribunal des conflits**) when there have been conflicting judgments by the ordinary and the administrative courts.
- **JURIDICTION** – **conflit de juridictions** – conflicting decisions relating to jurisdiction (conflict of jurisdiction), ie where two different courts both claim or decline to exercise jurisdiction to decide a case; conflict of jurisdiction between the courts of two or more different countries.
- **LOI** – **conflit de lois** – conflict of laws; choice of law; private international law.
  - •• **DROIT des conflits de lois** – private international law; conflict (of laws); rules governing choice of law.
- **NÉGATIF** – see ATTRIBUTION above.
- **POSITIF** – see ATTRIBUTION above.
- **RÈGLE de conflit (de lois) (règle sur les conflits)** – rule of private international law; choice-of-law rule.
- **SOCIAL** – **conflits sociaux** – labour disputes; industrial disputes.
- **TRANCHER un conflit** – settle a dispute.
- **TRAVAIL** – **conflit du travail** – industrial dispute; labour dispute.
- **TRIBUNAL des conflits** – court for settling questions of jurisdiction and inconsistent judgments between administrative courts on the one hand and ordinary courts on the other; Jurisdiction Court.

CONFONDRE
- **SE confondre** – be merged.

CONFORME
- **À** – **conforme à** – compatible with.
  - •• **LOI** – **conforme à la loi** – lawful; in accordance with law.

CONFORMER
- **SE conformer à** – comply with.

CONFORMITÉ
- **USAGE** – **conformité à l'usage envisagé par les parties** – fitness (ie for the purpose known to the vendor).

CONFUSION – merger.
- **PART** – **confusion de part** – inability to assign paternity owing to a conflict of two legal presumptions of paternity of two successive husbands of the same woman.
- **PEINE** – **confusion des peines** – concurrent sentences.

- **POUVOIR** – **confusion des pouvoirs** – failure to observe the principle of the separation of powers.

CONGÉ – notice; leave.
- **BAIL** – **congé de bail** – notice to terminate; notice to quit.
- **PÉNITENTIAIRE** – **congé pénitentiaire** – prison leave.

CONGÉDIEMENT – dismissal; termination of a contract of employment.

CONGRÉGATION – religious order.

CONGRÈS – joint meeting of both chambers of the French parliament to pass an Act amending the Constitution.

CONJOINT
- **CODÉBITEURS conjoints** – persons severally liable (each for his share).
- **DEMANDE conjointe** – joint petition for divorce or judicial separation (by both parties).
- **DIFFÉRENDS entre conjoints** – marital disputes.
- **OBLIGATION conjointe** – several liability.
- **REQUÊTE conjointe** – joint application (method of commencing contentious proceedings by parties agreeing to submit their dispute to the court).
- **SURVIVANT** – **conjoint survivant** – surviving spouse.

CONJOINTEMENT – jointly; together.

CONJUGAL consortium.
- **DEVOIR conjugal** – duty to have sexual relations with one's spouse.
- **DOMICILE conjugal** – matrimonial home.
- **UNION conjugale** – consortium.

CONNAISSANCE
- **CESSION** – **connaissance spéciale et personnelle de la première cession** – actual notice of the first assignment.
- **PRENDRE connaissance du dossier** – inspect the file.

CONNAISSEMENT – bill of lading.
- **CHEF** – **connaissement chef** – captain's copy of the bill.
- **DESTINATAIRE** – **connaissement destinataire** – consignee's copy of a bill of lading.
- **FLUVIAL** – **connaissement fluvial** – river bill of lading.
- **INTRANSMISSIBLE** – **connaissement intransmissible** – non-negotiable bill of lading.

- **NET** – **connaissement net** – clean bill of lading.
- **ORDRE** – **connaissement à ordre** – order bill of lading.
- **PORTEUR** – **connaissement au porteur** – bearer bill of lading.

CONNAÎTRE
- **DE** – **connaître de** – hear; deal with; hear and determine; entertain; take cognisance of.
  - •• **AFFAIRE** – **connaître d'une affaire** – (have jurisdiction to) hear a case; deal with a case.
  - •• **APPELER** – **qui sont appelés à connaître des affaires de divorce** – which try divorce cases.
  - •• **DEMANDE** – **connaître de la demande** – entertain the proceedings (the claim).
  - •• **FOND** – **connaître du fond d'une affaire** – deal with the merits of a case.
  - •• **POUVOIR connaître de** – have jurisdiction to decide.
  - •• **PROCÉDURE** – **connaître de procédures** – entertain proceedings.
- **DROIT** – **que connaît le droit allemand** – existing in (recognised by (in)) German law.

CONNEXE
- **À** – **connexe à** – arising from the same transaction; related to; closely connected with.

CONNEXITÉ – the relationship existing between two or more cases or offences which justifies their being joined and tried together; close connection.
- **EXCEPTION de connexité** – defence that related proceedings are pending in another court (lis alibi pendens).

CONNIVENCE – collusion.

CONSANGUIN – of the half blood on the father's side.

CONSEIL – council; board; commission; guardian; adviser; counsel.
- **ADMINISTRATION** – **conseil d'administration** – board of directors.
- **CABINET** – **conseil de cabinet** – meeting of the government chaired by the Prime Minister.
- **CHAMBRE du conseil** – judge's chambers; (Belg) Court in Chambers (which, inter alia, decides whether to commit for trial).

•• **EN chambre du conseil** – in private; in chambers; the court in chambers.

• **CONSTITUTIONNEL** – **Conseil constitutionnel** – Constitutional Council.

• **COURONNE** – **Conseil de la couronne** – (British) Privy Council.

• **ÉDUCATION** – **Conseil supérieur de l'Éducation nationale** – National Education Council (advisory body attached to the Ministry of Education).

• **ENQUÊTE** – **conseil d'enquête** – commission of inquiry.

• **ENTREPRISE** – **conseil d'entreprise** – works council.

• **ÉTAT** – **Conseil d'État** – highest administrative court and government adviser on questions arising in connection with legislation (not usually translated); State Council.

• **FAMILLE** – **conseil de famille** – family council.

• **GÉNÉRAL** – **conseil général** – Département Council; County Council.

• **GUERRE** – **conseil de guerre en campagne** – field court martial.

• **JUDICIAIRE** – **conseil judiciaire** – judicial guardian (appointed by the court to assist feeble-minded persons, alcoholics and spendthrifts); supervisor (appointed by the court).

• **JURIDIQUE** – **conseil juridique** – (formerly) legal adviser; legal representative; legal assistance.

•• **ADJOINDRE un conseil juridique à quelqu'un** – provide with legal assistance.

• **JUSTICE** – **conseil de justice** – naval court martial with jurisdiction over lesser offences committed by the NCOs and crew of a man-of-war.

• **MAGISTRATURE** – **Conseil supérieur de la magistrature** – Judicial Service Commission.

• **MINISTRE** – **conseil des ministres** – (meeting of the) Cabinet presided over by the President of the Republic (if he is not present, the expression used is **conseil de cabinet**).

• **MUNICIPAL** – **conseil municipal** – district council.

• **ORDRE** – **conseil de l'ordre (des avocats, des médecins, etc)** – Bar Council, General Medical Council, etc.

• **PRÉFECTURE** – **conseil de préfecture** – administrative court.

• **PRISE** – **conseil des prises** – prize court.

• **PRUD'HOMME** – **conseil de prud'hommes** – industrial (relations) tribunal; Labour Court.

• **RÉVISION** – **conseil de révision** (mil) – (formerly) recruitment board.

• **SURVEILLANCE** – **conseil de surveillance** (translation of German **Aufsichtsrat**) – supervising board.

• **SYNDICAL** – **conseil syndical** – managing committee elected by the co-owners of a building to assist the manager.

• **TUTELLE** – **conseil de tutelle** – committee of guardians; guardianship council; (UN) Trusteeship Council.

CONSEILLER – judge (of a superior or administrative court); (legal) adviser.

• **ÉTAT** – **conseiller d'État** – member (judge) of the Conseil d'État.

• **GÉNÉRAL** – **conseiller général** – département (county) councillor.

• **JURIDIQUE** – **conseiller juridique** – legal adviser.

• **MISE EN ÉTAT** – **conseiller de la mise en état** – judge directing the preparations for trial.

• **RAPPORTEUR** – **conseiller rapporteur** – reporting judge (ie judge who prepares a report on a case for a court).

• **RÉFÉRENDAIRE** – **conseiller référendaire** – auxiliary judge (of the Court of Cassation); middle-ranking member of the Auditor-General's Department (**Cour des comptes**).

CONSEILLER-MAÎTRE – senior member of the Auditor-General's Department (**Cour des Comptes**); senior auditor.

CONSENSUALISME

• **PRINCIPE de consensualisme** – rule that the simple agreement of the parties without any further formalities is sufficient to establish a contract.

CONSENTEMENT – consent.

• **VICE du consentement** – defect in consent (ie error, fraud or duress); vitiated consent; absence of consent.

CONSENTIR – grant (a lease).

CONSERVATEUR

• **HYPOTHÈQUE** – **conservateur des hypothèques** – Chief Registrar of the Mortgage Registry (of the Land (Charges) Registry); Mortgage Registrar; Land Registrar.

CONSERVATION

- **DROIT** – **conservation des droits** – preservation of rights.
- **HYPOTHÈQUE** – **conservation des hypothèques** – Mortgage (Land (Charges)) Registry.
- **VALEUR** – **conservation des valeurs** – safe custody of securities.

CONSERVATOIRE

- **MESURES conservatoires** – steps (measures) to preserve rights, property, evidence, the status quo, the present position; temporary administrative measures; protective measures; precautionary measures; interim (provisional) measures.
- **SAISIE conservatoire** – preventive attachment, ie an attachment before the creditor has obtained judgment in order to prevent the debtor rendering his property inaccessible to execution by dissipating or transferring his assets. (Cf Mareva injunction (asset-freezing order).)

CONSIDÉRANT (QUE) – whereas.

CONSIDÉRANTS – reasons; grounds; recitals.

CONSIDÉRATION – (in plural) reasons; grounds; recitals.

- **MORAL** – **jouir de la plus haute considération morale** – be of high moral character.

CONSIDÉRER – hold.

CONSIGNATAIRE – depositary.

CONSIGNATION – deposit.

- **JUDICIAIRE** – **consignation judiciaire** – payment into court.
- **JUSTICE** – **consignation en justice** – payment into court; placing in the custody of the court.

CONSIGNER – enter.

CONSILIUM FRAUDIS – awareness on the part of a debtor and the person with whom he is dealing that the transaction will increase the extent of his insolvency.

CONSOLIDATION – merger.

- **USUFRUIT** – **consolidation d'usufruit** – merger of the usufruct (life interest) in the fee simple or other estate out of which it issues.

CONSOLIDER – confirm (eg a right) by satisfying a condition precedent.

CONSOMMABLE

- **BIEN** – **biens consommables** – consumable articles or goods.

CONSOMMATION – completion (of an offence).

- **CRÉDIT à la consommation** – consumer credit.
- **CRÉDIT** – **état de consommation des crédits** – (statement of the) amount of appropriations used; (statement of) utilisation of appropriations.
- **DROIT de consommation** – excise duty.
- **MARIAGE** – **consommation de mariage** – consummation of marriage.
- **PRÊT de consommation** – loan of money (or other fungible or consumable goods) of which the borrower is under an obligation to restore an equivalent quantity; money loan.

CONSOMMER – complete (an offence).

CONSOMPTIBLES – consumable goods.

CONSTANT – established.

- **JURISPRUDENCE constante** – established case-law; established precedents.

CONSTAT – finding; hearing; taking of evidence; report as to the existence of certain facts; formal record(ing) of evidence by a bailiff.

- **ADULTÈRE** – **constat d'adultère** – report establishing adultery.
- **HUISSIER** – **constat d'huissier** – bailiff's official report (on some matter of fact).
- **JUDICIAIRE** – **constat judiciaire** – taking of evidence.
- **POLICE** – **constat de police** – police report.

CONSTATATION – placing on record (eg in a contract or judgment); recording; finding; declaration; (in plural) (of a court) obtaining evidence of facts from an expert witness.

- **ACTION en constatation** – declaratory action; action for a declaration; action to establish the facts.
- **DROIT** – **conclusions en constatation de droit** – application for a declaratory judgment.
- **FAIT** – **constatation matérielle des faits par le juge** – ascertainment of the facts by the court (in person or through an expert).

- **IDENTITÉ** – **constatation d'identité** – finding or establishment of a person's identity; finding that two things are identical.
- **INFRACTION** – **constatation de l'infraction** – finding of guilt.
- **INFRACTION** – **constatation d'une infraction** – finding (decision) that an offence has been committed.

CONSTATER – find; make a finding; record; ascertain; establish; report; evidence; become apparent to; state.
- **ÉCRIT constatant la créance** – writing evidencing (the right to obtain payment of) the debt, obligation, claim, etc.
- **INFRACTION** – **constater une infraction** – find (decide) that an offence has been committed.

CONSTITUANT – person creating a right in rem; settlor; grantor of a usufruct, easement, etc.
- **ASSEMBLÉE constituante** – constituent assembly.
- **GAGE** – **constituant de gage** – pledgor.

CONSTITUER
- **AVOCAT** – **constituer avocat** – instruct counsel to defend (or conduct) proceedings (equivalent to acknowledging service of a writ and giving notice of intention to defend (formerly entering an appearance)).
- **AVOUÉ** – **constituer avoué** – instructing a solicitor to defend (or conduct) proceedings in the Court of Appeal.
- **DEMEURE** – **constituer en demeure** – give notice to pay or perform.
- **MANDATAIRE** – **constituer un mandataire** – appoint an agent or attorney.
- **PARTIE CIVILE** – **se constituer partie civile** – sue for damages in criminal proceedings.
- **PRISONNIER** – **se constituer prisonnier** – give oneself up.
- **SÛRETÉ** – **constituer une sûreté** – give security.

CONSTITUT
- **POSSESSOIRE** – **constitut possessoire** – agreement by which the vendor recognises that he holds the property in the thing sold on behalf of the purchaser; transfer of the ownership of property of which the vendor retains possession as bailee.

CONSTITUTIF – creating or altering rights or status.
- **ACTE** – **acte constitutif** – instrument or legal transaction creating or altering rights.

- •• **GAGE** – **acte constitutif de gage** – contract of pledge.
- •• **HYPOTHÈQUE** – **acte constitutif d'hypothèque** – mortgage (referring to the instrument).
- •• **INFRACTION** – **acte constitutif de l'infraction** – actus reus.
- **ÉLÉMENT constitutif** – (factual) ingredient.
  - •• **INFRACTION** – **élément constitutif de l'infraction** – essential element, condition, requirement or ingredient of the offence.
- **JUGEMENT constitutif** – judgment in rem, effective against the whole world (erga omnes), creating or altering a status.

CONSTITUTION
- **AVOCAT** – **constitution d'avocat** – instructing counsel to defend (or conduct) proceedings (equivalent to acknowledging service of a writ and giving notice of intention to defend (formerly entering an appearance)).
- **AVOUÉ** – **constitution d'avoué** – instructing a solicitor to defend (or conduct) proceedings in the Court of Appeal.
- **SOCIÉTÉ** – **constitution d'une société** – founding (formation) of a partnership or company.
- **USUFRUIT** – **constitution d'usufruit** – grant of a usufruct (life estate); settlement.

CONSTRUIRE
- **PERMIS de construire** – building licence.

CONSULTATIF
- **VOIX** – **avec voix consultative** – non-voting.

CONSULTATION – opinion on facts at issue given by an expert witness commissioned by the court after an examination in the presence of the parties but without an extensive investigation.
- **DOSSIER** – **consultation du dossier** – inspection of the file
- **JURIDIQUE** – **consultation juridique** – legal opinion; legal advice.

CONSULTER
- **DOSSIER** – **consulter le dossier** – inspect the file.

CONTENANCE (d'un terrain) – area.

CONTENTIEUX (adj) – disputed; judicial; adjudicative.

- **COMPTE** – **sommes prises en compte contentieux** – disputed claims.
- **RECOURS contentieux** – recourse to the courts; court (legal) proceedings.

CONTENTIEUX (noun) – contentious proceedings; type of case; branch of litigation; actions; cases.

- **ADMINISTRATIF** – **contentieux administratif** – administrative proceedings.
  - ** **TRIBUNAUX du contentieux administratif** – administrative courts.
- **ANNULATION** – **contentieux de l'annulation** – proceedings to set aside an administrative decision.
- **ASSEMBLÉE du contentieux (du Conseil d'État)** – Combined Court of the (Conseil d'État).
- **ÉCONOMIQUE** – **contentieux économique** – commercial litigation.
- **EXCÈS DE POUVOIR** – **contentieux de l'excès de pouvoir** – proceedings based on grounds such as lack of jurisdiction, error of procedure, misapplication of the law, misuse of a discretion or ultra vires (exceeding or misusing one's authority); judicial review (of administrative action).
- **NON-VALEUR** – **contentieux et mise en non-valeur** – disputed items and bad debts.
- **OBJECTIF** – **contentieux objectif** – proceedings based on an infringement of the law not involving an individual right (proceedings in rem).
- **RÉPRESSION** – **contentieux de la répression** – proceedings relating to administrative offences.
- **SECTION du contentieux (du Conseil d'État)** – Litigation (Judicial) Division (of the Conseil d'État).
- **SERVICE du contentieux** – litigation department; legal department.
- **SUBJECTIF** – **contentieux subjectif** – proceedings based on the infringement of an individual right.

CONTESTATION – objection; application to set aside; dispute.

- **ÉLEVER** – **aucune contestation n'ayant été élevée contre cette décision** – this decision having gone unchallenged.
- **ÉTAT** – **action en contestation d'état** – action to disprove one's descent from one's ostensible parents; action to disprove a person's apparent status, descent or nationality.
- **LÉGITIMITÉ** – **contestation de la légitimité** – action to have a person declared

illegitimate.

CONTESTER – dispute; apply to set aside; deny; put in issue.

CONTIGU – adjacent.

- **FONDS contigu** – adjacent premises, property, land.

CONTINGENT

- **IMMIGRATION** – **contingent d'immigration** – immigration quota.

CONTINGENTEMENT

- **DEVISE** – **contingentement de devises** – exchange control.

CONTONDANT

- **ARME contondante** – blunt instrument.
- **OBJET contondant** – blunt instrument.

CONTRACTANT – contracting party.

CONTRACTER

- **ENGAGEMENT** – **contracter un engagement** – enter into a commitment or obligation.

CONTRACTUEL – (adj) in contract; (noun) temporary public servant.

CONTRADICTION

- **POSSESSION** – **contradiction de la possession** – denial of the right to possess.

CONTRADICTOIRE – involving the participation, representation or hearing of both parties; in the presence of the accused or both parties; adversarial; inter partes; normal; ordinary. (May sometimes be omitted in translation where it is obvious from the context that the proceedings are inter partes.)

- **NON contradictoire** – ex parte.
- **PRINCIPE du contradictoire (de la contradiction)** – the rule that both parties shall be heard (auditur et altera pars); adversarial principle. (Each party should have an opportunity of presenting his case and be fully informed of the case (documents, evidence, arguments, etc) relied on by his opponent, and the judgment must not be based on a point which has not been argued in court.)
- **RÉPUTÉ** – **jugement réputé contradictoire** – judgment deemed to have been given in proceedings in which both sides were represented (after both parties had been heard).

CONTRADICTOIREMENT – in the presence of (with the participation of, after hearing) both parties; inter partes; on equal terms; on an equal footing.

- **NON contradictoirement** – ex parte.

CONTRAIGNANT – coercive; binding.

- **CIRCONSTANCES contraignantes** – compelling circumstances.

CONTRAINTE – coercion; duress; order to pay issued by various authorities, esp. the collector of taxes, with statutory authority; (means of) enforcement; (translation of German **Haftung**) liability.

- **CORPS** – contrainte par corps – enforcement against the person; civil imprisonment; imprisonment for debt; imprisonment in default (for non-payment) (of a fine etc).
- **MESURE de contrainte** – coercive measure.
- **SANS contrainte** – unenforceable.
- **URBANISME** – contraintes d'urbanisme – (town-)planning requirements.

CONTRARIÉTÉ

- **JUGEMENT** – contrariété de jugements – conflicting (incompatible) judgments (if they are in the same case, this constitutes a ground for an appeal in law to the Court of Cassation); procedure whereby a litigant can obtain a decision from the Jurisdiction Court (**Tribunal des conflits**) when there have been conflicting judgments by the ordinary and the administrative courts.
- **MOTIF** – contrariété de motifs – inconsistent reasons in a judgment.

CONTRARIO – see A CONTRARIO.

CONTRAT

- **ACCESSOIRE** – contrat accessoire – collateral contract.
- **ADDITIONNEL** – contrat additionnel – supplementary contract.
- **ADHÉSION** – contrat d'adhésion – standard-form contract (imposed by the stronger party).
- **ADMINISTRATIF** – contrat administratif – contract subject to the jurisdiction of the Administrative Courts and governed by administrative law.
- **ALÉATOIRE** – contrat aléatoire – contract involving a risk or hasard for one or both parties, eg insurance, wager or life annuity.
- **AMODIATION** – contrat d'amodiation – lease in which the rent is calculated as a proportion of the produce of the land.

- **BIENFAISANCE** – contrat de bienfaisance – contract without consideration.
- **BIÈRE** – contrat de bière – exclusive supply contract.
- **BONNES MŒURS** – see MŒURS below.
- **COLLECTIF** – contrat collectif (de travail) – collective (labour) agreement.
- **COMMUTATIF** – contrat commutatif – contract based on an exchange of benefits; commutative contract.
- **COURTAGE** – contrat de courtage – brokerage contract.
- **DIRIGÉ** – contrat dirigé – controlled contract.
- **EMPHYTÉOSE** – contrat d'emphytéose – long lease.
- **ENTREPRISE** – contrat d'entreprise – contract for services (by an independent contractor and sometimes involving the supply of materials), eg with a dentist, taxi-driver, cabinet-maker, garage owner or tailor; locatio operis.
- **GRATUIT** – contrat à titre gratuit – contract without consideration.
- **GRÉ À GRÉ** – contrat de gré à gré – informal contract; freely negotiated contract.
- **GROSSE** – contrat à la grosse – bottomry bond.
- **IMPOSÉ** – contrat imposé – contract imposed by law.
- **INNOMMÉ** – contrat innommé – innominate (unnamed) contract, ie not belonging to a type governed by specific legal rules but devised by the parties for their own purposes.
- **INSTANTANÉ** – contrat instantané – contract of immediate execution.
- **JEU** – contrat de jeu – gaming contract; wagering contract.
- **JUDICIAIRE** – contrat judiciaire – settlement in court; judicial settlement.
- **LÉONIN** – contrat léonin – unconscionable bargain; contract conferring all the advantages on one party.
- **LICENCE** – contrat de licence – licence (eg to exploit a patent).
- **LOCATION-VENTE** – contrat de location-vente – hire-purchase contract.
- **LOUAGE**
  - **SERVICE** – contrat de louage de services – service contract; employment contract.
- **MANDAT** – contrat de mandat – agency contract.

- **MARIAGE** – **contrat de mariage** – marriage contract; marriage settlement.
- **MŒURS** – **contrat contraire aux bonnes mœurs** – immoral contract.
- **NOMMÉ** – **contrat nommé** – contract regulated by legislation; nominate contract.
- **NOTAIRE** – **contrat par-devant notaire** – contract recorded by a solicitor; notarial contract.
- **NOVATOIRE** – **contrat novatoire** – (contract created by) novation.
- **ONÉREUX** – **contrat onéreux** – contract involving consideration.
- **PIGNORATIF** – **contrat pignoratif** – loan disguised as a sale with an option to repurchase; contract whereby a debtor transfers the possession of one of his assets to the creditor as a security, eg pledge.
- **PRIMITIF** – **contrat primitif** – original contract.
- **PROMESSE de contrat** – pre-contract (eg option agreement, pre-emption agreement).
- **RÉEL** – **contrat réel** – real contract, ie a contract which requires for its formation the effective delivery of the thing to which it refers in addition to the agreement of the parties, eg deposit or loan for use. (Distinguish from real contracts in English law, which are contracts referring to real property, eg a lease.)
- **RELATIVITÉ** – **principe de la relativité des contrats** – privity of contract (rule) (ie a contract is binding only on the parties and does impose burdens or confer benefits on third parties)
- **RÉSILIER un contract** – terminate a contract.
- **ROMPRE un contract** – break a contract.
- **RUPTURE de contract** – breach of contract.
- **SERVICE** – **contrat de service** – service contract; employment contract.
- **SOCIÉTÉ** – **contrat de société** – articles of partnership; memorandum and articles of association of a company.
- **SOLENNEL** – **contrat solennel** – authenticated contract; solemn form contract; officially recorded contract.
- **SUCCESSIF** – **contrat successif** – contract involving successive performance; continuing contract.
- **SYNALLAGMATIQUE** – **contrat synallagmatique** – reciprocal contract; bilateral contract; contract involving obligations on both sides.

- **TACITE** – **contrat tacite** – implied contract; inferred contract.
- **TARIFAIRE** – **contrat tarifaire** – wage agreement.
- **TERME** – **contrat à terme** – a contract whose effect is suspended for a certain time or until the happening of some event.
- **TITRE** – **contrat de titres** – contract note.
- **TITULAIRE de contrat** – contractor.
- **TRANSPORT** – **contrat de transport** – contract of carriage.
- **TRAVAIL** – **contrat de travail** – contract of service (service contract); contract of employment (employment contract).
- **TYPE** – **contrat-type** – model contract; standard-form contract; standard contract.
  - •• **LOCATION** – **contrat-type de location** – uniform (standard) tenancy agreement.
  - •• **TRAVAIL** – **contrat-type de travail** – standard service contract (agreement).
- **UNILATÉRAL** – **contrat unilatéral** – unilateral contract.
- **VERBAL** – **contrat verbal** – oral contract; parol contract.
- **VIOLATION de (du) contrat** – breach of contract.

CONTRAVENTION – petty offence; summary offence.
- **POLICE** – **contravention de simple police** – petty offence; summary offence.
- **VOIRIE** – **contravention de grande voirie** – administrative offence of damaging or obstructing the highway.

CONTRAVENTIONNALISER – reduce to a petty offence.

CONTRE-ASSURANCE – reinsurance; reciprocal insurance.

CONTRE-CAUTION – surety for a surety; further or additional surety.

CONTRE-DÉNONCIATION (AU TIERS SAISI) – notice of validation proceedings to the garnishee.

CONTREDIT – procedure for raising a question of jurisdiction in the Court of Appeal; objection (to a payment order); objection to the judge's decision in insolvency proceedings.

CONTRE-ENQUÊTE – hearing evidence in reply; hearing the other party's evidence; bringing evidence to disprove the evidence adduced by the plaintiff.

CONTRE-EXPERT – expert called by the other side.

CONTRE-EXPERTISE – expert opinion submitted in reply, by the other side; second expert opinion.

CONTREFAÇON – forgery.
- **BREVET** – **contrefaçon de brevets** – infringement of patents.
- **DESSIN** – **contrefaçon de dessins** – infringement of registered designs.
- **ÉCRITURE** – **contrefaçon d'écritures** – forgery of documents.
- **LITTÉRAIRE** – **contrefaçon littéraire** – infringement of copyright.
- **MARQUE** – **contrefaçon de marques de fabrique** – infringement of registered trade marks.
- **MONNAIE** – **contrefaçon de monnaies** – making counterfeit coinage; coinage offences; forging coins.

CONTRE-LETTRE – secret document setting out the true facts of a fictitious transaction; modification of a marriage contract (marriage settlement).

CONTREPARTIE – consideration; equivalent; remuneration; opposing party (in this sense also **contrepartiste**).

CONTREPARTISTE – other (opposing) party.
- **PORTER** – **se porter contrepartiste** – (of an agent) contract with himself.

CONTRE-PASSATION – cross-entry; reversal; contra (entry).

CONTREPASSER – reverse or cancel an entry.

CONTREPRESTATION – consideration.

CONTRE-PREUVE – rebutting evidence.

CONTRE-SEING – countersignature.

CONTRESTARIES – demurrage.

CONTRE-SURESTARIES – demurrage.

CONTREVENANT – (petty offence) defendant; offender.

CONTREVENTION – petty offence.

CONTRIBUABLE – taxpayer.

CONTRIBUTION – procedure for the distribution between the creditors of the proceeds of an attachment in proportion to the amounts due to them.
- **APPEL de contributions** – call for contributions.
- **DETTE** – **contribution à la dette** – procedure by which a person who has paid a sum for which he is not ultimately liable obtains contribution or indemnity from those ultimately liable.
- **DIRECT** – **contribution directe** – direct taxation.
- **GUERRE** – **contribution de guerre** – war levy; special tax to meet the cost of a war.
- **PATENTE** – **contribution des patentes** – (formerly) trading-licence tax; trade tax.

CONTRÔLE
- **ACCORD de contrôle** – supervision agreement.
- **AGENT de contrôle** – supervising officer; checking officer.
- **A POSTERIORI** – **contrôle a posteriori** – subsequent (ex post facto) inspection (check, control, review).
- **A PRIORI** – **contrôle a priori** – previous inspection (check, control, review).
- **CHANGE** – **contrôle des changes** – exchange control.
- **COMPTABLE** – **contrôle comptable** – audit.
- **COMPTABILITÉ** – **contrôle de la comptabilité** – audit.
- **DEVISE** – **contrôle des devises** – exchange control.
- **DOUANE** – **contrôle de la douane** – customs inspection.
- **DROIT de contrôle** – right of supervision.
- **EFFECTIF** – **contrôle d'effectifs** – attendance check.
- **EXTERNE** – **contrôle externe** – external audit.
- **IDENTITÉ** – **contrôle d'identité** – identity check.
- **IMPÔT** – **contrôle de l'impôt** – tax inspection.
- **JUDICIAIRE** – **contrôle judiciaire** – judicial supervision; court supervision (of accused persons pending trial); judicial review.
- **JURIDICTIONNEL** – **contrôle juridictionnel** – judicial review of a decision etc; control by the courts of administrative decisions.

- **LÉGALITÉ** – **contrôle de la légalité** – review of (the) legality (lawfulness) (of proceedings etc).
- **NOMINATIF** – **contrôle nominatif** – nominal roll.
- **POSTAL** – **contrôle postal** – postal censorship.

CONTRÔLER – review; check; supervise; control; audit; inspect.

CONTRÔLEUR – (tax etc) inspector.
- **FINANCIER** – **contrôleur financier** – financial controller.

CONTUMACE – (of an accused) refusing (failure) to appear for trial; unlawful absence; wilful non-appearance.
- **ÉLÉMENTS constitutifs de la contumace** – requirements of unlawful absence.
- **JUGEMENT par contumace** – judgment concerning or trial of a serious indictable offence (felony) in absentia.
- **PURGE de la contumace** – retrial after conviction in absentia.

CONTUMAX – person convicted of a serious indictable offence (felony) in absentia; absent accused.

CONVAINCRE
- **S'ESTIMER convaincu** – be satisfied.
- **INTIMEMENT convaincu** – satisfied.

CONVENANCE
- **DE convenance** – conventional.

CONVENANT – lease at will in which the tenant is entitled to retain ownership of his erections and crops.

CONVENTION – agreement.
- **ARBITRAGE** – **convention d'arbitrage** – arbitration agreement. This covers both a **compromis**, ie an agreement to submit to arbitration when a dispute has already arisen, and a **clause compromissoire**, an agreement to submit future differences to arbitration.
- **ASSISTANCE**
  - **MARITIME** – **convention d'assistance maritime** – salvage agreement.
- **CADRE** – **convention-cadre** – outline convention.
- **COLLECTIF** – **convention collective** – collective (labour) agreement.
  - **EXTENSION d'une convention collective** – extension of a collective agreement (to cover a branch of industry or a region).
- **DOUBLE IMPOSITION** – see IMPOSITION below.
- **ÉCONOMIE d'une convention** – structure (scheme, logic) of a convention.
- **ENTREPRISE** – **convention d'entreprise** – works agreement.
- **ÉTABLISSEMENT** – **convention d'établissement** – establishment convention; convention on establishment.
- **EXPRESSE** – **convention expresse** – express agreement.
- **EXTRADITION** – **convention d'extradition** – extradition treaty.
- **GRÉ À GRÉ** – **convention de gré à gré** – private treaty (as opposed to public auction).
- **HÉRÉDITÉ** – **convention d'hérédité** – inheritance agreement.
- **IMPOSITION** – **convention sur la double imposition** – double taxation agreement.
- **INDIVISION** – **convention d'indivision** – agreement to continue co-ownership.
- **INTÉRÊT** – **convention d'intérêts** – agreement to pay interest.
- **LIBERTÉ des conventions** – freedom of contract.
- **MARIAGE** – **convention de mariage** – marriage contract; marriage settlement.
- **MATRIMONIAL** – **convention matrimoniale** – marriage contract; marriage settlement.
- **NON-RESPONSABILITÉ** – **convention de non-responsabilité** – agreement excluding (exempting from) liability.
- **SYNALLAGMATIQUE** – **convention synallagmatique** – reciprocal agreement; bilateral agreement.
- **TACITE** – **convention tacite** – implied agreement.
- **TARIFAIRE** – **convention tarifaire** – wage agreement; customs tariff convention.
- **TEMPS** – **convention à temps** – time charter.
- **TYPE** – **convention-type** – standard agreement; model agreement.
- **VERBAL** – **convention verbale** – oral agreement; parol agreement.
- **VOYAGE** – **convention au voyage** – voyage charter.

CONVENTIONNÉ – approved.

CONVENTIONNEL – based on or arising out of an agreement, contract or treaty.

- **DROIT INTERNATIONAL conventionnel** – treaty law (as opposed to customary international law); (sometimes referred to as) conventional international law.
- **VALEUR** – **avoir valoir conventionnelle** – rank as (be treated as) part of a convention, treaty, etc.

CONVICTION

- **ÉLÉMENT** – **faute d'éléments suffisants de conviction** – where the evidence is inconclusive.
- **EMPORTER la conviction du juge** – satisfy the court.
- **INTIME conviction** – being satisfied beyond reasonable doubt; evidence satisfying the court; personal conviction of the court (after considering all the evidence).
- **PIÈCE à conviction** – evidence; real evidence; exhibit (in a criminal case).

CONVOCATION – summons; notice; calling; convocation.

- **ASSEMBLÉE** – **convocation d'une assemblée** – calling of a meeting.
- **CORPS ÉLECTORAL** – **convocation du corps électoral** – (issuing of a) writ for elections.
- **PROCÈS-VERBAL** – **convocation avec procès-verbal** – summons with a statement of charges (method of commencing criminal proceedings without a judicial preliminary inquiry).

CONVOL

- **CLAUSE de non-convol** – clause forbidding marriage; celibacy clause.

CONVOQUER – summons; call; convene.

- **COMPARAÎTRE** – **convoquer à comparaître** – issue a summons to appear; summons to appear.

COOBLIGÉ (adj) – jointly liable.

COOBLIGÉ (noun) – co-obligor; person jointly liable with another.

- **SOLIDAIRE** – **coobligé solidaire** – person jointly and severally liable.

COOPÉRATEUR – member of co-operative society.

COOPÉRATISME – the co-operative movement.

COOPÉRATIVE – co-operative society.

- **ACHAT** – **coopérative d'achat** – purchasing co-operative.
- **PLACEMENT** – **coopérative de placement** – investment trust.
- **VENTE** – **coopérative de vente** – marketing co-operative.

COOPTATION – co-option.

COORDONNER

- **LOI** – **lois coordonnées (Belg)** – consolidated Acts.

COPARTAGEANT – person participating in a partition of assets; partitioner.

COPERMUTANT – party to a exchange.

COPIE

- **AUTHENTIQUE** – **copie authentique** – officially recorded copy; authenticated copy; office copy.
- **CERTIFIÉ** – **copie certifiée** – certified (true) copy.
  - **CONFORME** – **copie certifiée conforme** – certified (true) copy; office copy.
- **EXÉCUTOIRE** – **copie exécutoire** – execution copy of a judgment, ie a copy endorsed with authority to execute (with a writ of execution).

COPOSSESSION – possession in common; co-possession; joint possession.

COPRÉVENU – co-defendant or co-accused (charged with a petty offence or a misdemeanour).

COPROPRIÉTAIRE – co-owner; tenant in common.

COPROPRIÉTÉ – ownership in common, each owner being notionally entitled to a share; co-ownership in undivided shares.

- **APPARTEMENT** – **copropriété par appartements** – individual ownership of flats with co-ownership of the remaining parts of the building.
- **HORIZONTAL** – **copropriété horizontale** – co-ownership of several buildings erected on land owned in common.
- **VERTICAL** – **copropriété verticale** – co-ownership of a building in storeys.

CORDON

- **SANITAIRE** – **cordon sanitaire** – sanitary cordon.

CORESPONSABILITÉ – joint liability.

CORESPONSABLE – jointly liable.

CORPORATIF – representing sectional or professional interests.

CORPORATION – guild; professional association.
- **ARTISANAL** – **corporation artisanale** – trade guild; trade association.

CORPOREL – material; tangible; corporeal.
- **OBJET corporel** – material object.
- **DOMMAGE corporel** – personal (physical, bodily) injury.

CORPS
- **ASSURANCE sur corps** – ship policy.
- **CERTAIN** – **corps certain** – specific goods.
- **DUR** – **corps durs** – solid objects.
- **ÉLECTORAL** – **corps électoral** – electorate.
- **JUSTICE** – **corps de justice** – the judiciary.
- **LÉGISLATIF** – **corps législatif** – legislature.
- **MUNICIPAL** – **corps municipal** – district council; borough council.
- **SOCIAL** – **corps social** – social entity.

CORPUS – the physical aspect of possession, ie factual power exercised over an object.

CORRECTION
- **MAISON de correction** – detention centre; reformatory.

CORRECTIONNALISATION
- **JUDICIAIRE** – **correctionnalisation judiciaire** – trial of a felony as a misdemeanour.
- **LÉGAL** – **correctionnalisation légale** – reduction of felonies to misdemeanours by statute.

CORRECTIONNALISER – reduce felonies to misdemeanours by statute; prosecute for (charge with) a misdemeanour on facts which would support prosecution for felony.

CORRECTIONNEL
- **APPEL** – **chambre des appels correctionnels** – Criminal Appeals Chamber (Division); Criminal Chamber (Division) of the Court of Appeal.
- **CHAMBRE correctionnelle** – Criminal Section (Chamber).
- **TRIBUNAL correctionnel** – (regional) Criminal Court (for the trial of misdemeanours).

CORRUPTION
- **ACTIF** – **corruption active** – bribery.
- **MAGISTRAT** – **corruption de magistrat** – bribing of a judge or prosecutor.

- **PASSIF** – **corruption passive** – accepting or soliciting bribes.

CORSAIRE – privateer.

COTE – quotation on the stock exchange.
- **ADMIS à la cote (officielle)** – quoted.
  - •• **NON admis à la cote (officielle)** – unlisted.
- **HORS-cote** – (adj) unlisted; not officially quoted; (noun) unlisted security.
- **IMPÔT** – **cote d'impôt** – tax assessment.
- **MOBILIER** – **cote mobilière** – tenancy tax.

COTER – quote; list.
- **BOURSE** – **coté en bourse** – quoted.
- **NON coté** – unlisted.

COTISATION – contribution.

COTISER – pay contributions.

COTUTELLE – joint guardianship.

COTUTEUR – joint guardian; deputy guardian.

COUCHER
- **TESTAMENT** – **coucher sur un testament** – mention in a will.

COUP
- **AGGRAVANT** – **coups et blessures avec circonstances aggravantes** – dangerous wounding.
- **BLESSURE** – **coups et blessures** – assault and battery; assault; wounding (in serious cases).
- **MORT** – **coups et blessures ayant entraîné la mort sans intention de la donner** – wounding causing death; manslaughter.
- **TOMBER sous le coup de** – fall within (the ambit of); be covered (caught) by.

COUPABLE – guilty.
- **GRAND coupable** – principal offender.
- **PRINCIPAL** – **coupable principal** – principal offender.

COUPE-FILE – official pass (permit).

COUPON
- **ARRIÉRÉ** – **coupon arriéré** – coupon in arrear.
- **SOUFFRANCE** – **coupons en souffrance** – outstanding coupons.

COUPURE – banknote; currency note.

COUR

- **APPEL** – cour d'appel – Court of Appeal.
  - **ADMINISTRATIF** – **cour administrative d'appel** – Administrative Court of Appeal.
- **ARBITRAGE** – **Cour d'arbitrage** (Belg) – court deciding questions of administrative jurisdiction and legislative procedure; (Administrative) Jurisdiction and Procedure Court.
- **ASSISE** – **cour d'assises** – Assize Court.
- **CASSATION** – **Cour de cassation** – Court of Cassation, which decides appeals on points of law and procedure, either upholding the judgment or setting it aside and remitting the matter to a court of appeal for retrial.
- **COMPTE** – **Cour des comptes** – Auditor-General's Department.
- **DISCIPLINE BUDGÉTAIRE** – **Cour de discipline budgétaire et financière** – Disciplinary Offences (Budget and Finance) Court.
- **HAUT** – **Haute Cour de justice** – special court for the trial of the President of the Republic and ministers for treason or other offences committed in the exercise of their office.
- **PRISE** – **cour des prises** – prize appeal court.
- **RENVOI** – **cour de renvoi** – court of appeal to which a case is referred for retrial by the Court of Cassation.
- **SÛRETÉ DE L'ÉTAT** – **Cour de sûreté de l'État** – (former) National Security Court.

COURRIER

- **CABINET** – **courrier de cabinet** – courier; diplomatic bag.
- **DIPLOMATIQUE** – **courrier diplomatique** – courier; diplomatic bag.

COURS

- **AUTHENTIQUE** – **cours authentique** – official rate; official price.
- **BILLET en cours** – valid currency note.
- **CHANGE** – **cours du change** – rate of exchange.
- **COMPENSATION** – **cours de compensation** – making-up price.
- **DEMANDE** – **cours demandé** – buying rate.
- **EAU** – **cours d'eau** – waterway; river.
- **ÉMISSION** – **cours d'émission** – issue price.
- **FORCÉ** – **cours forcé** – forced currency.
- **GARANTIE de cours** – price guarantee.

- **INTÉRÊT** – **le cours de leurs intérêts s'arrête** – interest ceases to run.
- **INTRODUCTION** – **cours d'introduction** – opening price.
- **LÉGAL** – **avoir cours légal** – to be legal tender.
- **OFFERT** – **cours offert** – selling rate; asked price.
- **TERME** – **cours à terme** – forward price, settlement price.

COURSE

- **GUICHET** – **course au guichet** – run on a bank.

COURTAGE – commission; brokerage.

COURTIER

- **VALEUR** – **courtier en valeurs** – outside broker.

COÛT

- **INDICE du coût de la vie** – cost-of-living index.

CO-UTILISATION – joint user.

COUTUME – custom; usage.

- **CERTIFICAT de coutume** – certificate of foreign law.
- **COMMERCIAL** – **coutume commerciale** – trade usage; mercantile custom; commercial usage.
- **CONSTITUTIONNEL** – **coutume constitutionnelle** – convention of the constitution.

COUTUMIER

- **DROIT coutumier** – customary law; custom.

COUVERTURE

- **ASSURANCE** – **couverture d'assurance** – insurance cover.
- **NOTE de couverture** – cover note; covering note.
- **NULLITÉ** – **couverture de la nullité** – remedying (curing) the nullity (a void transaction).

COUVRE-FEU – curfew.

COUVRIR

- **NULLITÉ** – **couvrir la nullité** – cure (remedy) the nullity (a void transaction).
- **RENONCIATION** – **ne peuvent être couverts par aucune renonciation** – may not be waived by any renuciation.
- **SE couvrir** – be covered.

- **VICE** – **couvrir un vice** – cure a defect.

COVENDEUR – co-vendor; joint seller.

CPS = Code pénal suisse.

CRAINTE
- **RÉVÉRENTIEL** – **crainte révérentielle** – parental (etc) influence.

CRAPULEUX – committed from base motives, eg for pecuniary gain, or in a barbaric manner.
- **CRIME crapuleux** – felony committed from base motives, eg for pecuniary gain, or in a barbaric manner; sordid (barbaric) crime.
- **HOMICIDE crapuleux** – homicide committed from base motives, eg for pecuniary gain, or in a barbaric manner.

CRÉANCE – right to receive payment of a debt; right to receive the benefit or performance of a contract or other obligation; chose in action; right in personam; obligation; sum owed; contractual right; debt; claim.
- **ALIMENTAIRE** – **créance alimentaire** – (right to receive or claim) maintenance.
- **AMORTISSEMENT d'une créance** – extinction of a debt; writing off a debt.
- **CÉDÉ** – **créance cédée** – debt or chose in action which has been assigned.
- **CÉDER une créance** – assign a chose in action, ie the right to receive payment of a debt or performance of some other obligation.
- **CESSION de créance** – assignment of a chose in action, ie of the right to receive payment of a debt or performance of some other obligation.
- **CHIROGRAPHAIRE** – **créance chirographaire** – unsecured debt.
- **CIVIL** – **créance civile** – civil debt (ie governed by civil law).
- **COMMERCIAL** – **créance commerciale** – commercial debt (ie governed by commercial law).
- **COMPTABLE** – **créance comptable** – book debt (claim); account receivable.
- **CONTESTÉ** – **créance contestée** – disputed claim.
- **CONTREPARTIE** – **créance en contrepartie** – counterclaim.
- **DOMMAGES DE GUERRE** – **créance de dommages de guerre** – war-damage claim.
- **DOUTEUX** – **créance douteuse** – doubtful debt.
- **ÉCHU** – **créance échue** – due debt; debt accrued due; payable debt.

- **EXIGIBLE** – **créance exigible** – due debt; debt accrued due; payable debt.
- **FAILLITE** – **créance de faillite** – claim in bankruptcy.
- **FISCAL** – **créances fiscales** – tax claims; unpaid tax.
- **GAGE** – **créance donnée en gage** – debt or claim charged by way of security.
- **GAGÉ** – **créance gagée** – secured debt.
- **GARANTI** – **créance garantie** – secured debt.
- **GELÉ** – **créance gelée** – blocked (frozen) debt.
- **HONORAIRE** – **créance d'honoraires** – claim for fees; fees owing.
- **HYPOTHÉCAIRE** – **créance hypothécaire** – mortgage debt.
- **IMPÔT** – **créance d'impôt** – tax owing; tax claim(ed).
- **INCESSIBLE** – **créance incessible** – inalienable or non-negotiable claim.
- **INDEMNISATION** – **créance en indemnisation** – claim (right) to damages (compensation).
- **INDIVIS** – **créance indivise** – joint claim.
- **INTÉRÊT** – **créance d'intérêt** – claim for interest.
- **IRRÉCOUVRABLE** – **créance irrecouvrable** – bad debt.
- **LEGS de créance** – legacy of a chose in action (right to receive payment of a debt etc).
- **LETTRE de créance** – letters of credence; (a diplomat's) credentials; letter of credit.
- **LOYER** – **créance de loyers** – right to receive payment of rent.
- **MARCHANDISE** – **créance sur marchandises** – right to receive goods.
- **MASSE** – **créance contre la masse** – priority claim against the bankruptcy for costs, or obligations entered into by the trustee.
- **MONTANT RÉDUIT** – **créance d'un montant réduit** – small debt.
- **PRIX DE VENTE** – **créance de prix de vente** – right to receive the purchase money.
- **PRODUCTION d'une créance** – proof of a debt (in bankruptcy).
- **PRODUIRE une créance** – prove a debt (in bankruptcy).
- **RECOURS** – **créance en recours** – right to indemnity; right of recourse.
- **RECOUVRABLE** – **créance recouvrable** – recoverable debt.

- **RELIQUAT** d'une créance – balance or remainder of a debt; outstanding balance of a claim.
- **REPRISE** de créance – acceptance of the assignment of a chose in action (ie a claim to payment of a debt or performance of a contract).
- **RESTANT** de la créance – balance or remainder of the debt.
- **SAISI** – créance saisie – attached debt; garnished debt.
- **SAISI-ARRÊTÉ** – créance saisie-arrêtée – attached debt.
- **SUCCESSORAL** – créance successorale – right to a share in an estate.
- **TERME** – créance à terme – claim subject to a stipulation as to time.
- **TIERS** – créance d'un mineur contre un tiers – sum owed to a minor by a third person.
- **TRANSFERT (TRANSPORT)** de créance – assignment of a chose in action, ie of the right to receive payment of a debt or performance of some other obligation.

CRÉANCIER – creditor; (contracts) promisee; (obligations generally) obligee; the person entitled to receive the payment of a debt or the performance or the benefit of a contract or other obligation; person entitled to damages against a tortfeasor; party entitled.

- **ALIMENTAIRE** – créancier alimentaire – person entitled to maintenance.
- **ALIMENT** – créancier d'aliments – person entitled to maintenance.
- **ANTICHRÉSISTE** – créancier antichrésiste – mortgagee in possession (Welsh mortgagee).
- **APPEL** de créanciers – calling of a creditor's meeting.
- **CHANGE** – créancier de change – holder of a bill of exchange.
- **CHIROGRAPHAIRE** – créancier chirographaire – unsecured creditor.
- **COMITÉ** des créanciers – committee of inspection (in bankruptcy).
- **COMMISSION** des créanciers – committee of inspection (in bankruptcy).
- **CONCORDATAIRE** – créancier concordataire – creditor under a composition or scheme of arrangement.
- **CONCOURS** de créanciers – rule that creditors bear the loss (arising from an insolvency) in proportion to the amount of their claims.

- **DÉSINTÉRESSER** un créancier – satisfy, pay off or buy out a creditor.
- **DROIT RÉEL** – créanciers détenteurs de droits réels – secured creditors.
- **FAILLITE** – créancier de la faillite – creditor in the bankruptcy
- **GAGISTE** – créancier gagiste – pledgee
- **GARANTI** – créancier garanti – secured creditor.
- **HÉRÉDITAIRE** – créancier héréditaire – creditor of the estate.
- **HYPOTHÉCAIRE** – créancier hypothécaire – mortgagee.
- **INSCRIT** – créancier inscrit – proving creditor.
- **MASSE** – créancier de la masse – creditor of the bankruptcy.
- **NANTI** – créancier nanti – secured creditor.
- **NAVIRE** – créancier du navire – holder of a bottomry bond or person entitled to an unregistered lien on a ship.
- **OBLIGATAIRE** – créancier obligataire – debenture holder.
- **POURSUIVANT** – créancier poursuivant – judgment creditor; execution creditor.
- **PRIVILÉGIÉ** – créancier privilégié – preferred or secured creditor; preferential creditor (in bankruptcy).
- **PRODUISANT** – créancier produisant – proving creditor.
- **RENTE** – créancier de rente – annuitant.
- **RETARDATAIRE** – créancier retardataire – dilatory creditor.
- **SAISISSANT** – créancier saisissant – execution creditor.
- **SOCIAL** – créancier social – creditor of the partnership or company; partnership creditor.
- **SOLIDAIRE** – créancier solidaire – joint and several creditor.
- **SUCCESSION** – créancier de la succession – creditor of the (deceased's) estate.

CRÉATION

- **DROIT** – création du droit – formation of law.
- **SOCIÉTÉ** – création d'une société – formation of a partnership or company.

CRÉDIBILITÉ

- **SERMENT** de crédibilité – oath by an alleged debtor's surviving spouse or heirs that they are unaware of the existence of a debt or other relevant matter.

CRÉDIRENTIER – person entitled to a rentcharge; annuitant.

CRÉDIT – credit; appropriation.
- **ASSURANCE crédit** – credit insurance.
- **ATTEINTE au crédit de l'État** – disparagement of public credit.
- **ATTRIBUTION de crédits** – allocation of appropriations; attribution of expenditure to appropriations.
- **AVAL** – **crédit d'aval** – guaranteed credit.
- **BLANC** – **crédit blanc** – clean credit; open credit.
- **BLOCAGE de crédits** – blocking (freezing) of appropriations.
- **BUDGÉTAIRE** – **crédit budgétaire** – appropriation.
- **CAHIER de crédits** – supplementary estimates.
- **CAISSE** – **crédit de caisse** – overdraft facility.
- **CAUTION** – **crédit de caution** – guaranteed credit.
- **CAUTIONNEMENT** – **crédit de cautionnement** – guaranteed credit.
- **CONSOMMATION** – **crédit à la consommation** – consumer credit.
- **DEMANDE de crédit (supplémentaire)** – (supplementary) estimate.
- **ÉTABLISSEMENT de crédit** – financial institution.
- **IMPÔT** – **crédit d'impôt** – tax credit.
- **INSTITUTION de crédit** – financial institution.
- **MODIFIÉ** – **crédit modifié** – amended appropriation.
- **OUVRIR un crédit** – vote an appropriation.
- **OUVRIR des crédits de paiement** – appropriate funds.
- **PROJET de crédit** – proposal for an appropriation.
- **REPORT de crédit** – carry-over of an appropriation.
- **SUPPLÉMENTAIRE** – **crédit supplémentaire** – supplementary appropriation.
- **TITRE de crédit** – credit instrument; security.
- **VIREMENT de crédit** – virement; transfer (from one head of the estimates to another).

CRÉDIT-BAIL – leasing.

CRÉDITÉ – borrower.

CRÉDIRENTIER

CRÉDITEUR – creditor; person entitled to a credit balance.

CRÉDULITÉ
- **SERMENT de crédulité** – oath by an alleged debtor's surviving spouse or heirs that they are unaware of the existence of a debt or other relevant matter.

CRÉER
- **EFFET** – **créer un effet** – draw a bill.

CRIÉE
- **AUDIENCE des criées** – session for sale of real property by the court by auction; court auction.
- **VENTE à la criée** – sale of movables or immovables by public auction.

CRIME – felony (offence of the most serious category); serious indictable offence.
- **CRAPULEUX** – **crime crapuleux** – felony committed from base motives, eg for pecuniary gain, or in a barbaric manner; sordid (barbaric) crime.
- **DÉLIT** – **crimes et délits** – indictable offences; felonies and misdemeanours.
- **PASSIONNEL** – **crime passionnel** – offence motivated by jealousy; crime passionnel.
- **SANG** – **crimes de sang** – murder and similar crimes.

CRIMINALISATION – conversion of misdemeanours into felonies by statute; creation of an offence; making (certain acts) an offence.

CRIMINALISER – convert a misdemeanour into a felony by statute; create an offence; make (certain acts) an offence.

CRIMINALISTE – expert in criminal law or police science; criminal lawyer.

CRIMINALISTIQUE – police science; criminal science; criminalistics.

CRIMINALITÉ
- **AFFAIRE** – **criminalité des affaires** – economic crime; white-collar crime; business crime.

CRIMINEL – (of imprisonment) long-term.
- **ÉTAT** – **le criminel tient le civil en état** – when the same act involves criminal and civil proceedings, the civil court must await the decision of the criminal court before deciding the case.

CRISE
- **ÉTAT de crise** – state of emergency.
- **MESURE de crise** – emergency provision; special measure.

CROUPIER – person who shares the interest of a partner without being a member of the firm; purchaser of a partner's share; occult partner.

CULPABILITÉ
- **DÉCLARATION de culpabilité** – finding of guilt; verdict of guilty.
- **RECONNAISSANCE de culpabilité** – admission of guilt.
- **SENTENCE de culpabilité** – finding of guilt; verdict of guilty.

CUMUL – (tax) aggregation.
- **INFRACTION**
  - **IDÉAL** – cumul idéal d'infractions – position where a single act constitutes more than one offence.
  - **RÉEL** – cumul réel d'infractions – position where the offender has committed several acts each of which constitutes an offence.
- **PEINE** – cumul des peines – consecutive (aggregated) sentences.

CUMULATIF – (of sentences) consecutive.
- **JEU cumulatif** – concurrent application (effect).

CUMULATIVEMENT – (of sentences) to run consecutively.

CUPIDITÉ
- **PAR cupidité** – from avarice; for gain.

CURATELLE – administration; supervision; temporary guardianship.
- **ABSENCE** – curatelle d'absence – administration of the property of absent or missing persons.
- **SUCCESSION** – curatelle de succession – provisional administration of an estate.

CURATEUR – administrator; custodian; supervisor.
- **AD LITEM** – curateur ad litem – next friend; guardian ad litem.

D

DAMNUM EMERGENS – loss (and damage) suffered ; damnum emergens.

DANGER – threat; risk.
- **FUITE** – danger de fuite – danger of absconding.
- **MINEUR** – mineurs en danger – minors at risk.
- **PUBLIC** – danger public – public emergency.

DATE
- **CERTAIN** – date certaine – authenticated date, ie certified by a court, notary or official. The date may be considered as authenticated or certain as a result of registration, mention in an officially recorded document or the death of one of the parties.
- **ÉCHÉANCE** – date d'échéance – due date.
- **ÉMISSION** – date d'émission – date of issue.
- **FIXE** – procédure d'urgence à date fixe – fixed-date urgent proceedings.
- **RÉFÉRENCE** – date de référence – appointed day or date; prescribed date.
- **VALEUR** – date de valeur – value date.

DATION
- **GAGE** – dation en gage – pledging; charging.
- **NANTISSEMENT** – dation en nantissement – pledging; charging.
- **PAIEMENT** – dation en paiement – satisfaction; accord and satisfaction.

DÉBALLAGE
- **VENTE** au déballage – special-offer sale (from temporary premises).

DÉBAT
- **RESTREINT** – débat restreint – parliamentary debate in which speaking time is limited.

DÉBAT(S) – hearing; trial; proceedings.
- **CLÔTURE** des débats – termination of the hearing.
- **MAXIME** des débats (Sw) – rule that the parties control the (subject-matter of) the proceedings (and may present the case as they see fit).
- **ORAL** – débats oraux – hearing.
- **PROCÈS-VERBAL** des débats – record of the proceedings; transcript of the trial.
- **PUBLICITÉ** des débats – (requirement of, right to) a public hearing.

DÉBATTRE
- **PRINCIPAL** – débattre au principal – dispute the main issue; argue the merits.

DÉBAUCHAGE – enticement to quit employment; inducing breach of contract (of employment).

DÉBAUCHE – sexual immorality, including homosexual practices.
- **EXCITATION (des mineurs) à la débauche** – incitement (of minors) to immorality; depravation (of minors).

DÉBAUCHER – entice to quit employment; induce breach of contract (of employment).

DEBELLATIO – conquest.

DÉBET
- **ARRÊT** de débet – restitution order; repayment order (referring to a deficit in an account).
- **PROCÉDURE** de débet – proceedings for restitution or repayment by the accountant of the deficit in an account.

DÉBIRENTIER – person liable to pay an annuity, rentcharge, etc.

DÉBITEUR – debtor; promisor; obligor; tortfeasor; person liable.
- **ALIMENT** – débiteur d'aliments – person liable to pay maintenance.
- **ASSIGNÉ** – débiteur assigné – debtor against whom proceedings are pending.
- **CAMBIAIRE** – débiteur cambiaire – person liable on a bill.
- **CÉDÉ** – débiteur cédé – person liable to pay a debt or perform an obligation which has been assigned.
- **DÉFAILLANT** – débiteur défaillant – insolvent debtor; defaulter.
- **FAILLI** – débiteur failli – bankrupt.
- **GAGISTE** – débiteur gagiste – pledgor.
- **HYPOTHÉCAIRE** – débiteur hypothécaire – mortgagor.

- **INTÉRÊTS débiteurs (au compte profits et pertes d'un fonds)** – interest owing to the fund.
- **MALHEUREUX** – débiteur malheureux et de bonne foi – honest but unfortunate debtor.
- **NÉGLIGENT** – débiteur négligent – dilatory debtor.
- **OBLIGATAIRE** – débiteur obligataire – person liable on a negotiable security.
- **PRESTATION** – débiteur d'une prestation – person liable to confer a benefit; person liable to perform a contract; promisor.
- **RENTE** – débiteur d'une rente – person liable to pay an annuity, rentcharge, etc.
- **SAISI** – débiteur saisi – judgment debtor against whom attachment has issued, whose goods have been seized in execution.
- **SOLIDAIRE** – débiteur solidaire – person jointly and severally liable on a debt or other obligation; joint debtor etc.
- **SUCCESSION** – débiteur de la succession – debtor of the estate.
- **TIERS débiteur** – debtor of a debtor; garnishee.

DÉBLOCAGE – release; decontrol; unfreezing.

DÉBLOQUER – release; decontrol; unfreeze.

DÉBOURS – disbursements; outgoings.

- **TARIFÉ** – débours tarifés – disbursements allowed on taxation (eg transport, postage, telephone).

DÉBOUTÉ – court's dismissal of an application addressed to it.

- **JUGEMENT de débouté** – judgment dismissing an action.
- **OPPOSITION** – débouté d'une opposition – dismissal of an application to set aside.

DÉBOUTER – dismiss (an appeal etc).

- **DE** – être débouté de sa demande – lose one's case; have one's claim dismissed (application refused); have the court find against one.

DÉCAISSEMENT – disbursement; out-of-pocket expenses.

DÉCENTRALISATION – transfer of powers from central government to independent (local) authorities; devolution.

DÉCERNER

- **MANDAT** – décerner un mandat d'arrêt – issue an arrest warrant.

DÉCÈS

- **ACTE de décès** – death certificate; record of death.
- **ALLOCATION de (au) décès** – death grant.
- **ASSURANCE décès (en cas de décès)** – (whole) life assurance.
- **CERTIFICAT de décès** – (doctor's) death certificate.

DÉCHARGE – release (discharge) of a trustee, administrator, receiver, etc.

- **CONVENTIONNEL** – décharge conventionnelle – contractual discharge; remission of a debt.
- **DONNER décharge de sa gestion** – discharge in respect of his management.
- **FAIT à décharge** – exonerating evidence.
- **TÉMOIN à décharge** – defence witness.

DÉCHARGER – discharge; release.

DÉCHÉANCE – loss; deprivation; disentitlement; disqualification (for public office after a conviction); lapse; forfeiture; termination (of a right); avoidance (of a procedure etc.); being barred from proceeding for failure to comply with a time-limit; being out of time.

- **AUTORITÉ PARENTALE** – déchéance de l'autorité parentale – loss or deprivation of parental authority.
- **BREVET** – déchéance du brevet – revocation of a patent; expiry of a patent.
- **CLAUSE de déchéance** – forfeiture clause.
- **DROIT** – déchéance d'un droit – forfeiture of a right; loss of a right.
  - **CIVIQUE** – déchéance des droits civiques – deprivation of civic rights (disqualification from exercising certain rights on conviction).
  - **PENSION** – déchéance de la pension – loss or deprivation of pension rights.
- **FONCTION** – déchéance des fonctions – loss of office.
- **MANDAT** – déchéance du mandat – withdrawal or termination of authority or power of attorney.
- **NATIONALITÉ** – déchéance de la nationalité – loss or deprivation of citizenship (nationality).

- **PEINE** – sous peine de déchéance – to be valid.
- **PENSION** – déchéance de la pension (du droit à pension) – loss or deprivation of pension rights.
- **PUISSANCE PATERNELLE (now replaced by autorité parentale)** – déchéance de la puissance paternelle – loss or deprivation of paternal (parental) authority.
- **RELÈVEMENT de déchéance** – restoration of a right which has lapsed or of which a person has been deprived; termination of a disqualification.
- **TERME** – déchéance du terme – fact that all debts become immediately payable on insolvency, failure to provide security or acts by the debtor reducing the value of the security given.
- **TOMBER en déchéance** – lapse owing to non-user.
- **USUFRUIT** – déchéance de l'usufruit – termination of the usufruct (life estate, life tenancy).

DÉCHOIR – lapse; lose; be deprived of.
- **NATIONALITÉ** – déchoir de la nationalité – deprive of citizenship (nationality).

DÉCISION – decision; judgment.
- **ARBITRAGE** – décision d'arbitrage, décision arbitrale – (arbitral, arbitration) award.
- **ASSEMBLÉE** – décision prise en assemblée plénière – decision by the full court etc.
- **ATTAQUÉ** – décision attaquée – decision appealed against; decision of the court below (lower court or authority); impugned decision; decision being challenged.
- **CLASSEMENT** – décision de classement – decision to discontinue the proceedings (not to proceed, not to prosecute).
- **DÉFINITIF** – décision définitive – final decision.
- **ENTREPRENDRE une décision** – appeal against (attack, challenge) a decision or judgment.
- **EXÉCUTOIRE** – décision exécutoire – (immediately) enforceable decision.
- **EXPULSION** – décision d'expulsion – expulsion warrant (order); deportation order.
- **FOND** – décision au fond – decision on the merits; decision on the substance.
- **GRACIEUX** – décision gracieuse – decision (judgment) in a non-contentious matter; decision of an administrative nature by a judge.

- **HOMOLOGATION** – décision de homologation – confirmation; confirmatory decision.
- **INCRIMINÉ** – décision incriminée – decision appealed against; decision of the court below (lower court or authority); impugned decision; decision being challenged.
- **INTERNEMENT** – décision d'internement – detention order.
- **JUDICIAIRE** – décision judiciaire – judgment; court decision.
- **JUSTICE** – décision de justice – court decision; judgment; court order.
- **MOTIVÉ** – décision motivée – decision giving reasons; reasoned decision.
- **MOTIVER une décision** – give reasons (furnish grounds) for a judgment.
- **POUVOIR de décision propre** – personal discretion.
- **PRÉALABLE** – décision préalable – previous administrative decision which is an essential step in bringing a case in an Administrative Court or an appeal to the Conseil d'Etat; preliminary decision on the merits leaving the damages to be assessed later.
- **PRÉJUDICIEL** – décision préjudicielle – decision (ruling) on a preliminary question (point, issue) (by another court); preliminary ruling.
- **PRÉVISIONNEL** – décision prévisionnelle (Sw) – injunction; mandatory injunction; provisional order.
- **PRINCIPE** – décision de principe – leading case; authoritative decision; decision establishing an important principle.
- **PROVISOIRE** – décision provisoire – injunction; mandatory injunction; provisional order.
- **QUITUS** – décision de quitus – discharge; release.
- **RECOURS** – décision rendue sur recours – decision on appeal.
- **RENVOI** – décision de renvoi – committal for trial; reference, remission or transfer to another court.
- **TAXATION** – décision de taxation – taxation of costs.

DÉCISOIRE
- **SERMENT décisoire** – oath which a party is required to take by his opponent in order to decide the matter at issue between them.

DECISORIA LITIS – merits (as opposed to procedure).

DÉCLARANT – person making a customs declaration or reporting a birth or death to the registrar; declarant.

DÉCLARATIF
- **DROIT** – déclaratif de droits – declaratory (judgment, order).

DÉCLARATION (English often prefers to use a verb like declare, enter, file, report, register) declaration; notice; certificate; statement; report; entry; filing; advice; finding; deposition; address; announcement.
- **ABANDON** – déclaration d'abandon – declaration of abandonment (of ship or cargo).
  - •• **JUDICIAIRE** – déclaration judiciaire d'abandon – court declaration that a child has been abandoned.
- **ABSENCE** – déclaration d'absence – declaration of (prolonged) absence; declaration that a person is missing (and presumed dead).
- **ADHÉSION** – déclaration d'adhésion – declaration of accession.
- **ADJUDICATAIRE** – déclaration d'adjudicataire – naming one's principal at an auction held by a court.
- **APPEL** – déclaration d'appel – notice of appeal.
- **BIEN** – déclaration des biens – declaration or return of assets.
- **CESSION** – déclaration de cession – notice of assignment.
- **COMMAND** – déclaration de command – statement exercising the right of an ostensible purchaser to substitute the true purchaser for whom he was acting as an agent; naming one's principal at or after an auction.
- **CONFISCATION** – déclaration de confiscation – confiscation order.
- **DÉCÈS** – déclaration de décès – reporting or registering a death; declaration of death by a court.
  - •• **REQUÊTE** de déclaration de décès – application to register a death.
- **FAILLITE** – déclaration de faillite – (by the court) adjudication; (by the debtor) application for the commencement of bankruptcy proceedings.
- **FOI DU SERMENT** – déclaration sous la foi du serment – sworn declaration (statement); affidavit.
- **FORTUNE** – déclaration de fortune – return of capital; return of assets (for tax purposes).

- **IMPÔT** – déclaration d'impôts – tax return.
- **INCOMPÉTENCE** – déclaration d'incompétence – finding of lack of jurisdiction.
- **INDIGENCE** – déclaration d'indigence – certificate of lack of means (financial hardship).
- **INTENTION** – déclaration d'intention – statement of intention; declaration of intent.
- **JUGEMENT COMMUN** – déclaration de jugement commun – judgment binding on a party who has been joined to the proceedings by third-party notice.
- **MODÈLE** – déclaration de modèle – application to register a design.
- **NAISSANCE** – déclaration de naissance – reporting or registration of a birth.
- **NULLITÉ** – action en déclaration de nullité – action to set aside, avoid, declare void.
- **OUÏR** – la Cour a ouï dans leurs déclarations – the Court heard addresses by.
- **POURVOI** – déclaration de pourvoi – (filing) notice of appeal to the Court of Cassation or Conseil d'État.
- **RECOURS** – déclaration d'un recours – entry or filing of an appeal.
- **SOUMISSION** – déclaration de soumission d'enlèvement – (customs) statement that a bond (security) has been given permitting withdrawal of the merchandise.
- **SURENCHÈRE** – déclaration de surenchère – filing or entering a higher bid after completion of an auction. This procedure, the object of which is to ensure a fair price, leads to a second auction if there are any bidders. (See also SURENCHÈRE.)
- **TAXE** de déclaration – registration fee.
- **URGENCE** – déclaration d'urgence – declaration by the government enabling the Prime Minister to call for the establishment of a joint committee (**commission mixte paritaire**) after only one reading in each house instead of two.
- **UTILITÉ PUBLIQUE** – déclaration d'utilité publique – declaration that land is required for public purposes, which takes the form of an Act or a decree of the Conseil d'État. It constitutes the first stage in expropriation (and some other) proceedings.
- **VOLONTÉ** – déclaration de volonté – statement (declaration, manifestation) of intent(ion).

DÉCLARER – report; declare; state; enter; file; find; order; certify.

- **COUPABLE** – **déclarer coupable** – find guilty.

DÉCLASSEMENT – downgrading; release (from some specified category); transfer of property from the category of "public property" (**domaine public**) to that of "private property" (**domaine privé**).

DÉCLINATOIRE

- **COMPÉTENCE** – **déclinatoire de compétence** – objection to jurisdiction.
- **CONNEXITÉ** – **déclinatoire de connexité** – objection that related proceedings are pending in another court.
- **LITISPENDANCE** – **déclinatoire de litispendance** – (preliminary) objection that proceedings on the same issue are pending in another court (lis alibi pendens).

DÉCLINER – decline; refuse to accept (a nationality to which one is entitled, responsibility).

- **CHOSE JUGÉE** – **décliner l'autorité de la chose jugée** – refuse to accept that one is bound by a judgment.
- **COMPÉTENCE** – **décliner compétence** – refuse to assume jurisdiction; decline to exercise jurisdiction.
- **NATIONALITÉ** – **décliner la nationalité** – renounce one's nationality.
- **NOM** – **décliner ses nom et qualités** – give one's personal particulars.

DÉCOMPTER

- **ÊTRE** **décompté à partir de** – (of time) run from.

DÉCONCENTRATION – delegation of authority from superior (central) to subordinate (local) authorities of central government; devolution (of authority); decentralisation; decartelisation.

DÉCONCENTRÉ – central government working through local organs.

DÉCONFITURE – a state of insolvency (the equivalent of bankruptcy in persons who are not traders).

DÉCOTE – marginal tax relief (for persons whose income just reaches the point where it becomes taxable).

DÉCOULANT

- **DE** – **découlant de** – under.

DÉCOUPAGE

- **CIRCONSCRIPTION** – **découpage de circonscriptions** – drawing (ie fixing) of constituency boundaries.

DÉCOUVERT – overdraft.

- **A découvert** – without cover; without security.
- **LOI DE FINANCES** – **découvert de la loi de finances** – budget deficit.

DÉCRET – (governmental or presidential) decree or order; regulations.

- **APPLICATION** – **décret d'application** – implementing decree, order or instrument; implementing regulations.
- **AVANCE** – **décret d'avances** – supplementary budget appropriations which may be ordered by the government in precisely specified exceptional circumstances subject to subsequent ratification by parliament.
- **EXCEPTION** – **décret d'exception** – emergency regulations.
- **NATURALISATION** – **décret de naturalisation** – naturalisation order or certificate.
- **NOMINATION** – **décret de nomination** – instrument of appointment.
- **PÉNAL** – **décret pénal** – summary order imposing a fine which the defendant may have set aside if he wishes to have a full trial; sentence order.
- **RÈGLEMENT D'ADMINISTRATION PUBLIQUE** – **décret pris dans la forme des règlements d'administration publique** – (formerly) decree made by the Prime Minister after consultation of the full Conseil d'État.
- **UTILITÉ PUBLIQUE** – **décret d'utilité publique** – order (made in the public interest) approved by the Conseil d'État and signed by the Prime Minister.

DÉCRET-LOI – legislative decree (enacted by the government under the authority of an Act and having the effect of an Act, ie modifying existing legislation).

DE CUJUS – deceased.

DÉCUMUL – (tax) disaggregation.

DÉDIT – renunciation; repudiation; penalty; refusal to perform; right of promisor not to perform his obligation; sum payable by a promisor who avails himself of this right.

DÉDOMMAGEMENT – damages; compensation; indemnity; reparation.

DÉDOMMAGER – indemnify; compensate; pay damages.

DÉDOUBLEMENT
- **FONCTIONNEL** – dédoublement fonctionnel – plurality of functions.

DÉDUCTION
- **BASE** – déductions à la base – (tax) allowances.
- **CHARGE** – déduction pour charges de famille – family or dependants allowance.
- **FAMILIAL** – déductions familiales – family or dependants allowances.
- **SALAIRE** – déduction du salaire – deduction from wages.
- **VIEUX AU NEUF** – déduction du vieux au neuf – deduction to compensate for the increased value when an insurer replaces a damaged old object by a new one; new-for-old deduction.

DÉFAILLANCE – default; failure to pay or perform; failure to appear.

DÉFAILLANT – person who fails to pay (perform, appear or comply with a rule); party in default.
- **ÊTRE défaillant** – fail to appear to a writ; fail to comply with a formality:

DÉFAILLIR (of a condition) – fail.

DÉFALCATION
- **DETTE** – défalcation des dettes – deduction of debts.

DÉFAUT – fault; defect; absence; default; failure to appear, file pleadings or to make submissions.
- **ATTENTION** – défaut d'attention – lack of care or diligence.
- **CACHÉ** – défaut caché – hidden (latent) defect.
- **COMPARUTION** – défaut de comparution – failure to appear; default of appearance.
- **COMPÉTENCE** – défaut de compétence – lack of jurisdiction.
- **CONDAMNATION par défaut non frappée d'opposition** – conviction in absentia for a misdemeanour where no application has been made to set the conviction aside.
- **CONDITION** – une des conditions fait défaut – one of the conditions is not satisfied.

- **CONFORMITÉ** – défaut de conformité – state of affairs incompatible with a contract, treaty, etc.
- **CONGÉ** – défaut congé – striking out for failure to proceed (by the plaintiff).
- **CONTENANCE** – défaut de contenance – deficiency in the acreage sold.
- **DÉCLARATION** – défaut de déclaration – failure to report.
- **DISCERNEMENT** – défaut de discernement – lack of discretion.
- **DONNER défaut** – to record non-appearance by the defendant; give judgment by default.
- **EXPLOITATION** – défaut d'exploitation – non-user; failure to work a patent; failure to operate (a mine) at the agreed level of production; insufficient operation.
- **FAIRE défaut** – fail to appear.
- **FAUTE**
  - **ACCOMPLIR** – défaut faute d'accomplir les actes de procédure – failure to prosecute the proceedings.
  - **COMPARAÎTRE** – défaut faute de comparaître – failure to appear; default of appearance.
  - **CONCLURE** – défaut faute de conclure – (default by) failing to file pleadings (submissions).
- **FORME** – défaut de forme – formal defect; procedural defect.
- **JUGEMENT par défaut** – (civ) judgment by default; (crim) judgment in absentia (misdemeanours and petty offences).
- **MANIFESTE** – pour défaut manifeste de fondement – as manifestly ill-founded.
- **MOTIF** – défaut de motif(s) – inadequate (absence of) reasons (for a judgment).
- **NOTIFICATION** – défaut de notification – failure to serve or give notice.
- **NOUVELLE** – défaut de nouvelles – (prolonged) absence of news (in cases of disappearance).
- **PARTIE** – défaut d'une partie – failure of a party to appear.
- **PRESTATION** – défaut de prestation – failure to perform.
- **PREUVE** – défaut de preuve – absence (lack) of or insufficient evidence (proof).
- **PRONONCER (le) défaut** – give judgment by default.

- **RABATTEMENT de défaut** – setting aside a judgment (obtained) by default (where the defendant appears before the end of the hearing).

DÉFENDEUR (DÉFENDERESSE) –
defendant; respondent (divorce etc).

- **APPEL** – **défendeur en appel** – respondent.
- **CITÉ** – **défendeur cité** – defendant (who has been) served with a writ.
- **GOUVERNEMENT défendeur** – respondent government.

DÉFENDRE

- **CAUSE** – **défendre sa propre cause** – present one's own case.
- **JUSTICE** – **défendre en justice** – defend (legal proceedings).
- **SE défendre** – conduct one's own case.

DÉFENSE

- **CONCLUSIONS en défense** – defence (pleadings).
- **DROIT** – **défense des droits** – protection of the rights.
- **DROITS de la défense** – right of *both* parties to put forward their case and be informed of their opponent's case (including freedom to choose one's legal representative); right to a fair hearing (trial); due process; rights of the defence.
- **EN défense** – as defendant (respondent).
- **FAIRE VALOIR** – **a fait valoir des défenses au fond** – has a defence on the merits.
- **FOND** – **défense au fond** – defence on the merits.
- **LÉGITIME défense** – self-defence. (A defence to a prosecution for manslaughter or proceedings for assault; if the defence fails, the excuse of provocation can still be pleaded. The concept includes the defence of other persons and of property.)
  - •• **ABUS de la légitime défense** – use of disproportionate force in self-defence.
- **LIBERTÉ de la défense** – see DROITS above.
- **MOYENS de défense** – submissions; arguments; grounds of defence; defence.
- **SOCIAL** – **défense sociale** – social protection (ie against crime).
  - •• **COMITÉ de défense sociale** (Belg) – mental health area board.

DÉFENSEUR – defence counsel; counsel (representing either party).

- **AGRÉE** – **défenseur agréé** – approved representative in the Commercial Court.
- **OFFICE** – **défenseur d'office** – official (officially assigned) defence counsel.

DÉFÉRER – bring before; refer to.

- **COUR** – **déféré à la cour** – brought before the court.
- **INSTRUCTION** – **déférer à une instruction** – comply with a direction.
- **JUSTICE** – **déférer à la justice** (of the police) bring before the court; bring to court.
- **PARQUET** – **déférer au parquet** – bring (offender, suspect) before the public prosecutor; refer (case) to the Prosecutor's Department.
- **SERMENT** – **déférer le serment à quelqu'un** – require a person to take an oath; put a person to his oath.

DÉFIANCE

- **MOTION de défiance** – motion of no confidence.
- **VOTE de défiance** – vote of no confidence.

DÉFICIENT

- **MENTAL** – **déficient mental** – mentally deficient or disordered person; person of unsound mind; mental patient.

DÉFICIT

- **EXPLOITATION** – **déficit d'exploitation** – trading loss.

DÉFINITIF – final.

- **JUGEMENT définitif** – final judgment.

DÉGRADATION

- **BORNE** – **dégradation de bornes** – damaging boundary stones.
- **CIVIQUE** – **dégradation civique** – loss of civic rights; loss of political rights and functions following a conviction for felony; disqualification from holding office, voting, etc.
- **LIMITE** – **dégradation de limites** – damaging boundary stones.
- **MONUMENT** – **dégradation de monuments** – criminal damage to monuments or buildings.

DEGRÉ

- **DEUX** – **instruction à deux degrés** – investigation by both the investigating judge and thereafter the Indictments Chamber (compulsory in all cases of felony (**crime**)).
- **DOUBLE** – **droit à un double degré de juridiction** – right to an appeal (two-tier proceedings, a system of appeal courts).

- **PREMIER** degré – court below; trial court.
  - **DE premier degré** – of first instance.
- **SECOND** – **jurisdiction de second degré** – court with jurisdiction to hear appeals; appeal court.
- **SUCCESSIBLE** – **degré successible** – relationship entitling to succeed to an estate.
  - **AU degré successible** – entitled to inherit.

DÉGREVABLE – entitling to, qualifying for, tax relief.

DÉGRÈVEMENT – tax relief.

- **TOTAL** – **dégrèvement total** – exemption from tax.

DÉGUERPIR – quit; abandon ownership of property.

- **SOMMATION de déguerpir** – notice (summons) to quit.

DÉGUERPISSEMENT – abandonment of the mortgaged property to the mortgagee.

DÉGUISEMENT – simulation with the object of hiding the true nature of an instrument or one of its terms, eg the price paid.

DÉJUDICIARISATION – arrangements for treating out of court; diversion.

DÉJUGER

- **SE déjuger** – abandon an argument or submission; contradict oneself; come to a different decision.

DÉLAI – time-limit; period; time (allowed for doing something); adjournment.

- **ABANDON** – **délai d'abandon** – time allowed for making a declaration of abandonment.
- **AJOURNEMENT** – **délai d'ajournement** – time fixed for appearance.
- **APPEL** – **délai d'appel** – time for entering, filing or lodging notice of appeal.
- **ATTENTE** – **délai d'attente** – waiting period; qualifying period.
- **BREF** – **à bref délai** – speedily; promptly.
- **CADUCITÉ** – **délai de caducité** – period after which notice of appeal etc lapses if not followed up (eg by an application for listing).
- **CARENCE** – **délai de carence** – waiting time (period during which an insurer does not pay compensation); waiting period; qualifying period.
- **CIRCULATION** – **délai de circulation** – currency (of a bill etc); period of validity.

- **COMPARAÎTRE** – **délai pour comparaître** – time fixed for (entering an) appearance.
- **COMPARUTION** – **délai de comparution** – time fixed for (entering an) appearance.
- **COURIR** – **faire courir un délai** – start a period running; start time running.
- **DANS le délai de trois ans** – within three years.
- **DÉNONCIATION** – **délai de dénonciation** – period of notice to terminate.
- **DISTANCE** – **délai de distance** – extra time allowed for distance.
- **ÉCHÉANCE** – **délai d'échéance** – due date; date payable; date of expiry (expiration); maturity; date on which an obligation must be performed.
- **ÉCHÉANCE du délai** – expiry of the term or time(-limit).
- **ENLÈVEMENT** – **délai d'enlèvement** – time-limit for collection.
- **ÉPREUVE** – **délai d'épreuve** – trial period.
- **ÉVACUATION** – **délai d'évacuation** – (notice or order giving) time to quit.
- **EXÉCUTION** – **délai d'exécution** – time for performance.
  - **DROIT** – **délai d'exécution du droit** – time within which the right must be exercised.
- **EXERCICE** – **délai d'exercice** – time-limit for exercising a right etc.
- **EXPIRATION du délai** – expiry of the term or time(-limit).
- **EXPULSION** – **délai d'expulsion** – time to quit.
- **FIXATION d'un délai** – fixing a time-limit.
- **FIXER** – **délai fixé par le juge** – time-limit fixed by the court (judge).
- **FORCLUSION** – **délai de forclusion** – extinctive time-limit.
- **FRANC** – **délai franc** – time-limit starting from the first full day of the period and ending on the day after the last day of the period, ie measured in clear days.
- **GARANTIE** – **délai de garantie** – period covered by a guarantee or warranty.
- **GRÂCE** – **délai de grâce** – extension of time for payment etc granted by the court.
- **HORS délai** – out of time.
- **IMPARTIR un délai** – fix a time-limit.
  - **LOI** – **délai imparti par la loi** – statutory time-limit or period.
- **INOBSERVATION du délai** – failure to observe the time-limit.

- **INTENTER** – délai pour intenter une action – time within which proceedings must be taken.
- **INTERRUPTION des délais** – interruption of the limitation or prescription period, after which time begins to run afresh, ie the whole period recomences from the beginning. (Cf SUSPENSION below.)
- **JUDICIAIRE** – délai judiciaire – time-limit fixed by the court (judge).
- **LÉGAL** – délai légal – statutory time-limit or period.
- **MORATOIRE** – délai moratoire – extension of time for payment.
- **NON-RESPECT du délai** – failure to observe the time-limit.
- **OCTROI d'un délai** – granting of time.
- **OPPOSITION** – délai d'opposition – time-limit for lodging an application to set aside or raising an objection.
- **PÉREMPTION** – délai de péremption – strict time-limit (after which, eg, an instrument becomes ineffective (without destroying the underlying right) or an application may be made to strike out proceedings which have not been pursued for two years); fixed term.
- **PLANCHE** – délai de planche – lay days.
- **PRÉCLUSION** – délai de préclusion (Sw) – strict time-limit.
- **PRÉFIX** – délai préfix – predetermined time-limit; strict time-limit.
- **PRESCRIPTION**
  - •• **ACQUISITIF** – délai de prescription acquisitive – prescription period; period of adverse possession.
  - •• **EXTINCTIF** – délai de prescription extinctive – limitation period.
  - •• **PEINE** – délai de prescription de la peine – limitation period after which sentences may no longer be enforced.
- **PRÉSENTATION** – délai pour la présentation des motifs – time for filing grounds of appeal.
- **PRESTATION** – délai de prestation – time for performance.
- **PROLONGATION d'un délai** – extension of time.
- **PROROGATION d'un délai** – extension of time.
- **RECONNAÎTRE** – le délai que lui sera reconnu pour – the time he will be allowed for.
- **RECOURS** – délai de recours – time for appealing (entering an appeal).

- **REPRÉSENTATION** – délai de représentation – period within which a person (or object) shall again be brought before the court.
- **RIGUEUR** – délai de rigueur – strict time-limit.
- **SANS délai** – without time-limit; forthwith.
- **SURSIS** – délai de sursis – (crim) period of probation; (civ) extension of time for payment.
- **SUSPENSION des délais** – suspension of the limitation or prescription period, after which it continues to run again from the point reached when the suspension began. (Cf INTERRUPTION above.)
- **UTILE** – était encore dans le délai utile pour le faire – was still in time to do so.
- **VIDUITÉ** – délai de viduité – period of 300 days during which a woman may not remarry (after the death of her husband or the cessation of co-habitation preceding divorce).

DÉLAI-CONGÉ – period of notice required to terminate an employment contract.

DÉLAISSEMENT – right to claim full compensation for a ship on abandoning the wreck to the underwriters.
- **HYPOTHÈQUE** – délaissement pour hypothèque – abandonment of land on account of a mortgage.

DÉLAISSER – abandon (a ship to underwriters); desert (one's wife and family).

DÉLATEUR – informer.

DÉLATION
- **SERMENT** – délation du serment – requiring a party to take an oath; putting a party to his oath.

DÉLÉGALISATION – delegation of legislative power by Parliament to the executive.

DÉLÉGATAIRE – person in whose favour a debtor instructs his debtor to make a payment.

DÉLÉGATION – operation whereby a debtor (promisor) instructs a third person (normally his own debtor) to pay a debt or perform a contract for his creditor (promisee) in his place; a species of novation by change of debtor (promisor).
- **EMPLOI** – délégation à l'emploi – Labour Department in the Ministry of Labour.
- **IMPARFAIT** – délégation imparfaite – **délégation** (qv) in which the original

debtor (promisor) remains liable as well as the person he has instructed to pay (or perform) on his behalf.

- **MARCHÉ** – **délégation de marché** – charging the benefit of a public works contract by way of security in order to obtain a bank credit.
- **MUNICIPAL** – **délégation municipale** – interim managing committee (to perform the current administrative tasks of a town council which has been dissolved or has resigned en bloc).
- **PARFAIT** – **délégation parfaite** – **délégation** (qv) in which the person instructing his debtor to pay his creditor himself ceases to be liable.
- **PAIEMENT** – **délégation de paiement** – order (instruction) to pay (usually addressed to a banker).
- **SIGNATURE** – **délégation de signature** – (administrative law) delegation of powers to another public officer.
- **SOLDE** – **délégation de solde** – order to pay one's salary directly to one's dependants.
- **SOMME** – **délégation de sommes** – transfer by court order of sums due to one person to another (eg a husband's earnings to his wife); transfer order; assignment order.
- **SPÉCIAL** – **délégation spéciale** – interim managing committee (to perform the current administrative tasks of a town council which has been dissolved or has resigned en bloc).
- **VOTE** – **délégation de vote** – proxy.

DÉLÉGUÉ

- **PROBATION** – **délégué à la probation** – probation officer.
- **SÉCURITÉ** – **délégué à la sécurité** – security commissioner.
- **SÉNATORIAL** – **délégué sénatorial** – senatorial elector.
- **SYNDICAL** – **délégué syndical** – person representing a union in dealings with the head of a business; trade union's management representative.

DÉLIBÉRATIF

- **VOIX** – **avec voix délibérative** – with a right to vote; entitled to vote; voting.

DÉLIBÉRATION – resolution taken after discussion; discussion; deliberation; decision.

DÉLIBÉRÉ – consideration of a judgment by the judges in chambers; deliberation(s).

- **JUGE** – **renvoi au délibéré d'un juge** – arranging for the addresses to be heard by a single judge, who then discusses the case with the other two members of the bench (optional practice in the Commercial Court).
- **METTRE en délibéré** – deliberate; discuss; withdraw to deliberate; reserve a judgment.
- **RAPPORT** – **délibéré sur rapport** – considered judgment; judgment after deliberation; reserved judgment.
- **SIÈGE** – **délibéré sur le siège** – extempore judgment, ie where the court gives judgment without retiring after consultation on the bench.

DÉLICAT

- **QUESTION délicate** – difficulty; ticklish, nice question.

DÉLICTUEL – in tort; tortious.

- **QUASI** – **responsabilité quasi délictuelle** – liability for negligence (non-intentional tort).

DÉLIMITATION

- **COMMISSION de délimitation** – boundary commission; frontier commission.

DÉLINQUANCE

- **JUVENILE** – **délinquance juvénile** – juvenile delinquency.

DÉLINQUANT – offender.

- **ACCIDENTEL** – **délinquant accidentel** – casual offender.
- **DIFFICILE** – **délinquant difficile** – hardcore offender.
- **MINEUR délinquant** – juvenile delinquent.
- **PRIMAIRE** – **délinquant primaire** – first offender; person prosecuted for the first time.

DÉLIT – (crim) (generally) offence; (specifically) misdemeanour; lesser indictable offence; (civ) tort; (more specifically) intentional tort as opposed to negligent or inadvertent tort (**quasi-délit**).

- **ACCIDENTEL** – **délit accidentel** – casual offence.
- **AUDIENCE** – **délit d'audience** – the offence of disturbing judicial proceedings.
- **CIVIL** – **délit civil** – intentional tort; tort.
- **COMMISSION** – **délit de commission** – offence committed by an act (as opposed to an omission).
- **CONSCIENCE** – **délit de conscience** – "crime" of conscience.
- **CONSOMMÉ** – **délit consommé** – completed offence.

- **CORRECTIONNEL** – délit correctionnel – misdemeanour; lesser indictable offence.
- **DROIT COMMUN** – délit de droit commun – non-political offence; ordinary offence; criminal offence.
- **EXTRADITIONNEL** – délit extraditionnel – extraditable offence.
- **FLAGRANT** délit – offence discovered while it is being committed or immediately afterwards.
  - •• **ENQUÊTE de flagrant délit** – expedited police investigation; on-the-spot investigation (involving extended police powers).
  - •• **PRENDRE en flagrant délit** – arrest while committing an offence (in the act, red-handed, flagrante delicto).
- **FUITE** – délit de fuite – hit-and-run offence; failure to stop and give particulars after an accident.
- **IMPRUDENCE** – délit d'imprudence – offence not requiring mens rea; non-intentional offence; (tort of) negligence; negligent tort.
- **INITIÉ** – délit d'initié – insider dealing (trading).
- **INSTANTANÉ** – délit instantané – offence committed in a single act, ie non-recurrent and non-continuous.
- **MATÉRIEL** – délit matériel – offence which is only constituted if the act or omission produced a specified result; strict-liability offence (not requiring proof of criminal intent (mens rea)).
- **OPINION** – délit d'opinion – (if it is not possible to say: punished, prosecuted, etc for his opinions) offence of opinion; thought-crime.
- **PÉNAL** – délit pénal – misdemeanour; lesser indictable offence; (more generally) criminal offence (as opposed to a civil tort).
- **POLICE CORRECTIONNELLE** – délit de police correctionnelle – misdemeanour; lesser indictable offence.
- **PRESSE** – délit de presse – offence against the legislation on the press.
- **TENTÉ** – délit tenté – attempt.

DÉLIVRANCE – issue; delivery; duty of the vendor to place the goods sold at the disposal of the purchaser.

- **ACTION personnelle en délivrance** – action in personam to be put into possession of a usufruct (life tenancy, life interest).
- **BREVET** – délivrance d'un brevet – grant of a patent.

- **LEGS** – délivrance d'un legs – payment of a legacy.
- **EXEQUATUR** – délivrance de l'exequatur – registration of a foreign judgment; grant of authority to execute.

DÉLIVRER
- **PERSONNE** – délivré à personne – personally served.

DÉLOGEMENT – quitting; ejectment.

DÉLOGER – quit; eject.

DÉLOYAL – unfair.

DEMANDE – action; application; statement of claim; request.

- **ADDITIONNEL** – demande additionnelle – supplementary statement of claim.
- **CAUSE de la demande** – facts and rule of law on which a party founds his case; cause of action.
- **CHIFFRE de la demande** – amount involved (in the case); amount of the claim.
- **COMMUNICATION** – demande de communication de pièces – application for production or handing over of documents for inspection (application for discovery).
- **CONJOINT** – demande conjointe – joint petition for divorce or judicial separation (by both parties).
- **CONNEXE** – demande connexe – associated (related, closely connected) action, claim or application.
- **CRÉDIT** – demande de crédit (supplémentaire) – (supplementary) estimate.
- **DIVISIONNAIRE** – demande divisionnaire – action, claim or application limited to part of the subject-matter.
- **EN demande** – as plaintiff (petitioner).
- **EXEQUATUR** – demande d'exequatur – action to register and enforce a foreign judgment; application for authority to execute.
- **EXPULSION** – demande d'expulsion – action for possession.
- **EXTRADITION** – demande d'extradition – extradition request.
- **GARANTIE** – demande en garantie – action to enforce a guarantee.
- **INCIDENT** – demande incidente – additional (supplementary, interlocutory) application (by one of the parties or a third party in the course of the proceedings); motion; summons.

•• **GARANTIE** – demande incidente en garantie – third-party proceedings against a guarantor.

• **INDÉTERMINÉ** – demande indéterminée – subject-matter of indeterminate value.

• **INITIAL** – demande initiale – writ; statement of claim; originating summons or application.

• **INSCRIPTION** – demande à fin d'inscription – application for registration.

• **INSCRIPTION** – demande d'inscription à l'ordre du jour – motion (application, request) for an item to be included in the agenda.

• **INTERDICTION** – demande en interdiction – application for an administration order and guardianship (for a person incapable of managing his own affairs); application for a person to be declared of unsound mind (declaration of legal incapacity).

• **INTERVENTION**
    •• **FORCÉ** – demande en intervention forcée – third-party notice.
    •• **VOLONTAIRE** – demande en intervention (volontaire) – application to be joined in (the) proceedings.

• **INTRODUCTIF D'INSTANCE** – demande introductive d'instance – writ; statement of claim; originating summons or application; request (of the European Commission of Human Rights bringing a case before the European Court of Human Rights).

• **INVALIDATION** – demande d'invalidation – election petition.

• **JUSTICE** – demande en justice – writ; action; proceedings; statement of claim; claim.

• **MAINLEVÉE** – demande en mainlevée – application for release from (termination of) an attachment etc.

• **MONTANT** de la demande – amount involved (in the case); amount of the claim.

• **NOUVEAU** – demande nouvelle – extension of the statement of claim.

• **OBJET** de la demande – aim (purpose) of the claim or proceedings; subject(-matter) of the claim or proceedings.

• **OFFRE** – demande d'offres – call (advertisement) for tenders.

• **ORDRE DU JOUR** – demande d'inscription à l'ordre du jour – motion (application, request) for an item to be included on the agenda.

• **PRÉJUDICIEL** – demande préjudicielle – application for the decision of a preliminary question (point, issue) (for a preliminary ruling).

• **RECONVENTIONNEL** – demande reconventionnelle – counter-claim; cross-action; (divorce) cross-petition.

• **REJETER** une demande – dismiss an action or claim; reject an application.

• **REPOUSSER** une demande – dismiss an action or claim; reject an application.

• **RETIRER** une demande – withdraw or discontinue an action, claim or application.

• **SUITE** – donner suite à une demande – allow an application.

DEMANDER – apply for; ask for; request.

• **DIVORCE** – demander le divorce – petition for divorce.

DEMANDEUR – plaintiff; petitioner (divorce etc); applicant.

DÉMARCHAGE – selling from door to door; doorstep selling.

DÉMARCHE – step; measure; representation.

DÉMATÉRIALISATION

• **VALEUR** – dématérialisation des valeurs – representing and dealing with securities exclusively by means of entries on a computer account; dematerialisation.

DÉMEMBREMENT

• **PROPRIÉTÉ** – démembrement de (la) propriété – separation of one of the attributes (usus, fructus, abusus) of ownership; one of the attributes so separated.

• **PUISSANCE PUBLIQUE** – démembrements de la puissance publique – collective term covering local and territorial authorities, public corporations, etc.

DÉMENCE – mental disorder.

DEMEURE – place of residence; seat (registered office) of a company.

• **MISE** en demeure – notice to pay or perform; notice to remedy a certain state of affairs; default notice; notice to proceed or to comply (with an order, instruction, formality, etc); notice.

• **PERPÉTUEL** – perpétuelle demeure – permanent attachment to the soil.

DEMI-DROIT – half fee.

DÉMISSION
- **BLANC** – **démission en blanc** – undated letter of resignation.

DÉMOCRATIE
- **MÉDIATISÉ** – **démocratie médiatisée** – system in which, owing to the large number of parties, the head of government is not chosen by the electorate but by negotiations between the parties.

DÉMORALISATION
- **ENTREPRISE de démoralisation de l'armée** – undermining the morale of the troops.

DÉNATURATION – misinterpretation; erroneous interpretation; interpretation of or refusal to apply a clause which is clear and requires no interpretation; misconstruction of a clause in a contract or of foreign law or a legally relevant fact (ground of appeal to the Court of Cassation).

DÉNATURER – misinterpret.

DÉNI
- **JUSTICE** – **déni de justice** – refusal to do justice; refusal to decide a case; (more generally) miscarriage of justice; denial of justice.

DÉNOMINATION – name (of a company etc).
- **COMMERCIAL** – **dénomination commerciale** – trade name; brand.
- **PROFESSIONNEL** – **dénomination professionnelle** – professional description (name).
- **SOCIAL** – **dénomination sociale** – business name; firm name.

DÉNONCER – report (a fact or an offence); give notice of; make a complaint; lay an information; complain of; object to.
- **INSTANCE** – **dénoncer l'instance** – give third-party notice; give notice of proceedings.
- **JUSTICE** – **dénoncer en justice** – report to the prosecuting authorities.
- **TRAITÉ** – **dénoncer un traité** – denounce a treaty.

DÉNONCIATION – report; complaint; information; denunciation (of a treaty); notice (of process given to a third party).
- **ACTE de dénonciation** – formal written notice; notice of attachment.
- **CALOMNIEUX** – **dénonciation calomnieuse** – malicious accusation; bringing false accusations; malicious prosecution.
- **CLAUSE de dénonciation** – denunciation clause; termination clause.
- **EXPLOIT** – **dénonciation de l'exploit de saisie-arrêt** – notice to a judgment debtor of the garnishment (attachment) of a debt in the hands of the garnishee (**tiers saisi**).
- **FACULTÉ de dénonciation** – right to (give notice to) terminate; right to denounce a treaty.
- **FAUX** – **dénonciation en faux** – (defence or objection based on) an allegation of forgery.
- **INSTANCE** – **dénonciation d'instance** – third-party notice; notice of proceedings.
- **NOUVEL ŒUVRE** – see ŒUVRE below.
- **ŒUVRE** – **dénonciation de nouvel œuvre** – application for an injunction to stop building works; proceedings for a quia timet injunction, ie to prevent anticipated damage interfering with enjoyment (possession) of property.
- **SAISIE** – **dénonciation de la saisie** – notice of attachment.
- **SURENCHÈRE** – **dénonciation de la surenchère** – filing or entering a higher bid after completion of an auction. This procedure, the object of which is to ensure a fair price, leads to a second auction if there are any bidders. (See also SURENCHÈRE.)

DENRÉE
- **PÉRISSABLE** – **denrées périssables** – perishable goods.

DÉONTOLOGIQUE
- **CODE déontologique** – code of conduct, ethics or professional etiquette.

DÉPART
- **ASSOCIÉ** – **départ d'un associé** – resignation of a partner.
- **INDEMNITÉ de départ** – compensation for loss of employment; redundancy payment; leaving (severance) allowance.

DÉPARTEMENT – county; département.
- **POLITIQUE** – **département politique** (Sw) – (formerly) Foreign Office.

DÉPARTITEUR – umpire.
- **JUGE départiteur** – judge with a casting vote.

DÉPASSEMENT
- **POUVOIR** – **dépassement des pouvoirs** – exceeding one's powers; acting outside or beyond one's authority.

DÉPENDANCE

- **NÉCESSAIRE** – dépendances nécessaires – necessary appurtenances.
- **RAPPORT** de dépendance – dependent condition; state of dependence.

DÉPENS – costs.

- **COMPENSATION** des dépens – order that each party shall bear its own costs.
- **CONDAMNATION** – demander la condamnation de son adversaire aux dépens – ask for costs.
- **CONDAMNER** aux dépens – award costs against.
- **DISTRACTION** des dépens – right of the successful party's legal representative to recover his disbursements directly from the unsuccessful party.
- **ÉTAT** des dépens – bill of costs; statement of expenditure.
- **INSTANCE** – dépens de l'instance – costs of the proceedings, of the hearing.
- **LIQUIDATION** des dépens – taxation (assessment) of costs; settlement (payment) of costs.
- **TAXATION** dépens – taxation of costs.
- **VÉRIFICATION** des dépens – review by the registrar of his (or the court's) original assessment (**liquidation**) of costs. (If the litigant is still not satisfied he may apply to the president of the court for an order fixing the costs.)

DÉPENSE – expenditure.

- **ARTICLE** de dépense – item of expenditure.
- **BUDGET** des dépenses – expenditure budget.
- **CHAPITRE** des dépenses – head of expenditure.
- **COMPTE** de dépenses – expenditure account.
- **EFFECTIF** – dépenses effectives – actual expenditure.
- **ENGAGÉ** – dépenses engagées – committed expenditure.
- **ÉTABLISSEMENT** – dépenses d'établissement – formation expenses; promotion expenses; capital expenditure.
- **EXÉCUTION** de dépenses – discharge of liabilities.
- **FONCTIONNEMENT** – dépenses de fonctionnement – running expenses.
- **FONDATION** – dépenses de fondation – formation expenses; promotion expenses; capital expenditure.

- **IMPÔT** sur les dépenses – luxury (expenditure) tax (ie calculated on what a person spends).
- **INITIATIVE** des dépenses – the right to initiate (introduce) legislation involving expenditure.
- **OBLIGATOIRE** – dépenses ayant un caractère obligatoire – expenditure of a binding nature; mandatory expenditure.
- **PAIEMENT** de dépenses – discharge of liabilities.
- **PRÉVISIONS** de dépenses – estimated expenditure.
- **PROFESSIONNEL** dépenses professionnelles – (deductible) business or professional expenditure.
- **RÉEL** – dépenses réelles – actual expenditure.
- **TITRE** de dépense – head of expenditure; expenditure vote.

DÉPISTAGE

- **CRIMINALITÉ** – dépistage de la criminalité – crime detection.

DÉPLACEMENT

- **ADMINISTRATIF** – déplacement administratif – transfer.
- **BORNE** – déplacement de bornes – moving boundary stones.
- **DISCIPLINAIRE** – déplacement par mesure disciplinaire – disciplinary transfer.
- **DROIT** – déplacement d'un droit – transfer of a right.
- **INDEMNITÉ** de déplacement – travelling and subsistence allowance; relocation (removal, displacement) allowance.
- **SERVICE** – déplacement de service – official journey.

DE PLANO – without further authority; without further formalities or consideration

DÉPORT – backwardation; refusal to act by an arbitrator; withdrawal by a judge.

DÉPORTATION – deportation; displacement; transportation; conscription for labour abroad by an occupying power.

DÉPORTÉ – deportee; offender sentenced to transportation; displaced person.

DÉPORTER

- **SE déporter** – (of a judge) withdraw (on account of a personal interest in the proceedings).

DÉPOSANT – depositor; customer (of a bank).

DÉPOSER – give evidence; deposit; depose; make a statement; file (a document) in the court registry; table (a motion etc); issue (a writ).

- **ACTE** – déposer un acte introductif d'instance – issue a writ.
- **BILAN** – déposer son bilan – file one's statement of affairs (balance sheet) at the beginning of bankruptcy proceedings.
- **CONCLUSION** – déposer ses conclusions – file a pleading, petition, application or statement of claim; file pleadings; make an application.
- **EXPLOIT** – déposer un exploit d'assignation – issue a writ.
- **JUSTICE** – déposer en justice – give evidence.
- **PIÈCE** – déposer des pièces – produce or file documents.
- **PLAINTE** – déposer une plainte – report an offence to the prosecuting authorities; lay an information; make a complaint.
- **RATIFICATION** – déposer un instrument de ratification – deposit an instrument of ratification.
- **REFUS** de déposer – refusal to give evidence.

DÉPOSITAIRE – depositary.

- **AUTORITÉ PUBLIQUE** – dépositaire de l'autorité publique – person exercising public authority.
- **JUSTICE** – dépositaire de justice – official or statutory depositary.

DÉPOSITION – statement (given in evidence); evidence given by a witness; deposition.

- **RECEVOIR** une déposition – examine (a witness); take a statement (deposition) (from a witness).

DÉPOSSÉDER – dispossess; oust; evict.

DÉPOSSESSION – dispossession; eviction; parting with possession.

DÉPÔT – deposit; account; prison; filing of a document in the registry; tabling.

- **ACTION** – dépôt de l'action – issue of a writ; commencement of proceedings.

- **BILAN** – dépôt du bilan – filing one's statement of affairs (balance sheet) at the beginning of bankruptcy proceedings.
- **CERTAIN** – dépôt certain de titres – individual deposit of securities in safe custody (as opposed to collective deposit).
- **CERTIFICAT** de dépôt – deposit receipt.
- **COMPTE** de dépôt – current account.
- **COMPTE** – dépôt en compte – placing or holding money on a current account.
- **DÉCOUVERT** – dépôt à découvert – articles or certificates deposited with a bank otherwise than in sealed packets or an individual safe; unsealed deposit.
- **DEMANDE** – dépôt de la demande – filing an application or statement of claim.
- **DOUANE** – dépôt de douane – customs warehouse; bonded warehouse.
- **ÉCHÉANCE** – dépôt à échéance fixe – fixed(-term) deposit.
- **FONDS** en dépôt – amounts held (funds placed) on deposit.
- **GARANTIE** – dépôt de garantie – sum deposited as a guarantee.
- **INACTIF** – dépôt inactif – stationary account.
- **IRRÉGULIER** – dépôt irrégulier – deposit where the depositary acquires the ownership of the things deposited and is merely required to return an equivalent number or amount of articles of the same kind, eg money deposited in a bank account; general deposit.
- **JUDICIAIRE** – dépôt judiciaire – lodging in court or payment into court or according to the directions of the court; placing in the custody of the court.
- **JUSTICE** – dépôt en justice – lodging in court or payment into court or according to the directions of the court; placing in the custody of the court.
- **LÉGAL** – dépôt légal – legal deposit or filing (delivery) of copies of publications.
  - **BIBLIOTHÈQUE** de dépôt légal – copyright (deposit) library; legal deposit library.
- **MANDAT** de dépôt – order of a court or investigating judge to a prison governor to to admit and detain an accused; committal warrant; detention order.
- **MARQUE** – dépôt d'une marque – registration of a trademark.
- **MENDICITÉ** – dépôt de mendicité – vagrancy centre.

- **MODÈLE** – dépôt d'un modèle – registration of a design.
- **NÉCESSAIRE** – dépôt nécessaire – bailment of necessity (depositum miserabile).
- **NUIT** – dépôt de nuit – night safe.
- **PLAINTE** – dépôt de plainte – reporting an offence to the prosecuting authorities; laying an information; making a complaint.
- **PRÉAVIS** – dépôt à sept jours de préavis – deposit at seven days' notice.
- **RÉCÉPISSÉ de dépôt** – deposit receipt.
- **RECONNAISSANCE de dépôt** – deposit receipt.
- **REFUS du dépôt** – refusal by the registrar to accept an application for registration.
- **REGISTRE des dépôts** – register of documents deposited in the mortgage registry.
- **RÉGULIER** – dépôt régulier – deposit in which the depositary is obliged to return the actual articles deposited; special deposit.
- **TERME** – dépôt à terme – time deposit.
  - **FIXE** – dépôt à terme fixe – fixed (-term) deposit.
- **TITRES en dépôt** – securities held on deposit.
- **USAGE** – dépôt d'usage – deposit for use.

DÉPRÉCIATION
- **INDEMNITÉ de dépréciation** – compensation for wear and tear.

DÉPUTATION
- **CANDIDAT à la députation** – parliamentary candidate.
- **PERMANENT** – députation permanente – standing committee; (Belg) provincial council.

DÉRÈGLEMENT
- **MŒURS** – dérèglement des mœurs – immorality.

DÉRIVÉ
- **DROIT dérivé** – subordinate legislation.

DÉROGATION – partial repeal; creation of an exception; exclusion from the effect of a provision; exemption; repeal; exception.
- **LÉGAL** – sauf dérogation légale – unless otherwise provided (by law).
- **PAR dérogation à** – as an exception to.

DÉROGATOIRE
- **RÈGLE** – des règles dérogatoires du droit commun – exceptions to the general law.

DÉROGER
- **À** – déroger à – exclude the operation of a rule etc; create an exception from; vary from; depart from.

DÉROULEMENT
- **INSTANCE** – déroulement de l'instance – (course or conduct of the) proceedings.
- **PROCÉDURE** – déroulement normal de la procédure – proper conduct of the proceedings.

DÉROULER
- **AFFAIRE** – l'affaire se déroulera – the case will proceed.
- **SE dérouler** – (of proceedings) be conducted.

DÉSACCORD – dissent.
- **PERSISTANT** – désaccord persistant – deadlock.

DÉSAFFECTATION – abandonment, eg of a public right of way; change of category from public to private.

DÉSAFFECTER – exclude from the category of public state property.
- **NE PAS** – tant qu'ils n'ont pas été désaffectés – so long as they remain public state property.

DÉSAVEU – action to disclaim acts by a bailiff, notary, etc done without, or in excess of, his client's authority.
- **PATERNITÉ** – désaveu de paternité – action to disclaim paternity.

DESCENDANCE – issue; descendants.
- **LÉGITIME** – descendance légitime – birth in wedlock; legitimate descent.

DESCENTE
- **JUSTICE** – descente de justice – inspection of the premises (by the court); visit to the locus (in quo).
- **LIEU** – descente sur les lieux – visit to the locus (in quo), site of the crime, etc; inspection.

DÉSERTION
- **COMPLOT** – désertion avec complot – conspiracy and desertion.

DÉSHÉRENCE – failure of issue on intestacy.

- **SUCCESSION en déshérence** – failure of heirs; unclaimed estate; vacant succession, ie where there is no heir or no heir willing to take the estate, no surviving spouse and no universal (ie residuary) legatee.
- **TOMBER en déshérence** – escheat; revert to the state or the Crown.

DÉSIGNATION – nomination; appointment; description; right to appoint a representative to the supervisory board of a company.
- **DROIT de désignation** – right of appointment or nomination; right to appoint a representative to the supervisory board of a company.
- **ORIGINE** – désignation d'origine – indication or warranty of origin.
- **PROFESSIONNEL** – désignation professionnelle – professional description; job description.

DÉSIGNER – (in statutory definitions) to mean.

DÉSINTÉRESSER – satisfy; pay off; buy out.

DÉSINVESTITURE – removal from office.

DÉSISTEMENT – renunciation, waiver (of a right); abandonment or withdrawal (of proceedings or a candidature); discontinuance.
- **ACTION** – désistement de l'action – waiver of a right of action.
- **INSTANCE** – désistement d'instance – discontinuance or withdrawal of the proceedings only (not implying waiver of one's right of action).
- **VOLONTAIRE** – désistement volontaire – volontary abandonment of an intended offence before it is committed.

DÉSISTER
- **ACTION** – se désister d'une action – withdraw or discontinue an action.
- **CONTRAT** – se désister d'un contrat – terminate a contract.
- **SE désister** – withdraw.

DÉSPÉCIALISATION – extension by a lessee of commercial premises of his business to activities not contemplated by the lease.

DESSAISI – (of an official) (has) ceased to deal with (been taken off) a case; (of a court) (is) functus officio.

DESSAISINE-SAISINE – conveyance.

DESSAISIR – render functus officio; take (investigating judge, police officer, etc) off a case.
- **DROIT** – dessaisi de l'exercice de ses droits – excluded from exercising his rights.
- **GESTION** – le débiteur ne sera plus dessaisi de la gestion de son entreprise – the debtor will no longer be prohibited from managing his business.
- **SE dessaisir** – (of a court) stop dealing with a case; relinquish jurisdiction; decide one has no jurisdiction to hear.
  - **DE** – se dessaisir de quelque chose – relinquish something.
- **TRIBUNAL** – dessaisir un tribunal d'une affaire – remove a case from a court for lack of jurisdiction; terminate the authority of a court; render a court functus officio.

DESSAISISSEMENT – removal of a case from a court; deprival of possession; (in relation to a bankrupt) deprival of the right to administer or alienate his property; (of a court) fact of being functus officio; relinquishment of jurisdiction.

DESSERTE
- **VOIRIE** – desserte de voirie – available roads; access by road.

DESSIN
- **INDUSTRIEL** – dessins ou modèles industriels – industrial drawings and designs.

DESTINATAIRE – consignee; addressee; person being (to be) served; recipient.
- **RÈGLE** – destinataire d'une règle juridique – person to whom a rule of law is directed or addressed.

DESTINATION – use or purpose for which something is intended; normal use.
- **DÉCLARÉ** – destination déclarée – declaration of intended use.
- **PÈRE DE FAMILLE** – destination du père de famille – use by owner of two tenements of one for the benefit of the other in such a way that an easement or profit arises when one of the tenements passes into different hands; state of affairs which would constitute an easement if the dominant and servient tenements were owned by different persons; quasi-easement.

DESTITUER – dismiss (a person from a post).

DESTITUTION – dismissal (of a person from a post).

DÉSUÉTUDE
- **TOMBER en désuétude** – become obsolete through non-user.

DÉTACHÉ – seconded.

DÉTACHEMENT – secondment.

DÉTAIL
- **APPLICATION – détails d'application** – implementing regulations or arrangements.
- **EXÉCUTION – détails d'exécution** – implementing regulations or arrangements.

DÉTAXE – return or remission of tax, duties, dues, fees, etc.

DÉTAXÉ – tax-free; with reduced tax.

DÉTENIR – hold.

DÉTENTEUR – possessor; holder; bearer; custodian; occupier; bailee.
- **ACTUEL – détenteur actuel** – current holder.
- **GAGISTE – détenteur gagiste** – pledgee.

DÉTENTION – custody; keeping; imprisonment; (more particularly) imprisonment for political offences; detention; control; occupation.
- **ARBITRAIRE – détention arbitraire** – arbitrary, illegal imprisonment; false imprisonment.
- **CRIMINEL – détention criminelle** – imprisonment for political offences.
- **INJUSTIFIÉ – détention injustifiée** – wrongful detention.
- **MAINTIEN en détention** – continued detention (on remand); remand (in custody).
- **MATÉRIEL – détention matérielle** – physical control.
- **PRÉCAIRE – détention précaire** – occupation of another's property by virtue of an agreement with the owner (eg as a tenant).
- **PRÉVENTIF – détention préventive** (Belg) – detention on remand; remand (in custody); detention pending investigation or trial; custody (for short periods).
- **PROVISOIRE – détention provisoire** – detention on remand; remand (in custody); detention pending investigation or trial; pre-trial detention; custody (for short periods).
- **STUPÉFIANT – détention de stupéfiants** – possession of drugs.
- **TITRE de détention** – committal order.

DÉTENU – prisoner.
- **CONTRAIGNABLE – détenu contraignable** – debtor liable to imprisonment.
- **PRIMAIRE – détenu primaire** – first offender.

DÉTÉRIORATIONS – (of a tenant for life etc) waste (dilapidations).
- **RÉPONDRE – il ne répond pas des détériorations** – he is not liable for waste (dilapidations).

DÉTERMINÉ – specified.
- **TEL – telle personne déterminée** – a specified person.

DÉTERMINER – assess.

DÉTOURNEMENT – conversion; fraudulent conversion; embezzlement; misappropriation.
- **ACTIF – détournement d'actifs** – concealment of assets by a debtor or bankrupt.
- **CLIENTÈLE – détournement de clientèle** – enticement of another's customers.
- **FONDS – détournement de fonds** – embezzlement (in the case of a clerk or servant); fraudulent conversion; misappropriation (of money or funds).
- **GAGE – détournement de gage** – fraudulent conversion of securities or pledges.
- **MINEUR – détournement de mineur** – abduction of a minor.
- **OBJET SAISI – détournement d'objets saisis** – fraudulent removal or conversion of attached property (goods seized).
- **PIÈCE – détournement de pièces** – suppression of documents or documentary evidence.
- **POUVOIR – détournement de pouvoir** – abuse (misuse, misapplication) of a power, authority or discretion; improper exercise of authority; misfeasance (in (public) office).

DÉTRUIRE – rebut (a presumption).

DETTE – liability; obligation; debt.
- **ACTIF – dette active** – right to receive payment of a debt.
- **ALIMENTAIRE – dette alimentaire** – liability to pay maintenance; maintenance obligation.
- **ALIMENT – dette d'aliments** – liability to pay maintenance; maintenance obligation.
- **ALTERNATIF – dette alternative** – alternative obligation.
- **CADUC – dette caduque** – statute-barred debt.
- **CAMBIAIRE – dette cambiaire** – sum due on a bill of exchange.

- **COMMUNAUTÉ** – dette de la communauté – debt of the (marital) community.
- **COMPTE** – dette du compte courant – debit balance on current account.
- **CORPS CERTAIN** – dette de corps certain – obligation to transfer specific goods.
- **DEVISE** – dette en devises étrangères – foreign-currency debt.
- **ÉCHU** – dette échue – debt due, payable.
- **EMPRUNT** – dette d'emprunt – funded debt.
- **ESPÈCE** – dette d'espèce – obligation to sell or deliver specific goods.
- **EXEMPT de dettes** – free of debts; unencumbered.
- **EXIGIBLE** – dette exigible – debt due, payable.
- **FINANCIER** – dette financière – financial obligation.
- **FLOTTANT** – dette flottante – floating debt; unfunded debt.
- **FONCIER** – dette foncière – charge on land, ie a capital-sum payment of which (together with costs and interest if stipulated) is charged on land. No consideration is stated in the transaction, which, unlike a mortgage, does not purport to be the security for the repayment of a loan.
- **GAGE** – dette gagée – secured debt.
- **GENRE** – dette de genre – obligation to transfer generic goods.
- **HYPOTHÉCAIRE** – dette hypothécaire – mortgage debt.
- **IMMOBILIER** – dette immobilière – encumbrance; charge on land.
- **IMPÔT** – dette d'impôt – tax owing; tax arrears.
- **JEU** – dette de jeu – gaming debt.
- **MARCHANDISE** – dette sur marchandises – obligation to transfer or deliver goods.
- **MASSE** – dette de la masse – debt of the bankruptcy arising out of the obligations entered into by the trustee while administering the assets and payable out of the bankrupt's assets or estate before distribution to the creditors.
- **MOBILIER** – dette mobilière – debt secured on movables.
- **NANTISSEMENT** – dette garantie par nantissement – debt guaranteed by (collateral) securities.
- **OBLIGATAIRE** – dette obligataire – debenture debt; bond.

- **PASSIF** – dette passive – debt; liability to pay a debt.
- **PORTABLE** – dette portable – debt payable at the creditor's residence or place of business.
- **PRISE EN CHARGE d'une dette** – assumption of liability for the obligation or debt of another.
- **PROMESSE de dette** – formal unilateral obligation to pay or perform for which consideration is not required and usually not mentioned.
- **QUÉRABLE** – dette quérable – debt payable at the debtor's residence or place of business.
- **RAPPORT des dettes** – operation whereby an heir deducts from his share of the estate his debts to the deceased or a coheir.
- **RECONNAISSANCE de dette** – formal acknowledgement of a duty to pay or perform for which consideration is not required and usually not mentioned.
- **REMISE de dette** – release from or waiver of a debt.
- **REPRENDRE une dette** – undertake to satisfy the debt or perform the obligation of another.
- **REPRISE de dette** – undertaking to satisfy the debt or perform the obligation of another.
- **SOCIAL** – dette sociale – partnership or company debt.
- **SOLIDAIRE** – dette solidaire – debt or obligation for which several persons are jointly and severally liable.
- **SUBROGÉ à la dette** – person assuming the liability to pay the debt or perform the obligation of another.
- **SUCCESSORAL** – dette successorale – debt of the (deceased's) estate.
- **VIAGER** – dette viagère – liability to pay an annuity.

DETTIER – person imprisoned for failing to pay a fine or taxes.

DEUXIÈME
- **CHANGE** – deuxième de change – second of exchange.

DÉVIANCE – deviant behaviour.

DEVIS – (detailed) estimate.

DEVISE – national or foreign currency; for exchange control purposes, any instrument entitling to payment in a foreign currency.

- **ALLOCATION** en devises – exchange control allowance, permission, allocation.
- **APPRÉCIÉ** – **devise appréciée** – hard currency.
- **ATTRIBUTION** de devises – exchange control allowance (allocation) or permission.
- **CONTINGENTEMENT** de devises – exchange control.
- **CRÉANCE** en devises étrangères – right to receive payment in foreign currency.
- **FORT** – **devise forte** – hard currency.
- **OCTROI** de devises – exchange control permission; currency allowance.
- **OPÉRATION** sur devises – currency transaction.
- **RENTRÉE** de devises – foreign-currency receipts (payments received).

DEVISE-TITRE – foreign-currency security.

DEVOIR

- **ATTENTION** – **devoir d'attention** – duty of care.
- **CHARGE** – **devoirs de sa charge** – official duties; official functions.
- **CONJUGAL** – **devoir conjugal** – duty to have sexual relations with one's spouse.
- **DILIGENCE (ET PRUDENCE)** – **devoir de diligence (et prudence)** – duty of care.
- **OMISSION** – **devoir d'omission** – duty to abstain from doing something.
- **SECOURS** – **devoir de secours** – duty of assistance (owed to a spouse).
- **VIOLATION** du devoir professionnel – breach of professional (official) duty.

DÉVOLUTIF

- **EFFET** dévolutif – (of an application to set aside) effect of bringing a default judgment back to the court by which it was originally decided; transfer of all issues of fact and law to a (higher) court (eg on appeal).
  - **NORMAL** – **effet dévolutif normal** – the normal transfer of jurisdiction.

DÉVOLUTION – passing; transfer; devolution; transmission, in particular with regard to the right of the paternal or maternal relations to succeed to the whole of the estate on the failure of the other line.

- **COMPÉTENCE** – **dévolution de compétence** – transfer of jurisdiction or powers.
- **HÉRÉDITAIRE** – **dévolution héréditaire** – succession to an estate.
- **SUCCESSION** – **dévolution de la succession** – order of devolution of property.

DIES

- **AD QUEM** – **dies ad quem** – final day of a time-limit.
- **A QUO** – **dies a quo** – day on which a thing is done or an instrument becomes operative (formerly excluded when calculating a time-limit) : the old rule still applies to time-limits calculated in days; dies a quo.

DIÈTE

- **FÉDÉRAL** – **Diète fédérale** – (German) Federal Parliament (**Bundestag**).
- **PROVINCIAL** – **Diète provinciale** – (Austrian or German) Land Parliament (**Landtag**).

DIFFAMATION – defamation; libel; slander; criminal libel.

DIFFÉREND – dispute.

- **COLLECTIF** – **différend collectif (de travail)** – labour (industrial) dispute.
- **JUSTICIABLE** – **différend justiciable** – legal dispute; dispute falling within the jurisdiction of the courts.
- **TRAVAIL** – **différend du travail** – labour (industrial) dispute.
- **VIDER** un différend – settle a dispute.

DIFFICULTÉ

- **EXÉCUTION** – **difficultés d'exécution d'un jugement** – points (difficulties) arising on the execution of a judgment.

DIFFORME – inconsistent; having a different content.

DILATOIRE

- **APPEL** dilatoire – appeal entered to gain time.
- **EXCEPTION** dilatoire – defence raised to gain time, eg so as to decide whether to accept a succession or give third-party notice to a guarantor; application to stay the proceedings to allow time to make a decision or comply with a formality.
- **INTÉRÊT** – **dans un intérêt dilatoire** – with a view to protracting the proceedings; as a delaying tactic.
- **MANŒUVRES** dilatoires – delaying tactics.
- **PROCÉDÉS** dilatoires – delaying tactics.

DILIGENCE – care; (in plural) steps in the proceedings.

- **À** – **est fait à la diligence du juge** – must be done by the judge.

- **DEVOIR de diligence (et prudence)** – duty of care.
- **FAIT – diligences faites** – steps taken.
- **MANIFESTER la diligence voulue** – exercise due care (and attention to duty, including the duty to proceed expeditiously); show proper (due) diligence.
- **PARTIE – diligence de la partie** – system in which the initiative in commencing and pursuing the proceedings lies with the parties.

DILIGENTER – introduce or conduct proceedings.

DIMINUTIF – lesser claim.

DIMINUTION
- **ACTION en diminution** – action by the purchaser for a reduction in the price of goods.
- **CAPACITÉ – diminution de la capacité de travail** – loss of earning capacity.

DIPLÔMÉ (adj) – qualified; certificated; state certified; state registered.

DIRE – (of a court) hold (rule); written objection entered by counsel relating to the terms and conditions of a sale by the court; (in plural) allegations.
- **DIRE pour droit** – rule; hold; find.
- **DROIT – dire le droit** – hear and determine cases.
- **EXPERT – à dire d'experts** – according to expert opinion or evidence.
- **REQUÉRANT – le requérant dit** – the applicant alleges.

DIRECT
- **RÈGLES directes** – (private international law) substantive rules.

DIRECTEMENT
- **APPLICABLE – directement applicable** – directly applicable; self-executing.

DIRECTES – income-tax department; inland revenue.

DIRECTEUR – manager (of a company); Deputy (Under-)Secretary; head of department; director.
- **GÉNÉRAL – directeur général** – general manager; Deputy (Under-)Secretary; head of department; director.
- **POLICE URBAINE – Directeur départemental des polices urbaines** – County Commissioner of Municipal (City) Police; Chief Constable.

- **POLITIQUE – Directeur politique** – Political Director.

DIRECTION
- **AGENT de direction** – senior executive.
- **DÉBAT – direction des débats** – conduct (control) of the proceedings.
- **INTELLECTUEL – direction intellectuelle** – non-physical control of an object, eg by the owner of a chauffeur-driven car; right to give orders relating to the thing in question.
- **MATÉRIEL – direction matérielle** – physical control.

DIRECTOIRE – management (of a company); managing board.

DIRIGISME – planning; planned economy.
- **ÉTATIQUE – dirigisme étatique** – state planning.

DIRIMANT – (of an objection etc) fatal (to an argument, case, etc).
- **EMPÊCHEMENT dirimant** – impediment entailing nullity or voidability of a marriage celebrated in spite of the impediment; absolute impediment.

DISCERNEMENT – understanding.
- **ÂGE de discernement** – age of discretion.

DISCIPLINAIRE
- **POUVOIRS disciplinaires** – (of a chairman, speaker, etc) powers for the maintenance of order.

DISCIPLINE
- **CONSEIL de discipline** – disciplinary committee (board).
- **FAUTE contre la (faute de) discipline** – disciplinary offence.
- **GROUPE – discipline de groupe** – (in parliament) obligation to vote on party lines; the party whip.
- **VOTE – sans discipline de vote** – in a free vote.

DISCONTINUATION
- **POURSUITE – discontinuation des poursuites** – abandonment (discontinuation) of the prosecution; decision to offer no evidence.

DISCOUNT – sale at abnormally low prices.

DISCOURS
- **COURONNE (TRÔNE) – discours de la couronne (du trône)** – speech from the throne.

DISCRÉTIONNAIRE

- **POUVOIR discrétionnaire** – (unfettered) discretion or (unlimited) power.
  - **PRÉSIDENT – pouvoir discrétionnaire du président** – power of the president of an assize court to take all such measures as he may consider useful for ascertaining the truth.

DISCRÉTIONNAIREMENT – in the exercise of one's own unfettered discretion.

DISCUSSION

- **BÉNÉFICE de discussion** – surety's right to require execution to be directed against the principal debtor before the creditor levies execution on the surety.

DISCUTER – attach and sell the goods of a debtor.

- **QUESTION – où la question n'avait pas été expressément discutée** – (proceedings) in which the point was not argued (expressly raised).

DISJOINDRE – separate (sever) (proceedings).

DISJONCTION – separation (severance) (of proceedings).

- **DEMANDE de disjonction** – application for a separate trial.

DISPACHE – average adjustment.

DISPARITION – disappearance in circumstances which render survival improbable.

DISPENSE – exemption; dispensation.

- **ÂGE – dispense d'âge** – exemption from the rule as to age (age requirement).
- **BAN – dispense de bans** – dispensation from publication of the banns.
- **CAUTION – dispense de caution** – exemption from the requirement of giving security.
- **EMPÊCHEMENT DE MARIAGE – dispense des empêchements de mariage** – exemption (dispensation) from impediments to marriage.
- **PEINE – dispense de peine** – discharge (without imposing a penalty on an accused who has committed an offence but appears unlikely to commit further offences).
  - **CONDITIONNEL – dispense de peine conditionnelle** – conditional discharge.

DISPENSER

- **DE – dispenser de** – exempt from.

- **PEINE – dispenser de peine** – discharge.

DISPONIBILITÉ

- **CRÉDIT – disponibilité d'un crédit** – availability of funds under an appropriation.
- **EN disponibilité** – on half pay, ie available for service.
- **TRÉSORERIE – disponibilités de trésorerie** – available funds; liquid assets; cash resources.

DISPONIBLE

- **AFFECTATION – disponible sans affectation** – uncommitted.
- **QUOTITÉ disponible** – portion of his estate over which a testator can dispose freely; disposable portion.

DISPOSANT – person alienating; donor; testator.

DISPOSER

- **CAPACITÉ de disposer** – capacity to alienate.
- **DE – disposer de** – alienate.
  - **DROIT des peuples à disposer d'eux-mêmes** – right of self-determination.
- **VIF – disposer entre vifs** – alienate inter vivos.

DISPOSITIF (adj)

- **PRINCIPE dispositif** – rule governing civil proceedings requiring the court to make a decision on all the questions submitted to it and on nothing else.

DISPOSITIF (noun) – (of a statute or decree) enacting clauses (body, purview).

- **JUGEMENT – dispositif d'un jugement** – (formal) order (setting out the effect of a judgment); operative words (provisions) (of a judgment).
- **PRINCIPE du dispositif** – rule that the parties control the course of civil proceedings.

DISPOSITION – alienation; provision.

- **ACTE de disposition** – instrument or legal transaction disposing of rights or property; disposal; conveyance; deed of gift.
- **APPLICATION – disposition d'application** – implementing provision.
- **CAUSE DE MORT** – see MORT below.
- **COMMUN – dispositions communes** – provisions covering a number of different cases; common provisions.

- **CONTRAIRE** – sauf disposition contraire – unless otherwise provided.
- **DÉCÈS** – disposition en cas de décès – donation mortis causa.
- **DERNIÈRE VOLONTÉ** – see VOLONTÉ below.
- **DROIT de disposition** – right to alienate; right of disposal.
- **EXÉCUTION** – disposition d'exécution – implementing provision.
- **FACULTATIF** – disposition facultative – optional provision.
- **GOUVERNEMENT** – mise à la disposition du gouvernement (Belg) – placing at the disposal of the government (system for dealing with habitual offenders involving preventive detention combined with conditional release adjusted to the requirements of the individual concerned).
- **GRATUIT** – disposition à titre gratuit – transfer without consideration (gift or legacy).
- **IMPÉRATIF** – disposition impérative – mandatory provision.
- **LÉGAL** – disposition légale – statutory provision.
- **LÉGISLATIF** – disposition législative – statutory provision.
  - •• **RÉGLEMENTAIRE** – dispositions législatives et réglementaires – statutes and regulations.
- **MORT** – disposition à cause de mort – testamentary disposition.
- **PÉNAL** – disposition pénale – criminal provision.
- **POSTHUME** – disposition posthume – testamentary provision.
- **POTESTATIF** – disposition potestative – optional or non-mandatory provision.
- **POUVOIR de disposition** – power of alienation; power of disposal.
- **PRÉLIMINAIRE** – disposition préliminaire – introductory provision.
- **PROCÉDURE** – disposition de procédure – procedural provision.
- **PROHIBITIF** – disposition prohibitive – prohibition.
- **PROTECTEUR** – disposition protectrice – protective provision.
- **RÉGLEMENTAIRE** – disposition réglementaire – regulation.
- **SAUVEGARDE** – disposition de sauvegarde – protective provision.
- **TRANSITOIRE** – disposition transitoire – transitional provision.

- **VIF** – disposition entre vifs – conveyance or donation inter vivos.
- **VOLONTÉ** – disposition de dernière volonté – testamentary disposition.

DISQUALIFIER
- **VICE DE FOND** – disqualifier un vice de fond en vice de forme – redefine (downgrade, construe) an essential defect as a formal (merely procedural) defect.

DISSIDENT – dissenting; voting against; opposing; dissentient.

DISSIMULATION – concealment.
- **BIEN** – dissimulation de biens – concealment of assets.

DISSOLUTION – winding-up; dissolution (of Parliament); termination of a status or institution.
- **MARIAGE** – dissolution du mariage – divorce; dissolution of marriage.

DISSOUDRE – wind up (a company); dissolve (a partnership).

DISTINCTION
- **HONORIFIQUE** – distinction honorifique – honour.

DISTRACTION
- **DEMANDE en distraction** – claim to the ownership of goods or property seized by a third party made during the execution proceedings.
- **DÉPENS** – distraction des dépens – anyone's right, with the permission of the court, to sue the opposing party for the costs one has advanced (usually exercised by counsel of the successful party).
- **DROIT de distraction** – right of third parties to withdraw their property from the assets in bankruptcy.
  - •• **CRÉANCIER de droit de distraction** – third party having the right to withdraw his property from the assets in bankruptcy.
- **FRAIS** – distraction des frais – deduction of expenses.

DISTRIBUER – allocate (a case to a court).

DISTRIBUTION
- **CHAMBRE** – distribution d'une affaire à une chambre – allocation of a case to a particular court (chamber) for trial.

- **CONTRIBUTION** – **distribution par contribution** – procedure for the pro-rata apportionment between the creditors of the proceeds of the sale of a debtor's attached assets together with any sums of money which may have been garnished; apportionment of the proceeds of execution (in the UK the rule "first come first served" applies except in bankruptcy).
- **ÉTAT de distribution** – distribution scheme; apportionment plan; plan of distribution; distribution of work.
- **EXPRÈS** – **distribution par exprès** – special delivery.
- **PROCÉDURE de distribution** – distribution or apportionment proceedings.

DISTRICT – district union.
- **AFFERMÉ** – **district affermé** – leased preserve.
- **CHASSE** – **district de chasse** – hunting preserve.
- **PÊCHE** – **district de pêche** – fishery.

DIVERTIR – misappropriate.

DIVERTISSEMENT – misappropriation; fraudulent conversion.

DIVIDENDE
- **ACOMPTE sur dividende** – interim dividend.
- **ACTION** – **dividende des actions ordinaires** – ordinary dividend.
- **BLOCAGE des dividendes** – dividend stop; dividend freeze.
- **PASSER le dividende** – pay no dividend; pass the dividend.
- **PERÇU**
  - •• **NON** – **dividende non perçu** – unclaimed dividend.
- **PRIORITAIRE** – **dividende prioritaire** – preference dividend.
- **PROVISOIRE** – **dividende provisoire** – interim dividend.

DIVIS – separate.

DIVISION
- **BÉNÉFICE de la division** – right of one of the sureties to limit his liability to his share subject to his having to assume his part of the share of any surety who becomes insolvent.

DIVORCE
- **ACTION en divorce** – divorce petition; divorce proceedings.

- **CAUSE de divorce** – ground of divorce.
- **DEMANDE en divorce** – divorce petition.
  - •• **RECONVENTIONNEL** – **demande reconventionnelle en divorce** – respondent's petition; cross-petition.
- **FAILLITE** – **divorce faillite** – divorce based on the breakdown principle.
- **FAIT RECONNU** – **divorce pour faits reconnus par les deux époux** – divorce on grounds of facts admitted by both parties.
- **FAUTE** – **divorce sans faute** – no-fault divorce.
- **INSTANCE**
  - •• **DE** – **être en instance de divorce** – to be engaged in divorce proceedings.
  - •• **EN** – **instance en divorce** – divorce proceedings.
- **JUGEMENT de divorce** – decree of divorce.
- **MIGRATOIRE** – **divorces migratoires** – forum shopping (in divorce proceedings).
- **MOTIF de divorce** – ground of (for) divorce.
- **PRONONCER un divorce** – pronounce a decree of divorce; grant a divorce; dissolve (terminate) a marriage.
- **REMÈDE** – **divorce remède** – divorce based on the breakdown principle.
- **SANCTION** – **divorce sanction** – divorce for a matrimonial offence.
- **TORT**
  - •• **EXCLUSIF** – **divorce prononcé aux torts exclusifs du mari** – divorce (decree) granted against the husband.
  - •• **RÉCIPROQUE** – **divorce prononcé aux torts réciproques** – divorce based on the fault of both parties; divorce granted to both parties; divorce on grounds of mutual fault.

DIVULGATION – publication; revelation; disclosure.

DOCTRINAL
- **OPINION doctrinale dominante** – most authorities.

DOCTRINE – legal opinion; legal theory; legal writers; doctrine; authorities.
- **CONSTANT** – **il est de doctrine constante** – it is well established.
- **DOMINANT** – **doctrine dominante** – prevailing (better, accepted) opinion; most writers (authorities).

DOCUMENT

- **BORD** – documents de bord – ship's papers.
- **COMPTABLE** – document comptable – accounting document; voucher.
- **EMBARQUEMENT** – document d'embarquement – shipping document.
- **EXPORTATION** document d'exportation – export permit.
- **FAUX** document – forged document.
- **PARLEMENTAIRE** – documents parlementaires – parliamentary papers.
- **PRIMITIF** – document primitif – original document.
- **PROBATOIRE** – document probatoire – written evidence; documentary evidence.
- **SERVICE** – document de service – official document.
- **VOYAGE** – document de voyage – travel document.

DOIT

- **AVOIR** – doit et avoir – debit and credit.

DOL – deceit; fraud; tortious intent; malicious intent; intentional fault.

- **ÉVENTUEL** – dol éventuel – rashness; temerity; recklessness.
  - •• **PAR** dol éventuel – rashly; recklessly.
- **EXCEPTION** de dol – defence alleging fraud on the part of the plaintiff.
- **GÉNÉRAL** – dol général – consciousness of committing an unlawful act; guilty mind; mens rea.
- **INCIDENT** – dol incident – deceit as to a matter not essential to the contract or actually influencing the victim's decision.
- **INDÉTERMINÉ** – dol indéterminé – malicious intent without contemplating a specific result.
  - •• **PAR** dol indéterminé – recklessly.
- **PRINCIPAL** – dol principal – deceit going to the root of the contract (ie decisive in causing the other party to enter into the contract); deceit actually influencing the victim.
- **SPÉCIAL** – dol spécial – special intent.

DOLOSIF – intentional (eg breach of contract).

DOLOSIVEMENT

- **AGIR** dolosivement – act with fraudulent, tortious or malicious intent or with intent to deceive or defraud.

DOMAINE – landed property; real estate; scope; ambit; state (Crown) land(s).

- **AÉRIEN** domaine aérien airspace.
- **AGRICOLE** – domaine agricole – farm; agricultural holding.
- **APPLICATION** – domaine d'application – scope; field of application; ambit.
- **COMPÉTENCE** – domaine de compétence – jurisdiction.
- **CONGÉABLE** – bail à domaine congéable – short-term agricultural tenancy in which the tenant retains ownership of (or is entitled to compensation for) his erections, plantations and crops and also has a right of pre-emption.
- **COURONNE** – domaine de la couronne (Belg etc) – Crown land(s).
- **LOI** – domaine de la loi – parliamentary legislative sphere (ie matters exclusively reserved for parliamentary legislation in France).
- **PRIVÉ** – domaine privé – private property of the state or public authorities (ie property not specifically earmarked for public purposes and governed by private law); private state property.
- **PUBLIC** – domaine public – public property of the state or public authorities (ie property specially earmarked for public purposes and governed by public law); national domain; public state property.
  - •• **DU** domaine public – free (out) of copyright and other similar restrictions; non-copyright.
  - •• **TOMBÉ** dans le domaine public – having become public property; in the public domain; on which the patent has expired or the copyright has lapsed.
- **SOUTERRAIN** – domaine souterrain – ownership of the subsoil.
- **TERRITORIAL** – domaine territorial – area of application; territorial jurisdiction.

DOMANIALITÉ – quality of being state (Crown) land.

DOMANIER – tenant in a short-term lease (**bail à domaine congéable**).

DOMESTICITÉ – household servants.

DOMICILE – ordinary residence; principal residence; official place of residence; habitual residence; permanent residence; home; address. ("Domicile" should not be used as a translation unless it clear that the word is being used in the English sense of "a system of law by which a person is governed".)

- **ABANDON** du domicile conjugal – desertion (of the matrimonial home).
- **ADMISSION** à domicile – special residence permit.
- **ASSIGNATION** à domicile – house arrest.
- **CERTAIN** – domicile certain – fixed abode.
- **COLLECTE** à domicile – house-to-house collection.
- **COMMERCIAL** – domicile commercial – registered office.
- **CONJUGAL** – domicile conjugal – matrimonial home.
- **ÉLECTION** – domicile d'élection – residence for the purpose of performance and jurisdiction (venue); address for service.
- **ÉLECTION** de domicile – choice of jurisdiction; choice of venue; jurisdiction clause; clause giving an address for service.
- **ÉLU** – domicile élu – residence for the purpose of performance and jurisdiction (venue); address for service.
- **ÉTAT** du domicile – state of ordinary residence (see DOMICILE).
- **FICTIF** – domicile fictif – notional residence.
- **FISCAL** – domicile fiscal – residence for tax purposes.
- **FIXE** – domicile fixe – fixed abode.
  - •• **SANS** domicile fixe – of no fixed abode.
- **INVIOLABILITÉ** du domicile – inviolability of a person's residence; sanctity of the home.
- **JURIDICTION** – domicile attributif de juridiction – residence for the purpose of determining jurisdiction.
- **MATRIMONIAL** – domicile matrimonial – district in which a person's marriage may lawfully be celebrated.
- **MENDICITÉ** à domicile – house-to-house begging.
- **MULTIPLE** – domicile multiple – more than one residence.
- **PERMANENT** – domicile permanent – permanent residence.
- **POLICE** – domicile de police – registered address (ie with the police).
- **QUÊTE** à domicile – house-to-house collection.
- **RÉGULIER** – domicile régulier (Sw) – ordinary residence.
- **SECOURS** – domicile de secours – permanent residence for assistance purposes; place where a person is entitled to receive social-security benefits.

- **SOCIAL** – domicile social – registered office of a company or partnership; place where an individual is entitled to receive social-security benefits.
- **SOCIÉTÉ** de domicile – company having only its registered office in a given country.
- **TRANSFERT (TRANSLATION)** de domicile – change of permanent residence.
- **VIOLATION** de domicile – violation of the privacy (sanctity) of the home; trespass on domestic premises; violation of domestic privacy; unlawful entry of a person's home.

DOMICILIATAIRE – paying agent.

DOMICILIATION – domiciliation (indication of place of payment).
- **VISA** de domiciliation – certificate of domiciliation.

DOMMAGE – damage; injury.
- **ACCIDENT** – dommage résultant d'accident – accident damage.
- **ANIMAL** – dommage causé par les animaux – damage caused by animals (eg cattle trespass).
- **ATTROUPEMENT** – dommage causé par les attroupements – riot damage.
- **AUTEUR** du dommage – tortfeasor; person causing the damage.
- **AVARIE** – dommage d'avarie – average.
- **AVIS** de dommage – notice of damage.
- **BIEN** – dommage aux biens – material damage; damage to property.
  - •• **REQUISITIONNÉ** – dommage aux biens requisitionnés – damage to requisitioned property.
- **CONSÉCUTIF** – dommage consécutif – consequential damage; further damage arising after a lapse of time.
- **CONSTATATION** du dommage – assessment of damage; statement of damage.
- **CORPOREL** – dommage corporel – personal (physical, bodily) injury.
- **CULTURE** – dommage aux cultures – damage to crops.
- **DÉCLARATION** de dommage – notice of damage.
- **ÉVALUATION** du dommage – assessment of damage.
- **EXCESSIF** – dommage excessif – exceeding the limit of noise, smoke, etc normally acceptable between neighbours; nuisance.
- **GUERRE** – créance de dommage de guerre – war-damage claim.

- **INTÉGRAL** – dommage intégral – total loss.
- **INTENTION de causer un dommage** – intention to injure.
- **MATÉRIEL** – dommage matériel – damage to property; pecuniary (material) damage.
- **MORAL** – dommage moral – non-pecuniary (non-material) damage.
- **OBJET du dommage** – thing (property) damaged.
- **OCCUPATION** – dommage d'occupation – occupation damage, ie damage caused by the occupying authorities or members of the occupation forces.
- **PATRIMONIAL** – dommage patrimonial – pecuniary damage; economic loss.
- **PÉCUNIAIRE** – dommage pécuniaire – pecuniary damage; pecuniary loss.
- **PERSONNE** – dommage aux personnes – personal (physical, bodily) injury.
- **PERSONNEL** – dommage personnel – personal (physical, bodily) injury.
- **RÈGLEMENT des dommages** – assessment of damages.
- **RESPONSABILITÉ pour les dommages** – liability for damage; damages.
- **RICOCHET** – dommage par ricochet – indirect damage suffered by dependants (or others similarly situated) from the death or injury of a victim.
- **SUBI** – dommage subi – damage suffered.
- **SURVENANCE d'un dommage** – occurrence of damage.
- **TIERS** – dommage aux tiers – damage caused to third parties.
- **VICTIME du dommage** – injured party.

DOMMAGEABLE – injurious; harmful.

DOMMAGES-INTÉRÊTS – damages; compensation; reparation.

- **ACTION en dommages-intérêts** – action for (in) damages.
- **COMPENSATOIRE** – dommages-intérêts compensatoires – damages for failure to perform; damages for breach of contract.
- **FIXATION des dommages-intérêts** – assessment of damages.
- **MORATOIRE** – dommages-intérêts moratoires – damages for late performance, for delay; default interest.

DON – gift; donation.

- **ARGENT** – don en argent – money gift; gift of money.

- **MANUEL** – don manuel – gift from hand to hand.

DONATAIRE – donee.

DONATEUR – donor.

DONATION – gift; donation; voluntary settlement.

- **ACTE de donation** – instrument (deed) of gift; settlement.
- **BIEN** – donation de biens à venir – settlement of future assets.
- **CHARGE** – donation avec charge – gift with a condition attached; gift subject to a condition or obligation.
- **CONTRAT de donation** – contract of gift; voluntary settlement.
- **DÉGUISÉ** – donation déguisée – simulated transaction (eg a sale) concealing a gift.
- **MANUEL** – donation manuelle – gift from hand to hand.
- **MUTUEL** – donation mutuelle – reciprocal donation; mutual gifts.
- **OBLIGATOIRE** – donation obligatoire – gift made in fulfilment of a moral obligation.
- **ONÉREUX** – donation onéreuse – gift with a condition attached; gift subject to a condition or obligation.
- **PERSONNE INTERPOSÉE** – donation par personne interposée – indirect donation.
- **PRÉCIPUTAIRE** – donation préciputaire – money, chattels or land which the surviving spouse is entitled to take from the community property before partition.
- **PROPTER NUPTIAS** – donation propter nuptias – donation in consideration of marriage by the future spouse or a third-party.
- **RÉMUNERATOIRE** – donation rémunératoire – gift in consideration of past services.
- **RÉVOCATION de (d'une) donation** – revocation of a gift.
  - **ACTION en révocation de (d'une) donation** – action to revoke a gift.
- **TESTAMENTAIRE** – donation testamentaire – testamentary gift; gift by will.
- **USAGE** – donation d'usage – customary (traditional) gift.
- **VIF** – donation entre vifs – donation inter vivos (between living persons).

DONATION-PARTAGE – inter vivos distribution of the estate among the presumptive heirs.

DONNER – create or transfer a right in rem.

- **ACTE** – **donner acte de** – (officially, formally) confirm; take formal note of; note a declaration on the record.
- **OBLIGATION de donner** – obligation to transfer property or a right in rem.
- **SUITE** – **donner suite à** – allow (a claim, an application, etc).

DONNEUR

- **AVAL** – **donneur d'aval** – guarantor of a bill.
- **GAGE** – **donneur de gage** – pledgor; mortgagor.
- **ORDRE** – **donneur d'ordre** – employer of an independent contractor; principal; especially, a person instructing a banker or stockbroker.

DOSSIER – file; documentation; case; matter; case-file.

- **COMMUNICATION du dossier** – making the file available for inspection; producing the file for inspection; right of civil servant etc to see his personal file.
- **EXAMEN du dossier** – inspection of the file.
- **PROCÈS** – **dossier du procès** – case file.

DOT – dowry; wife's settled property (administered by the husband for the benefit of the marriage); husband's settled property; gift in consideration of marriage.

- **CONSTITUTION de dot** – marriage settlement on the wife or husband.

DOTATION – endowment; grant; appropriation; civil list; subsidy; subvention.

- **PROVISIONNEL** – **dotation provisionnelle** – reserve; transfer to reserve.

DOTER – make a marriage settlement (especially on a woman); endow.

DOUAIRE – dower (widow's right to the income of her late husband's property).

DOUANE

- **ACQUIT de douane** – customs receipt; customs release.
- **COMMISSIONNAIRE en douane** – customs agent.
- **ENTREPÔT de douane** – bonded warehouse; bond; customs warehouse.
- **PRÉPOSÉ des douanes** – customs official.
- **RAYON de douane** – (customs) frontier zone.

DOUBLE (adj)

- **DEGRÉ** – **droit à un double degré de juridiction** – right to an appeal (two-tier proceedings, a system of appeal courts).
- **IMPOSITION** – **double imposition** – double taxation.
- **INCRIMINATION** – **double incrimination** – (extradition) requirement that the offence committed should be an offence in both countries; requirement of dual criminal liability.

DOUBLE (noun) – second original (of a contract etc).

DOUTE

- **BÉNÉFICE** – **au bénéfice du doute** – for lack of evidence.

DOUZIÈME

- **PROVISOIRE** – **douzième provisoire** – provisional monthly appropriation pending the adoption of the budget.

DOYEN – eldest or senior member of a body.

- **ÂGE** – **doyen d'âge** – oldest member present; provisional chairman (president).
- **CORPS DIPLOMATIQUE** – **doyen du corps diplomatique** – dean or doyen of the diplomatic corps, ie senior ambassador or nuncio accredited in a given capital.

DROIT – law; right; claim; due; duty; charge; title.

- **ABUS de droit** – abuse of rights.
- **ACCESSION** – **droit d'accession** – right of the owner of property to all it produces and everything which becomes united to it, ie (1) all produce (periodical or other), (2) in the case of ownership of the surface, all that lies above or below it, (3) everything that becomes incorporated in it, (4) water springing from or flowing over the soil; right of accession or accretion.
- **ACCISE** – **droit d'accise** – excise duty.
- **ACCROISSEMENT** – **droit d'accroissement** – right of accretion.
- **ACHAT** – **droits d'achat** – purchase options.
- **ACQUIS** – **droit acquis** – vested right; established right.
  - •• **FOI** – **droit acquis de bonne foi** – right acquired in good faith (bona fide).

- **ACQUISITION** – droit en cours d'acquisition – inchoate right.
- **ACQUITTER** un droit – pay dues or charges.
- **ACTION** – droit d'action – cause of action.
- **ADHÉRER** – droit d'adhérer – right to accede to.
- **ADMINISTRATIF** – droit administratif – administrative law.
- **ADMISSION** – droit d'admission – admission fee; entrance money.
- **AÉRIEN** – droit aérien – air law.
- **AFFOUAGE** – droit d'affouage – right to take wood for household use; common of estovers.
- **AGIR** – droit d'agir en justice – right to bring proceedings; right to sue.
- **ALERTE** – droit d'alerte – a right to convey a warning of a danger or of an economically disturbing position directly to an employer or the directors or members of a company etc.
- **ALIÉNABLE** – droit aliénable – alienable right.
- **ALPAGE** – droit d'alpage – right to summer pastures in the mountains.
- **ANCIEN** droit – pre-revolutionary law.
- **ANGARIE** – droit d'angarie – right of angary; right of a belligerent to seize neutral ships in its territorial waters.
- **ANNEXE** – droit annexe – accessory or ancillary right.
- **ANTÉRIORITÉ** – droit d'antériorité – right of prior user; right of priority.
- **APPORT** – droit d'apport – tax on assets brought into a company or partnership.
- **APPUI** – droit d'appui – right of support; easement of support.
- **ARRESTATION** – droit d'arrestation – right to arrest.
- **ASILE** – droit d'asile – right of asylum.
- **ASSOCIATION** – droit d'association – right of association.
- **ASSOCIATION** – droit des associations – law of clubs and associations.
- **ASSURANCE** – droit d'assurance – insurance premium.
- **ATTACHÉ** – droit attaché – cum rights; cum new.
  - •• **PERSONNE** – droit attaché à la personne – strictly (exclusively) personal right; easement in gross.
- **ATTEINTE** aux droits – infringement (violation, impairment) of or interference with rights.

- •• **AUTEUR** – atteinte au droit d'auteur – infringement of copyright.
- **ATTERRISSAGE** – droit d'atterrissage – landing rights.
- **AUTEUR** – droit d'auteur – copyright.
- **AUTEUR** – droits d'auteur – royalties.
- **AUTODÉTERMINATION** – droit d'autodétermination – right of self-determination.
- **BAIL** – droit au bail – tenant's right to a lease.
- **BALANCE** – droit de balance – weighing charge.
- **BANAL** – droit banal – feudal monopoly.
- **BANCAIRE** – droit bancaire – banking law.
- **BASE** – droit de base – basic customs tariff.
- **BATTRE** – droit de battre monnaie – right of coinage.
- **BIEN** – droit des biens – the law of property.
  - •• **MATRIMONIAL** – droit des biens matrimoniaux – the law of matrimonial property.
- **BREVET** – droit des brevets – patent law.
- **CABOTAGE** – droit de cabotage – right to engage in, or monopoly of, coastal trade.
- **CAMBIAIRE** – droit cambiaire – the law of negotiable instruments.
- **CANON** – droit canon – canon law.
- **CESSIBLE** – droit cessible – assignable (transferable) right.
- **CESSION** de droits – assignment of rights.
- **CHANCELLERIE** – droit de chancellerie – office fee; consular fee.
- **CHANGE** – droit du change – the law of negotiable instruments.
- **CHASSE** – droit de chasse – shooting rights; shooting licence.
- **CHOSE** – droit des choses – the law governing real property and chattels.
- **CIRCULATION** – droit de la circulation – the law relating to road traffic; road-traffic law.
- **CITOYEN** – droits du citoyen – civic rights.
- **CIVIL** – droit civil – civil law, ie non-commercial private law.
- **CIVIL ET POLITIQUE** – droits civils et politiques – right to vote and hold public office; civic rights.
- **CIVIQUE** – droits civiques – right to vote and hold public office; civic rights.

- **COALITION** – droit de coalition – right of association.
- **COERCITION** – droit de coercition – right of enforcement; right to enforce.
- **COGESTION** – droit de cogestion – (workers') right of joint management.
- **COLLATION** – droit de collation – right of appointment.
- **COMMERCE** – droits hors (du) commerce – rights which cannot form the subject-matter of a legal transaction.
- **COMMERCIAL** – droit commercial – commercial law; business law.
  - •• **COUTUMIER** – droit commercial coutumier – customary commercial law; mercantile custom; the law merchant; trade custom; commercial practice.
- **COMMISSION** – droit de commission – (broker's etc) commission.
- **COMMUN** – droit commun – general law; ordinary or existing law.
  - •• **DE** droit commun – ordinar(il)y; de droit commun celui qui veut obtenir l'annulation d'un acte – the general rule is that someone seeking to have a transaction set aside.
  - •• **EXORBITANT** du droit commun – going beyond (falling outside the scope of) (the rights conferred by) the general (ordinary) law; creating or constituting an exception to the general law, eg a clause in a government contract excluding the jurisdiction of the ordinary courts.
  - •• **JURIDICTION** de droit commun – ordinary court; ordinary jurisdiction.
  - •• **PROCÉDURE** – droit commun de la procédure – the ordinary rules of procedure.
  - •• **RECOURS** de droit commun – ordinary remedy.
  - •• **TRIBUNAL** – tribunaux de droit commun – the ordinary (and administrative) courts (ie excluding the specialised courts of limited jurisdiction).
- **COMMUNICATION** – droit de communication – right to have documents, accounts, etc made available for inspection.
- **COMMUNICATION** – droit des communications – transport law.
  - •• **AÉRIEN** – droit des communications aériennes – the law of air transport.
- **COMPENSATEUR** – droit compensateur – compensating, equalising tariff; countervailing duty.
- **COMPENSATION** – droit de compensation – (right to) set-off.
- **COMPTANT** – droits au comptant – taxes subject to immediate collection.
- **CONCURRENCE** – droit de la concurrence – competition law; the law of competition; the law prohibiting restraint of trade.
- **CONFLIT** de droits – conflicting claims; alternative grounds of claim.
- **CONFLIT DE LOIS** – droit des conflits de lois – private international law; conflict (of laws); rules governing choice of law.
- **CONSENTEMENT** – droit de consentement – right to sanction taxation etc.
- **CONSERVATION** des droits – preservation of rights.
- **CONSOMMATION** – droit de consommation – excise duty.
- **CONSOMMATION** – droit de la consommation – consumer law.
- **CONSTATÉ** – droits constatés – taxes not subject to immediate collection.
- **CONSTITUTIONNEL** – droit constitutionnel – constitutional law.
  - •• **COUTUMIER** – droit constitutionnel coutumier – customary constitutional law; conventions of the constitution.
- **CONSTRUIRE** – droit de construire – right to build.
- **CONTRACTER MARIAGE** – droit de contracter mariage – right to marry.
- **CONTRAINTE** – droit de contrainte – right to enforce.
- **CONTRAIRE** – droit contraire – opposing right; conflicting right.
- **CONTRE-VALEUR** – droit à contre-valeur – right to an equivalent; right to the proceeds of.
- **CONTRÔLE** – droit de contrôle – right of supervision or inspection.
- **CONVENANCIER** – droits convenanciers – compensation for erections, plantations and crops payable to a short-term tenant of an agricultural holding (cf BAIL À DOMAINE CONGÉABLE).
- **CONVENTIONNEL** – droit conventionnel – right based on contract; contractual right; agreed rate of duty; treaty law.
- **COPROPRIÉTÉ** – droit de copropriété – co-ownership; ownership in common.
- **CORPORATIF** – droit corporatif – the law of guilds and professional associations.

- **CORPOREL** – droit corporel – property right; right to a tangible object.
- **CORRECTION** – droit de correction – right to inflict corporal punishment.
- **COURTAGE** – droit de courtage – (broker's) commission.
- **CO-UTILISATION** – droit de co-utilisation – right of joint user.
- **COUTUMIER** – customary law; custom.
  - •• **INTERNATIONAL** – droit coutumier international – customary international law.
- **CRÉANCE** – droit de créance – right to receive payment of a debt or performance of an obligation; chose in action; claim; right in personam; obligation.
  - •• **IMMOBILIER** – droit de créance immobilière – chose in action appurtenant to immovable property.
- **CRIÉE ET BOUGIE** – droit de criée et de bougie – fee for an auction conducted by the court.
- **CRIMINEL** – droit criminel – criminal law.
- **CRITIQUE** – droit de critique autorisée – (right of, defence of) fair comment.
- **CULTE** – droit de culte privé – right to hold services in an embassy.
- **DE**
  - •• **PLEIN** – see PLEIN below.
  - •• **QUI** – à qui de droit – to the person entitled; to whom it may concern.
- **DÉCHÉANCE** d'un droit – loss (forfeiture) of a right.
- **DÉCISION** – droit de décision – power of decision.
- **DÉCOUVERTE** – droit de découverte – the law relating to finder's rights.
- **DÉDOMMAGEMENT** – droit à dédommagement – right to compensation.
- **DÉDOUANEMENT** – droit de dédouanement – clearance fee.
- **DÉFENSE** – droits de la défense – right of *both* parties to put forward their case and be informed of their opponent's case (including freedom to choose one's legal representative); right to a fair hearing (trial); due process; rights of the defence.
- **DÉNIER** un droit à quelqu'un – refuse someone a right; hold that someone is not entitled to a right; reject (dismiss, disallow) a claim.
- **DÉRIVÉ** – droits dérivés – derivative rights.
- **DÉSIGNATION** – droit de désignation – right of appointment or nomination; right to appoint a representative to the supervisory board of a company.
- **DESSAISI** de l'exercice de ses droits – excluded from exercising his rights.
- **DÉVELOPPEMENT** du droit – development of the law.
- **DIFFUSION** – droit de diffusion – right to publicise, broadcast, disseminate.
- **DIRE** le droit – do justice; act as a court; enforce (state, declare) the law (as it is).
- **DIRE** pour droit – rule; find; hold.
- **DIRECTION** – droit de direction – right of control (over a thing).
- **DISCIPLINAIRE** – droit disciplinaire – disciplinary regulations; standing orders.
- **DISJONCTION** – droit de disjonction (Sw) – right to withdraw one's property from the operation of bankruptcy.
- **DISPENSE** – droit de dispense – right to grant dispensations (exemptions); dispensing power.
- **DISPOSER** – droit des peuples à disposer d'eux-mêmes – right of self-determination.
- **DISPOSITION** – droit de disposition – right to alienate; right of disposal.
- **DOUBLE** droit – double fee (charge).
- **ÉCONOMIQUE** – droit économique – business law; the law relating to economic crime.
- **ÉCOULEMENT** – droit d'écoulement des eaux de pluie – (easement conferring a) right to discharge rain-water (over the servient tenement).
- **ÉCRIT** – droit écrit – written law (ie as opposed to customary law and conventions); statute; statute law.
  - •• **NON** – droit non écrit – unwritten law (ie customary law and conventions as opposed to statutes etc).
- **ÉDITION** – droit d'édition – the law of publishing; copyright.
- **ÉLECTORAL** – droit électoral – right to vote; franchise; the law governing elections; electoral law.
- **ÉLECTORAT** – droit d'électorat – right to vote; franchise; the law governing elections; electoral law.
- **ÉLIGIBILITÉ** – droit d'éligibilité – right to stand for election.
- **EN** droit de – entitled to.
- **ENCAISSEMENT** – droit d'encaissement – collection charge.

- **ENREGISTREMENT** – droit d'enregistrement – registration fee.
- **ENTENDU** – droit d'être entendu (par un juge) – right to judicial proceedings; right to a fair trial (hearing).
- **ENTRÉE** – droit d'entrée – right of entry; entrance; charge; import duty.
- **ENTREPÔT** – droit d'entrepôt – warehouse charges.
- **ÉPAVE** – droit d'épave – the law relating to unclaimed movables.
- **ÉPUISÉ** – droit épuisé – ex rights.
- **ESPÉRANCE** – droit en espérance – expectation (right in spe).
- **ESTER** – droit d'ester en justice – right to take part in court proceedings; standing (before the court); locus standi.
- **ESTIVAGE** – droits d'estivage – charges for summer pasture.
- **ÉTABLISSEMENT** – droit d'établissement – right to settle (take up residence); right of establishment.
- **ÉTAPE** – droit d'étape – right of troops to pass through foreign territory.
- **ÉTRANGER** – droit des étrangers – the law relating to aliens (foreign nationals).
- **ÊTRE** en droit de – be entitled to.
- **ÉTROIT** – de droit étroit – to be strictly (restrictively, narrowly) interpreted.
- **ÉVENTUEL** – droit éventuel – contingent right.
- **ÉVOCATION** – droit d'évocation – superior court's power to order pending proceedings to be transferred to itself for decision.
- **EXAMEN** – droit d'examen – examination fee.
- **EXCEPTION** – droit d'exception – rule creating an exception.
- **EXCLUSIVITÉ** – droit d'exclusivité – sole (exclusive) right.
- **EXERCÉ** – droit exercé – ex rights.
- **EXERCICE** – droit d'exercice – right to practise (a profession).
- **EXHAUSSEMENT** – droit d'exhaussement – right to build higher.
- **EXPÉDITION** – droit d'expédition – fee for a certified copy.
- **EXPERTISE** – droit d'expertise – fee for an expert opinion.
- **EXPLOITATION** – droit d'exploitation – operating right; mining concession.
  - •• **FORESTIER** – droit d'exploitation forestière – forestry concession.
- **EXPROPRIATION** – droit d'expropriation – right to expropriate.

- **EXTRACTION** – droit d'extraction – mining right.
- **EXTRAPATRIMONIAL** – droit extrapatrimonial – non-pecuniary (non-proprietorial, non-proprietary) right.
- **FACTAGE** – droit de factage – cartage; delivery charge.
- **FAIRE** droit à une demande – allow (grant) an application.
- **FAIRE VALOIR** un droit – put forward (advance, submit) a claim; claim (assert) a right.
- **FAMILLE** – droit de la famille – family law.
- **FISCAL** – droit fiscal – tax law.
- **FISCAL** – droits fiscaux – taxes and duties.
- **FIXE** – droit fixe – fixed charge, due, duty.
- **FONCTION PUBLIQUE** – droit de la fonction publique – civil-service law.
- **FORFAITAIRE** – droit forfaitaire – fixed (flat-rate) charge.
- **FRAPPE** – droit de frappe – right of coinage.
- **FRAUDÉ** – droit fraudé – evading payment of a fee.
- **FUTUR** – droit futur – future right.
- **GAGE** – droit de gage – creditor's right to retain, sell and pay himself out of the proceeds of the object pledged; pledgee's rights; lien; pledge; security.
  - •• **BAILLEUR** – droit de gage du bailleur – landlord's lien for rent.
  - •• **GÉNÉRAL** – un droit de gage général sur le patrimoine de son débiteur – a "floating" charge over the debtor's property, ie the creditor's right to enforce his claim against the debtor's entire property.
  - •• **IMMOBILIER** – droit de gage immobilier – real security; charge on real property.
- **GARANTIE** – droit de garantie – guarantee commission.
- **GARDE** – droit de garde – storage charge (customs etc); safe-custody charge (bank etc); right to control and care (physical custody) of a child.
- **GENS** – droit des gens – public international law; jus gentium; the law of nations.
- **GLOBAL** – droit global – standard charge; inclusive charge.
- **GRÂCE** – droit de grâce – prerogative of mercy.

- **GRADUÉ** – droit gradué – graduated tax or charge.
- **GREFFE** – droit de greffe – registry fee (eg for copies).
- **GUERRE** – droit de la guerre – the law(s) of war.
- **HABITATION** – droit d'habitation – civil-law right of habitation, ie the right to live in a house belonging to another without charge, usually for life.
- **HÉBERGEMENT** – droit d'hébergement – right to receive visits from a child in the care (custody) of another; staying access.
- **HÉRÉDITAIRE** – droit héréditaire – right to succeed to an estate; hereditary right.
- **HÉRÉDITÉ** – droit d'hérédité – right to succeed to an estate.
- **HOMME** – droits de l'homme – human rights.
- **HORS (DU) COMMERCE** – see COMMERCE above.
- **HUMANITAIRE** – droit humanitaire – humanitarian law (ie law relating to the victims of armed conflicts).
- **IMMOBILIER** – droit immobilier – the law of real property; right relating to an immovable (land).
- **IMMUNITÉ** – droit d'immunité – immunity.
- **IMPÉRATIF** – droit impératif – mandatory law (provisions).
  - **NON** – droit non impératif – non-mandatory law (provisions).
- **IMPOSITION** – droit d'imposition – right to raise (impose) taxes.
- **INALIÉNABLE** – droit inaliénable – inalienable right.
- **INCORPOREL** – droit incorporel – right other than that of ownership; right relating to something other than a physical object; intangible right.
- **INDEMNISATION** – droit à indemnisation – right to damages (compensation).
- **INDIVIDU** – droit de l'individu – personal right; individual right.
- **INDIVIDUEL** – droit individuel – personal right; individual right.
- **INITIATIVE** – droit d'initiative parlementaire – right of members of Parliament to initiate (introduce) legislation.
- **INJONCTION** – droit d'injonction – right of an administrative authority to give instructions (directions).
- **INSCRIPTION** – droit d'inscription – enrolment fee; registration fee.
- **INSÉCURITÉ du droit** – uncertainty of the law.
- **INSPECTION** – droit d'inspection – right to inspect, control or supervise.
- **INTÉGRITÉ** – droit à l'intégrité physique et morale – right to protection from physical and mental injury
- **INTELLECTUEL** – droit intellectuel – intellectual-property right.
- **INTERMÉDIAIRE** – droit intermédiaire – transitional law; revolutionary law (covering the period between 1789 and the Code Napoléon); the law applying in an intermediate period.
- **INTERNATIONAL**
  - **CONVENTIONNEL** – droit international conventionnel – treaty law (as opposed to customary international law); (sometimes referred to as) conventional international law.
  - **ÉCRIT** – droit international écrit – treaty law.
  - **PRIVÉ** – droit international privé – private international law; conflict of laws.
  - **PUBLIC** – droit international public – public international law.
  - **VOISINAGE** – droit international de voisinage – international law of frontier relations; international law of nuisance.
- **INTERNE** – droit interne – internal (municipal, domestic, national) law.
- **INTERPELLATION** – droit d'interpellation – right to put parliamentary questions.
- **INTERPRÈTE** – droit de l'interprète – performer's right (copyright).
- **INTERVENTION** – droit d'intervention – right to intervene.
- **INVENTION** – droits d'invention – inventor's rights.
- **INVOQUER un droit** – rely on, advance, submit a right, claim, or argument.
- **JOUISSANCE** – droit de jouissance – right to use and enjoy property; usufruct; beneficial interest; right to rents and profits; right to receive dividends without the corresponding voting rights.
- **JUDICIAIRE** – droit judiciaire (privé) – (civil) procedure.
- **LÉGATION**
  - **ACTIF** – droit de légation actif – right to send diplomatic missions to other states.

●● **PASSIF** – droit de légation passif – right to receive diplomatic missions from other states.

● **LÉGIFÉRER** – droit de légiférer – right to legislate.

● **LÉSER les droits** – interfere with, violate or infringe a person's rights.

● **LÉSION dans les droits** – interference with, violation or infringement of a person's rights.

● **LICENCE** – droit de licence (d'exploitation) – licence (to operate a mine, trade or manufacture or use a patent, copyright, etc); licence fee; royalty.

● **LICENCIEMENT** – droit de licenciement – right to dismiss.

● **LITIGIEUX** – droit litigieux – disputed claim.

● **LIVRAISON** – droit à livraison – right to receive delivery.

● **LOCATION DE CHASSE** – droit de location de chasse – the law of shooting rights.

● **MAGASINAGE** – droit de magasinage – depository fee; warehouse (warehousing) charge; storage charge.

● **MAINTIEN DANS LES LIEUX** – droit du maintien dans les lieux – right to remain in occupation.

● **MARIAGE** – droit du mariage – the law of marriage.

● **MARITIME** – droit maritime – maritime law.

●● **INTERNATIONAL** – droit maritime international – the law of the sea.

● **MATÉRIEL** – droit matériel – substantive law (as opposed to procedure).

● **MOBILE** – droits mobiles – sliding-scale tariff (customs).

● **MOBILIER** – droit mobilier – right relating to a movable.

● **MORAL** – droit moral de l'auteur – non-pecuniary, special (personal) right of an author, artist, etc in his work; non-pecuniary (attributes of) copyright.

● **MOYEN de droit** – ground based on law; point of law.

●● **PUR** – moyen de pur droit – legal ground resulting implicitly from the facts as presented to the court.

● **MUTATION** – droit de mutation – capital transfer tax; transfer duty.

●● **DÉCÈS** – droit de mutation par décès – succession duty; inheritance tax.

● **NATUREL** – droit naturel – natural law (a system of law based on reason and human nature as opposed to actual (positive) law).

● **NAVIGATION AÉRIENNE** – droit de navigation aérienne – air law; the law of air transport.

● **NÉGOCIATION** – droit de négociation (Sw) – turnover tax.

● **NEUTRALITÉ** – droit de la neutralité – law of neutrality.

● **NOM** – droit au nom – right to one's name.

● **NOMINATION** – droit de nomination – right to appoint.

● **OBJECTIF** – droit objectif – the rules of law; the law (as opposed to **droit subjectif**).

● **OBLIGATION** – droit des obligations – law of obligations; contract and tort. It also includes quasi-contract (restitution, unjust enrichment, etc) and statutory obligations (eg maintenance).

● **OCCUPATION** – droit d'occupation – right to occupy; right to take possession of ownerless property; occupation law, ie that imposed by an occupying power.

● **OPPOSITION** – droit d'opposition – right to object; right to apply to have a decision set aside.

● **OPTION** – droit d'option – option.

● **OUVRIR (un) droit** – entitle; grant (confer) a right.

● **PANAGE** – droit de panage – right to pasture swine in a forest.

● **PARCOURS** – droit de parcours – right of common (for pasturing animals).

● **PART RÉSERVATAIRE** – droit à part réservataire – right to a reserved portion in a parent's estate.

● **PASSAGE** – droit de passage – right of way.

● **PATRIMONIAL** – droits patrimoniaux – pecuniary rights; property rights; proprietorial (proprietary) rights; economic rights.

● **PÂTURE** – (droit de) vaine pâture – right of common; common of pasture exercisable after mowing or harvest.

● **PAVILLON** – droit de pavillon – the law of the flag.

● **PAYER** – droit de se payer – right to obtain satisfaction or payment.

● **PÉAGE** – droit de péage – toll.

● **PÊCHE** – droit de pêche – fishing rights; (right of) fishery.

● **PÉNAL** – droit pénal – (the) criminal law.

●● **PRÉMIAL** – droit pénal prémial – criminal law based on rewards instead of punishment; recompensive criminal law.

- **PÉNITENTIAIRE – droit pénitentiaire –** prison law.
- **PENSION – droit à une pension de retraite –** pension entitlement.
- **PERDRE – perdre des droits –** forfeit rights.
- **PERQUISITION – droit de perquisition –** right of search.
- **PERSONNALITÉ – droits de la personnalité –** non-pecuniary personal rights other than family rights; personality rights (name, reputation, privacy, etc); strictly personal rights.
- **PERSONNE – droit attaché à la personne –** strictly (exclusively) personal right; easement in gross.
- **PERSONNE – droits de la personne (Can) –** human rights.
- **PERSONNE – droit des personnes –** law of persons.
- **PERSONNEL – droit personnel –** (pecuniary) right in personam; obligation; chose in action; claim.
- **PERTE du droit –** loss or forfeiture of a right or claim.
- **PEUPLE – droit des peuples à disposer d'eux-mêmes –** right of self-determination.
- **PLAIDOIRIE – droit de plaidoirie –** counsel's hearing fee.
- **PLEIN – de plein droit –** by operation of law; ipso jure; as a matter of law (ie without the need for any application or stipulation); as of right; of itself; as full members; ex officio; as ex-officio members.
- **POINT de droit –** point of law; question of law.
- **PORT – droits de port –** harbour dues.
- **POSITIF – droit positif –** positive law, ie the law as it actually exists, as opposed to natural law.
- **POURSUITE – droit de poursuite –** right to prosecute; right of (hot) pursuit.
- **PRÉCAIRE – droit précaire –** revocable right, ie subject to revocation by the grantor.
- **PRÉÉMINENCE du droit –** rule of law.
- **PRÉEMPTION – droit de préemption –** right of pre-emption; option to purchase in preference to others.
- **PRÉFÉRENCE – droit de préférence –** right (of a mortgagee or person entitled to a statutory priority, preference or lien (**privilège**)) to be paid in preference to other creditors; preferential right.
- **PRÉFÉRENTIEL – droit préférentiel –** right (of a mortgagee or person entitled to statutory priority, preference or lien (**privilège**)) to be paid in preference to other creditors; preferential right; preferential (customs) duty.
- **PRESCRIPTION d'un droit –** lapse (barring) of a right by statutory limitation.
- **PRÉSÉANCE – droit de préséance –** right of precedence.
- **PRÉSENTATION – droit de présentation –** right to name a successor for appointment to certain professional offices, such as those of bailiff, registrar, stockbroker or auctioneer.
- **PRÊT – droit de prêt public –** public lending right.
- **PRÉTORIEN – droit prétorien –** judge-made law.
- **PREUVE – faire la preuve de son droit –** establish one's title.
- **PRIMAUTÉ du droit –** rule of law.
- **PRINCIPAL – droit principal –** independent (non-accessory) right.
- **PRISE – droit des prises –** prize law.
- **PRISÉE – droit de prisée –** appraisement fee; valuation fee.
- **PRIVATIF – droit privatif –** exclusive right.
- **PRIVATION des droits civiques –** disqualification from exercising the franchise and holding public office imposed on certain convicts.
- **PRIVÉ – droit privé –** private law.
- **PRIVILÈGE – droit de privilège –** statutory lien or privilege giving a right to be paid in preference to other creditors.
  - **SPÉCIAL – droit de privilège spécial –** lien on certain movables or immovables giving a right to preferential payment.
- **PROCÉDURE – droit de la procédure –** procedure; procedural law; law of procedure.
- **PROCÉDURE – droit de procédure –** trial fee; court fee.
- **PROCESSUEL – droit processuel –** (the study of) (the law governing) procedure.
- **PROPORTIONNEL – droit proportionnel –** proportional tax; graduated tax.
- **PROPRIÉTÉ – droit de propriété –** ownership; property right; right in property.
  - **INDUSTRIEL – droit de propriété industrielle –** industrial-property right, eg patent, trademark.
- **PROSPECTION – droit de prospection –** prospecting right.

- **PROTECTION** – **droit de protection** – legal provision(s) whose object is to protect certain persons; protective provision(s).
- **PROUVÉ** – **droit prouvé** – established right.
- **PUBLIC** – **droit public** – public law.
  - •• **CHAMBRE de droit public** – public-law division.
  - •• **RECOURS de droit public** – public-law appeal.
- **PUISAGE** – **droit de puisage** – right to draw water from a well.
- **PURGE** – **droit de purge** – purchaser's right to redeem charges (mortgages) for the price paid or the present value. It may only be exercised by a purchaser not personally liable on the mortgage.
- **QUAI** – **droit de quai** – wharfage.
- **QUESTION** – **droit de question** – right to put questions, to interrogate.
- **RACHAT** – **droit de rachat** – right of (option to) repurchase; vendor's right of pre-emption.
- **RAPPEL** – **droit de rappel** – right to recall.
- **RAPPEL de droits** – supplementary assessment.
- **RÉCEPTION du droit** – reception (adoption) of a foreign, eg Roman, law.
- **RECETTE** – **droit de recette** – collection charge.
- **RECHERCHE** – **droit de recherche** – search fee.
- **RECOMMANDATION** – **droit de recommandation** – charge for registering (a letter etc).
- **RECONNAISSANCE de droit** – de jure recognition.
- **RECOURS** – **droit de recours** – right of appeal; right of recourse.
- **RECOUVREMENT** – **droits mis en recouvrement** – entitlements called in.
- **RECOUVRER** – **droits à recouvrer** – entitlements; sums due.
  - •• **RESTER** – **droits restant à recouvrer** – entitlements outstanding.
- **RÉCUSATION** – **droit de récusation** – right of challenge.
- **RÉDUIRE**
  - •• **PEINE** – **droit de réduire une peine** – right to remit or commute a sentence.
- **RÉEL** – **droit réel** – right in rem.
  - •• **BIEN** – **droit réel sur un bien de son débiteur** – right in rem over one of his debtor's assets.

- **RÉFORMATION** – **droit de réformation** – right to set aside or alter the judgment of a lower court.
- **REGARD** – **droit de regard** – right of inspection or supervision.
  - •• **GESTION** – **droit de regard sur la gestion** – right to be informed about the management.
- **RÈGLE de droit** – legal norm (rule); the law; rule of law.
- **RÉINTEGRATION dans ses droits** – reinstatement in one's rights.
- **RELATIF** – **droit relatif** – right binding only on a specific person or persons, eg a promisor, debtor or tortfeasor; right in personam.
- **REMBOURSEMENT** – **droit à remboursement** – right to be reimbursed.
- **REMBOURSEMENT** – **droit de remboursement** – collection fee; COD charge.
- **RÉMÉRÉ** – **droit de réméré** – option or right to repurchase.
- **REMISE**
  - •• **DOMICILE** – **droit de remise à domicile** – delivery charge.
- **RENONCIATION** – **droit de renonciation** – right to waive (relinquish, renounce, abandon) a right, privilege, etc.
- **RÉPARATION** – **droit à réparation** – right to compensation (damages, reparation).
- **RÉPARATOIRE** – **droits réparatoires** – compensation for erections, plantations and crops payable to a short-term tenant of an agricultural holding (cf BAIL À DOMAINE CONGÉABLE).
- **REPENTIR** – **droit de repentir** – right to rescind (withdraw from a contract).
- **RÉPLIQUE** – **droit de réplique** – right of reply; right of rectification.
- **RÉPONSE** – **droit de réponse** – right of reply; right of rectification.
- **REPRÉSENTATION** – **droit de représentation** – counsel's fee (for the hearing); performing right.
- **REPRISE** – **droit de reprise** – landlord's right in certain circumstances to recover premises in spite of the tenant's right to an extension of the lease; landlord's right to re-occupy demised premises because he needs them for himself.
- **RÉSERVATAIRE** – **droits réservataires** – statutory right to a share in the estate of a parent; reserved portion.

- **RÉSILIATION** – droit de résiliation – right to terminate a contract.
- **RÉSOLUTION** – droit de résolution – right to rescind (set aside, annul, cancel).
- **RESTAURATION** d'un droit – restitution of a right.
- **RÉTENTION** – droit de rétention – lien; right to retain or remain in possession; right of retention, ie a right to withhold property until a debt is paid.
- **RÉTORSION** – droits de rétorsion – customs duties imposed as a measure of retortion.
- **RETOUR** – droit de retour – donor's contingent reversion in the event of the donee's dying before him. (In some cases the right passes to the donor's heirs.)
- **RETRAIT** – droit de retrait – right to buy out or redeem; right to retain certain property together on the termination of the community; right to stop working if one has reasonable grounds for believing that the situation involves a serious and immediate danger to life or health; right to rescind (withdraw from a contract).
- **RETRAITE** – droit à la retraite – right to receive a pension.
- **RÉUNION** – droit de réunion – right of assembly.
- **RÉVERSIBLE** – droit réversible – revertible right; right capable of passing to a survivor, eg a pension.
- **RÉVOCATION** – droit de révocation – right to revoke (a will etc); right to dismiss or remove from office.
- **RIVERAINETÉ** – droit de riveraineté – rights of adjoining (abutting) owners; riparian rights.
- **ROUTIER** – droit routier – the law relating to road traffic; road-traffic law.
- **RURAL** – droit rural – the law governing agricultural property and holdings and the status of farmers.
- **SAISIE** – droit de saisie – right to seize (in connection with certain offences).
  - •• **GAGE** – droit de saisie du gage – right to attach property as a security for payment.
- **SANG** – droit du sang (jus sanguinis) – rule that nationality is conferred by descent.
- **SAUVETAGE** – droit de sauvetage – salvage (money).
- **SCEAU** – droit de sceau – stamp duty.
- **SECONDAIRE** – droit secondaire – subordinate legislation.

- **SÉJOUR** – droit de séjour – right to temporary residence (to remain temporarily).
- **SERVITUDE** – droit de servitude – easement; servitude.
- **SOCIAL** – droit social – welfare legislation; social law; labour law; the law of industrial relations.
- **SOCIÉTÉ** – droit des sociétés – company law; partnership law.
- **SOI** – en droit soi – in his own right.
- **SOL** – droit du sol (jus soli) – rule that nationality is acquired by birth on the territory of the state concerned.
- **SOURCES** du droit – sources of law.
- **SOUSCRIPTION**
  - •• **IRRÉDUCTIBLE** – droit de souscription à titre irréductible – irrevocable right to subscribe for shares.
- **SOUVERAIN** – droit souverain – sovereign (absolute, unrestricted, unfettered) right or power.
- **SOUVERAINETÉ** – droit de souveraineté – sovereign right; sovereignty.
- **SPÉCIAL** – droit spécial – particular right; privilege; particular provisions.
- **STATIONNEMENT** – droit de stationnement – right to station troops.
- **STRICT** – droit strict – mandatory law.
- **SUBJECTIF** – droit subjectif – right conferred on or exercised by an individual; individual (personal, private) right (as opposed to **droit objectif**).
- **SUBSTANTIEL** – droit substantiel – substantive right forming the subject-matter of litigation; substantive law.
- **SUCCESSIBILITÉ** – droit de successibilité – right to inherit (succeed to) property; inheritance right.
- **SUCCESSIF** – droit successif – right to inherit (succeed to) property; inheritance right; the law of succession (inheritance).
  - •• **VENTE** de droits successifs – sale of one's right to an inheritance; sale of an expectancy.
- **SUCCESSION** – droit de succession – the law of succession (inheritance); right to inherit (succeed to) property; (usually in plural) inheritance tax; succession duty.
- **SUCCESSION** – droit des successions – the law of succession (inheritance).
- **SUCCESSORAL** – droit successoral – the law of succession (inheritance); inheritance

right; (usually in plural) inheritance tax; succession duty.

- **SUFFRAGE** – **droit de suffrage** – suffrage; right to vote.
- **SUITE** – **droit de suite** – right to trace or follow property into the hands of a third person; mortgagee's right to attach the mortgaged property and have it sold to answer the mortgage debt into whoever's hands it may have passed; right of persons entitled to a **privilège** (right to preferential payment) to follow property; right of a secured creditor to take possession of the security even if in the possession of a third party; (bankruptcy) right of stoppage in transitu; (copyright) right of an author to a percentage of the sale price of his work (over which he may not dispose inter vivos or by will and to which his heirs are entitled for a period of fifty years after his death, subject to a life interest of the surviving spouse); reserved royalties; right of an artist to a percentage of the price of his picture every time it is sold by an auctioneer or art dealer; surviving right; inheritable royalty; surviving royalty; resale right.
- **SUJET de droit** – person (entity) recognised by law or a particular system of law as capable of owning and exercising rights and being subject to obligations; person, ie as having legal personality; legal person; (in an international context) subject of law.
  - •• **INTERNATIONAL** – **sujet de droit international** – person recognised by international law as having rights and duties (having legal personality); subject of (international) law.
- **SUPERFICIE** – **droit de superficie** – surface rights (in a piece of land containing minerals); right in rem to buildings and plantations on the land of another; surface owner's rights; building owner's rights; building lease.
- **SUPPLÉTIF** – **droit supplétif** – non-mandatory rules of law, eg expressing the presumed intention of the parties to a contract.
- **SURVEILLANCE** – **droit de surveillance** – right of supervision.
- **SURVOL** – **droit de survol** – right to fly over national territory.
- **SYNDICAL** – **droit syndical** – right of association; right to organise; right to form trade unions; trade-union law.
- **SYNDICAL** – **droits syndicaux** – trade-union rights.

- **TERRITORIAL** – **droits territoriaux** – territorial rights.
- **TESTAMENTAIRE** – **droit testamentaire** – law of wills.
- **TESTER** – **droit de tester** – right to make a will (transfer property by will).
- **TIMBRE** – **droit de timbre** – stamp duty.
  - •• **PASSEPORT** – **droit de timbre sur les passeports** – passport fee.
- **TIRAGE** – **droit de tirage spécial** – special drawing right.
- **TITRE** – **droit né du titre** – right incorporated in a security, eg bearer securities.
- **TITULAIRE** d'un **droit** – person entitled to (owner, holder of) a right.
- **TOUR** – **droit (servitude) de tour d'échelle** – easement entitling the owner of the dominant property to place ladders on the servient property.
- **TRANSCRIT** – **droit transcrit** – registered right or interest.
- **TRANSITOIRE** – **droit transitoire** – transitional provisions; transitional legislation.
- **TRANSMISSION** – **droit de transmission** – transfer duty.
- **TRANSPARENCE** – **droit de transparence** – right of access to official documents etc (corresponding to a duty of disclosure).
- **TRAVAIL** – **droit du travail** – labour law.
- **TRÉMATAGE** – **droit de trématage** – priority of passage through a lock.
- **UNIQUE** – **droit unique** – standard charge.
- **URGENCE** – **droit d'urgence** – emergency provisions.
- **USAGE** – **droit d'usage** – right of user; right in rem to use the property of another to satisfy one's personal needs and those of one's family for life; usus.
- **USUFRUIT** – **droit de l'usufruit** – usufruct; right in rem to use and enjoy the property of another to the same extent as an owner but without altering the substance (functionally equivalent to a life tenancy).
- **VAINE PÂTURE** – see PÂTURE above.
- **VARIABLE** – **droit variable** – variable rate of tax etc.
- **VIAGER** – **droit viager** – right (to something) for life.
- **VIDUITÉ** – **droit de viduité** – widow's right to maintenance from her late husband's estate for a limited period.

- **VISITE** – droit de visite – right to inspect; right of search; right to stop and search; right of access.
- **VOIE de droit** – legal channel; legal action; legal procedure; remedy; appeal; proceedings.
  - •• **TOUT** – toute voie de droit – any legally permissible means, eg procedure, form of evidence.
- **VOISINAGE** – droit de voisinage – law governing the rights and duties of adjacent owners.
- **VUE** – droit de vue – right to have an opening in a wall at less than the statutory distance from an adjoining property; right to inspect (accounts, documents, etc).

DTS = droit de tirage spécial.

DUCROIRE – del credere.

DUPLICATA – second copy; duplicate.

DUPLIQUE – rejoinder (defendant's reply to the plaintiff's reply).

DURÉE – time spent.
- **BAIL** – durée du bail – term (period) of the lease.
- **CIRCULATION** – durée de circulation – currency of a bill.
- **CONTRACTUEL** – durée contractuelle – length (term, period) of the contract.
- **CONTRAT** – durée du contrat – length (term, period) of the contract.
- **ÉCHÉANCE** – durée d'échéance – currency (of a bill).
- **EMPLOI** – durée d'emploi – length of employment.
- **EXPIRATION de la durée** – expiration of time; expiration of the period.
- **FONCTION** – durée des fonctions – length (period, term) of office.
- **MANDAT de durée déterminée** – fixed term of office.
  - •• **ÉLECTIF** – durée du mandat électif – period for which a person is elected; term of office.
- **PEINE** – durée de la peine – length of the sentence.
- **PROLONGATION de la durée** – extension of time.
- **SERVICE** – durée des services – length of service.
- **VALIDITÉ** – durée de validité – (period of) validity; currency.

DURETÉ
- **CLAUSE de dureté** – hardship clause.

—

E

EAU
- **ADJACENT** – **eaux adjacentes** – coastal waters.
- **CÔTIER** – **eaux côtières** – coastal waters.
- **INTÉRIEUR** – **eaux intérieures** – national or domestic waters, ie waters within the baseline of the territorial sea.
- **RÈGLEMENT d'eau** – apportionment (allocation) of water rights (between riparian owners); water regulations.
- **TERRITORIAL** – **eaux territoriales** – territorial waters.
  - •• **CONTIGU** – **eaux territoriales contiguës** – contiguous (adjoining) territorial waters.

ÉBRANLEMENT
- **LIEN CONJUGAL** – **ébranlement du lien conjugal** – weakening of the marriage bond; breakdown of the marriage.

ÉCARTER – (of a presumption) rebut.
- **DEMANDE** – **écarter une demande** – dismiss an application.
- **RÈGLE** – **les règles de droit commun sont écartées pour les notifications entre avocats** – the general rules do not apply to simplified service (of documents) between counsel.

ÉCHANGE
- **SOULTE** – **échange avec soulte** – exchange with payment of the difference.

ÉCHANTILLON – sample.
- **VENTE sur échantillon** – sale by sample.

ÉCHÉANCE – due date; date payable; date of expiry (expiration); maturity; date on which an obligation must be performed.
- **DÉLAI** – **échéance du délai** – expiry of the term or time(-limit).
- **DÉTERMINÉ** – **à une échéance déterminée** – at a fixed date.
- **MOYEN** – **échéance moyenne** – average due date.
- **PROROGATION d'échéance** – extension of time.
- **REMBOURSEMENT** – **échéance de remboursement** – date of repayment.
- **TERME** – **échéance du terme** – expiry of the term or time(-limit); becoming due (of a debt, bill, etc).

- **TERME d'échéance** – date of payment.

ÉCHEC – breakdown (of marriage).

ÉCHEL(L)AGE – easement entitling the owner of the dominant property to place ladders on the servient property.

ÉCHELLE
- **MOBILE** – **échelle mobile des peines** – graduated scale of sentences.

ÉCHELON
- **ANCIENNETÉ** – **échelon d'ancienneté** – seniority; salary step; increment.
- **HIÉRARCHIQUE** – **échelon hiérarchique** – rank; grade.

ÉCHELONNEMENT
- **PAIEMENT** – **échelonnement des paiements** – payment by instalments.

ÉCHEVIN – alderman; (Belg) deputy mayor; (Can) town councillor. (Also used in translations to designate the non-professional members of a court or tribunal.)

ÉCHEVINAL
- **FORMATION** – **en formation échevinale** – (of a court) sitting with non-professional members.

ÉCHOUER – fail.

ÉCLAIRER
- **JURIDICTION** – **lorsque la juridiction s'estime éclairée** – when the court considers it is sufficiently informed.

ÉCOLE
- **MAGISTRATURE** – **École nationale de la magistrature** – Legal Service Training College.

ÉCONOMIE – structure (scheme, logic) (of a convention); tenor (of a provision).

ÉCOT (Sw) – bill of costs.

ÉCRIT
- **DIFFAMATOIRE** – **écrit diffamatoire** – libel.

- **PRIVÉ** – **écrit privé** – signed writing (not officially recorded); private document.
- **SEING PRIVÉ** – **écrit sous seing privé** – signed writing (not officially recorded); private document.

ÉCRITURE

- **ALTÉRATION** d'écritures – forgery.
- **COMPARAISON** d'écritures – comparison or proof of handwriting.
- **CONTREFAÇON** d'écritures – forgery of documents.
- **CRÉDIT** – **écriture au crédit** – credit entry.
- **EXPERT** en écritures – handwriting expert.
- **FALSIFICATION** d'écritures – forgery or falsification of documents.
- **FAUX** en écriture(s) – forgery.
- **FICTIF** – **écriture fictive** – disguised handwriting; fictitious entry.
- **FRAIS** d'écritures – copying (typing) fees charged by the registry as an item of costs.
- **PASSATION** en écritures – posting (entry) in an account.
- **PRIVÉ** – **écriture privée** – private document (not officially recorded).
- **PUBLIC** – **écritures publiques** – public documents.
- **REDRESSEMENT** – **écriture de redressement** – rectifying entry.
- **VÉRIFICATION** d'écriture – proof of handwriting.

ÉCROU – arrest.

- **ACTE** d'écrou – memorandum of imprisonment.
- **EXTRADITIONNEL** – **écrou extraditionnel** – custody pending extradition.
- **FORMALITÉS** d'écrou – admission formalities (fingerprinting, registration, etc).
- **LEVÉE** d'écrou – release; release order.
- **ORDRE** d'écrou – committal order (warrant).
- **REGISTRE** d'écrou – prison register.
- **TITRE** d'écrou – committal order (warrant).

ÉCROUER – arrest; imprison.

ÉDICTER – enact; prescribe; establish; lay down.

ÉDIFICE

- **SUPERFICIE** – **édifices et superficies** – erections, plantations and crops.

ÉDITION

- **AUTEUR** – **édition à compte d'auteur** – publication at the author's expense.

- **CONTRAT** d'édition – publishing contract.
- **DROIT** d'édition – the law of publishing; copyright.

ÉDUCATION

- **CORRECTIF** – **institution d'éducation corrective** – reformatory.
- **SURVEILLÉ** – **institution d'éducation surveillée** – approved school.
- **SURVEILLÉ** – **maison d'éducation surveillée** – reformatory; approved school; Borstal institution.

EFFET – bill of exchange (promissory note, cheque, etc); effect.

- **ACCEPTATION** d'un effet – acceptance of a bill.
- **ACCEPTÉ** – **effet accepté** – accepted bill.
- **ACTION** en paiement d'un effet – action on (to enforce) a bill.
- **CAVALERIE** – **effet de cavalerie** – accommodation bill; kite.
- **CHANGE** – **effet de change** – bill of exchange.
- **CHOSE JUGÉE** – **effet de la chose jugée** – res judicata.
- **CIRCULATION** – **effet de circulation** – finance bill; bank bill; accommodation bill.
- **COMMANDITE** – **effet en commandite** – finance bill.
- **COMMERCE** – **effets de commerce** – negotiable instruments.
- **COMPLAISANCE** – **effet de complaisance** – accommodation bill.
- **CONSTITUTIF** – **effet constitutif** – effect in rem, ie altering status or rights.
- **COURS** – **effet en cours** – current bill; circulating bill.
- **CRÉER** un effet – draw a bill.
- **CROISÉ** – **effets croisés** – accommodation bills drawn on each other by two traders in difficulties.
- **DATE** – **effet à un certain délai de date** – time bill; bill payable (so many days) after date.
- **DÉCLARATIF** – **effet déclaratif** – declaratory effect.
- **DEHORS** – **effet sur le dehors** – non-local bill; out-of-town bill; foreign bill; country bill.
- **DÉPLACÉ** – **effet déplacé** – non-local bill; out-of-town bill; foreign bill; country bill.
- **DÉVOLUTIF** – **effet dévolutif** – (of an application to set aside) effect of bringing a

default judgment back to the court by which it was originally decided; transfer of all issues of fact and law to a (higher) court (eg on appeal).

•• NORMAL – effet dévolutif normal – the normal transfer of jurisdiction.

• DOMICILIE – effet domicilié – domiciled bill.

• ÉCHÉANCE – effet à échéance – bill payable on a fixed day.

• ÉCHU – effet échu – matured bill.

• ÉMETTEUR d'un effet – issuer (drawer) of a bill.

• ENCAISSEMENT – effet à l'encaissement – bill for collection.

• ERGA OMNES – effet erga omnes – effect binding on everyone (the whole world); effect in rem (erga omnes).

• ESCOMPTE – effet à l'escompte – bill for discount.

• ESCOMPTÉ – effet escompté – discounted bill.

• ÉTRANGER – effet à l'étranger – foreign bill.

• FICTIF – effet fictif – accommodation bill; kite.

• FINANCIER – effet financier – accommodation bill; finance bill.

• INTÉRIEUR – effet sur l'intérieur – inland bill; domestic bill.

• INTER PARTES – effet inter partes – effect as between the parties.

• IRRÉCOUVRABLE – effet irrécouvrable – irrecoverable bill.

• LIBÉRATOIRE – effet libératoire – effect of releasing from liability.

• LONGUEUR d'un effet – currency of a bill.

• MATÉRIEL – effet matériel – substantive effect (cet avant-acte ne peut produire aucun effet matériel – this precontract has no substantive effect).

• MOBILIER – effets mobiliers – movables; chattels.

• MOBILISATION – effet de mobilisation – finance bill.

• NANTISSEMENT – effet en nantissement – bill deposited as a security; pawned bill.

• NOURRICE – effet en nourrice – bill deposited as a security; pawned bill.

• PAYER – effets à payer – bills payable.

• PENSION – effet en pension – bill deposited as a security; pawned bill.

• PERSONNEL – effets personnels – personal effects.

• PLACE – effet sur place – local bill; town bill.

• PRIVÉ d'effet – ineffectual; unenforceable.

• PROROGATION d'un effet – extension of a bill.

• PROTESTÉ – effet protesté – protested bill.

• PROTESTER un effet – protest a bill.

• PROTÊT d'un effet – protest.

• PUBLIC – effets publics – government securities.

• RECOUVREMENT d'un effet – collection of a bill.

• RECOUVRER – effet à recouvrer – bill for collection.

• RELATIF – effet relatif – effect as between the parties.

•• CONTRAT – effet relatif des contrats – (doctrine of) privity of contract, ie a contract is binding only on the parties to it and does not impose burdens or confer benefits on third parties.

• RENOUVELLEMENT d'un effet – renewal (extension) of a bill.

• RÉSOLUTOIRE (RÉSOLUTIF) – effet résolutoire (résolutif) – effect of annulling (cancelling, rescinding) a contract.

• RETIRER un effet – withdraw a bill.

• RETOUR d'effets – redraft; re-exchange.

• RETRAIT d'effet – withdrawing a bill.

• RÉTROACTIF – effet rétroactif – retrospective effect.

• SORTIR ses effets – become effective.

• SOUFFRANCE – effet en souffrance – bill held over; overdue bill.

• SUSPENSIF – effet suspensif – suspensive effect.

• TIRER un effet – draw a bill.

•• COMPTE – effet tiré pour compte – bill drawn on a bank on behalf of another (eg a documentary credit).

• TRÉSOR – effet du Trésor – Treasury bill.

• UTILE – principe de l'effet utile – the principle of effectiveness (ut res magis valeat quam pereat); the principle that where possible a transaction or document should be interpreted in a manner that renders it effective.

• VUE – effet à vue – sight bill.

EFFECTIF

• PERSONNEL – effectif réel du personnel – staff in service.

EFFRACTION – breaking (into premises).

- **VOL avec effraction** – housebreaking; burglary.

ÉGALITÉ

- **ACCÈS** – **programme d'accès à l'égalité** – affirmative-action programme (human rights).
- **ARME** – **égalité des armes** – equality of arms.
- **VOIX** – **s'il y a égalité des voix** – where the votes are equal.

ÉLARGIR – set free; release.

ÉLARGISSEMENT – release.

ÉLECTEUR – elector.

- **CONSULAIRE** - **électeur consulaire** – person entitled to elect judges to the Commercial Court.
- **DEGRÉ** – **électeur du premier degré** – person entitled to vote for an elector in a two-tier system.
- **INSCRIT** – **électeur inscrit** – voter on the register; registered elector.
- **PREMIER DEGRÉ** – see DEGRÉ above.
- **GRAND électeur** – (second-degree) elector in a two-tier system.
- **PRIMAIRE** – **électeur primaire** – person entitled to vote for an elector in a two-tier system.

ÉLECTION

- **AMI** – **élection d'ami** – declaration by a (commission) agent stating the name of his principal.
- **COMPLÉMENTAIRE** – **élection complémentaire** – by-election.
- **CONSULAIRE** – **élection consulaire** – election of judges of the Commercial Court.
- **DOMICILE** – **élection de domicile** – choice of jurisdiction; choice of venue; jurisdiction clause; clause giving an address for service.
- **PARTIEL** – **élection partielle** – by-election.
- **PRUD'HOMAL** – **élection prud'homale** – election of the judges of the industrial relations tribunal (Labour Court).
- **TRIANGULAIRE** – **élection triangulaire** – three-cornered election.

ÉLECTORAL

- **LOI électorale** – Electoral Provisions Act; Representation of the People Act.

ÉLECTORAT – franchise; electorate.

ÉLÉMENT – (in plural) evidence; material.

- **ACTIF** – **élément actif** – asset.

- **APPRÉCIATION** – **éléments d'appréciation** – evidence; factors to be taken into account.
- **CONSTITUTIF** – **élément constitutif** – (factual) ingredient.
  - •• **INFRACTION** – **élément constitutif de l'infraction** – essential element, condition, requirement or ingredient of the offence.
- **CONVICTION** – **faute d'éléments suffisants de conviction** – where the evidence is inconclusive.
- **ESSENTIEL** – **éléments essentiels du contrat** – essentials of the contract.
- **FAISCEAU d'éléments concordants** – (number of) facts pointing in the same direction.
- **FAIT** – **éléments de fait** – facts; factual circumstances.
- **MORAL** – **élément moral** – mental element.
- **PLAIDANT** – **éléments plaidant contre** – evidence against.
- **PREUVE** – **éléments de preuve** – evidence; proof.
- **RATTACHEMENT** – **élément de rattachement** – connecting factor.
- **SUBSTANTIEL** – **élément substantiel du contrat** – essential (material) part of the contract.
- **TRAIN DE VIE** – **éléments de train de vie** – standard-of-living criteria.

ÉLEVER

- **CONFLIT** – **élever un conflit** – raise a conflict of jurisdiction (by means of an application by the Prefect to have the case transferred from the ordinary courts to the administrative courts).
- **S'élever contre** – to dispute.

ÉLIGIBILITÉ

- **DROIT d'éligibilité** – right to stand for election.

ÉLIRE

- **DOMICILE** – **élire domicile** – to stipulate or agree upon a person's permanent residence, usually in a contract, for the purpose of conferring jurisdiction on a particular court or providing an address for service; accept the jurisdiction of; confer jurisdiction upon.

ÉLOIGNEMENT
- **INDEMNITÉ d'éloignement** – expatriation allowance; foreign-service (foreign-residence) allowance.

ÉLU – member of Parliament or of a local authority; elected representative.

ÉLUDER
- **LOI** – éluder la loi – evade the law.

ÉMANCIPATION – declaration that a minor shall be regarded as of full age and capacity; emancipation.

ÉMANCIPER – declare of full age; free of incapacities imposed by minority; treat as being of full age; emancipate.

ÉMARGEMENT – initials or signature in the margin or a column; marginal entry or signature.

ÉMARGER – sign or initial in a column or margin; receive money.

EMBARRAS
- **VOIE PUBLIQUE** – embarras de la voie publique – obstructing the highway.

ÉMENDER
- **JUGEMENT** – émender un jugement – vary a judgment.

ÉMETTRE – issue.
- **CAVALERIE** – émettre de la cavalerie – fly a kite; issue bad bills.
- **CHÈQUE** – émettre un chèque – draw a cheque.

ÉMEUTE – riot; rout; disturbance.

ÉMIGRATION
- **CAPITAL** – émigration de capitaux – flight of capital.

ÉMISSION – issue.
- **BANQUE d'émission** – issuing bank; issuing house.
- **CHÈQUE** – émission de chèque sans provision – issuing a bad (worthless) cheque.

ÉMOLUMENT – scale fee of an officer of the court (barrister, bailiff, etc); allowance paid to a witness or expert.
- **BÉNÉFICE d'émolument** – limitation of a spouse's liability for the community debts to his or her share of the community assets.
- **JUSTICE** – émolument de justice (Sw) – court fees.

EMPÊCHEMENT – impediment; bar; hindrance; disability.
- **CAUSE d'empêchement** – ground of impediment.
- **DIRIMANT** – empêchement dirimant – impediment entailing nullity or voidability of a marriage celebrated in spite of the impediment; absolute impediment.
- **DISPENSE des empêchements de mariage** – exemption (dispensation) from impediments to marriage.
- **LÉGAL** – empêchement légal – statutory impediment.
- **LÉGITIME** – empêchement légitime – lawful impediment (objection).
- **LIVRAISON** – empêchement à la livraison – ground for refusing delivery.
- **MARIAGE** – empêchement au mariage – impediment (to marriage).
- **PROHIBITIF** – empêchement prohibitif – impediment which does not render void or voidable a marriage celebrated in spite of the impediment.

EMPHYTÉOSE – long lease conferring a right in rem.

EMPHYTÉOTE – lessee under a long lease conferring a right in rem.

EMPIÈTEMENT – trespass; infringement; encroachment.
- **FONCTION** – empiètement de fonctions – exceeding one's authority.

EMPLOI – post; office; duty; employment; use; utilisation; purchase of property with available capital.
- **ABUSIF** – emploi abusif – misuse; improper use.
- **BUDGÉTAIRE** – emploi budgétaire – established post.
- **FAIRE emploi du prix de vente** – reinvest the proceeds of sale.
- **FORCE** – emploi de la force – use of force.
- **LUCRATIF** – emploi lucratif – paid employment; gainful employment; profitable use.
- **MI-TEMPS** – emploi à mi-temps – part-time employment.
- **OCCUPER un emploi public** – hold public office.
- **PRIORITÉ de l'emploi** – prior right of employment.
- **PRISE d'emploi** – assumption (taking up) of duties.

EMPLOYÉ

- **PROLONGATION d'emploi** – continued employment.
- **RETRAIT d'emploi** – removal from office; dismissal.
- **VACANCE d'emploi** – vacant post.

EMPLOYÉ – clerk; servant; salaried employee.

EMPREINTE

- **DIGITAL** – empreinte digitale – fingerprint.

EMPRISE – (illegal) expropriation; possession; taking possession; (legal or illegal) dispossession by the authorities; encroachment.

- **TOTAL** – réquisition d'emprise totale – application for the compulsory purchase of property rendered unusable by the expropriation of the rest of the building or land in question.

EMPRISONNEMENT

- **CELLULAIRE** – emprisonnement cellulaire – solitary (cellular) confinement (detention).
- **COMMUN** – emprisonnement en commun – group detention.
- **CORRECTIONNEL** – emprisonnement correctionnel – imprisonment for misdemeanour.
- **CRIMINEL** – emprisonnement criminel – imprisonment for felony.
- **INDIVIDUEL** – emprisonnement individuel – solitary confinement.
- **POLICE** – emprisonnement de police – imprisonment for a petty offence.
- **PRÉVENTIF** – emprisonnement préventif (Belg) – detention on remand.
- **SUBSIDIAIRE** – emprisonnement subsidiaire (Belg) – imprisonment in default (of payment of a fine).

EMPRUNT

- **AMORTISSABLE** – emprunt amortissable – redeemable loan.
- **AMORTISSEMENT d'emprunt** – redemption of (paying off) a loan.
- **CAPITAL d'emprunt** – outside capital; borrowed capital.
- **CAUTIONNÉ** – emprunt cautionné – guaranteed loan; secured loan.
- **CONSOLIDATION** – emprunt de consolidation – funding loan.
- **CONVENTION d'emprunt** – loan agreement.
- **CONVERSION** – emprunt de conversion – conversion loan.

- **DÉNONCIATION d'emprunt** – calling in a loan.
- **GAGÉ** – emprunt gagé – secured loan.
- **HYPOTHÉCAIRE** – emprunt hypothécaire (sur hypothèque) – mortgage (loan).
- **LOT** – emprunt à lots – lottery loan.
- **MONNAIE** – emprunt (libellé) en monnaie étrangère – foreign-currency loan.
- **OBLIGATAIRE** – emprunt obligataire – debenture loan.
- **OBLIGATION** – emprunt par obligations (Sw) – debenture loan.
- **PERPÉTUEL** – emprunt perpétuel – irredeemable loan.
- **PRIME** – emprunt à prime – premium loan.
- **PRODUIT de l'emprunt** – proceeds of the loan.
- **REVALIDATION** – emprunt de revalidation – redemption loan.
- **TRANCHE d'emprunt** – block of debentures, consols, etc.
- **VALEUR STABLE** – emprunt à valeur stable – fixed-value loan.

EMPRUNTEUR – borrower.

ENCAISSE – cash in hand.

ENCAISSEMENT – collection; cashing; payment.

- **CHÈQUE à l'encaissement** – cheque for collection.

ENCAISSER

- **CHÈQUE** – encaisser un chèque – collect a cheque.

ENCEINTE

- **TRIBUNAL** – enceinte du tribunal – courtroom; precinct of the court.

ENCHANNEMENT

- **CONTRAT d'enchaînement** – tied-house contract.

ENCHÈRE

- **FORT** – plus forte enchère – highest bid.
- **FOU** – folle enchère – frivolous (sham) bid (at an auction).
- **MINIMUM** – enchère minimum – lowest bid; lowest price.
- **VENDRE aux enchères** – sell by auction.

ENCHÉRIR – bid; increase the price of.

ENCHÉRISSEUR – bidder.

- **DERNIER** enchérisseur – highest bidder.
- **FORT** – plus fort enchérisseur – highest bidder.
- **FOU** – fol enchérisseur – sham bidder.

ENCLAVANT
- **FONDS** enclavant – land surrounding an enclave.

ENCLAVER – surround so as to create an enclave.

ENCLORE – enclose.

ENCLOS – enclosure; enclosed field or property; curtilage.

ENCOURIR – incur; be liable to.

ENDETTÉ – in debt.

ENDETTEMENT – indebtedness; debts.
- **COEFFICIENT** d'endettement – borrowing-to-capital ratio; debt ratio.
- **IMMOBILIER** – endettement immobilier – mortgage debts.
- **RATIO** d'endettement – borrowing-to-capital ratio; debt ratio.

ENDOS – endorsement.
- **PROCURATION** – endos de procuration – endorsement signed by an agent or manager.

ENDOSSABLE – endorsable; negotiable.

ENDOSSATAIRE – endorsee.

ENDOSSEMENT – endorsement.
- **BLANC** – endossement en blanc – blank endorsement.
- **COMPLET** – endossement complet – full endorsement.
- **EFFET PROTESTÉ** – endossement d'un effet protesté – endorsement after protest; subsequent endorsement.
- **GARANTIE** – endossement à titre de garantie – endorsement by way of security.
- **PERSONNE**
  - •• **DÉNOMMÉ** – endossement à personne dénommée – endorsement to a specified person; full endorsement.
- **PIGNORATIF** – endossement pignoratif – endorsement by way of security.
- **PORTEUR** – endossement au porteur – endorsement to the bearer; endorsement in blank.
- **PROCURATION** – endossement de procuration – endorsement signed by an agent or manager.

ENDOSSER – endorse.

ENDOSSEUR – endorser.
- **PRÉCÉDENT** – endosseur précédent – previous endorser.

ENFANCE
- **ABANDONNÉ** – enfance moralement abandonnée – neglected children.
- **ASSISTANCE** à l'enfance – child welfare.
- **COUPABLE** – enfance coupable – juvenile delinquents.
- **DÉLINQUANT** – enfance délinquante – juvenile delinquents.
- **MORALEMENT ABANDONNÉ** – see ABANDONNÉ above.

ENFANT
- **ABANDON** d'enfant – abandonment (exposure) of a child.
- **ABANDON** d'enfants – deserting one's children.
- **ADULTÉRIN** – enfant adultérin – adulterine child.
- **CHARGE** – enfant à charge – dependant child.
- **CONÇU** – enfant conçu – unborn child; child en ventre sa mère.
- **CONSANGUIN** – enfant consanguin – child of the same father.
- **LIT**
  - •• **AUTRE** – enfant d'un autre lit – stepchild.
  - •• **PREMIER** – enfant du premier lit – child of the first marriage.
- **SUBSTITUTION** d'enfant – substitution of a child.
- **SUPPOSITION** d'enfant – attributing a child to an imaginary woman or to a woman who has not conceived; passing off a child.
- **SUPPRESSION** d'enfant – causing the disappearance of a new-born child (charge brought where nothing more can be proved); concealment of birth.
- **UTÉRIN** – enfant utérin – child of the same mother.

ENFREINDRE – infringe; violate; be in breach of.

ENGAGEMENT – appointment; pledging; mortgaging; pawning; undertaking; obligation; commitment; liability.
- **BILAN** – engagement hors bilan – liability not appearing on the balance sheet.
- **CAMBIAIRE** – engagement cambiaire – liability under a bill of exchange.

- **CAUTIONNÉ** – **engagement cautionné** – secured liability or obligation.
- **CHANGE** – **engagement de change** – undertaking to surrender foreign currency.
- **COMMERCIAL** – **engagement commercial** – business commitment or obligation.
- **CONTRACTER un engagement** – enter into a commitment or obligation.
- **DÉPENSE** – **engagement de dépenses** – commitment of expenditure.
- **EMPLOI** – **engagement d'emploi** – undertaking as to the application of funds.
- **ESSAI** – **engagement à l'essai** – appointment on probation.
- **GARANTIE** – **engagement de garantie** – obligation to provide a guarantee or security.
- **HORS BILAN** – see BILAN above.
- **LOCATIF** – **engagement locatif** – tenant's obligation(s).
- **PAIEMENT** – **engagement de paiement** – obligation or liability to pay.
- **SANS engagement** – conditional (offer); without commitment.
- **SERVICE** – **engagement de service** – employment contract; obligation to serve; compulsory service.
- **SOLIDAIRE** – **engagement solidaire** – joint and several undertaking.
- **TERME** – **engagement à terme** – future commitment.
- **TRAVAIL** – **engagement de travail** – employment contract; obligation to serve; compulsory service.
- **UNILATÉRAL** – **engagement unilatéral** – unilateral undertaking.
- **VUE** – **engagement à vue** – sight liability.

ENGAGER – commit.

- **DÉPENSE** – **engager des dépenses** – commit or incur expenditure or funds.
- **ORGANISATION** – **engager l'organisation** – commit the organisation.
- **POURSUITE** – **engager des poursuites** – commence a prosecution.
- **PROCÉDURE** – **engager une procédure** – begin (start, commence) proceedings; bring an action; initiate a procedure.
- **RESPONSABILITÉ**
  - **LE** – **engager la responsabilité de** – render (someone) liable.
  - **SON** – **engager sa responsabilité** – incur liability; assume responsibility.

ENJEU – stake.

ENJOINDRE

- **À** – **enjoindre à** – order.

ENLÈVEMENT

- **ENFANT** – **enlèvement d'enfant** – abduction of a child.

ÉNONCÉ

- **FAIT** – **énoncé des faits** – (statement of) the facts.

ENQUÊTE – investigation; inquiry; taking of evidence.

- **CHAMP** – **enquête sur le champ** – taking evidence on the spot in civil proceedings (a judge or the court may take evidence in this way at any time provided both sides are represented).
- **COMMISSION d'enquête** – commission of inquiry; fact-finding committee; investigating committee.
- **COMMODO ET INCOMMODO** – **enquête de commodo et incommodo** – (formerly) administrative inquiry to ascertain the possible effects of proposed public works.
- **COMPLÉMENT d'enquête** – further investigations; further inquiries (into the facts).
- **CONSEIL d'enquête** – commission of inquiry.
- **FLAGRANT** – **enquête de flagrant délit** – expedited police investigation; on-the-spot investigation (involving extended police powers).
- **GOUVERNEMENTAL** – **enquête gouvernementale** – government inquiry.
- **INCIDENT** – **enquête incidente** – taking of evidence in the course of proceedings.
- **ORDINAIRE** – **enquête ordinaire** – taking of evidence (before a single judge).
- **PARCELLAIRE** – **enquête parcellaire** – inquiry as to the property to be expropriated (compulsorily acquired).
- **PAVILLON** – **enquête de pavillon** – establishing a ship's nationality.
- **PÉNAL** – **enquête pénale** (Sw) – criminal investigation.
- **PERSONNALITÉ** – **enquête de personnalité** – character report on an accused by the welfare officer.
- **PLACE** – **enquête sur place** – (criminal) investigation on the spot (on the scene of the crime, in loco).

- **POLICE** – enquête de police – police investigation.
- **PRÉLIMINAIRE** – enquête préliminaire – preliminary police investigation.
- **RESPECTIF** – enquête respective – taking evidence of the facts alleged by the defendant; bringing evidence which does not simply consist in countering evidence brought by the plaintiff.
- **SOCIAL** – enquête sociale – investigation by the welfare authorities; social inquiry report.
- **SOMMAIRE** – enquête sommaire – taking of evidence by the trial court itself (an exceptional procedure).

ENQUÊTEUR – detective constable; investigator.

ENREGISTREMENT – registration.
- **DÉBET** – enregistrement en débet – registration of the case file with the fees being payable later.
- **DROIT** d'enregistrement – registration fee.
- **NUMÉRO** d'enregistrement – registration number.

ENRICHISSEMENT
- **CAUSE** – enrichissement sans cause – unjust enrichment.
- **ILLÉGITIME** (Sw) – enrichissement illégitime – unjust enrichment.

ENRÔLEMENT – registration; filing; entering a case in the court register.
- **EFFECTUER** – dans la mesure où l'enrôlement au secrétariat-greffe n'a pas été effectué – if they have not been filed in the registry.

ENSEIGNEMENT
- **LIBERTÉ** d'enseignement – freedom of instruction; freedom to impart knowledge.

ENTACHER – vitiate.
- **ARBITRAIRE** – entaché d'arbitraire – arbitrary.
- **ERREUR** – entaché d'erreur – erroneous.
- **INCERTITUDE** – entaché d'incertitude – contingent.
- **NULLITÉ** – entaché de nullité – void.

ENTAMER
- **PROCÈS** – entamer un procès – commence proceedings.

ENTENTE – formal or informal agreement in restraint of trade.

- **AMIABLE** – entente amiable – friendly settlement.
- **DÉLICTUEUX** – entente délictueuse – conspiracy.
- **INDUSTRIEL** – entente industrielle – industrial combine; cartel.
- **PRÉALABLE** – entente préalable – prior agreement (consent).
- **TERRAIN** d'entente – common ground.

ENTÉRINEMENT – confirmation; endorsement.

ENTÉRINER – confirm; endorse.

EN-TÊTE
- **JUGEMENT** – en-tête du jugement – heading of the judgment.

ENTIERCEMENT – deposit of a pledge in the hands of a third party.

ENTITÉ
- **JURIDIQUE** – entité juridique – legal entity; juridical person; corporation.

ENTÔLAGE – theft by a prostitute from a customer.

ENTRAIDE
- **ADMINISTRATIF** – entraide administrative – mutual assistance in administrative matters.
- **JUDICIAIRE** – entraide judiciaire – mutual assistance between courts; judicial co-operation.
- **JURIDIQUE** – entraide juridique – mutual assistance in legal matters.

ENTRAVE – obstacle; hindrance; impediment.
- **JUSTICE** – entrave au fonctionnement de la justice – contempt of court; interference with the administration of justice.
- **LIBERTÉ**
  - **ENCHÈRE** – entrave à la liberté des enchères – interference with (the proper conduct of) an auction and fair bidding.
  - **TRAVAIL** – entrave à la liberté du travail – interference with freedom of employment.
- **NAVIGATION** – entrave à la navigation – interference with navigation.

ENTRÉE
- **ASSOCIÉ** – entrée d'un associé – entry of a partner into a firm.
- **FONCTION** – entrée en fonctions – assumption of duties, office, etc.

- **FRANCHISE** – **entrée en franchise** – entry of goods free of customs.
- **JOUISSANCE** – **entrée en jouissance** – taking possession; entry on (commencement of the enjoyment of) the benefits, fruits, rents and profits of property; entry into possession of a usufruct.
- **MATIÈRE** – **discussion de l'entrée en matière** (Sw) – preliminary discussion to decide whether a matter should be pursued further.
- **POSSESSION** – **entrée en possession** – taking possession.
- **VIGUEUR** – **entrée en vigueur** – (Act) entry (coming) into force; (regulations, rules, etc) coming into operation; (Act, regulations, rules, etc) commencement.

ENTREPÔT

- **COLLECTIF** – **entrepôt collectif** – collective storage.
- **CONSTITUER en entrepôt** – bring into bond.
- **DOUANE** – **entrepôt de douane** – bonded warehouse; bond; customs warehouse.
- **FICTIF** – **entrepôt fictif** – private bonded warehouse.
- **RÉCÉPISSÉ d'entrepôt** – warehouse receipt; deposit warrant.
- **RÉEL** – **entrepôt réel** – bonded warehouse; bond.
- **SPÉCIAL** – **entrepôt spécial** – bonded warehouse; bond.

ENTREPRENDRE

- **JUGEMENT** – **entreprendre un jugement** – appeal against (attack, challenge) a judgment.

ENTREPRENEUR – entrepreneur; contractor; employer; industrialist; operator; manufacturer; merchant; businessman; producer; independent contractor (in contract for services).

- **PRIVÉ** – **entrepreneur privé** – private contractor etc.
- **RESPONSABILITÉ de l'entrepreneur** – employer's liability; manufacturer's liability ; producer's liability.

ENTREPRISE – firm; enterprise; business; concern; works; undertaking.

- **ACCONAGE** – **entreprise d'acconage** – lighterage company.
- **ACCORD d'entreprise** – works agreement; staff agreement.
- **AGRICOLE** – **entreprise agricole** – farm.

- **ANONYME** – **entreprise anonyme** – joint-stock company.
- **ARTISANAL** – **entreprise artisanale** – manual trade.
- **BUT LUCRATIF** – **entreprise à but lucratif** – profit-making enterprise; enterprise with a view to gain.
- **CAISSE d'entreprise** – works provident fund.
- **COMITÉ d'entreprise** – works council; works committee.
- **CONCÉDÉ** – **entreprise concédée** – concessionnaire; undertaking operating a concession.
- **CONCESSIONNAIRE** – **entreprise concessionnaire** – concessionaire; undertaking operating a concession.
- **CONTRAT d'entreprise** – contract for services (by an independent contractor and sometimes involving the supply of materials), eg with a dentist, taxi-driver, cabinet-maker, garage owner or tailor; locatio operis.
- **CONVENTION d'entreprise** – works agreement; staff agreement.
- **DÉFICITAIRE** – **entreprise déficitaire** – losing business; business operating at a loss.
- **DÉMORALISATION** – **entreprise de démoralisation de l'armée** – undermining the morale of the troops.
- **INDIVIDUEL** – **entreprise individuelle** – independent business.
- **LIBRE entreprise** – free enterprise.
- **MOYEN** – **entreprise moyen** – medium-sized firm etc.
- **PERTE** – **entreprise travaillant à perte** – losing business; business operating at a loss.
- **RÈGLEMENT d'entreprise** – works regulations; staff regulations.
- **RESPONSABLE d'entreprise** – (in some contexts) worker's representative; shop steward.
- **SUCCESSORAL** – **entreprise successorale** – successor concern.
- **SYNDICAT d'entreprise** – local or works union.

ENTRER

- **FONCTION** – **entrer en fonctions** – assume office; take up duties.
- **LIQUIDATION** – **entrer en liquidation** – go into liquidation; be wound up.
- **VIGUEUR** – **entrer en vigueur** – (Act) enter (come) into force; (regulations, rules, etc)

come into operation; (Act, regulations, rules, etc) commence.

ENTRETENIR – provide maintenance; maintain; pay maintenance.

ENTRETIEN
- **OBLIGATION d'entretien** – duty to maintain a person or keep a building in repair.
- **REFUS d'entretien** – refusal to pay maintenance (to maintain).

ÉNUMÉRATION
- **PIÈCE** – **énumération des pièces** – listing of documents (with a view to obtaining discovery).

ENVELOPPE
- **BUDGÉTAIRE** – **enveloppe budgétaire** – budget package.

ENVOI
- **ACTE d'envoi en possession** – authority to take possession of an estate (document).
- **FORCÉ** – **vente par envoi forcé** – unsolicited postal sale.
- **FRAIS d'envoi** – forwarding expenses.
- **POSSESSION PROVISOIRE** – **envoi en possession provisoire** – provisional authority to take possession.
- **REBUT** – **envoi tombé en rebut** – undeliverable (dead) letter.
- **REMBOURSEMENT** – **envoi contre remboursement** – cash on delivery.

ENVOYÉ
- **EXTRAORDINAIRE** – **envoyé extraordinaire** – special envoy; envoy extraordinary.

ENVOYER
- **POSSESSION** – **envoyer en possession** – put in possession of an estate.

ÉPARGNE
- **LIVRET d'épargne** – (savings) passbook.
- **MATRIMONIAL** – **épargnes matrimoniales** – savings during the marriage (forming part of the matrimonial property).

ÉPAVE – lost (but not abandoned) movable property; wreck; remnant; object abandoned by its owner.

ÉPOQUE
- **FAIT** – **à l'époque des faits** – at the material time.

ÉPOUSE – wife, spouse.
- **DIVORCÉ** – **épouse divorcée** – divorced wife.

ÉPOUX – husband; spouse; party to a marriage.
- **ABANDONNÉ** – **époux abandonné** – deserted spouse.
- **COMMUN** – **époux commun (en biens)** – spouse living in community of property.
- **COMMUNAUTÉ entre époux** – community of property (between spouses); marital community.
- **DÉFENDEUR** – **époux défendeur** – respondent (divorce proceedings).
- **DEMANDEUR** – **époux demandeur** – petitioner (divorce proceedings).

ÉPREUVE
- **INÉVITABLE** – **épreuve inévitable** – unavoidable hardship.
- **MISE à l'épreuve** – probation.

ÉPUISEMENT
- **RECOURS**
  - **INTERNE** – **épuisement des recours internes** – exhaustion of domestic remedies.
  - **VOIE** – **épuisement des voies de recours** – exhaustion of the (available) remedies.

ÉQUIPOLLENT
- **THÉORIE des équipollents** – rule that a prescribed formality may be replaced by something equivalent.

ÉQUITABLE – fair; reasonable.

ÉQUITÉ – fairness; reasonableness; taking account of the particular circumstances of the individual case; equity in the non-technical sense.
- **JUGER en équité** – decide on equitable principles (ex aequo et bono).

ÉQUIVALENCE
- **TITRE** – **équivalence de titres** – equivalence of qualifications.

ÉQUIVOQUE – uncertainty or ambiguity (eg as to the date in a document); ambiguous nature (eg of acts performed by a person apparently in possession).

ERGA OMNES – erga omnes; (effective) against the whole world; in rem.

ERREUR – mistake; error.
- **APPRÉCIATION** – **erreur d'appréciation** – error (in assessing evidence or exercising a discretion).

- **COMMUN** – **erreur commune** – mistake common to both parties; common mistake.
- **CONVENU** – **erreur convenue** – mistake going to the root of the contract.
- **DIRIMANT** – **erreur dirimante** – mistake rendering the transaction voidable.
- **DROIT** – **erreur de droit** – mistake of law.
- **ÉVALUATION** – **erreur d'évaluation** – mistake as to the value of the subject-matter.
- **FAIT** – **erreur de fait** – mistake of fact.
- **JUDICIAIRE** – **erreur judiciaire** – miscarriage of justice.
- **LÉSIONNAIRE** – **erreur lésionnaire** – gross error as to the value of the subject-matter of a contract.
- **MATÉRIEL** – **erreur (purement) matérielle** – factual error (eg a false entry in an account); clerical error.
- **MOBILE (MOTIF)** – **erreur sur le mobile (motif)** – mistake affecting the motive (in principle not sufficient to render a contract voidable).
- **PERSONNE** – **erreur sur la personne** – mistake as to the person of the other contracting party.
- **SUBSTANTIEL** – **erreur substantielle** – mistake relating to the essential nature (essential properties) of the subject-matter (of a contract).
  - •• **NON** – **erreur sur les qualités non substantielles** – mistake relating to non-essential properties of the subject-matter (of a contract).
- **VALEUR** – **erreur sur la valeur** – mistake as to the value of the subject-matter.
- **VERSER dans l'erreur** – err.

ERRONÉ – erroneous; wrong (in law).

ÈS
- **QUALITÉ** – **ès qualités** – in that capacity; in the exercise of one's functions; in one's official capacity; ex officio.

ESCROC – swindler; cheat.
- **MARIAGE** – **escroc au mariage** – marriage impostor.

ESCROQUER – obtain by false pretences; cheat; defraud.

ESCROQUERIE – obtaining by false pretences; fraud; deceit.
- **ASSURANCE** – **escroquerie à l'assurance** – insurance fraud.
- **MÉTIER** – **escroquerie par métier** – earning one's living by fraud; professional fraud.

ESPACE
- **AÉRIEN** – **espace aérien** – airspace.
  - •• **INTERDIT** – **espace aérien interdit** – prohibited airspace.

ESPÈCE – case; (in plural) cash; coins.
- **APPORT en espèces** – cash brought in; assets brought in in cash.
- **AVANCE en espèces** – cash advance.
- **CONSIGNATION d'espèces** – deposit of cash by way of security.
- **EN espèces** – in cash.
- **EN l'espèce** – in the instant (present) case.
- **MONNAYÉ** – **espèces monnayées** – coins.
- **PRESTATION en espèces** – payment in cash; cash benefit.
- **VERSEMENT en espèces** – payment in cash.

ESPÉRANCE
- **SUCCESSORAL** – **espérance successorale** – expectancy.

ESSAI
- **CONCILIATION** – **essai de conciliation** – attempted reconciliation.
- **VENTE à l'essai** – sale on approval; sale or return.

ESSARTEMENT
- **SERVITUDE d'essartement** – forest owner's duty to leave a clear space of 20 metres on either side of the highway.

ESTER
- **CAPACITÉ d'ester en justice** – right to take part in court proceedings; standing (before the court); locus standi.
- **DROIT d'ester en justice** – right to take part in court proceedings; standing (before the court); locus standi.
- **INCAPACITÉ d'ester en justice** – lack of standing (before the court); incapacity to take part in court proceedings.
- **JUGEMENT** – **ester en jugement** – take part in court proceedings; appear and plead before a court.
- **JUSTICE** – **ester en justice** – take part in court proceedings; appear and plead before a court.

ESTIMABLE – capable of assessment.

ESTIMATION – assessment; valuation; estimate.

- **CONTRADICTOIRE** – estimation contradictoire – assessment in the presence of the parties.
- **JUDICIAIRE** – estimation judiciaire – assessment by the court; judicial assessment.
- **PRIX** d'estimation – estimated price.
- **VALEUR** d'estimation – estimated price.

ESTIMATOIRE

- **ACTION** estimatoire – action for the reduction of the price of goods sold, on account of defects.

ESTIMER – (of a court) hold.

ÉTABLIR – establish; prove; show; make out; substantiate.

- **JUSTICE** – établir en justice – prove in court.

ÉTABLISSEMENT – (place of) business; institution; settlement; premises; establishment; corporation.

- **ACCORD** (collectif) d'établissement – works agreement.
- **ASSIETTE**
  - **IMPÔT** – établissement de l'assiette de l'impôt – tax assessment; basis of assessment.
- **AUTORISATION** d'établissement – permission to settle (take up residence).
- **BIENFAISANCE** – établissement bienfaisance – charitable institution; charitable corporation; charity.
- **CENTRAL** – établissement central – principal office; principal place of business.
- **CLASSE** – établissement classé – classified premises.
- **CONVENTION** d'établissement – convention on establishment; establishment convention.
- **CRÉDIT** – établissement de crédit – financial institution.
- **DANGEREUX** – établissement dangereux, incommode et insalubre – dangerous, offensive (noxious) or unhealthy works (premises).
- **DÉPENSES** d'établissement – formation expenses; promotion expenses; capital expenditure.
- **DROIT** d'établissement – right to settle (take up residence); right of establishment.
- **ENFANT** – établissement d'un enfant – setting up a child; conferring a portion on a child.

- **IMPÔT** – établissement de l'impôt – tax assessment.
- **INDUSTRIEL** – établissement industriel – industrial premises.
- **INTÉRÊT PUBLIC** – établissement d'intérêt public – public-service corporation.
- **LIBERTÉ** d'établissement – freedom to settle (take up residence); freedom of establishment.
- **LIEU** d'établissement – place of residence; place of business.
- **PÉNITENTIAIRE** – établissement pénitentiaire – prison.
- **PERMIS** d'établissement – residence (establishment) permit; authority to settle (take up residence).
- **PERSONNEL** – établissement en nom personnel – private firm (business); one-man firm (business).
- **PRÊT SUR GAGES** – établissement de prêt sur gages – pawnbroker.
- **PRINCIPAL** – établissement principal – principal office; principal place of business.
- **PROFESSIONNEL** – établissement professionnel – office; practice; place of business.
- **PUBLIC** – établissement public – public institution; public corporation.
- **REDRESSEMENT** – établissement de redressement – reformatory; approved school; borstal institution.
- **STABLE** – établissement stable – business premises; industrial premises; works; plant; fixed assets.
- **TRAITÉ** d'établissement – establishment treaty.
- **UTILITÉ PUBLIQUE** – établissement d'utilité publique – public corporation promoting the public interest; charitable corporation.

ÉTAGE

- **PROPRIÉTAIRE** d'étage – owner of a floor (storey) in a building.
- **PROPRIÉTÉ** d'étage – ownership of a floor (storey) in a building.

ÉTALON

- **MÉTALLIQUE** – étalon métallique – metal (currency) standard.
- **MONÉTAIRE** – étalon monétaire – monetary standard.
- **OR** – étalon (d')or – gold standard.

ÉTAT – state; central government; status; register; statement; list.

- **ACCUSATION** – être en état d'accusation – be the subject of a prosecution; have proceedings taken against one.
- **ACTION** d'état – action to establish, contest or change one's personal status (descent, marriage, etc); status action.
- **AFFAIRE** en état – case ready for hearing, ready for trial.
- **AGENT** d'État – civil servant; state employee.
- **BELLIGÉRANCE** – état de belligérance – state of belligerency.
- **BELLIGÉRANT** – État belligérant – belligerent state.
- **BLOCUS** – état de blocus – blockade.
- **CARENCE** – état de carence – absence of goods capable of being attached.
- **CAUSE** – en tout état de cause – at any stage of the proceedings.
- **CHARGE** – état de charges – list of encumbrances.
- **CIVIL** – état civil – civil status; registry of births, deaths and marriages; population register; marital status.
  - •• **ACTE** de l'état civil – civil-status record (entry) or certificate.
  - •• **EXTRAIT** de l'état civil – civil-status certificate.
  - •• **FALSIFICATION** de l'état civil – forgery or falsification of civil-status certificates (documents or records relating to civil status).
  - •• **OFFICIER** de l'état civil – registration officer; registrar.
  - •• **PIÈCE** d'état civil – civil-status certificate.
  - •• **REGISTRE** d'état (de l'état) civil – population register; register of births, deaths and marriages.
- **COLLOCATION** – état de collocation – list of creditors, debts and available assets (in bankruptcy); order of preference in bankruptcy.
- **COMPTABLE** – état comptable – statement of accounts.
- **CONSEIL** d'État – highest administrative court and government adviser on questions arising in connection with legislation (not usually translated); State Council.
- **CONSOMMATION**
  - •• **CRÉDIT** – état de consommation des crédits – (statement of the) amount of appropriations used; (statement of) utilisation of appropriations.
- **CONTESTATION** – action en contestation d'état – action to disprove one's descent from one's ostensible parents; action to disprove a person's apparent status, descent or nationality.
- **CONTRACTANT** – État contractant – contracting state.
- **CRISE** – état de crise – state of emergency.
- **DÉPENS** – état des dépens – bill of costs; statement of expenditure.
- **DESCRIPTIF** – état descriptif – description.
  - •• **DIVISION** – état descriptif de division – description of the division of the property.
- **DETTE** – état des dettes – statement or list of debts.
- **DISTRIBUTION** – état de distribution – distribution scheme; apportionment plan; plan of distribution; distribution of work.
- **DOMICILE** – État du domicile – state of ordinary residence (see DOMICILE).
- **DROIT** – État de droit – (state governed by) the rule of law.
- **ÉGLISE** – État de l'Église – Vatican City State.
- **EN** état – ready for decision; ready for trial.
  - •• **TENIR** – le criminel tient le civil en état – civil proceedings for damages arising out of a criminal offence must await the outcome of the criminal trial.
- **EN** l'état – as matters stand (stood); as the case stands (stood).
  - •• **IRRECEVABLE** en l'état – inadmissible in the current state of the file.
- **ENTRETIEN** – état d'entretien – state of repair.
- **ENVOI** – État d'envoi – sending state.
- **ÉTABLISSEMENT** – État d'établissement – state in which a person has established his residence.
- **EXCEPTION** – état d'exception – state of emergency; martial law.
- **EXÉCUTOIRE** – état exécutoire – enforceable order for costs.
- **FAIRE** état de – rely on; establish.
  - •• **ATTITUDE** – faire état de cette attitude comme constituant – treat this attitude as constituting.
- **FAIT** – état de faits – facts; statement of facts; factual situation.
- **FONCTIONNAIRE** d'État – civil servant.
- **FONDS** de l'État – public money.

- **FONDS d'État** – government bonds (securities, stock).
- **FRAIS** – état de frais – statement of costs; order for costs.
- **HYPOTHÉCAIRE** – état hypothécaire – statement (list) of mortgages.
- **INVENTORIÉ** – état inventorié – inventory.
- **LIEU** – État du lieu de la situation – state in which the object is situated.
- **LIEU** – état des lieux – state of the premises; inventory of fixtures.
- **LIMITROPHE** – État limitrophe – neighbouring (bordering) state; border (frontier) state.
- **LIQUIDATIF** – état liquidatif – statement of amount due; settlement statement; final scheme of division in a partition.
- **MANDATAIRE** – État mandataire – mandatory state, ie a state holding a League of Nations mandate.
- **MEMBRE** – État membre – member state.
- **METTRE en état** – prepare (a case) for trial; make (a case) ready for hearing; put in order; put (premises) into repair.
  - •• **SE mettre en état** – (as required of a convicted offender who is appealing on points of law) surrender to custody.
- **MEUBLE** – état de meubles – list of movable property.
- **MISE en état** – preparation (of a case) for trial; making (a case) ready for hearing; putting in order; putting (premises) into repair; (required of a convicted offender who is appealing on points of law) surrender(ing) to custody.
- **MI-SOUVERAIN** – État mi-souverain – semi-sovereign state.
- **NÉANT** – état néant – negative report; nil return.
- **NÉCESSITÉ** – état de nécessité – (state of) necessity; defence of necessity.
- **NEUTRE** – État neutre – neutral state.
- **NOMINATIF** – état nominatif – list of names; nominal roll.
  - •• **ÉMARGEMENT** – état nominatif d'émargement – list of names with a column for signatures.
- **NUMÉRIQUE** – état numérique – numerical return.
- **PARCELLAIRE** – état parcellaire – copy of the official plan and description of a piece of land.
- **PAVILLON** – État du pavillon – state whose flag is flown by a ship or aircraft; state

of the flag.
- **PERSONNE** – état des personnes – civil (personal, family status).
- **PONTIFICAL** – États pontificaux – Papal States.
- **POSSESSION** – état de possession – position established by actual occupation.
- **POSSESSION d'état** – actual enjoyment of a certain civil (personal, family) status; public acceptance of a person's status; factual possession of status; de facto enjoyment of a certain status, eg the prerogatives of citizenship; enjoyment of status by repute.
- **PRÉVISION**
  - •• **DÉPENSE** – état de prévision de dépenses – estimate of future expenditure.
  - •• **RECETTE** – état de prévision de recettes – estimate of future revenue.
- **PRÉVISIONNEL** – état prévisionnel – budget estimates; estimates; budget.
- **PROTECTEUR** – État protecteur – protecting state; protecting power.
- **PROTÉGÉ** – État protégé – protected state; protectorate.
- **QUESTION d'état** – matter relating to civil (personal, family) status.
- **RÉCLAMATION** – (action en) réclamation d'état – action to establish descent from a parent (legitimacy).
- **RECTIFICATIF** – état rectificatif – corrigendum.
- **RENTE sur l'État** – state annuity; state pension.
- **RÉPARTITION** – état de répartition – apportionment plan.
- **REQUÉRANT** – État requérant – applicant state; requesting state.
- **REQUIS** – État requis – requested state.
- **RÉSIDENCE** – État de résidence – state of residence.
- **REVERSEMENT** – état de reversement – enforceable repayment order.
- **RIVERAIN** – État riverain – riparian state.
- **SÉCURITÉ de l'État** – national security.
- **SÉJOUR** – État de séjour – state of temporary residence.
- **SERVICE** – état de services – record of service.
- **SIÈGE** – état de siège – martial law; state of emergency.

•• **PROCLAMER** l'état de siège – proclaim martial law or a state of emergency.

• **SITUATION** – état de situation – statement of affairs; return.

•• **BANQUE** – état de situation de banque – bank's statement of its affairs.

• **SOUS-JACENT** – État sous-jacent – state whose territory is being flown over; overflown state.

• **SOUVERAIN** – État souverain – sovereign state.

• **SUCCESSEUR** – État successeur – successor state.

• **SURVOLÉ** – État survolé – state whose territory is being flown over; overflown state.

• **TAMPON** – État tampon – buffer state.

• **TENIR** en état – (of criminal proceedings in relation to civil proceedings) require to be stayed (pending the outcome of the criminal proceedings); take precedence (priority) over.

•• **CRIMINEL** – le criminel tient le civil en état – civil proceedings for damages arising out of a criminal offence must await the outcome of the criminal trial.

• **TRANSITÉ** – État transité – state over whose territory a right of passage or transit is exercised.

• **UNION** d'États – union between states; union of two or more states.

• **UNITAIRE** – État unitaire – unitary state; centrally governed state.

• **URGENCE** – état d'urgence – state of emergency.

• **USURPATION** d'état civil – assumption of false name or identity.

ÉTATIQUE – state (adj).

ÉTATISATION – placing under direct state control (ie with less independence than a nationalised undertaking).

ÉTATISER – place under direct state control.

ÉTEINDRE

• **ACTION PUBLIQUE** – l'action publique se trouve éteinte – the prosecution is (statute-)barred (has lapsed).

• **DETTE** – éteindre une dette – extinguish a debt.

• **S'éteindre** – lapse.

ÉTENDRE – extend.

ÉTRANGER – alien; foreigner; foreign national; abroad.

• **À** – étranger à – not connected with; alien to; a stranger to.

•• **GIBRALTAR** – étranger à Gibraltar – non-Gibraltarian.

• **AVOIRS** à l'étranger – accounts, deposits or assets abroad.

• **BIENS** à l'étranger – assets abroad.

• **CAUSE** étrangère – external (outside) cause; cause for which the promisor (defendant) is not liable; cause which cannot be imputed to the promisor (defendant) or person whose animal or thing caused the damage.

• **COMPTE** à l'étranger – foreign account.

• **POLICE** des étrangers – immigration department.

• **REGISTRE** des étrangers – aliens register.

• **REPRÉSENTATION** à l'étranger – diplomatic representation abroad.

ÉTUDE

• **NOTAIRE** – étude de notaire – solicitor's (notary's) office (practice).

ÉVACUATION

• **ACTION** en évacuation – action for possession.

• **DÉLAI** d'évacuation – (notice or order giving) time to quit.

ÉVADÉ – escaped prisoner.

ÉVALUATION – assessment; valuation; basis of calculation; estimated amount.

• **CONTRADICTOIRE** – évaluation contradictoire – assessment in the presence of the parties.

• **DÉPENSE** – évaluation de la dépense – estimated amount of expenditure.

• **DOMMAGE** – évaluation des dommages – assessment of the damages.

• **FISCAL** – évaluation fiscal – tax or duty valuation; tax rating.

• **FORFAITAIRE** – évaluation forfaitaire – lump-sum estimate.

• **PROVISOIRE** – évaluation provisoire – provisional estimate.

• **VENTE** sur évaluation – sale at an estimated price.

ÉVASION – escape.

• **CAPITAL** – évasion des capitaux – flight of capital.

• **FISCAL** – évasion fiscale – tax avoidance.

ÉVÉNEMENT

- **CASUEL** – événement casuel – fortuitous event; accident.
- **DOMMAGEABLE** – événement dommageable – cause of damage.

ÉVENTUALITÉ – contingency; risk.

- **MOMENT** – le moment où l'éventualité se produit – the time when the contingency occurs.

ÉVENTUEL

- **PUREMENT** éventuel – contingent.

ÉVICTION – dispossession (of a purchaser etc) by a person exercising a superior right.

- **GARANTIE contre l'éviction** – covenant for peaceful possession.

ÉVINCER – dispossess by virtue of a superior right; oust; deprive of a right; defeat by superior title.

ÉVOCATION – order of a superior court bringing before itself for decision a case pending in a lower tribunal; transfer order; decision on the merits by a court of appeal after it has decided an appeal on a point of procedure.

ÉVOLUTIF

- **INTERPRÉTATION** évolutive – progressive (evolutive) interpretation by the courts.
- **JURISPRUDENCE** évolutive – progressive (evolutive) interpretation by the courts.

ÉVOLUTION

- **LITIGE** – évolution du litige – development in the legal position occurring in a case (either at the trial or at a later stage which justifies giving third-party notice on appeal).

ÉVOQUER – issue a transfer order (see ÉVOCATION); (of a superior court) transfer to itself.

EXACTITUDE – correctness.

EXAMEN

- **APTITUDE** – examen d'aptitude – aptitude test; qualifying examination.
- **COMMISSION d'examen** – board of examiners.
- **COMPAGNONNAGE** – examen de compagnonnage – journeyman's test; skilled workman's test.
- **DOSSIER** – examen du dossier – inspection of the file.
- **DROIT d'examen** – examination fee.

- **FOND** – examen au fond – consideration of the merits.
- **INTERMÉDIAIRE** – examen intermédiaire – intermediate examination.
- **MAÎTRISE** – examen de maîtrise – master craftsman's examination.
- **NOUVEAUTÉ** – examen de nouveauté – examination as to novelty (patents).
- **PERSONNALITÉ** – examen de personnalité – report on the accused's personality (compulsory in cases of felony).
- **PROBATOIRE** – examen probatoire – aptitude test.

EXAMINER – examine; test; consider; investigate.

EXCÉDENT

- **BUDGÉTAIRE** – excédent budgétaire – budget surplus.
- **CAISSE** – excédent de caisse – cash surplus.
- **CHARGE** – excédent de charge – overloading; excess weight.
- **COMPTABLE** – excédent comptable – accounting surplus.
- **POIDS** – excédent de poids – overloading; excess weight.

EXCÉDENTAIRE – showing a surplus.

EXCÉDER

- **POUVOIR** – excéder ses pouvoirs – act beyond (exceed) one's authority.

EXCEPTER – make an exception.

EXCEPTION – exception; defence; objection (constituting a temporary obstacle to proceedings); preliminary issue or objection.

- **ANTÉRIORITÉ** – exception d'antériorité – defence of prior right, user, etc (which renders void an industrial property right).
- **CHOSE JUGÉE** – exception de chose jugée – defence of res judicata.
- **COMMUNICATION** – exception de communication de pièces – objection which can be raised requesting the court to stay proceedings so long as the opposite party refuses to make his documents available.
- **COMPENSATION** – exception de compensation – (defence of) set-off.
- **CONNEXITÉ** – exception de connexité – defence that related proceedings are pending in another court (lis alibi pendens).
- **CONTREPARTIE** – exception de contrepartie – defence based on the agent's

option himself to assume the liability of the undisclosed principal.

- **DÉCLINATOIRE** – **exception déclinatoire** – defence, objection or plea that the court has no jurisdiction to hear a case; objection to jurisdiction.
- **DILATOIRE** – **exception dilatoire** – defence raised to gain time, eg so as to decide whether to accept a succession or give third-party notice to a guarantor; application to stay the proceedings to allow time to make a decision or comply with a formality.
- **DISCUSSION** – **exception de discussion** – defence raised by a guarantor or surety requiring the principal debtor to be sued first.
- **DOL** – **exception de dol** – defence alleging fraud on the part of the plaintiff.
- **EXTRANÉITÉ** – **exception d'extranéité** – defence alleging that the plaintiff is an alien.
- **GARANTIE** – **exception de garantie** – defence alleging the existence of a guarantee.
- **ILLÉGALITÉ** – **exception d'illégalité** – defence that the contract relied on by the plaintiff is illegal or that the administrative regulation on which the prosecution is based is unlawful.
- **INCOMPÉTENCE** – **exception d'incompétence** – defence, objection or plea that the court has no jurisdiction to hear a case; objection to jurisdiction.
- **INEXÉCUTION** – **exception d'inexécution** – defence that the plaintiff has not performed his part of the contract.
- **IRRECEVABILITÉ** – **exception d'irrecevabilité** – objection to admissibility (particularly in the case of private member's Bill or amendment which is not in accordance with the Constitution).
- **JEU** – **exception de jeu** – defence alleging that the contract etc relied on by the plaintiff is void as a wager.
- **JURIDICTION d'exception** – (1) court of limited jurisdiction; specialised court, ie any court other than the **Tribunal de grande instance** and the Court of Appeal, eg the **tribunal d'instance**, the **tribunal de commerce**, and the **conseil de prud'hommes**; (2) specialised criminal court, eg the **juridictions pour mineurs**, the **tribunaux aux armées** and the **Haute Cour de justice**; (3) (Belg) special court (ie set up to deal with an individual case or cases).
- **LÉGISLATION d'exception** – emergency legislation.
- **LITISPENDANCE** – **exception de litispendance** – (preliminary) objection that a matter is pending before another competent court (lis alibi pendens).
- **LOI d'exception** – Emergency Provisions Act.
- **MESURE d'exception** – emergency provision; special measure.
- **NON ADIMPLETI CONTRACTUS** – **exception "non adimpleti contractus"** – defence that the plaintiff has not performed his part of the contract.
- **NULLITÉ** – **exception de nullité** – defence that the transaction etc relied on by the plaintiff is void; application for a step in the proceedings (writ, pleading, etc) to be struck out (set aside) on grounds of nullity.
- **PÉREMPTOIRE** – **exception péremptoire** – absolute defence; defence which goes to the root of and destroys the plaintiff's case.
- **PLURIUM CONCUBENTIUM** – **exception plurium concubentium** – defence alleging that the mother has had relations with persons other than the alleged father during the conception period.
- **PRÉJUDICIEL** – **exception préjudicielle** – preliminary question which must be referred to another court after the proceedings have been stayed.
- **PRÉLIMINAIRE** – **exception preliminiaire** – preliminary objection; preliminary point.
- **PREUVE** – **exception relative à la preuve** – objection relating to the evidence.
- **PROPOSER une exception** – raise an objection; plead (put forward, raise) a defence.
- **RÉGLEMENTATION d'exception** – emergency regulations.
- **REJETER une exception** – dismiss an objection; reject a defence.
- **SIMULATION** – **exception de simulation** – defence alleging that the transaction relied on is fictitious.
- **SOULEVER une exception** – raise an objection; plead (put forward, raise) a defence.
- **TRIBUNAL d'exception** – see JURIDICTION above.
- **VOIE** – **par voie d'exception** – as a defence or an objection.

EXCÈS – abuse; excess.

- **OBLIGATION** – **excès des obligations (ordinaires) de voisinage** – nuisance.

- **POUVOIR** – excès de pouvoir – abuse (misuse) of authority; acting in excess of authority (jurisdiction); acting ultra vires.
  - •• **COMMETTRE un excès de pouvoir** – exceed one's jurisdiction.
  - •• **RECOURS (en annulation) pour excès de pouvoir** – application to an administrative court to set aside an administrative decision on grounds such as lack of jurisdiction, error of procedure, misapplication of the law, misuse of a discretion or ultra vires (exceeding or misusing one's authority); application for judicial review.
- **VITESSE** – excès de vitesse – exceeding the speed-limit; speeding.
- **VOISINAGE** – see OBLIGATION above.

EXCESSIF – unreasonable.

EXCIPER
- **BONNE FOI** – see FOI below.
- **DE** – exciper de – rely on; plead in one's defence.
  - •• **DIVORCE** – l'époux prétendu bigame peut exciper d'un divorce régulier – an allegedly bigamous spouse may rely on the defence of a divorce in due form.
- **DROIT** – exciper de son droit – rely on a right.
- **FOI** – exciper de sa bonne foi – plead one's good faith.
- **PRESCRIPTION** – exciper de la prescription – raise the defence of limitation; plead limitation.

EXCIPIENS – person raising the defence that the plaintiff has not performed his part of the contract.

EXCITATEUR – trouble-maker; agitator.

EXCITATION
- **DÉBAUCHE** – excitation (des mineurs) à la débauche – incitement (of minors) to immorality; depravation (of minors).

EXCLURE
- **MUTUELLEMENT** – qui s'excluent mutuellement – contradictory.

EXCLUSION
- **JUGEMENT** d'exclusion – order excluding claims not lodged within the appointed time.
- **RESPONSABILITÉ** – exclusion de la responsabilité – exclusion of liability.

EXCLUSIVITÉ – exclusive rights.

- **CLAUSE** d'exclusivité – exclusive-rights clause.
- **DROIT** d'exclusivité – sole (exclusive) right.

EX-CONJOINT – former spouse.

EXCUSE – ground of excuse.
- **ABSOLUTOIRE** – excuse absolutoire – statutory ground for exemption from punishment.
- **ATTÉNUANT** – excuse atténuante – ground for mitigating sentence, eg provocation or the fact that the accused is under age.

EX-DROIT – ex rights; ex new.

EXÉCUTER – perform; fulfil; execute; carry out; enforce.
- **DÉBITEUR** – le débiteur doit exécuter – the obligor (promisee etc) is under an duty to perform his obligation.
- **OBLIGATION** – exécuter une obligation – perform an obligation.
- **PEINE** – (faire) exécuter une peine – enforce a sentence.

EXÉCUTEUR
- **TESTAMENTAIRE** – exécuteur testamentaire – executor.

EXÉCUTIF – the executive (as opposed to the legislative and the judiciary).

EXÉCUTION – fulfilment; performance; execution; enforcement.
- **ACCORD** d'exécution – administration agreement; administrative agreement.
- **ACTE** d'exécution – execution (enforcement) measure; measure of execution.
- **ACTE** – exécution d'un acte – execution of an instrument.
- **ANTICIPÉ** – exécution anticipée de peines (Sw) – advance enforcement of sentences (ie starting before the sentence becomes final).
- **BUDGET** – exécution du budget – implementation of the budget.
- **CHOSE JUGÉE** – exécution tardive de la chose jugée – late compliance with a court order.
- **CONTRAT** – exécution du contrat – performance of the contract.
- **DÉLAI** d'exécution – time for performance.
- **DIFFICULTÉS** d'exécution d'un jugement – points arising on the execution of a judgment.

- **ÉTAT PRÉVISIONNEL** – **exécution de l'état prévisionnel** – implementation of the budget.
- **FÉDÉRAL** – **exécution fédérale** – coercion exercised by the federal authorities against a member state of the federation; federal coercion.
- **FORCÉ** – **exécution forcée** – execution by force or threat of force; enforcement; execution.
  - •• **NATURE** – **exécution forcée en nature** – enforcing specific performance.
  - •• **SUSCEPTIBLE d'exécution forcée** – capable of being enforced.
- **IMPOSSIBILITÉ d'exécution** – impossibility of performance (this is judged by an objective standard and not by the defendant's personal inability to perform).
- **JUGE de l'exécution** – judge of the Regional Court with jurisdiction to decide questions relating to the execution of civil judgments; execution(s) judge.
- **JUGEMENT** – **exécution du jugement** – enforcement of the judgment, order or sentence.
- **LIEU d'exécution** – place of performance (of a contract).
- **LOYAL** – **exécution loyale** – correct (punctual, full) performance.
- **MANDAT d'exécution** – instruction to levy execution given by the judgment creditor to the bailiff; writ of execution.
- **MESURE d'exécution** – form or measure of execution (enforcement); execution (enforcement) measure; implementing measure (which may take the form of implementing regulations).
- **METTRE en exécution** – enforce.
- **MINUTE** – **exécution sur minute** – immediate execution, ie on the authority of the original written judgment, without having to serve an execution copy (**grosse**).
- **MODALITÉ d'exécution** – implementing regulation, provision, etc.
- **NATURE** – **exécution en nature** – specific performance.
- **OFFICE** – **exécution d'office** – execution by the authorities at the expense of the person concerned; ex-officio execution of administrative decisions by the authorities.
- **ORDRE d'exécution** – writ of execution endorsed on an order to pay.
- **ORGANE d'exécution** – executive organ (body).
- **ORGANISME d'exécution** – executive organ (body).
- **PARTIEL** – **exécution partielle** – part performance.
- **PEINE** – **exécution d'une peine** – enforcement of (serving) a sentence.
- **POURSUIVRE l'exécution** – levy execution.
- **POUVOIR d'exécution** – power (authority) to enforce (execute); executive power.
- **PROCÉDURE d'exécution** – execution proceedings; execution procedure.
- **PROMESSE** – **exécution d'une promesse** – fulfilment of a promise.
- **PROMESSE** – **promesse d'exécution** – formal undertaking to perform the obligation of another.
- **PROVISION** – **exécution par provision** – order making a judgment immediately enforceable notwithstanding the lodging of an appeal; order annulling the suspensive effect of an appeal.
- **PROVISOIRE** – **exécution provisoire** – order making a judgment immediately enforceable notwithstanding the lodging of an appeal; order annulling the suspensive effect of an appeal.
- **RECEVOIR exécution** – be put into effect.
- **REFUS d'exécution** – refusal to perform; repudiation.
- **RÈGLEMENT d'exécution** – implementing regulations.
- **REPRISE d'exécution** – undertaking the performance of another's obligation but not the obligation itself; agreement whereby a third party agrees with the debtor (promisor) to perform the latter's obligation, the creditor (promisee) not being a party to the agreement; agreement for vicarious performance.
- **RETARD dans l'exécution** – delay in performance; late performance.
- **SAISIE** – **exécution de la saisie** – execution of writ of fi fa; attachment; seizure.
- **SUCCESSIF** – **contrat à exécution successive** – continuing contract.
- **SURSEOIR à l'exécution** – stay execution.
- **SURSIS à l'exécution** – stay of execution.
- **VOIE d'exécution** – (method of) execution; (in plural) execution (enforcement) procedure.
- **VOLONTAIRE** – **exécution volontaire** – voluntary performance.

EXÉCUTOIRE (adj) – enforceable; operative.
- **DIVORCE exécutoire** – decree absolute.
- **FORCE exécutoire** – enforceability.
  - **AVOIR force exécutoire** – be enforceable (by execution).
- **MINUTE – exécutoire sur minute** – enforceable immediately, ie on the authority of the original written judgment, without having to serve an execution copy (**grosse**).
- **PROVISION – exécutoire par provision** – immediately enforceable.
- **VALEUR – avoir valeur exécutoire** – including an authority to execute; be enforceable by execution.

EXÉCUTOIRE (noun) – order fixing the amount of costs; order for costs.
- **PRENDRE l'exécutoire** – make an order for costs.

EXÉGÈSE – interpretation.

EXEMPT
- **CHARGE – exempt de charges** – unencumbered; free from encumbrances.
- **IMPÔT – exempt d'impôt(s)** – tax-free; free of tax; not liable to tax.

EXEQUATUR – (decision conferring) authority to execute (a judgment or arbitral award); registration for enforcement; official confirmation; exequatur (for a consul).
- **DÉLIVRER l'exequatur** – register a foreign judgment for execution; grant authority to execute.
- **INSTANCE en exequatur** – application for authority to enforce a foreign judgment.

EXERCER
- **ACTION – exercer une action** – bring an action.
- **COMPÉTENCE – exercer sa compétence** – entertain proceedings; exercise jurisdiction.
- **RECOURS – exercer un recours** – bring (enter) an appeal; exercise (have recourse to) a remedy.

EXERCICE – accounting year; financial year.
- **BUDGÉTAIRE – exercice budgétaire** – accounting year; financial year.
- **CAPACITÉ d'exercice** – independent capacity to exercise one's own rights without any form of representation, assistance or authorisation; legal capacity.
- **CLOS – exercice clos** – past (previous) financial year.
- **DÉLAI d'exercice** – time-limit for exercising a right etc.

- **ÉCOULÉ – exercice écoulé** – past (previous) financial year.
- **EN exercice** – serving; present; acting; in charge; on duty; in office; for the time being.
- **FISCAL – exercice fiscal** – tax year; year of assessment.
- **INCAPACITÉ d'exercice** – incapacity to exercise one's own rights without some form of representation, assistance or authorisation; absence of legal capacity.
- **MANDAT – exercice d'un mandat** – acting as an agent; acting under a power of attorney; fulfilling instructions.
- **SOCIAL – exercice social** – (company's) accounting (financial) year.

EXHAUSSEMENT – increase in height of a wall or building.

EXHÉRÉDATION – depriving of a right of inheritance.
- **CAUSE d'exhérédation** – ground for depriving of a right of inheritance.

EXIGER
- **DOMMAGES-INTÉRÊTS – exiger des dommages-intérêts** – claim damages.

EXIGIBILITÉ – current liability.
- **CONDITION d'exigibilité** – condition on which payment may be demanded.
- **OBLIGATION – exigibilité de l'obligation** – existence of a cause of action.

EXIGIBLE – due; payable.

EXONÉRATION – exemption from liability, tax, etc.
- **CAUSE d'exonération** – ground of exemption.
- **FISCAL – exonération fiscale** – exemption from tax.
- **IMPÔT – exonération d'impôt(s)** – exemption from tax.
- **RESPONSABILITÉ – exonération de la responsabilité** – exemption from liability.

EXONÉRÉ – free from liability.

EXONÉRER – exempt from tax; remit tax.

EXORBITANT
- **DROIT COMMUN – exorbitant du droit commun** – going beyond (falling outside the scope of) (the rights conferred by) the general (ordinary) law; creating or constituting an exception to the general law, eg a clause

in a government contract excluding the jurisdiction of the ordinary courts.

EXPÉDIENT
- **PASSER** expédient – admit the plaintiff's statement of claim.

EXPÉDITION – dispatch; office copy; duplicate; execution copy (of a judgment).
- **AUTHENTIQUE – expédition authentique** – office copy.
- **AVIS** d'expédition – notice (advice) of dispatch.
- **BULLETIN d'expédition** – dispatch note or slip.
- **DEUXIÈME** expédition – second copy.
- **PAPIERS** d'expédition – shipping documents; consignment note.
- **PREMIER – première expédition** – top copy.
- **SIMPLE** expédition – plain copy (ie not endorsed with an authority to execute).

EXPERT – expert witness.
- **CONSULTANT – expert consultant** – consultant.
- **ÉCRITURE – expert en écritures** – handwriting expert.
- **JUDICIAIRE – expert judiciaire** – court expert.
- **JURÉ – expert juré** – sworn expert.
- **MINORITÉ – expert de minorité** – expert appointed by the court to examine certain transactions of a company on the application of minority shareholders.
- **RAPPORT** d'expert – expert opinion; auditor's report.
- **TRIBUNAL – expert près les tribunaux** – court expert.

EXPERTISE – expert opinion (report).

EXPIATION – retribution.

EXPIRATION
- **DÉLAI – expiration du délai** – expiration of the term or time(-limit).
- **DURÉE – expiration de la durée** – expiration of time; expiration of the period.

EXPIRER – lapse; expire; run out.

EXPLICATION
- **VOTE – explication de vote** – statement of one's reasons for voting.

EXPLICITE – express.

EXPLICITEMENT – expressly.

EXPLOIT – process served by a bailiff.
- **AJOURNEMENT – exploit d'ajournement** – writ or summons (served on the defendant).
- **COMPARUTION – exploit à fin de comparution** – summons.
- **DÉNONCIATION** de l'exploit de saisie-arrêt – notice to a judgment debtor of the garnishment (attachment) of a debt in the hands of the garnishee (**tiers saisi**).
- **HUISSIER – exploit d'huissier** – instrument (process) served by a bailiff.
- **INTRODUCTIF D'INSTANCE – exploit introductif d'instance** – writ of summons.
- **NOTIFICATION – exploit de notification** – record of service made by a process-server.
- **OPPOSITION – exploit d'opposition** – notice of application to set aside.
- **SAISIE-ARRÊT – exploit de saisie-arrêt** – notice of garnishment (attachment) of a debt served on a debtor to prevent him paying the judgment debtor.
- **SIGNIFICATION – exploit de signification** – record of service made by a process-server.

EXPLOITANT
- **FORESTIER – exploitant forestier** – forestry contractor.

EXPLOITATION
- **AGRICOLE – exploitation agricole** – agricultural holding; farm.
  - **FAMILIAL – exploitation agricole à caractère familial** – family farm; family holding.
- **CAPITAL** d'exploitation – working capital.
- **DÉFAUT** d'exploitation – non-user; failure to work a patent; failure to operate (a mine) at the agreed level of production; insufficient operation.
- **DROIT** d'exploitation – operating right; mining concession.
- **LICENCE** d'exploitation – licence to operate a mine, trade or manufacture; licence to use a patent or copyright; operating licence; trade licence.
- **PERMIS** d'exploitation – mining licence.
- **VICE** d'exploitation – faulty organisation.

EXPONSE – surrender of a lease to avoid future liability for rent.

EXPOSÉ
- **DROIT – exposé de droit** – legal argument.

- **FAIT** – exposé des faits – the facts.
- **MOTIF** – exposé des motifs – statement of reasons; explanatory memorandum; objects and reasons.

EXPOSER – incur (costs).

EXPOSITION

- **ENFANT** – exposition d'enfant – exposure of a child.

EXPROPRIANT – expropriating authority.

EXPROPRIATION – compulsory purchase; expropriation.

- **ARRÊTÉ d'expropriation** – expropriation order; compulsory-purchase order.
- **CONDITIONNEL – expropriation conditionnelle** – expropriation authorised on condition that the cost does not exceed a specified figure.
- **DEMANDE d'expropriation** – application for expropriation.
- **DROIT d'expropriation** – right to expropriate.
- **INDEMNITÉ d'expropriation** – compensation for compulsory purchase (expropriation).
- **INSALUBRITÉ – expropriation pour cause d'insalubrité** – expropriation on grounds of unfitness for human habitation.
- **PLUS-VALUE – expropriation pour cause de plus-value** – expropriation of adjacent land because it has appreciated in value.
- **UTILITÉ PUBLIQUE – expropriation pour cause d'utilité publique** – expropriation in the public interest.

EXPROPRIÉ – expropriated person.

EXPULSÉ – expelled person; person expelled from his homeland.

EXPULSION – expulsion; deportation; eviction.

- **ACTION en expulsion** – action for possession.
- **ARRÊTÉ d'expulsion** – expulsion warrant (order); deportation order.
- **DÉCISION d'expulsion** – expulsion warrant (order); deportation order.
- **DÉLAI d'expulsion** – time to quit.
- **DEMANDE d'expulsion** – action for possession.
- **ORDONNANCE d'expulsion** – order for possession; writ of possession.

EXTENSION

- **ARRÊTÉ d'extension** – declaration that something is of general application.

- **COMPÉTENCE – extension de compétence** – extension of jurisdiction.
- **CONVENTION**
  - **COLLECTIF – extension d'une convention collective** – declaration that the terms of a collective agreement are of general application.

EXTÉRIORISER

- **S'extérioriser** – be outwardly evident.

EXTÉRIORITÉ – extraneous cause.

EXTERRITORIALITÉ – exterritorial status.

EXTINCTIF

- **CONDITION extinctive** – condition subsequent (of (in) a contract etc, to a transaction etc).

EXTINCTION

- **DROIT – extinction d'un droit** – lapse or extinction of a right.
- **INSTANCE – extinction de l'instance** – (premature) termination of the proceedings.

EXTORQUER – obtain by threats or menaces, by blackmail.

EXTORSION

- **AVEU – extorsion d'aveux** – obtaining a confession by threats.
- **FONDS – extorsion de fonds** – obtaining money by threats; blackmail; extortion.
- **SIGNATURE – extorsion d'une signature** – obtaining a signature by duress.

EXTOURNE – reverse entry.

EXTRA-CONJUGAL – extra-matrimonial; outside marriage.

EXTRACONTRACTUEL – non-contractual; tortious; in tort.

EXTRACTION

- **DROIT d'extraction** – mining right.
- **PERMIS d'extraction** – mining licence.

EXTRADÉ – extradited person.

EXTRADITION

- **DEMANDE d'extradition** – extradition request.
- **ÉTAT qui demande l'extradition** – requesting state.
- **TRANSIT – extradition en transit (extradition par voie de transit)** – granting transit facilities for the purpose of extradition.

EXTRAIT – short-form certificate.

- **CADASTRE** – **extrait du cadastre** – copy of a section of the property register (official plan) relating to a plot or plots of land.
- **CASIER JUDICIAIRE** – **extrait du casier judiciaire** – copy of a person's criminal (police) record.
- **ÉTAT CIVIL** – **extrait de l'état civil** – civil-status certificate.
- **MATRICULAIRE** – **extrait matriculaire** – copy of a person's prison record.
- **NAISSANCE** – **extrait de naissance** – birth certificate.
- **REGISTRE**
  - **COMMERCE** – **extrait du registre du commerce** – copy of an entry or entries in the commercial register.
  - **FONCIER** – **extrait du registre foncier** (Sw) – copy of an entry or entries in the land register; copy of the land certificate.

EXTRAJUDICIAIRE – out of court; extrajudicial.

- **ACTE extrajudiciaire** – extrajudicial process or formality (eg formal demand for payment, protest).

EXTRAJUDICIAIREMENT – out of court; extrajudicially.

EXTRA-LÉGAL – illegal; contrary to law.

EXTRANÉITÉ – foreign origin; status of being an alien; state of being a stranger to a contract or other legal instrument.

- **FACTEUR** – **affecté d'un facteur d'extranéité** – involving a foreign element.

EXTRAPATRIMONIAL – non-pecuniary (non-material).

EXTRA-TERRITORIAL – extraterritorial.

~

F

FABRICANT
- **MONNAIE** – **fabricant de fausse monnaie** – forger; coiner.

FABRICATION
- **MONNAIE** – **fabrication de fausse monnaie** – counterfeiting coinage; forgery.
- **SECRET de fabrication** – manufacturing secret.

FABRIQUE
- **MARQUE de fabrique** – trade mark.
- **SECRET de fabrique** – manufacturing secret.

FACERIE – pasturing agreement.

FACILITÉ
- **CAISSE** – **facilités de caisse** – short-term bank credits; overdraft facility.

FACTIEUX – (violent) agitator.

FACTURATION – invoicing.

FACTURE – bill; invoice.
- **ACCEPTÉ** – **facture acceptée** – accepted invoice.
- **ACQUITTÉ** – **facture acquittée** – receipted invoice.
- **FICTIF** – **facture fictive** – pro-forma invoice.
- **SIMULÉ** – **facture simulée** – fictitious invoice; pro-forma invoice.

FACTURE-CONGÉ – consignment note issued against security.

FACTURIER – invoice book.

FACULTATIF – optional; discretionary.

FACULTÉ – right; power; option; (in plural) goods; cargo.
- **ABANDON** – **faculté d'abandon de mitoyenneté** – right to give up one's rights in a party wall (fence, ditch, etc).
- **ACTION** – **faculté d'action** – cause of action; right to bring an action.
- **AVOIR la faculté de** – be open to (someone to do something).
- **CONTRIBUTIF** – **faculté contributive** – taxable capacity.
- **DÉCIDER** – **laisse au juge la faculté de décider** – gives the court power to decide.
- **DÉNONCIATION** – **faculté de dénonciation** – right to (give notice to) terminate; right to denounce (a treaty).
- **DROIT** – **faculté de droit** – law faculty; school of jurisprudence.
- **OPTION** – **faculté d'option** – option.
- **PROPORTION** – **à proportion de leurs facultés respectives** – according to their respective resources.
- **PUR** – **de pure faculté** – in the exercise of one's own right.
- **RACHAT** – **faculté de rachat** – right of (option to) repurchase; vendor's right of pre-emption.
- **RENONCIATION** – **faculté de renonciation** – right or power to renounce (waive).

FAIBLE
- **ESPRIT** – **faible d'esprit** – imbecile; mentally deficient; feeble-minded.

FAILLI – bankrupt.
- **CONCORDATAIRE** – **failli concordataire** – bankrupt who has entered into a composition with his creditors.

FAILLITE – bankruptcy (of a trader); compulsory liquidation of a company.
- **ASSIGNATION en déclaration de faillite** – presentation of a bankruptcy petition.
- **CRÉANCIER de la faillite** – creditor in the bankruptcy.
- **DÉCLARATION de faillite** – (by the court) adjudication; (by the debtor) application for the commencement of bankruptcy proceedings.
- **FAIRE faillite** – become, be declared, bankrupt; (of a company) be in compulsory liquidation.
- **MASSE de la faillite** – bankrupt's assets; estate of a deceased bankrupt; assets of a company in compulsory liquidation.
- **OFFICE des faillites** (Sw) – execution and bankruptcy department (for persons engaged in trade).
- **OUVERTURE de la faillite** – commencement of bankruptcy.
- **PERSONNEL** – **faillite personnelle** – culpable bankruptcy (involving sanctions imposed personally in bankruptcy on dishonest or rashly imprudent traders or company

directors and consisting of various disqualifications and prohibitions); (Belg) personal bankruptcy (the expression does not seem to imply culpability in Belgium).
- **SYNDIC de la faillite** – trustee in bankruptcy; liquidator.

FAIRE
- **APPEL** – **faire appel** – appeal; lodge an appeal; give (enter) notice of appeal.
- **FOI** – **faire foi** – be authoritative (authentic); be good evidence.
- **JUSTICE** – **faire justice d'un grief** – remedy (redress) a complaint.
- **OBLIGATION de faire** – obligation to do something other than transfer a right in rem.
  - •• **NE PAS** – **obligation de ne pas faire** – obligation to abstain (refrain) from doing something.
- **VALOIR** – **faire valoir** – raise; claim; submit; argue; assert; put forward; advance; plead (in one's defence); adduce; sue for; present (one's case); exercise; enforce.

FAISCEAU
- **ÉLÉMENT** – **faisceau d'éléments concordants** – (number of) facts pointing in the same direction.

FAIT – act; fact; evidence; (in plural) evidence.
- **ACTIF** – **fait actif** – positive action.
- **APPRÉCIATION du fait** – assessment of (decision on) the facts.
- **ARRESTATION sur le fait** – arrest while actually committing the offence; in the act; red-handed; in flagrante delicto.
- **ASSOCIATION de fait** – de facto association; de facto partnership.
- **CAUSE** – **faits de la cause** – the facts; the merits.
- **CHARGE** – **fait(s) à charge** – incriminating fact or evidence; evidence against the accused; evidence for the prosecution.
- **CHOSE** – **fait des choses** – damage caused by inanimate objects.
- **CONNEXE** – **fait connexe** – closely connected (related) act or fact.
- **CONSTANT** – **fait constant** – established fact.
- **CONSTITUTIF** – **fait constitutif d'une infraction** – act constituting an element (ingredient) of an offence.
- **CRÉATEUR** – **fait créateur de droit** – fact (state of affairs) creating or giving rise to a right.
- **DÉCHARGE** – **fait à décharge** – exonerating fact or evidence; evidence for the defence.

- **DÉLICTUEUX** – **fait délictueux** – offence; tortious act; tort.
- **DIFFAMATOIRE** – **fait diffamatoire** – defamation; defamatory allegation.
- **ERREUR de fait** – error of fact.
- **ÉTAT de faits** – facts; statement of facts; factual situation.
- **EXPOSÉ des faits** – (statement of) the facts.
- **GUERRE** – **fait de guerre** – act of war; enemy action.
- **ILLICITE** – **fait illicite** – illegal act; tortious act; tort.
- **IMPRESCRIPTIBLE** – **fait imprescriptible** – offence not subject to limitation.
- **IMPUTÉ** – **fait imputé à charge** – offence charged.
- **INCRIMINÉ** – **fait incriminé** – offence charged.
- **JUGE du fait** – court deciding on the facts; lower court; trial court; court assessing the facts; tribunal of fact.
- **JURIDIQUE** – **fait juridique** – legally relevant fact, event or situation; facts having a legal effect. (Most facts mentioned in a legal context fall into this category and are in English simply referred to as "facts".)
- **JUSTIFICATIF** – **fait justificatif** – justification.
- **MATÉRIEL** – **fait matériel** – act (ie actus reus of a criminal offence).
- **NOTOIRE** – **fait notoire** – matter of common knowledge.
- **NOUVEAU** – **fait nouveau** – new fact; fresh fact; fresh evidence.
- **PRINCE** – **fait du prince** – act of state.
- **PROUVER** – **fait à prouver** – fact to be established.
- **PUNISSABLE** – **fait punissable** – offence; punishable offence.
- **RÉPRÉHENSIBLE** – **fait répréhensible** – offence; punishable offence.
- **RÉSISTANCE** – **fait de résistance** – act of resisting authority; obstructing the police.
- **TIERS** – **fait d'un tiers** – act of a third party.
- **VOIE de fait** – assault; trespass to the person; patently illegal action by an administrative authority affecting the fundamental freedoms or property of an individual.

FALSIFICATEUR – forger; counterfeiter.

FALSIFICATION – forgery; counterfeiting; adulteration.

- **DOCUMENT – falsification de documents** – forgery of documents.
- **ÉCRITURE – falsification d'écritures** – forgery or falsification of documents.
- **ÉTAT CIVIL – falsification de l'état civil** – forgery or falsification of civil-status certificates (documents or records relating to civil status).
- **IDENTITÉ – falsification d'identité (de papiers d'identité)** – forgery of identity documents.
- **MARCHANDISE – falsification de marchandises** – adulteration or dishonest presentation of goods for sale.
- **MONNAIE – falsification de monnaie** – counterfeiting (coin(age)); forging notes.
- **SCEAU – falsification de sceaux** – forgery of seals, dies, etc.

FALSIFIER – forge; counterfeit; falsify; adulterate or present for sale in a dishonest fashion.

FAMILLE

- **ABANDON de famille** – wilful neglect to maintain; wilful neglect or desertion.
- **ARRANGEMENT de famille** – transfer of land to a descendant in consideration of the latter's paying the transferor's debts.
- **BIEN de famille** – reserved family property (not liable to attachment or capable of being mortgaged); hereditary farm; long-standing family property; homestead.
- **CONSEIL de famille** – family council.
- **LIVRET de famille** – family civil-status book; family record book; family (civil-status) registration book.
- **SUBSISTANCE de famille** – family maintenance.

FANTAISIE

- **PASSEPORT de fantaisie** – bogus passport.

FANTAISISTE

- **RECOURS d'inspiration fantaisiste** – frivolous application.

FARDAGE – dishonest presentation of goods for sale.

FARDE (Belg) – file.

FARDEAU

- **PREUVE – fardeau de la preuve** – burden (onus) of proof.

FASCICULE

- **BREVET – fascicule de brevet** – patent specification.

FAUSSAIRE – forger; counterfeiter.

FAUTE – fault (the term covers both deliberate action and negligence); misconduct; misfeasance; culpability; error; tortious intent. (Where the context shows that negligence is intended, this is the best translation).

- **ABSENCE de faute** – absence of fault; absence of intention or negligence.
- **ADMINISTRATIF – faute administrative** – administrative error.
- **AUTRUI – faute d'autrui** – negligence of another.
- **AVEU de faute** – admission of a fault.
- **CARACTÉRISÉ – faute caractérisée** – definite (specific) fault.
- **COLLECTIF – faute collective** – collective guilt.
- **COMMUN – faute commune** – joint negligence; contributory negligence.
- **CONTRACTUEL – faute contractuelle** – culpable or negligent breach of contract.
- **DÉLIBÉRÉ – faute délibérée** – deliberate tortious intent.
- **DÉLICTUEL – faute délictuelle** – intentional tort; tortious conduct; tortious intent.
  - **QUASI – faute quasi délictuelle** – negligence.
- **DÉTACHABLE – faute détachable** – fault or error committed by a public servant not intrinsically connected with the performance of his duties and for which he is accordingly personally liable in the ordinary courts.
- **DISCIPLINAIRE – faute disciplinaire** – disciplinary offence.
- **FORME – faute de forme** – formal defect; error of form.
- **GRAVE – faute grave** – serious negligence; misconduct.
- **IMPUTER – être imputé à faute** – be treated as improper.
- **IN ABSTRACTO – faute in abstracto** – failure to observe the standard of reasonable care.
- **IN CONCRETO – faute in concreto** – failure to observe the standard of care one applies in one's own affairs.
- **INEXCUSABLE – faute inexcusable** – gross negligence; inexcusable conduct.

- **INTENTIONNEL** – **faute intentionnelle** – deliberate tortious intent.
- **LÉGER** – **faute légère** – slight negligence.
  - ●● **TRÈS** – **faute très légère** – very slight negligence.
- **LOURD** – **faute lourde** – gross negligence.
- **LUCRATIF** – **faute lucrative** – tort which is profitable to the tortfeasor; profitable tort.
- **NAUTIQUE** – **faute nautique** – navigational error.
- **OBJECTIF** – **faute objective** – failure to observe the standard of reasonable care.
- **PARTAGE** – **faute partagée** – joint negligence; contributory negligence.
- **PERSONNEL** – **faute personnelle** – personal fault; fault or error committed by a public servant not intrinsically connected with the performance of his duties and for which he is accordingly personally liable in the ordinary courts.
- **PRÉSOMPTION** de faute – presumption of fault.
- **PROFESSIONNEL** – **faute professionnelle** – professional misconduct.
- **RESPONSABILITÉ**
  - ●● **POUR** – **responsabilité pour faute** – liability for intention or negligence; fault liability.
  - ●● **SANS** – **responsabilité sans faute** – liability without fault (ie without either intention or negligence); strict liability; absolute liability; risk liability; no-fault liability.
- **SERVICE** – **faute de service** – administrative (official) error; fault committed by a public servant in the performance of his duties for which he is not liable in the ordinary courts.
  - ●● **PUBLIC** – **faute du service public** – error occurring in the public service; official error.
- **SIMPLE** – **faute simple** – negligence.
- **TECHNIQUE** – **faute technique** – professional negligence.
- **VICTIME** – **faute de la victime** – contributory negligence.

FAUTEUR

- **DÉSORDRE** – **fauteur de désordre** – disturber of the peace; agitator.

FAUTIF – negligent; improper; unsatisfactory; wrongful.
- **ÉTAT fautif** – offending state.

FAUX (adj)

- **CLÉ** - **fausse clé** – skeleton key; master key.
- **FRAIS** – **faux frais** – expenses; disbursements; overheads.
- **FRET** – **faux fret** – half freight or forfeit freight payable on abandoning a charter.
- **MÉNAGE** – **faux ménage** – concubinage; extramarital cohabitation.
- **SERMENT** – **faux serment** – perjury by a party; false declaration (on a form etc).
- **TÉMOIGNAGE** – **faux témoignage** – perjury (by a witness); false evidence (when given by an accused not under oath).

FAUX (noun) – forgery.

- **ARGUER** de faux – allege that a document is forged; challenge the authenticity of a document.
- **DOCUMENTAIRE** – **faux documentaire** – forgery of documents.
- **ÉCRITURE** – **faux en écriture(s)** – forgery of documents.
- **IMMATÉRIEL** – **faux immatériel** – causing an official to issue false certificates or to make false records, eg by giving false information.
- **INCIDENT** – **faux incident civil** – interlocutory civil proceedings to decide on the authenticity of a document.
- **INSCRIPTION** de faux – (independent or interlocutory) civil proceedings to challenge the authenticity of a document or prove it is a forgery.
- **INSCRIRE** – **s'inscrire en faux** – allege that a document is forged; challenge the authenticity of a document.
- **INTELLECTUEL** – **faux intellectuel** – giving false information for inclusion in a document.
- **MATÉRIEL** – **faux matériel** – physical alteration of a text.
- **MOYENS** de faux – grounds on which it is alleged that a document is not genuine (forged).
- **PRINCIPAL** – **faux principal** – forgery of documents.
- **SERMENT** – **faux serment** – perjury by a party.
- **USAGE** de faux – uttering; making use of forged documents with intent to defraud.

FAVORISER

- **NATION** – **clause de la nation plus favorisée** – most-favoured-nation clause.

FÉDÉRATIF – federal.

FEMME

- **COMMUN** – **femme commune en biens** – wife in community of property.
- **DOTAL** – **femme dotale** – woman benefiting from a marriage settlement in her favour.
- **SEUL** – **femme seule** – woman living alone.

FENTE – division of a succession in equal halves between the ascendants of the maternal and paternal lines.

FÉRIÉ

- **POURSUITE** – **jours fériés en matière de poursuites** – days on which execution cannot be levied.

FERMAGE – lease.

FERME – farm; agricultural holding.

- **BAILLEUR à ferme** – lessor; landlord.
- **PRISON ferme** – immediate (ie non-suspended) imprisonment; affirmative sentence.

FERMETURE

- **CHASSE** – **fermeture de la chasse** – beginning of the close season.
- **DOUANIER** – **fermeture douanière** – customs seal.
- **ENTREPRISE** – **fermeture d'office d'une entreprise** – compulsory closure of an undertaking.

FERMIER – lessee; tenant.

FÊTE

- **LÉGAL** – **fête légale** – statutory holiday; bank holiday.

FEUILLE

- **ACCIDENT** – **feuille d'accident** – accident report form.
- **AUDIENCE** – **feuille d'audience** – record (of the proceedings).
- **AVIS** – **feuille d'avis** – gazette; bulletin.
  - **JUDICIAIRE** – **feuille d'avis judiciaires** – court gazette; newspaper publishing court notices.
- **DÉCLARATION** – **feuille de déclaration** – report form.
- **DÉPOUILLEMENT** – **feuille de dépouillement** – tally sheet.
- **IMPÔT** – **feuille d'impôt(s)** – tax return; (notice of) tax assessment.

- **MALADIE** – **feuille de maladie** – medical form, card or record; case notes; (social security) treatment form.
- **PAIE** – **feuille de paie** – pay slip.
- **PAPIER**
  - **TIMBRÉ** – **feuille de papier timbré** – sheet of stamped paper on which certain legal documents are required to be written.
- **POINTAGE** – **feuille de pointage** – tally sheet.
- **ROUTE** – **feuille de route** – waybill.
- **SOIN** – **feuille de soins** – (social security) treatment form.

FIANÇAILLES – engagement.

FICHE

- **ANTHROPOMÉTRIQUE** – **fiche anthropométrique** – fingerprint form; physical identification form.

FICHIER

- **IMMOBILIER** – **fichier immobilier** – Land Registry index.

FICTIF – notional; fictitious.

FICTION – fiction; assumption.

- **JURIDIQUE** – **fiction juridique** – legal fiction.
- **LÉGAL** – **fiction légale** – statutory fiction.
- **LOI** – **fiction de loi** – statutory fiction.

FIDÉICOMMIS – life estate followed by a remainder but without the machinery of a settlement (no trustee).

- **FONDATEUR d'un fidéicommis** – settlor.

FIDÉIJUSSEUR – surety; guarantor.

FIDÉIJUSSION – guarantee.

- **BANQUE** – **fidéijussion d'une banque** – bank guarantee.

FIDUCIAIRE) – (adj) fiduciary; trust; (noun) life tenant under a **fidéicommis**.

FIDUCIE – transfer of ownership of property as security for a debt; trust.

FILATURE – shadowing (of a suspect) by the police.

FILIALE – branch; subsidiary.

FILIATION – descent; relationship by descent; relationship to one's father or parents; lawful descent.

- **ADULTÉRIN** – filiation adultérine – adulterine descent.
- **ÉTABLISSEMENT de la filiation** – proof of relationship by descent; proof of paternity.
- **LÉGITIME** – filiation légitime – legitimate descent; birth in wedlock.
- **NATUREL** – filiation naturelle – natural descent; birth out of wedlock.
- **PROCÈS en filiation** – proceedings to establish legitimacy or paternity.

FILLE

- **CARTE** – fille en carte – supervised prostitute.
- **PUBLIC** – fille publique – common prostitute.
- **SOUMIS** – fille soumise – supervised prostitute.

FILOUTERIE – petty fraud.

- **ALIMENT** – filouterie d'aliments – obtaining credit (ie a meal) by fraud.
- **LOGEMENT** – filouterie de logement – obtaining credit (ie lodging) by fraud.
- **TRANSPORT** – filouterie de transport – obtaining credit (ie transport) by fraud; travelling without a ticket.

FIN

- **LUCRATIF** – à fin lucrative – with a view to gain or profit.
- **NON-RECEVOIR** – fin de non-recevoir – application to strike out on grounds such as one of the following: failure to pursue, disclosing no cause of action, lack (want) of standing, limitation, res judicata; objection to admissibility; preliminary objection; ground of inadmissibility; objection to jurisdiction.
  - •• **HEURTER** – se heurter à une fin de non-recevoir – be inadmissible.
  - •• **OPPOSER à un requérant une fin de non-recevoir** – refuse to entertain an application.
- **NON-VALOIR** – see NON-RECEVOIR above.
- **RENVOYER des fins de la poursuite** – acquit.

FINANCE

- **LOCAL** - finances locales – local-government finances.
- **LOI de finances** – Budget Act (covering both expenditure (Appropriation Act) and revenue (Finance Act)).
- **RECEVEUR des finances** – collector of taxes.

FINANCIER

- **JURIDICTION financière** – court exercising jurisdiction in tax matters; tax court.

FIRME

- **CONCURRENT** – firme concurrente – competing business.

FISC – tax authorities; state authorities in their public capacity.

FISCAL

- **ADMINISTRATION fiscale** – tax authorities; Revenue.

FISCALITÉ – tax system; tax legislation.

FIXATION – fixing.

- **ACTION en fixation** – action for a declaration (declaratory judgment).
- **AUDIENCE** – fixation d'audience – fixing a day for hearing (for trial).
- **AUDIENCE de fixation** – hearing at which the president of the court discusses the presentation of the case with counsel; hearing for directions.
- **PEINE** - fixation de la peine – determination of the sentence.
- **PRIX** – fixation du prix – price-fixing.

FIXE – fixed salary.

FLAGRANCE

- **ENQUÊTE de flagrance** – expedited police investigation; on-the-spot investigation (involving extended police powers).

FLAGRANT

- **DÉLIT** – flagrant délit – offence discovered while it is being committed or immediately afterwards.
  - •• **ENQUÊTE de flagrant délit** – expedited police investigation; on-the-spot investigation (involving extended police powers).
  - •• **PRENDRE en flagrant délit** – arrest while committing an offence (in the act, red-handed, flagrante delicto).

FLEUVE

- **FRONTIÈRE** – fleuve frontière – river constituting the border; frontier river.
- **INTERNATIONAL** - fleuve international – international river.

FOI

- **BON** – bonne foi – good faith; honest dealing in legal transactions; erroneous but not negligent belief in the existence of a fact, right or rule of law.

- **EN foi de quoi** – in witness whereof.
- **FAIRE foi** – be authentic (authoritative); be good evidence.
- **MAUVAIS** – **mauvaise foi** – bad faith; tortious intent; criminal intent; malice; mens rea.
- **PUBLIC** – **la foi publique** – public confidence.

FONCIER (adj) – relating to land; real; immovable; landed.
- **PRÊT foncier** – mortgage loan.

FONCIER (noun) – (in a **bail à domaine congéable**) landowner; landlord.

FONCTION
- **DÉCHÉANCE des fonctions** – loss of office.
- **DURÉE des fonctions** – length (period, term) of office.
- **EN fonction** – in office; in charge; acting.
- **ENTRÉE en fonctions** – assumption of duties, office, etc.
- **EXERCICE** – **dans l'exercice de ses fonctions** – in the course of his employment; in the execution (performance) of his duties.
- **FAIRE fonction de** – represent; act for; act as.
- **GOUVERNEMENTAL** – **fonction gouvernementale** – power of government; right to govern (rule); executive power.
- **IMMUNITÉ de fonctions** – immunity by virtue of one's office; official immunity.
- **INDEMNITÉ de fonction(s)** – official expenditure allowance; acting allowance; duty allowance; allowance for extra duties.
- **INSIGNE de fonctions** – badge of office.
- **INVESTIR** – **être investi d'une fonction publique** – hold (a) public office.
- **JUDICIAIRE** – **fonction judiciaire** – judicial office; legal office; legal functions. (The term includes the office of prosecutor as well as that of judge in certain contexts.)
- **JURIDICTIONNEL** – **fonction juridictionnelle** – judicial power; jurisdiction; the judiciary.
- **LÉGISLATIF** – **fonction législative** – legislative power.
- **OCCUPER une fonction publique** – hold (a) public office.
- **PRISE de fonctions** – assumption of duties (office).
- **PUBLIC** – **fonction publique** – civil and local-government service; public office.

- **RELÈVEMENT de fonctions** – removal from office.
- **STATUT de la fonction publique** – Civil Service Act and Regulations.
- **SUSPENSION de fonctions** – suspension from office.
- **TITULAIRE d'une fonction publique** – holder of (a) public office.
- **USURPATION de fonctions** – usurpation (illegal exercise) of office.

FONCTIONNAIRE – civil servant; public servant; official; local-government officer.
- **AUTORITÉ** – **fonctionnaire d'autorité** – official with power to make decisions.
- **CARRIÈRE** – **fonctionnaire de carrière** – established or career civil servant.
- **COMMUNAL** – **fonctionnaire communal** – local-government officer.
- **CONTRACTUEL** – **fonctionnaire contractuel** – temporary civil servant; government employee.
- **CONTRIBUTION** – **fonctionnaire des contributions** – tax official.
- **CORRUPTION de fonctionnaire** – bribery of a civil servant, official, etc.
- **DISPONIBILITÉ** – **fonctionnaire en disponibilité** – civil servant not actively employed but available for service, sometimes on half pay; temporarily retired.
- **ÉTAT** – **fonctionnaire d'État** – civil servant.
- **HAUT fonctionnaire** – senior official; senior civil servant.
- **INAMOVIBLE** – **fonctionnaire inamovible** – official who cannot be removed from office.
- **MUNICIPAL** – **fonctionnaire municipal** – local-government officer.
- **OUTRAGE à fonctionnaire** – insulting an official or civil servant or officer.
- **RÉAFFECTATION** – **fonctionnaire en instance de réaffectation** – (redundant) civil servant awaiting reappointment.
- **SERMENT des fonctionnaires** – official oath.
- **STAGIAIRE** – **fonctionnaire stagiaire** – civil servant on probation.
- **SUBALTERNE** – **fonctionnaire subalterne** – subordinate official.
- **TITULAIRE** – **fonctionnaire titulaire** – established civil servant.
  - **NON** – **fonctionnaire non titulaire** – temporary, non-established civil servant.

FONCTIONNEMENT

- **DÉPENSES de fonctionnement** – running expenses.
- **JUSTICE – fonctionnement de la justice** – course of justice; functioning (operation) of the judicial system.
  - •• **SEREIN – fonctionnement serein de la justice** – proper (unimpeded, smooth) operation of the courts.

FOND – substance; merits; subject-matter.

- **CONCLURE au fond** – plead on the merits.
- **DE fond** – substantive; relating to the merits.
  - •• **MOYEN – tout moyen de fond étant réservé** – liberty to bring further argument on the merits; without prejudging (prejudice to) the merits.
  - •• **RÈGLES de fond** – substantive rules.
  - •• **VICE de fond** – essential defect; substantive defect.
- **DROIT – fond du droit** – substance; merits.
- **JUGE – juges du fond** – trial and appeal courts; courts below.
- **JUGEMENT au (sur le) fond** – judgment on the merits; trial of the merits.
- **LITIGE – fond du litige** – gist (merits, substance) of the dispute; subject-matter; cause of action.
- **REJET au fond** – dismissal on the merits.
- **RENVOYER pour le fond** – refer (to a committee) for report.
- **RÉSERVE – fonds de réserve** – reserve fund.
- **TRIBUNAL du fond** – trial court; tribunal of fact; (in plural) trial and appeal courts; courts below.

FONDATEUR – promoter; settlor; person establishing; founder.

- **FIDÉICOMMIS – fondateur d'un fidéicommis** – settlor.
- **PART de fondateur** – founder's share; promoter's share.

FONDATION – foundation; settlement; charitable settlement; charitable trust; founding; promotion.

- **DÉPENSES de fondation** – formation expenses; promotion expenses; capital expenditure.
- **PRIVÉ – fondation privée** – private trust.
- **PUBLIC – fondation publique** – charitable trust.
- **QUALIFIÉ – fondation qualifiée** – special formation of a company, ie in which the promoters enter into "dangerous agreements"

that may prejudice the interests of subsequent shareholders or of the creditors.

FONDÉ (adj) – well-founded.

- **MAL fondé** – ill-founded; unfounded; without foundation.
- **NON fondé** – unfounded; without foundation; ill-founded.

FONDÉ (noun)

- **POUVOIR – fondé de pouvoir** – attorney; authorised agent or manager.
- **PROCURATION – fondé de procuration** – authorised agent or manager (employed by a business).

FONDEMENT

- **DÉNUÉ de fondement** – without foundation; unmeritorious.
- **JURIDIQUE – fondement juridique** – legal basis (foundation).

FONDER – found; set up; create; establish; settle.

- **DROIT – fondé en droit** – well-founded.
  - •• **RAISON – pour une raison fondée en droit** – for a legally valid reason.
- **ÊTRE fondé à** – have good cause to.

FONDS – land; piece of land; property; business; fund.

- **ABONNEMENT – fonds d'abonnement** – prefect's special expense allowance.
- **AMORTISSEMENT – fonds d'amortissement** – sinking fund.
- **APPEL de fonds** – call on not fully paid-up shares; call on shareholders etc.
- **ASSUJETTI – fonds assujetti** – servient tenement.
- **AUTOMOBILE – fonds de garantie automobile** – fund which compensates the victims of accidents caused by uninsured drivers.
- **AUTRUI – fonds d'autrui** – another's land.
- **BAILLEUR de fonds** – person providing finance; money-lender.
- **BUDGÉTAIRE – fonds budgétaires** – appropriations.
- **CESSION d'un fonds** – sale (transfer) of a business.
- **CESSIONNAIRE d'un fonds** – purchaser of a business.
- **COMMERCE – fonds de commerce** – business; goodwill.

•• **CLAUSE de fonds de commerce** – clause in a marriage contract (marriage settlement) whereby a business belonging to one of the spouses is settled on the survivor or the survivor authorised to purchase the business.

• **COMPENSATION** – **fonds de compensation** – equalisation fund; clearing fund.

• **CONTREPARTIE** – **fonds de contrepartie** – counterpart fund.

• **DÉBITEUR** – **fonds débiteur de la servitude** – servient tenement.

• **DÉPÔT** – **fonds en dépot** – amounts held (funds placed) on deposit.

• **DÉTOURNEMENT de fonds** – embezzlement (in the case of a clerk or servant); fraudulent conversion; misappropriation (of money or funds).

• **DOMINANT** – **fonds dominant** – dominant tenement.

• **DOTAL** – **fonds dotal** – dowry; nuptial settlement.

• **ÉGALISATION** – **fonds d'égalisation des changes** – currency equalisation fund.

• **ENCLAVÉ** – **fonds enclavé** – enclave.

• **ÉTAT** – **fonds de l'État** – public money.

• **ÉTAT** – **fonds d'État** – government bonds (securities, stock).

• **EXPLOITATION** – **fonds d'exploitation** – working capital.

• **EXTORSION de fonds** – obtaining money by threats; blackmail; extortion.

• **GREVÉ** – **fonds grevé** – servient tenement.

• **HYPOTHÉQUÉ** – **fonds hypothéqué** – land subject to a mortgage.

• **INDEMNISATION** – **fonds d'indemnisation** – compensation fund.

• **MARIN** – **fonds marins** – sea-bed.

• **MISE de fonds** – capital investment.

• **PERDU** – **fonds perdu** – life annuity.

•• **À fonds perdu(s)** – non-repayable; non-returnable; non-redeemable.

•• **CONTRIBUTION à fonds perdu(s)** – irredeemable contribution.

•• **INVESTIR (PLACER) à fonds perdu(s)** – take out (purchase) a life annuity.

•• **PLACEMENT à fonds perdu(s)** – doubtful investment.

•• **PRÊT à fonds perdu(s)** – irredeemable loan.

•• **PRÊTER à fonds perdu(s)** – lend money without security.

•• **VENTE à fonds perdu(s)** – sale for a rentcharge.

• **PRÊTEUR de fonds** – money-lender; person providing finance.

• **PUBLIC** – **fonds publics** – public securities; public funds.

• **RÉSERVE** – **fonds de réserve** – reserve fund.

• **RETRAITE** – **fonds de retraite** – pension fund.

• **ROULEMENT** – **fonds de roulement** – working capital.

• **SERVANT** – **fonds servant** – servient tenement.

• **SOCIAL** – **fonds social** – capital of a company or partnership; partnership funds.

• **TERRE** – **fonds de terre** – plot (parcel) of land.

• **TUTELLE** – **fonds de tutelle** – trust funds.

• **VOISIN** – **fonds voisin** – adjacent property.

FONGIBILITÉ – quality (state) of being fungible; fungibility.

FONGIBLE – fungible; interchangeable; non-specific; generic.

FOR – court; jurisdiction; (Sw) place where a court having jurisdiction in a given matter is situated, eg the court of the defendant's place of residence.

FORÇAT – convict.

FORCE

• **CHOSE JUGÉE** – **force de chose jugée** – res judicata, ie the quality (state) of having been finally decided.

•• **ACQUÉRIR (COULER en, PASSER en, PRENDRE) force de chose jugée** – become final (of a judgment).

•• **AYANT (COULÉ en, PASSÉ en, PRIS) force de chose jugée** – final (of a judgment).

• **EXÉCUTOIRE** – **force exécutoire** – enforceability.

•• **AVOIR force exécutoire** – be enforceable (by execution).

• **LÉGISLATIF** – **force législative** – force of law.

• **LOI** – **ayant force de loi** – legally binding; having statutory force (force of law).

• **MAJEUR** – **force majeure** – force majeure; vis major.

• **OBLIGATOIRE** – **force obligatoire** – binding force; the quality of being binding.

• **ORDRE** – **forces de l'ordre** – police; law-enforcement agencies.

- **PROBANT** – **force probante** – conclusiveness; evidential value; weight as evidence.
- **PUBLIC** – **force publique** – police; law-enforcement agencies.
  - •• **AGENT de la force publique** – police officer; constable; member of the police force.
  - •• **RÉBELLION contre la force publique** – forcefully resisting or obstructing the police.
- **RECOURS à la force** – use of force; resorting to force.

FORCÉ

- **ADMISSION forcée** – compulsory admission.
- **RECOUVREMENT forcé** – enforcement of debts.

FORCEMENT

- **CONSIGNE** – **forcement de consigne** – disobedience to orders (military offence).

FORCER

- **BLOCUS** – **forcer le blocus** – run the blockade.

FORCEUR

- **BLOCUS** – **forceur de blocus** – blockade-runner.

FORCLORE – exclude; preclude; extinguish.

FORCLOS – statute-barred; lapsed; out of time; extinct.

- **À** – **forclos à contester** – estopped from contesting.
- **DE** – **forclos de** – debarred from.
- **SANS être forclos** – without being out of time.

FORCLUSION – (operation of) an extinctive time-limit; extinction; lapse; loss of rights for failure to observe a time-limit; estoppel; being out of time (and thus barred from proceeding further with the application in question).

- **DÉLAI de forclusion** – extinctive time-limit.
- **ÉCOULEMENT** – **l'écoulement de ce délai entraîne la forclusion** – after the expiry of this time-limit the (remedy etc) is barred.
- **EXCEPTION susceptible de forclusion** – defence or objection liable to be ruled out of time.
- **FRAPPÉ de forclusion** – out of time.
- **JUGEMENT de forclusion** – order excluding claims not lodged within the appointed time.

- **PEINE** – **à peine de forclusion** – if it is not to be out of time.
- **RELEVÉ (RELÈVEMENT) de forclusion** – leave to proceed (appeal etc) out of time; extension of time for appealing.
- **RELEVER de la forclusion** – give leave to proceed (appeal etc) out of time; extend time for appealing.

FORÊT

- **DOMANIAL** – **forêt domaniale** – state forest; national forest.

FORFAIT – crime; lump sum; lump-sum compensation; agreed sum; fixed rate or amount; agreed approximate assessment or basis of assessment.

- **À forfait** – globally; inclusive.
  - •• **ADJUDICATION à forfait** – adjudication (knocking down) at an inclusive or lump-sum price.
  - •• **IMPÔT à forfait** – lump-sum tax; tax based on a notional assessment.
- **COMMUNAUTÉ** – **forfait de communauté** – clause authorising one of the spouses to take the whole community assets on termination of the community in return for a lump sum.
- **DÉCLARER forfait** – withdraw; abandon; waive one's rights.
- **IMPÔT** – **forfait d'impôt** – lump-sum assessment; assessment in a notional amount.
- **INDEMNITÉ** – **forfait d'indemnité** – liquidated damages.
- **VERSER un forfait** – pay a fixed or agreed sum.

FORFAITAIRE – global; inclusive; lump-sum; wholesale; in a lot; pre-established; flat-rate; fixed-rate; fixed-scale; fixed.

- **ÉVALUATION sur bases forfaitaires** – on a fixed scale.
- **MÉTHODE forfaitaire** – blanket assessment.
- **PARTICIPATION forfaitaire** – fixed contribution.
- **TAUX forfaitaire** – flat rate.

FORFAITAIREMENT – globally; inclusively; for a lump sum; for an agreed sum.

FORFAITURE – any kind of serious abuse of office by a civil servant or member of the armed forces; felony committed by a public officer in the exercise of his functions; malfeasance.

FORMALISER
- **APPEL** – **formaliser un appel** – bring (enter, lodge) an appeal.

FORMALISME
- **INSTANCE** – **le formalisme de l'instance** – the (procedural) formalities.

FORMALITÉ
- **ACCESSOIRE** – **formalité accessoire** – subsidiary (inessential) formality.
- **HABILITANT** – **formalités habilitantes** – formalities enabling a contract to be made on behalf of an incapable; enabling formalities.
- **ORDRE PUBLIC** – **formalité d'ordre public** – mandatory requirement; mandatory formality.
- **REJET de la formalité** – refusal by the Mortgage Registrar to register a document containing an error. If the applicant corrects the error within a month of receiving notice of it, the document will be registered as of the date of its original deposit.
- **SECONDAIRE** – **formalité secondaire** – subsidiary (inessential) formality.
- **SUBSTANTIEL** – **formalité substantielle** – essential formality.

FORMATION
- **DROIT** – **formation du droit** – creation (shaping) of the law.
- **JUGEMENT** – **formation de jugement** – trial bench.
- **RÉDUIT** – **en formation réduite** – with a reduced bench; with fewer judges.

FORME – (in plural) procedure.
- **ACCOMPLIR** – **formes à accomplir** – (necessary) formalities (procedural steps).
- **BON** – **en bonne et due forme** – in order; in proper form; in the prescribed form.
- **CONDITION de forme** – requirement as to form; formal requirement; formality.
- **DANS les formes** – in accordance with formal requirements.
- **DÉFAUT de forme** – formal defect; failure to comply with the rules of form or procedure.
- **HABILITANT** – **forme habilitante** – enabling formality.
- **INOBSERVATION des formes** – failure to comply with essential formalities (ground for an appeal in law to the Court of Cassation).
- **IRRÉGULARITÉ de forme** – formal defect; failure to comply with the rules of procedure.
- **JURIDIQUE** – **forme juridique** – legal form; statutory form.

- **LOCAL** – **forme locale** – form required by the local law (by the lex situs).
- **OLOGRAPHE** – **dans la forme olographe** – in the testator's own handwriting; holograph.
- **PRESCRIPTION de forme** – formal requirement; provision as to form; procedural provision.
- **RÈGLE de forme** – procedural rule.
- **SANS forme** – informal; without formal requirements.
- **SUBSTANTIEL** – **forme substantielle** – essential formal requirement (formality).
- **VICE de forme** – formal (procedural) defect (error, irregularity).
- **VIOLATION des formes** – failure to comply with formal (procedural) requirements.

FORMEL – express; technical; procedural.

FORMELLEMENT – formally; expressly; strictly; procedurally.
- **INTERDIT** – **formellement interdit** – strictly forbidden.

FORMER
- **ACTION** – **former une action** – bring proceedings (an action).
- **APPEL** – **former un appel** – bring (enter, lodge) an appeal.
- **OPPOSITION** – lodge an objection or application to set aside.

FORMULAIRE – form; precedent; precedent book; book of precedents.

FORMULE – form; wording.
- **DEMANDE** – **formule de demande** – application form.
- **EXÉCUTOIRE** – **formule exécutoire** – (clause conferring) authority to execute (enforce); writ of execution (endorsed on a judgment).
- **LÉGAL** – **la formule légale** – the wording of the Act (statute).
- **SERMENT** – **formule de serment** – form of oath; wording of an oath.

FORTERESSE
- **ARRÊTS de forteresse** (mil) – detention in a fortress.

FORTUIT – purely accidental (ie without fault).
- **CAS fortuit** – unforeseen (unforeseeable) accident; accidental occurrence

•• **PAR** cas fortuit – accidentally.

FORTUNE – assets; property; fortune; capital.

• **IMMOBILIER** – **fortune immobilière** – immovable assets; landed property.

• **IMPOSABLE** – **fortune imposable** – taxable assets.

• **IMPÔT** sur la fortune – capital tax; property tax; wealth tax.

• **MER** – **fortune de mer** – that part of a shipowner's fortune which consists of the ship and freight; the hazards of the sea.

• **MOBILIER** – **fortune mobilière** – movable assets.

• **SITUATION** de fortune – financial position.

• **TERRE** – **fortune de terre** – a shipowner's assets exclusive of the ship and freight.

FORUM – court; jurisdiction; (Sw) place where a court having jurisdiction in a given matter is situated, eg the court of the defendant's place of residence.

FOSSE

• **MITOYEN** – **fosse mitoyenne** – common ditch separating adjacent properties; party ditch.

FOU

• **APPEL** – **fol appel** – frivolous or vexatious appeal.

•• **AMENDE** de fol appel – fine for lodging a frivolous appeal.

• **ENCHÈRE** – **folle enchère** – frivolous (sham) bid (at an auction).

FOUILLE – search; (in plural) excavations.

• **CORPOREL** – **fouille corporelle** – personal search; search of the person.

•• **RAPPROCHÉ** – **fouille corporelle rapprochée** – intimate body search.

• **CORPS** – **fouille à corps** – personal search; search of the person; (prisons) body search.

FOURNIR

• **VALOIR** – **clause de fournir et faire valoir** – del credere clause.

FOURNISSEMENT – contribution; action for partition.

FOURNISSEUR

• **GROS** – **fournisseur en gros** – wholesaler.

FOURNITURE – (in plural) supplies.

• **CONTRAT** de fourniture – supply contract.

FOURRIÈRE – pound (for stray animals or impounded vehicles).

FOYER – home.

• **ABANDON** de foyer – desertion and failure to maintain.

• **DOMESTIQUE** – **foyer domestique** – family home; matrimonial home.

FRACTION

• **INDEMNITÉ** – **fraction d'indemnité** – part compensation.

• **PARLEMENTAIRE** – **fraction parlementaire** – parliamentary party or group.

FRACTIONNEMENT

• **PEINE** – **fractionnement de la peine** – court's order that a sentence shall be enforced in instalments.

FRACTURER – break open.

FRAI – wear (of coins).

FRAIS – costs; expenditure; disbursements; charges; fees.

• **AGIR** à ses propres frais – proceed at one's own expense.

• **ANNULATION** des frais – disallowance of costs.

• **BANQUE** – **frais de banque** – bank charges.

• **CHARGE** des frais – burden of costs.

• **CHÔMAGE DE WAGON** – **frais de chômage de wagon** – demurrage.

• **CONSERVATION** – **frais de conservation** – cost of preservation.

• **CONSULAIRE** – **frais consulaires** – consular fees.

• **CRÉANCE** pour frais – claim for costs.

• **DÉPLACEMENT** – **frais de déplacement** – travel and subsistence expenses.

• **ÉCRITURE** – **frais d'écritures** – copying fees (typing) fees charged by the registry as an item of costs.

• **ENCAISSEMENT** – **frais d'encaissement** – collection charges.

• **ENTRETIEN** – **frais d'entretien** – cost of maintenance.

• **ENVOI** – **frais d'envoi** – forwarding expenses.

• **ÉTABLISSEMENT** – **frais d'établissement** – promotion expenses; formation expenses.

• **FAUX** frais – incidental expenses; necessary incidental costs; overheads.

• **FONDATION** – **frais de fondation** – promotion expenses; formation expenses.

- **FRUSTRATOIRE** – frais frustratoires – arbitrary and unnecessary or unauthorised costs (which are borne by the barrister etc by whom they are incurred).
- **FUNÉRAIRE** – allocation pour frais funéraires – death grant; death allowance.
- **GARDE** – frais de garde – expenses of (charges for) storage or safe keeping.
- **JUSTICE** – frais de justice – court fees.
- **JUSTICIAIRE** – frais justiciaires – court fees.
- **LIQUIDÉ** – frais liquidés – taxed costs; ascertained costs.
- **MÉDICAL** – frais médicaux – medical expenses.
- **MISE EN ÉTAT** – frais de mise en état – expense of restoring (premises etc) to their original condition.
- **MISSION** – frais de mission – official journeys allowance.
- **MOINS** – frais en moins – less costs.
- **NÉCESSAIRE** – frais nécessaires – costs necessarily incurred.
- **OCCUPATION** – frais d'occupation – occupation costs
- **PLUS** – frais en plus – plus costs.
- **POURSUITE** – frais de poursuite – court fees; prosecution costs.
- **PRINCIPAL** – les frais suivent le principal – costs follow the event.
- **PROFESSIONNEL** – frais professionnels – professional expenses (deductible for tax purposes).
- **RÉCUPÉRABLE** – frais récupérables – recoverable costs.
- **RÉGIE** – frais de régie – management expenses; overheads.
- **RÈGLEMENT** – frais de règlement – cost of assessing damages.
- **RELÂCHE** – frais de relâche – port dues (in a port of refuge).
- **REMPLACEMENT** – frais de remplacement – cost of replacing; cost of obtaining a substitute.
- **REPRÉSENTATION** – frais de représentation – entertainment expenses; cost of obtaining a representative (being represented).
- **SAISIE** – frais de saisie – execution costs; costs of attachment.
- **TAXATION** des frais – taxation of costs; fixing of costs.
- **VEXATOIRE** – frais vexatoires – expenditure caused with malicious intent; vexatious costs.

FRANC

- **AVARIE** – franc d'avarie – free of average.
  - •• **ÉCHOUEMENT** – franc d'avarie sauf échouement – free of average unless the vessel be stranded.
  - •• **PARTICULIER** – franc d'avaries particulières absolument – free of particular average absolutely.
- **ÉMOLUMENT** – franc d'émolument (Sw) – free of charge.
- **HUITAINE** – à huitaine franche – in eight clear days.
- **HYPOTHÈQUE** – franc d'hypothèques – unencumbered; free of encumbrances; free of mortgages.
- **IMPÔT** – franc d'impôt – tax-free; free of tax.
- **JOUR** – à cinq jours francs – in five clear days.
- **QUINZAINE** – à quinzaine franche – in fifteen clear days.
- **QUITTE** – franc et quitte de toute dette – free of all debts and obligations.

FRANCHISAGE – franchising.

FRANCHISE – franchising; (insurance) excess.

- **ASSURANCE** – franchise d'assurance – self-insurance; being one's own insurer; excess.
- **CONVENTIONNEL** – franchise conventionnelle – agreed self-insurance; contractual self-insurance.
- **DIPLOMATIQUE** – franchise diplomatique – diplomatic exemption from customs and taxes.
- **ENTRÉE** en franchise – entry of goods free of customs.
- **HÔTEL** – franchise d'hôtel – inviolability of embassy premises and ambassador's residence.
- **RESPONSABILITÉ** – franchise de responsabilité – exemption from liability.
- **RISQUE**
  - •• **GUERRE** – franchise de risques de guerre – excluding war risks.
- **TAXE** – franchise de taxe – exemption from taxation or fees.
- **TIMBRE** – franchise de timbre – exemption from stamp duty.
- **TOTAL** – franchise totale – total exemption.

FRANCHISSEMENT

- **FRONTIÈRE – franchissement irrégulier de la frontière** – illegal entry; illegally crossing the frontier.

FRANCISATION – registration of a ship in France.

- **ACTE de francisation** – French ship's registration certificate.

FRANCO

- **BORD – franco de bord** – free on board (fob).
- **FRAIS – franco de tous frais** – free of all charges.

FRAPPER

- **ALIGNEMENT – frapper d'alignement** – impose a building line.
- **IMPOSITION – frapper d'une imposition** – tax.
- **NULLITÉ – frapper de nullité** – render void.
  - •• **RADICAL – frappé d'une nullité radicale** – absolutely void.
- **USUFRUIT – frappé d'un usufruit** – subject to a usufruct (life interest).

FRAUDE – fraud.

- **CIVIL – fraude civile** – evading the rules of civil law.
- **FISCAL – fraude fiscale** – tax evasion.
- **LOI – fraude à la loi** – fraudulent evasion of statutory provisions (of the law).
- **PAULIEN – fraude paulienne** – defrauding one's creditors.
- **QUALITÉ – fraude sur la qualité des marchandises** – passing off inferior goods.

FREINTE

- **ROUTE – freinte de route** – loss (wastage) in transit.

FRELATER – adulterate.

FRÈRE

- **CONSANGUIN – frère consanguin** – half-brother on the father's side.
- **GERMAIN – frère germain** – full brother.
- **UTÉRIN – frère utérin** – half-brother on the mother's side.

FRET – freight.

- **PRIX du fret** – freight.
- **TEMPS – fret à (au) temps** – time freight.

FRÉTEUR – shipowner.

FRONTALIER – person living near the border or crossing the border frequently for purposes of employment, trade, etc.

- **NON frontalier** – inland.

FRONTIÈRE

- **DIFFÉREND de frontière** – boundary dispute.
- **PETIT – régime de petite frontière** – local frontier traffic

FRUIT – (in plural) things produced by property at regular intervals and in principle without reducing its substance; periodical produce (crops, young of animals, rents and profits)

- **CIVIL – fruits civils (fructus civiles)** – income from property, ie rents, profits, dividends, interest, etc.
- **IMMOBILISATION – immobilisation des fruits** – effect of the seizure of land in execution of a judgment, ie the produce is treated as part of the land for the purposes of the execution and the proceeds of its sale divided among the mortgagees and preferential creditors.
- **INDUSTRIEL – fruits industriels (fructus industriales)** – produce resulting from the labour and industry of the occupant, eg cultivated crops.
- **NATUREL – fruits naturels (fructus naturales)** – things produced naturally by the land without cultivation, eg wool, metal, milk and the young of animals.
- **PARTAGE des fruits** – apportionment of produce.
- **PENDANT – fruits pendants (par branches ou par racines)** – unsevered fruits or produce; growing (standing) crops.
- **PERÇU – fruits perçus** – severed fruits or produce.

FRUSTRATOIRE

- **ACTE frustratoire** – invalid or defective process, document, formality or step in the proceedings.
- **FRAIS frustratoires** – arbitrary and unnecessary or unauthorised costs (which are borne by the barrister etc by whom they are incurred).

FUGITIF – escaped prisoner.

FUITE – flight; escape; absconding; abscondance.

- **CAPITAL – fuite des capitaux** – flight of capital.

FUSION

- **DÉLIT** de fuite – hit-and-run offence; failure to stop and give particulars after an accident.
- **FISCAL** – fuite fiscale – tax evasion.
- **PRENDRE** la fuite – abscond.

FUSION – merger; amalgamation.

- **ACCORD** de fusion – merger agreement.

FUTAIE

- **BOIS** de haute futaie – timber.

FUTURUM

- **MESURE** d'instruction in futurum – order (measure ordered) to facilitate possible future proceedings, eg by preserving evidence.

—

G

GAGE – pledge; pawn; security.

- **ACTE constitutif de gage** – contract of pledge.
- **AVANCE sur gage** – loan on the security of a pledge.
- **BAILLEUR de gage** – pledgor.
- **CONSTITUANT de gage** – pledgor.
- **CONSTITUER un gage** – make or give a pledge (security).
- **CRÉANCIER – gage des créanciers** – security of one's creditors.
- **DÉTENTEUR de gage** – pledgee.
- **DONNER en gage** – pledge.
- **DONNEUR de gage** – pledgor.
- **DROIT de gage** – creditor's right to retain, sell and pay himself out of the proceeds of the object pledged; pledgee's rights; lien; pledge; security.
  - **BAILLEUR – droit de gage du bailleur** – landlord's lien for rent.
  - **GÉNÉRAL – un droit de gage général sur le patrimoine de son débiteur** – a "floating" charge over the debtor's property, ie the creditor's right to enforce his claim against the debtor's entire property.
- **HYPOTHÉCAIRE – gage hypothécaire** – mortgage.
- **IMMOBILIER – gage immobilier** – real security; mortgage.
- **LETTRE de gage** – pledge certificate.
- **MISE en gage** – pledging; pawning; giving as security.
- **MOBILIER – gage mobilier** – movable security; security in the form of movables; pledge; pawn.
- **OBJET de (en) gage** – thing pledged or pawned.
- **PRÊTER sur gage** – lend on the security of pledges.
- **PRÊTEUR sur gage** – pawnbroker; person who lends on the security of pledges.
- **PRISE en gage** – taking something as a pledge or security.
- **RÉALISATION du gage** – sale of the pledge; realisation of the security.
- **RETIRER un gage** – redeem a pledge.
- **TITRE de gage** – document of title to a pledge.

GAGISTE – pledgee.

GAGNANT

- **PARTIE gagnante** – successful party.

GAGNER

- **MANQUE à gagner** – loss of earnings or profit (lucrum cessans).

GAIN

- **CAPITAL – gain en capital** – capital gain.
- **CAUSE – avoir gain de cause** – win (a case).
- **FORTUNE – gain de fortune** – increase in one's assets (fortune).
- **HORAIRE – gain horaire** – hourly remuneration (wage).
- **PERTE de gain (Sw)** – loss of earnings.
- **SURVIE – gain de survie** – advantage accruing to the survivor.

GARANT – surety; guarantor.

- **PORTER – se porter garant de** – stand surety for; go bail for; guarantee.

GARANTI – person for whom a security or guarantee is given.

GARANTIE – guarantee; warranty; security; safeguard; (insurance) cover.

- **ABSTRAIT – garantie abstraite** – security without possession.
- **ACCORD de garantie** – guarantee agreement.
- **ACTION en garantie** – action to enforce a guarantee or warranty; share certificate deposited as a security.
- **APPEL en garantie** – proceedings against the guarantor which may take the form of giving third-party notice.
- **APPELER en garantie** – have recourse to (proceed against) the guarantor.
- **ASSIGNATION en garantie** – action to enforce a guarantee or warranty.
- **BANCAIRE – garantie bancaire** – bank guarantee.
- **CLAUSE de garantie** – guarantee clause; warranty.
- **COLLATÉRAL – garantie collatérale** – collateral guarantee; collateral warranty.
- **DÉLAI de garantie** – period covered by a guarantee or warranty.

- **DEMANDE en garantie** – action to enforce a guarantee or warranty.
- **DÉPÔT de garantie** – sum deposited as a guarantee.
- **DROIT** – **garantie des droits** – inclusion of a guarantee of human rights in a state's constitution.
- **ÉVICTION** – **garantie contre l'éviction** – covenant for peaceful possession.
- **FORMEL** – **garantie formelle** – guarantee in which the guarantor is obliged not only to indemnify the person guaranteed but also to take steps to prevent the loss or damage occurring.
- **HYPOTHÉCAIRE** – **garantie hypothécaire** – mortgage security.
- **IMMOBILIER** – **garantie immobilière** – real security; mortgage security.
- **INCIDENT** – **garantie incidente** – joinder of guarantor (in pending proceedings).
- **LOCATIF** – **garantie locative** – security of tenure.
- **MOBILIER** – **garantie mobilière** – security consisting of a charge on movables; security based on movables.
- **PÉCUNIAIRE** – **garantie pécuniaire** – pecuniary security.
- **PERSONNEL** – **garantie personnelle** – personal security.
- **PROCÉDURE** – **garanties de procédure** – procedural safeguards.
- **PROMESSE de garantie** – indemnity; guarantee.
- **PROVENANCE** – **garantie de provenance** – warranty of origin.
- **RECOURS en garantie** – action to enforce a guarantee or warranty.
- **RÉEL** – **garantie réelle** – security other than personal, ie on land or movables.
- **REPRÉSENTATION** – **garanties de représentation** – bail.
- **RESSOURCE** – **garantie de ressources** – unemployment benefit for persons losing or giving up their employment after the age of 60 (70% of previous earnings).
- **RISQUE** – **garantie d'un risque** – insurance against a risk.
- **SIMPLE** – **garantie simple** – guarantee in which the guarantor's duty is limited to indemnifying the person guaranteed.
- **TRANSFERT** – **garantie de transfert** – guarantee of the right to transfer profits.
- **TRANSFERT en garantie** – transfer of ownership (but not possession) by way of guarantee.

- **TROUBLE** – **garantie des troubles** – covenant or warranty for peaceful possession.
- **VICE** – **garantie des vices** – warranty that goods or animals sold are free of faults or defects.

GARANTIR
- **BIEN** – **garantir les dommages aux biens** – provide insurance against (cover for) damage to goods (property).

GARDE – (physical) custody; care; power of direction and control over an object.
- **DROIT de garde** – storage charge (customs etc); safe-custody charge (bank etc); right to control and care (physical custody) of a child.
- **ENFANT** – **garde d'un enfant** – right to control and care (physical custody) of a child.
- **FRAIS de garde** – expenses of (charges for) storage or safe keeping.
- **JURIDIQUE** – **garde juridique** – custody; guardianship.
- **MATÉRIEL** – **garde matérielle** – (physical) custody; care.
- **RÉTABLISSEMENT de la garde** – restoration of custody.
- **SCEAU** – **Garde des Sceaux** – Minister of Justice.
- **VUE** – **garde à vue** – police custody.

GARDER
- **VUE** – **garder à vue** – keep in police custody.

GARDIEN – holder; custodian; keeper; person having the custody and care of; person responsible for; person in charge of, ie having the use, direction and control of an object causing damage.
- **ANIMAL** – **gardien d'un animal** – owner or other person responsible for an animal (as a rule a person who in some way makes use of the animal).
  - **RESPONSABILITÉ du gardien d'un animal** – liability of the owner or other person responsible for an animal for the damage it causes.
- **JUDICIAIRE** – **gardien judiciaire** – curator (guardian) appointed by the court.
- **PAIX** – **gardien de la paix** – (police) constable; police officer.
- **SCELLÉ** – **gardien des scellés** – person in charge of or responsible for the safe keeping of sealed objects or premises.

GARDIENNAGE – guarding; caretaking; custody.
- **SOCIÉTÉ de gardiennage** – security firm.

GENDARMERIE – military organisation with police functions; constabulary; gendarmerie.

GÊNER – prejudice.

GENS
- **LOI** – gens de loi – (practising) lawyers; the legal community (profession(s)).
- **MAISON** – gens de maison – domestic servants.

GÉRANCE
- **LIBRE** – gérance libre – leasing of a business.
- **SALARIÉ** – gérance salariée – appointment of a paid manager to run a business.

GÉRANT – (business) manager.
- **AFFAIRE** – gérant d'affaires (sans titre) (negotiorum gestor) – one who in the absence of another looks after his affairs or interests or acts as his agent without previous authority; self-appointed (unauthorised, purported) agent.
- **IMMEUBLE** – gérant d'immeubles – estate (property) manager; rent collector.

GERMAIN – (relation) of the full blood.

GESTION
- **AFFAIRE** – gestion d'affaires (sans titre) – agency without authority, ie looking after another's affairs or interests in his absence without previous authority.
- **BON** – bonne gestion – sound management.
- **COMPTE** de gestion (budgétaire) – (budgetary) management account.
- **DÉCHARGE** – donner décharge de sa gestion – discharge in respect of his management.
- **DÉLOYAL** – gestion déloyale – dishonest management.
- **FAIT** – gestion de fait – unauthorised agency; acting as agent without authority.
- **OCCULTE** – gestion occulte – unauthorised agency; acting as an agent without authority.
- **TRÉSORERIE** – gestion de la trésorerie – treasurer's management account.

GOUVERNEMENT – government; executive.
- **ACCÉDANT** – acceding government.
- **ACTE de gouvernement** – certain acts falling within the government's prerogative which cannot be questioned by legal proceedings; prerogative act; exercise of the government's prerogative; act of state.
- **AUTONOME** – gouvernement autonome – self-government.
- **COMMISSAIRE du gouvernement** – prosecutor in a court martial; law officer whose task it is to present a completely impartial report on a case to an administrative court, especially the Conseil d'État, or to the Jurisdiction Court (**Tribunal des conflits**); officer representing the point of view of a ministry in an administrative division of the Conseil d'État.
- **DE FACTO** – gouvernement de facto – de facto government.
- **DE FAIT** – gouvernement de fait – de facto government.
- **FANTOCHE** – gouvernement fantoche – puppet government.
- **INSURGÉ** – gouvernement insurgé – insurgent government.
- **INSURRECTIONNEL** – gouvernement insurrectionnel – insurgent government.
- **LÉGAL** – gouvernement légal – legitimate government.
- **REQUÉRANT** – gouvernement requérant – requesting government; applicant government.
- **REQUIS** – gouvernement requis – requested government.
- **UNION** – gouvernement d'union nationale – national government.

GRÂCE – pardon; prerogative of mercy.
- **AMNISTIANT** – grâce amnistiante – amnesty granted by the government which annuls the conviction; amnesty restricted to certain members of the category involved, specified by decree.
- **CONDITIONNEL** – grâce conditionnelle – conditional pardon.
- **DÉLAI de grâce** – extension of time for payment etc granted by the court.
- **DROIT de grâce** – prerogative of mercy.
- **INDIVIDUEL** – grâce individuelle – individual pardon.
- **RECOURS en grâce** – petition for (an exercise of the prerogative of) mercy; application (request) for pardon.

GRACIER – pardon.
- **COMPÉTENCE pour gracier** – prerogative of mercy.

- **POUVOIR de gracier** – prerogative of mercy.

GRACIEUX – free; non-contentious.
- **DÉCISION gracieuse** – decision (judgment) in a non-contentious matter; decision of an administrative nature by a judge.
- **PROCÉDURE (en matière) gracieuse** – non-contentious proceedings (procedure).
- **RECOURS gracieux** – application to the same administrative authority to reconsider its decision.

GRATIFICATION – gratuity; bonus; ex gratia payment.

GRATIFIÉ – beneficiary; donee.

GRATUIT
- **TITRE – à titre gratuit** – gratuitous; without consideration; free of charge.

GRÉ À GRÉ
- **ALIÉNATION de gré à gré** – sale to a willing purchaser (at arm's length); sale by private treaty (as opposed to an auction); sale on the open market.
- **TRAITER de gré à gré** – conclude a private agreement.
- **VENTE de gré à gré** – see ALIÉNATION above.

GREFFE – registry (of a court).
- **CORRECTIONNEL – greffe correctionnel** registry of the Criminal Court.
- **DROIT de greffe** – registry fee (eg for copies).
- **INSTANCE – greffe d'instance** – Regional Court registry.
- **MUNICIPAL – greffe municipal (Sw)** – local-government offices; town hall.

GREFFER
- **SE greffer sur** – be an adjunct of.

GREFFIER – registrar.
- **ASSUMÉ – greffier assumé (Belg)** – acting registrar.
- **CRIMINEL – greffier criminel** – registrar of a criminal court.

GRÈVE
- **AVERTISSEMENT – grève d'avertissement** – token strike.
- **BRAS CROISÉS – grève des bras croisés** – sit-down strike.
- **INSURRECTIONNEL – grève insurrectionnelle** – revolutionary strike.

- **PERLÉ – grève perlée** – go-slow (strike); slow-down.
- **PONCTUEL – grèves ponctuelles** – selective strikes.
- **RÈGLEMENT – grève du règlement** – work-to-rule.
- **TOURNANT – grève tournante** – staggered strike.
- **ZÈLE – grève du zèle** – work-to-rule.

GREVÉ (adj) – encumbered; mortgaged; charged; subject to; tenant for life; person holding subject to a charge, mortgage, etc.
- **FONDS grevé** – servient tenement.
- **HÉRITIER grevé** – heir who takes subject to (an obligation to pay) a legacy, or as a tenant for life (**usufruitier**) under a testamentary settlement (**fidéicommis**).

GREVÉ (noun)
- **RESTITUTION – grevé d'une restitution** – tenant for life under a will.
- **SUBSTITUTION – grevé de substitution** – tenant for life.
- **USUFRUIT – grevé d'usufruit** – property subject to a usufruct (life tenancy).

GREVER
- **DE – grever de** – subject to (rights in rem).
  - •• **HYPOTHÈQUE – grevé des hypothèques prises sur l'immeuble** – subject to the mortgages on the property; encumbered or charged with mortgages.

GRIEF – claim; complaint; cause of action; ground of appeal; prejudice; allegation; grievance.
- **ACCUSATION – griefs d'accusation** – charges; counts.
- **APPEL – griefs d'appel** – grounds of appeal.
- **CAUSER un grief à** – prejudice; injure; adversely affect.
- **FAIRE grief à** – adversely affect.
- **PREUVE – avoir à faire la preuve d'un grief** – prove that one has suffered a disadvantage (loss, harm, prejudice).
- **SUITE – donner suite à un grief** – allow a claim.

GRIVÈLERIE – obtaining credit by fraud in a hotel or restaurant.

GROS
- **OUVRAGE – gros ouvrage** – main walls and roof.

GROSSE – (former term for) execution copy of a judgment, ie a copy endorsed with authority to execute (with a writ of execution endorsed); instrument drawn by a solicitor (**notaire**) incorporating an authority to execute.

GROSSOYER – engross (prepare) the execution copy of a judgment or a notarial act incorporating an authority to execute.

GROUPE
- **DISCIPLINE de groupe parlementaire** – party discipline; party whip.
- **IMPÔT – groupe d'impôt** – tax category (eg single, married, married with one child).

GROUPEMENT – group or association of persons in the wide sense including **associations** (ie non-profit-making associations) and **sociétés** (profit-making partnerships and companies).
- **AGRICOLE**
  - •• **EXPLOITATION – groupement agricole d'exploitation en commun** – farming partnership.
  - •• **FONCIER – groupement agricole foncier** – agricultural land partnership.
- **COMMUNAL – groupement communal** – association of local authorities; district union.
- **COOPÉRATIF – groupement coopératif** – co-operative; professional association.
- **ILLICITE – groupement illicite** – unlawful association.
- **INTÉRÊT ÉCONOMIQUE – groupement d'intérêt économique** – agency of economic interest, eg a joint purchasing agency established by two or more companies; joint enterprise; consortium; (EU) economic interest grouping.
- **PATRONAL – groupement patronal** – employers association.
- **SYNDICAL – groupement syndical** – professional, trade or industrial association.

GUELTE – commission on sales.

GUERRE
- **CONTRIBUTION de guerre** – war levy; special tax to meet the cost of a war.
- **DROIT de la guerre** – the law(s) of war.
- **FAIT de guerre** – act of war; enemy action.
- **PRISE de guerre** – booty; prize.
- **PUISSANCE en guerre** – belligerent power.

~

H

HABILE
- **SUCCÉDER** – habile à succéder – having capacity to inherit.
- **TESTER** – habile à tester – capable of making a will.

HABILITANT – enabling.
- **FORMALITÉS habilitantes** – formalities enabling a contract to be entered into on behalf of an incapable; enabling formalities.

HABILITATION – authorisation enabling a person under an incapacity to do certain acts, or conferring an authority on an official.
- **LÉGISLATIF** – habilitation législative – statutory authorisation.
- **LOI d'habilitation** – Act authorising the government to legislate by regulation; enabling Act.

HABILITER – authorise a person to do something which he would otherwise be legally incapable of doing; empower; enable.
- **AGENTS spécifiquement habilités** – officers specifically authorised in that behalf (for that purpose).
- **SUCCÉDER** – habilité à succéder – having capacity to inherit.

HABITATION – occasional residence; right to occupy the house of another for the requirements of oneself and one's family (for life).
- **BON MARCHÉ** – see MARCHÉ below.
- **BOURGEOIS** – habitation bourgeoise – use as a private dwelling-house only.
- **LOCAL d'habitation** – living accommodation; dwelling.
- **LOYER**
  - **MODÉRÉ** – habitation à loyer modéré – low-rent flat; rent-controlled premises.
- **MARCHÉ** – habitation à bon marché – low-rent flat; rent-controlled premises.
- **MEUBLÉ** – habitation meublée – furnished premises.
- **USAGE** – à usage d'habitation – residential.

HABITUDE
- **COMMERCIAL** – habitude commerciale – commercial usage.
- **MALFAITEUR d'habitude** – habitual criminal (offender).

HALAGE
- **SERVITUDE de halage** – duty of a riparian owner to leave space for a towpath alongside a navigable waterway.

HANDICAPÉ – disabled.

HARMONIE
- **MISE en harmonie** – consequential amendment.

HAUTE COUR DE JUSTICE – see COUR.

HAUTE MER – see MER.

HAUTEUR
- **PROCÉDURE** – à toute hauteur de la procédure – at any stage of the proceedings.

HÉBERGE – height of the roof of the lower of two buildings separated by a wall.

HÉBERGEMENT
- **DROIT d'hébergement** – right to receive visits from a child in the care (custody) of another; staying access.

HÉRÉDITAIRE – hereditary; passing on succession.
- **CRÉANCIER héréditaire** – creditor of the estate.
- **RÉSERVE héréditaire** – reserved portion (of a deceased's estate).

HÉRÉDITÉ – succession; estate (of a deceased person).
- **ACTION**
  - **PÉTITION** – action en pétition d'hérédité – action to obtain possession of an estate from a person claiming to be the heir; action to claim (a share in) an estate.
  - **REVENDICATION** – action en revendication d'hérédité – action to obtain possession of an estate from a person not claiming as heir or under a will.
- **ADITION d'hérédité** – acceptance of a succession.
- **JACENT** – hérédité jacente – vacant succession; unclaimed estate.

- **PÉTITION d'hérédité** – action to obtain possession of an estate from a person claiming to be the heir; action to claim (a share in) an estate.
- **VENTE d'hérédité** – sale of an inheritance; sale of one's rights in an estate.

HÉRITAGE – succession; estate (of a deceased person); piece of land; hereditament; property; tenement.

- **CAPTATION d'héritage** – attempting to obtain a succession by illegal or immoral means; legacy hunting.
- **FAIRE un héritage** – inherit.
- **HYPOTHÉQUÉ** – **héritage hypothéqué** – piece of land subject to a mortgage.

HÉRITIER – heir; person entitled on an intestacy; next of kin.

- **AB INTESTAT** – **héritier ab intestat** – statutory heir; person entitled on a intestacy; next of kin.
- **APPARENT** – **héritier apparent** – ostensible heir.
- **APPELÉ** – **héritier appelé** – reversionary heir; remainderman; reversioner.
- **BÉNÉFICIAIRE** – **héritier bénéficiaire** – heir whose liability for the debts of the estate is limited to the amount of the net assets he actually receives.
- **COLLATÉRAL** – **héritier collatéral** – collateral heir.
- **COPARTAGEANT** – **héritier copartageant** – co-heir; joint heir.
- **GREVÉ** – **héritier grevé** – heir who takes subject to (an obligation to pay) a legacy, or as a tenant for life (**usufruitier**) under a testamentary settlement (**fidéicommis**).
- **INSTITUÉ** – **héritier institué** – heir appointed by will; testamentary heir.
- **LÉGAL** – **héritier légal** – statutory heir; person entitled on an intestacy; next of kin.
- **LÉGITIME** – **héritier légitime** – statutory heir; person entitled on an intestacy; next of kin.
- **LIGNE DIRECTE** – **héritier en ligne directe** – heir in the direct line (directly descended from the deceased).
- **NATUREL** – **héritier naturel** – illegitimate heir.
- **ORDRE** – **héritier du premier ordre** – heir belonging to the first class of entitled persons.
- **PRÉSOMPTIF** – **héritier présomptif** – heir presumptive, ie who will be heir if no nearer relative is born.

- **PUR ET SIMPLE** – **héritier pur et simple** – heir whose liability for the deceased's debts is not limited to the amount of the estate, and who has lost the right to refuse the estate.
- **RANG SUCCESSIBLE** – **héritier au rang successible** – person entitled on an intestacy.
- **RENONÇANT** – **héritier renonçant** – heir who has waived his right to the estate.
- **RÉSERVATAIRE** – **héritier réservataire** – heir statutorily entitled to a certain portion of the estate (reserved portion).
- **RÉSERVE** – **héritier à réserve** – heir statutorily entitled to a certain portion of the estate (reserved portion).
- **TESTAMENTAIRE** – **héritier testamentaire** – heir appointed by will; testamentary heir.
- **UNIVERSEL** – **héritier universel** – sole heir; heir to the entire estate.

HEURE

- **HEURE** – **d'heure à heure** – at an hour's notice.
- **LÉGAL** – **heures légales** – hours during which process may be served and judgments executed (7 – 21).
- **SERVICE** – **heures de service** – working hours; working time.
- **SUPPLÉMENTAIRE** – **heures supplémentaires** – overtime.

HEURTER

- **SE heurter à** – fall foul of.

HIATUS

- **JURIDIQUE** – **hiatus juridique** – gap or omission (lacuna) in the law.

HIÉRARCHIE

- **SALAIRE** – **hiérarchie des salaires** – salary scales (ie the wage and salary structure in an institution).

HIÉRARCHIQUE

- **RECOURS hiérarchique** – appeal to a higher administrative authority; application to a higher administrative authority to review the decision of a lower administrative authority; application for disciplinary proceedings.
- **SUPÉRIEUR hiérarchique** – official (immediate) superior; higher administrative officer; superior officer.

- VOIE – **par la voie hiérarchique** – through the usual (official) channels; through one's superior officer(s).

HIÉRARCHIQUEMENT – by reference to the higher authority; by seniority.

HISTORIQUE – background.
- PROCÉDURE – **historique de la procédure** – summary of the proceedings.

HOIRIE
- AVANCEMENT **d'hoirie** – advancement.

HOLDING – holding company.

HOMICIDE – homicide; person committing homicide.
- CRAPULEUX – **homicide crapuleux** – homicide committed from base motives, eg for pecuniary gain, or in a barbaric manner.
- IMPRUDENCE – **homicide par imprudence** – negligent homicide; causing death by negligence.
- INVOLONTAIRE – **homicide involontaire** – unintentional homicide; manslaughter.
- PRÉMÉDITÉ – **homicide prémédité** – premeditated homicide (with malice aforethought); murder.
- PRAETERINTENTIONNEL – **homicide praeterintentionnel** – unintentional homicide by wounding; causing death unintentionally by intentionally wounding (manslaughter or murder).
- VOLONTAIRE – **homicide volontaire** – intentional homicide.

HOMME
- CONFIANCE – **homme de confiance** – confidential adviser or agent.
- DROIT – **droits de l'homme** – human rights.
- LOI – **homme de loi** – (practising) lawyer; (in plural) the legal community (profession(s)).
- PAILLE – **homme de paille** – man of straw.

HOMOLOGATION – confirmation; approval; recognition.
- DÉCISION **d'homologation** – decision confirming.
- JUDICIAIRE – **homologation judiciaire** – judicial confirmation.
- JUGEMENT **d'homologation** – judgment confirming.
- JUSTICE – **homologation de justice** – judicial confirmation.

HOMOLOGUE – opposite number.

HOMOLOGUER – confirm; approve; recognise; sanction.

HONNEUR
- ACTE **contraire à l'honneur** – dishonourable act or conduct.
- ATTEINTE **à l'honneur** – insult; defamation; libel; slander.
- FAIRE **honneur à ses engagements** – honour one's obligations (commitments).
- JURIDICTION **d'honneur** – court of honour; disciplinary (professional) tribunal; jurisdiction of such a court or tribunal.
- MEMBRE **d'honneur** – honorary member.

HONORAIRES – fees.
- CRÉANCE **d'honoraires** – claim for fees; fees owing.
- LIQUIDATION **des honoraires** – fixing of fees; settling (payment) of fees.

HONORARIAT – honorary title conferred on retirement.

HORS
- CAUSE – **hors (de) cause** – not subject to (above, cleared of) suspicion; in the clear; cleared; exonerated.
- COMMERCE – **hors (du) commerce** – whose sale is prohibited by law; not subject to legal transactions; inalienable; not for sale.
  - •• DROITS **hors (du) commerce** – rights which cannot form the subject-matter of a legal transaction.
  - •• METTRE **hors (du) commerce** – prohibit the sale of; prohibit commercial transactions relating to; render inalienable.
- DÉLAI – **hors délai** – out of time.
- MARIAGE – **hors mariage** – extramarital; out of wedlock.
- PART – **(par préciput et) hors part** – (of a gift to an heir out of an estate) not subject to hotchpot; in addition to the heir's share of the estate.

HORS-COTE – (adj) not officially quoted; unlisted; (noun) unlisted security.

HÔTEL
- FRANCHISE **d'hôtel** – inviolability of embassy premises and ambassador's residence.
- JUGE – **hôtel du juge** – judge's private residence.
- MONNAIE – **Hôtel des monnaies** – Mint.

- **VENTE** – hôtel des ventes – auction rooms.

HUIS
- **CLOS**
  - •• **À huis clos** – in camera; in private.
  - •• **PRONONCER le huis clos** – exclude the public.

HUISSIER – bailiff.
- **AUDIENCIER** – huissier audiencier – court usher; tipstaff.
- **CONSTAT d'huissier** – bailiff's official report (on some matter of fact).

HUITAINE
- **FRANC** – à huitaine franche – in eight clear days.

HUMANITÉ
- **CLAUSE d'humanité** – hardship clause.

HYPOTHÉCAIRE – mortgage (adj); secured by mortgage.
- **PRÊT hypothécaire** – mortgage (loan).

HYPOTHÈQUE – mortgage.
- **ACTE d'hypothèque** – mortgage deed.
  - •• **CONSTITUTIF – acte constitutif d'hypothèque** – mortgage (referring to the instrument).
- **AÉRIEN – hypothèque aérienne (Sw)** – mortgage on an aircraft.
- **AÉRONEF – hypothèque sur aéronef** – mortgage on an aircraft.
- **AMÉLIORATION – hypothèque sur amélioration de terrains (Sw)** – land improvement charge.
- **AMORTISSABLE – hypothèque amortissable** – mortgage repayable in annual instalments.
- **BATEAU – hypothèque sur bateau** – mortgage on a ship.
- **BUREAU des hypothèques** – Mortgage Registry (Land (Charges) Registry).
- **CONSENTIR une hypothèque** – to mortgage; grant a mortgage on.
- **CONSERVATEUR des hypothèques** – Chief Registrar of the Mortgage Registry (of the Land (Charges) Registry); Mortgage Registrar; Land Registrar.
- **CONVENTIONNEL – hypothèque conventionnelle** – contractual mortgage.
- **EMPRUNTER sur hypothèque** – borrow on mortgage.
- **FLUVIAL – hypothèque fluviale** – mortgage of river craft.
- **FRANC d'hypothèques** – unencumbered; free of encumbrances; free of mortgages.

- **GARANTIE – hypothèque de garantie** – guarantee mortgage; mortgage which in every respect is strictly ancillary to the debt guaranteed.
- **GREVER – grevé d'une hypothèque** – subject to a mortgage.
- **INSCRIPTION d'une hypothèque** – registration of a mortgage.
- **INSCRIT – hypothèque inscrite** – registered mortgage.
- **JUDICIAIRE – hypothèque judiciaire** – mortgage or charge registered by order of the court as a measure of execution.
- **LÉGAL – hypothèque légale** – statutory mortgage; statutory charge.
- **LIBELLÉ – hypothèque libellée en monnaies étrangères** – foreign-currency mortgage.
- **LIBRE d'hypothèques** – unencumbered; free of encumbrances; free of mortgages.
- **MARITIME – hypothèque maritime** – mortgage on a ship.
- **OCCULTE – hypothèque occulte** – non-registered mortgage.
- **OCTROI d'hypothèques** – grant of mortgages.
- **PRENDRE une hypothèque sur** – to take a mortgage on.
- **PRÊT sur hypothèque** – mortgage (loan).
- **PURGE d'une hypothèque** – redemption or discharge of a mortgage; removal or cancellation of the entry of a mortgage in the register; (of a purchaser) paying off a mortgage.
- **PURGER une hypothèque** – (of a purchaser) pay off a mortgage.
- **RANG – hypothèque de second rang** – second mortgage.
- **REGISTRE des hypothèques** – mortgage register or registry.
- **SÛRETÉ – hypothèque de sûreté (Lux)** – guarantee mortgage, a mortgage the existence of which is in all respects bound up with that of the debt guaranteed.
- **TERRESTRE – hypothèque terrestre** – non-maritime mortgage.
- **TRANSCRIPTION d'une hypothèque** – registration of a mortgage.
- **TRANSCRIT – hypothèque transcrite** – registered mortgage.

HYPOTHÉQUER – mortgage.

HYPOTHÈSE – case; inference; assumption; eventuality.

I

IDÉAL – notional.
- **QUOTE-PART idéale** – notional share.

IDÉALEMENT – notionally.
- **CLOS** – (espace) idéalement clos – notionally enclosed (space).

IDENTIQUE
- **RÉEXPORTER à l'identique** – re-export unchanged (in the same condition).

IDENTITÉ
- **CONSTATATION d'identité** – finding or establishment of a person's identity; a finding that two things are identical.
- **CONTRÔLE d'identité** – identity check.
- **FALSIFICATION d'identité** – forgery of identity documents.
- **INTERROGATOIRE d'identité** – examination to establish identity; examination (questioning) as to one's personal particulars.
- **JUDICIAIRE** – (service de) l'identité judiciaire – criminal identification department; criminal records office.
- **JUSTIFIER de son identité** – prove one's identity.
- **RECONNAISSANCE d'identité** – establishment of a person's identity.
- **TITRE d'identité** – identity document.
- **VÉRIFICATION d'identité** – forcible checking of a person's identity by the police involving his detention on the premises during the process; identity check.

IGNORANCE
- **DROIT** – ignorance du droit – ignorance of the law.

ILLÉGAL – illegal; unlawful; (of a court decision) erroneous; wrong in law.

ILLÉGALEMENT – unlawfully; illegally.

ILLÉGALITÉ – illegality; unlawfulness; incorrectness (in law) of a court decision.
- **EXCEPTION d'illégalité** – defence or objection alleging (the) illegality (of an administrative regulation relied on by the other party).

ILLÉGITIME – unlawful; illegitimate.

ILLÉGITIMITÉ – unlawfulness; illegitimacy.

ILLICÉITÉ – unlawfulness; illegality.

ILLICITE – unlawful; illegal; wrongful.

ILLIMITÉ – perpetual.

IMMATRICULATION – registration (of a company, ship, etc).
- **PORT d'immatriculation** – home port.
- **REGISTRE**
  - •• **COMMERCE** – immatriculation au registre du commerce – registration in the commercial registry (register).

IMMATRICULE – number allotted to a bailiff when his name is entered on the roll.
- **HUISSIER** – immatricule d'huissier – bailiff's court-registration number.

IMMATRICULER – enter; register.

IMMEUBLE – immovable; plot; parcel; (piece of) land; hereditament; building; messuage; real property; (less technically) buildings.
- **CONSULAIRE** – immeuble consulaire – consulate building.
- **DESTINATION** – immeuble par destination – statutory immovable; chattel real.
- **DOMMAGES aux immeubles** – damage to land (and buildings).
- **DOTAL** – immeuble dotal – dowry land; spouse's settled land.
- **GÉRANT d'immeubles** – estate (property) manager; rent collector.
- **HABITATION** – immeuble à usage d'habitation – dwelling-house; residential premises.
- **RAPPORT** – immeuble de rapport – house let to tenants; rented house.

IMMOBILIER – immovable.
- **BIENS immobiliers** – immovable property; real estate.
- **CARACTÈRE** – avoir un caractère immobilier – be deemed to be land; be treated notionally as land.
- **DROIT immobilier** – the law of real property; right relating to an immovable (land).

IMMOBILISATION – (in plural) fixed assets; assets permanently employed in a business.

- **DURÉE** – **immobilisation à longue durée** – long-term investment; tying up capital for a long period.
- **FRUIT** – **immobilisation des fruits** – effect of the seizure of land in execution of a judgment, ie the produce is treated as part of the land for the purposes of the execution and the proceeds of its sale divided among the mortgagees and preferential creditors.
- **PARTICIPATION** – **immobilisations y compris participations** – fixed assets including investments.
- **VÉHICULE** – **immobilisation de véhicule** – punishment consisting of deprival of the use of one's vehicle for a period not exceeding six months.

IMMOBILISÉ – (of assets) fixed.

IMMOBILISER – convert into notional immovables; classify as fixed assets.

IMMORAL – immoral; contrary to morality.

IMMUABLE – unalterable.

IMMUNITÉ – immunity.
- **ARRESTATION** – **immunité d'arrestation** – immunity from arrest.
- **CONSULAIRE** – **immunités consulaires** – consular immunities.
- **DIPLOMATIQUE** – **immunité diplomatique** – diplomatic immunity.
- **DOUANIER** – **immunité douanière** – exemption from customs duties.
- **EXÉCUTION** – **immunité d'exécution** – immunity from execution.
- **FISCAL** – **immunité fiscale** – freedom from taxation.
- **FONCTION** – **immunité de fonctions** – immunity by virtue of one's office; official immunity.
- **JURIDICTION** – **immunité de juridiction** – immunity from jurisdiction; immunity from legal proceedings.
- **LEVÉE de l'immunité** – waiver (withdrawal, deprivation) of immunity, eg in the case of an MP who has committed an offence.
- **LEVER l'immunité** – withdraw immunity (from) (deprive of immunity) (eg an MP who has committed an offence); waive (a person's) immunity.
- **PARLEMENTAIRE** – **immunité parlementaire** – parliamentary immunity.
- **POURSUITE** – **immunité de poursuites** – immunity from prosecution.

IMMUTABILITÉ – unalterability.
- **DEMANDE** – **immutabilité de la demande** – rule that the petition or statement of claim cannot be amended or added to.
- **LITIGE** – **immutabilité du litige** – rule that the parties, the capacity in which they are proceeding and the cause of action may not be changed during the proceedings.

IMPARTAGEABLE – indivisible.

IMPARTIAL – impartial.

IMPARTIALITÉ – impartiality.
- **OBJECTIF** – **impartialité objective** (Belg) – outward appearance of impartiality.
- **SUBJECTIF** – **impartialité subjective** (Belg) – impartiality (ie mental attitude of the judge).

IMPARTIR
- **DÉLAI** – **impartir un délai** – set (fix) a time-limit.

IMPASSE
- **BUDGÉTAIRE** – **impasse budgétaire** – budget deficit to be covered by a loan or cash in the Treasury.

IMPENSE – expenditure on property; money spent on improvements (by a person in possession).
- **NÉCESSAIRE** – **impense nécessaire** – necessary expenditure.
- **UTILE** – **impense utile** – useful expenditure.
- **VOLUPTUAIRE** – **impense voluptuaire** – expenditure on luxuries.

IMPÉRATIF – mandatory; compelling.

IMPÉRIEUX – compelling.

IMPERIUM – court's administrative powers.

IMPÉTRANT – person who obtains something by applying for it.

IMPIGNORÉ – pledged; pawned.

IMPLANTATION – site; site plan; siting.

IMPLICITE – implied; tacit; implicit; inherent.

IMPLICITEMENT – impliedly; tacitly; implicitly; by implication.

IMPLIQUER – imply; entail; involve; mean.

IMPORT (Belg) – amount.
- **NOMINAL** – **import nominal** – nominal amount.

IMPORTATION
- **CONSIGNATION** – **importation en consignation** – import in bond.
- **FRANCHISE** – **importation en franchise** – duty-free import.

IMPOSABILITÉ – liability to tax.

IMPOSABLE – liable to tax; subject to tax.
- **NON-**imposable – not liable to tax.
- **PÉRIODE imposable** – assessment period; period of assessment.

IMPOSER – tax; subject to tax.
- **S'imposer à** – be binding on.

IMPOSITION – taxing; taxation; assessment.
- **ANNUEL** – **imposition annuelle** – annual assessment.
- **ASSIETTE d'imposition** – basis of assessment.
- **AVIS d'imposition** – assessment.
- **BASE d'imposition** – taxable (rateable) value; value for tax purposes; basis of assessment.
- **DÉCISION d'imposition** – assessment.
- **DOUBLE imposition** – double taxation.
- **DROIT d'imposition** – right to raise (impose) taxes.
- **FORFAITAIRE** – **imposition forfaitaire** – lump-sum assessment; assessment in a notional amount.
- **INTÉGRAL** – **imposition intégrale** – confiscatory taxation, ie 100% rate of tax.
- **LIMITE d'imposition** – limit of taxation; point at which a tax immunity ceases to apply.
- **PÉRIODE d'imposition** – assessment period; period of assessment.
- **SÉPARÉ** – **imposition séparée** – separate assessment.
- **SOURCE** – **imposition des revenus à la source** – deduction (of tax) at source; PAYE.
- **TARIF d'imposition** – rate of tax.
- **TAUX d'imposition** – rate of tax.
- **TRANCHE d'imposition** – "slice" of taxable income; income band.

IMPOSSIBILITÉ
- **EXÉCUTION** – **impossibilité d'exécution** – impossibility of performance (this is judged by an objective standard and not by the defendant's personal inability to perform).

- **RELATIF** – **impossibilité relative** – inability (personal to the promisor) to perform the obligation (which could be performed by others).

IMPÔT – tax.
- **ACCROISSEMENT**
  - **CAPITAL** – **impôt sur les accroissements du capital** – capital gains tax.
  - **FORTUNE** – **impôt sur l'accroissement de la fortune** – capital gains tax.
  - **VALEUR** – **impôt sur l'accroissement de la valeur** – capital gains tax.
- **AFFECTÉ** – **impôt affecté à une dépense déterminée** – special-purpose tax.
- **AMÉNAGEMENT** – **impôt d'aménagement** – improvement rate.
- **ANALYTIQUE** – **impôts analytiques** – specific taxes
- **ANTICIPÉ** – **impôt anticipé** (Sw) – advance tax.
- **ARRIÉRÉ d'impôt** – tax arrears.
- **ARRIÉRÉ** – **impôts arriérés** – tax arrears.
- **ASSUJETTI à l'impôt** – liable to tax; subject to tax.
- **ASSUJETTISSEMENT à l'impôt** – liability to taxation.
- **BARÈME de l'impôt sur les salaires** – salary-tax tables; (Schedule E) income-tax tables.
- **BÉNÉFICE** – **impôt sur les bénéfices** – profits tax.
  - **GUERRE** – **impôt sur les bénéfices de guerre** – war-profits tax; excess-profits tax.
  - **SOCIÉTÉ** – **impôts sur les bénéfices des sociétés** – corporation tax.
- **BOISSON** – **impôt sur les boissons** – beverage tax.
- **BON d'impôt** – tax-payment certificate; tax-reserve certificate.
- **BOURSE** – **impôt sur les opérations de bourse** – stamp duty on stock-exchange transactions (contracts).
- **CAPITAL** – **impôt sur le capital** – capital tax; property tax.
- **CÉDULAIRE** – **impôt cédulaire** – schedule(d) tax; tax applying to particular category of income.
- **CIRCULATION** – **impôts de circulation** – transfer taxes.
- **CODE général des impôts** – Taxation Act; Tax Code.

- **COLLECTIVITÉ** – impôt sur les collectivités (Lux) – corporation tax.
- **COMMUNAL** – impôt communal – local tax; rates.
- **COMPENSATAIRE** – impôt compensataire sur le revenu (Belg) – income tax.
- **COMPENSATOIRE** – impôt compensatoire (Sw) – equalisation tax.
- **CONSOMMATION** – impôt de consommation – excise duty; consumer tax.
- **CRÉANCE** d'impôt – tax owing; tax claim(ed).
- **DÉBIT** – impôt sur les débits de boissons – liquor licence (on and off).
- **DÉBITEUR** d'impôt – taxpayer.
- **DÉCLARATION** d'impôts – tax return.
- **DÉPENSE** – impôt sur les dépenses – luxury (expenditure) tax (ie calculated on what a person spends).
- **DETTE** d'impôt – tax owing; tax arrears.
- **ÉTABLISSEMENT** de l'impôt – (tax) assessment.
- **EXEMPT** d'impôt(s) – tax-free; free of tax; not liable to tax.
- **EXONÉRATION** d'impôt(s) – exemption from tax.
- **FEUILLE** d'impôt(s) – tax return; (notice of) tax assessment.
- **FONCIER** – impôt foncier – land tax.
- **FORFAIT** d'impôt – lump-sum assessment; assessment in a notional amount.
- **FORFAIT** – impôt à forfait – lump-sum tax; tax based on a notional assessment.
- **FORFAITAIRE** – impôt forfaitaire – lump-sum tax; tax on a notional assessment.
- **FORTUNE** – impôt sur la fortune – capital tax; property tax; wealth tax.
- **FRANC** d'impôt – tax-free; free of tax.
- **GÉNÉRAL** – impôt général sur le revenu – income tax.
- **GROUPE** d'impôt – tax category (eg single, married, married with one child).
- **IMMOBILIER** – impôt à base immobilière – real-property tax.
- **INDICIAIRE** – impôt indiciaire – indicator-based tax; apparent-wealth tax (based on external indications of wealth).
- **INDIRECT** – impôt indirect sur la consommation – indirect consumer tax; excise duty.
- **LEVER** un impôt – levy (raise, impose, collect) a tax.
- **LIQUIDATION** de l'impôt – (tax) assessment; fixing the amount of tax; payment of tax.

- **LOCAL** – impôts locaux – rates.
- **LOCATIF** – impôt locatif – rent tax; tax on income from rents.
- **LUXE** – impôt sur le luxe – luxury tax.
- **MAJORATION** de l'impôt – increase in the amount of tax due.
- **MONTANT** de l'impôt – amount of tax due.
- **MUNICIPAL** – impôt municipal – local tax; rates.
- **NATURE** – impôt en nature – tax(ation) in kind.
- **OPÉRATION DE BOURSE** – see BOURSE above.
- **PERCEVOIR** un impôt – levy (raise, impose, collect) a tax.
- **PROPRIÉTÉ BÂTIE** – impôt sur la propriété bâtie – built-up-property tax.
- **QUOTITÉ** – impôt de quotité – tax calculated at a certain rate on a certain quantity or amount; pro-rata tax.
- **RAPPEL** d'impôt – supplementary assessment; demand for arrears of tax.
- **RECETTES** d'impôt – tax revenue; revenue from taxation.
- **RECOUVREMENT** d'impôts – collection of taxes.
- **RÉEL** – impôts réels – non-personal property taxes (eg trade tax, land tax, dog tax).
- **REFUS** de l'impôt – refusal to pay taxes.
- **REMBOURSEMENT** d'impôts – repayment of taxes.
- **REMISE** d'impôt – tax remission.
- **RENDEMENT** de l'impôt – tax revenue; tax yield.
- **RENTRÉE** des impôts – collection (getting in) of taxes.
- **RENTRÉES** d'impôts (de l'impôt) – tax receipts; revenue received from taxes.
- **RETENUE** d'impôt – retention (deduction) of tax.
- **REVENU** – impôt sur le revenu – income tax.
  - **CAPITAL MOBILIER** – impôt sur le revenu des capitaux mobiliers – tax on income from securities; income tax on investments other than land.
  - **LOCATIF** – impôt sur le revenu locatif – rent tax; tax on income from rents.
  - **TRAVAIL** – impôt sur les revenus du travail – tax on individual earnings; tax on earned income.

- **SALAIRE** – **impôt sur les salaires** – salaries tax; wages tax; payroll tax.
- **SOCIÉTÉ** – **impôt sur les sociétés** – corporation tax.
- **SOMPTUAIRE** – **impôt somptuaire** – luxury tax.
- **SOURCE d'impôts** – source of tax.
- **SPECTACLE** – **impôt sur les spectacles** – entertainment tax.
- **SUCCESSION** – **impôt sur les successions** – inheritance tax; succession duty.
- **SUPERBÉNÉFICE** – **impôt sur les super-bénéfices** – excess-profits tax.
- **SUPPLÉMENTAIRE** – **impôt supplémentaire** – additional tax.
- **SYNTHÉTIQUE** – **impôts synthétiques** – general taxes; comprehensive taxes.
- **TRANSFERT** – **impôt sur les transferts de capital** – (capital) transfer tax; conveyancing duty.
- **TRANSMISSION** – **impôts sur les transmissions à titre onéreux** – (capital) transfer tax; conveyancing duty.
- **TRANSPORT** – **impôt sur les transports** – transport tax.
- **UNIQUE** – **impôt unique** – standard tax.
- **VERSEMENT des impôts** – payment of taxes.

IMPRESCRIPTIBILITÉ – non-applicability of statutory limitation; indefeasibility.

IMPRESCRIPTIBLE – not subject to limitation; not capable of being acquired by prescription; indefeasible.

IMPRÉVISIBILITÉ – unforeseeability.

IMPRÉVISIBLE – unforeseeable.

IMPRÉVISION – unforeseeability.
- **THÉORIE de l'imprévision** – doctrine permitting the modification of, or release from, a contract owing to an unforeseen and fundamental change of circumstances; frustration of a contract by unforeseen events.

IMPRÉVUS – contingencies.

IMPRUDENCE
- **BLESSURES par imprudence** – negligent injury.
- **DÉLIT d'imprudence** – offence not requiring mens rea; non-intentional offence; (tort of) negligence; negligent tort.
- **HOMICIDE par imprudence** – negligent homicide; causing death by negligence.

IMPUBÈRE – under marriageable age.

IMPUBERTÉ – being under marriageable age.

IMPUISSANCE – impotence.

IMPUTABILITÉ – the fact of requiring to be taken into account (eg in calculating a sentence); imputability.
- **NON-imputabilité** – absence of guilt; absence of criminal responsibility (owing to insanity or duress).

IMPUTABLE – requiring to be taken into account; imputable, ie for which a person may be called upon to answer.

IMPUTATION – taking into account; accusation; setting off (against); charging (to budget etc).
- **BUDGÉTAIRE** – **imputation budgétaire** – budgetary coding.
- **DIFFAMATOIRE** – **imputation diffamatoire** – defamatory allegation; innuendo.

IMPUTER – take into account; accuse; charge (to budget etc).
- **SUR** – **imputer sur** – set off against; charge to.

IN ABSTRACTO – according to an abstract standard; with reference to the ordinary man, reasonable contractor, etc.
- **APPRÉCIER** – **la faute du propriétaire est appréciée in abstracto** – the owner's fault is judged according to an objective standard (ie the conduct of a reasonable owner).

INADMISSIBLE – (of an administrative decision being challenged) unreasonable.

INALIÉNABILITÉ – inalienability.

INALIÉNABLE – inalienable.

INAMOVIBILITÉ – irremovability; security of office; fact of holding a life appointment (being irremovable). (In France this security is in fact not absolute but provides a guarantee against arbitrary removal, arbitrary posting, etc.)

INAMOVIBLE – irremovable; holding office for life.

INAPPLICATION – non-application.

INAPTE

- **SERVICE** – **inapte au service** – unfit for (military) service.

INAPTITUDE

- **TRAVAIL** – **inaptitude au travail** – (physical) incapacity for work; permanent disablement.

INATTAQUABLE – inappellable (unappealable); not subject to appeal; not liable to be set aside or declared void on grounds of fraud, error, duress, etc; unchallengeable.

INCAPABLE – incapable; lacking in legal capacity.

- **CONTRACTER** - **incapable de contracter** – incapable of contracting or entering into legal relations.

INCAPACITÉ – disability; incapacity; disqualification.

- **CERTIFICAT** **d'incapacité de travail** – certificate of unfitness for work.
- **CONTRACTER** – **incapacité de contracter** – incapacity to contract or enter into legal transactions.
- **ÉLECTORAL** – **incapacité électorale** – incapacity to vote or be elected; disqualification.
- **ESTER** – **incapacité d'ester en justice** – lack of standing (before the court); incapacity to take part in court proceedings.
- **EXERCICE** – **incapacité d'exercice** – incapacity to exercise one's own rights without some form of representation, assistance or authorisation; absence of legal capacity.
- **JOUISSANCE** – **incapacité de jouissance** – incapacity to hold (exercise) legal rights; absence of legal personality.
- **PERMANENT** – **incapacité permanente** – permanent disability; permanent unfitness for work.
- **PHYSIQUE** – **incapacité physique** – physical disability.
- **PROFESSIONNEL** – **incapacité professionnelle** – lack of professional qualification or capacity; professional disqualification.
- **RELATIF** – **incapacité relative** – incapacity to contract with certain specific persons.
- **SERVICE** – **incapacité de service** – unfitness for (military) service.
- **TEMPORAIRE** – **incapacité temporaire** – temporary disablement; temporary disability.
- **TRAVAIL** – **incapacité de travail** – unfitness for work; disablement.

INCARCÉRATION – imprisonment.

INCENDIAIRE – person committing arson; arsonist.

INCENDIE

- **INTENTIONNEL** – **incendie intentionnel** (Sw) – arson.
- **VOLONTAIRE** – **incendie volontaire** – arson.

INCENDIER – set on fire.

INCERTAIN (noun) – variable (movable) exchange.

- **DONNER l'incertain** – quote uncertain; quote variable exchange; quote in foreign currency.

INCESSIBLE – unassignable.

INCIDENT (adj)– interlocutory.

- **DEMANDE incidente** – additional (supplementary, interlocutory) application (by one of the parties or a third party in the course of the proceedings); motion; summons.
  - •• **GARANTIE** – **demande incidente en garantie** – third-party proceedings against a guarantor.
- **GARANTIE incidente** – joinder of guarantor (in pending proceedings).

INCIDENT (noun) – question or point (arising in the course of proceedings); particular point; interlocutory procedure; application; motion; summons; (in plural) (interlocutory) proceedings.

- **AUDIENCE** – **incident d'audience** – incident occurring during the trial.
- **COMPÉTENCE** – **incident de compétence** – summons (motion) to decide a question of jurisdiction.
- **CRIMINEL** – **incident criminel** – pleading a criminal offence during civil proceedings.
- **EXÉCUTION** – **incident d'exécution** – objection to execution.
- **INSTANCE** – **incident de l'instance** – incidental or interlocutory proceedings.
- **PROCÉDURE** – **incident de procédure** – procedural application; step in the procedure; interlocutory (incidental) application or proceedings.
- **PROCÈS** – **incidents du procès** – (interlocutory) procedural objections or applications.

INCITATION

- **CRIME** – **incitation au crime** – incitement to commit a felony (very serious offence).
- **FAUX TÉMOIGNAGE** – **incitation au faux témoignage** – subornation of perjury.
- **FISCAL** – **incitations fiscales** – tax inducements.
- **RÉVOLTE** – **incitation à la révolte** – incitement to rebellion (mutiny).

INCITER – incite; instigate; foment.

INCIVIQUE (Belg) – person disqualified from exercising certain civic rights as a punishment; collaborator.

INCIVISME – lack of patriotism; (Belg) collaboration with the enemy; treason.

INCOHÉRENCE – inconsistency.

INCOMBER – fall upon; be borne by.
- **DEVOIR qui lui incombe** – duty owed by him.
- **FRAIS** – **les frais incombent à cette partie** – the costs shall be borne by that party.

INCOMMODE – causing disturbance; offensive; noxious.
- **ÉTABLISSEMENT dangereux, incommode et insalubre** – dangerous, offensive (noxious) or unhealthy works (premises).

INCOMPATIBILITÉ – incompatibility; disability or disqualification (in matters of eligibility for office).
- **HUMEUR** – **incompatibilité d'humeur** – incompatibility of temperament.

INCOMPÉTENCE – lack of jurisdiction; incompetence.
- **DÉCLARATION d'incompétence** – finding of lack of jurisdiction.
- **EXCEPTION d'incompétence** – defence, objection or plea that the court has no jurisdiction; objection to jurisdiction.
- **FAIT** – **incompétence pour les faits qui s'étaient déroulés** – lack (want) of (had no) jurisdiction over matters occurring.
- **LIEU** – **incompétence à raison du lieu** – lack (want) of jurisdiction ratione loci, ie resulting from factors such as the defendant's place of residence or the situation of the subject-matter.
- **MATIÈRE** – **incompétence à raison de la matière** – lack (want) of jurisdiction ratione materiae, ie resulting from the nature of the subject-matter.

- **RATIONE LOCI** – see LIEU above.
- **RATIONE MATERIAE** – see MATIÈRE above.

INCOMPÉTENT – lacking jurisdiction.
- **DÉCLARER** – **se déclarer incompétent** – refuse (decline) jurisdiction.

IN CONCRETO – with reference to the particular person concerned (tortfeasor, victim, etc); subjective; in the particular case (circumstances).

INCONDUITE – misconduct; immorality.

INCONSCIENCE
- **TOTAL** – **inconscience totale** – complete unawareness of what one is doing.

INCONSOMPTIBLE – unconsumable, ie not destroyed by use.

INCORPORATION – (national service etc) call-up.
- **RÉSERVE** – **incorporation de réserves** – (increase of capital through) capitalisation of reserves.

INCORPOREL – incorporeal; intangible.

INCORPORER – incorporate; admit to membership.
- **CAPITAL** – **incorporer au capital** – add reserves to capital; capitalise reserves.

INCOTÉ – unquoted.

INCRIMINATION – offence; definition of an offence; creation of an offence; statute or regulation creating an offence.
- **DOUBLE** – **condition de la double incrimination** – (extradition) requirement that the offence committed should be an offence in both countries; requirement of dual criminal liability.

INCRIMINER – make an offence; create as a specific offence.
- **DÉCISION incriminée** – decision appealed against; decision of the court below (lower court or authority); impugned decision; decision being challenged.
- **FAIT incriminé** – offence charged; matter complained of.
- **JUGEMENT incriminé** – judgment appealed against.

INCULPATION – accusation; charge; notice of prosecution.

- **TARDIF** – **inculpation tardive** – error of an investigating judge who examines as a witness a person against whom there is serious evidence of guilt; delay in charging a suspect.

INCULPÉ – (in proceedings before the investigating judge) defendant; accused; person charged (with a criminal offence).

INCULPER – accuse; charge.

INDÉLICATESSE – misconduct; dishonest behaviour.

INDEMNISABLE – indemnifiable.

INDEMNISATION – compensation; damages; indemnity.

- **BARÈME d'indemnisation** – scale of compensation.
- **CRÉANCE en indemnisation** – claim (right) to damages (compensation).
- **DROIT à indemnisation** – right to damages (compensation).
- **ÉQUITABLE** – **indemnisation équitable** – fair compensation; just satisfaction.
- **SOUFFRANCE** – **indemnisation des souffrances (pretium doloris)** – (damages for) pain and suffering.
- **TARIF d'indemnisation** – scale (rate) of compensation.

INDEMNISER – indemnify; compensate.

INDEMNITÉ – compensation (moneys); damages; indemnity.

- **ABSENCE** – **indemnité d'absence** – separation allowance.
- **ACCESSOIRE** – **indemnité accessoire** – subsidiary or supplementary allowance.
- **ACCIDENT** – **indemnité en cas d'accident** – compensation for injuries (arising out of an accident).
- **ACCORDER une indemnité** – award damages; grant (award) compensation.
- **ACCOUCHEMENT** – **indemnité d'accouchement** – maternity grant.
- **ACTION en indemnité** – action for damages.
- **ALLAITEMENT** – **indemnité d'allaitement** – nursing allowance.
- **ALLOUER une indemnité** – award damages; grant (award) compensation.
- **ANCIENNETÉ** – **indemnité d'ancienneté** – seniority allowance.
- **ASSISTANCE** – **indemnité d'assistance** – salvage (money).

- **ASSURANCE** – **indemnité d'assurance** – insurance money(s); insurance compensation.
  - •• **INCENDIE** – **indemnité d'assurance contre l'incendie** – fire-insurance money(s).
- **ATTENTE** – **indemnité d'attente** – demurrage.
- **BASE** – **indemnité de base** – basic allowance.
- **CAISSE** – **indemnité (de déficit) de caisse** – indemnity for cashier's deficit.
- **CAPITAL** – **indemnité en capital** – lump-sum compensation; capital payment.
- **CHANGE** – **indemnité de change** – compensation for loss on exchange.
- **CHANGEMENT D'EMPLOI** – **indemnité de changement d'emploi** – compensation for change of employment.
- **CHARGE**
  - •• **ADMINISTRATIF** – **indemnité de charges administratives** – official-expenditure allowance.
  - •• **ENFANT** – **indemnité pour charge d'enfants (Lux)** – children's allowance.
- **CHERTÉ DE VIE** – **indemnité de cherté de vie** – cost-of-living allowance.
- **CHÔMAGE** – **indemnité de chômage** – unemployment benefit.
  - •• **MALADIE** – **indemnité de chômage pour cause de maladie** – sickness benefit.
- **COMPARUTION** – **indemnité de comparution** – witness allowance.
- **COMPENSATEUR** – **indemnité compensatrice** – equalisation allowance; hardship allowance.
  - •• **LOGEMENT** – **indemnité compensatrice de logement** – allowance in lieu of (official) accommodation.
- **COMPENSATOIRE** – **indemnité compensatoire** – equalisation allowance; hardship allowance.
- **COMPLÉMENTAIRE** – **indemnité complémentaire** – supplementary allowance.
- **CONGÉDIEMENT** – **indemnité de congédiement** – compensation for loss (termination) of employment; damages for dismissal; redundancy payment.
- **DÉCÈS** – **indemnité de décès** – death grant.
- **DÉCOUCHER** – **indemnité de découcher (Sw)** – night allowance.
- **DÉFICIT** – see CAISSE above.

- **DÉLAI-CONGÉ** – **indemnité de délai-congé** – payment (compensation) in lieu of notice.
- **DÉMÉNAGEMENT** – **indemnité de déménagement** – removal allowance.
- **DÉPART** – **indemnité de départ** – compensation for loss of employment; redundancy payment; leaving (severance) allowance.
- **DÉPLACEMENT** – **indemnité de déplacement** – travelling and subsistence allowance; relocation (removal, displacement) allowance.
- **DÉPRÉCIATION** – **indemnité de dépréciation** – compensation for wear and tear.
- **DIFFÉRENTIEL** – **indemnité différentielle** – equalisation allowance.
- **ÉLOIGNEMENT** – **indemnité d'éloignement** – expatriation allowance; foreign-service (foreign-residence) allowance.
- **ESPÈCE** – **indemnité en espèces** – compensation in cash.
- **ÉVICTION** – **indemnité d'éviction** – compensation for non-renewal of a business tenancy.
- **EXPATRIATION** – **indemnité d'expatriation** – expatriation allowance; foreign-service (foreign-residence) allowance.
- **EXPERTISE** – **indemnité d'expertise** – fee for an expert opinion; expert witness's fee.
- **EXPROPRIATION** – **indemnité d'expropriation** – compensation for compulsory purchase (expropriation).
- **FAMILIAL** – **indemnité familiale** (Belg) – family allowance.
- **FIN D'ANNÉE** – **indemnité de fin d'année** – Christmas gratuity.
- **FONCTION** – **indemnité de fonction(s)** – official expenditure allowance; acting allowance; duty allowance; allowance for extra duties.
- **FORFAITAIRE** – **indemnité forfaitaire** – lump-sum compensation.
- **FRAIS** – **indemnité pour frais** – expenditure allowance.
  - **DÉPLACEMENT** – **indemnité de frais de déplacement** – travelling and subsistance allowance.
  - **FUNÉRAIRE** – **indemnité pour frais funéraires** – funeral grant; death grant.
  - **PROFESSIONNEL** – **indemnité de de frais professionnels** – professional-expenditure allowance.
  - **ROUTE** – **indemnité de frais de route** – travelling allowance.
  - **SERVICE** – **indemnité de frais de service** – official-expenditure allowance.

- **FUNÉRAIRE** – **indemnité funéraire** (Sw) – funeral grant; death grant.
- **GLOBAL** – **indemnité globale** – general damages; inclusive damages.
- **GROSSESSE** – **indemnité de grossesse** – pregnancy grant.
- **HABILLEMENT** – **indemnité d'habillement** – clothing allowance.
- **HEURE SUPPLÉMENTAIRE** – **indemnité pour heures supplémentaires** – overtime.
- **JOURNALIER** – **indemnités journalières** – sick pay.
- **KILOMÉTRIQUE** – **indemnité kilométrique** – mileage allowance.
- **LICENCIEMENT** – **indemnité de licenciement** – compensation for loss (termination) of employment; damages for dismissal; redundancy payment.
- **LOGEMENT** – **indemnité de logement** – housing allowance; rent allowance.
- **LOUAGE** – **indemnité de louage** – rent allowance.
- **MANQUE À GAGNER** – **indemnité pour manque à gagner** – compensation for loss of earnings.
- **MÉNAGE** – **indemnité de ménage** (Sw) – household allowance.
- **MISE**
  - **ÉQUIPEMENT** – **indemnité de première mise d'équipement** – equipment allowance; capital allowance.
- **NATIONALISATION** – **indemnité de nationalisation** – compensation for nationalisation.
- **NATURE** – **indemnité en nature** – compensation (reparation) in kind.
- **NUIT** – **indemnité de nuit** (Sw) – night allowance.
- **OCCUPATION** – **indemnité d'occupation** – mesne profits.
- **PARLEMENTAIRE** – **indemnité parlementaire** – MP's allowances.
- **PARTIEL** – **indemnité partielle** – partial compensation.
- **PÉCUNIAIRE** – **indemnité pécuniaire** – pecuniary damages.
- **PERSONNEL** – **indemnité de caractère personnel** – strictly personal damages (pain and suffering, aesthetic damage, etc).
- **PERTE**
  - **GAIN** – **indemnité pour perte de gains** – compensation for loss of profit.

•• **SALAIRE** – **indemnité pour perte de salaires** – compensation for loss of wages (earnings).

• **PLUS-VALUE** – **indemnité de plus-value** – compensation for loss of betterment.

• **PRÉAVIS** – **indemnité de préavis** – payment (compensation) in lieu of notice.

• **PREMIÈRE MISE D'ÉQUIPEMENT** – see MISE above.

• **PRÉRÉQUISITION** – **indemnité de préréquisition** – compensation for loss of power of disposal over property reserved for requisition.

• **PRINCIPE** – **indemnité de principe** – nominal damages (compensation).

• **PRIVATION**

•• **JOUISSANCE** – **indemnité pour privation de jouissance** – compensation for loss of enjoyment of property.

• **PROCÉDURE** – **indemnité de procédure** (Belg) – preparation allowance (for preparing a case for trial).

• **PROVISIONNEL** – **indemnité provisionnelle** – provisional compensation.

• **RÉAPPRENTISSAGE** – **indemnité de réapprentissage** – conversion allowance; retraining allowance.

• **RÉINSTALLATION** – **indemnité de réinstallation** – resettlement allowance; relocation (removal, displacement) allowance.

• **RENCHÉRISSEMENT** – **indemnité de renchérissement** (Lux) – cost-of-living allowance.

• **RENVOI** – **indemnité de renvoi** – compensation for loss (termination) of employment; damages for dismissal; redundancy payment.

• **REPRÉSENTATION** – **indemnité de représentation** – entertainment allowance.

• **RÉQUISITION** – **indemnité de réquisition** – compensation for requisitioning.

• **RESPONSABILITÉ** – **indemnité de responsabilité** – liability allowance.

• **RISQUE** – **indemnité de risques** – danger money.

• **ROUTE** – **indemnité de route** (Sw) – travelling allowance.

• **RUPTURE**

•• **ABUSIF** – **indemnité de rupture abusive** – damages for wrongful dismissal.

•• **CONTRAT** – **indemnité de rupture de contrat** – damages for breach of contract.

• **SÉJOUR** – **indemnité de séjour** – subsistence allowance.

• **SINISTRE** – **indemnité de sinistre** – insurance money(s).

• **TÉMOIN** – **indemnité de témoin** – witness's allowance.

• **VIE CHÈRE** – **indemnité de vie chère** – cost-of-living allowance.

• **VOYAGE** – **indemnité de voyage** – travelling allowance.

INDÉPENDANT – self-employed.

INDICATION

• **PIÈCE** – **indication des pièces** – listing of documents (with a view to obtaining discovery).

• **RÉGLEMENTAIRE** – **indications réglementaires** – prescribed details (information).

INDICE – (fact forming the basis of an) inference; (in plural) (circumstantial) evidence; proof by inference from facts; indicia.

• **PONDÉRÉ** – **indice pondéré** – weighted index.

• **PREUVE par indices** – circumstantial evidence.

• **SÉRIEUX** – **indices sérieux** – strong circumstantial evidence.

INDICIAIRE

• **IMPÔT indiciaire** – indicator-based tax; apparent-wealth tax (based on external indications of wealth).

INDIFFÉRENT – irrelevant.

INDIGENCE

• **CERTIFICAT (DÉCLARATION) d'indigence** – certificate of lack of means (financial hardship).

INDIGÈNE – native.

INDIGNE

• **NATIONAL** – **indigne national** – citizen deprived of certain civic rights by way of punishment.

INDIGNITÉ – unfitness.

• **SUCCESSORAL** – **indignité successorale** – unworthiness to inherit.

INDIRECT – consequential.

• **RÈGLES indirectes** – (private international law) choice-of-law rules.

INDIRECTES – Commissioners of Excise; indirect-taxation department.

INDISPONIBILITÉ – status of an object which is not capable of being disposed of.

- **FILIATION** – indisponibilité des actions relatives à la filiation – the right of action relating to descent cannot be waived.
- **PÉNAL** – indisponibilité du procès pénal – rule that the public prosecutor does not exercise discretionary control over the course of criminal proceedings.
- **RÉEL** – indisponibilité réelle – inalienability in rem effective erga omnes; absolute inalienability.

INDISPONIBLE – not capable of being disposed of; which may not be freely disposed of; inalienable.

INDIVIDU
- **EXTRADÉ** – individu extradé – extradited person.

INDIVIDUALISÉ – specially identified (ie in the case of generic goods).

INDIVIDUEL
- **OPINIONS** individuelles – separate opinions; individual opinions.

INDIVIS
- **ACQUÉREURS** indivis – co-purchasers.
- **OBJET** indivis – object in joint ownership.
- **PAR** indivis – in undivided shares.
- **PART** indivise – undivided share.

INDIVISAIRE – owner of an undivided share; joint owner.

INDIVISIBILITÉ – indivisibility.

INDIVISÉMENT – jointly.

INDIVISIBLE – indivisible; (of clause in an illegal contract) not severable.

INDIVISION – ownership in common, each co-owner being notionally entitled to a share; co-ownership; ownership in undivided shares.
- **FORCÉ** – indivision forcée – obligatory co-ownership.
- **FRACTION** – indivision par fractions – tenancy in common.
- **HÉRÉDITAIRE** – indivision héréditaire – co-ownership of an estate (succession); (where apposite) co-parceny.
- **PERPÉTUEL** – indivision perpétuelle – permanent co-ownership.
- **SUCCESSORAL** – indivision successorale – co-ownership of an estate (succession); (where apposite) co-parceny.

INDU – not due; not owing; not reasonable; not justified.

- **PAIEMENT** de l'indu – payment in satisfaction of a non-existent obligation (which gives rise to a right to restitution – money had and received).
- **RÉPÉTITION** de l'indu – action for restitution of money paid (or things transferred) without legal cause (ie when not in fact owing); action for money had and received.
- **RESTITUTION** de l'indu – restitution of money paid (or things transferred) without legal cause.

INDUCTION – inference.

INDÛMENT – unreasonably; unlawfully; without legal cause.
- **PAYÉ** – indûment payé – paid in error; wrongly paid; overpaid.

INÉGALITÉ
- **TRAITEMENT** – inégalité de traitement – unequal treatment; discrimination.

INÉLIGIBLE – not entitled to stand for election.

INEXÉCUTABLE – which cannot be performed or fulfilled; which cannot be executed or enforced; unenforceable.

INEXÉCUTION – failure to perform; breach of contract.

INFAMANT
- **DÉLIT** infamant – dishonourable offence.

INFIRMATION – setting aside (a judgment).

INFIRMER – vary; set aside; reverse; weaken; invalidate; cancel.
- **JUGEMENT** – infirmer un jugement – set aside a judgment.

INFLATION
- **LÉGISLATIF** – inflation législative – plethora (proliferation) of legislation.
- **PÉNAL** – inflation pénale – plethora of criminal legislation.

INFLIGER – impose.
- **PEINE** – infliger une peine – impose (pass) a sentence.

INFORMATION – investigation; inquiry; collection of evidence by the police prior to the judicial (preliminary) investigation; police investigation; police inquiries; but more often used in the sense of **instruction**, ie judicial (preliminary) investigation.

- **COMMODO ET INCOMMODO** – **information de commodo et incommodo** – administrative inquiry to ascertain the possible effects of proposed public works.
- **OUVRIR une information** – commence investigations or a judicial (preliminary) investigation.

INFORMER – conduct or initiate an investigation (inquiry).

- **CONTRE** – **informer contre** – lay an information against; bring proceedings against.
- **ORDRE d'informer** – direction to commence a judicial (preliminary) investigation.

INFRACTION – offence; breach; infringement; violation.

- **ACTE constitutif de l'infraction** – actus reus.
- **COMMETTRE une infraction** – commit an offence.
- **CONCOURS d'infractions** – coincidence of several offences.
  - •• **IDÉAL** – **concours idéal d'infractions** – single act fulfilling the conditions required to constitute various offences; complex action which, though fulfilling the conditions required to constitute various offences, is nevertheless treated as a single offence owing to the presence of some unifying factor; notional plurality of offences.
  - •• **RÉEL** – **concours réel d'infractions** – plurality of offences dealt with in the same proceedings.
- **CONNEXITÉ d'infractions** – close connection or relationship between offences, eg so as to justify their being tried together.
- **CONSTATATION de l'infraction** – finding of guilt.
- **CONSTATATION d'une infraction** – finding (decision) that an offence has been committed.
- **CONSTATER une infraction** – find (decide) that an offence has been committed.
- **CONTINU** – **infraction continue** – continuing offence (eg abduction).
- **CONTINUÉ** – **infraction continuée** – planned series of offences.
- **CORPS de l'infraction** – corpus delicti; object on which a crime has been committed.
- **CUMUL**
  - •• **IDÉAL** – **cumul idéal d'infractions** – position where a single act constitutes more than one offence.

- •• **RÉEL** – **cumul réel d'infractions** – position where the offender has committed several acts each of which constitutes an offence.
- **DISCIPLINAIRE** – **infraction disciplinaire** – disciplinary offence.
- **DISCIPLINE** – **infraction à la discipline** – disciplinary offence.
- **DROIT COMMUN** – **infraction de droit commun** – ordinary offence; non-political offence; ordinary crime.
- **ÉCONOMIQUE** – **infraction économique** – economic offence; business crime.
- **FISCAL** – **infraction fiscale** – tax offence.
- **FLAGRANT** – **infraction flagrante** – offence discovered while it is being committed or immediately afterwards.
- **FORMEL** – **infraction formelle** – acts constituting an offence per se irrespective of their results.
- **INCRIMINÉ** – **infraction incriminée** – offence charged; charge.
- **INTENTIONNEL** – **infraction intentionnelle** – offence requiring proof of criminal intent (mens rea).
- **LOI** – **infraction à la loi** – breach (infringement, violation, contravention) of the law or an Act.
- **MATÉRIEL** – **infraction purement matérielle** – strict-liability offence (not requiring proof of criminal intent (mens rea)).
- **PERMANENT** – **infraction permanente** – instantaneous offence the effects of which continue as a result of the purely passive attitude of the offender (eg bigamy).
- **POLICE** – **infraction de simple police** – summary or petty offence.
- **PRAETERINTENTIONNEL** – **infraction praeterintentionnelle** – deliberate offence with consequences more serious than those contemplated by the offender.
- **PUREMENT MATÉRIEL** – see MATÉRIEL above.
- **RÈGLEMENT** – **infraction au règlement** – administrative offence; regulatory offence.
- **REPROCHÉ** – **infraction reprochée moins grave** – lesser charge.
- **SIMPLE POLICE** – see POLICE above.
- **VIE** – **infractions contre la vie et l'intégrité de la personne** – offences against the person (including homicide).

INGÉRENCE – interference.

INHIBITORIUM – clause in a garnishee order forbidding the judgment debtor to dispose of the debt which has been garnished.

INIMITIÉ – ill-will.

INIQUE – unjust; inequitable; unfair.

INIQUITÉ – injustice; inequity.

INITIAL
- **TEXTE initial** – original text.

INITIATIVE
- **DÉPENSE** – **initiative des dépenses** – right to initiate (introduce) legislation involving expenditure.
- **LÉGISLATIF** – **initiative législative** – right to initiate legislation.
- **LOI** – **initiative des lois** – right to initiate legislation.
- **PARLEMENTAIRE** – **initiative parlementaire** – parliamentary proposal for legislation.
  - •• **DROIT d'initiative parlementaire** – right of members of Parliament to initiate (introduce) legislation.
- **POPULAIRE** – **initiative populaire** – (Sw) request for a referendum; (with reference to Austria) proposal for legislation.

INITIÉ
- **DÉLIT d'initié** – insider dealing (trading).
- **OPÉRATIONS financières par les initiés** – insider dealing (trading).

INJONCTION – order; administrative direction (instruction); injunction.
- **PAIEMENT** – **injonction de paiement** – order to pay.
- **PAYER** – **injonction de payer** – (summary) payment order; order to pay.
- **POUVOIR d'injonction** – power to give directions.
- **PROCÉDURE d'injonction** – administrative enforcement procedure.

IN JUDICANDO – relating to the merits (substance).

INJURE – insult; (vulgar) abuse.
- **GRAVE** – **injures graves** – serious insults.

INJUSTE – wrongful.

INNAVIGABLE – unseaworthy.

INNOMMÉ
- **CONTRAT innommé** – contract not regulated by legislation, but devised by the parties for their specific purposes; innominate contract.

INNOVATION
- **MATÉRIEL** – **innovations matérielles** – physical alterations.

INOBSERVATION – failure to observe (comply with).
- **DÉLAI** – **inobservation du délai** – failure to observe the time-limit.
- **FORME** – **inobservation des formes** – failure to comply with essential formalities (ground for an appeal in law to the Court of Cassation).

INOFFENSIF
- **PASSAGE inoffensif** – innocent passage.

INOPÉRANT – ineffective.

INOPPORTUN – inexpedient; inadvisable; ill-advised.

INOPPOSABLE
- **À** – **inopposable à** – not binding on; which does not affect or prejudice the rights of; void against (eg a trustee in bankruptcy); voidable by; unenforceable against; not effective against; not able to be raised against (raised to defeat).

IN PROCEDENDO – relating to procedure.

INQUISITOIRE – inquisitorial.

INSAISISSABILITÉ – fact (state) of being exempt from (not subject to) execution or attachment; unseizability; freedom from attachment.

INSAISISSABLE – exempt from (not subject to) execution or attachment; unseizable.

INSALUBRITÉ
- **EXPROPRIATION pour cause d'insalubrité** – expropriation on grounds of unfitness for human habitation.

INSCRIPTION – registration; entry; inclusion.
- **COMPTE** – **inscription au compte** – entry in the account.
- **CRÉDIT** – **inscription au crédit** – credit entry.
- **DEMANDE à fin d'inscription** – application for registration.
- **DEMANDE d'inscription à l'ordre du jour** – motion (application, request) for an item to be included in the agenda.

- **DOSSIER** – inscription au dossier – entry on a person's personal file.
- **DROIT** d'inscription – enrolment fee; registration fee.
- **FAUX** – inscription de faux – (independent or interlocutory) civil proceedings to challenge the authenticity of a document or prove it is a forgery.
- **GRAND LIVRE** – see LIVRE below.
- **HYPOTHÉCAIRE** – inscription hypothécaire – registered mortgage.
- **HYPOTHÈQUE** – inscription d'hypothèque – registration of a mortgage; registered mortgage.
- **LIVRE** – inscription sur le grand livre – registered (state) annuity.
- **MARITIME** – inscription maritime – merchant seaman's registry.
- **MODIFICATIF** – inscription modificative – alteration of an entry in the register.
- **ORDRE DU JOUR** – inscription à l'ordre du jour – inclusion in the agenda.
- **PRÉALABLE** – inscription préalable – caution, ie an entry in the register to protect a contractual right to the transfer of an interest in land.
- **PROCÈS-VERBAL** – inscription au procès-verbal – inclusion in the record.
- **REGISTRE**
  - **COMMERCE** – inscription au registre du commerce – registration in the commercial registry (register).
  - **FONCIER** – inscription au registre foncier – registration in the land registry.
- **RENOUVELLEMENT** – inscription de renouvellement – renewal of registration of a mortgage.
- **RENTE** – inscription de rente – registered (state) annuity.
- **RÔLE** – inscription au rôle – entry in the list (of cases).

INSCRIRE – enter.
- **COMPTE** – inscrire au compte – enter in the account.
- **FAUX** – s'inscrire en faux – plead that a document is a forgery.

INSCRIT – person whose rights are entered in the register.
- **MARITIME** – inscrit maritime – registered seaman.

INSCRIVANT – person applying for registration.

INSÉCURITÉ
- **DROIT** – insécurité du droit – uncertainty of the law.
- **JURIDIQUE** – insécurité juridique – uncertainty of the law.

INSERTION – advertisement (in a newspaper, gazette, etc).

INSIGNE
- **SOUVERAINETÉ** – insigne de souveraineté – emblem of sovereignty; national emblem.

IN SOLIDUM
- **OBLIGATION** in solidum – type of restricted joint and several liability which applies, eg, in the case of joint tortfeasors or persons jointly liable on a bill of exchange. It does not include the effects based on the presumed mutual agency of the co-obligors.

INSOLVABILITÉ – insolvency.

INSOLVABLE – insolvent; unable to meet one's commitments as they arise.

INSOUMIS – person failing to report for duty; person refusing to perform military service.

INSOUMISSION – failure to report for duty; refusal to perform military service; non-compliance.
- **NÉGLIGENCE** – insoumission par négligence – negligent failure to report for duty.
- **ORDONNANCE** – insoumission à une ordonnance – non-compliance with an order.

INSPECTEUR – detective sergeant.
- **DIVISIONNAIRE** – inspecteur divisionnaire – detective chief inspector.
- **PRINCIPAL** – inspecteur principal – detective inspector.

INSPECTION
- **FINANCE** – inspection des finances – Treasury control; the Treasury.
- **LOCAL** – inspection locale (Sw) – inspection of the premises; visit to the locus (in quo).
- **MARITIME** – inspection maritime (Belg) – merchant seamen's registry.

INSTANCE – court; tribunal; level of proceedings; (first or last) instance; authority; level of jurisdiction; proceedings.
- **ACTE** introductif d'instance – writ; originating procedure.

- **ADMINISTRATIF** – **instance administrative** – (higher or lower) administrative level.
- **APPEL** – **instance d'appel** – appeal (appellate) court (tribunal, authority).
- **ARBITRAGE** – **instance d'arbitrage** – arbitral tribunal; arbitrator(s); arbitration.
- **ARBITRAL** – **instance arbitrale** – arbitral tribunal; arbitrator(s); arbitration.
- **CAUSES en instance** – pending cases.
- **CIVIL** – **instance civile** – civil proceedings.
- **COMMERCIAL** – **instance commerciale** – commercial proceedings.
- **CONTRÔLE** – **instance de contrôle** – supervising authority.
- **COURS** – **au cours de l'instance** – during the proceedings.
- **DÉCLARATION**
  - •• **DÉCÈS**– **instance en déclaration judiciaire de décès** – proceedings for declaration of death; application for a judicial declaration of death.
- **DÉNONCER l'instance** – give third-party notice; give notice of proceedings.
- **DÉNONCIATION d'instance** – third-party notice; notice of proceedings.
- **DÉPENSES de l'instance** – costs.
- **DERNIER** – **dernière instance** – last instance.
- **DÉSISTEMENT d'instance** – withdrawal or discontinuance of the proceedings only (not implying waiver of one's right of action).
- **DEUX instances** – courts of first instance and appeal.
- **DEVANT toutes les instances** – at every stage in the proceedings.
- **DIVORCE**
  - •• **DE** – **être en instance de divorce** – be engaged in divorce proceedings.
  - •• **EN** – **instance en divorce** – divorce proceedings.
- **ENGAGÉ** – **instance déjà engagée** – pending proceedings.
- **EN instance** – pending; awaiting trial or judgment.
- **EXEQUATUR** – **instance en exequatur** – application for authority to enforce a foreign judgment.
- **FORMALISME** – **le formalisme de l'instance** – the (procedural) formalities.
- **INTERMÉDIAIRE** – **instance intermédiaire** – intermediate court (tribunal, authority).
- **INTRODUCTION de l'instance** – commencement of (the) proceedings.

- **JUDICIAIRE** – **instance judiciaire** – court; judicial authority.
- **JUGEMENT en première instance** – decision at first instance.
- **JUSTICE** – **instance en justice** – action; court proceedings.
- **LIEN (juridique) d'instance** – procedural relationship (situation).
- **LIER l'instance** – begin the preparations for trial; commence proceedings.
- **MOMENT** – **à tout moment de l'instance** – at any stage of the proceedings.
- **OCCASION** – **à l'occasion d'une instance** – in the course of proceedings.
- **PÉNAL** – **instance pénale** – criminal court; criminal proceedings.
- **PRIMITIF** – **instance primitive** – original proceedings.
- **PRINCIPAL** – **instance principale** – main proceedings.
- **RECOURS**
  - •• **DE** – **instance de recours** – appeal (appellate) court (tribunal, authority).
  - •• **EN** – **instance en recours** – appeal proceedings.
- **RÉFÉRÉ** – **instance en référé** – summary application to a single judge for an interim order in an urgent case; urgent application (summons, motion).
- **REQUÊTE introductive d'instance** – writ; statement of claim; petition (eg in divorce); (original) application; originating summons.
- **RÉVISION** – **instance en révision** – retrial (proceedings).
- **SUPÉRIEUR** – **instance supérieure** – higher court (instance, tribunal, authority).
- **SUPRÊME** – **instance suprême** – highest court (instance, tribunal, authority).

INSTANTANÉ

- **CONTRAT instantané** – contract of immediate execution.

INSTIGATEUR – instigator; abettor; accessory (before the fact); person who incites.

INSTIGATION – incitement.

INSTITUER – prescribe; fix; appoint.
- **HÉRITIER** – **instituer un héritier** – appoint an heir.

INSTITUTION – special (set of) rules governing a specific area of the law; doctrine; figure of law; rule(s); institution; authority.

- **ASSISTANCE** – institution d'assistance – welfare institution (authority).
- **BIENFAISANCE** – institution de bienfaisance – charitable institution.
- **COMPENSATION** – institution de compensation – clearing-house.
- **COMPÉTENT** – institution compétente – (social security) competent institution.
- **CONTRACTUEL** – institution contractuelle – contractual appointment of an heir; contract without consideration disposing of one's estate on death.
- **CRÉDIT** – institution de crédit – financial institution.
- **DROIT INTERNATIONAL** – les institutions de droit international s'intéressant à l'homme – the rules of international law concerning the individual.
- **ÉDUCATION**
  - •• **SURVEILLÉ** – institution d'éducation surveillée – reformatory.
- **HÉRITIER** – institution d'héritier – appointment of an heir.
- **JUDICIAIRE** – institution judiciaire – judicial authority.
- **JURIDIQUE** – institution juridique – special set of rules governing a specific area of the law; doctrine; figure of law; legal rule(s); legal construction.
- **LIBRE** – institution libre – private school.
- **PARAÉTATIQUE** – institution paraétatique – semi-public institution.
- **PRÉVOYANCE** – institution de prévoyance – friendly society; provident society.
- **SOCIAL** – institution sociale – social-service institution (department, corporation); welfare institution.
- **UTILITÉ PUBLIQUE** – institution d'utilité publique – institution promoting the public interest; charitable institution.

INSTRUCTEUR

- **MAGISTRAT** instructeur – investigating judge.

INSTRUCTION – instruction; direction; directive; (crim) (judicial) investigation; examination; committal proceedings; (crim) inquiry into the facts; (civ) preparatory (interlocutory) stages of the proceedings; (civ) preparation (of a case) for trial.

- **ACTE** d'instruction – measure of investigation (investigative measure) taken or ordered by the investigating judge; procedural step in preparation for trial.

- **CHARGE ET DÉCHARGE** – instruction à charge et décharge – investigation of the cases for the prosecution and the defence.
- **CODE** d'instruction criminelle – Code of Criminal Procedure.
- **COMPLÉMENT** d'instruction – further investigations; further inquiries (into the facts).
- **DEGRÉ** – instruction à deux degrés – investigation by both the investigating judge and thereafter the Indictments Chamber (compulsory in all cases of felony (**crime**)).
- **DEMANDE** – instruction des demandes de permis – procedure for granting licences.
- **DISCIPLINAIRE** – instruction disciplinaire – disciplinary investigation.
- **IMPÉRATIF** – instruction impérative – mandatory instruction (direction).
- **INTERPRÉTATIF** – instruction interprétative – interpretative provision.
- **MESURE** d'instruction – measure of investigation (investigative measure); procedural step in preparation for trial; procedural measure (eg for preserving or establishing evidence).
  - •• **FUTURUM** – mesure d'instruction in futurum – order (measure ordered) to facilitate possible future proceedings, eg by preserving evidence.
  - •• **ORDONNER** des mesures d'instruction – (civ) give (procedural) directions; (crim) order investigations (inquiries into the facts).
- **MINISTÉRIEL** – instruction ministérielle – ministerial direction (circular).
- **PARTICULIER** – instruction particulière – individual instruction (directive).
- **PÉNAL** – instruction pénale – investigation of a criminal offence.
- **PRÉLIMINAIRE (PRÉPARATOIRE, PRÉALABLE)** – instruction préliminaire (préparatoire, préalable) – preliminary (judicial) inquiry; preliminary (judicial) investigation.
- **SERVICE** – instruction de service – service regulation; standing order; administrative instruction.

INSTRUIRE – investigate; inquire into an offence; try; (civ) prepare a case for trial.

- **DOSSIER** – instruire le dossier – prepare the case file; conduct the investigation (inquiry).

INSTRUMENT – instrument (in the sense of a document).

INSTRUMENTER – prepare (draw (up)) an officially recorded document.

INSUBORDINATION – disobedience.

INSUFFISANCE – shortfall.

- **ACTIF** – **insuffisance d'actif** – deficiency of assets.
- **ASSURANCE** – **insuffisance d'assurance** – underinsurance.
- **ÉVALUATION** – **insuffisance d'évaluation** – undervalue.
- **PROVISION** – **insuffisance de la provision** – insufficient cover.
- **RECETTE** – **insuffisance de recettes** – income shortfall; income deficiency.

INSULTE – insult; defamation; abuse; insulting language.

INSURGÉ – insurgent.

INSUSCEPTIBLE

- **RECOURS** – **insusceptible de (voie de) recours** – against which no appeal lies; not subject to appeal.

INTÉGRITÉ – integrity; inviolability (of territory, the person, premises, etc); sanctity (of the home).

- **PERSONNE**
  - **ATTEINTE à l'intégrité de la personne** – (assault causing) bodily harm.
  - **INFRACTIONS contre la vie et l'intégrité de la personne** – offences against the person (including homicide).
- **PHYSIQUE** – **atteinte à l'intégrité physique** – (assault causing) bodily harm.
  - **MORAL** – **atteinte à l'intégrité physique ou morale** – physical or psychological duress.
- **PHYSIQUE** – **droit à l'intégrité physique et morale** – right to protection from physical and mental injury.
- **PHYSIQUE** – **mettre en danger l'intégrité physique de** – constitute a threat to the person of.

INTELLIGENCE

- **ENNEMI** – **intelligences avec l'ennemi** – collusion (being in communication) with the enemy.
- **PUISSANCE ÉTRANGÈRE** – **intelligences avec (des agents d')une puissance étrangère** – being in communication with agents of a foreign power.

INTEMPESTIF

- **RECOURS intempestif** – misconceived application.

INTENTER

- **ACTION** – **intenter une action** – bring an action.

INTENTION – intention; intent; purpose; criminal intent to injure (damage).

- **COMMUN** – **intention commune** – joint (common) purpose.
- **COUPABLE** – **intention coupable** – mens rea; (guilty) intent.
- **CRIMINEL** – **intention criminelle** – felonious intent.
- **DÉLICTUEUX** – **intention délictueuse** – intent to commit an offence; criminal intent.
- **DOLOSIF** – **intention dolosive** – tortious intent.
  - **AVEC intention dolosive** – deliberately.
- **DOMMAGE** – **intention de causer un dommage** – intention to injure (damage).
- **FRAUDULEUX** – **intention frauduleuse** – intent to deceive (defraud); bad faith.
- **LETTRE d'intention** – letter of intent.
- **LIBÉRAL** – **intention libérale** – intention of making a gift; animus donandi.
- **NUIRE** – **intention de nuire** – intention to injure.

INTENTIONNEL – intentional; deliberate.

INTERDICTION – prohibition; rule forbidding; guardianship; declaration of legal incapacity; disqualification; injunction to restrain.

- **DEMANDE en interdiction** – application for an administration order and guardianship (for a person incapable of managing his own affairs); application for a person to be declared of unsound mind (declaration of legal incapacity).
- **DROIT d'interdiction** – the right to prohibit.
- **DROIT** – **interdiction des droits de l'article 42** – disqualifications in section 42.
- **JUDICIAIRE** – **interdiction judiciaire** – deprivation of legal capacity; guardianship (order).
- **LÉGAL** – **interdiction légale** – statutory disabilities imposed on conviction for certain offences; statutory disability of convicts.

- **LEVER** l'interdiction – terminate the guardianship order; terminate the state of legal incapacity; discharge the injunction.
- **MAINLEVÉE** d'interdiction – termination of a guardianship order; order terminating a state of legal incapacity; discharge of an injunction.
- **MOTIF** d'interdiction – reason for a prohibition.
- **RÉSIDENCE** – interdiction de résidence – order forbidding a person to reside in a particular area or areas; residence prohibition.
- **SÉJOUR** – interdiction de séjour – order forbidding a person to enter a particular area or areas.
- **ZONE** d'interdiction – prohibited area.

INTERDIT – person deprived of legal capacity; subject to (under) guardianship; person officially declared insane (of unsound mind).
- **LÉGAL** – interdit légal – person subject to penal incapacity.
- **SÉJOUR** – interdit de séjour – person forbidden to enter a particular area or areas.

INTÉRÊT
- **AGIR** – intérêt pour agir – capacity to take part in legal proceedings; standing; locus standi; interest enabling the person concerned to take or defend legal proceedings.
- **ARRIÉRÉ** des intérêts – arrears of interest.
- **ARRIÉRÉ** – intérêts arriérés – arrears of interest.
- **AVANCE** sans intérêt – interest-free loan.
- **CIVIL** – intérêt civil – civil claim; private-law claim.
- **COLLECTIF** – intérêts collectifs de la profession – the interests of the profession as a whole.
- **COMMUN** – intérêt commun – public (general) interest.
- **COMPENSATOIRE** – intérêts compensatoires – interest allowed as damages for breach of contract etc.
- **COMPOSÉ** – intérêts composés – compound interest.
- **CONSOLIDÉ** – intérêts consolidés – compound interest.
- **CONTRACTUEL** – intérêt contractuel – interest due under a contract or agreement; agreed interest.
- **CONVENTIONNEL** – intérêt(s) conventionnel(s) – interest due under a contract or agreement; agreed interest.
- **CONVENU** – intérêt convenu – interest due under a contract or agreement; agreed interest.
- **CORPORATIF** – intérêts corporatifs – professional interests.
- **COURS** – le cours de leurs intérêts s'arrête – interest ceases to run.
- **COURU** – intérêts courus – accrued interest.
- **CRÉANCE** d'intérêt – claim for interest.
- **DÉBITEUR** – intérêts débiteurs (au compte des profits et pertes) d'un fonds – interest owing to the fund.
- **DÉFAUT** d'intérêt – absence of any (legitimate) interest.
- **ÉCHU** – intérêt(s) échu(s) – interest due; accrued interest.
- **ÉVENTUEL** – intérêt éventuel – contingent interest.
- **EXEMPT** d'intérêt – interest-free.
- **GROUPE** – intérêts hors groupe – minority interests.
- **INVOQUER** un intérêt moral – claim a non-material interest.
- **JURIDIQUE** – intérêt (d'ordre) juridique – legal interest; legitimate interest.
- **LÉGAL** – intérêt légal – statutory (rate of) interest.
- **LÉGITIME** – intérêt légitime – legally protected interest.
- **LITIGIEUX** – intérêt litigieux – sum involved (in litigation).
- **MAJEUR** – intérêt majeur – overriding interest.
- **MORATOIRE** – intérêt(s) moratoire(s) – interest for delay; default interest.
- **NÉ ET ACTUEL** – intérêt né et actuel – existing pecuniary interest.
- **NOMINAL** – taux d'intérêt nominal – nominal interest.
- **PLACEMENT** à intérêt – interest-bearing investment.
- **PORTER** intérêt – bear interest.
- **PRIVÉ** – la nullité est d'intérêt privé – the (procedural) defect is not a matter of public policy (ie the proceedings are not void but only voidable).
- **PROMESSE** d'intérêt – undertaking to pay interest.
- **PUBLIC** – d'intérêt public – of (serving the) public (general) interest; charitable.
- **REMISE** d'intérêts – waiver of interest.
- **SERVIR** des intérêts – make interest payments; service a loan.
- **SPHÈRE** d'intérêt – sphere of influence.

- STATUTAIRE – **intérêt statutaire** – interest due under the statutes.
- STIPULATION **des intérêts** – provision for interest; interest clause.
- STIPULÉ – **intérêt stipulé** – agreed interest.
- SUPPRESSION **des intérêts** – cancellation of interest.
- TAUX **d'intérêt** – rate of interest.
  - NOMINAL – **taux d'intérêt nominal** – nominal interest.
- USUAIRE – **intérêt usuaire** – unconscionable rate of interest.

INTERGROUPE – inter-party group of MPs.

INTÉRIM – period during which an office is held by an acting office holder.
- AD **intérim** – acting.
- PAR **intérim** – acting.

INTERJETER
- APPEL – **interjeter appel** – appeal; lodge an appeal; give (enter) notice of appeal.

INTERLOCUTOIRE – interlocutory (interim, preliminary) decision.

INTERMÉDIAIRE – mediator; negotiator; intermediary; agent; middleman.
- DROIT **intermédiaire** – transitional law; revolutionary law (covering the period between 1789 and the Code Napoléon); the law applying in an intermediate period.
- RÉGIME **intermédiaire** – (prisons) intermediate treatment.

INTERNE
- DROIT **interne** – domestic (municipal, national, internal) law.

INTERNEMENT – (preventive) detention; (political) internment; (medical) confinement (in a mental hospital).
- ADMINISTRATIVE – **internement administrative** – restrictions on freedom of movement imposed by the administration (house arrest, internment, etc).
- ASILE – **internement dans un asile** – detention (confinement) in a mental hospital (asylum).
- MAISON **d'internement** – mental hospital; asylum.
- ORDRE **d'internement** – detention order; internment order.
- SÛRETÉ – **internement de sûreté** – preventive detention, ie detention of habitual offenders for the protection of the public.

INTERNONCE – internuncio.

INTERPELLANT – person asking a parliamentary question.

INTERPELLATEUR – person asking a parliamentary question.

INTERPELLATION – parliamentary question; notice; summons; member of parliament's right to introduce a debate (with a limited number of speakers) on a matter of general interest.
- DROIT **d'interpellation** – right to put parliamentary questions.

INTERPELLER – stop and question.

INTERPOSITION
- PERSONNE – **interposition de personne(s)** – position where a transaction ostensibly for the benefit of one person is in fact for the benefit of another; use of an intermediary.

INTERPRÉTATION
- AGRÉÉ – **interprétation agréée** – agreed interpretation (construction).
- ANALOGIE – **interprétation par voie d'analogie** – interpretation by (way of) analogy.
- CONVENU – **interprétation convenue** – agreed interpretation (construction).
- DOCTRINAL – **interprétation doctrinale** – interpretation (construction) supported by leading writers.
- ÉVOLUTIF – **interprétation évolutive** – progressive (evolutive) interpretation by the courts.
- EXTENSIF – **interprétation extensive** – broad (liberal) interpretation.
- JURISPRUDENTIEL – **interprétation jurisprudentielle** – judicial interpretation; interpretation by the courts.
- LÉGAL – **interprétation légale** – statutory interpretation, ie interpretation by a subsequent statute.
- LIBÉRAL – **trouver une interprétation plus libérale** – be interpreted more widely.
- RESTRICTIF – **interprétation restrictive** – strict (narrow) interpretation.
- STRICT – **interprétation stricte** – strict (narrow) interpretation; rule forbidding courts to extend the meaning of a criminal statute.

- **SYSTÉMATIQUE** – **interprétation systématique de la convention** – interpretation of the convention as a whole.
- **TÉLÉOLOGIQUE** – **interprétation téléologique** – teleological (purposive) interpretation, ie based on the purpose or intention of the enactment.

INTERPRÈTE
- **DROIT** de l'interprète – performer's right (copyright).
- **JURÉ** – **interprète juré** – sworn interpreter.

INTERPRÉTER – construe.

INTERROGATOIRE – examination.
- **FAITS ET ARTICLES** – **interrogatoire sur faits et articles** – (formerly) examining a party to civil proceedings on interrogatories.
- **FOND** – **interrogatoire sur le fond** – examination (questioning) on the merits (the subject-matter).
- **IDENTITÉ** – **interrogatoire d'identité** – examination to establish identity; examination (questioning) as to one's personal particulars.
- **PUBLIC** – **interrogatoire public** – public examination.

INTERROGER – examine; question; interrogate.

INTERROMPRE
- **PRESCRIPTION** – **interrompre la prescription** – interrupt the running of the limitation or prescription period (after which time begins to run afresh, ie the whole period recommences from the beginning).

INTERRUPTION – interruption (after which time begins to run afresh).
- **CIVIL** – **interruption civile** – legal interruption of prescription, ie interruption resulting from some legal act or transaction.
- **DÉLAI** – **interruption des délais** – interruption of the limitation or prescription period, after which time begins to run afresh, ie the whole period recommences from the beginning. (Cf SUSPENSION.)
- **INSTANCE** – **interruption de l'instance** – interruption of the proceedings, eg on the death of a party, change of counsel, etc, before the beginning of the hearing.
- **NATUREL** – **interruption naturelle** – factual interruption of prescription, eg by loss of possession.
- **PRESCRIPTION** – **interruption de la prescription** – interruption of the limitation or prescription period, after which time begins to run afresh, ie the whole period recommences from the beginning. (Cf SUSPENSION.)
- **SÉANCE** – **interruption de la séance** – interruption of the sitting.

INTERSESSION – period between two sessions; parliamentary recess.

INTERVALLE
- **LUCIDE** – **intervalle lucide** – lucid interval.

INTERVENANT – acceptor for honour; acceptor supra protest; intervening party; intervener; party applying to be joined to the proceedings.
- **ACCESSOIRE** – **intervenant accessoire** – person applying to be joined to proceedings as joint plaintiff or joint defendant.

INTERVENTION – intervention in proceedings; application to be joined to proceedings; acceptance for honour.
- **ACCEPTANCE par intervention** – acceptance for honour.
- **ACCESSOIRE** – **intervention accessoire** – application to be joined to proceedings as joint plaintiff or joint defendant.
- **DEMANDE en intervention** – application to be joined to proceedings.
- **FORCÉ** – **intervention forcée** – third-party notice; joinder of a third party.
- **PRINCIPAL** – **intervention principale** – application by a third party claiming ownership of the subject-matter of pending proceedings.
- **PROTÊT** – **intervention à protêt** – payment supra protest.
- **VOLONTAIRE** – **intervention volontaire** – application to be joined to proceedings; intervention in proceedings.

INTERVERSION
- **PRESCRIPTION** – **interversion de la prescription** – substitution of the general limitation period of thirty years for a shorter period after the latter has been interrupted by an acknowledgement etc.
- **TITRE** – **interversion de titres** – position where a person not previously holding in his own right now claims to do so in order to take advantage of prescription.

INTESTAT – see AB INTESTAT.

INTIMATION – service of notice of appeal on a respondent.

INTIME
- **CONVICTION** – **intime conviction** – reasonable conviction; reasonable certainty; state of being satisfied beyond reasonable doubt (personally convinced); personal conviction of the court (after considering all the evidence).

INTIMÉ – respondent; defendant.

INTITULÉ
- **JUGEMENT** – **intitulé du jugement** – heading of a judgment.

INTRANSMISSIBLE – not negotiable.
- **HÉRITAGE** – **intransmissible par voie d'héritage** – non-inheritable.

INTRA VIRES – expression indicating that an heir (legatee, partner) is not liable to pay debts except to the extent of the assets he has actually received from the estate etc. (NB not the sense in which the Latin term is used in English law.)

INTRINSÈQUE
- **PREUVE intrinsèque** – proof based on the instrument itself; proof appearing on the face of the document.

INTRODUCTIF
- **ACTE introductif d'instance** – writ; originating procedure.

INTRODUCTION
- **ACTION** – **introduction de l'action** – commencement of the action ((the) proceedings).
- **DEMANDE** – **introduction d'une demande** – making an application.
- **INSTANCE** – **introduction de l'instance** – commencement of (the) proceedings.
- **LOI d'introduction** – Introductory Act.
- **PREUVE** – **introduction des preuves** (Sw) – submission of evidence.

INTRODUIRE – lodge; file; bring; commence; take (proceedings).
- **ACTION** – **introduire une action** – commence an action (proceedings).
- **INSTANCE** – **introduire une instance** – commence (take) proceedings.
- **RECOURS** – **introduire un recours** – enter an appeal; take proceedings.

INTUITUS
- **PECUNIAE** – **intuitus pecuniae** – with a view to a pecuniary interest.

- **PERSONAE** – **intuitus personae** – personal relationship; involving consideration of the person.

INVALIDATION – declaration that an election etc. is invalid (void).
- **DEMANDE d'invalidation** – election petition.

INVALIDE – disabled person.
- **GRAND invalide** – severely disabled person.

INVALIDER – declare invalid (void).

INVALIDITÉ – disablement; invalidity; permanent incapacity to work; voidness; nullity.
- **ASSURANCE invalidité** – disablement insurance.
- **COMPLET** – **invalidité complète** – total disablement.
- **DEGRÉ d'invalidité** – degree of disablement.
- **PENSION d'invalidité** – disablement pension.
- **RENTE d'invalidité** – disablement pension.
- **RETRAITE d'invalidité** – disablement pension.

INVENTAIRE – inventory; taking of an inventory; statement of assets and liabilities.
- **LIVRE d'inventaires** – balance-sheet book.

INVENTEUR – finder of treasure trove or lost property.

INVENTION
- **BREVET d'invention** – patent.
- **BREVETABLE** – **invention brevetable** – patentable invention.
- **BREVETÉ** – **invention brevetée** – patented invention.
- **DROITS d'invention** – inventor's rights.
- **PERFECTIONNEMENT d'invention** – improvement.
- **SERVICE** – **invention faite dans le service** – employee's invention.

INVESTIR
- **DE** – **investi de** – exercising; endowed with.

INVESTISSEMENT
- **BIENS d'investissement** – capital goods; items of equipment.
- **ENCOURAGEMENT aux investissements** – investment incentives.

INVESTITURE – nomination of a candidate by a political party.

- **SCRUTIN d'investiture** – (formerly) vote in the National Assembly confirming the appointment of a Prime Minister by the President.

INVIOLABILITÉ

- **DOMICILE** – inviolabilité du domicile – inviolability of a person's residence; sanctity of the home.
- **PARLEMENTAIRE** – inviolabilité parlementaire – parliamentary immunity (from prosecution for offences not connected with parliamentary functions).

INVITATION

- **PAYER** – invitation à payer – summons to pay; request for payment.

INVITER

- **COMPARAÎTRE** – inviter à comparaître – summon to appear.

INVOLONTAIRE – unintentional.

- **BLESSURES involontaires** – unintentional injuries.
- **HOMICIDE involontaire** – unintentional homicide; manslaughter.

INVOQUER – rely on; plead; raise; put forward; cite; pray in aid.

- **COMPENSATION** – le débiteur doit invoquer la compensation – the debtor etc must plead the set-off.
- **DROIT** – invoquer un droit – rely on a right.

IRATO – see AB IRATO.

IRRACHETABLE – irredeemable.

IRRECEVABILITÉ – inadmissibility.

IRRECEVABLE – inadmissible.

- **DÉFENSE** – à peine d'être déclaré irrecevable dans sa défense – if he is not to be estopped from defending the proceedings.

IRRÉCOUVRABLE – irrecoverable.

IRRÉCUSABLE – not liable to be challenged.

IRRÉFRAGABLE – irrefragable; irrebuttable; impossible to refute.

IRRÉGULARITÉ – incorrectness; the fact of not being in proper form or not complying with (statutory) requirements; (procedural) defect; (in plural) misconduct.

- **FOND** – irrégularité de fond – essential defect (rendering proceedings void).
- **FORME** – irrégularité de forme – failure to satisfy formal requirements; formal defect.
- **SUBSTANTIEL** – irrégularité substantielle – essential (material) defect.

IRRÉGULIER – not in accordance with requirements; not in order; defective; inadmissible; unauthorised; unlawful.

- **SITUATION** – qui se trouve en situation irrégulière – not satisfying the requirements (in breach) of the law (statute, regulations, etc).

IRRÉMÉDIABLE – (breakdown of marriage) irretrievable.

IRRESPONSABILITÉ – freedom from (absence of) liability; (crim) absence of responsibility; absence of guilt.

- **CLAUSE d'irresponsabilité** – exemption clause; clause excluding liability.
- **PARLEMENTAIRE** – irresponsabilité parlementaire – parliamentary immunity for votes and words spoken in Parliament.
- **PÉNAL** – irresponsabilité pénale – absence of criminal responsibility; legal irresponsibility.

IRRESPONSABLE – not liable; not responsible for one's actions.

IRRÉTRACTABLE – irrevocable.

IRRÉVOCABLE – irrevocable.

ISOLÉ – (MP) independent.

ISOLEMENT

- **CELLULAIRE** – isolement cellulaire – solitary (cellular) confinement (detention).

ISOLÉMENT – by itself.

ISOLOIR – polling-booth.

ISSUE – egress; access.

- **VOIE PUBLIQUE** – issue insuffisante à la voie publique – insufficient access to the highway.

J

JARDIN
- **FAMILIAL** – **jardin familial** – allotment.
- **OUVRIER** – **jardin ouvrier** – allotment.

JAUGE – tonnage (burden) of a ship.

JAUGEAGE – measurement of a ship.

JET
- **IMMONDICE** – **jet d'immondices** – throwing filth (rubbish).
- **MER** – **jet à la mer** – jettison.

JETON
- **MONNAIE** – **jeton de monnaie** – coin; money token.
- **PRÉSENCE** – **jeton de présence** – (eg director's) attendance fee.

JEU – gaming.
- **BÉNÉFICE du jeu** – winnings.
- **DETTE de jeu** – gaming debt.
- **ÉCRITURE** – **jeu d'écritures** – transfer of entries.
- **HASARD** – **jeu de hasard** – game of chance.

JOINDRE
- **FOND** – **joindre au fond** – join to the merits.

JONCTION – joinder.
- **CAUSE** – **jonction de causes** – joinder of cases (actions).
- **DEMANDE** – **jonction de demandes** – joinder of cases (actions).
- **INSTANCE** – **jonction d'instances** – joinder of cases (actions).
- **POSSESSION** – **jonction de possessions** – joinder of successive periods of possession.

JOUIR – enjoy ((the benefit of) the rents and profits of property).
- **DROIT** – **jouir d'un droit** – exercise (have the benefit of) a right.
- **PÈRE DE FAMILLE** – **jouir en bon père de famille** – (obligation imposed on a tenant or hirer) to use rented etc property without damaging it, ie to keep the premises in good condition, fair wear and tear excepted.

JOUISSANCE – enjoyment; benefit; rents and profits of; right to receive the periodical (or other) produce of property either in kind or indirectly, having transferred the direct enjoyment to another; right to enjoy.
- **ABUS de jouissance** – excessive exploitation of a usufruct; waste; misuse.
- **ACTION de jouissance** – share whose capital has been repaid (on drawing of lots) but which is still entitled to dividends etc.
- **BON de jouissance** – certificate giving a right to a share in profits or on liquidation or to subscribe for shares; participation certificate (not identical with a **bon de participation**).
- **COMMUN** – **jouissance commune** – joint possession.
- **DROIT de jouissance** – right to use and enjoy property; usufruct; beneficial interest; right to rents and profits; right to receive dividends without the corresponding voting rights.
- **DROIT** – **jouissance d'un droit** – enjoyment of a right.
- **ENTRÉE en jouissance** – taking possession; entry on (commencement of the enjoyment of) the benefits, fruits, rents and profits of property; entry into possession (of a usufruct).
- **ENTRER en jouissance** – take (enter into) possession.
- **LÉGAL** – **jouissance légale** – parent's statutory right to child's income from property.
- **PAISIBLE** – **jouissance paisible et utile** – peaceful possession; lawful possession.
- **PERTE de jouissance** – loss of enjoyment; loss of possession.

JOUR – window or aperture admitting light and air but not allowing of a view. (Cf VUE.)
- **AMENDE** – **jour-amende** – day-fine.
- **AUDIENCE** – **jour d'audience** – day of trial (hearing).
- **CHÔMÉ** – **jour chômé** – non-working day.
- **ÉCHÉANCE** – **jour d'échéance** – due date; maturity.
- **FÉRIÉ** – **jour férié** – public holiday.
- **FIXE** – **assignation à jour fixe** – fixed-date proceedings.
- **FRANC** – **jour franc** – clear day (period of 24 hours starting at the beginning of the next day).

- **GRÂCE** – jour de grâce – day of grace.
- **OUVRABLE** – jour ouvrable – working day.
- **PLANCHE** – jour de planche – lay day.
- **RÉFÉRENCE** – jour de référence – appointed day; relevant day.
- **RETARD** – jour de retard – day late.
- **SOUFFRANCE** – jour de souffrance – closed window admitting light but not air.
- **TIRAGE** – jour de tirage – day of the draw.
- **TOLÉRANCE** – jour de tolérance – closed window admitting light but not air.
- **UTILE** – jour utile (Sw) – working day.

JOURNAL
- **ANNONCE**
  - •• **LÉGAL** – journal d'annonces légales – (official) gazette; newspaper carrying official announcements.
- **BORD** – journal de bord – ship's log.
- **OFFICIEL** – journal officiel – official gazette.

JUDICATURE – judicial office.

JUDICIAIRE – the judiciary; the courts; judicial; of the courts; appointed by the court; of the ordinary courts; court (adj).
- **FONCTION** judiciaire – judicial office; legal office; legal functions. (The term includes the office of prosecutor as well as that of judge in certain contexts.)
- **POLICE** judiciaire – (criminal) police (the adjective is usually unnecessary in English as the term "police" does not as in France extend to other administrative departments); criminal investigation department. (The term also includes other persons, such as mayors, who have certain functions in connection with the repression of crime.)
  - •• **OFFICIER** de police judiciaire – senior police officer, mayor, prefect, etc entitled to exercise special powers in connection with the repression of crime; senior law-enforcement officer.
- **PROTECTION** judiciaire – (court) protection order.

JUDICIARISATION – bringing (a matter) within the jurisdiction of the courts.

JUGE – judge; court.
- **AD HOC** – juge ad hoc – judge or court appointed to hear a specific case; ad hoc judge or court.
- **ADJOINT** – juge adjoint – additional judge (eg in special constitutional proceedings).

- **APPLICATION** – juge de l'application – see PEINE below.
- **A QUO** – juge a quo – court appealed against; court below.
- **ARBITRE** – juge-arbitre – arbitrator.
- **ASSESSEUR** – juge assesseur – (non-presiding) judge; judge acting as an assessor on a board or commission.
- **AUXILIAIRE** – juge auxiliaire – assistant (auxiliary) judge.
- **CANTONAL** – juge cantonal – (formerly) district judge (court); (Sw) cantonal judge (court).
- **CARRIÈRE** – juge de carrière – professional judge; legally qualified judge.
- **CIVIL** – juge civil – civil court(s) or judge.
- **COMMERCE** – juge de commerce – (non-professional) commercial judge; Commercial Court.
- **COMMERCIAL** – juge commercial – (non-professional) commercial judge; Commercial Court.
- **COMMIS** – juge commis – judge taking evidence on commission or performing some other function at the request of another court.
- **COMMISSAIRE** – juge commissaire – judge taking evidence on commission or performing some other function at the request of another court; bankruptcy judge.
- **CONCILIATEUR** – juge conciliateur – judge presiding over conciliation proceedings.
- **CONSULAIRE** – juge consulaire – (judge of the) Commercial Court.
- **DEGRÉ** – juge du deuxième degré – higher court; appeal court.
- **DÉLÉGUÉ** – juge délégué – member of a court entrusted with a particular task (eg hearing evidence) by the president of the court.
- **DÉPARTITEUR** – juge départiteur – judge with a casting vote.
- **DEUXIÈME DEGRÉ** – see DEGRÉ above.
- **DEVANT** ses juges – before the court.
- **DISCIPLINAIRE** – juge en matière disciplinaire – chairman or member of a disciplinary tribunal or committee; judge deciding on a disciplinary matter.
- **DROIT COMMUN** – juge de droit commun – ordinary court.
- **ENFANT** – juge des (pour) enfants – (judge of the) youth court (formerly juvenile court); children's judge.

- **EXÉCUTION** – **juge de l'exécution** – judge of the Regional Court with jurisdiction to decide questions relating to the execution of civil judgments; execution(s) judge.
- **EXPROPRIATION** – **juge de l'expropriation** – judge responsible for fixing the compensation payable on compulsory purchase.
- **EXTRAORDINAIRE** – **juge extraordinaire** (Sw) – special court or judge.
- **FAILLITE** – **juge de la faillite** – bankruptcy judge; bankruptcy court.
- **FAIT** – **juge du fait** – court deciding on the facts; lower court; trial court; court assessing the facts; tribunal of fact.
- **FOND** – **juges du fond** – trial and appeal courts; courts below.
- **GRAND juge** (Sw) – court president.
- **HONORAIRE** – **juge honoraire** – unremunerated or retired judge.
- **INSTANCE** – **juge d'instance** – district judge (court).
  - **GRAND** – **juge de grande instance** – (judge of the) Regional Court.
  - **PREMIER** – **juge de première instance** – court of first instance; (Belg) (judge of the) Regional Court.
- **INSTRUCTION** – **juge d'instruction** – investigating judge; examining judge.
  - **MILITAIRE** – **juge d'instruction militaire** – investigating officer; judge advocate.
- **JUDICIAIRE** – **juge judiciaire** – ordinary court(s).
- **LIVRE FONCIER** – **juge du livre foncier** – Land Registry judge.
- **MATRIMONIAL** – **juge délégué aux affaires matrimoniales (JAM)** – judge with jurisdiction for divorce by consent and ancillary matters in matrimonial causes.
- **MILITAIRE** – **juge militaire** – member of a court martial; judge advocate.
- **MISE EN ÉTAT** – **juge de la mise en état** – judge (master) directing (in charge of) preparations for trial.
- **NATUREL** – **juge naturel** – pre-existing court, as opposed to a court established ad hoc to try a particular case; court which would lawfully exercise jurisdiction over a person; lawful judge; judge established (appointed, specified) by (the) law; statutory judge; rightful judge; normal judge; lawfully established court; regular judge.
- **ORDRE** – **juge aux ordres** – judge responsible for supervising the distribution of the proceeds of sale between the mortgagees or other preferential creditors.
- **PAIX** – **juge de paix** – (formerly) district judge (court).
- **PEINE** – **juge de l'application des peines** – judge responsible for the execution of sentences.
- **PÉNAL** – **juge pénal** – criminal court(s) or judge.
- **POLICE** – **juge de simple police** – judge exercising summary jurisdiction; court of summary jurisdiction.
- **PREMIER juge** – court below; trial court.
- **RAPPORTEUR** – **juge rapporteur** – reporting judge (ie judge who prepares a report on a case for a court); (in the Commercial Court) judge who directs preparations for trial.
- **RÉCUSÉ** – **juge récusé** – judge who has been challenged, eg for bias.
- **RÉFÉRÉ** – **juge des référés** – urgent applications judge (with jurisdiction to make interim orders and issue injunctions).
- **RÈGLEMENT de juges** – procedure for settling conflicts of jurisdiction between different courts in criminal matters.
- **RÉPRESSIF** – **juge répressif** – criminal court(s) or judge.
- **REQUIS** – **juge requis** – judge taking evidence on commission or performing some other function at the request of another court.
- **RÉSIDENT** – **juge résident** – judge who never sits away from his own court.
- **SIMPLE POLICE** – see POLICE above.
- **SUPPLÉANT** – **juge suppléant** – substitute judge.
- **TRIBUNAL MILITAIRE** – **juge au tribunal militaire** – judge advocate.
- **TUTELLE** – **juge des tutelles** – guardianship judge.
- **UNIQUE** – **juge unique** – single judge.

JUGE-ARBITRE – arbitrator.

JUGEMENT – judgment; trial; decision; proceedings.

- **ABSOLUTION** – **jugement d'absolution** – conviction without punishment; discharge (after conviction).
- **ACCORD** – **jugement d'accord** – consent judgment; consent order.
- **ACQUITTEMENT** – **jugement d'acquittement** – acquittal.

- **ACTION en déclaration de jugement commun** – third-party notice.
- **ADJUDICATION** – jugement d'adjudication – allocation of property.
- **ANNULER un jugement** – set a judgment aside.
- **APPEL** – jugement d'appel – appeal judgment; judgment on appeal.
- **APPELER d'un jugement** – appeal against a judgment.
- **ARBITRAIRE** – jugement arbitraire – arbitrary decision.
- **ARBITRAL** – jugement arbitral – (arbitral) award.
- **ATTAQUÉ** – jugement attaqué – judgment appealed against.
- **ATTAQUER un jugement** – appeal against a judgment.
- **AUDIENCE de jugement** – reading of the judgment.
- **AVANT DIRE (FAIRE) DROIT** – see DROIT below.
- **CHOSE JUGÉE** – jugement passé en force de chose jugée – final judgment.
- **CIVIL** – jugement civil – civil judgment, decision or proceedings.
- **COLLECTIF** – jugement collectif – judgment or proceedings affecting a number of persons.
- **COMMERCIAL** – jugement commercial – judgment in a commercial case; commercial decision.
- **COMMINATOIRE** – jugement comminatoire – order containing a revocable penalty for non-compliance with its terms.
- **COMMUN** – jugement commun – judgment binding on a party who has been joined to the proceedings by third-party notice.
- **CONDAMNATION** – jugement de condamnation – conviction and sentence.
- **CONFIRMATIF** – jugement confirmatif – judgment upholding (confirming, affirming) the decision of the court below.
- **CONFLIT de jugements** – procedure whereby a litigant can obtain a decision from the Jurisdiction Court (**Tribunal des conflits**) when there have been conflicting judgments by the ordinary and the administrative courts.
- **CONSTITUTIF** – jugement constitutif – judgment in rem, effective erga omnes (creating or altering status).
  - •• **DROIT** – jugement constitutif de droit – judgment altering (ie creating, terminating or varying) the rights of the parties, eg divorce.
  - •• **ÉTAT** – jugement constitutif d'état – judgment in rem (effective erga omnes, creating or altering status).
- **CONTENTIEUX** – jugement contentieux – judgment in contentious proceedings.
- **CONTRADICTOIRE** – jugement contradictoire – judgment after hearing the (both) parties; proceedings in which both parties are heard.
- **CONTRARIÉTÉ de jugements** – conflicting (incompatible) judgments (if they are in the same case, this constitutes a ground for an appeal in law to the Court of Cassation); procedure whereby a litigant can obtain a decision from the Jurisdiction Court (**Tribunal des conflits**) when there have been conflicting judgments by the ordinary and the administrative courts.
- **CONTUMACE** – jugement par contumace – judgment concerning or trial of a serious indictable offence (felony) in absentia; conviction in absentia in proceedings for felony.
- **CONVENU** – jugement convenu – consent judgment, decree or order.
- **CORRECTIONNEL** – jugement correctionnel – judgment concerning or trial of a lesser indictable offence (misdemeanour); criminal judgment; criminal trial.
- **DÉCLARATIF** – jugement déclaratif (de droit) – declaratory judgment.
  - •• **ABSENCE** – jugement déclaratif d'absence – judgment establishing that a person has disappeared and cannot be traced.
  - •• **DÉCÈS** – jugement déclaratif de décès – declaration of death.
  - •• **FAILLITE** – jugement déclaratif de faillite – adjudication in bankruptcy.
  - •• **FILIATION** – jugement déclaratif de filiation – judgment establishing descent.
  - •• **NAISSANCE** – jugement déclaratif de naissance – judgment establishing date of birth.
  - •• **NULLITÉ** – jugement déclaratif de nullité – judgment establishing nullity; judgment declaring (a transaction, contract, etc) void; (marriage) decree of nullity.
- **DÉCLARATOIRE** – jugement déclaratoire (de droit) – declaratory judgment.

- **DÉFAUT** – jugement par défaut – (civ) judgment in default; default judgment; (crim) judgment in absentia.
- **DÉFINITIF** – jugement définitif – final judgment.
- **DERNIER RESSORT** – see RESSORT below.
- **DISPOSITIF** d'un jugement – (formal) order (setting out the effect of a judgment); operative words (provisions) (of a judgment).
- **DIVORCE** – jugement de divorce – decree of divorce.
- **DONNER (DONNÉ) ACTE** – jugement de donner (donné) acte – (judgment confirming the) entry of a fact in the record.
- **DROIT** – jugement avant dire (faire) droit – interlocutory decision or order.
- **EN-TÊTE** du jugement – heading of the judgment.
- **ERRONÉ** – jugement erroné – erroneous judgment.
- **ESTER** en jugement – take part in court proceedings; appear and plead before a court.
- **ÉTAT** – jugement d'état – judgment in rem (effective erga omnes, creating or altering status).
- **ÉTRANGER** – jugement rendu à l'étranger – foreign judgment; judgment of a foreign court.
- **EXCLUSION** – jugement d'exclusion – order excluding claims not lodged within the appointed time.
- **EXÉCUTION** du jugement – enforcement of the judgment.
- **EXÉCUTOIRE** – jugement exécutoire – enforceable judgment, order or sentence.
- **EXEQUATUR** – jugement d'exequatur – (decision conferring) authority to enforce (execute).
- **EXPÉDIENT** – jugement d'expédient – consent judgment, order or decree.
- **EXPÉDITION** du jugement – execution copy of the judgment.
- **EXPROPRIATION** – jugement d'expropriation – expropriation order; compulsory purchase order.
- **FAILLITE** – jugement de faillite – adjudication in bankruptcy.
- **FINAL** – jugement final – final judgment.
- **FOND** – jugement au fond – judgment on the merits.
- **FORCE** – jugement passé en force (Sw) – final judgment.
- **FORCLUSION** – jugement de forclusion – order excluding claims not lodged within the appointed time.
- **GRACIEUX** – jugement gracieux – decision in non-contentious proceedings (sometimes on an ex parte application).
- **HOMOLOGATION** – jugement d'homologation – order confirming or approving.
- **INCIDENT** – jugement sur incident – interlocutory order.
- **INFIRMER** un jugement – set aside a judgment.
- **INSTANCE** – jugement en première instance – judgment, trial or proceedings at first instance.
- **INTERDICTION** – jugement d'interdiction – order depriving a person of his legal capacity; guardianship order; order declaring a person legally incapable.
- **INTERLOCUTOIRE** – jugement interlocutoire – interlocutory order.
- **INTERPRÉTATIF** – jugement interprétatif – judgment interpreting a previous judgment.
- **IRRÉVOCABLE** – jugement irrévocable – final judgment; irrevocable judgment.
- **JONCTION** – jugement de jonction – order for the joinder of proceedings.
- **JURIDICTION** de jugement – trial court.
- **LEVER** un jugement – obtain a copy of the judgment endorsed with authority to execute; obtain the execution copy of the judgment; obtain a writ of execution (endorsed on the judgment).
- **MINUTE** du jugement – original judgment signed by the registrar and the president of the court. (The copy for execution is called the **grosse**.)
- **MIXTE** – jugement mixte – final interlocutory judgment, eg a judgment which decides the question of liability and appoints an expert to assess the damages.
- **OBTENIR** un jugement – obtain a judgment.
- **OPPOSITION** – jugement frappé d'opposition – judgment in default which the defendant has applied to set aside; judgment subject to an application to set aside.
- **PASSÉ EN FORCE** – see FORCE above.
  - •• **CHOSE JUGÉE** – see CHOSE JUGÉE above.
- **PÉNAL** – jugement pénal – criminal judgment; criminal trial.
- **PIÈCE** – jugement sur pièces – judgment given on the pleadings (on the written evidence, on the file).

- **PREMIÈRE INSTANCE** – see INSTANCE above.
- **PREMIER RESSORT** – see RESSORT below.
  - **DERNIER** – see RESSORT below.
- **PRENDRE un jugement** – obtain a judgment.
- **PRÉPARATOIRE** – **jugement préparatoire** – interlocutory order.
  - **ABSENCE** – **jugement préparatoire d'absence** – intermediate order in proceedings to declare that a person has disappeared and cannot be traced; tracing order.
- **PRONONCÉ du jugement** – reading (giving, delivery) of a judgment.
- **PROVISOIRE** – **jugement provisoire** – judgment ordering a provisional or procedural measure; interlocutory judgment or order.
- **RADIATION** – **jugement de radiation** – striking out.
- **RECEVABILITÉ** – **jugement sur la recevabilité** – decision on admissibility.
- **RÉCOGNITIF** – **jugement récognitif** – judgment based on the defendant's admission of the plaintiff's claim.
- **RECONNAISSANCE D'ÉCRITURE** – **jugement de reconnaissance d'écriture** – judgment incorporating the defendant's recognition of the genuineness of a document or signature.
- **RÉFORMATION d'un jugement** – setting aside, (partial) alteration (variation, rectification) or reversal of a judgment (by a higher court).
- **RÉFORMATOIRE** – **jugement réformatoire** – decision varying the judgment of the court below.
- **RELAXE** – **jugement de relaxe** – acquittal.
- **RENDRE un jugement** – give or deliver a judgment.
  - **MAL** – **jugement mal rendu** – erroneous judgment.
- **RENVOI** – **jugement de renvoi** – order transferring the proceedings.
- **REPORT DE LA FAILLITE** – **jugement de report de la faillite** – retrospective adjudication in bankruptcy.
- **RÉPRESSIF** – **jugement répressif** – criminal judgment.
- **RESCINDANT** – **jugement du rescindant** – (formerly) judgment declaring an application for retrial admissible.
- **RÉSOLUTION** – **jugement de résolution** – judgment setting aside (annulling) a contract.
- **RESSORT**
  - **DERNIER** – **jugement en dernier ressort** – judgment against which no appeal lies; judgment, trial or proceedings at last instance; last-instance decision.
  - **PREMIER** – **jugement en premier ressort** – judgment, trial or proceedings at first instance; first-instance decision.
  - **PREMIER ET DERNIER** – **jugement en premier et dernier ressort** – judgment, trial or proceedings at first instance against which no appeal lies.
- **SÉPARATION DE CORPS** – **jugement de séparation de corps** – decree of judicial separation.
- **SIGNIFICATION du jugement** – service of the judgment (by a bailiff).
- **TRANSLATIF DE PROPRIÉTÉ** – **jugement translatif de propriété** – court order transferring ownership.
- **VALIDITÉ** – **jugement de validité** – judgment confirming the validity of a garnishee order (ie an attachment of a debt) and transferring the title to the debt to the attaching creditor.
- **VÉRIFICATION D'ÉCRITURE** – **jugement de vérification d'écriture** – decision on the genuineness of a document (in contentious proceedings).

JUGER

- **ÉQUITÉ** – **juger en équité** – decide on equitable principles (ex aequo et bono).
- **FAIRE** – **entendre faire juger** – seek a ruling that.
- **FOND** – **juger au fond** – decide on the merits.
- **PIÈCE** – **juger sur pièces** – decide (a matter) on the pleadings (on the written evidence, on the file).

JURÉ – juryman; member of the jury; (in plural) jury.

- **EXPERT** – **juré-expert** – (sworn) expert witness.
- **SUPPLÉANT** – **juré suppléant** – substitute juryman.

JURIDICITÉ – (of a problem etc) amenability to being settled by legal means; legal nature.

JURIDICTION – court; jurisdiction; tribunal.

- **ADMINISTRATIF** – juridiction administrative – administrative court; administrative jurisdiction; the administrative courts.
- **APPEL** – juridiction d'appel – appeal (appellate) court.
- **ARBITRAL** – juridiction arbitrale – arbitration tribunal; arbitration.
- **ATTRIBUTION** – juridiction d'attribution – administrative court with specialised jurisdiction.
- **AVOIR** juridiction – have or exercise jurisdiction.
- **BORD** – juridiction de bord – maritime (naval) court martial.
- **CAPITULAIRE** – juridiction capitulaire – exterritorial or consular jurisdiction formerly exercised in Turkey, Morocco, China, etc.
- **CIVIL** – juridiction civile – civil court; civil jurisdiction; the civil courts.
  - •• **ORDRE** des juridictions civiles – the civil courts.
- **COLLÉGIAL** – juridiction collégiale – bench of judges; court; full court.
- **COMMERCIAL** – juridiction commerciale – commercial court; commercial jurisdiction; the commercial courts.
- **COMPÉTENCE** de pleine juridiction – power to make any order required by the justice of a case (to deal with all aspects of a case).
- **COMPÉTENT** – juridiction compétente – court having jurisdiction; competent court.
- **CONFLIT** de juridictions – conflicting decisions relating to jurisdiction (conflict of jurisdiction), ie where two different courts both claim or decline to exercise jurisdiction to decide a case; conflict of jurisdiction between the courts of two or more different countries.
- **CONSTITUTIONNEL** – juridiction constitutionnelle – jurisdiction to decide questions of constitutional law; constitutional jurisdiction.
- **CONSULAIRE** – juridiction consulaire – commercial court; commercial jurisdiction; the commercial courts; (formerly) consular court (jurisdiction).
- **CONTENTIEUX** – juridiction contentieuse – contentious jurisdiction.
- **CORPORATIF** – juridiction corporative – jurisdiction of a professional (disciplinary) tribunal.
- **CORRECTIONNEL** – juridiction correctionnelle – criminal court (for offences of medium gravity); criminal jurisdiction.

- **CRIMINEL** – juridiction criminelle – criminal court (for the most serious offences); criminal jurisdiction.
- **DEGRÉ**
  - •• **DOUBLE** – (garantie du) double degré de juridiction – right of appeal to a higher court (this guarantees a complete rehearing, including admission of fresh evidence, arguments, etc).
  - •• **SECOND** – juridiction de second degré – court with jurisdiction to hear appeals; appeal court.
- **DISCIPLINAIRE** – juridiction disciplinaire – disciplinary court, tribunal or committee; disciplinary jurisdiction.
- **DROIT COMMUN** – juridiction de droit commun – ordinary court; ordinary jurisdiction; the ordinary courts.
- **ENFANT** – juridiction pour enfants – youth court; (formerly) juvenile court.
- **ÉTRANGER** – juridiction étrangère – foreign court.
- **EXCEPTION** – juridiction d'exception – (1) court of limited jurisdiction; specialised court, ie any court other than the **Tribunal de grande instance** and the Court of Appeal, eg the **tribunal d'instance**, the **tribunal de commerce**, and the **conseil de prud'hommes**; (2) specialised criminal court, eg the **juridictions pour mineurs**, the **tribunaux aux armées** and the **Haute Cour de justice**; (3) (Belg) special court (ie set up to deal with an individual case or cases).
- **EXTRATERRITORIAL** – juridiction extraterritoriale – extraterritorial jurisdiction.
- **FINANCIER** – juridiction financière – court exercising jurisdiction in tax matters; tax court.
- **FISCAL** – juridiction (en matière) fiscale – jurisdiction in tax matters.
- **GRACIEUX** – juridiction gracieuse – non-contentious jurisdiction.
- **HONNEUR** – juridiction d'honneur – court of honour; disciplinary (professional) tribunal; jurisdiction of such a court or tribunal.
- **IMMUNITÉ** de juridiction – immunity from jurisdiction; immunity from legal proceedings.
- **INCOMPÉTENT** – juridiction incompétente – court without (lacking) jurisdiction; incompetent court.

- **INSTRUCTION** – **juridiction d'instruction** – the investigating courts (ie the investigating judge and the Indictments Chamber).
- **INTERNATIONAL** – **juridiction internationale** – international court or tribunal; international jurisdiction.
- **INTERNE** – **juridiction interne** – domestic court.
- **JUDICIAIRE** – **juridiction judiciaire** – ordinary court; ordinary jurisdiction; the ordinary courts.
- **JUGEMENT** – **juridiction de jugement** – trial court; court trying (hearing) the case.
- **MARITIME** – **juridiction maritime** – admiralty court; admiralty jurisdiction; the admiralty courts.
- **MILITAIRE** – **juridiction militaire** – court martial; jurisdiction in military matters.
- **OBLIGATOIRE** – **juridiction obligatoire** – compulsory jurisdiction.
- **OCCUPATION** – **juridiction d'occupation** – occupation court; jurisdiction of the occupation courts.
- **ORDRE**
  - •• **ADMINISTRATIF** – **juridiction de l'ordre administratif** – administrative court.
  - •• **JUDICIAIRE** – **juridiction de l'ordre judiciaire** – ordinary court.
- **PÉNAL** – **juridiction pénale** – criminal court; criminal jurisdiction; the criminal courts.
- **PLEIN**
  - •• **COMPÉTENCE de pleine juridiction** – power to make any order that may be required by the justice of a case (to deal with all aspects of a case).
  - •• **RECOURS de pleine juridiction** – application to an administrative court to find that the applicant is entitled to a claim against the state or to set aside or vary an administrative act which does not fall within the scope of an action for misuse or abuse of authority (**excès de pouvoir**) (usually a contract with a public authority); application to an administrative court for damages or recognition and enforcement of a right; administrative-law action.
- **PLÉNITUDE de juridiction** – power to make any order that may be required by the justice of a case (to deal with all aspects of a case); power of the ordinary courts in certain cases to hear matters falling within the jurisdiction of the specialised courts; (used

of a court of appeal) indicates that if a case which was wrongly brought before the Commercial Court instead of the ordinary court comes before the Court of Appeal, the error is deemed to be cured once the appeal has been decided by the Court of Appeal. (The same applies to felonies (**crimes**) which the Assize Court holds to be misdemeanours (**délits**).)

- •• **JOUIR** – **jouissant de la plénitude de la juridiction** – competent to deal with all aspects of a case.
- **POUVOIR de juridiction** – the judiciary (the courts) (in the theory of the separation of the powers).
- **PROFESSIONNEL** – **juridiction professionnelle** – professional tribunal; jurisdiction of a professional tribunal.
- **PROROGATION (volontaire) de juridiction** – extension of a court's ordinary jurisdiction (by agreement of the parties).
- **PRUD'HOMAL** – **juridiction prud'homale** – industrial tribunal(s); labour court(s); jurisdiction of such tribunals (courts).
- **RELEVER d'une juridiction** – to fall under or within (be subject to) the jurisdiction of a court or other authority.
- **RENVOI** – **juridiction de renvoi** – court to which a case is referred or transferred for hearing and decision.
- **RÉPRESSIF** – **juridiction répressive** – Criminal Court; criminal jurisdiction.
- **SAISI** – **juridiction saisie** – court dealing with a case (before which a case has been brought); court in which proceedings are pending.
- **SPÉCIAL** – **juridiction spéciale** – special court.
- **VOLONTAIRE** – **juridiction volontaire** – non-contentious proceedings.

JURIDICTIONNEL – judicial; relating to jurisdiction; jurisdictional; relating to courts other than the ordinary courts; quasi-judicial.

- **DÉCISION d'ordre juridictionnel** – quasi-judicial decision, eg by a disciplinary committee.
- **PROCÉDURE juridictionnelle** – judicial or quasi-judicial proceedings; legal proceedings.

JURIDIQUE – legal.

- **CONSEIL juridique** – legal adviser; legal representative; legal assistance.

- **NORME** juridique – rule of law; legal rule.
- **ORDRE** juridique – legal system (order); branch of law.
- **PROTECTION** juridique – access to (protection of) the courts; legal protection.
- **RÉGIME** juridique – rules governing.
  - •• **PARTICULIER** – **régime particulier juridique** – special legal arrangements; special rules.

JURIDIQUEMENT
- **CONTRAIGNANT** – **juridiquement contraignant** – legally binding.

JURIMÉTRIE – jurimetrics (use of scientific methods to study legal questions).

JURISCONSULTE – jurist; legal adviser.

JURISDICTIO – the courts' judicial (as opposed to their administrative) functions.

JURIS ET DE JURE – (of a presumption) absolute (irrebuttable, irrefutable).

JURISPRUDENCE – case-law; established precedents; decided cases; decisions; previous (earlier) decisions; leading cases; line of authority; authorities; line of cases; the courts; judicial doctrine; position adopted by the courts.
- **ADMINISTRATIF** – **jurisprudence administrative** – the decisions of the administrative courts.
- **ALLEMAND** – **jurisprudence allemande** – the German courts.
- **CAS** de jurisprudence – leading case; precedent; authority.
- **CONSTANT** – **jurisprudence constante** – established precedents; long line of decisions (decided cases).
  - •• **ABSOLUMENT** – **la jurisprudence est absolument constante en ce sens** – the precedents are unanimous on this point; this is unanimously confirmed by the courts; the courts have consistently so held.
- **DOMINANT** – **jurisprudence dominante** – the prevalent opinion; the balance of judicial opinion; most authorities.
- **ÉTABLI** – **jurisprudence bien établie** – well-established line of decisions.
- **ÉVOLUTIF** – **jurisprudence évolutive** – progressive (evolutive) interpretation by the courts.
- **FAIRE** jurisprudence – establish a precedent.
- **INTERNATIONAL** – **jurisprudence internationale** – the decisions (doctrine) of

international courts; international precedents (case-law).
- **RECUEIL** de jurisprudence – law reports; collection of decisions.
- **RELATIF** – **jurisprudence relative à** – the cases on.
- **RENVERSEMENT (REVIREMENT) de jurisprudence** – (decision making a) change of (in) judicial doctrine or policy; new line of decisions; new precedent; reversal of precedent; departure from (abandonment of) existing precedents (previously established doctrine).
- **TOURNANT** de jurisprudence – turning-point in the doctrine of the courts (in the case-law).

JURISPRUDENTIEL
- **INTERPRÉTATION jurisprudentielle** – judicial interpretation; interpretation by the courts.
- **TENDANCE jurisprudentielle** – line or trend of judicial reasoning, doctrine or practice; the courts have inclined to the view.

JURIS TANTUM – (of a presumption) rebuttable (refutable).

JURISTE – lawyer; legal expert.

JURY
- **EXPROPRIATION** – **jury d'expropriation** – (former) tribunal to fix the amount of compensation to be paid for expropriated property; expropriations valuation tribunal.
- **HONNEUR** – **jury d'honneur** – court of honour; professional disciplinary committee.
- **JUGEMENT** – **jury de jugement** – jury (which decides both the question of guilt and the sentence to be imposed).

JUSTICE – the courts; the judicial system; justice.
- **ACTION** en justice – action; legal proceedings.
- **ACTIONNER** en justice – sue; bring an action or (legal) proceedings against.
- **ADMINISTRATIF** – **justice administrative** – the administrative courts; administrative jurisdiction.
- **AGIR** en justice – bring legal proceedings.
- **ALLER** en justice – bring legal proceedings.
- **ASSIGNATION** en justice – issuing a summons or writ against; bringing proceedings against.

- **ASSIGNER (ATTAQUER) en justice** – sue; issue a summons or writ against; bring proceedings against.
- **AUTORISATION de justice** – permission of (authorisation by) the court; leave of the court.
- **AUTORITÉ** – **par autorité de justice** – by the court.
- **BON** – **bonne justice** – proper administration of justice.
- **CITATION en justice** – writ; (originating) summons; subpoena; summons (to appear before the court).
- **CIVIL** – **justice civile** – the civil courts; civil jurisdiction.
- **CODE de justice militaire** – Army Act; Military Criminal Code.
- **CONSIGNATION en justice** – payment into court; placing in the custody of the court.
- **CRIMINEL** – **justice criminelle** – the Criminal Courts; criminal jurisdiction.
- **DÉCISION de justice** – court decision; judgment; court order.
- **DÉFENDRE en justice** – defend (legal proceedings).
- **DÉLÉGUÉ** – **justice déléguée** – delegated jurisdiction.
- **DEMANDE en justice** – writ; action; proceedings; statement of claim; claim.
- **DÉNI de justice** – refusal to do justice; refusal to decide a case; (more generally) miscarriage of justice; denial of justice.
- **DÉNONCER en justice** – report to the prosecuting authorities.
- **DÉPÔT en justice** – lodging in court or payment into court or according to the directions of the court; placing in the custody of the court.
- **DESCENTE de justice** – inspection of the premises (by the court); visit to the locus (in quo).
- **EMPÊCHER que justice ne soit faite** – impede the course of justice.
- **ESTER en justice** – take part in court proceedings; appear and plead before a court.
- **FAIRE**
  - •• **GRIEF** – **faire justice d'un grief** – remedy (redress) a complaint.
  - •• **SE faire justice à soi-même** – take the law into one's own hands.

- **FONCTIONNEMENT de la justice** – course of justice; functioning (operation) of the judicial system.
  - •• **SEREIN** – **fonctionnement serein de la justice** – proper (unimpeded, smooth) operation of the courts.
- **MARCHE** – **bonne marche de la justice** – due course of justice; proper functioning of the judicial system.
- **RAPPORTER** – **s'en rapporter à la justice du tribunal** – leave the matter to the discretion of the court.
- **RENDRE la justice** – do justice.
- **SÉRÉNITÉ** – **troubler la sérénité de la justice** – interfere with the proper conduct of proceedings.
- **TRANSPORT de justice** – inspection of the site, locus (in quo), scene of the crime or premises by the court.

JUSTICIABILITÉ – state of being able to be enforced by the courts; enforceability.

JUSTICIABLE – subject to the jurisdiction of the courts; litigant; the public; plaintiff; defendant; person on trial.
- **ACCÈS des justiciables aux tribunaux** – public access to the courts.
- **APPEL** – **justiciable de l'appel** – subject to appeal.

JUSTIFIABLE
- **VOIE de recours** – **justifiable de cette voie de recours** – subject to this remedy.

JUSTIFICATIF – supporting document.

JUSTIFICATION – proof; evidence; vouchers; reasons.
- **FORMALITÉ** – **justification de l'accomplissement de la formalité** – proof (evidence) that the formality (requirement) has been complied with.
- **ORDONNANCE de justification** – show cause order.

JUSTIFIÉ
- **RAPPORT justifié** – report stating reasons.

JUSTIFIER – establish; prove.
- **PROCURATION** – **à condition de justifier d'une procuration** – if he is able to produce (show he possesses) an authority.
- **TITRE** – **justifier par titres** – produce documentary evidence (to establish) that.

—

L

LABEL – term for certain trade marks belonging to an association or other group of persons.

LACÉRATION
- **AFFICHE** – lacération d'affiches – damaging notices or posters.

LACUNE
- **DROIT** – lacune de droit – lacuna (gap, omission) in the law; matter not provided for by law; absence of legal provision; (legal) loophole.

LAÏC – secular; non-denominational.

LAIS
- **RELAIS** – lais et relais de la mer – land formed by the gradual action of the sea, alluvion (alluvio maris). (This becomes the private property of the state.)

LAISSE
- **MER** – laisse de basse mer – lowest line of ebb tide.

LAISSÉ-POUR-COMPTE – term used to describe goods in carriage that have been so damaged that they can no longer be used: the carrier must pay their full value in damages and the consignee is entitled to refuse delivery; left on hand; refused.

LAISSEZ-PASSER – (in particular) pass for the transport of certain wines and spirits on which tax is not due; cart note; transire.

LARCIN – theft.

LATITUDE – discretion.

LECTURE – reading; delivery.
- **ADOPTER** – être adopté en première lecture – be given a first reading.

LÉGAL – in accordance with law; legal; based on law; prescribed by law; statutory.
- **HYPOTHÈQUE** légale – statutory mortgage; statutory charge.
- **PSYCHIATRE** légal – court (ie appointed by the court) psychiatrist.
- **PSYCHIATRIE** légale – forensic psychiatry.
- **VOIE** – selon les voies légales – in accordance with a procedure prescribed by law; through prescribed channels.

LÉGALEMENT – by operation of law; legally; lawfully.
- **ADMISSIBLE** – légalement admissible – which the law allows.

LÉGALISATION – certification that the signatures appended to a document are genuine and that the persons signing hold the offices they purport to hold; authentication; (in the case of documents from abroad or intended for use abroad) legalisation.

LÉGALISER – give statutory form to.

LÉGALISTE – legalistic; formalistic.

LÉGALITÉ – legality; lawfulness.
- **POURSUITE** – légalité des poursuites – mandatory (compulsory) prosecution; legal basis for or requirement of prosecution.
- **PRINCIPE de (la) légalité** – rule requiring conformity with statute; strict compliance with the law; rule of law; obligatory prosecution; rule requiring that offences and punishments shall be strictly defined by law.
- **VEILLER au respect de la légalité** – ensure compliance with the law.

LÉGATAIRE – legatee or devisee or person entitled to a share of an estate.
- **PARTICULIER** – légataire à titre particulier – person entitled to an individual legacy, ie a specific or pecuniary legacy or a devise.
- **UNIVERSEL** – légataire universel – person to whom a testator leaves the whole or a share of his estate, possibly subject to legacies; universal legatee; residuary legatee. (If a universal legatee or the persons entitled to the reserved portions (**héritiers réservataires**) disappear, the remaining universal legatees become entitled to his or their share(s).)
  - **TITRE** – légataire à titre universel – person to whom the testator bequeathes or devises a share of his estate. (Such a share may be a share of the whole, all the real property, all the movables, a share of the real property or a share of the movables.)

LÉGATION – seat of a diplomatic mission.

- **DROIT**
  - **ACTIF** – **droit de légation actif** – right to send diplomatic missions to other states.
  - **PASSIF** – **droit de légation passif** – right to receive diplomatic missions from other states.

LEGE FERENDA – legislative policy.

LEGE LATA – existing law.

LÉGIFÉRER – legislate.

LÉGISLATEUR – this term is used more frequently than "legislator" in English. It may sometimes be translated as: Act; regulations; legislation; legislature; Parliament.

LÉGISLATIF – legislative (does not normally include subordinate legislation, ie regulations etc); statutory.
- **TEXTES législatifs** – statute law; legislation (usually excluding subordinate legislation).
- **TEXTES législatifs ou réglementaires** – statutes and regulations.

LÉGISLATION – legislation (does not normally include subordinate legislation, ie regulations etc).
- **CHANGE** – **législation sur le contrôle des changes** – exchange-control legislation.
- **EXCEPTION** – **législation d'exception** – emergency legislation.
- **INTERNE** – **législation interne** – national (internal, domestic) legislation.
- **NATIONAL** – **législation nationale** – national (internal, domestic) legislation.
- **OCCUPATION** – **législation d'occupation** – occupation law.
- **PÉNAL** – **législation pénale** – criminal legislation.
- **RÉGLEMENTATION** – **législation et réglementation** – statutes and regulations.
- **SOCIAL** – **législation sociale** – welfare legislation.
- **STUPÉFIANT** – **législation sur les stupéfiants** – legislation on dangerous drugs (narcotics).
- **SUBSIDIAIRE** – **législation subsidiaire de caractère générale** – delegated legislation of general application.
- **TARIFAIRE** – **législation tarifaire** – legislation on collective agreements.

LÉGISLATURE – legislature; period for which a parliament is elected; life of a parliament.

LÉGISTIQUE – science of preparing legislation; legal or parliamentary drafting (draughtsmanship).

LÉGITIMATION – legitimation; authority.
- **ADOPTIF** – **légitimation adoptive** – prior to 1966 (in France) a form of adoption giving the adopted child a status more akin to that of a child born in wedlock than an ordinary adoption.
- **JUDICIAIRE** – **légitimation par voie judiciaire** – legitimation by order of the court; judicial legitimation.
- **MARIAGE** – **légitimation par mariage subséquent** – legitimation by subsequent marriage. In France it is necessary that the child should have been recognised by its parents prior to their marriage.
- **"POST NUPTIAS"** – **légitimation "post nuptias" par décision judiciaire** – legitimation after marriage by a court decision.
- **PRINCE** – **légitimation par le fait du prince** – legitimation by act of the executive.
- **SANS MARIAGE** – **légitimation sans mariage** – legitimation without marriage. (This was exceptionally permitted (in France) in the case of war victims when it was established that the parties would have married if the father had not been killed.)

LÉGITIME – legitimate; lawful.
- **DÉFENSE** – **légitime défense** – self-defence. (A defence to a prosecution for manslaughter or proceedings for assault; if the defence fails, the excuse of provocation can still be pleaded. The concept includes the defence of other persons and of property.)
  - **ABUS de la légitime défense** – use of disproportionate force in self-defence.
- **EMPÊCHEMENT légitime** – lawful impediment (objection).
- **MOTIF** – **sans motif légitime** – without lawful cause, reason or intent.

LÉGITIMEMENT – properly; reasonably; legitimately.
- **CROIRE** – **se croire légitimement propriétaire** – believe oneself to be the true owner.

LÉGITIMER – legitimate; justify.

LÉGITIMITÉ
- **CONTESTATION de la légitimité** – action to have a person declared illegitimate.

LEGS – legacy.

- **ALTERNATIF** – **legs alternatif** – alternate legacy (ie giving the legatee a choice between two or more alternatives; once made the choice is final).
- **CHARGE** – **legs avec charge** – legacy conditional on performing an obligation imposed by the testator.
- **CHOSE D'AUTRUI** – **legs de la chose d'autrui** – legacy of something not belonging to the testator. (In principle this is void, but if the testator has some right over the thing in question, the legacy is valid. The same applies if the legacy consists of a certain quantity of generic goods not contained in the estate.)
- **CRÉANCE** – **legs de créance** – legacy of a chose in action (right to receive payment of a debt etc).
- **DE RESIDUO** – **legs "de residuo"** – legacy subject to the requirement that the legatee shall leave what remains of the legacy on his death to a specified person.
- **GENRE** – **legs d'un genre de choses** – legacy of generic (unspecific) goods.
- **LIBÉRATION** – **legs de libération** – testamentary provision releasing the debtor from a debt he owes the testator.
- **PARTICULIER** – **legs (à titre) particulier** – individual legacy (ie a specific or pecuniary legacy, bequest or devise).
- **UNIVERSEL** – **legs universel** – the whole or a share of a testator's estate, possibly subject to legacies; universal legacy; residuary legacy. (In the case of a share, if the other persons entitled to like shares and those entitled to the reserved portions (**héritiers réservataires**) disappear, the universal legatee becomes entitled to the whole.)
  - •• **TITRE** – **legs à titre universel** – legacy, bequest or devise of a share of an estate. (Such a share may be a share of the whole, all the real property, all the movables, a share of the real property or a share of the movables.)
- **USUFRUIT** – **legs en usufruit** – life interest in property under a will.

LÉGUER – bequeath; devise; give a legacy.

LÉONIN – unconscionable.

LÉSER – injure; wrong; aggrieve; infringe.

LÉSION – loss caused to one of the parties by a contract; excessive loss; inadequate consideration; unfair price. In certain cases it constitutes a ground for rescinding the contract: (1) on a sale of real property where the seller has lost more than seven-twelfths of the value; (2) on accepting an estate (of a deceased person) where the estate is reduced by more than half on the discovery of a will unknown at the date of acceptance; (3) in a partition where one of those entitled suffers a loss of more than a quarter; (4) on the assignment of a literary or artistic copyright if the author or artist suffers a loss of more than seven-twelfths; (5) in legal transactions where one of the parties is a minor.

- **CORPOREL** – **lésion corporelle** – physical (personal, bodily) injury.
- **DROIT** – **lésion dans les (des) droits** – infringement of rights.
- **MOITIÉ** – **lésion de plus de la moitié** – loss of more than half the value.

LÉSIONNAIRE – unequal; unfair; with inadequate consideration; unconscionable.

- **ERREUR lésionnaire** – gross error as to the value of the subject-matter of a contract.

LETTRE

- **CHANGE** – **lettre de change** – bill of exchange, ie a written instruction by the drawer (**tireur**) to the drawee (**tiré**) to pay the payee (**preneur** or **bénéficiaire**).
- **CHARGÉ** – **lettre chargée** – insured letter containing money or valuables.
- **CONVOCATION** – **lettre de convocation** – letter inviting to attend a meeting etc; notice of a meeting etc.
- **COUVERTURE** – **lettre de couverture** – cover note (insurance).
- **CRÉANCE** – **lettre de créance** – letters of credence; (a diplomat's) credentials; letter of credit.
- **GAGE** – **lettre de gage** – bond.
  - •• **HYPOTHÉCAIRE** – **lettre de gage hypothécaire** – mortgage bond.
- **INTENTION** – **lettre d'intention** – letter of intent.
- **MISSIVE** – **lettre missive** – personal letter; letter, card, etc sent through the post or by messenger.
- **RAPPEL** – **lettres de rappel** – (ambassador's) letters of recall.
- **RÉCRÉANCE** – **lettres de récréance** – (ambassador's) letters of recall.
- **TRANSPORT**
  - •• **AÉRIEN** – **lettre de transport aérien** – air freight warrant; air consignment

note (equivalent to a bill of lading at sea).
- **VOITURE** – **lettre de voiture** – consignment note; waybill.

LEVÉ – survey of land.

LEVÉE – removal (of an impediment); termination or lifting (of an attachment); discharge (of an injunction or other judicial order); exercise (of an option); withdrawal (of a reservation); raising (of recruits).
- **ÉCROU** – **levée d'écrou** – release.
- **IMMUNITÉ** – **levée de l'immunité** – waiver (withdrawal, deprivation) of immunity, eg in the case of an MP who has committed an offence.
- **MASSE** – **levée en masse** – final resistance to an invading army by the whole population.
- **RÉQUISITION** – **levée de la réquisition** – lifting (termination) of the requisitioning.
- **SCELLÉ** – **levée de scellés** – (official) removal of seals (eg when making an inventory).
- **SÉQUESTRE** – **levée du séquestre** – termination of a stakeholding, custodianship or temporary administration of property.

LEVER – remove; terminate; lift; discharge (an injunction or other judicial order); exercise or take up (an option); withdraw (a reservation); raise (recruits).
- **ÉCROU** – **lever l'écrou** – release.
- **IMMUNITÉ** – **lever l'immunité** – withdraw immunity (from) (deprive of immunity) (eg an MP who has committed an offence); waive (a person's) immunity.
- **IMPÔT** – **lever un impôt** – levy (raise, impose, collect) a tax.
- **JUGEMENT** – **lever un jugement** – obtain a copy of the judgment endorsed with authority to execute; obtain the execution copy of the judgment; obtain a writ of execution (endorsed on the judgment).
- **SCELLÉ** – **lever les scellés** – (officially) remove the seals (eg when making an inventory).

LIAISON
- **INSTANCE** – **liaison de l'instance** – hearing at which submissions are first exchanged and after which objections may no longer be raised.

LIBELLÉ – wording.

- **ALIGNER** **le libellé** – make the wording (of two documents) agree.
- **EXPLOIT** – **libellé de l'exploit** – statement of claim.

LIBELLER
- **ÊTRE** **libellé** – (of a document) read (eg as follows).

LIBÉRAL
- **INTERPRÉTATION** – **trouver une interprétation plus libérale** – be interpreted more widely.

LIBÉRALISME – liberal attitude (of the courts etc).

LIBÉRALITÉ – gift; donation; transaction without consideration; voluntary disposition (of property).
- **CHARGE** – **libéralité avec charge** – gift subject to an obligation (to be fulfilled by the donee).
- **RÉMUNÉRATOIRE** – **libéralité rémunératoire** – gift in consideration of past services.
- **TESTAMENTAIRE** – **libéralité testamentaire** – testamentary gift.

LIBÉRATION – release; payment; discharge.
- **ACTION** – **libération d'actions** – paying up (not fully paid up) shares.
- **ANTICIPÉ** – **libération anticipée** – release before completion of one's sentence; early release.
- **COMMISSION** **de libération** – release board.
- **CONDITIONNEL** – **libération conditionnelle** – release on parole (licence) (from prison); conditional release (from detention on remand). (Misconduct may entail a return to prison.)
- **PUR ET SIMPLE** – **libération pure et simple** – unconditional release.

LIBÉRATOIRE – resulting in release (discharge) from an obligation.
- **ÊTRE** – **ne serait pas libératoire** – would not constitute a discharge.
- **PAIEMENT** **libératoire** – payment effected in accordance with the conditions required by law for the discharge of the debtor.

LIBÉRÉ
- **ENTIÈREMENT** **libéré** – fully paid up.

LIBÉRER – pay up (of shares)
- **SE libérer** – escape liability.

LIBERTÉ

- **ACTION** – **liberté d'action** – freedom to act according to one's own discretion.
- **APPRÉCIATION** – **pleine liberté d'appréciation** – freedom to form an opinion on the facts (without being restricted by the technical rules of evidence).
- **CIRCULATION** – **liberté de circulation** – freedom of movement.
- **CIVIL** – **liberté civile** – freedom to do anything not forbidden by law.
- **CONCURRENCE** – **liberté de concurrence** – free competition, ie the opposite of restraint of trade.
- **CONTRACTUEL** – **liberté contractuelle** – freedom of contract; freedom to contract; freedom to choose the law governing the contract.
- **CONVENTION** – **liberté des conventions** – freedom of contract.
- **DÉFENSE** – **liberté de la défense** – right of both parties to proceedings to be heard and to choose their own counsel.
- **ENCHÈRE** – **entrave à la liberté des enchères** – interference with (the proper conduct of) an auction and fair bidding.
- **ENSEIGNEMENT** – **liberté d'enseignement** – freedom to impart knowledge according to one's own discretion.
- **ÉTABLISSEMENT** – **liberté d'établissement** – freedom to settle (take up residence); freedom of establishment.
- **INDIVIDUEL** – **liberté individuelle** – personal freedom, ie freedom to make one's own decisions and come and go as one chooses (including freedom of movement, freedom to demonstrate and freedom of one's private life); liberty of the subject; (in plural) liberties of the subject.
- **PAROLE** – **liberté de la parole** – freedom of speech.
- **PRIVATIF** – **peine privative de liberté** – custodial sentence; imprisonment.
- **PROVISOIRE** – **mise en liberté provisoire** – provisional release from detention on remand; (release on) bail; release pending trial.
- **PUBLIC** – **libertés publiques** – fundamental rights and freedoms; individual freedoms; civil liberties; civil rights.
- **RÉUNION** – **liberté de réunion** – freedom of assembly.
- **SÉJOUR** – **liberté de séjour** – freedom of movement (residence).
- **SURVEILLÉ** – **liberté surveillée** – freedom subject to supervision (by a social worker); release under supervision. (This may be ordered against a minor pending proceedings or after a sentence or other measure has been imposed and may continue until the minor comes of age; it may also be imposed on minors who are vagrants.)
- **SYNDICAL** – **liberté syndicale** – freedom to fix rates (charges, prices).
- **TARIFAIRE** – **liberté tarifaire** (Sw) – freedom to negotiate wage agreements.
- **TRAVAIL** - **entrave à la liberté du travail** – interference with freedom of employment.

LIBRE

- **CHARGE** – **libre de toutes charges** – free of all encumbrances.
- **DROIT** – **libre de tous droits** – free of all rights; free of all charges.
- **HYPOTHÈQUE** – **libre d'hypothèques** – free of mortgages.
- **PREUVE** – **la preuve de la cause est libre** – the consideration (legal basis) may be proved by any kind of evidence.
- **SALAIRE DE LA FEMME MARIÉE** – **libre salaire de la femme mariée** – married woman's free earnings. The wife is entitled to administer and dispose of her earnings and the movables and immovables purchased therewith although these remain part of the community (of property). Often known as "reserved property".

LICÉITÉ – lawfulness.

LICENCE – permission; licence.

- **CABARETAGE** – **licence de cabaretage** (Lux) – on-licence for wines and spirits.
- **COLPORTAGE** – **licence de colportage** – hawker's licence; pedlar's licence.
- **CONCESSION de licence** – granting (grant) of a licence.
- **CONCESSIONNAIRE de licence** – licensee.
- **DÉBIT DE BOISSON** – **licence de débit de boisson** – liquor licence.
- **DROIT de licence (d'exploitation)** – licence (to operate a mine, trade or manufacture or use a patent, copyright, etc); licence fee; royalty.
- **EXCLUSIF** – **licence exclusive** – exclusive licence (to operate a mine, trade or manufacture or use a patent, copyright, etc).
- **EXERCICE** – **licence de plein exercice** – on-licence for wines and spirits.

- **EXPLOITATION** – **licence d'exploitation** – licence to operate a mine, trade or manufacture; licence to use a patent or copyright; operating licence; trade licence.
- **GRAND** – **grande licence** – on-licence for wines and spirits.
- **OBLIGATOIRE** – **licence obligatoire** – compulsory licence. (If the owner fails to use his patent anyone may apply to him for a licence. If he does not grant it, application may be made to the Regional Court for a non-exclusive compulsory licence.)
- **OCTROI de licence** – grant(ing) of a licence.
- **PLEIN EXERCICE** – see EXERCICE above.
- **PRENEUR de licence** – licensee.
- **PROFESSIONNEL** – **licence professionnelle** – licence to exercise a trade or profession.
- **RESTREINT** – **licence restreinte** – restricted licence (ie conveying part of the rights conferred by a patent or copyright; or a licence to sell liquor subject to certain restrictions).
- **RETRAIT de licence** – withdrawal of a licence.
- **SIMPLE** – **licence simple** – ordinary (non-exclusive) licence.
- **SPÉCIAL** – **licence spéciale** – special licence. (If patents relating to drugs or other remedies are so used by the holder of the patent that the products in question do not reach the public in sufficient quantity or quality or the price is too high, special licences can be granted to other manufacturers by the Ministry of Health.)
- **TITULAIRE de licence** – licensee; licence-holder.
- **TRANSFERT** – **licence de transfert** – consent to assign.
- **VOLONTAIRE** – **licence volontaire** – licence granted by mutual agreement; contractual licence.

LICENCIÉ – licensee; licence-holder.

LICENCIEMENT – dismissal; termination of services.

- **AVIS de licenciement** – notice of dismissal; letter of dismissal.
- **IMMÉDIAT** – **licenciement immédiat** – dismissal without notice.
- **INDEMNITÉ de licenciement** – compensation for loss (termination) of employment; damages for dismissal; redundancy payment.

LICENCIER – dismiss; terminate the services of.

LICITATION – sale by public auction, usually of immovable property in joint ownership which cannot practically be partitioned; sale by auction of property owned in common. (The expression may, however, refer to movables and to property which is not in joint ownership.)

- **AMIABLE** – **licitation amiable** – auction by mutual agreement.
- **JUDICIAIRE** – **licitation judiciaire** – auction by the court (to which recourse is had where the parties cannot agree or some of them are absent, under age, etc.).
- **VOLONTAIRE** – **licitation volontaire** – auction by mutual agreement.

LICITE – lawful; permitted.

LICITER – to sell by public auction (generally property which it is not practical to partition among co-owners – see LICITATION).

LIÉ

- **AFFAIRE** – **l'affaire est liée** – the case is ready to proceed (ready for trial).

LIEN

- **CAUSALITÉ** – **lien de causalité** – causal relationship (link); relationship of cause and effect; (chain of) causation.
- **CONJUGAL** – **lien conjugal** – marital relationship (bond).
- **DROIT** – **lien de droit** – legal relationship.
- **INSTANCE** – **lien (juridique) d'instance** – procedural relationship (situation).
- **PARENTÉ** – **lien de parenté** – relationship.

LIER

- **INSTANCE** – **lier l'instance** – begin the preparations for trial; commence proceedings.

LIEU

- **EXÉCUTION** – **lieu d'exécution** – place of performance (of a contract).
- **IMMATRICULATION** – **lieu d'immatriculation** – place of registration.
- **INFRACTION** – **lieu de l'infraction** – place where the offence was committed.
- **LOUÉ** – **lieux loués** – demised premises.
- **MAINTIEN dans les lieux** – tenant's statutory right to remain in occupation after termination of the tenancy; statutory tenancy.
- **POURSUITE** – **lieu de la poursuite** – place of trial; venue.

- **PUBLIC** – lieu public – public place, including places which by reason of their purpose are freely open to the public (roads, squares, stations, cemeteries, etc) and also places of a private nature which are open to the public by virtue of the intention of their owners (cafés etc).
- **TRANSPORT sur les lieux** – inspection of the site, locus (in quo), scene of the crime or premises by the court.
- **VIDER les lieux** – quit the premises.
- **VISITE des lieux** – inspection of the site, locus (in quo), scene of the crime or premises by the court.

LIGUE
- **RECONSTITUTION de ligue dissoute** – reconstituting a proscribed organisation.

LIMITATIF – exhaustive.

LIMITATION
- **RESPONSABILITÉ – limitation de la responsabilité** – limitation of liability.
- **SAISIE – limitation de la saisie** – limitation of the attachment.

LIMITATIVEMENT – exhaustively.
- **ÉNONCÉ – limitativement énoncé** – specifically enumerated.

LIMITE – boundary.
- **ASSIGNÉ – limites assignées à** – restrictions on.
- **BASSES EAUX** – see EAU below.
- **CHARGE – limite de charge** – maximum load.
- **EAU – limite des basses eaux** – low-water mark.
- **ÉTAT – limite d'État** – state frontier.
- **IMPOSITION – limite d'imposition** – limit of taxation; point at which a tax immunity ceases to apply.

LIMITÉ – qualified.

LIMITROPHE
- **ÉTAT limitrophe** – neighbouring (bordering) state; border (frontier) state.

LIQUIDATEUR – liquidator.
- **AMIABLE – liquidateur amiable** – liquidator appointed by mutual agreement.
- **JUDICIAIRE – liquidateur judiciaire** – liquidator appointed by the court.

LIQUIDATIF
- **ÉTAT liquidatif** – statement of amount due; settlement statement; final scheme of division in a partition.

LIQUIDATION – liquidation; fixing; calculation; assessment; settlement; payment.
- **BIEN – liquidation de biens** – compulsory winding-up order; judicial liquidation.
- **DÉPENS – liquidation des dépens** – taxation (assessment) of costs; settlement (payment) of costs.
- **DOMMAGE – liquidation des dommages** – assessment of damages.
- **ENTRER en liquidation** – go into liquidation; be wound up.
- **FORCÉ – liquidation forcée** – compulsory liquidation (winding-up).
- **HONORAIRE – liquidation des honoraires** – fixing of fees; settling (payment) of fees.
- **IMPÔT – liquidation de l'impôt** – (tax) assessment; fixing the amount of tax; payment of tax.
- **JUDICIAIRE – liquidation judiciaire** – (formerly) a procedure less rigorous than bankruptcy (**faillite**), now replaced in France by the **règlement judiciaire**.
- **PENSION – liquidation de la pension** – calculation of the amount of the pension.
- **PIÈCES de liquidation** – documents required for the purpose of settlement.
- **PRODUIT de la liquidation** – proceeds of the liquidation; proceeds on winding-up.
- **SUCCESSION – liquidation de la succession** – division of the estate between the heirs.
- **TERME de (la) liquidation** – date for settlement.

LIQUIDE – liquid; in an immediately available form; certain and of a fixed amount; assessed at a fixed amount.

LIQUIDER – liquidate; realise; assess; calculate.
- **ASTREINTE – liquider une astreinte** – fix the amount payable as a coercive fine.

LIQUIDITÉ – liquidity; in an immediately available form; of a definitely ascertained amount; (in plural) cash reserves.

LISTE
- **BLOQUÉ – liste bloquée** – a list to be accepted or rejected in toto (in a vote).
- **ÉMARGEMENT – liste d'émargement** – column on the electoral list for recording that the elector has voted.

- **SCRUTIN de liste** – election in which the voter votes for a party list and not for an individual candidate.
- **TÊTE de liste** – candidate whose name appears at the top of the party list; party's leading candidate.

LITIGE – dispute; case; cause; issue; proceedings.

- **CIVIL** – litige civil – civil action.
- **INSTANCE** – litige en instance – pending case.
- **JUDICIAIRE** – litige judiciaire – court proceedings.
- **MATRIMONIAL** – litige matrimonial – matrimonial cause (proceedings, dispute).
- **OBJET du (en) litige** – subject-matter of the proceedings.
- **PARTIE au litige** – party to the proceedings; litigant.
- **POINTS en litige** – points in (at) issue.
- **RÈGLEMENT d'un litige** – settlement of an action (case).
- **SOMME en litige** – amount in dispute.
- **SUCCESSORAL** – litige successoral – proceedings concerning a disputed inheritance.
- **VALEUR en (du) litige** – value of the subject-matter; sum involved; amount in dispute.
- **VIDER le litige** – settle a case.

LITIGIEUX – disputed; in (at) issue; complained of; impugned.

- **DÉCISION litigieuse** – decision appealed against.
- **ÉPOQUE des faits litigieux** – the material time.
- **PROCÉDURE litigieuse** – proceedings complained of.
- **RETRAIT litigieux** – exercise by the defendant of his right, in a case where the plaintiff has sold his right against the defendant (with which the pending proceedings are concerned) to another, to acquire this right from the purchaser on reimbursing him what he paid for it; right of a debtor sued by the assignee of a debt to settle the proceedings by paying the assignee the amount for which he purchased the debt together with the costs of the assignment and interest.

LITISCONSORT – co-plaintiff or co-defendant.

LITISPENDANCE – lis alibi pendens. (When two actions between the same parties relating to the same subject-matter and based on the same grounds are brought before two different courts each having jurisdiction, it is for the higher or else the second court to say whether there is sufficient identity between the proceedings to justify a preliminary objection of lis alibi pendens.)

- **DÉCLINATOIRE de litispendance** – (preliminary) objection that proceedings on the same issue are pending in another court (lis alibi pendens).
- **EXCEPTION de litispendance** – (preliminary) objection that a matter is pending before another competent court (lis alibi pendens).

LIVRAISON – delivery.

LIVRE – (code) book. The French, Belgian and Luxembourg Civil Codes are divided into **livres** (books), **titres** (parts), **chapitres** (chapters), **sections** (sections) and **articles** (articles). The Swiss Civil Code is divided into **livres** (books), **parties** (parts), **titres** (sections), **chapitres** (chapters) and **articles** (articles).

- **BORD** – livre de bord – (ship's) log-book.
- **COMMERCE** – livres de commerce – books (of account).
- **DISCIPLINE** – livre de discipline – (ship's) punishment book.
- **FONCIER** – livre foncier – land register; Land Registry.
- **INVENTAIRE** – livre d'inventaire (des inventaires) – balance-sheet book.
- **PUBLIC** – livre public – public register.

LIVRER

- **VENTE à livrer** – sale for delivery (ie within a stated period).

LIVRET

- **CAISSE D'ÉPARGNE** – livret de caisse d'épargne – savings (bank) book.
- **ÉTRANGER** – livret pour étranger (Sw) – alien's identity card.
- **FAMILLE** – livret de famille – family civil-status book; family record book; family (civil-status) registration book.
- **IDENTITÉ** – livret d'identité – identity card.
- **INDIVIDUEL** – livret individuel – military-service certificate (certifying that the person concerned has performed military service).
- **MATRICULE** – livret matricule – military-service certificate.

- **MILITAIRE** – livret militaire – soldier's pay-book.

LOCAL

- **COMMERCIAL** – local (à usage) commercial – business premises.
- **DISCIPLINAIRE** – local disciplinaire – punishment cell.
- **HABITATION** – local (à usage) d'habitation – residential premises; dwelling; accommodation.
- **NU** – local nu – unfurnished premises.
- **PROFESSIONNEL** – local (à usage) professionnel – business premises.

LOCATAIRE – tenant; lessee.

- **PRINCIPAL** – locataire principal – sublessor.

LOCATION – tenancy; lease.

- **MEUBLÉ** – location en meublé – furnished tenancy.
- **VERBAL** – location verbale – parol tenancy; oral tenancy.

LOCATION-GÉRANCE – leasing of a business in which the lessee runs the business on his own account and at his own risk.

LOCATION-VENTE – hire-purchase.

LOGEMENT

- **AFFECTATION** de logement – allocation of accommodation.
- **ALLOCATION** de logement – rent allowance (mortgage interest allowance).
- **ENTREPRISE** – logement d'entreprise – house or flat provided by the employing business.
- **FAMILIAL** – logement familial – matrimonial home.
- **FAMILLE** – logement de famille – matrimonial home.
- **FONCTION** – logement de fonction – official residence; premises occupied in connection with an employment.
- **INDEMNITÉ** de logement – housing allowance; rent allowance.
- **OCCUPÉ**
  - •• **INSUFFISAMENT** – logement insuffisamment occupé – under-occupied accommodation.

LOI – Act; the law in the sense of all written law emanating directly or indirectly from the legislature.

- **ABROGATION** – loi d'abrogation – repealing Act.

- **ABROGER** une loi – repeal an Act.
- **ADDITIONNEL** – loi additionnel – supplementary Act.
- **ADOPTER** une loi – pass an Act; enact a statute.
- **APPLICATION** – loi d'application – implementing Act.
- **APPROBATION** – loi d'approbation – approving Act.
- **AUTONOMIE** – loi d'autonomie – rule of private international law that contracts are governed by the law expressly or tacitly chosen by the parties.
- **BUDGET** – loi de budget – Appropriation Act (expenditure).
- **BUDGÉTAIRE** – loi budgétaire – Appropriation Act (expenditure).
- **CIRCONSTANCE** – loi de circonstance – special Act.
- **COMPÉTENT** – loi compétente – proper law.
- **COMPTE** – loi de comptes (Belg) – Finance Act.
- **CONFLIT** de lois – conflict of laws; choice of law; private international law.
- **CONFORME** à la loi – lawful; in accordance with law.
- **CONFORMÉMENT** – ordonnance rendue conformément à la loi – lawful order.
- **COORDONNÉ** – lois coordonnées (Belg) – consolidated Acts.
- **DISPOSITIF** – loi dispositive – statutory provision which can be displaced by even the implied intention of the parties; non-mandatory legislation.
- **DOMICILE** – loi du domicile – law of a person's ordinary or habitual place of residence.
- **ÉLECTORAL** – loi électorale – Electoral Provisions Act; Representation of the People Act.
- **ÉLUDER** la loi – circumvent (evade) the law.
- **ENSEMBLE** – loi d'ensemble – general Act.
- **EXCEPTION** – loi d'exception – special Act; emergency legislation.
- **EXÉCUTION** – loi d'exécution – implementing Act (legislation).
- **FACULTATIF** – loi facultative – non-mandatory legislation.
- **FINANCE** – loi de finances – Budget Act (covering both expenditure (Appropriation Act) and revenue (Finance Act)).

- **FISCAL** – loi fiscale – Tax Act; taxing statute; tax legislation.
- **FONDAMENTAL** – loi fondamentale – basic Act; basic law.
- **FORCE** – ayant force de loi – legally binding; having statutory force (the force of law).
- **FORMEL** – loi au sens formel – Act of Parliament.
- **FORMEL** – loi formelle – legislation in the formal or procedural sense, ie an enactment which has passed through the forms prescribed by constitutional law.
- **FRAUDE à la loi** – fraudulent evasion of statutory provisions (of the law).
- **GIGOGNE** – loi gigogne – Miscellaneous Provisions Act.
- **HABILITATION** – loi d'habilitation – Act authorising the government to legislate by regulation; enabling Act.
- **HOMMES de loi** – the legal community; the profession; (practising) lawyers.
- **IMPÉRATIF** – loi impérative – mandatory Act (legislation, provisions), ie based on considerations of public policy.
- **INFRACTION à la loi** – breach (infringement, violation, contravention) of the law or an Act.
- **INITIATIVE des lois** – right to initiate legislation.
- **INTERDICTION** – loi d'interdiction – Act containing prohibitions.
- **INTERPRÉTATIF** – loi interprétative – Act interpreting a previous Act (not "Interpretation Act", which lays down certain general rules of interpretation and a number of definitions of general application).
- **JUGE SAISI** – loi du juge saisi – lex fori (ie national law of the court trying the case).
- **LIEU**
  - **ACTE** – loi du lieu de l'acte – law of the place where the act was committed or done (lex actus).
  - **CONTRAT** – loi du lieu du contrat – law of the place where the contract was made (lex loci actus).
- **MARTIAL** – loi martiale – Revolutionary law authorising local authorities to make use of the military to maintain order, now replaced by the **lois sur l'état de siège** and **sur l'état d'urgence**; martial law.
- **MILITAIRE** – loi militaire – military law; Army Act.
- **MODIFICATIF** – loi modificative – amendment Act.
- **MUNICIPAL** – loi municipale – Local Government Act.
- **NATIONAL** – loi nationale – national (municipal, domestic) law.
- **NATUREL** – loi naturelle – natural law, ie law based on reason and the nature of man as opposed to law as it actually exists.
- **ORDRE PUBLIC** – loi d'ordre public – mandatory Act (legislation, provisions), ie based on considerations of public policy.
- **ORGANIQUE** – loi organique – State Authorities Act; Act, not forming part of the Constitution, laying down the principles governing the organisation or structure of organs of government or other public authorities; Institutional Act; Act establishing; (with reference to Spain) implementing Act.
- **ORGANISATION MUNICIPALE** – loi sur l'organisation municipale – Local Government Act.
- **ORIENTATION** – loi d'orientation – General Principles Act; Outline Act.
- **OUVRIER** – loi ouvrière – Workmen's Protection Act.
- **PARTICULIER** – loi particulière – special Act; special provision.
- **PLEIN POUVOIR** – see POUVOIR below.
- **POLICE** – loi de police – public order Act.
- **POUVOIR** – loi de pleins pouvoirs – Act authorising the government to legislate by regulations; enabling Act.
- **PROCÉDURE** – loi de procédure – Code of Procedure; Procedure Act; procedural provisions.
- **PROGRAMME** – loi de programme – Act authorising the government to take measures involving expenditure covering several financial years.
- **PROJET de loi** – (government) Bill.
- **PROPOSITION de loi** – (private member's) Bill.
- **RECETTE** – loi de recettes – Finance Act.
- **REDRESSEMENT** – loi de redressement (Belg) – consolidating Act; Law Revision Act.
- **REPRÉSENTANTS de la loi** – law-enforcement agencies.
- **RÉPRESSIF** – loi répressive – penal statute (Act); penal legislation.
- **SOUVERAINETÉ de la loi** – supremacy of the law.
- **SUPPLÉTIF** – loi (purement) supplétive – statutory provisions displaced only by the express intention of the parties; non-mandatory provisions.

- **TALION** – **loi du talion** – principle of retaliation (an eye for an eye).
- **TARIFAIRE** – **loi tarifaire** – Customs Tariff Act; (Sw) Collective (Wage) Agreements Act.
- **TERRITORIAL** – **loi territoriale** – territorial legislation (ie applying only to acts committed in a certain territory).
- **TOURNER la loi** – evade the law.
- **TRANSITION** – **loi de transition** – Transitional Provisions Act; transitional legislation.
- **TYPE** – **loi type** – model law.
- **UNIFORME** – **loi uniforme** – uniform law (ie enacted in several countries in the same form).
- **VALIDÉ** – **loi validée** – validated Act (ie one that was originally invalid).
- **VIGUEUR** – **loi en vigueur** – existing Act (legislation); law currently in force (in force at the time).
- **VIOLATION de la loi** – error of law (ground of appeal to the Court of Cassation).
- **VOTER une loi** – pass an Act; enact a statute.

LOI-CADRE – Act laying down the general principles governing some field of legislation; General Principles Act; Outline Act.

LOISIBLE – permissible.
- **À** – **il est loisible au requérant de** – the applicant is entitled to (may); it is open to the applicant to.

LONGUEUR
- **EFFET** – **longueur d'un effet** – currency of a bill of exchange.

LOTIR – divide a piece of land up into building plots.

LOTISSEMENT – the dividing up of land into plots for building or other purposes; building estate; division into plots or parcels; industrial (building) estate.

LOTISSEUR – (building) estate owner.

LOUAGE
- **CHEPTEL** – **louage à cheptel** – hiring of a herd of cattle.
- **CHOSE** – **louage de chose** – hiring, letting or leasing of property.
- **DOMAINE CONGÉABLE** – **louage à domaine congéable** – short-term agricultural tenancy in which the tenant retains ownership of (or is entitled to compensation for) his erections, plantations and crops and also has a right of pre-emption.
- **EMPHYTÉOTIQUE** – **louage emphytéotique** – long lease of land in which the tenant is given a right in rem in the property.
- **INDUSTRIE** – **louage d'industrie** – contract for services, ie to make or do something as an independent contractor, eg make a suit or fill a tooth.
- **NOURRITURE** – **louage à nourriture** – agreement to provide a person with board and lodging in return for periodical payments or a capital sum.
- **OUVRAGE** – **louage d'ouvrage** – contract for services; contract for work (and materials). (Comprises both **louage de services** (service contract; employment contract) and **louage d'industrie** (contract for services, ie to make or do something as an independent contractor, eg make a suit or fill a tooth).)
- **SERVICE** – **louage de services** – service contract; employment contract.

LOUER – let; rent; hire.

LOYAUTÉ – (duty of) fairness.

LOYER – rent; hire-purchase instalments; interest charge.
- **ACOMPTE sur loyer** – advance payment of rent.
- **ALLOCATION de loyer** – rent allowance.
- **ARGENT** – **loyer de l'argent** – interest.
- **BAILLEUR à loyer** – landlord; lessor.
- **CRÉANCE de loyers** – right to receive payment of rent.
- **PRINCIPAL** – **loyer principal** – rent payable to the superior landlord.
- **TRIMESTRIEL** – **loyer trimestriel** – quarterly rent.

LUCRATIF
- **OCCUPATION lucrative** – remunerated (gainful) employment.

LUCRUM CESSANS – loss of profit or earnings (lucrum cessans).

M

MAGASIN
- **GÉNÉRAL** – magasins généraux – state depository.
- **PUBLIC** – magasin public – public warehouse.

MAGASINAGE – depository fee(s); warehouse (warehousing) charge(s); storage charge(s).
- **DROIT de magasinage** – depository fee; warehouse (warehousing) charge; storage charge.
- **TAXE de magasinage** – depository fee; warehouse (warehousing) charge; storage charge.

MAGISTRAT – member of the national legal service, ie either a judge or a law officer (member of the Attorney-General's Department, State Counsel (prosecutor)); member of the court.
- **ASSIS** – magistrat assis – judge.
- **CONSULAIRE** – magistrat consulaire – member of the Commercial Court; Commercial Court judge.
- **DEBOUT** – magistrat debout – law officer; prosecutor; State Counsel; State prosecutor; member of the Attorney-General's Department.
- **INSTRUCTEUR** – magistrat instructeur – investigating judge.
- **MILITAIRE** – magistrat militaire – judge advocate.
- **MUNICIPAL** – magistrat municipal – generic term for the senior members of a town (city) council, ie the mayor and his immediate assistants (**adjoints** – aldermen).
- **SIÈGE** – magistrat du siège – judge.
- **TAXATEUR** – magistrat taxateur – taxing master.

MAGISTRATURE – national legal service; judiciary.
- **CONSEIL supérieur de la magistrature** – Judicial Service Commission.
- **DEBOUT** – magistrature debout – the law officers; Attorney-General's department.
- **ÉCOLE supérieure de la magistrature** – Legal Service Training College.
- **INDÉPENDANCE de la magistrature** – independence of the judiciary.
- **SIÈGE** – magistrature du siège – the judges; the judiciary.

MAIN
- **ARMÉ** – attaque à main armée – armed assault.
- **AUX mains de** – in the power of.
- **COMMUN** – main commune – clause by which (the) spouses agree that the community shall be administered jointly.
- **COURANT** – main courante – register of offences recorded by the police; (police) notebook.
- **JUSTICE** – placer sous main de justice – have (order to be) administered by the court.
- **LEVÉ** – vote à main levée – vote by show of hands.

MAINLEVÉE – lifting (of an attachment etc); discharge (of a court order); termination; (Swiss execution procedure) setting aside the debtor's objection.
- **ACTION en mainlevée du séquestre** – action to obtain release of property from judicial custody.
- **AMIABLE** – mainlevée amiable – termination (lifting) of an attachment by agreement between the parties.
- **INSCRIPTION**
  - **HYPOTHÉCAIRE** – mainlevée d'inscription hypothécaire – cancellation of (the entry of) a mortgage (in the Land Registry (land register)).
- **INTERDICTION** – mainlevée de l'interdiction – release from guardianship; restoration of full capacity.
- **JUDICIAIRE** – mainlevée judiciaire – termination (lifting) of an attachment by court order.
- **MANDAT**
  - **DÉPÔT** – mainlevée du mandat de dépôt – cancellation of the arrest warrant.
- **MESURE**
  - **EXÉCUTION** – mainlevée des mesures d'exécution – stopping (lifting) of measures of execution.
- **SAISIE** – mainlevée de la saisie – lifting of the attachment.
- **SÉQUESTRE** – mainlevée du séquestre – release of property from judicial custody, compulsory administration, seizure, attachment or (in some cases) sequestration.

MAINMISE

- **JUSTICE** – mainmise de la justice – attachment; seizure.

MAINMORTE – mortmain.

MAINTENANCE – lump-sum provision on divorce.

MAINTENIR

- **ÉTAT** – maintenir en état – keep in repair.

MAINTENUE

- **POSSESSOIRE** – maintenue possessoire – court order that property be restored to the state it was in prior to the interference with possession complained of.

MAINTIEN – continuation.

- **DÉTENTION** – maintien en détention – continued detention (on remand); remand (in custody).
- **ÉTAT** – maintien en état – keeping in repair.
- **LIEU** – maintien dans les lieux – order staying execution of a writ of possession; statutory right to remain in occupation after the termination of a tenancy; statutory tenancy.
- **ORDRE PUBLIC** – maintien de l'ordre public – keeping the peace.
- **VIGUEUR** – maintien en vigueur – keeping or remaining in force.

MAISON

- **ARRÊT** – maison d'arrêt – short-stay prison; remand prison.
- **CENTRAL** – maison centrale (de force (correction)) – prison.
- **CORRECTION** – maison de correction – reformatory; detention centre.
- **ÉDUCATION** – maison d'éducation corrective (surveillée) – reformatory.
- **FORCE** – maison de force – prison.
- **HABITATION** – maison d'habitation – dwelling-house.
- **INTERNEMENT** – maison d'internement – mental hospital; asylum.
- **JUSTICE** – maison de justice – remand prison.
- **PÉNITENTIAIRE** – maison pénitentiaire – prison.
- **PRÊT SUR GAGE (NANTISSEMENT)** – maison de prêts sur gage (nantissement) – pawnbroker (the only such establishments allowed are those run by a local authority (**crédits municipaux**) and state depositories (**magasins généraux**)).

- **RÉCLUSION** – maison de réclusion – prison.
- **REDRESSEMENT** – maison de redressement – reformatory.
- **REFUGE** – maison de refuge – assistance home (for persons dependent on some form of national assistance, eg vagrants); shelter (for battered wives etc).
- **SOCIAL** – maison sociale – registered office (headquarters) of a company.

MAÎTRE

- **BIEN** sans maître – res nullius; ownerless (unclaimed) goods.
- **MUR** – maître du mur – owner of the wall.
- **ŒUVRE** – maître d'œuvre – architect or building contractor.
- **ŒUVRE** – maître de l'œuvre – client; owner; person for whom the house etc is being built.
- **OUVRAGE** – maître de l'ouvrage – client; owner; person for whom the house etc is being built.
- **REQUÊTE** – maître des requêtes – legal adviser at the Conseil d'État, junior to the judges (**conseillers**) and senior to the legal assistants (**auditeurs**).

MAÎTRE CHANTEUR – blackmailer; extortioner.

MAJEUR – (adj) of (full) age; (noun) person of full age.

MAJORATION

- **RETARD** – majoration de retard – penalty (surcharge) for late payment of tax.

MAJORITÉ – full age; majority.

- **ABSOLU** – majorité absolue – absolute majority (more than half the votes).
- **CIVIL** – majorité civile – full age; majority.
- **ÉLECTORAL** – majorité électorale – age at which one is entitled to vote; voting age.
- **MATRIMONIAL** – majorité matrimoniale – age at which one is entitled to marry; marriageable age.
- **PÉNAL** – majorité pénale – age (18) at which one is criminally responsible.
- **QUALIFIÉ** – majorité qualifiée – special majority (ie a majority greater than an absolute majority).
- **RELATIF** – majorité relative – relative majority (more votes than any other candidate).
- **SIMPLE** – majorité simple – simple majority (more votes than any other candidate).

MALADIE

- **CAISSE de maladie** – sickness fund; health-insurance fund (association).
- **FEUILLE de maladie** – medical form, card or record; case notes; (social security) treatment form.
- **PROFESSIONNEL** – maladie professionnelle – occupational disease.

MALFAITEUR – criminal.

- **ASSOCIATION de malfaiteurs** – criminal association; conspiracy.
- **HABITUDE** – malfaiteur d'habitude – habitual criminal (offender).
- **RECEL de malfaiteur** – harbouring a criminal.

MAL-FONDÉ – (of a judgment) absence of legal basis; erroneous assumption.

MALHONNÊTE – fraudulent.

MALICIEUX – wilful.

MAL-JUGÉ – incorrect (erroneous) judgment (decision); judicial error.

MALVEILLANCE – malice; evil intention.

MALVERSATION – misconduct; misappropriation.

MANDANT – principal (of an agent).

MANDAT – contract of agency; power of attorney; authority; terms of reference; contract whereby one person confers on another the power to enter into legal transactions on his behalf; mandate; warrant.

- **AD LITEM** – mandat ad litem – (barrister's) authority to act for (his) client in litigation.
- **AMENER** – mandat d'amener – warrant to bring a suspect or an accused before the investigating judge or public prosecutor immediately.
- **APPARENT** – mandat apparent – allowing a person to hold himself out as one's agent.
- **ARRÊT** – mandat d'arrêt – arrest warrant; warrant to arrest and imprison a fugitive offender, suspect or accused.
- **COMPARUTION** – mandat de comparution – summons (to appear before the investigating judge).
- **CONVENTIONNEL** – mandat conventionnel – contract of agency.
- **DÉCERNER un mandat d'arrêt** – issue an arrest warrant.

- **DÉPÔT** – mandat de dépôt – order of a court or investigating judge to a prison governor to admit and detain an accused; committal warrant; detention order.
- **DOMESTIQUE** – mandat domestique – (formerly) wife's right (authority) to represent her husband in household matters and pledge his credit for household necessaries. (Since 1965 she has been considered not as representing her husband but as acting directly on behalf of the community in such matters.)
- **DURÉE** – mandat de durée déterminée – fixed term of office.
- **DURÉE du mandat électif** – period for which a person is elected; term of office.
- **ÉCROU** – mandat d'écrou – committal warrant.
- **ÉLECTIF** – mandat électif – right (and duty) to represent one's electors; electoral mandate.
- **EXCÉDER son mandat** – exceed one's authority.
- **EXÉCUTION** – mandat d'exécution – instruction to levy execution given by the judgment creditor to the bailiff; writ of execution.
- **FICTIF** – mandat fictif – payment order relating to a fictitious debt.
- **GÉNÉRAL** – mandat général – general power of attorney.
- **IMPÉRATIF** – mandat impératif – system under which a Member of Parliament's right to represent his electors depends on his complying with their instructions.
- **JUDICIAIRE** – mandat judiciaire – authority conferred by the court.
- **LÉGAL** – mandat légal – authority conferred by statute; statutory authority.
- **OCCASIONNEL** – mandat occasionnel – ad hoc terms of reference.
- **ORAL** – mandat oral – oral authority.
- **PAIEMENT** – mandat de paiement – warrant or authority to pay issued by a Treasury official.
- **PARLEMENTAIRE** – mandat parlementaire – right to sit in Parliament.
- **PERQUISITION** – mandat de perquisition – search warrant.
- **RECOUVREMENT** – mandat de recouvrement – authority to collect debts (for another).
- **REPRÉSENTATION** – mandat sans représentation – agent acting for an undisclosed principal.

- **RÉPRESSION** – mandat de répression (Sw) – sentence order.
- **SÉNATORIAL** – mandat sénatorial – right to sit in the Senate.
- **SOUS** mandat – territoire sous mandat – mandate; mandated territory.
- **SPÉCIAL** – mandat spécial – special power of attorney.
- **TACITE** – mandat tacite de la femme mariée – (formerly) wife's right (authority) to represent her husband in household matters and pledge his credit for household necessaries. (Since 1965 she has been considered not as representing her husband but as acting directly on behalf of the community in such matters.)
- **TERRITOIRE** sous mandat – mandate; mandated territory.
- **VERBAL** – mandat verbal – oral authority.
- **VIREMENT** – mandat de virement – transfer order.

MANDATAIRE – agent; attorney; representative.
- **AD LITEM** – mandataire ad litem – barrister authorised to act for (his) client in litigation.
- **CONSTITUER** un mandataire – appoint an agent or attorney.
- **GÉNÉRAL** – mandataire général – person holding a general power of attorney (a general authority) to act on behalf of another.
- **JUDICIAIRE** – mandataire judiciaire – administrator or curator appointed by the court.
- **LÉGAL** – mandataire légal – agent appointed by statute; statutory agent.
- **SOCIAL** – mandataire social – agent or attorney of a company or partnership.
- **VOTE** – mandataire d'un droit de vote – proxy.

MANDATER – appoint as agent, attorney or representative.

MANDEMENT – court order.
- **JUSTICE** – mandement de justice – court order.

MANIFESTATION
- **VÉRITÉ** – manifestation de la vérité – discovery of the truth (in criminal proceedings).
- **VOIE PUBLIQUE** – manifestation sur la voie publique – street demonstration.

MANIFESTER
- **DILIGENCE** – manifester la diligence voulue – exercise due care (and attention

to duty, including the duty to proceed expeditiously); show proper (due) diligence.

MANŒUVRE – unskilled workman; deceitful act; dishonest conduct (intended to deceive).
- **CRIMINEL** – manœuvres criminelles – criminal acts.
- **DILATOIRE** – manœuvres dilatoires – delaying tactics.
- **DOLOSIF** – manœuvres dolosives – fraudulent practices; deceit; fraud.
- **FRAUDULEUX** – manœuvres frauduleuses – fraudulent practices; false pretences; deception; fraud.
- **RETARDEMENT** – manœuvres de retardement – delaying tactics.

MANQUE
- **DISCERNEMENT** – manque de discernement – lack of discernment (discretion) (especially in a child).
- **GAGNER** – manque à gagner – loss of earnings or profit (lucrum cessans).
- **PREUVE** – manque de preuve – absence of proof.

MANQUEMENT – omission; fault; breach; infringement; violation; wrong.
- **CONVENTION** – manquement à la Convention – breach of the Convention.
- **DEVOIR** – manquement à son devoir – failure to comply with one's obligations.
- **DISCIPLINE** – manquement à la discipline – disciplinary offence.

MANU MILITARI – with the assistance of the police (including the use of physical force).

MARAUDAGE – stealing unpicked fruit or standing crops in small quantities; theft of unseparated crops.

MARC
- **FRANC** – au marc le franc – in proportionate shares; pro rata.

MARCHAND (adj) – merchantable.

MARCHAND (noun) – trader.
- **AMBULANT** – marchand ambulant – hawker.
- **BIEN** – marchand de biens – estate agent.

MARCHANDAGE – subcontracting (building work).

MARCHANDISE

- **CRÉANCE sur marchandises** – right to receive goods.
- **DETTE sur marchandises** – obligation to transfer or deliver goods.
- **LOYAL ET MARCHAND** – **marchandise loyale et marchande** – goods of merchantable quality.

MARCHE

- **INSTANCE** – **marche de l'instance** – conduct of the proceedings; course of the proceedings.
- **JUSTICE** – **bonne marche de la justice** – due course of justice; proper functioning of the judicial system.
- **MISE en marche des autorités pénales** – institution of criminal proceedings.

MARCHÉ

- **APPEL D'OFFRES** – **marché par appel d'offres** – contract by advertisement (call) for tenders (invitation to tender); putting a contract out to tender.
- **COMPTANT** – **marché au comptant** – spot transaction.
- **ENTENTE DIRECTE** – **marché par entente directe** – sale by private treaty.
- **FORFAIT** – **marché à forfait** – agreement by a contractor to do the work in question for a fixed sum.
- **FOURNITURE** – **marché de fournitures** – contract for the supply of goods.
- **GRÉ À GRÉ** – **marché de gré à gré** – sale by private treaty.
- **PUBLIC** – **marché public** – public works or supply contract.
- **TERME** – **marché à terme** – forward transaction.

MARCHEPIED

- **SERVITUDE de marchepied** – duty of a riparian owner to leave space alongside a navigable waterway for necessary manœuvring on land by boat crews.

MARIAGE

- **ANNULATION du mariage** – granting a decree of nullity; annulment of (a) marriage.
- **APTITUDE au mariage** – capacity to marry.
- **BIGAMIQUE** – **mariage bigamique** – bigamous marriage.
- **BOITEUX** – **mariage boiteux** – marriage recognised in one country but not in another.
- **CÉLÉBRATION du mariage** – solemnisation of marriage.
- **COMPARUTION**
  - **•• PERSONNEL** – **mariage sans comparution personnelle** – proxy marriage.
- **CONSENTEMENT au mariage** – consent to marriage.
- **CONSOMMÉ** – **mariage consommé** – consummated marriage.
- **CONTRAT de mariage** – marriage contract; marriage settlement.
- **DISSOLUTION du mariage** – divorce; dissolution of marriage.
- **EMPÊCHEMENT au mariage** – impediment (to marriage).
- **NULLITÉ du mariage** – nullity (of marriage).
- **OFFICIER DE L'ÉTAT CIVIL** – **mariage devant l'officier de l'état civil** – marriage in the registry office (by the mayor).
- **PROCUREUR** – **mariage par procureur** – proxy marriage.
- **PUBLICATION de mariage** – notice of marriage; (in a church etc) (marriage) banns.
- **PUTATIF** – **mariage putatif** – putative marriage.

MARIN

- **FONDS marins** – sea-bed.

MARINIER – waterman.

MARITALEMENT – as man and wife; in concubinage (cohabitation).

MARQUE – trade mark.

- **CONNU** - **marque notoirement connue** – well-known trade mark.
- **DÉCLARATION de marque de fabrique** – trade-mark application; application for registration of a trade mark.
- **DÉPOSÉ** – **marque déposée** – registered trade mark.
- **DÉPÔT d'une marque** – registration of a trade mark.
- **ENREGISTREMENT d'une marque** – registration of a trade mark.
- **FABRIQUE** – **marque de fabrique** – trade mark.
- **NOTOIRE(MENT CONNU)** – **marque notoire(ment connue)** – well-known trade mark.
- **PRODUIT** – **marque de produit** – trade name; trade description; descriptive mark.
- **RENOMMÉE** – **marque de haute renommée** – famous trade mark (brand (name)).

- **SOUVERAINETÉ** – **marque de souveraineté** – national emblem; symbol of sovereignty.

MARQUE-LABEL – quality mark.

MASSE – pool; common fund; assets (in bankruptcy); creditors (in bankruptcy).
- **BIEN** – **masse de biens** – group of assets.
- **CRÉANCE contre la masse** – priority claim against the bankruptcy for costs, or obligations entered into by the trustee.
- **CRÉANCIER de la masse** – creditor of the bankruptcy.
- **CRÉANCIER** – **masse des créanciers** – ordinary creditors (of a bankrupt); the assets; the bankruptcy; the general body of creditors.
- **DETTE de la masse** – debt of the bankruptcy arising out of the obligations entered into by the trustee while administering the assets and payable out of the bankrupt's assets or estate before distribution to the creditors.
- **FAILLITE** – **masse de la faillite** – bankrupt's assets; estate of a deceased bankrupt; assets of a company in compulsory liquidation.
- **FRAIS DE GESTION de la masse de la faillite** – expenses of administering the assets.
- **PARTAGE** – **masse de partage** – assets to be divided.
- **SORTIE** – **masse de sortie** – (prisoner's) release savings.
- **SUCCESSION** – **masse de la succession** – the assets of the estate.
- **SUCCESSORAL** – **masse successorale** – the assets of the estate.

MATÉRIALISER
- **SE matérialiser** – take material form in; be identified with.
  - •• **CRÉANCE** – **une créance se matérialise dans le titre au porteur qui la constate** – a right in personam becomes identified with the bearer security by which it is evidenced.

MATÉRIEL – factual; substantive; physical; not requiring criminal intent.
- **ACTE matériel** – physical act.
- **AUTEUR** – **lorsque l'instituteur est l'auteur matériel du préjudice** – where the teacher himself (personally, physically) causes the damage.
- **COMPÉTENCE matérielle** – jurisdiction of a criminal court to try felonies or misde-

meanours or petty offences, as the case may be.
- **DÉLIT matériel** – offence which is only constituted if the act or omission produced a specified result; strict-liability offence (not requiring proof of criminal intent (mens rea)).
- **DISPARITION** – **la seule disparition matérielle de l'État de l'enclave** – the mere physical disappearance of the enclave.
- **ERREUR (purement) matérielle** – factual error (eg a false entry in an account); clerical error.
- **EXISTENCE** – **l'existence matérielle de la clôture** – the physical existence of the enclosure.
- **FAIT matériel** – act (ie actus reus of a criminal offence).
- **INFRACTION purement matérielle** – strict-liability offence (not requiring proof of criminal intent (mens rea)).
- **ORDRE** – **d'ordre matériel** – of a factual nature.

MATÉRIELLEMENT
- **CAUSER** – **dommages causés matériellement par les élèves** – damage caused by the pupils themselves (personally, physically).

MATERNITÉ – legal relationship between a mother and her child.

MATIÈRE
- **CIVIL** – **matière civile** – civil case.
- **CONTENTIEUX** – **matière contentieuse** – contentious matter.
- **GRACIEUX** – **matière gracieuse** – non-contentious matter.
- **IMPOSABLE** – **matière imposable** – property subject to tax.
- **LITIGIEUX** – **matière litigieuse** – matter at issue; subject-matter.
- **PÉNAL** – **matière pénale** – criminal case.
  - •• **EN matière pénale** – in criminal cases; in criminal law.
- **PROCÈS** – **matière d'un procès** – subject-matter of proceedings.
- **SOMMAIRE** – **matière sommaire** – short civil or commercial case.

MATRIMONIAL
- **ÉPARGNES matrimoniales** – savings during the marriage (forming part of the matrimonial property).
- **LITIGE matrimonial** – matrimonial cause (proceedings, dispute).

- **RÉGIME matrimonial** – system (regime) of matrimonial (marital) property.
- **REGISTRE matrimonial** – register of systems (regimes) of matrimonial property.

MAUVAIS
- **FOI** – **mauvaise foi** – bad faith; tortious intent; criminal intent; malice; mens rea.
- **TRAITEMENT** – **mauvais traitements** – cruelty; ill-treatment.

MAXIMA – see A MAXIMA.

MÉCONNAISSANCE – disregard; failure to comply with; non-compliance; violation; infringement; breach.
- **DROIT** – **méconnaissance du droit** – (in addition to the meanings given above) misinterpretation (misreading) of the law.

MÉCONNAÎTRE – infringe; violate; fail to apply.
- **DROIT** – **méconnaître un droit** – infringe a right.

MÉDECIN
- **LÉGISTE** – **médecin légiste** – forensic medical examiner (formerly – and in common parlance still – police surgeon); court medical officer; pathologist.
- **MARRON** – **médecin marron** – unqualified (quack) or unscrupulous doctor, eg one who who signs certificates to suit the convenience of his patients.
- **OFFICIEL** – **médecin officiel** – (government) medical officer.
- **TRAITANT** – **médecin traitant** – (a party's) own (family) doctor.

MÉDECIN-CONSEIL – medical officer working for a public or private body, eg social-security office or an insurance company.

MÉDECINE
- **LÉGAL** – **médecine légale** – forensic (legal) medicine.

MÉDIATEUR – Parliamentary Commissioner (for Administration); ombudsman.

MÉDIATION – mediation.

MÉDICO-LÉGAL
- **INSTITUT médico-légal** – forensic mortuary.

MÉMOIRE – memorial; pleading; observations; statement of grounds of appeal.
- **AMPLIATIF** – **mémoire ampliatif** – supplementary memorial; further pleadings.

- **FRAIS** – **mémoire des frais** – bill of costs.
- **INTERVENTION** – **mémoire d'intervention** – application to be joined in the proceedings.
- **INTRODUCTIF D'INSTANCE** – **mémoire introductif d'instance** – application; statement of claim; writ; opening memorial; originating summons.
- **POUR mémoire** – token entry.
- **RÉPONSE** – **mémoire en réponse** – memorial in reply; observations in reply.

MÉMORANDUM
- **ACCORD** – **mémorandum d'accord** – memorandum of agreement.

MÉMORIAL
- **LE** Mémorial (Lux) – (Luxembourg) Official Gazette.

MENACE
- **ORDRE PUBLIC** – **menace pour l'ordre public** – threat to the peace (public order, public policy).

MÉNAGE
- **BESOINS courants de la ménage** – household necessaries.
- **BIENS du ménage** – matrimonial property.
- **FAIT** – **ménage de fait** – extramarital cohabitation; concubinage.
- **FAUX ménage** – concubinage; extramarital cohabitation.

MENÉES – subversion; disloyal behaviour.

MENEUR – ringleader.

MENSUALISATION – deduction of tax or payment of salary on a monthly basis (certain privileges are associated with this type of salary payment).

MENTAL
- **TROUBLES mentaux** – mental disorder.

MENTION – (in plural) particulars (in a document).
- **DOSSIER** – **mention au dossier** – entry in the file.
- **MARGE** – **mention en marge** – marginal entry.
- **ORDRE** – **mention à ordre** – order clause on a cheque, bill, etc.

MENU
- **OUVRAGE** – **menus ouvrages** – building work other than the main walls and the roof.

MÉPRIS
- **LOI** – au mépris d'une loi – in disregard (defiance) of a statute.

MER
- **FERMÉ** – mer fermée – enclosed sea.
- **HAUT** – haute mer – high sea(s).
- **LIBRE** – mer libre – open sea.
- **TERRITORIAL** – mer territoriale – territorial sea; territorial waters.

MERCURIALE – speech by a representative of the Attorney-General's Department at the ceremony marking the beginning of the judicial year.

MÈRE
- **NATUREL** – mère naturelle – mother of an illegitimate child (natural mother).

MESURE
- **APPLICATION** – mesure d'application – implementing measure.
- **CLÉMENCE** – mesure de clémence – act of clemency.
- **COERCITIF** – mesure coercitive – coercive mesure.
- **COERCITION** – mesure de coercition – coercive mesure.
- **COMMINATOIRE** – mesure comminatoire – coercive measure (ie involving a threat of legal sanctions).
- **CONSERVATOIRE** – mesures conservatoires – steps (measures) to preserve rights, property, evidence, the status quo, the present position; temporary administrative measures; protective measures; precautionary measures; interim (provisional) measures.
- **CRISE** – mesure de crise – emergency provision; special measure.
- **DÉPLACEMENT par mesure disciplinaire** – disciplinary transfer.
- **EXCEPTION** – mesure d'exception – emergency provision; special measure.
- **EXÉCUTION** – mesure d'exécution – form or measure of execution (enforcement); execution (enforcement) measure; implementing measure (which may take the form of implementing regulations).
- **INSTRUCTION** – mesure d'instruction – measure of investigation (investigative measure); procedural step in preparation for trial; procedural measure (eg for preserving or establishing evidence).
  - •• **ORDONNER des mesures d'instruction** – give procedural directions.
- **LÉGISLATIF** – mesures législatives et réglementaires – statutes and regulations.

- **PRÉVENTION** – mesure de prévention – preventive measure.
- **RÉFÉRÉ** – mesure de référé – injunction; mandatory injunction.
- **REPRÉSAILLES** – mesures de représailles – measure of reprisal; reprisals.
- **SUBSTITUTION** – mesure de substitution – alternative (measure).
- **SÛRETÉ** – mesure de sûreté – social-protection order; preventive measure; measure which can be imposed by the court on an offender not as a punishment but for the protection of society. (Such measures include detention of insane offenders, prohibition of residence in certain places, various disqualifications, compulsory treatment of alcoholics or drug addicts and the supervision of minors.)

MÉTAYAGE – tenancy of an agricultural holding in which the rent is paid in produce (in the absence of contrary agreement the landlord receives one-third).

MÉTIER
- **CHAMBRE des métiers** – chamber (association) of (manual) trades; trades association; guild; corporation.

METTRE
- **ADJUDICATION** – mettre en adjudication – advertise (call) for (invite) tenders.
- **APPLICATION** – mettre en application – bring into operation.
- **CAUSE** – mettre en cause – serve third-party notice on; implicate.
  - •• **ÊTRE mis en cause** – have proceedings brought against one; be implicated.
  - •• **MIS en cause** – against which the claim is directed; respondent (adj).
- **CONCOURS** – mettre en concours – advertise (call) for (invite) tenders.
- **DÉLIBÉRÉ** – mettre en délibéré – deliberate; discuss; withdraw to deliberate; reserve a judgment.
- **DEMEURE** – mettre en demeure – give notice to pay or perform (to remedy a certain state of affairs, to proceed or to comply (with an order, instruction, formality etc)); give (default) notice.
- **ENCHÈRE** – mettre aux enchères – auction.
- **ÉTAT** – mettre en état – prepare (a case) for trial; make (a case) ready for hearing; put in order; put (premises) into repair.

•• **SE mettre en état** – (as required of a convicted offender who is appealing on points of law) surrender to custody.

• **LIBERTÉ** – **mettre en liberté** – release.

• **PIED** – **mettre à pied** – suspend (from duty) on disciplinary grounds; lay off (employees); suspend a contract of employment for economic reasons.

• **RECOUVREMENT** – **mettre en recouvrement** – take steps to collect debts or taxes.

• **RETRAITE** – **mettre à la retraite** – retire (a person).

• **SCELLÉ** – **mettre sous scellés** – place seals on (place under seal) (eg pending an inventory).

• **SECRET** – **mettre au secret** – place in solitary confinement; hold incommunicado; prohibit communications.

• **VIGUEUR** – **mettre en vigueur** – bring into force.

MEUBLE – movable (property).

• **ANTICIPATION** – **meubles par anticipation** – things such as minerals and crops which it is intended to separate from the soil and which for some purposes are treated as movables prior to separation.

• **CORPOREL** – **meubles corporels** – corporeal movables; goods; tangible movables.

• **DÉTERMINATION DE LA LOI** – **meubles par détermination de la loi** – statutory movables: incorporeal assets, rights or choses in action, including in most cases rights in rem over corporeal movables but not the ownership of a corporeal movable where this is deemed to merge with the movable itself.

• **INCORPOREL** – **meubles incorporels** – incorporeal movables.

• **MEUBLANT** – **meubles meublants** – furniture.

• **NATURE** – **meubles par leur nature** – corporeal movables; goods; chattels. (Things which move (animals) or can be moved from place to place, eg boats, furniture, gas, electric current and bearer certificates not centrally deposited.)

MEUBLÉ – furnished premises.

MEURTRE – unlawful killing without aggravating circumstances; manslaughter (ie the actus reus of murder but without malice aforethought, eg if there is provocation). (The three elements of the French crime are (1) an act causing death; (2) the victim must be a living person already born; and (3) an intention to kill. If the intention was only to injure and the victim subsequently dies, the offence is only wounding (**coups et blessures**).)

• **JUDICIAIRE** – **meurtre judiciaire** – judicial murder (manslaughter).

MIEUX

• **ACHAT au mieux** – purchase at the best available price.

MILICE – vigilante group.

MILICIEN (Belg) – national serviceman; conscript.

MILIEU

• **FERMÉ** – **en milieu fermé** – custodial.

MINES – minerals; mines.

MINEUR – minor; juvenile; infant; under age.

• **DANGER** – **mineurs en danger** – minors at risk.

• **DE** – **mineur de dix-huit ans** – minor under 18.

• **DÉLINQUANT** – **mineur délinquant** – juvenile delinquent.

• **DÉTOURNEMENT de mineur** – abduction of a minor.

• **ÉMANCIPÉ** – **mineur émancipé** – minor declared of full age and capacity (emancipated minor).

MINIMA – see A MINIMA.

MINISTÈRE

• **AVOCAT** – **le ministère (obligatoire) d'avocat ou d'avoué alourdirait la procédure** – (compulsory) representation by a barrister or solicitor would make the proceedings cumbersome; legal representation.

• **PUBLIC** – **ministère publique** – the prosecution; (Principal) State (Crown) Counsel's Office (Department); (Principal) Legal Adviser's Office (Department); (in general or civil context) Attorney-General's Department; State (Crown, Public) Prosecutor's Office (Department); the public prosecutor; the prosecuting authorities; State (Crown) Prosecution Service; legal department; the law officers.

MINISTÉRIEL

• **OFFICE ministériel** – one of certain offices – such as those of bailiff, solicitor (**notaire**) and stockbroker – the holders of which are officially appointed, though their relationship with their clients is in most cases that of a professional adviser or agent; professional office.

- **OFFICIER ministériel** – member of one of certain professions (eg bailiff, solicitor (**notaire**) or stockbroker) whose members are officially appointed, though their relationship with their clients is in most cases that of a professional adviser or agent; professional officer.

MINISTRE

- **ADJOINT** – **ministre adjoint** – deputy minister.
- **CONSEIL des ministres** – (meeting of the) Cabinet presided over by the President of the Republic (if he is not present, the expression used is **conseil de cabinet**).
- **DÉLÉGUÉ** – **ministre délégué** – minister delegated by the Prime Minister to perform a specific task or mission; Minister of State; assistant minister.
- **ÉTAT** – **Ministre d'État** – Secretary of State; Minister.
- **PLÉNIPOTENTIAIRE** – **ministre plénipotentiaire** – minister plenipotentiary.

MINORITÉ – minority (also in the sense of being under age).

- **FAVEUR** – **minorité de faveur** – sufficient minority (in a jury) to bring about an acquittal.
- **PÉNAL** – **minorité pénale** – age up to 18 when a child is not (or not fully) criminally responsible.

MINUTE – (official) record; original document; original judgment.

- **(ACTE en) minute** – the original instrument kept by the solicitor (**notaire**) in his archives. (The execution copy of a directly enforceable instrument is known as the **grosse** and other copies are called **expéditions**.)
- **DRESSER minute** – execute an instrument the original of which is to be kept by the solicitor (**notaire**) as a **minute**.
- **EXÉCUTOIRE sur minute** – enforceable immediately, ie on the authority of the original written judgment, without having to serve an execution copy (**grosse**).
- **JUGEMENT** – **minute du jugement** – original judgment signed by the registrar and the president of the court. (The copy for execution is called the **grosse**.)
- **PASSER minute** – execute an instrument

the original of which is to be kept by the solicitor (**notaire**) as a **minute**.

MISE

- **ACCUSATION** – **mise en accusation** – decision to prefer an indictment to the Assize Court made by the Indictments Chamber (**chambre d'accusation**); committal for trial.
- **ADJUDICATION** – **mise en adjudication (publique)** – putting out to tender; advertisement (call) for tenders.
- **CAUSE** – **mise en cause** – third-party notice.
  - **DÉBITEUR** – **mise en cause du débiteur** – joinder of the debtor.
  - **RESPONSABILITÉ** – **mise en cause de la responsabilité de quelqu'un** – raising the question of someone's liability.
  - **RUINER la mise en cause du requérant** – destroy the case against the applicant.
- **CAUSE** – **mise hors cause** – discharge; (more generally) elimination from an inquiry; exoneration.
- **COMMERCE** – **mise hors (du) commerce** – prohibition of dealing in or sale of.
- **CONCOURS** – **mise en concours** – putting out to tender; advertisement (call) for tenders.
- **DÉLIBÉRÉ** – **mise en délibéré** – decision to give a considered judgment; reserving judgment.
- **DEMEURE** – **mise en demeure** – notice to pay or perform; notice to remedy a certain state of affairs; default notice; notice to proceed or to comply (with an order, instruction, formality, etc); notice.
  - **ACQUÉRIR** – **mise en demeure d'acquérir** – notice to purchase.
  - **ARRÊTÉ de mise en demeure** – official order to put an end to a given state of affairs.
- **ÉPREUVE** – **mise à l'épreuve** – (putting on) probation.
- **ÉTAT** – **mise en état** – preparation (of a case) for trial; making (a case) ready for hearing; putting in order; putting (premises) into repair; (required of a convicted offender who is appealing on points of law) surrender(ing) to custody.

•• JUGE de la mise en état – judge directing (in charge of) the preparation of a case for trial.

• FERMAGE – mise en fermage – letting of an agricultural holding.

• FONDS – mise de fonds – capital contribution to a partnership etc.

   •• NATURE – mise de fonds en nature – contribution in kind.

• GAGE – mise en gage – pledging; pawning; giving as security.

• GARDE – mise en garde – state of national emergency not involving a declaration of martial law.

• HARMONIE – mise en harmonie – consequential amendment.

• INDEX – mise à l'index – blacklisting.

• JOUR – mise à jour du registre foncier – rectification of the land register.

• INTERDIT – mise en interdit – blacklisting.

• LIBERTÉ – mise en liberté – release.

   •• CAUTION – mise en liberté sous caution – release on bail.

   •• PROVISOIRE – mise en liberté provisoire – provisional release from remand; (release on) bail; release pending trial.

• NOMINATIF – mise au nominatif – conversion into registered shares, debentures, etc.

• OBSERVATION – mise en observation – detention for observation.

• PIED – mise à pied – disciplinary suspension; laying off (lay-off) (of employees); suspension of a contract of employment for economic reasons.

• PRIX – mise à prix – opening or reserve price (in an auction).

• RECOUVREMENT – mise en recouvrement – (steps taken for the) collection of debts or taxes.

• RÉGIE – mise en régie – conversion into a state-run service.

• RETRAITE – mise à la retraite d'office – compulsory retirement.

• RÔLE – mise au rôle – entering in the court register.

• SCELLÉ – mise sous scellés – placing under seal (eg pending inventory).

• SECRET – mise au secret – (placing in) solitary confinement; holding incommunicado; prohibition of communications.

• SUPÉRIEUR – mise supérieure – higher bid.

• VIGUEUR – mise en vigueur – bringing into force; commencement.

MISSION
• CHARGÉ de mission – special adviser; special consultant.

MISSIVE
• LETTRE missive – personal letter; letter, card, etc sent through the post or by messenger.

MITOYEN
• MUR mitoyen – party wall.

MITOYENNETÉ – joint ownership of party walls, ditches, fences, etc, to which a number of special rules and presumptions apply.
• CESSION de mitoyenneté – assignment of party rights in a wall, fence, ditch, etc.

• CLÔTURE – mitoyenneté des clôtures – co-ownership of party walls, fences, etc; party rights.

MIXTE
• JUGEMENT mixte – final interlocutory judgment, eg a judgment which decides the question of liability and appoints an expert to assess the damages.

MOBILE – motive.
• ERREUR sur le mobile – mistake affecting the motive (in principle not sufficient to render a contract voidable).

MOBILIER – movable; personal (property).

MODALITÉ – details; various matters; arrangements; varieties; manner; procedure for.
• APPLICATION – modalités d'application – implementing provisions (regulations).

• EXÉCUTION – modalités d'exécution – implementing provisions (regulations).

• PAIEMENT – modalités de paiement – conditions of payment.

• PROCÉDURE – modalités de la procédure – forms of procedure.

MODÈLE – design.
• DÉCLARATION de modèle – application to register a design.

• DÉPÔT d'un modèle – registration of a design.

• INDUSTRIEL – modèle industriel – industrial design.

• UTILITÉ – modèle d'utilité – registered design.

MODÉRATION

- ORGANE de modération (Sw) – agency for arbitrating professional fees.

MODIFICATIF – amending provision.

MODIFICATION – amendment; alteration; modification.

- STATUTAIRE – modification statutaire – alteration of the statutes.

MODIFIER – amend; alter; modify; vary.

MŒURS

- ATTENTAT aux mœurs – sexual offence.
- BON – bonnes mœurs – morality.
- DÉRÈGLEMENT des mœurs – immorality.
- NATURE – mœurs contre nature – sexual perversion.

MOMENT – stage in the proceedings.

MONÉTAIRE

- CLAUSE monétaire – monetary correction clause; escalator clause.

MONNAIE

- ALTÉRATION de monnaie – debasing currency.
- APPOINT – monnaie d'appoint – small change which is legal tender only up to a prescribed amount.
- BILLON – monnaie de billon – small change which is legal tender only up to a prescribed amount.
- CONTREFAIT – monnaie contrefaite – counterfeit coin(age); forged notes.
- FALSIFICATION de monnaie – counterfeiting (coin(age)); forging notes.
- FICTIF – monnaie fictive – inconvertible currency.
- FIDUCIAIRE – monnaie fiduciaire – inconvertible currency.
- LÉGAL – monnaie légale – legal tender.
- SCRIPTURAL – monnaie scripturale – bank or other forms of financial credit; bank money.

MONNAIE-MATIÈRE – token money.

MONNAYAGE

- FAUX monnayage – forging (counterfeiting) currency.

MONOPOLE

- PAVILLON – monopole de pavillon – types of navigation reserved for national ships, eg coastal trade and coastal shipping.

MONTANT

- COMPENSATOIRE – montant compensatoire – compensating amount (countervailing charge).
- COMPTE – montant du compte – state of (balance on) an account.
- CRÉANCE – montant de la créance – amount of the claim.
- DEMANDE – montant de la demande – amount involved (in the case); amount of the claim.
- EXONÉRÉ – montant exonéré – (tax-free) allowance.
- FORFAITAIRE – montant forfaitaire – fixed sum; lump sum.
- IMPOSÉ
  - •• NON – montant non imposé – (tax-free) allowance.
- PEINE – montant de la peine – length of the sentence.

MONT-DE-PIÉTÉ – pawnbroker. (In France such business may now only be transacted by the crédit municipal or the magasins généraux.)

MORAL – non-material (damage); juridical (person); non-pecuniary (compensation or damage).

- DROIT
  - •• AUTEUR – droit moral de l'auteur – non-pecuniary, special (personal) right of an author, artist, etc in his work; non-pecuniary (attributes of) copyright.
- ÉLÉMENT moral – mental element.
- PERSONNE morale – legal entity; corporation; legal (juridical) person.
  - •• DROIT PRIVÉ – personne morale de droit privé – private-law corporation.
  - •• DROIT PUBLIC – personne morale de droit public – public-law corporation.

MORALITÉ

- TÉMOIN de moralité – witness to prove character.

MORATOIRE – moratorium.

MORT

- CIVIL – mort civile – civil death. Forfeiture of all civil rights formerly imposed on felons.

MOTIF – ground (of divorce or appeal); reason (for a judgment); motive (for entering into a contract); cause; justification.
- **ACCUSATION** – **motif d'accusation** – count (charge) in an indictment.
- **APPEL** – **motif d'appel** – ground of (for) appeal.
- **ARRESTATION** – **motif d'arrestation** – ground (reason) for arrest.
- **CONTRARIÉTÉ de motifs** – inconsistent reasons in a judgment.
- **DÉCISOIRE** – **motifs décisoires** – grounds of a judgment which are treated as having effect as if included in the formal order (operative words).
- **DÉFAUT de motif(s)** – inadequate (absence of) reasons (for a judgment).
- **DIVORCE** – **motif de divorce** – ground of (for) divorce.
- **EMPÊCHEMENT** – **motif d'empêchement** – obstacle; impediment.
- **ERREUR sur le motif** – mistake affecting the motive (in principle not sufficient to render a contract voidable).
- **EXPOSÉ des motifs** – explanatory memorandum; (statement of) objects and reasons.
- **JUGEMENT** – **motifs du jugement** – reasons for the judgment.
- **NULLITÉ** – **motif de nullité** – ground of nullity.
- **RETENU** – **motifs retenus** – reasons (given by a court for its judgment).
- **SANS motif sérieux** – without reasonable cause.

MOTION – (Sw) parliamentary motion (requiring government to legislate) (as opposed to **postulat**).
- **ACCUSATION** – **motion d'accusation** – motion for impeachment.
- **DÉFIANCE** – **motion de défiance** – motion of no confidence.
- **ORDRE** – **motion d'ordre** – point of order.
- **PROCÉDURE** – **motion de procédure** – (procedural) application.

MOTIVATION
- **APPEL** – **motivation de l'appel** – (lodging the) grounds of the appeal.
- **BREF** – **une brève motivation** – brief statement of reasons.

MOTIVÉ – containing grounds (reasons).
- **JUGEMENT motivé** – reasoned judgment; judgment giving reasons.

MOTIVER – furnish with reasons; give reasons for.
- **DÉCISION** – **motiver une décision** – give reasons for a decision (judgment).

MOUVEMENT
- **COLLECTIF** – **mouvement collectif** – (prison) mutiny.

MOYEN – cause of action; defence; ground of defence or claim; procedure; argument; allegation; type of evidence; point; submission; plea; ground of (for) appeal.
- **APPEL** – **moyen d'appel** – ground of (for) appeal.
- **BUDGÉTAIRE** – **moyen budgétaire** – budget provision.
- **CAUSE** – **moyen se trouvant dans la cause** – ground inherent in the facts as presented though not relied on by the parties.
- **COERCITION** – **moyen de coercition** – means of coercion or pressure.
- **DÉFENSE** – **moyens de défense** – grounds of defence.
- **DILATOIRE** – **moyen dilatoire** – application whose (sole) object is to retard the proceedings; means of retarding the proceedings; delaying tactic.
- **DROIT** – **moyen de droit** – ground based on law; point of law.
  - **PUR** – **moyen de pur droit** – legal ground resulting implicitly from the facts as presented to the court.
- **EXISTENCE** – **moyens d'existence** – means of subsistence (support).
- **FAIT** – **moyen de fait** – ground based on fact.
- **FAUX** – **moyen de faux** – allegation of forgery; grounds on which it is alleged a document is forged.
- **FINANCIER** – **moyens financiers** – financial resources.
- **FOND** – **tout moyen de fond étant réservé** – liberty to bring further argument on the merits; without prejudging (prejudice to) the merits.
- **NULLITÉ** – **moyen de nullité** – ground of nullity.
- **OBLIGATION de moyens** – obligation to use one's best endeavours (ie skill, care and diligence); duty to exercise skill and care; best-endeavours obligation.
- **OFFICE** – **moyen pris (relevé) d'office** – point (ground) raised by the court of its own motion (ex officio).

- **ORDRE PUBLIC** – moyen d'ordre public – ground involving a question of public policy (which the court must raise of its own motion at any stage of the proceedings).
- **PAIEMENT** – moyen de paiement – means of payment.
- **PRÉSENTATION de moyens nouveaux** – submission of new grounds.
- **PREUVE** – moyen de preuve – (piece of) evidence; proof.
- **PREUVE par tous les moyens** – all types of evidence.
  - •• **POSSIBLE** – la preuve serait alors possible par tous les moyens – in that case any kind of evidence would be admissible (could be adduced).
- **PROBATOIRE** – moyen probatoire – evidence; proof.
- **RÉCUSATION** – moyen de récusation – ground for challenging (a judge, juror, etc).
- **RÉSERVÉ** – see FOND above.
- **SUPPLÉER** – le tribunal ne peut suppléer d'office ce moyen – the court cannot raise this defence of its own motion (ex officio).
- **TARDIVETÉ** – moyen de tardiveté – submission that an application etc is out of time.
- **TOUS les moyens** – any type of evidence.
- **VALOIR** – faire valoir ses moyens – present one's case.

MULTIPROPRIÉTÉ – time-sharing.

MULTIRÉCIDIVISTE – persistent offender.

MUNICIPALITÉ – local-government district; township; town council; local authority.

MUR
- **MITOYEN** – mur mitoyen – party wall.

MÛREMENT
- **RÉFLÉCHI** – mûrement réfléchi – considered.

MUTATION – transfer (of property or employee); posting (of a civil servant); change of ownership.
- **DROIT de mutation** – capital transfer tax; transfer duty.
  - •• **DÉCÈS** – droit de mutation par décès – succession duty; inheritance tax.
- **FONCIER** – mutation foncière – entry of a transfer (of ownership) in the land register.
- **OFFICE** – mutation d'office – disciplinary transfer (posting).
- **PROPRIÉTÉ** – mutation de propriété – change (transfer) of ownership.
  - •• **TAXE sur les mutations de propriété** – conveyancing duty.
- **SERVICE** – mutation de service – posting (transfer).
- **TAXE de mutation** – transfer tax.

MUTUALITÉ (MUTUELLE) – friendly society; mutual insurance company.

MUTUUM – loan of money (or other fungible or consumable goods) of which the borrower is under an obligation to return an equivalent quantity; money loan.

N

NAISSANCE
- **ILLÉGITIME** – naissance illégitime – birth out of wedlock.
- **LÉGITIME** – naissance légitime – birth in wedlock.

NAISSANT – incipient; at an early stage.

NANTISSEMENT – pledge; mortgage; contract by virtue of which the debtor delivers something to his creditor as a security (in the case of a movable, this constitutes a pledge (**gage**); in the case of an immovable, a sort of mortgage in which the mortgagee in possession receives the produce or rents which are set off against the interest and principal of the debt (**antichrèse**); but the term **nantissement** is now also employed in a number of cases where the object charged remains in the possession of the chargor, eg charges on a business (**fonds de commerce**), agricultural equipment, oil stocks, a motor vehicle or professional installation or equipment); charge; bill of sale.
- **EFFET** en nantissement – bill deposited as a security; pawned bill.
- **FONDS DE COMMERCE** – nantissement sur fonds de commerce – charge on a business.
- **MARCHANDISE** – nantissement sur marchandises – pledge of goods.
- **TITRE** – nantissement sur titres – pledge of securities.

NATION
- **FAVORISÉ** – clause (traitement) de la nation la plus favorisée – most-favoured-nation clause (treatment).

NATIONALITÉ
- **DÉCHOIR** de la nationalité – deprive of citizenship (nationality).
- **DÉCLINER** la nationalité – renounce one's nationality.
- **ORIGINE** – nationalité d'origine – nationality of origin; nationality by birth.

NATURALISATION
- **GRAND** – grande naturalisation (Belg) – naturalisation conferring full civic rights.
- **PETIT** – petite naturalisation (Belg) – naturalisation without full civic rights.

NATURALISÉ – naturalised person.

NATURE
- **APPORT** en nature – contribution in kind.
- **AVANTAGE** en nature – benefit in kind.
- **BAIL** en nature – tenancy in which the rent is paid in kind.
- **EXÉCUTION** en nature – specific performance.
- **INDEMNITÉ** en nature – compensation (reparation) in kind.
- **JURIDIQUE** – nature juridique – legal nature.
- **RESTITUTION** en nature – restoration of the previous state of affairs (as opposed to money compensation); restitution in kind.

NATUREL – illegitimate; out of wedlock; natural; non-marital.
- **JUGE** naturel – pre-existing court, as opposed to a court established ad hoc to try a particular case; court which would lawfully exercise jurisdiction over a person; lawful judge; judge established (appointed, specified) by (the) law; statutory judge; rightful judge; normal judge; lawfully established court; regular judge.

NAVETTE
- **PARLEMENTAIRE** – navette parlementaire – (of a Bill) movement to and fro between the upper and lower chambers of Parliament.

NAVIGABILITÉ – seaworthiness; airworthiness.

NAVIGATION
- **RÉSERVÉ** – navigation réservée – shipping reserved for vessels flying the (French) flag, eg coastal trade.

NAVIRE – seagoing ship.

NEC BIS IN IDEM – rule that a person must not be tried twice for the same offence; non bis in idem.

NÉCESSITÉ
- **ÉTAT** de nécessité – (state of) necessity; defence of necessity.

NÉGATOIRE

- **ACTION négatoire** – action to establish the non-existence of an easement, profit, servitude, etc.

NÉGOCIATION – transfer free of equities.

- **COLLECTIF** – **négociation collective** – collective bargaining.
- **COMPTANT** – **négociation au comptant** – cash bargain; cash transaction.
- **PRIME** – **négociation à prime** – option bargain; option deal.
- **TERME** – **négociation à terme** – bargain for account.

NET

- **IMPÔT** – **net d'impôts** – free of tax.

NEUTRALITÉ

- **JUGE** – **neutralité du juge** – neutrality of the court (implying that control of the proceedings and of the presentation of the subject-matter is exercised by the parties).
- **STATUT de neutralité** – neutral status.

NEUTRE – neutral.

NOLIS – freight.

NOLISSEMENT – chartering; affreightment.

NOM

- **COLLECTIF** – **société en nom collectif** – commercial partnership.
- **COMMERCIAL** – **nom commercial** – business name.
- **EMPRUNT** – **nom d'emprunt** – assumed name.
- **GUERRE** – **nom de guerre** – pseudonym.
- **PATRONYMIQUE** – **nom patronymique** – surname; family name.
- **PERSONNEL** – **établissement en nom personnel** – private firm (business); one-man firm (business).
- **PROPRE** – **en nom propre** – in his own right.
- **SOCIAL** – **nom social** – business name.

NOMADE – person having (of) no fixed abode.

NOMINAL – nominal value.

NOMINATIF – (shares) registered.

NOMMÉ

- **CONTRAT nommé** – contract regulated by legislation; nominate contract.

NON-APPEL

- **CERTIFICAT de non-appel** – certificate by the registrar that there has been no appeal from, or application to set aside, a judgment or order.

NON BIS IN IDEM – rule that a person must not be tried twice for the same offence; non bis in idem.

NONCE – nuncio.

NON-CONCILIABILITÉ – incompatibility.

NON-CONCURRENCE

- **CLAUSE de non-concurrence** – agreement not to compete.

NON-CUMUL

- **PEINE** – **non-cumul des peines** – rule that where a person has committed several offences, consecutive sentences are not imposed. Instead the court pronounces the severest of the penalties available for one of the individual offences.

NON-EXÉCUTION – failure to perform.

NON-IMMIXTION – non-interference; non-intervention.

NON-IMPOSABLE – not liable to tax.

NON-IMPUTABILITÉ – absence of guilt; absence of criminal responsibility (owing to insanity or duress).

NON-INSCRIT – independent (MP).

NON-LIEU – discharge (by the investigating judge) of the accused; termination of the proceedings, ie when the accused is not committed for trial.

NON-PRÉCARITÉ – (holding something) in one's own right.

NON-RECEVABLE

- **ÊTRE** – **est non-recevable** – (of an appeal) does not lie.

NON-RÉEMBAUCHAGE

- **CLAUSE de non-réembauchage** – clause undertaking not to work for a competitor.

NON-REFOULEMENT – non-return (to the persecuting country); non-repatriation (ie provisional admission or transfer to a country willing to accept).

NON-REPRÉSENTATION

- **ENFANT** – **non-représentation d'enfant** – (criminal offence of) failure to hand over a child to the person(s) entitled to its custody.

NON-RESPECT – failure to comply.

- **DÉLAI** – **non-respect du délai** – failure to observe the time-limit.

NON-RESPONSABILITÉ – freedom or exemption from liability.

- **CLAUSE** de non-responsabilité – exemption clause; clause excluding liability.
- **CONVENTION** de non-responsabilité – agreement excluding (exempting from) liability.

NON-RÉTABLISSEMENT

- **CLAUSE** de non-rétablissement – clause undertaking not to enter into competition with the purchaser of a business etc.

NON-USAGE – non-user.

NON-VALEUR

- **METTRE** en instance de non-valeur – classify (credit entry) as doubtful.
- **MISE** en instance de non-valeur – amount awaiting a decision as to write-off.

NONCE – nuncio.

NORMATIF – law-making; rule-making.

- **CLAUSE normative** – rule-making clause; substantive clause.
- **FORME** – **sous forme normative** – in prescriptive form.

NORME – legal rule; norm; standard.

- **FONDAMENTAL** – **norme fondamentale** – basic (fundamental) norm (translation of German **Grundnorm** in Kelsen's theory).
- **INTERNATIONAL** – **norme internationale** – rule of international law.
- **JURIDIQUE** – **norme juridique** – rule of law; legal rule.

NOSTRIFICATION – naturalisation; recognition of a foreign qualification etc.

NOTAIRE – solicitor. (This is the general functional equivalent but there are many differences when it comes to details of practice and scope of function; in some contexts "notary" should be used, but care should be taken to avoid confusion with the considerably narrower English profession of notary public.)

- **ACTE devant notaire** – officially (ie notarially) recorded instrument; notarial act; docu-

ment drawn by a solicitor. (Cf an English deed.)
- **CHAMBRE des notaires** – law society.
- **CLERC de notaire** – legal executive; solicitor's (notary's) clerk.
- **ÉTUDE de notaire** – solicitor's (notary's) office (practice).
- **TARIF des notaires** – scale of solicitors' charges.

NOTARIAT – solicitor's (notary's) profession; (Lux, Sw) solicitor's office (practice).

NOTARIÉ – officially (ie notarially) recorded; notarial.

NOTATION – assessment (of an official's performance).

NOTE

- **AMENDEMENT** – **note d'amendement** – assessment of improvement (on a prisoner's personal file).
- **AUDIENCE** – **note d'audience** – court record; record of the hearing.
- **CIRCULAIRE** – **note circulaire** – circular.
- **COUVERTURE** – **note de couverture** – cover note; covering note.
- **DÉLIBÉRÉ** – **note en délibéré** – note sent by a party to a court when it is deliberating.
- **FRAIS** – **note de frais** – bill of costs.
- **ORIENTATION** – **note d'orientation** – briefing.
- **PAYÉ** – **note payée** – receipted invoice.
- **PLAIDOIRIE** – **note de plaidoirie** – written submissions summarising counsel's address.
- **PROTESTATION** – **note de protestation** – protest note.
- **SERVICE** – **note de service** – office circular.

NOTIFICATION – service; notification.

- **ACTE DE PROCÉDURE** – **notification des actes de procédure** – service of process.
- **ACTION** – **notification de l'action** – service of the writ, summons, etc.
- **DÉFAUT de notification** – failure to serve or give notice.
- **DOMICILE** – **notification à domicile** – service at a person's ordinary residence.
- **EXPLOIT de notification** – record of service made by a process-server.
- **MAIN PROPRE** – **notification en main(s) propre(s)** – personal service.

- **PERSONNE** – notification à personne – personal service.
- **PROCÉDURE** – notification des actes de procédure – service of process.
- **SUBSIDIAIRE** – notification subsidiaire – substituted service.

NOTIFIER – serve; notify.

NOTOIRE – (matter) of common knowledge; (facts) of which judicial notice is taken (ie which do not require to be proved).

NOTORIÉTÉ
- **ACTE** de notoriété – officially recorded document containing statements by a number of persons as to matters of common knowledge.
- **ÊTRE** de notoriété (publique) – to be a matter of common knowledge.

NOURRITURE
- **LOUAGE** à nourriture – agreement to provide a person with board and lodging in return for periodical payments or a capital sum.

NOVATION – novation.

NOVER – replace by a fresh obligation (novation).

NU – unfurnished.

NUANCER – qualify (reasons, a decision).

NUBILE – marriageable.

NUE-PROPRIÉTÉ – remainder.

NUIRE
- **BUT** – sans nuire au but – without prejudice to the purpose.

NUISANCE – disturbance; inconvenience; nuisance; harmful effect of industrial or technical development.

NUL – void.
- **AVENU** – nul et non avenu – null and void.
- **EFFET** – nul et de nul effet – null and void.

NULLITÉ – nullité.
- **ABSOLU** – nullité absolue – incurable nullity; state of being (absolutely) void. (English prefers the adjective to the noun.)
- **ACTION** en nullité – action to set aside (declare void).
- **CAUSE** de nullité – ground of nullity.
- **COUVRIR** la nullité – cure (remedy) the nullity (a void transaction).

- **DROIT** – nullité de droit – mandatory nullity, ie not in the discretion of the court.
- **ENTACHÉ** de nullité – void.
  - **RELATIF** – entaché de nullité relative – voidable (by the person the law seeks to protect).
- **EXCEPTION** de nullité – defence that the transaction etc relied on by the plaintiff is void; application for a step in the proceedings (writ, pleading, etc) to be struck out (set aside) on grounds of nullity.
- **FRAPPER** de nullité – render void.
  - **RADICAL** – frappé d'une nullité radicale – absolutely void.
- **JUGEMENT** déclaratif de nullité – judgment establishing nullity; judgment declaring (a transaction, contract, etc) void; (marriage) decree of nullity.
- **MARIAGE** – nullité du mariage – nullity (of marriage).
- **MISE EN ŒUVRE** de la nullité – procedure for establishing nullity.
- **MOTIF** de nullité – ground of nullity.
- **MOYEN** de nullité – ground of nullity.
- **ORDRE PUBLIC** – nullité d'ordre public – absolute (essential) nullity.
- **PEINE** – à (sous) peine de nullité – cannot validly; to be valid.
  - **OBLIGATION** – l'obligation n'est pas prescrite à peine de nullité de la décision – failure to comply does not mean that the decision is void.
  - **PRESCRIPTIONS** qui doivent être observées à peine de nullité – requirements failure to observe which makes the judgment etc void.
- **PRIVÉ** – nullité de caractère privé – voidability.
- **PROPOSER** une nullité – raise an objection (defence) on the ground that the action etc is void.
- **RELATIF** – nullité relative – state of being voidable (by the person the law seeks to protect); voidability; curable nullity.
- **TEXTUEL** – nullité textuelle – nullity which can be declared by a court only on the basis of an express statutory provision.
- **VIRTUEL** – nullité virtuelle – nullity which can be declared by a court even in the absence of an express statutory provision.

NUMÉRAIRE – cash.
- **AVOIRS** en numéraire – cash in hand.

NUMÉRO

- **CADASTRAL** – numéro cadastral – land-plan number; plot number on index map.
- **MINÉRALOGIQUE** – numéro minéralogique – motor-vehicle number.

- **ORDRE** – numéro d'ordre – serial number.

NUNCUPATIF – nuncupative; oral.

NU-PROPRIÉTAIRE – remainderman.

—

O

OBJECTIF
- **RESPONSABILITÉ objective** – strict liability; absolute liability; liability without fault; risk liability.

OBJET
- **APPROPRIATION d'objet trouvé** – stealing by finding; conversion of property by a finder.
- **CONTRAT** – **objet d'un contrat** – subject-matter of the contract; thing to which the contract relates; transaction which the contract is intended to bring about, eg a sale.
- **DEMANDE** – **objet de la demande** – aim (purpose) of the claim or proceedings; subject(-matter) of the claim or proceedings.
- **DÉTOURNEMENT d'objets saisis** – fraudulent removal or conversion of attached property (goods seized).
- **DOMMAGE** – **objet du dommage** – thing (property) damaged.
- **GAGE** – **objet de (en) gage** – thing pledged or pawned.
- **INDIVIS** – **objet indivis** – object in joint ownership.
- **LITIGE** – **objet du (en) litige** – subject-matter of the proceedings.
- **LITIGIEUX** – **objet litigieux** – object in dispute.
- **MOBILIER CORPOREL** – **objets mobiliers corporels** – goods; movables; chattels.
- **OBLIGATION** – **objet de l'obligation** – thing(s) to which the obligation relates; subject-matter of the obligation, ie the act of performance contemplated.
- **PREUVE** – **objet de la preuve** – thing (matter) to be proved.
- **RECOURS** – **objet du recours** – subject-matter of the appeal.
- **SAISI** – **objet saisi** – thing (property) attached.
- **SOCIAL** – **objet social** – the objects of a company or partnership.

OBLIGATAIRE – debenture-holder.

OBLIGATION – obligation, ie a legal relationship by virtue of which one person (the obligee, eg a promisee) may avail himself of the means of coercion put at his disposal by the law to ensure that another person (the obligor, eg a promisor) transfers the property in some thing, or does something or refrains from doing something; legal relationship of a pecuniary nature between two or more persons, by virtue of which the one (the obligor) is bound to perform something for the benefit of the other (the obligee); obligation; right in personam; chose in action; liability; debt; duty; debenture; bond.

- **ABSTENIR** – **obligation de s'abstenir** – obligation to refrain (from doing something).
- **ACCESSOIRE** – **obligation accessoire** – collateral obligation, understanding or agreement.
- **ALIMENTAIRE** – **obligation alimentaire** – (statutory) obligation to maintain (a person); maintenance obligation.
- **ALTERNATIF** – **obligation alternative** – obligation in which the promisor etc is bound to do one of two alternative things either at his choice or at that of the promisee etc.
- **CIVIL** – **obligation civile** – obligation non-performance of which entails a legal sanction.
- **CONJOINT** – **obligation conjointe** – several liability.
- **CONJONCTIF** – **obligation conjonctive** – obligation by virtue of which the promisor etc is bound to accomplish two or more different acts of performance.
- **CONTRACTER** – **obligation de contracter** – (statutory) obligation to contract.
- **CONTRACTUEL** – **obligation contractuelle** – liability (obligation) in contract; contractual obligation, ie an obligation arising out of a contract.
- **CONVENTIONNEL** – **obligation conventionnelle** – liability (obligation) in contract; contractual obligation, ie an obligation arising out of a contract.
- **CONVERTIBLE** – **obligations convertibles (en actions)** – convertible debentures.
- **CULTURE** – **obligation de culture** – obligation to cultivate land.
- **DÉLICTUEL** – **obligation délictuelle** – liability for intentional tort; tort (whether intentional or negligent); obligation in tort.
  - **QUASI** – **obligation quasi délictuelle** – liability for negligent tort; liability for negligence.

- **DÉTERMINÉ** – **obligation déterminée** – obligation to produce a specific result.
- **DETTE** – **obligation à la dette (aux dettes)** – liability for the debt(s) (of another, of a deceased person).
- **DOMMAGES-INTÉRÊTS** – **obligation à dommages-intérêts** – liability in damages.
- **DONNER** – **obligation de donner** – obligation to transfer property or a right in rem.
- **DROIT** **des obligations** – the law of obligations; contract and tort. It also includes quasi-contract (restitution, unjust enrichment, etc) and statutory obligations (eg maintenance).
- **ENTRETIEN** – **obligation d'entretien** – obligation to maintain a person or keep a building in repair.
- **ÉVENTUEL** – **obligation éventuelle** – contingent obligation; contingent liability.
- **EXTRAPATRIMONIAL** – **obligation extrapatrimoniale** – obligation of a non-pecuniary nature (though it has a pecuniary value).
- **FACULTATIF** – **obligation facultative** – obligation relating to a single act of performance from which the performer may be released by performing something else.
- **FAIRE** – **obligation de faire** – obligation to do something other than transfer a right in rem.
    - ●● **NE PAS** – **obligation de ne pas faire** – obligation to abstain (refrain) from doing something.
- **FONCIER** – **obligation foncière** – mortgage debenture secured on land.
- **GARANTIE** – **obligation de garantie** – (seller's) statutory warranty.
- **HYPOTHÉCAIRE** – **obligation hypothécaire** – mortgage debenture; mortgage bond.
- **IN SOLIDUM** – **obligation in solidum** – type of restricted joint and several liability which applies, eg, in the case of joint tortfeasors or persons jointly liable on a bill of exchange. It does not include the effects based on the presumed mutual agency of the co-obligors.
- **JURIDIQUE** – **obligation juridique** – legal duty; legal obligation.
- **MOYEN** – **obligation de moyens** – obligation to use one's best endeavours (ie skill, care and diligence); duty to exercise skill and care; best-endeavours obligation.
- **NATUREL** – **obligation naturelle** – natural obligation (obligation which cannot be enforced but is valid and cannot be set aside if voluntarily performed).
- **NON-CONCURRENCE** – **obligation de non-concurrence** – obligation not to compete.
- **PLURAL** – **obligation plurale** – obligation with several obligors or several obligees.
- **PORTEUR** – **obligation au porteur** – bearer debenture.
- **PROPTER REM** – **obligation propter rem** – obligation binding on the owner of a hereditament.
- **PRUDENCE** – **obligation de prudence et de diligence** – duty of care; duty to exercise care and diligence; duty to use one's best endeavours.
    - ●● **GÉNÉRAL** – **obligation générale de prudence** – general duty of care.
- **QUASI DÉLICTUEL** – see DÉLICTUEL above.
- **RÉEL** – **obligation réelle** – obligation secured in rem; secured obligation; obligation binding on the owner of a hereditament as such.
- **RÉSERVE** – **obligation de réserve** – obligation to treat the court with respect; obligation of judge or civil servant to refrain from any actions or expression of opinions incompatible with his functions or loyalty to the state; obligation to exercise reserve; duty of discretion.
- **RÉSULTAT** – **obligation de résultat** – obligation to produce a specific result; absolute obligation.
- **SÉCURITÉ** – **obligation de sécurité** – duty of care for the safety of others (implied by case-law in certain contracts).
- **SOLIDAIRE** – **obligation solidaire** – joint and several obligation.
- **STATUTAIRE** – **obligation statutaire** – duty imposed by (the) statute(s), regulations, etc.
- **SUCCESSORAL** – **obligation successorale** – liability of the estate.
- **TRÉSOR** – **obligation du Trésor** – treasury bond.
- **VALEUR** – **obligation de valeur** – fixed-value debt.
- **VOISINAGE** – **obligations (ordinaires) de voisinage** – duties owed to neighbours.
    - ●● **EXCÈS des obligations (ordinaires) de voisinage** – nuisance.

OBLIGATOIRE – binding; compulsory; obligatory.

- **VALEUR** obligatoire – binding effect.

OBLIGÉ – obligor; promisor.

OBSERVATION – (in plural) comments; representations; observations; submissions.
- **COMPLÉMENTAIRE** – observations complémentaires – further observations.

OBSERVER – comply with; follow.

OBSTACLE
- **FAIT** – obstacle de fait – material hindrance.

OBTEMPÉRER
- **À** – obtempérer à – comply with.

OBTENTION
- **VÉGÉTAL** – obtention végétale – creation of new plant species.

OCCUPANT – occupier; possessor; occupying forces (or power).
- **TITRE** – occupant sans titre – unlawful occupier; squatter.

OCCUPATION – (military) occupation; original acquisition of ownerless property; occupation of previously unclaimed territory; assuming ownership of ownerless property by taking possession; occupation.
- **DOMMAGE** d'occupation – occupation damage, ie damage caused by the occupying authorities or members of the occupation forces.
- **JURIDICTION** d'occupation – occupation court; jurisdiction of the occupation courts.
- **LÉGISLATION** d'occupation – occupation law.
- **LUCRATIF** – occupation lucrative – remunerated (gainful) employment.
- **SOL** – plan d'occupation des sols – local development plan; land-use plan.
- **TRIBUNAL** d'occupation – occupation court.

OCCUPER
- **POUR** – occuper pour – (of an **avoué**) act for.

ŒUVRE (fem) – charity.
- **ADOPTION** – œuvre d'adoption – adoption society.
- **BIENFAISANCE** – œuvre de bienfaisance – charitable institution.
- **ESPRIT** – droits sur œuvres de l'esprit – right to the fruits of mental activity (products of the mind, creative work, intellectual property).

- **PRIVÉ** – œuvre privée – private charity.
- **SOCIAL** – œuvre sociale – welfare institution.

ŒUVRE (masc)
- **NOUVEAU** – dénonciation de nouvel œuvre – application for an injunction to stop building works; proceedings for a quia timet injunction, ie to prevent anticipated damage interfering with enjoyment (possession) of property.

OFFENSE – insult; abuse; insulting (a head of state).

OFFICE
- **BONS** offices – good offices.
- **D'office** – ex officio; of its own motion; proprio motu.
  - •• **AVOCAT** d'office – official (officially assigned) defence counsel.
  - •• **DÉFENSEUR** d'office – official (officially assigned) defence counsel.
  - •• **RELEVER** d'office – (of a court) raise of its own motion (ex officio).
- **FAILLITE** – office des faillites (Sw) – execution and bankruptcy department for persons engaged in trade.
- **PLACEMENT** – office de placement de main-d'œuvre – labour exchange.
- **PUBLIC OU MINISTÉRIEL** – office public ou ministériel – one of certain offices – such as those of bailiff, solicitor (**notaire**) and stockbroker – the holders of which are officially appointed, though their relationship with their clients is in most cases that of a professional adviser or agent; professional office.

OFFICIER
- **DÉFENSEUR** – officier défenseur – defending officer (before a court martial).
- **ÉTAT CIVIL** – officier de l'état civil – registration officer; registrar.
- **JUSTICE** – officier de justice – court officer.
- **MINISTÉRIEL** – officier ministériel – member of one of certain professions (eg bailiff, solicitor (**notaire**) or stockbroker) whose members are officially appointed, though their relationship with their clients is in most cases that of a professional adviser or agent; professional officer.
- **PAIX** – officier de paix – (police) sergeant.

•• **PRINCIPAL** – officier de paix princi-pal – (police) inspector.

• **POLICE** – officier de police – senior (uni-formed) police officer (**officier de paix** or **commandant**).

•• **JUDICIAIRE** – officier de police ju-diciaire – senior police officer, mayor, prefect, etc entitled to exercise special powers in connection with the repression of crime; senior law-enforcement officer.

• **PUBLIC** – officier public – person entitled to make officially recorded documents (the general term is sometimes used where the context shows that, for example, a solicitor (**notaire**) or bailiff is intended); holder of a professional office; professional officer.

OFFICIEUX – semi-official; non-statutory; extra-statutory; unofficial.

OFFRANT

• **PLUS** – le plus offrant – the highest bidder.

OFFRE – offer (the first step towards a con-tract, which is completed by "acceptance").

• **CONCOURS** – offre de concours – offer to contribute to the cost of public works by an interested party (a contract governed by public law).

• **DEMANDE** d'offres – call (advertisement) for tenders.

• **DEMANDE** – offre et demande – supply and demand.

• **ESPÈCE** – offre en espèces – cash offer.

• **PREUVE** – offre de preuve – offer or application to produce or bring evidence.

•• **PRÉSENTER** des offres de preuve – submit evidence.

• **RÉEL** – offres réelles – (formal) tender of performance or payment, ie tender of the sum due by a person with capacity to pay to a creditor with capacity to receive (or to a person entitled to receive it on his behalf). (To be valid the sum must be presented by a bailiff or solicitor at the place prescribed for payment. If refused the sum is paid into court.)

OLOGRAPHE – holograph (will), ie entirely in the testator's handwriting.

OMISSION

• **STATUER** – omission de statuer – failure (by a court) to decide a point raised in the pleadings. (This may constitute a ground for appeal to the Court of Cassation or for an application to the trial court to retry the

issue in question (**recours en révision**, formerly **requête civile**).)

OMNES – see ERGA OMNES.

ONÉREUX

• **TITRE** – à titre onéreux – for (valuable) consideration; for payment; non-gratuitous; for value.

OPÉRATION – transaction.

• **BOURSE** – opération de bourse – stock-exchange transaction (contract).

•• **IMPÔT** sur les opérations de bourse – stamp duty on stock-exchange transac-tions.

• **ÉLECTORAL** – opérations électorales – holding of an election.

• **FICTIF** – opération fictive – fictitious transaction.

• **LIÉ** – opération liée – connected or collat-eral transaction; combined transaction.

OPINION

• **ABSTRAIT** – opinion abstraite – the gen-eral view; the opinion of the reasonable man.

• **COMMUN** – opinion commune – joint opinion.

• **CONCORDANT** – opinion concordante – concurring opinion.

• **DISSIDENT** – opinion dissidente – dissent-ing opinion.

• **DOMINANT** – opinion dominante – pre-dominant view (opinion); better opinion.

• **INDIVIDUEL** – opinion individuelle – sep-arate opinion.

• **PARTAGE** d'opinions – equality of votes; evenly split.

• **SÉPARÉ** – opinion séparée – separate opin-ion.

OPPORTUNITÉ – expediency; desirability; discretion.

• **ACTE ADMINISTRATIF** – l'opportunité d'un acte administratif – expediency of (the way a discretion has been exercised in arriv-ing at) an administrative decision.

• **POURSUITE** – principe de l'opportunité des poursuites – rule that whether a prose-cution should be brought is a matter within the discretion of the prosecuting authorities; principle of discretionary prosecution.

OPPOSABLE

- **À** – opposable à – binding on; enforceable against; effective against; capable of being raised against;
  capable of operating against.
  - •• **TIERS** – opposable aux tiers – valid vis-à-vis third parties; effective against third parties; binding on (applicable to) third parties (eg strangers to a contract).

OPPOSANT – person applying to set aside (a judgment by default or in absentia); person placing a stop on a negotiable instrument; objector.

OPPOSER – raise the defence; plead in defence; reply; object; set up (against).

- **ACTE** – opposer un acte – rely on a document made by the other party.
  - •• **PRÉTENDRE** opposer un acte – seek (purport) to allege the validity of an act (transaction).
- **S'opposer** – son droit interne s'oppose à – its domestic law prevents.

OPPOSITION – application to a court to set aside a judgment it has given by default or in the absence of an accused and rehear the case; objection; (negotiable instrument) stop; notice to a debtor not to pay his creditor; notice of attachment of a debt.

- **ACTE** d'opposition – application to set aside.
- **CONTRAINTE** – opposition à contrainte – application to set aside (objection to) an order to pay.
- **DÉBOUTÉ** d'une opposition – dismissal of an application to set aside.
- **DÉFAUT** – opposition sur défaut – application to set aside a judgment by default.
- **DÉLAI** d'opposition – time-limit for lodging an application to set aside or raising an objection.
- **EXPLOIT** d'opposition – notice of application to set aside.
- **FAIRE (FORMER)** opposition – lodge (file) an application to set aside; lodge (file) an objection; put a stop on a negotiable instrument.
- **INCIDENT** – opposition incidente – see TIERCE below.
- **MARIAGE** – opposition à mariage – prevention by certain persons of the celebration of a marriage.
- **SUSCEPTIBLE** d'opposition – la décision qui ordonne une mesure d'instruction n'est pas susceptible d'opposition – an application may not be brought to set aside a decision ordering a procedural measure.
- **TIERCE** opposition – application by a third party (ie a person not represented in the proceedings) to set aside a judgment adversely affecting his interests.
  - •• **INCIDENT** – tierce opposition incidente – application by a third party incidental to pending proceedings to set aside a judgment.
  - •• **PRINCIPAL** – tierce opposition principale – application by a third party independent of pending proceedings to set aside a judgment.

OPTION

- **LEVÉE** de l'option – exercise of the option.
- **LEVER** une option – exercise an option.
- **PLACE** – option de place – right to choose place of payment.

ORALITÉ

- **DÉBAT** – oralité des débats – (requirement of) a(n oral) hearing.

ORDONNANCE – order (certain provisional orders of a legislative nature made by the government in connection with the budget or the introduction of special programmes of legislation; certain orders made by a single judge, especially those connected with the investigation of an offence); warrant (authority) authorising payment by the Treasury.

- **ACCORD** – ordonnance rendue sur la base d'un accord – consent order.
- **APPLICATION** – ordonnance d'application – implementing regulations.
- **CLÔTURE** – ordonnance de clôture – order by which an investigating judge closes an investigation (ie discharge or committal for trial).
- **COMPARUTION** – ordonnance de comparution – summons (to appear before the court making the order).
- **CONTRAINTE** – ordonnance de contrainte – warrant to bring before the court.
- **CONTUMACE** – ordonnance de contumace – order to present oneself for trial within ten days.
- **DESSAISISSEMENT** – ordonnance de dessaisissement – order transferring a case to another investigating judge.
- **EXEQUATUR** – ordonnance d'exequatur – authority to execute (enforce) a judgment.

- **EXPROPRIATION** – **ordonnance d'expropriation** – expropriation (compulsory purchase) order.
- **EXPULSION** – **ordonnance d'expulsion** – order for possession; writ of possession.
- **INCOMPÉTENCE** – **ordonnance d'incompétence** – finding by an investigating judge that he lacks jurisdiction to deal with the case.
- **INTERNEMENT** – **ordonnance d'internement** – detention order; internment order.
- **JUSTICE** – **ordonnance de justice** – court order; judge's order.
- **JUSTIFICATION** – **ordonnance de justification** – show cause order.
- **NON-LIEU** – **ordonnance de non-lieu** – discharge (by the investigating judge).
- **NON-RECEVABILITÉ** – **ordonnance de non-recevabilité** – ruling (by the investigating judge) that the conditions for opening an investigation are not satisfied.
- **PÉNAL** – **ordonnance pénale** – summary order imposing a fine which the defendant may have set aside if he wishes to have a full trial; sentence order.
- **PRENDRE** **une ordonnance** – make or issue an order.
- **PREUVE** – **ordonnance de preuves (Sw)** – order for evidence to be taken.
- **PRISE DE CORPS** – **ordonnance de prise de corps** – arrest warrant issued by the Indictments Chamber.
- **RÉFÉRÉ** – **ordonnance de référé (sur référé)** – provisional (interim) order made by a single judge, usually the president of the court, in an urgent matter; (judge's) order (on an application in urgent proceedings).
- **REFUS D'INFORMER** – **ordonnance de refus d'informer** – ruling (by the investigating judge) that the conditions for opening an investigation are not satisfied.
- **RÈGLEMENT** – **ordonnance de règlement** – order by which an investigating judge closes an investigation (ie discharge or committal for trial).
- **RENDRE** – **ordonnance rendue conformément à la loi** – lawful order.
- **RENVOI** – **ordonnance de renvoi** – committal for trial.
- **REQUÊTE** – **ordonnance sur requête** – order made by the president of the court or a single judge on an ex parte application.
- **SAISIE-ARRÊT** – **ordonnance de saisie-arrêt** – (formerly) garnishee order nisi.

- **SÉQUESTRE** – **ordonnance de séquestre (Sw)** – provisional attachment order.
- **SOIT-COMMUNIQUÉ** – **ordonnance de soit-communiqué** – order by the investigating judge closing an investigation, transmitting the file and informing the public prosecutor's office that the case is ready for further action; notification to proceed (with a prosecution).
- **TAXE** – **ordonnance de taxe** – order fixing the costs; certificate of taxed costs; allocatur; taxation of costs (by the president of the court on an appeal from a taxation (**vérification des dépens**) by the registry).
- **TRANSMISSION (DE PIÈCES)** – **ordonnance de transmission (de pièces)** – order by the investigating judge closing an investigation and sending the file to the Principal Public Prosecutor's Office (Attorney-General's Department) for submission to the Indictments Chamber of the Court of Appeal.

ORDONNANCEMENT
- **DÉPENSE** – **ordonnancement des dépenses** – warrant (issued by the minister personally) authorising payment by the Treasury; authorisation of settlement.

ORDONNATEUR – minister or civil servant entitled to authorise the payment and receipt of public moneys; commitments officer.

ORDONNER – order.

ORDRE
- **AVOCAT** – **ordre des avocats** – bar (association).
- **BILLET** **à ordre** – promissory note
- **CHÈQUE** **à ordre** – order cheque.
- **CLAUSE** **à ordre** – order clause written on a cheque or bill (ie the words "or order"). (A bill of exchange is transferable by endorsement even without an express order clause unless it contains words expressly excluding such transfer.)
- **CONNAISSEMENT** **à ordre** – order bill of lading.
- **CONSEIL** **de l'ordre (des avocats, des médecins, etc** – Bar Council, General Medical Council, etc.
- **CONSTITUTIONNEL** – **ordre constitutionnel** – the existing constitutional order (system).

- **CRÉANCIER** – **ordre entre créanciers** – procedure for the distribution of the proceeds of sale of real property among the privileged and secured creditors according to the priority of their liens, rights to prior payment (preferences) and mortgages.
- **ÉCROU** – **ordre d'écrou** – committal order (warrant).
- **ENCAISSEMENT** – **ordre d'encaissement** – order (authority) to collect a debt.
- **EXÉCUTION** – **ordre d'exécution** – writ of execution endorsed on an order to pay.
- **EXPULSION** – **ordre d'expulsion** – expulsion order; deportation order; order for possession; writ of possession.
- **HÉRITIER** – **ordre d'héritiers** – order of succession.
- **INFORMER** – **ordre d'informer** – direction to commence a judicial (preliminary) investigation.
- **INTERNEMENT** – **ordre d'internement** – detention order; internment order.
- **JUDICIAIRE** – **ordre judiciaire** – (ordinary) courts; judiciary.
- **JURIDICTION** – **ordre de juridiction** – type (class) of court (jurisdiction) (eg civil, criminal or administrative).
- **JURIDIQUE** – **ordre juridique** – legal system (order); branch of law.
- **MÉDECIN** – **ordre des médecins** – medical association.
- **MENACE pour l'ordre public** – threat to the peace (public order, public policy).
- **MENTION à ordre** – order clause on a cheque, bill, etc.
- **NORMATIF** – **ordre normatif** – system of rules.
- **PAIEMENT** – **ordre de paiement** – payment order; order to pay.
- **PAPIER à ordre** – order security.
- **PUBLIC** – **ordre public** – public policy; public order; ordre public. (In French private international law, public policy excludes the application of foreign law if it is contrary to the fundamental principles of French civilisation. Freedom of contract is subject to the condition that the agreement entered into is not contrary to public policy or morality.)
  - •• **D'ordre public** – a matter of public policy and hence mandatory.
- **RECOUVREMENT** – **ordre de recouvrement** – collection order; order to collect; payment demand note.
- **RÈGLE d'ordre public** – mandatory rule of law; rule of public policy.

- **SUCCESSORAL** – **ordre successoral** – order of succession.

ORGANE – organ, in the sense of a person or body through the instrumentality of which a function is performed; responsible body; responsible person; agency; organ; institution; authority; competent person.
- **DIRECTION** – **organe de direction** – governing body (organ).
- **EXÉCUTION** – **organe d'exécution** – executive organ (body).
- **JURIDICTIONNEL** – **organe juridictionnel** – court; tribunal; judicial organ; quasi-judicial body (organ).
- **LÉGISLATIF** – **organe legislatif** – legislative body; legislature; parliament.
- **RÉVISION** – **organe de révision** – auditor; board of auditors.

ORGANIGRAMME – organisation(al) chart; establishment chart; organigramme.

ORGANIQUE – institutional; constitutional; quasi-constitutional.
- **LOI organique** – State Authorities Act; Act, not forming part of the Constitution, laying down the principles governing the organisation or structure of organs of government or other public authorities; institutional Act; Act establishing; (with reference to Spain) implementing Act.

ORGANISATION
- **JUDICIAIRE** – **organisation judiciaire** – administration of justice; organisation of the courts; judicature.
- **SUCCESSORAL** – **organisation successorale** – successor organisation.

ORGANISME
- **ARBITRAL** – **organisme arbitral** – arbitral tribunal.
- **AUTONOME** – **organisme autonome** – self-governing body.
- **CONSULTATIF** – **organisme consultatif** – advisory body.
- **EXÉCUTION** – **organisme d'exécution** – executive organ (body).

ORIENTATION
- **AGRICOLE** – **orientation agricole** – agricultural planning.
- **FONCIER** – **orientation foncière** – land planning.
- **NOTE d'orientation** – briefing.

OUÏR

- **DÉCLARATION** – la Cour a ouï dans leurs déclarations – the Court heard addresses by.

OUTRAGE – insult; abuse (especially insulting persons holding official positions).

- **AGENT** – outrage à agent – insulting a constable.
- **BONNES MŒURS** – see MŒURS below.
- **DERNIER** – subir les derniers outrages – be raped.
- **MŒURS** – outrage aux bonnes mœurs – offence against morality; immoral publications (especially those of an obscene or erotic nature); obscene publications, songs, cries or advertisements.
- **MORALITÉ PUBLIQUE** – outrage à la moralité publique – causing offence by indecent behaviour or exposure.
- **PUDEUR** – outrage public à la pudeur – indecent behaviour or exposure in public; gross indecency.

OUTREPASSER

- **POUVOIR** – outrepasser ses pouvoirs – exceed one's powers (one's authority).

OUVERT

- **ACTION** – aussi l'action restera-t-elle ouverte bien au-delà de trois ans – the action will therefore remain available for much longer than three years (eg because time does not run during the plaintiff's minority).
- **VILLE** ouverte – (international law) open (ie undefended) city.

OUVERTURE – commencement; grounds; eligibility; entitlement; cases in which an action or appeal is available.

- **ACTION PÉNALE** – ouverture de l'action pénale – institution (commencement) of criminal proceedings.
- **CASSATION** – ouverture à cassation – grounds on which an appeal to the Court of Cassation may be based.
- **CONDITIONS** d'ouverture du droit aux prestations – conditions of entitlement to benefit.
- **CRÉDIT** – ouverture de crédit – agreement whereby a a bank agrees to place certain sums at the disposal of a client for a specified period.
- **DÉBAT** – ouverture des débats – stage of a trial which commences when the plaintiff's counsel begins speak.
- **DONNER** ouverture à réparation – afford a claim in damages.
- **DROIT** – ouverture d'un droit – grounds on which a claim or right is based; granting of a right.
  - **PRESTATION** – ouverture du droit aux prestations – eligibility for benefit.
- **FAILLITE** – ouverture de la faillite – commencement of bankruptcy.
- **RÉPARATION** – donnant ouverture à réparation – affording a claim in damages.
- **SUCCESSION** – ouverture de la succession – moment when the succession takes place; passing of the estate to the heirs.
- **USUFRUIT** – ouverture de l'usufruit – commencement of the usufruct (life tenancy).

OUVRAGE

- **GROS** ouvrage – main walls and roof.
- **LOUAGE** d'ouvrage – contract for services; contract for work (and materials). (Comprises both **louage de services** (service contract; employment contract) and **louage d'industrie** (contract for services, ie to make or do something as an independent contractor, eg make a suit or fill a tooth).)

OUVRIR

- **ACTION** – ouvrir une action – give (make available) a cause of action.
- **CASSATION** – la voie de cassation est ouverte contre – an appeal on points of law lies against.
- **CRÉDIT** – ouvrir un crédit – vote an appropriation.
- **DROIT** – ouvrir (un) droit – entitle; grant (confer) a right.
- **INFORMATION** – ouvrir une information – commence a judicial investigation.
- **INSTRUCTION** – ouvrir une instruction – commence a judicial investigation.

OYANT

- **COMPTE** – oyant compte – person to whom an account is rendered.

P

PACAGE – right to pasture sheep; common of pasture.
- **SERVITUDE de pacage** – profit of pasture.

PACTE
- **COMMISSOIRE** – **pacte commissoire** – foreclosure clause in a pledge or mortgage; clause permitting the pledgee or mortgagee to keep the object pledged or mortgaged in case of non-repayment; (more generally) rescission clause.
- **MATRIMONIAL** – **pacte matrimonial** – marriage contract.
- **PRÉFÉRENCE** – **pacte de préférence** – pre-emption agreement.
- **QUOTA LITIS** – **pacte de quota litis** – agreement authorising another to pursue an action on one's behalf in return for a share of the proceeds; champertous agreement (if entered into by a lawyer).
- **RACHAT** – **pacte de rachat** – redemption clause; clause giving a vendor the right to repurchase property (within five years).
- **RÉMÉRÉ** – **pacte de réméré** – redemption clause; clause giving a vendor the right to repurchase property (within five years).
- **SOCIAL** – **pacte social** – articles of association or partnership.
- **SUCCESSION FUTURE** – **pacte sur succession future** – agreement on the succession of a living person.

PAIEMENT – performance of an obligation (payment of a debt) and more particularly performance of an obligation to pay money.
- **ANTICIPATION** – **paiement par anticipation** – payment in advance.
- **CESSATION de(s) paiement(s)** – cessation (suspension) of (a debtor's) payments (state preceding bankruptcy); inability to meet current liabilities; insolvency.
- **COMPENSATOIRE** – **paiement compensatoire** – equalisation payment; deficiency payment.
- **DATION en paiement** – satisfaction; accord and satisfaction.
- **DÉLÉGATION de paiement** – order (instruction) to pay (usually addressed to a banker).
- **ÉCHELONNÉ** – **paiement échelonné** – payment by instalments.

- **ÉCHU** – **paiement échu** – payment due.
- **ESPÈCE** – **paiement en espèces** – payment in cash.
- **FICTIF** – **paiement fictif** – notional payment.
- **FRACTIONNÉ** – **paiement fractionné** – payment by instalments.
- **INDU** – **paiement de l'indu** – payment in satisfaction of a non-existent obligation (which gives rise to a right to restitution – money had and received).
- **INTÉRIEUR** – **paiement intérieur** – inland payment.
- **INTERVENTION** – **paiement par intervention** – payment for honour.
- **LIBÉRATOIRE** – **paiement libératoire** – payment effecting a discharge (from an obligation).
- **NUMÉRAIRE** – **paiement en numéraire** – payment in cash.
- **PRÉSENTATION au paiement** – presentation for payment.
- **PROVISIONNEL** – **paiement provisionnel** – payment of an advance.
- **SOMMATION de paiement** – official demand for payment by the bailiff.
- **SOUFFRANCE** – **paiement en souffrance** – overdue payment.
- **SURSIS de paiement** – extension of time for payment.
- **TEMPÉRAMENT** – **paiement à tempérament** – payment by instalments.
- **TROP** – **paiement en trop** – overpayment.

PAIR
- **AU pair** – at par.

PAISSON – right of pasture for pigs.

PANACHAGE – the inclusion by a voter of candidates selected from different party lists in his voting-paper.

PAPIER – bill of exchange.
- **COMPLAISANCE** – **papier de complaisance** – accommodation bill.
- **DOMESTIQUE** – **papiers domestiques** – family papers, eg diaries.
- **FAIT** – **papier fait** – bill with three signatures accepted for rediscount by the Bank of France.

- **ORDRE** – **papier à ordre** – order security.
- **PORTEUR** – **papier au porteur** – bearer security.
- **TIMBRÉ** – **papier timbré** – stamped paper, ie paper bearing a revenue stamp on which certain documents must be written.

PARADIS

- **FISCAL** – **paradis fiscal** – tax haven.

PARAÉTATIQUE – partly state-owned (or controlled).

PARAFISCAL – extra-budgetary.

PARAJUDICIAIRE – quasi-judicial.

PARALÉGAL – quasi-statutory.

PARAPHER – initial the text of a treaty to show it has been provisionally agreed. This does not in any way bind the negotiating states.

PARAPHERNAL

- **BIENS paraphernaux** – separate property of the wife under the dotal system of marital property (abolished in France with respect to future marriages as from 1965) which does not form part of her settled property (**biens dotaux**).

PARASTATAL – partly state-owned (or controlled).

PARCELLAIRE

- **PLAN parcellaire** – registered plan; index map (showing plots of land).
- **REMEMBREMENT parcellaire** – consolidation of smallholdings.

PARCELLE – plot (parcel) (of land).

- **CADASTRAL** – **parcelle cadastrale** – plot on a registered plan.

PARCOURS

- **DROIT de parcours** – right of common (for pasturing animals).
- **LIBRE parcours** – free passage.

PAREATIS (Belg) – authority to execute (enforce).

PARENT

- **CONSANGUIN** – **parents consanguins** – relations of the half-blood on the father's side.
- **GERMAIN** – **parents germains** – relations of the full blood.
- **UTÉRIN** – **parents utérins** – relations of the half-blood on the mother's side.

PARENTÈLE – family group consisting of a person and his issue; stirps; stock.

PARER

- **GRIEF** – **parer à un grief** – redress a complaint.

PARÈRE – written statement confirming the existence of a trade custom.

PARI – bet; wager.

PARITAIRE – equi-representational; joint.

PARITÉ – official rate of exchange.

PARJURE – perjury; perjurer.

PARQUET – State (Crown) Counsel's Office (Department); Attorney-General's Department; State (Crown, Public) Prosecutor's Office (Department); the prosecution; the prosecuting authorities.

- **GÉNÉRAL** – **parquet général** – Principal State (Crown) Counsel's Office (Department); Attorney-General's Department; Principal State (Crown, Public) Prosecutor's Office (Department); the prosecution; the prosecuting authorities.
- **PRATIQUE des parquets** – prosecution practice.

PART – portion; share; newly born infant.

- **ASSOCIÉ** – **part d'associé** – share in a partnership.
- **FONDATEUR** – **part de fondateur** – founder's share; promoter's share.
- **HORS** – **(par préciput et) hors part** – (of a gift to an heir out of an estate) not subject to hotchpot; in addition to the heir's share of the estate.
- **INDIVIS** – **part indivise** – undivided share.
- **INTÉRÊT** – **part d'intérêt** – partnership share; non-negotiable share.
- **PRÉCIPUTAIRE** – **part préciputaire** – gift to an heir out of an estate in addition to his share.
- **SOCIAL** – **part sociale** – share in a partnership, business or private company.
- **SUBSTITUTION de part** – substitution of a child.
- **SUCCESSORAL** – **part successorale** – share in an estate; share on (an) intestacy.
- **SUPPOSITION de part** – attributing a child to an imaginary woman or to a woman who has not conceived; passing off a child.
- **SUPPRESSION de part** – causing the disappearance of a new-born child (charge

brought where nothing more can be proved); concealment of birth.

- VIRIL – **part virile** – separate share; equal share.

PARTAGE – partition.

- ASCENDANT – **partage d'ascendant** – division of an estate by a parent or ancestor among his children or issue to avoid subsequent litigation.
- CONJONCTIF – **partage conjonctif** – division by the father and mother of their estate among all their issue.
- JUDICIAIRE – **partage judiciaire** – partition by the court.
- NATURE – **partage en nature** – partition in kind.
- OPINION – **partage d'opinions** – equality of votes; evenly split.
- PROVISIONNEL – **partage provisionnel** – provisional partition (esp where there is a usufruct (life interest) pending the final division of the property).
- SOUCHE – **partage par souche(s)** – division per stirpes.
- SOULTE – **partage avec soulte** – partition with payment of compensation.
- TESTAMENTAIRE – **partage testamentaire** – division by will.
- TÊTE – **partage par tête** – division per capita.
- VOIX – **partage des voix** – equality of votes; tie; if the votes are equal.

PARTAGEABLE – divisible.

PARTAGEANT – person entitled to a share on partition.

PARTENAIRE – the other party (to a contract).

- SOCIAL – **partenaires sociaux** – management and labour; both sides of industry; partners in industry; employers and labour.

PARTI

- SANS **parti** – independent.

PARTIAIRE

- COLON **partiaire** – tenant who pays his rent in produce.

PARTIAL – biased; partial.

PARTIALITÉ – bias.

PARTICIPATION

- ACQUÊT – **participation aux acquêts** – sharing of after-acquired property. (System of marital property under which each spouse keeps his own property and at the end of the marriage each takes half the other's after-acquired property.)
- BON de participation – participation certificate giving a right to share in profits or on liquidation or to subscribe for shares (not identical with a **bon de jouissance**).
- CRIMINEL – **participation criminelle** – complicity (in a felony).
- FORFAITAIRE – **participation forfaitaire** – fixed contribution.
- MAJORITAIRE – **participation majoritaire** – majority holding.
- SOCIÉTÉ en participation – partnership with a sleeping partner or undisclosed partnership.

PARTICULIER – private individual.

- TRANSMISSION à titre particulier – transfer of (succession to) one or more specific items of property (not subject to the personal debts of one's predecessor in title).

PARTIE – (code) part. The Swiss Civil Code is divided into **livres** (books), **parties** (parts), **titres** (sections), **chapitres** (chapters) and **articles** (articles).

- ADVERSE – **partie adverse** – the other side; opposite (opposing) party (it may be preferable to specify "the plaintiff", "the respondent", etc).
- APPELANT – **partie appelante** – appellant.
- ASSIGNÉ – **partie assignée** – party on whom a writ has been served, ie the defendant.
- ASSISTANCE JUDICIAIRE – **partie admise à l'assistance judiciaire** – legally aided party.
- BELLIGÉRANT – **partie belligérante** – belligerent.
- CAUSE – **partie en cause** – party to the proceedings.
  - •• METTRE – **partie mise en cause** – respondent.
- CITÉ – **partie citée** – party on whom a writ of summons has been served, ie the defendant.

- **CIVIL** – **partie civile** – party claiming damages (in criminal proceedings); (sometimes) complainant.
- **COMMUN** – **parties communes** – parts of a building and its surroundings in the joint ownership of the co-owners.
- **COMPARANT** – **partie comparante** – party before the court.
- **CONSTITUTIF** – **partie constitutive** – constituent part; essential part.
- **CONTRACTANT** – **(haute) partie contractante** – (high) contracting party.
- **DÉBOUTÉ** – **partie déboutée** – unsuccessful (losing) party.
- **DÉFAILLANT** – **partie défaillante** – party failing to appear.
- **DÉFENDEUR** – **partie défenderesse** – defendant; respondent.
- **DEMANDEUR** – **partie demanderesse** – plaintiff.
- **DIFFÉREND** – **partie au différend** – litigant.
- **GAGNANT** – **partie gagnante** – successful party.
- **INDIGENT** – **partie indigente** – poor party.
- **INTÉGRANT** – **partie intégrante** – essential component.
- **INTERVENANT** – **partie intervenante** – third party; intervening party; intervener.
- **INTIMÉ** – **partie intimée** – respondent.
- **JOINT** – **partie jointe** – co-plaintiff or co-defendant; party joined as plaintiff or defendant; associated party; status of State Counsel when he intervenes in civil proceedings to submit his observations to the court.
  - • **ÊTRE** – **lorsqu'il est partie jointe** – when he is joined in the proceedings.
- **LÉSÉ** – **partie lésée** – injured party.
- **LITIGE** – **partie au litige** – party to the proceedings; litigant.
- **OPPOSANT** – **partie opposante** – objecting party.
- **PERDANT** – **partie perdante** – unsuccessful (losing) party.
- **PLAIGNANT** – **partie plaignante** – complainant.
- **POURSUIVANT** – **partie poursuivante** – plaintiff; applicant; prosecutor.
- **PRENANT** – **partie prenante** – party entitled to receive payment.
- **PRÉSENT** – **partie présente** – party before the court.
- **PRINCIPAL** – **partie principale** – State

Counsel when he takes part in civil proceedings as plaintiff or defendant.
- **PRIVATIF** – **parties privatives** – parts of a building in co-ownership occupied exclusively by the various co-owners.
- **PROCÈS** – **partie au procès** – party to the proceedings; litigant.
- **PUBLIC** – **partie publique** – Attorney-General's Department; the prosecution.
- **RÉCLAMANT** – **partie réclamante** – complainant; applicant.
- **REQUÉRANT** – **partie requérante** – plaintiff; applicant.
- **SUCCOMBANT** – **partie succombante** – unsuccessful (losing) party.

PAS-DE-PORTE – premium payable for the right to occupy business premises; premium for goodwill.

PASSAGE – right of way.
- **DROIT** de passage – right of way.
- **INOFFENSIF** – **passage inoffensif** – innocent passage.
- **USAGE** – **le passage a fait l'objet de trente ans d'usage** – the right of way has been exercised for thirty years.

PASSATION
- **ACTE** – **passation d'un acte** – execution of a legal instrument.
- **ÉCRITURE** – **passation en écritures** – posting (entry) in an account.
- **POUVOIR** – **passation des pouvoirs** – transfer of power; handing over of office (functions).

PASSAVANT – excise pass (for the transport of wines and spirits and other merchandise); transire.

PASSE-DROIT – dispensation.

PASSEPORT
- **SERVICE** – **passeport de service** – service passport.

PASSER – enter into; conclude.
- **ACTE** – **passer un acte** – execute a legal instrument.
- **OUTRE** – **passer outre** – continue (proceedings) in spite of an objection etc.

PASSIBLE
- **DE** – **passible de** – subject (liable) to.

PASSIF – liabilities.
- **ÉLÉMENT** de passif – liability.

- **HYPOTHÉCAIRE** – **passif hypothécaire** – mortgage debts.
- **SUJET passif (d'un droit, d'une obligation)** – person against whom a right may be enforced; obligor; promisor; debtor; tortfeasor; person bound by (liable to perform) an obligation.

PASSIONNEL

- **CRIME passionnel** – offence motivated by jealousy; crime passionnel.

PATENTE – trade tax; traders tax; licence (to practise a profession, sell liquor, etc).

- **NET** – **patente nette** – clean bill of health.

PATERNITÉ

- **ACTION en recherche de paternité** – affiliation proceedings; action to establish paternity.

PATRIMOINE – assets; fortune; fund; property; goods; possessions; collection of assets and liabilities attached to a person.

- **AFFECTATION** – **patrimoine d'affectation** – collection of assets and liabilities allocated or reserved for a special purpose; special-purpose fund.
- **MORAL** – **patrimoine moral** – strictly personal property; strictly personal rights; non-material rights.
- **SOCIAL** – **patrimoine social** – partnership or company assets.

PATRIMONIAL – pecuniary; economic.

- **DROITS patrimoniaux** – pecuniary rights; property rights; proprietorial (proprietary) rights; economic rights.

PATRON – employer.

PATRONAGE (Sw) – supervision of released prisoners.

- **COMITÉ de patronage** – prisoners aid committee.

PATRONAL – employers'.

PATRONYMIQUE

- **NOM patronymique** – surname; family name.

PÂTURE

- **SERVITUDE de pâture** – profit of pasture; right to pasture cattle or sheep.
- **VAIN** – **(droit de) vaine pâture** – right of common; common of pasture exercisable after mowing or harvest.

PAULIEN

- **ACTION paulienne** – action by which a creditor can have declared void certain transactions by a debtor with third parties prejudicial to his interests.

PAUMER (Belg) – sell land through a solicitor (**notaire**) to the person making the best offer (not an auction).

PAVILLON – a ship's flag in the sense of its nationality.

- **COMPLAISANCE** – **pavillon de complaisance** – flag of convenience.
- **PARLEMENTAIRE** – **pavillon parlementaire** – flag of truce.

PAYS

- **ACCUEIL** – **pays d'accueil** – host country.
- **JURIDICTION** – **pays de juridiction** – country with jurisdiction; (formerly) country in which consular juridiction is exercised over foreign nationals.
- **MANDAT** – **pays de mandat** – (League of Nations) mandated territory; mandate.
- **REQUÉRANT** – **pays requérant** – applicant country; requesting country.
- **REQUIS** – **pays requis** – country receiving the application; requested country.

PÉAGE – toll.

PÊCHE – fishery.

- **PETIT** – **petite pêche** – right to fish in coastal waters.

PÉCULAT (Sw) – embezzlement of public funds.

PÉCULE – prisoner's earnings.

- **LIBÉRATION** – **pécule de libération** – (prisoner's) release savings.

PEINE – punishment; sentence; penalty; sanction.

- **À peine de** – failing which (it will be); if it is not to be.
  - **IRRECEVABILITÉ** – **à peine d'irrecevabilité** – if it is not to be declared inadmissible; will be inadmissible unless.
  - **NULLITÉ** – **à peine de nullité** – cannot validly; to be valid.
- **ACCESSOIRE** – **peine accessoire** – ancillary (accessory) penalty (measure).

- **ADOUCISSEMENT de peine** – mitigation of penalty.
- **AFFLICTIF** – **peine afflictive et infamante** – penalty imposed for a felony (life or fixed-term imprisonment coupled with banishment and civic disqualification).
- **AGGRAVATION de peine** – aggravation of penalty.
- **AJOURNEMENT (du prononcé) de (la) peine** – deferment of sentence.
- **ATTÉNUATION de peine** – mitigation of penalty.
- **CERTITUDE de la peine** – fixed penalties; fixed sentences.
- **COMMUER une peine** – commute a sentence.
- **COMPLÉMENTAIRE** – **peine complémentaire** – additional penalty (measure).
- **CONFUSION des peines** – concurrent sentences.
- **CORPOREL** – **peine corporelle** – (formerly) (penalty entailing) corporel punishment; (occasionally used in the sense of) custodial sentence.
- **CORRECTIONNEL** – **peine correctionnelle** – penalty for a misdemeanour (lesser indictable offence).
- **CRIMINEL** – **peine criminelle** – penalty for a felony (serious indictable offence).
- **CUMUL des peines** – consecutive (aggregated) sentences.
- **DISPENSE de peine** – discharge.
  - **CONDITIONNEL** – **dispense de peine conditionnelle** – conditional discharge.
- **DROIT** – **peine de droit** – statutory penalty.
  - **COMMUN** – **peine de droit commun** – sentence (penalty) imposed under the ordinary criminal law.
- **ENCOURIR une peine** – incur (become liable (subject) to) a penalty.
- **ENSEMBLE** – **peine d'ensemble (Sw)** – consolidated sentence, ie for several offences.
- **EXÉCUTION d'une peine** – enforcement (serving) of a sentence.
- **INDÉTERMINÉ** – **peine à durée indéterminée** – indeterminate sentence; sentence of unspecified duration.
- **INFAMANT** – **peines infamantes** – penalties imposed for a felony (ie banishment and civic disqualification).
- **LIBERTÉ** – **peine privative de liberté** – custodial sentence; imprisonment.
- **NON-CUMUL des peines** – rule that where a person has committed several

offences, consecutive sentences are not imposed. Instead the court pronounces the severest of the penalties available for one of the individual offences.

- **PATRIMONIAL** – **peine patrimoniale** – pecuniary penalty.
- **PERPÉTUEL** – **peine perpétuelle** – life sentence.
- **POLICE** – **peine de (simple) police** – penalty for summary (petty) offence.
- **PRESCRIT** – **peine prescrite** – lapsed penalty; statute-barred penalty.
- **PRINCIPAL** – **peine principale** – primary (principal) penalty (measure).
- **PRIVATIF** – **peine privative de liberté** – custodial sentence; imprisonment.
- **PRONONCÉ des peines** – sentencing.
- **PURGER une peine** – serve a sentence.
- **QUANTUM de la peine** – length of sentence; amount of a fine.
- **REMETTRE une peine** – remit a sentence.
- **REMPLACEMENT** – **peine de remplacement** – substitute (alternative) penalty.
- **SECONDAIRE** – **peine secondaire** – accessory penalty (measure).
- **SOUS peine de** – failing which (it will be); if it is not to be.
  - **MESURE** – **sous peine de mesures disciplinaires** – under threat (on pain) of disciplinary sanctions.
  - **NULLITÉ** – **sous peine de nullité** – cannot validly; to be valid.
- **SUBIR une peine** – serve a sentence.
- **SUBSTITUTION** – **peine de substitution (à l'emprisonnement)** – alternative to imprisonment.

PÉNAL – criminal; penal.
- **ÂGE pénal** – age at which a person becomes criminally liable.
- **MATIÈRE pénale** – criminal case.
  - **EN matière pénale** – in criminal cases; in criminal law.
- **POURSUITE(S) pénale(s)** – criminal proceedings; prosecution.

PÉNALITÉ – imposition of punishments; punishment; penalty.
- **CONVENTIONNEL** – **pénalité conventionnelle** – contractual penalty (penalty clause).
- **DÉLAI** – **pénalité de délai** – penalty for late performance.

PENDANT – pending.

PÉNÉTRATION
- **IRRÉGULIER** – pénétration irrégulière – unauthorised entry.

PÉNITENTIAIRE – prisons; penological; correctional.
- **ÉTABLISSEMENT** pénitentiaire – prison.

PENSION – periodical payments.
- **ALIMENTAIRE** – pension alimentaire – maintenance; alimony (judicial separation only).
- **CENT POUR CENT** – pension à cent pour cent – full pension.
- **DÉCHÉANCE** de la pension (du droit à pension) – loss or deprivation of pension rights.
- **DIFFÉRÉ** – pension à jouissance différée – deferred pension.
- **EFFET** en pension – bill deposited as a security; pawned bill.
- **LIQUIDATION** de la pension – calculation of the amount of the pension.
- **RÉFORME** – pension de réforme – invalidity pension.
- **RÉVERSION** – pension de réversion – widows' and orphans' pension; survivor's pension; dependant's pension; reversionary pension.
- **VIAGER** – pension viagère – life annuity.

PERCEPTION – separation (of periodical produce (**fruits**) from the soil).
- **IMMÉDIAT** – perception immédiate – on-the-spot payment of fines.

PERCEVOIR – collect (taxes).
- **INDEMNITÉ** – percevoir une indemnité sociale – draw a social-security benefit.

PERDU – irredeemable.

PÈRE DE FAMILLE
- **BON** père de famille – reasonable, prudent man; careful, diligent owner.
  - **JOUIR** en bon père de famille – (obligation imposed on a tenant or hirer) to use rented etc property without damaging it, ie to keep the premises in good condition, fair wear and tear excepted.
- **DESTINATION** du père de famille – use by the owner of two tenements of one for the benefit of the other in such a way that an easement or profit arises when one of the tenements passes into different hands; state of affairs which would constitute an easement

if the dominant and servient tenements were owned by different persons; quasi-easement.

PÉREMPTION – expiring of a time-limit; lapse by expiry of a time-limit (and failure to take action, eg failing to prosecute an action, appeal, etc).
- **DÉLAI** de péremption – strict time-limit (after which, eg, an instrument becomes ineffective (without destroying the underlying right) or an application may be made to strike out proceedings which have not been pursued for two years); fixed term.
- **FRAPPER** – être frappé de péremption – lapse.
- **INSTANCE** – péremption d'instance – lapse of an action for want of prosecution (this does not take effect ipso jure and an application to strike out is required); striking out a case for failure to prosecute the proceedings (for inaction).
- **JUGEMENT** – péremption du jugement – lapse of a judgment by default for failure to serve it within six months.

PÉREMPTOIRE – mandatory; absolute.
- **CAUSE** péremptoire de divorce – absolute ground of divorce.
- **EXCEPTION** péremptoire – absolute defence; defence which goes to the root of and destroys the plaintiff's case.
- **RÉCUSATION** péremptoire – challenge without cause; peremptory challenge.

PÉRÉQUATION – equalisation.
- **PRÉLÈVEMENT** de péréquation – equalisation tax, charge or contribution.

PÉRIL
- **ARRÊTÉ** de péril – danger notice.

PÉRIMER – lapse (for want of prosecution).

PÉRIMÈTRE
- **DÉFENSE** – périmètre de mise en défense – (hunting or fishing) preserve.
- **PROSPECTION** – périmètre de prospection – (licensed) prospecting claim.
- **PROTECTION** – périmètre de protection – protected area.
- **REMEMBREMENT** – périmètre de remembrement – land-consolidation area (for the purpose of consolidating smallholdings).

PÉRIODE

- **CELLULAIRE** – période cellulaire (Sw) – solitary confinement.
- **COMPLÉMENTAIRE** – période complémentaire – complementary period.
- **CONSIDÉRER** – période à considérer – material time.
- **FONCTION** – période de fonctions – term of office.
- **IMPOSABLE** – période imposable – assessment period; period of assessment.
- **IMPOSITION** – période d'imposition – assessment period; period of assessment.
- **RÉFLEXION** – période de réflexion – (house-to-house sales) cooling-off period.
- **SÛRETÉ** – période de sûreté – period of unconditional imprisonment (during which no form of release can be granted).
- **SUSPECT** – période suspecte – period of relation back (doubtful period) from adjudication in bankruptcy to the date on which the debtor first ceased to meet his obligations. (The debtor's transactions during this period may be challenged by the creditors, acting through the trustee in bankruptcy.)

PERMANENCE

- **JURIDIQUE** – permanence juridique – legal advice office.

PERMIS – licence; permit.

- **ASSIGNER** – permis d'assigner – (divorce) leave to bring proceedings (this must be applied for to the president of the court by the petitioner in person).
- **BÂTIR** – permis de bâtir – building permit; planning permission.
- **CIRCULATION** – permis de circulation – vehicle licence, eg for seagoing pleasure boats.
- **CITER** – permis de citer – leave to bring proceedings.
- **COLPORTGE** – permis de colportage – hawker's licence.
- **CONDUIRE** – retrait du permis de conduire – withdrawal (deprivation) of one's driving licence; disqualification from driving.
- **CONSTRUIRE** – permis de construire – building permit; planning permission.
- **ÉTABLISSEMENT** – permis d'établissement – residence (establishment) permit; authority to settle (take up residence).
- **EXPLOITATION** – permis d'exploitation – mining licence (take up residence).
- **EXPROPRIER** – permis d'exproprier – authority for compulsory purchase.
- **EXTRACTION** – permis d'extraction – mining licence.
- **PROSPECTION** – permis exclusif de prospection – exclusive prospecting licence.
- **RECHERCHE** – permis exclusif de recherche – exclusive prospecting licence.
- **SÉJOUR** – permis de séjour – residence permit.
- **STATIONNEMENT** – permis de stationnement – permission to occupy or erect movable structures on part of the highway or in some other public place, eg for a café to put chairs on the pavement.

PERMISSION

- **VOIRIE** – permission de voirie – unilateral grant by an administrative authority of the right to occupy part of the highway or some other public place.

PERPÉTUEL

- **DEMEURE** – perpétuelle demeure – permanent attachment to the soil.

PERPÉTUITÉ

- **RÉCLUSION** à perpétuité – life imprisonment.

PERQUISITION – (entry and) search.

- **DOMICILIAIRE** – perquisition domiciliaire – (house) search.

PERQUISITIONNER – search.

PERSONNALISABLE

- **MATIÈRE** personnalisable (Belg) – matter on which a Belgian citizen is entitled to correspond with the authorities in his mother tongue anywhere in the country.

PERSONNALISÉ – constituting a juridical person.

PERSONNALISER – confer legal personality on.

PERSONNALITÉ

- **ACTIF** – personnalité active – capacity to bring proceedings.
  - **COMPÉTENCE** de la personnalité active – jurisdiction based on the nationality (or domicile) of the offender or tortfeasor.
- **CIVIL** – personnalité civile – legal personality (ie being entitled to rights and subject to obligations).

- **DOTÉ** de la personnalité – possessing legal personality.
- **DROIT DES GENS** – **personnalité morale du droit des gens** – legal personality in international law (ie being entitled to rights and subject to obligations in international law).
- **DROITS** de la personnalité – non-pecuniary personal rights other than family rights; personality rights (name, reputation, privacy, etc); strictly personal rights.
- **INTERNATIONAL** – **personnalité internationale** – international personality (ie being entitled to rights and subject to obligations in international law).
- **JURIDIQUE** – **personnalité juridique** – legal personality (ie being entitled to rights and subject to obligations).
- **MORAL** – **personnalité morale** – legal personality (ie being entitled to rights and subject to obligations).
- **PASSIF** – **personnalité passive** – capacity to defend proceedings.
- **PEINE** – **personnalité des peines** – rule that punishment should be applied to the offender only and not to other persons, eg his family or heirs.
- **PRINCIPE** de la personnalité – rule that a person is governed by his personal law (ie by the system of law to which he as a person belongs).

PERSONNE

- **ACTIF** – **personne active** – member of the working population.
- **ACTION** (exclusivement) attachée à la personne – strictly (purely) personal action; non-pecuniary action.
- **AUTONOME** – **personne morale autonome** – self-governing (independent) corporation.
- **CHARGE** – **personne à charge** – dependant; person for whose maintenance one is liable (the term does not usually include a widow).
- **CIVILEMENT RESPONSABLE** – see RESPONSABLE below.
- **DÉLIVRER** – **délivré à personne** – personally served.
- **DÉPLACÉ** – **personne déplacée** – displaced person.
- **DISPARU** – **personne disparue** – missing person; person who cannot be traced.
- **DOMMAGE** aux personnes – personal (physical, bodily) injury.

- **DROIT** attaché à la personne – strictly (exclusively) personal right; easement in gross.
- **DROIT** des personnes – law of persons.
- **DROITS** de la personne (Can) – human rights.
- **ÉTAT** des personnes – civil (personal, family) status.
- **FUTUR** – **personne future** – person not yet in existence.
- **INTERPOSÉ** – **personne interposée** – man of straw; intermediary.
- **JURIDIQUE** – **personne juridique** – person recognised by law as being entitled to rights and subject to obligations.
- **LÉSÉ** – **personne lésée** – injured person.
- **MORAL** – **personne morale** – legal entity; corporation; legal (juridical) person.
  - **DROIT PRIVÉ** – **personne morale de droit privé** – private-law corporation.
  - **DROIT PUBLIC** – **personne morale de droit public** – public-law corporation.
- **PHYSIQUE** – **personne physique** – natural person; individual.
- **PUBLIC** – **personne (morale) publique** – public corporation, eg the state or a local authority.
- **REPROCHABLE** – **personne reprochable** – person who may be challenged (as being biased or unsuitable).
- **RESPONSABLE** – **personne civilement responsable** – person liable in damages.
- **SOCIÉTÉ** de personnes – partnership (but the term also includes the **société à responsabilité limitée**).
- **TOUT** – **à l'encontre de toutes personnes** – as against the whole world (everyone); erga omnes.

PERSONNEL (adj)

- **DROIT** personnel – (pecuniary) right in personam; obligation; chose in action; claim.
- **FAILLITE** personnelle – culpable bankruptcy (involving sanctions imposed personally in bankruptcy on dishonest or rashly imprudent traders or company directors and consisting of various disqualifications and prohibitions); (Belg) personal bankruptcy (the expression does not seem to imply culpability in Belgium).
- **TITRE** – **à titre personnel** – in his (her, their) personal capacity (capacities).

PERSONNEL (noun) – staff.

- **STATUT** du personnel – staff regulations.
- **SUPÉRIEUR** – **personnel supérieur** – senior staff; (industry) managerial or executive-grade staff; (civil service) administrative-grade staff.

PERSONNIFICATION

- **CIVIL** – **personnification civile** (Belg) – legal (juridical) personality.

PERTE

- **FORTUIT** – **perte fortuite** – purely accidental loss (ie without fault).
- **GAIN** – **perte de gain** (Sw) – loss of earnings.
- **SALAIRE** – **perte de salaire** – loss of earnings.

PERTINENCE – relevance (of evidence).

PÉTITION

- **HÉRÉDITÉ** – **(action en) pétition d'hérédité** – action to obtain possession of an estate from a person claiming to be the heir; action to claim (a share in) an estate.
- **REMISE** – **pétition en remise** – application for remission of tax.

PÉTITIONNAIRE – petitioner.

PÉTITOIRE – (action) to establish ownership or another right in rem.

- **ACTION pétitoire** – action to establish ownership or another right in rem.

PHASE

- **PROCÉDURE** – **phase de la procédure** – stage in the proceedings.

PHILOSOPHIE

- **DROIT** – **philosophie du droit** – jurisprudence.

PHYSIQUE

- **PERSONNE physique** – natural person; individual.

PIÈCE – document; coin; exhibit.

- **CAISSE** – **pièce de caisse** – voucher.
- **COMMUNICATION**
  - •• **DEMANDE de communication de pièces** – application for production of documents for inspection (application for discovery).
  - •• **EXCEPTION de communication de pièces** – objection which can be raised requesting the court to stay proceedings so long as the opposite party refuses to make his documents available.

- **CONVICTION** – **pièce à conviction** – evidence; real evidence; exhibit (in a criminal case).
  - •• **RÉGLER le sort des pièces à conviction** – dispose of the exhibits.
- **DOSSIER** – **pièces du dossier** – evidence (in the file).
- **ÉNUMÉRATION des pièces** – listing of documents (with a view to obtaining discovery).
- **ÉTAT CIVIL** – **pièce d'état civil** – civil-status certificate.
- **FAUX** – **pièce arguée de faux** – document alleged to be false (forged).
- **INDICATION des pièces** – listing of documents (with a view to obtaining discovery).
- **JUSTIFICATIF** – **pièce justificative** – documentary evidence.
- **LIQUIDATION** – **pièces de liquidation** – documents required for the purpose of settlement.
- **PROCÉDURE** – **pièces de la procédure** – case file; documents on the file.
- **PRODUCTION de(s) pièces** – production of documents.
- **SOMMATION de communiquer les pièces** – summons to make documents available (for discovery and production of documents).
- **STATUER sur pièces** – decide the case on the pleadings (on the written evidence, on the file).
- **TERRAIN** – **pièce de terrain** – plot of land.

PIGNORATIF – by way of security.

- **CONTRAT pignoratif** – loan disguised as a sale with an option to repurchase; contract whereby a debtor transfers the possession of one of his assets to the creditor as a security, eg pledge.

PILLAGE – looting.

PILOTE

- **ARRÊT pilote** – leading case.

PLACER – invest.

PLACET – application for a case to be entered in the list; application for a case to be heard as an urgent application (**référé sur placet**); copy writ (or originating summons).

PLAGIAT – plagiarism.

PLAIDER – argue; maintain.

- **COUPABLE** – **plaider coupable** – plead guilty.
- **PERSONNE** – **plaider en personne** – conduct one's case in person.

PLAIDEUR – party; litigant.

PLAIDOIRIE – (counsel's) address; argument(s).
- **AUDIENCE des plaidoiries** – hearing; trial.
- **DROIT de plaidoirie** – counsel's hearing fee.
- **STADE des plaidoiries** – trial stage (of the proceedings).

PLAIDOYER – (defence counsel's) address.

PLAIGNANT – complainant.

PLAINTE – complaint (to the prosecuting authorities); information.
- **DÉPOSER une plainte** – report an offence to the prosecuting authorities; lay an information; make a complaint.
- **INCONNU** – **plainte contre inconnu** – complaint (information) against a person or persons unknown.
- **PORTER plainte** – report an offence to the prosecuting authorities; lay an information; make a complaint.

PLAIRE
- **BIEN** – **à bien plaire** – ex gratia; without obligation.
- **DIRE** – **plaise à la Cour dire** – the Court is requested to hold.

PLAN
- **ALIGNEMENT** – **plan d'alignement** – alignment plan.
- **AMÉNAGEMENT** – **plan d'aménagement** – development plan.
- **CADASTRAL** – **plan cadastral** – index map (showing plots); official plan; registered plan; land survey.
- **DÉVELOPPEMENT** – **plan de développement** – national economic plan.
- **OCCUPATION** – **plan d'occupation des sols** – local development plan; land-use plan.
- **PARCELLAIRE** – **plan parcellaire** – registered plan; index map (showing plots of land).
- **URBANISME** – **plan d'urbanisme** – development plan; structure plan.

PLANO – see DE PLANO.

PLAQUE
- **IMMATRICULATION** – **plaque d'immatriculation** – (vehicle) number-plate.

PLATEAU
- **CONTINENTAL** – **plateau continental** – continental shelf.

PLAUSIBLE
- **RAISONS plausibles** – good reasons.

PLÉNIER – full; plenary.

PLÉNITUDE
- **COMPÉTENCE** – **plénitude de compétence** – see JURIDICTION below.
- **JURIDICTION** – **plénitude de juridiction** – power to make any order that may be required by the justice of a case (to deal with all aspects of a case); power of the ordinary courts in certain cases to hear matters falling within the jurisdiction of the specialised courts; (used of a court of appeal) indicates that if a case which was wrongly brought before the Commercial Court instead of the ordinary court comes before the Court of Appeal, the error is deemed to be cured once the appeal has been decided by the Court of Appeal. (The same applies to felonies (**crimes**) which the Assize Court holds to be misdemeanours (**délits**).)
  - •• **JOUIR** – **jouissant de la plénitude de juridiction** – competent (having jurisdiction) to deal with all aspects of a case.

PLI
- **JUDICIAIRE** – **pli judiciaire** (Belg) – judicial recorded delivery.

PLUMITIF – (former name of) registrar's notes (record) of the hearing.

PLUS-VALUE – increase in value; appreciation; capital gain.

POIDS
- **PREUVE** – **poids d'un élément de preuve** – evidential value; weight of evidence.

POINÇON – hallmark; inspection stamp.

POINT
- **ATTACHE** – **point d'attache** – connecting factor.
- **LITIGIEUX** – **point litigieux** – point in (at) issue.

POLICE – administration; (uniformed) police; policing; public order; responsibility for keeping order; (insurance) policy.

- **ADMINISTRATIF** – police administrative – administrative authorities; administrative procedure; maintaining public order and safety; policing.
- **AGENT de police** – police officer; constable; member of the police force.
- **AMENDE de simple police** – fine for a summary (petty) offence.
- **ASSEMBLÉE** – police de l'assemblée – (responsibility for) keeping order in Parliament and other assemblies.
- **AUDIENCE** – police de l'audience – (responsibility for) keeping order in court.
- **BÂTIMENT** – police des bâtiments – building-regulations authority.
- **COMMISSAIRE de police** – police superintendent.
- **COMMISSARIAT de police** – police station.
- **CORPS** – police sur corps – comprehensive insurance.
- **CORRECTIONNEL** – police correctionnelle – (court) jurisdiction over misdemeanours (lesser indictable offences).
- **CRIMINEL** – police criminelle – (criminal) police; criminal investigation department.
- **ÉTRANGER** – police des étrangers – immigration department.
- **JUDICIAIRE** – police judiciaire – (criminal) police (the adjective is usually unnecessary in English as the term "police" does not as in France extend to other administrative departments); criminal investigation department. (The term also includes other persons, such as mayors, who have certain functions in connection with the repression of crime.)
  - •• **OFFICIER de police judiciaire** – senior police officer, mayor, prefect, etc entitled to exercise special powers in connection with the repression of crime; senior law-enforcement officer.
- **MUNICIPAL** – police municipale – local administration; city (municipal) police.
- **ROULAGE** – police du roulage – traffic police or policing.
- **RURAL** – police rurale – rural administration; rural police.
- **SANITAIRE** – police sanitaire – health administration; health authority.
- **SOUSCRIPTEUR de police** – the insured; policyholder.
- **TRIBUNAL de (simple) police** – court of summary jurisdiction; police court; district court.

- •• **CORRECTIONNEL** – tribunal de police correctionnelle – (regional) Criminal Court (for the trial of misdemeanours).

POLLICITANT – offeror.

POLLICITATION – offer; offer of reward; unilateral promise.

POLLUTION
- **MER** – pollution des mers – marine pollution.

PONCTUEL
- **GRÈVES ponctuelles** – selective strikes.

POPULATION
- **ACTIF** – population active – working population.

PORT
- **IMMATRICULATION** – port d'immatriculation – home port (ie port where a ship is registered).

PORTABILITÉ – (of a debt) the fact of being payable at the creditor's residence or place of business.

PORTABLE – (of a debt) payable at the creditor's residence or place of business.

PORTÉE – effect; scope.
- **GÉNÉRAL** – avoir une portée générale – be of general application.

PORTE-FORT – person who guarantees that another will do a specific thing (generally ratify a contract entered into on his behalf).
- **PROMESSE de porte-fort** – undertaking to ensure that a third party performs his obligation.

PORTE-PAROLE – spokesman.

PORTER
- **AFFAIRE** – l'affaire sera portée devant un juge unique – the case will be taken (heard) by a single judge.
- **ATTEINTE** – porter atteinte à – infringe; violate; interfere with; undermine; adversely affect.
- **FORT** – se porter fort pour un tiers – undertake that someone else will do something.
- **REMÈDE** – porter remède à – redress.
- **TRANSFERT** – portant transfert de propriété – transferring (passing of) ownership (property).

PORTEUR – holder; bearer.
- **ACTION au porteur** – bearer share; share warrant; bearer stock.
- **CHÈQUE** – **porteur d'un chèque** – holder of a cheque.
- **CLAUSE au porteur** – bearer clause.
- **CONNAISSEMENT au porteur** – bearer bill of lading.
- **ÊTRE au porteur** – made out to bearer.
- **OBLIGATION** – **porteur d'obligation** – debenture holder.
- **PAPIER au porteur** – bearer security.
- **PART** – **porteur de parts** – participant (investment funds); shareholder.
- **PETIT porteur** – small shareholder.
- **POLICE** – **porteur de police** – policyholder.
- **POUVOIR** – **porteur de pouvoir** – holder of a power of attorney; attorney.

PORTION
- **DISPONIBLE** – **portion disponible** – portion of his estate which a testator may dispose of freely.
- **HÉRÉDITAIRE** – **portion héréditaire** – share of an estate devolving on an heir.
- **SAISISSABLE** – **portion saisissable** – attachable portion, eg of earnings.
- **VIRIL** – **portion virile** – one of several equal shares in an estate.

POSITIF
- **DROIT positif** – positive law, ie the law as it actually exists, as opposed to natural law.

POSITIVISME
- **JURIDIQUE** – **positivisme juridique** – positivism (theory which rejects the concept of natural law and maintains that the only law is the law actually in force at a given time – positive law).

POSSÉDER
- **PRÉCAIRE** – **posséder à titre précaire** – occupy, possess or hold under (in the right of, on behalf of, under the authority of) another (and not in one's own right); have custody of.

POSSESSEUR
- **ANTÉRIEUR** – **possesseur antérieur** – previous holder; previous occupant.
- **FOI** – **possesseur de bonne foi** – bona fide holder; holder in good faith; bona fide occupant.
- **PRÉCAIRE** – **possesseur précaire** – person occupying, possessing or holding under (in

the right of, on behalf of, under the authority of) another (and not in his own right); custodian.

POSSESSION – possession; holding; occupation; factual exercise of the rights pertaining to ownership.
- **BONNE FOI** – see FOI below.
- **ENTRÉE en possession** – taking possession.
- **ÉQUIVOQUE**
  - **NON** – **possession non équivoque** – unequivocal (undisputed) possession.
- **ÉTAT de possession** – position established by actual occupation.
- **ÉTAT** – **possession d'état** – actual enjoyment of a certain civil (personal, family) status; public acceptance of a person's status; factual possession of status; de facto enjoyment of a certain status, eg the prerogatives of citizenship; enjoyment of status by repute.
- **FOI** – **possession de bonne foi** – bona fide possession or occupation.
- **PAISIBLE** – **possession paisible** – peaceable possession.
- **TROUBLE de la possession** – trespass; nuisance; interference with (a person's) possession (quiet enjoyment).
- **UTILE** – **possession utile** – valid (effective) possession.
- **VÉRITABLE** – **présomption de possession véritable** – presumption that the possessor is the true owner.
- **VICE de la possession** – defect in possession.

POSSESSOIRE
- **ACTION possessoire** – action to protect or recover possession; possessory action. There are three types: **complainte** – trespass, ie when possession is disturbed by some factual or legal action; **dénonciation de nouvel œuvre**, when works are commenced completion of which would interfere with possession; and **réintégrande**, where a person has been deprived of possession.

POSTE – item (in an account, budget, etc).

POSTERIORI – see A POSTERIORI.

POSTÉRITÉ – descendants; issue.

POSTPÉNITENTIAIRE
- **ASSISTANCE postpénitentiaire** – aftercare.

POSTULANT – applicant for a post.

POSTULAT (Sw) – parliamentary motion (requesting the government to legislate) (as opposed to **motion**).

POSTULATION – pre-trial work, eg advising on evidence, drawing pleadings, preparing for trial; taking procedural steps on behalf of a client (as opposed to representing him in court).

POSTULER – represent a client and conduct proceedings other than in court; take procedural steps on behalf of a client (as opposed to representing him in court).

POT-DE-VIN – bribe.

POTESTATIF – potestative; depending on the free will of one of the parties.
- **PRESCRIPTION potestative** – provision whose application is discretionary.

POURCENTAGE
- **COUVERTURE – pourcentage de couverture** – (currency) cover ratio.

POURSUITE(S) – proceedings; prosecution; search for an offender; civil proceedings.
- **ACTE de poursuite** – step in criminal proceedings.
- **CHAUD – poursuite à chaud** – hot pursuit.
- **DISCIPLINAIRE – poursuite disciplinaire** – disciplinary proceedings.
- **DROIT de poursuite** – right to prosecute; right of (hot) pursuit.
- **ENGAGER des poursuites** – commence a prosecution.
- **EXTINCTION des poursuites** – (premature) termination of the proceedings.
- **IMMUNITÉ de poursuites** – immunity from prosecution.
- **INSTANCE – poursuite de l'instance** – continuation of the proceedings; conduct of the proceedings.
- **JUDICIAIRE – poursuite judiciaire** – court proceedings.
- **LÉGALITÉ des poursuites** – mandatory (compulsory) prosecution; legal basis for or requirement of prosecution.
- **OFFICE des poursuites** (Sw) – execution department (responsible for conducting executions against persons not engaged in trade).
- **OPPORTUNITÉ – (principe de) l'opportunité des poursuites** – rule that whether a prosecution should be brought is a matter within the discretion of the prosecuting authorities; principle of discretionary prosecution.

- **PÉNAL – poursuite(s) pénale(s)** – prosecution.
- **RENVOI des fins de la poursuite** – acquittal.
- **RESPONSABILITÉ – poursuite en responsabilité** – action for damages (in tort or contract).
- **SUSPENSION des poursuites individuelles** – stay (suspension) of individual actions (consequence of bankruptcy).

POURSUIVANT (adj)
- **PARTIE poursuivante** – plaintiff; applicant; prosecutor.

POURSUIVANT (noun) – applicant; plaintiff; prosecutor.

POURSUIVRE – sue; prosecute; take proceedings.
- **DETTE – poursuivi en paiement de sa dette, le débiteur...** – when sued for his debt, the debtor...
- **EXÉCUTION – poursuivre l'exécution** – levy execution.
- **INFRACTION – poursuivi pour une infraction** – charged with an offence.
- **JUSTICE – poursuivre en justice** – sue; bring (take) to court.
- **RÈGLEMENT – poursuivre le règlement de** – (seek to) settle (eg a conflict of juridiction).

POURVOI – appeal on points of law (on a point of law, in law) (to the Court of Cassation or, in the case of an administrative appeal, to the Conseil d'État); application for retrial.
- **ACTE de pourvoi** – notice of appeal; grounds of appeal.
- **CASSATION – pourvoi en cassation** – appeal on points of law (on a point of law, in law) (to the Court of Cassation or the Conseil d'État).
- **CAUSES du pourvoi** – grounds of appeal.
- **DÉCLARATION de pourvoi** – (filing) notice of appeal to the Court of Cassation or the Conseil d'État.
- **EXCÈS – pourvoi pour excès de pouvoir** – appeal to the Court of Cassation by the Attorney-General's Department, acting on the instructions of the Minister of Justice, against a decision by which the courts have exceeded their jurisdiction by purporting to exercise legislative or executive powers.

- **INCIDENT** – **pourvoi incident** – cross-appeal.
- **LOI** – **pourvoi dans l'intérêt de la loi** – appeal by the Attorney-General's Department to the Court of Cassation against a decision contravening a statutory provision. The result does not affect the decision appealed against as far as the parties are concerned.
- **MOYEN de pourvoi** – ground of appeal.
- **NULLITÉ** – **pourvoi en nullité** (Sw) – appeal on points of law (on a point of law, in law).
- **PROVOQUÉ** – **pourvoi provoqué** – cross-appeal by a party against whom the original appeal was not directed (ie a third party affected by the proceedings, eg a guarantor).
- **RÉVISION** – **pourvoi en révision** – application for a retrial.
- **SUSPENSIF** – **pourvoi suspensif** – appeal having the effect of a stay of execution.

POURVOIR

- **SE pourvoir** – appeal; enter an appeal; seek to have set aside.

POUVOIR – power; authority; power of attorney; power to exercise the rights of others; power to take proceedings (on behalf of an incapable or juridical person); authority to act (for a client) in legal proceedings.

- **ABUS de pouvoir** – abuse (misuse) of (official) authority; acting in excess of one's authority or discretion.
- **APPRÉCIATION** – **pouvoir d'appréciation** – discretion; power (freely) to evaluate (assess) (evidence etc).
- **COMMANDEMENT** – **pouvoir de commandement** – factual power (not necessarily founded in law) to give orders relating to a thing.
- **CONFUSION des pouvoirs** – failure to observe the principle of the separation of powers.
- **CONSTITUANT** – **pouvoir constituant** – power to make a constitution.
- **CONSTITUTIONNEL** – **pouvoir constitutionnel** – power to make a constitution.
- **DÉCISION** – **pouvoir de décision propre** – personal discretion.
- **DÉTOURNEMENT de pouvoir** – abuse (misuse, misapplication) of a power, authority or discretion; improper exercise of authority; misfeasance (in (public) office).
- **DISCRÉTIONNAIRE** – **pouvoir discrétionnaire** – (unfettered) discretion or (unlimited) power.
  - •• **PRÉSIDENT** – **pouvoir discrétionnaire du président** – power of the president of an assize court to take all such measures as he may consider useful for ascertaining the truth.
- **DISPOSITION** – **pouvoir de disposition** – power of alienation; power of disposal.
- **EXCEPTIONNEL** – **pouvoirs exceptionnels** – emergency powers exercised by the President of the Republic.
- **EXCÈS de pouvoir** – abuse (misuse) of authority; acting in excess of authority (jurisdiction); acting ultra vires.
  - •• **COMMETTRE un excès de pouvoir** – exceed one's jurisdiction.
- **EXÉCUTION** – **pouvoir d'exécution** – power (authority) to enforce (execute); executive power.
- **GRACIER** – **pouvoir de gracier** – prerogative of mercy.
- **HIÉRARCHIQUE** – **pouvoir hiérarchique** – disciplinary control; power of direction and control over subordinates.
- **INJONCTION** – **pouvoir d'injonction** – power to give directions.
- **JUDICIAIRE** – **pouvoir judiciaire** – courts; judiciary.
- **LIBÉRATOIRE** – **avoir pouvoir libératoire** – (of money) to be legal tender.
- **PASSATION des pouvoirs** – transfer of power; handing over of office (functions).
- **PLEINS pouvoirs** – full powers; full authority.
  - •• **LOI de pleins pouvoirs** – Act authorising the government to legislate by regulations; enabling Act.
- **PUBLIC** – **pouvoir public** – the executive; the authorities; public authorities.
- **RÉGLEMENTAIRE** – **pouvoir réglementaire** – power to make regulations.
- **REMISE des pouvoirs** – submission of credentials.
- **SÉPARATION des pouvoirs** – separation of powers.
- **SUBSTITUTION** – **pouvoir de substitution** – power to appoint a sub-agent; right of a superior authority to take measures in the place and on behalf of a subordinate authority.
- **TUTELLE** – **pouvoir de tutelle** – supervising authority; guardianship authority.

- **VALIDATION des pouvoirs** – ratification of credentials; validation of the appointment.
- **VÉRIFICATION des pouvoirs** – examination of credentials.

PRATIQUE

- **ÉTAT** – **pratique des États** – state practice.
- **PROCÉDURE** – **la pratique de la procédure** – practice.
- **TRIBUNAL** – **pratique des tribunaux** – practice; court practice.

PRÉALABLE – previous.

- **QUESTION préalable** – preliminary question (point, issue) to be decided by the court trying the main issue.

PRÉAMBULE – preamble.

PRÉAVIS – notice; warning.

- **INDEMNITÉ de préavis** – payment (compensation) in lieu of notice.

PRÉAVISER – give notice.

PRÉCAIRE – provisional; in the right of another.

- **DÉTENTION précaire** – occupation of another's property by virtue of an agreement with the owner (eg as a tenant).

PRÉCARITÉ – the fact of holding or occupying property in (by virtue of) the right of another (eg as a tenant).

- **EXEMPT de précarité** – not holding in the right of another.

PRÉCÉDENT – precedent.

PRÉCIPUT – clause in a marriage contract whereby the surviving spouse has a right to receive a sum of money or certain chattels before the partition of the community property; right to receive something in advance before the division of an estate or thing so received.

- **PART** – **préciput hors part** – gift to an heir out of the estate in addition to his share.
  - •• **PAR préciput et hors part** – (of a gift to an heir out of an estate) not subject to hotchpot; in addition to the heir's share of the estate.

PRÉCIS – specific.

PRÉCISER – specify.

PRÉCOMPTE – advance payment; salary deduction for the purpose of paying an employee's social-security contributions; deduction at source.

- **IMMOBILIER** – **précompte immobilier** (Belg) – advance on income tax payable on immovable property.

PRÉCONTRACTUEL

- **PÉRIODE précontractuelle** – period preceding the contract.

PRÉÉMINENCE

- **DROIT** – **prééminence du droit** – rule of law.
  - •• **ADHÉRER** – **adhérant à la prééminence du droit** – subscribing to the rule of law.

PRÉEMPTION – preemption; first option to purchase.

PRÉFÉRENCE

- **DROIT de préférence** – right (of a mortgagee or person entitled to a statutory priority, preference or lien (**privilège**)) to be paid in preference to other creditors; preferential right; preferential duty.

PRÉFET – prefect; chief administrative officer in a département (county).

- **MARITIME** – **préfet maritime** – admiral in charge of a coastal district.
- **POLICE** – **préfet de police** – (Paris) Metropolitan Police Commissioner; Commissioner of Police for the Metropolis.
- **RÉGION** – **préfet de région** – regional prefect; chief administrative officer in a region.

PRÉJUDICE – damage; injury; loss; harm.

- **AGRÉMENT** – **préjudice d'agrément** – loss of amenity.
- **CHEF de préjudice** – head of damage.
- **MATÉRIEL** – **préjudice matériel** – pecuniary (material) damage.
- **MORAL** – **préjudice moral** – non-pecuniary (non-material) damage.
- **PATRIMONIAL** – **préjudice patrimonial** – pecuniary damage; economic loss.
- **PÉCUNIAIRE** – **préjudice pécuniaire** – pecuniary damage.
- **PERSONNEL** – **préjudice de caractère personnel** – loss of amenity, pain and suffering and aesthetic damage.
- **PORTER préjudice** – cause damage.
  - •• **PRINCIPAL** – **ne portent pas préjudice au principal** – without prejudice to (without affecting) the merits.
- **RICOCHET** – **préjudice par ricochet** – indirect damage suffered by dependants (or

others similarly situated) from the death or injury of a victim.

- **SANS** préjudice de – subject to; without prejudicing (prejudice to); without prejudging.
- **SOCIAL** – **préjudice social** – loss or damage suffered by a company, (professional or other) association, trade union, etc.
- **VOISINAGE** – **préjudice excédant la mesure ordinaire des obligations de voisinage** – nuisance.

PRÉJUDICIABLE – harmful.

PRÉJUDICIEL

- **DÉCISION préjudicielle** – decision (ruling) on a preliminary question (point, issue) (by another court); preliminary ruling.
- **DEMANDE préjudicielle** – application for the decision of a preliminary question (point, issue) (for a preliminary ruling).
- **QUESTION préjudicielle** – preliminary question (issue); preliminary point of law (pending the decision of which by another court the proceedings are stayed); case stated.
    - •• **ACTION** – **question préjudicielle à l'action** – preliminary question (point, issue) to be decided before an action can be brought.
    - •• **JUGEMENT** – **question préjudicielle au jugement** – preliminary question (point, issue) to be decided before judgment can be given.
- **RENVOI préjudiciel** – reference of a preliminary question (point, issue) to another court for decision or for a ruling.

PRÉJUDICIER – harm; damage.

PRÉJUGER – make a preliminary, provisional or interlocutory decision; decide on (admit) in advance.

PRÉLEGS – preferential legacy.

PRÉLÈVEMENT – deduction before partition; deduction; tax; contribution; levy; withdrawal.

- **PÉRÉQUATION** – **prélèvement de péréquation** – equalisation tax, charge or contribution.
- **SOURCE** – **prélèvement à la source** – deduction at source; PAYE.

PRÉLIMINAIRE

- **CONCILIATION** – **préliminaire de conciliation** – conciliation proceedings.

PREMIER

- **CHANGE** – **première de change** – first of exchange.
- **DEGRÉ** – **premier degré** – court below; trial court; first instance.
- **INSTANCE** – **première instance** – first instance.
- **JUGE** – **premier juge** – the court below; trial court; first instance.
    - •• **TRIBUNAL** – **premier juge du tribunal de grande instance** – senior judge of the Regional Court.
- **PRÉSIDENT** – **premier président** – President (of the Court of Appeal or Court of Cassation).

PRENDRE

- **ACTE** – **prendre acte de** – take formal note of; take official notice of.
- **CONCLUSION** – **prendre des conclusions** – file pleadings; make an application (in court proceedings).
- **FUITE** – **prendre la fuite** – abscond.
- **JUGEMENT** – **prendre un jugement** – obtain a judgment.
- **PAROLE** – **prendre la parole** – address (the court).
- **RANG** – **prendre rang avant** – take precedence of.

PRENEUR – purchaser; payee; tenant; lessee.

- **LICENCE** – **preneur de licence** – licensee.

PRÉNOM – forename; first name; Christian name.

PRÉPARATOIRE

- **JUGEMENT préparatoire** – interlocutory decision.

PRÉPOSÉ – servant, ie a person under one's direction and control, employed to perform a task and for whose faults one is vicariously liable; person who works under the direction of another.

- **DOUANE** – **préposé des douanes** – customs official.
- **REGISTRE** – **préposé au registre du commerce** (Sw) – officer in charge of the Commercial Registry; Commercial Registrar.

PRÉPOSITION – position of a superior entitled to give orders to subordinates (ie master-and-servant relationship).

- **RAPPORT de préposition** – master-and-servant relationship.

PRÉRÉQUISITION – period between receiving notice of a requisition and its execution.

PRÉROGATIVE – particular right.

- **EXORBITANT** – prérogatives exorbitantes du droit commun – powers not subject to (falling outside the scope of) the general (ordinary) law, creating or constituting an exception from the general law, eg a clause in a government contract excluding the jurisdiction of the ordinary courts.
- **PROPRIÉTAIRE** – prérogatives du propriétaire – owner's (accessory) rights.
- **PROPRIÉTÉ** – prérogatives du droit de propriété – owner's rights ; rights of ownership.

PRÈS

- **COUR (TRIBUNAL)** – près la cour (le tribunal) – (of a prosecutor, expert, etc) at the court.

PRESCRIPTIBILITÉ – fact of being subject to limitation or prescription.

PRESCRIPTIBLE – subject to limitation or prescription.

PRESCRIPTION – instruction; prescription; limitation; provision; means of acquiring property and rights (prescription) or freeing oneself of obligations (limitation); (crim) time-limit after which an offence cannot be prosecuted or a sentence enforced.

- **ABRÉGÉ** – prescription abrégée – short limitation period.
- **ACQUISITIF** – prescription acquisitive – (positive or acquisitive) prescription (as a means of acquiring rights); adverse possession (as a means of acquiring property).
- **ACTION PÉNALE** – see ACTION PUBLIQUE below.
- **ACTION PUBLIQUE** – prescription de l'action publique – time-limit after which a prosecution may not be brought.
- **ADMINISTRATIF** – prescription administrative – administrative direction or regulation.
- **ARRÊTER** le cours de la prescription – stop time running.
- **CRIMINEL** – prescription criminelle – time-limit for (bringing a) prosecution; time-limit for enforcing a sentence.
- **DÉLAI** de prescription – (acquisitive) prescription period; period of adverse possession; (extinctive) limitation period.

- •• **PEINE** – délai de prescription de la peine – limitation period after which sentences may no longer be enforced.
- **DÉROGATOIRE** – prescription dérogatoire – exception.
- **DROIT** – prescription d'un droit – lapse (barring) of a right by statutory limitation.
- **EXCIPER** de la prescription – raise the defence of limitation; plead limitation.
- **EXPIRATION** de la prescription – completion of the prescription or limitation period; expiry of the time-limit for prosecution or enforcement of a sentence.
- **EXTINCTIF** – prescription extinctive – limitation (less frequently referred to as negative prescription) (which extinguishes or renders unenforceable rights and the corresponding obligations).
- **FORME** – prescription de forme – formal or procedural requirement.
- **IMPÉRATIF** – prescription impérative – mandatory provision.
- **INTERRUPTION** de la prescription – interruption of the limitation or prescription period, after which time begins to run afresh, ie the whole period recommences from the beginning. (Cf SUSPENSION below.)
- **INTERVERSION** – interversion de la prescription – substitution of the general limitation period of thirty years for a shorter period after the latter has been interrupted by an acknowledgement etc.
- **LÉGAL** – prescriptions légales – statutory requirements.
- **LIBÉRATOIRE** – prescription libératoire – limitation.
- **OBLIGATOIRE** – prescription obligatoire – mandatory provision.
- **PEINE** – prescription de la peine – (expiry of) time-limit for the enforcement of a sentence.
- **POTESTATIF** – prescription potestative – provision whose application is discretionary.
- **POURSUITE** – prescription des poursuites – (expiry of) time-limit for prosecuting an offence.
- **PRISE** – donner prise à la prescription – be subject to limitation.
- **SANCTIONNÉ**
  - •• **NON** – prescription non sanctionnée – provision carrying no penalty for non-compliance.
- **SUSPENSION** de la prescription – suspension of the limitation or prescription

period, after which it continues to run again from the point reached when the suspension began. (Cf INTERRUPTION above.)

PRESCRIRE – make regulation etc; obtain (acquire) by prescription.

- **POSSESSEUR** – **le tiers possesseur prescrit à la fois contre l'usufruitier et contre le nu-propriétaire** – time runs in favour of the occupier against both the life tenant (usufructuary) and the remainderman.
- **SE prescrire** – lapse by limitation; be subject to limitation.

PRESCRIT – statute-barred; time-barred; barred by limitation.

PRÉSÉANCE – precedence.

PRÉSENCE – (in plural) attendance register.

- **JETON de présence** – (eg director's) attendance fee.

PRÉSENT

- **USAGE** – **présents d'usage** – traditional gifts.

PRÉSENTATION

- **DROIT de présentation** – right to name a successor for appointment to certain professional offices, such as those of bailiff, registrar, stockbroker or auctioneer.
- **PAIEMENT** – **présentation au paiement** – presentation for payment.
- **VOLONTAIRE** – **présentation volontaire** – voluntary appearance of the parties (means of commencing proceedings before the district court (**tribunal d'instance**)).

PRÉSENTER – submit; move; file.

- **AMENDEMENT** – **présenter un amendement** – move (table) an amendment.
- **DUPLIQUE** – **présenter une duplique** – file a rejoinder.
- **SE présenter spontanément** – report voluntarily.

PRÉSIDENT

- **ÂGE** – **président d'âge** – oldest member (of a committee etc) acting as chairman (president) ad interim.
- **CHAMBRE** – **président de chambre** – president of a division of the Court of Appeal or Court of Cassation.
- **EXERCICE** – **président en exercice** – chairman(-in-office); president(-in-office).
- **HONNEUR** – **président d'honneur** – honorary president (chairman).

- **INTÉRIM** – **président par intérim** – acting chairman (president).
- **PREMIER président** – President (of the Court of Appeal or Court of Cassation).

PRÉSIDENT-DIRECTEUR GÉNÉRAL – chairman and general manager (managing director).

PRÉSOMPTIF

- **HÉRITIER présomptif** – heir presumptive, ie who will be heir if no nearer relative is born.

PRÉSOMPTION – presumption, ie the inference of an unproved fact from a fact already established; inference; some (prima facie) evidence; indication.

- **ABSOLU** – **présomption absolue** – irrebuttable (irrefutable) presumption.
- **HOMME** – **présomption de l'homme** – presumption of fact; supporting evidence; rebuttable (refutable) presumption; evidence tending to prove.
- **INFRACTION** – **présomption d'infraction** – prima facie offence.
- **IRRÉFRAGABLE** – **présomption irréfragable** – irrebuttable (irrefutable) presumption.
- **JURIS ET DE JURE** – **présomption juris et de jure** – absolute (irrebuttable, irrefutable) presumption.
- **JURISPRUDENTIEL** – **présomption jurisprudentielle** – presumption established by case-law.
- **JURIS TANTUM** – **présomption juris tantum** – rebuttable (refutable) presumption; statutory rebuttable presumption.
- **LÉGAL** – **présomption légale** – statutory presumption; presumption of law.
- **POSSESSION** – **présomption de possession véritable** – presumption that the possessor is the true owner.
- **RÉGULARITÉ** – **présomption de régularité** – presumption that proceedings have have been properly conducted.
- **RELATIF** – **présomption relative** – rebuttable (refutable) presumption.
- **SIMPLE** – **présomption simple** – rebuttable (refutable) presumption.
- **TOMBER** – **faire tomber une présomption** – rebut (refute) a presumption.
- **VIE** – **présomption de vie** – presumption that a person is alive.

PRESSE

- **DÉLIT de presse** – offence against the legislation on the press.

PRESSION

- **EXERCER** – tendant à exercer des pressions – prejudicial.
- **TÉMOIN** – pression sur les témoins – intimidation of witnesses.

PRESTATAIRE – person performing or liable to perform an obligation; promisor; person from whom something is requisitioned.

PRESTATION – thing or service promised in a contract; fulfilment (performance, execution) of this promise; (promised) benefit; subject-matter of the contract; act of performance forming the subject-matter of an obligation; thing, service or payment which the obligor is bound to transfer, furnish or make for the benefit of the obligee; thing etc promised; performance; (social-security) benefit; (in plural) acts of performance.

- **ACCESSOIRE** – prestation accessoire – collateral benefit.
- **BÉNÉFICIAIRE d'une prestation** – beneficiary; person receiving a benefit; promisee.
- **COMPENSATOIRE** – prestation compensatoire – pecuniary provision on divorce (intended to equalise the position of the ex-spouses).
- **DÉBITEUR d'une prestation** – person liable to confer a benefit; person liable to perform a contract; promisor.
- **DÉLAI de prestation** – time for performance.
- **DÛ** – prestation due – thing or service owed.
- **ESPÈCE** – prestation en espèces – payment in cash; cash benefit.
- **FAMILIAL** – prestations familiales – family allowances.
- **MATERNITÉ** – prestation de maternité – maternity benefit.
- **NATURE** – prestation en nature – benefit in kind.
- **SERMENT** – prestation de serment – taking an oath.
- **SERVICE** – prestation de service – performing a service.
- **SOCIAL** – prestations sociales – social-security benefits.
- **SUCCESSIF** – prestations successives – performance in instalments.
- **SÛRETÉ** – prestation de sûreté – giving security.

PRÊT – loan.

- **AVENTURE** – prêt à l'aventure (à la grosse aventure) – bottomry loan.
- **BONIFIÉ** – prêt bonifié – interest rebate loan; soft loan.
- **CONSOMMATION** – prêt de consommation) – loan of money (or other fungible or consumable goods) of which the borrower is under an obligation to restore an equivalent quantity; money loan.
- **CONVENTIONNEL** – prêt conventionnel – contractual loan.
- **CORPS** – prêt sur corps – bottomry loan.
- **FONCIER** – prêt foncier – mortgage loan; (to a company) mortgage debenture.
- **FONDS PERDU** – prêt à fonds perdu(s) – irredeemable loan.
- **GAGE** – prêt sur gage – loan secured by a pledge.
- **GROS** – prêt à la grosse (aventure) – bottomry loan.
- **HYPOTHÉCAIRE** – prêt hypothécaire – mortgage (loan).
- **HYPOTHÈQUE**
  - •• **PREMIER** – prêt en première hypothèque – loan secured by a first mortgage.
  - •• **SUR** – prêt sur hypothèque – mortgage (loan).
- **USURAIRE** – prêt usuraire – loan at an unconscionable rate of interest.

PRÊTE-NOM – agent who acts in his own name; man of straw; nominee; factor; agent of a principal whose name is not disclosed.

PRÉTENDRE – claim; maintain; submit; allege.

- **POUVOIR** – pouvoir prétendre à – be qualified for.

PRÉTENDU

- **ÉGALITÉ** – prétendue égalité des contractants – notional (ostensible) equality of the contracting parties.

PRÉTENDUMENT – allegedly.

PRÉTENTION – claim; allegation; cause of action; allegation in pleadings; ground of defence; submission; pleading.

- **ALIMENTAIRE** – prétention alimentaire (Sw) – maintenance claim.
- **CHIFFRER ses prétentions** – quantify one's claims.

- **EXPOSER** ses prétentions – present one's case.
- **REJETER** une prétention – dismiss a claim.

PRÊTEUR

- **FONDS** – prêteur de fonds – money-lender; person providing finance.

PRÉTEXTE

- **SOUS** prétexte que – on the ground that.

PRETIUM DOLORIS – (damages for) pain and suffering.

PRÉTOIRE – courtroom; court; disciplinary court for offences committed by a prisoner serving a sentence; disciplinary board (in a prison); board of visitors.

- **DEHORS** – en dehors du prétoire – out of court.

PRÉTORIEN – judicial; judge-made.

PRÊT-RELAIS – bridging loan.

PREUVE – proof; evidence.

- **ACTE DE NOTORIÉTÉ** – preuve par acte de notoriété – proof by declaration (affidavit) relating to a matter of common knowledge.
- **ADMINISTRER** une (la) preuve (des preuves) – adduce evidence; bring evidence to establish; (of procedure in court) take evidence.
- **APPRÉCIATION** des preuves – assessment of (the) evidence.
- **CHARGE** de la preuve – burden (onus) of proof.
- **COMMENCEMENT** de preuve par écrit – signed writing rendering admissible confirmatory oral evidence or presumptions which would otherwise be excluded; writing admitting oral evidence; some evidence in writing; prima facie case.
- **COMMUNE RENOMMÉE** – see RENOMMÉE below.
- **COMPLÉMENTAIRE** – preuve complémentaire – further evidence.
- **COMPLET** – preuve complète – full proof.
- **CONSERVATION** de la preuve – preservation of evidence.
- **CONTRAIRE** – preuve contraire – proof of the contrary; refuting evidence.
  - •• **DÉTRUIRE** – susceptible d'être détruit par la preuve contraire – (of evidence) rebuttable.

- **CONTRAIRE** – jusqu'à preuve du contraire – until the contrary has been proved, ie prima facie.
- **DÉFAUT** de preuve – absence (lack) of or insufficient evidence (proof).
- **DISPARAÎTRE** – faire disparaître des preuves – suppress evidence.
- **ÉCRIT** – preuve par écrit – documentary evidence.
- **ÉLÉMENTS** de preuve – evidence; proof.
- **ÉVIDENT** – preuve évidente – convincing proof.
- **FARDEAU** de la preuve – burden (onus) of proof.
- **FAUTE** de preuve – for lack of evidence (proof).
- **INDICE** – preuve par indices – circumstantial evidence.
- **INTRINSÈQUE** – preuve intrinsèque – proof based on the instrument itself; proof appearing on the face of the document.
- **LÉGAL** – preuve légale – statutory proof.
  - •• **FORMEL** – preuve légale et formelle – (proof according to the) strict rules of evidence.
- **LIBRE** – la preuve de la cause est libre – the consideration (legal basis) may be proved by any kind of evidence.
- **LITTÉRAL** – preuve littérale – documentary evidence.
- **MANQUE** de preuve – absence (lack) of or insufficient evidence (proof).
- **MATÉRIEL** – preuve matérielle – real evidence.
- **MODE** de preuve – mode of proof; type of evidence.
- **MOYEN** de preuve – (piece of) evidence; proof.
- **MOYEN** – preuve par tous les moyens – all types of evidence.
  - •• **POSSIBLE** – la preuve serait alors possible par tous les moyens – in that case any kind of evidence would be admissible (could be adduced).
- **NORMES** relatives à la preuve – rules of evidence.
- **OBJET** de la preuve – thing (matter) to be proved.
- **OFFRE** de preuve – offer or application to produce or bring evidence.
  - •• **PRÉSENTER** des offres de preuve – submit evidence.
- **ORDONNANCE** de preuves (Sw) – order for evidence to be taken.

- **PRÉCONSTITUÉ** – preuve préconstituée – proof by documents prepared for that purpose.
- **PRODUIRE des preuves** – adduce (bring) evidence.
- **RAPPORTER la preuve** – establish by evidence; prove.
- **RECHERCHE** – recherche de preuves – obtaining evidence.
- **RÉGIME des preuves** – rules of evidence.
- **RÈGLE de preuve** – rule of evidence.
- **RENOMMÉE** – preuve par commune renommée – evidence of common repute.
- **SOLIDITÉ des preuves** – reliability of the evidence.
- **SÛRETÉ** – mise en sûreté de la preuve – preservation of evidence.
- **TESTIMONIAL** – preuve testimoniale – oral evidence.
- **TITRE** – preuve par titres – documentary evidence.

PRÉVALOIR

- **NULLITÉ** – se prévaloir de la nullité par voie d'action ou par voie d'exception – base one's action or defence on a nullity.
- **SE prévaloir de** – rely on.

PRÉVARICATION – abuse of official authority; misfeasance in public office.

PRÉVENTIF

- **DÉTENTION (PRISON) préventive** (Belg) – detention on remand; remand (in custody); detention pending investigation or trial; custody (for short periods).

PRÉVENTION – detention on remand; charge.

- **CHEF de prévention** – charge; count.
- **MESURE de prévention** – preventive measure.
- **RETENIR une prévention** – (of a court) find a charge has been proved.
- **SITUATIONNEL** – prévention situationnelle – target hardening.

PRÉVENTIONNAIRE – remand prisoner.

PRÉVENTIVE (Belg) – see PRÉVENTIF and PRISON.

PRÉVENU – accused (defendant) appearing before a criminal court other than a court of assize; accused (defendant) charged with a misdemeanour or summary offence; remand prisoner; untried prisoner.

- **LIBRE** – prévenu libre – accused (defendant) on bail or released pending trial.

PRÉVISION

- **DÉPENSE** – prévisions de dépenses – estimated expenditure.

PRÉVISIONNEL

- **ÉTAT prévisionnel** – budget estimates; estimates; budget.

PRÉVOIR

- **LOI** – prévu par la loi – statutory.

PRIMAIRE

- **DÉTENU primaire** – first offender.

PRIMAUTÉ

- **DROIT** – primauté du droit – rule of law.

PRIME – premium; bonus; allowance; option; profit; grant.

- **ACCOUCHEMENT** – prime d'accouchement – maternity grant.
- **BONIFICATION de la prime** – return of the premium.
- **ÉMISSION avec prime** – issue at a premium (above par).
- **MARCHÉ à prime** – option.

PRIMER – take precedence over.

PRIMITIF

- **INSTANCE primitive** – original proceedings.
- **PROJET primitif** – rough draft; first draft.

PRIMITIVEMENT – originally; in the first place.

- **TRIBUNAL ayant primitivement statué** – the court which originally dealt with the proceedings.

PRINCE

- **FAIT du prince** – act of state.

PRINCIPAL – capital of a debt etc; subject-matter of proceedings as defined by the pleadings.

- **AU principal** – in the main proceedings; on the merits.
- **DÉBATTRE au principal** – dispute the main issue; argue the merits.
- **FRAIS** – les frais suivent le principal – costs follow the event.
- **STATUER au principal** – try the main issue; hear and decide the case; try the case; decide (give judgment in) the main proceedings; determine the merits of a case.

PRINCIPE – rule; principle; general rule.

- **DÉCISION de principe** – leading case; authoritative decision; decision establishing an important principle.
- **INDEMNITÉ de principe** – nominal damages (compensation).

PRIORITÉ

- **ACTION de priorité** – preference share.
- **TOUR de priorité** – (right of) precedence.

PRISE – prize.

- **BÉNÉFICE – prise de bénéfice** – taking a profit.
- **CHARGE – prise en charge** – acceptance of responsibility for; taking into custody.
  - •• **DETTE – prise en charge d'une dette** – assumption of liability for the obligation or debt of another.
  - •• **FRAIS – prise en charge des frais** – acceptance of liability for costs.
- **CONSEIL des prises** – prize court.
- **CORPS – ordonnance de prise de corps** – arrest warrant issued by the Indictments Chamber.
- **COUR des prises** – prize appeal court.
- **DÉCLARER bonne prise** – declare good prize.
- **EAU – prise d'eau fondée en titre** – established right to take water.
- **FONCTION – prise de fonctions** – assumption of duties (office).
- **GAGE – prise en gage** – taking something as a pledge or security.
- **GARDE – prise en garde** – taking something into one's custody.
- **GUERRE – prise de guerre** – booty; prize.
- **LIVRAISON – prise de livraison** – taking delivery.
- **MARITIME – prise maritime** – prize.
- **PARTIE – prise à partie** – action for damages against a judge for misuse of his authority.

PRISÉE – valuation.

PRISON

- **BRIS de prison** – escape.
- **FERME – prison ferme** – immediate imprisonment (ie not suspended); affirmative sentence.
- **PRÉVENTIF – prison préventive (Belg)** – detention on remand; remand (in custody); detention pending investigation or trial; custody (for short periods).

PRISONNIER

- **CONSTITUER – se constituer prisonnier** – give oneself up.
- **DROIT COMMUN – prisonnier de droit commun** – ordinary prisoner (as opposed to a political prisoner).

PRIVATIF – exclusive; in exclusive ownership; individual.

- **LIBERTÉ – peine privative de liberté** – custodial sentence; imprisonment.

PRIVATISTE – expert in private law.

PRIVATION

- **DROIT**
  - •• **CIVIQUE – privation des droits civiques** – civic disqualification; deprivation of civic rights.
- **INDEMNITÉ pour privation de jouissance** – compensation for loss of enjoyment of property.

PRIVILÈGE – right of certain classes of creditors to be paid in preference to others (including the secured creditors); right to preferential payment; preference; lien; licence; exemption.

- **BAILLEUR – privilège du bailleur** – landlord's right of distress.
- **BOUILLEUR DE CRU – privilège des bouilleurs de cru** – distiller's licence.
- **DIPLOMATIQUE – privilège diplomatique** – diplomatic privilege.
- **FAILLITE – privilège en cas de faillite** – right to preferential payment in bankruptcy.
- **GÉNÉRAL – privilège général** – right to preferential payment out of the debtor's entire assets or estate.
- **IMMOBILIER**
  - •• **GÉNÉRAL – privilège immobilier général** – right to preferential payment out of all the debtor's immovables.
  - •• **SPÉCIAL – privilège immobilier spécial** – right to preferential payment attaching to specific immovables.
- **JURIDICTION – privilège de juridiction** – exemption from jurisdiction.
- **MOBILIER**
  - •• **GÉNÉRAL – privilège mobilier général** – right to preferential payment out of all the debtor's movables.
  - •• **SPÉCIAL – privilège mobilier spécial** – right to preferential payment attaching to specific movables.

- **PAVILLON** – privilège de pavillon – flag discrimination, ie reserving rights of fishery or coastal trade to national ships.

PRIVILÉGIÉ – preferential creditor;
- **CRÉANCIER** privilégié – secured or preferred creditor; preferential creditor (in bankruptcy).

PRIX
- **AMATEUR** – prix d'amateur – collector's (connoisseur's, fancy price).
- **BAIL** – prix du bail – rent.
- **FAIT** – prix fait – agreed price.
- **FORFAITAIRE** – prix forfaitaire – inclusive price.
- **LOYER** – prix du loyer – rent.

PROBANT
- **MANIÈRE** – de manière probante – reliably.
- **VALEUR** probante – evidential value; probative value.
  - **ÉLÉMENT** – valeur probante des éléments – weight of evidence.

PROBLÈME – question; issue.

PROCÉDÉ
- **BREVET** de procédé – process patent.
- **COERCITIF** – procédé coercitif – means of coercion.
- **CONTRAINTE** – procédé de contrainte – means of coercion.
- **SIGNIFICATION** – procédés de signification des actes de procédure – procedure for (manner of) serving judicial process (by a bailiff).

PROCÉDURAL
- **SCHÉMA** procédural – form of procedure.

PROCÉDURE – proceedings; procedure; process; case file; police report.
- **ABRÉGÉ** – procédure abrégée – shortened form of procedure.
- **ACCÉLÉRÉ** – procédure accélérée – shortened form of procedure.
- **ACCUSATOIRE** – procédure accusatoire – adversarial proceedings.
- **ACTE** de procédure – step in judicial proceedings (writ, pleading, application, etc); procedural formality; process; procedural document; procedural step; procedural measure.
  - **NOTIFICATION** des actes de procédure – service of process.

- **SIGNIFICATION** des actes de procédure – service of judicial process (by a bailiff).
- **ADMINISTRATIF** – procédure administrative – administrative procedure.
  - **JURIDICTIONNEL** – procédure administrative juridictionnelle – administrative-court procedure.
- **ADMINISTRATION DE LA PREUVE** – procédure d'administration d'une (de la) preuve (des preuves) – taking (bringing, adducing) evidence.
- **ALERTE** – procédure d'alerte – procedure enabling an auditor or works council to call for explanations from the managers when the economic position of a business appears precarious.
- **ANNULER** la procédure – set the proceedings aside.
- **ARTIFICE** de procédure – procedural device.
- **CONCORDAT** – procédure de concordat – composition or arrangement with creditors (approved by the court).
- **CONFLIT** – procédure de conflit – procedure for settling conflicts of jurisdiction.
- **CONTENTIEUX** – procédure contentieuse – contentious proceedings.
  - **CONTRADICTOIRE** – procédure contentieuse contradictoire – ordinary (ie inter partes) contentious proceedings.
- **CONTRADICTOIRE** – procédure contradictoire – proceedings involving the participation, representation or hearing of both parties; inter partes (ie ordinary) proceedings.
- **CONTRAINTE** – procédure de contrainte – coercive measures.
- **CONTUMACE** – procédure par contumace – trial in absentia.
- **DÉBET** – procédure de débet – proceedings for restitution or repayment by the accountant of the deficit in an account.
- **DÉFAUT** – procédure par défaut – (civ) default proceedings; (crim) trial in absentia.
- **DÉLAI** de procédure – procedural time-limit.
- **DÉROULEMENT** de la procédure – course of the proceedings.
- **DISPOSITION** de procédure – procedural provision.
- **DROIT** de la procédure – procedure; procedural law; law of procedure.
- **DROIT** de procédure – trial fee; court fee.

- **ÉLEVER**
  - **S'élever contre la procédure** – complain of the procedure.
- **ENGAGER une procédure** – begin (start, commence) proceedings; bring an action; initiate a procedure.
- **ENQUÊTE – procédure d'enquête** – investigation(s).
- **EXÉCUTION - procédure d'exécution** – execution proceedings; execution procedure.
- **FOND – procédure sur le fond** – trial on the merits; trial of the principal issue.
- **FORCÉ – procédure forcée** – coercive measures.
- **FRUSTRATOIRE – procédure frustratoire** – obstructive tactics.
- **GRACIEUX – procédure (en matière) gracieuse** – non-contentious proceedings (procedure).
- **INCIDENT de procédure** – procedural application; step in the procedure; interlocutory (incidental) application or proceedings.
- **INDEMNITÉ de procédure (Belg)** – preparation allowance (for preparing a case for trial).
- **INJONCTION – procédure d'injonction** – administrative enforcement procedure.
- **INQUISITOIRE – procédure inquisitoire** – inquisitorial procedure (the investigation is in the hands of the court and conducted in secret with special rules of evidence and no confrontation of prosecution and accused on equal terms).
- **INSTANCE – procédure en instance** – pending proceedings.
- **INSTRUCTION – procédure d'instruction** – preliminary inquiry; investigation proceedings.
- **INTRODUIRE une procédure** – bring proceedings (an action etc).
- **INVESTIGATION – procédure d'investigation** – investigations; investigation procedure.
- **JOUR – procédure à jour fixe** – fixed-date (expedited) proceedings.
- **JUDICIAIRE – procédure judiciaire** – court proceedings; legal proceedings; judicial proceedings.
- **JURIDICTIONNEL – procédure juridictionnelle** – judicial or quasi-judicial proceedings; legal proceedings.
- **LOI de procédure** – Code of Procedure; Procedure Act; procedural provisions.
- **MODALITÉS de la procédure** – forms of procedure.
- **MOTION de procédure** – (procedural) application.
- **NOTIFICATION – procédure de notification** – service of process; service.
- **ORAL – procédure orale** – (oral) hearing.
- **ORDRE – procédure d'ordre** – procedure for distributing the proceeds of sale of real property among the preferential and secured creditors, according to the priority of their liens, preferential rights and mortgages.
- **PARTIE ADVERSE – procédure sans citation de la partie adverse** – ex parte proceedings.
- **PÉNAL – procédure pénale** – criminal procedure.
- **PIÈCES de la procédure** – case file; documents on the file.
- **POLICE – procédures de police spéciales** – special administrative proceedings.
- **PRENDRE – s'en prendre à la procédure** – complain of the procedure.
- **RÈGLE de procédure** – rule of court; procedural rule; rule of procedure.
- **RÉOUVERTURE de la procédure** – reopening of the proceedings.
- **RÉPRESSION – procédure de répression d'une infraction** – procedure for dealing with an offence.
- **REQUÊTE – procédure sur requête** – ex parte proceedings.
- **SUSPENDRE la procédure** – stay the proceedings.
- **URGENCE – procédure d'urgence** – (procedure for) urgent cases.
  - **DATE – procédure d'urgence à date fixe** – fixed-date urgent proceedings.
- **VICE – procédure entachée d'un vice** – invalid proceedings.
- **VICE de procédure** – procedural defect (error, irregularity).

PROCÉDURIER – (adj) litigious; (noun) litigant who takes undue advantage of procedural devices (niceties); vexatious litigant.

PROCÈS – proceedings, trial.
- **DIRECTION d'un procès** – conduct (control) of the proceedings.
- **DOSSIER d'un procès** – case file.
- **ENGAGER un procès** – begin (start, commence) proceedings; bring an action.
- **ÉQUITABLE – procès équitable** – fair trial.

- **FILIATION** – procès en filiation – proceedings to establish legitimacy or paternity.
- **FORME** – procès en bonne et due forme – properly conducted trial.
- **GAGNER** un procès – win a case.
- **INSTANCE** – procès en instance – pending proceedings.
- **INTENTER** un procès – begin (start, commence) proceedings; bring an action.
- **MARCHE** d'un procès – course of proceedings.
- **MENER** un procès – conduct proceedings.
- **PERDRE** un procès – lose a case.

PROCESSIF – procedural; (of a litigant) vexatious; (of other persons) litigious.

PROCESSUEL – procedural.
- **DROIT** processuel – procedure.

PROCÈS-VERBAL – (official) record or report; minute; police report; memorandum (minutes) of proceedings; record of acts performed by a bailiff (eg service or attachment); (parking etc) ticket.
- **AUDIENCE** – procès-verbal d'audience – record of the hearing.
- **AUDITION** – procès-verbal d'audition – deposition; record of evidence taken from a witness.
- **CAISSE** – procès-verbal de caisse – certificate of verification of cash.
- **CARENCE** – procès-verbal de carence – official report (affidavit) of failure to attend or failure to perform some obligation or to do some specific thing; bailiff's return that there is no property to be seized (nulla bona).
- **DÉBAT** – procès-verbal des débats – record of the proceedings; transcript of the trial.
- **DRESSER** – il en est dressé procès-verbal – the proceedings are recorded.
- **INTÉGRAL** – procès-verbal intégral – verbatim record.
- **RÉSUMÉ** – procès-verbal résumé – summary record.

PROCURATION – power of attorney; authority; counsel's authority to act (for a client).
- **ACTE** de procuration – power of attorney; authority.
- **DÉFAUT** de procuration – lack of authority.
- **ÉLECTORAL** – procuration électorale – authority to vote on behalf of another; proxy.
- **ENDOS(SEMENT)** de procuration – endorsement signed by an agent or manager.

- **GÉNÉRAL** – procuration générale – general power of attorney; general authority.
- **NOTARIÉ** – procuration notariée – officially recorded power of attorney.
- **RÉVOCATION** d'une procuration – revocation of a power of attorney.
- **SPÉCIAL** – procuration spéciale – special power of attorney.
- **VENTE** – procuration pour la vente – authority to sell.
- **VOTE** par procuration – proxy vote; vote given by a proxy.

PROCUREUR – public prosecutor; State prosecutor (Counsel); Legal Adviser; (Belg) Crown prosecutor (Counsel).
- **ÉTAT** – procureur d'État (Lux) – State prosecutor (Counsel).
- **GÉNÉRAL** – procureur général – Principal State Prosecutor (Counsel); Attorney-General; Principal Legal Adviser; (Belg) Principal Crown Prosecutor (Counsel).
- **RÉPUBLIQUE** – procureur de la République – public prosecutor; State prosecutor (Counsel).
- **ROI** – procureur du Roi (Belg) – public prosecutor; Crown prosecutor (Counsel).

PRO DEO (Belg) – legal aid; in forma pauperis; poor persons'.

PRODIGALITÉ – extravagance.

PRODIGUE – extravagant person; spendthrift.

PRODUCTEUR – manufacturer; producer.

PRODUCTION – production (disclosure) (of documents etc); proving (proof) (of debts or claims in bankruptcy and similar proceedings).
- **ACTE** – production d'actes – production of documents (in evidence, for inspection).
- **BIENS** de production – capital goods.
- **CRÉANCE** – production d'une créance – proof of a debt (in bankruptcy).
- **JUSTICE** – production en justice – production in evidence.

PRODUIRE – produce (disclose) (documents etc); (of evidence) adduce (bring); (of a debt or claim in bankruptcy) prove.
- **CRÉANCE** – produire une créance – prove a debt (in bankruptcy).
- **JUSTICE** – produire en justice – produce in evidence.

- **PIÈCE** – **produire des pièces** – produce documents (in evidence, for inspection).
- **TÉMOIN** – **produire des témoins** – call evidence (witnesses).

PRODUIT – produce; product; proceeds; (in plural) things produced by property at irregular intervals and causing a reduction in its substance.
- **FINANCIER** – **produit financier** – cash yield.
- **LIQUIDATION** – **produit de la liquidation** – proceeds of the liquidation; proceeds on winding-up.
- **LOCATIF** – **produit locatif** – rental.

PROFESSION
- **AMBULANT** – **profession ambulante** – itinerant trade or occupation.
- **ARTISANAL** – **profession artisanale** – manual trade.
- **LIBÉRAL** – **profession libérale** – (independent) profession.

PROFESSIONNEL
- **ASSOCIATION professionnelle** – trade association.

PROHIBER – forbid; declare illegal.

PROHIBITIF
- **EMPÊCHEMENT prohibitif** – impediment which does not render void or voidable a marriage celebrated in spite of the impediment.

PROJET
- **AMENDEMENT** – **projet d'amendement** – draft amendment.
- **BUDGET** – **projet de budget** – estimates.
- **CRÉDIT** – **projet de crédit** – proposal for an appropriation.
- **LOI** – **projet de loi** – (government) Bill.
- **PRIMITIF** – **projet primitif** – rough draft; first draft.
- **RÈGLEMENT** – **projet de règlement** – suggestion for a solution or settlement; draft regulation(s).
- **RÉSOLUTION** – **projet de résolution** – draft resolution.

PROLONGATION – extension of time (of a time-limit).

PROMESSE
- **BÉNÉFICIAIRE d'une promesse** – promisee.
- **CONTRACTER** – **promesse de contracter** (Sw) – preliminary contract; pre-contract.
- **CONTRAT** – **promesse de contrat** – pre-contract (eg option agreement, pre-emption agreement).
- **DETTE** – **promesse de dette** – formal unilateral obligation to pay or perform for which consideration is not required and usually not mentioned.
- **EXÉCUTION d'une promesse** – **exécution d'une promesse** – fulfilment of a promise.
- **EXÉCUTION** – **promesse d'exécution** – formal undertaking to perform the obligation of another.
- **GARANTIE** – **promesse de garantie** – indemnity; guarantee.
- **PORTE-FORT** – **promesse de porte-fort** – undertaking to ensure that a third party performs his obligation.
- **POST MORTEM** – **promesse post mortem** – clause providing that the obligations in agreement shall only be performed on the death of one of the parties.
- **SEING PRIVÉ** – **promesse sous seing privé** – written promise.
- **VENTE** – **promesse de vente** – (preliminary) contract of sale; promise to sell.

PROMETTANT – promisor.

PROMOTEUR – property developer.

PROMOTION
- **SOCIAL** – **promotion sociale** – social advancement.

PROMULGATION – promulgation; (loosely) publication.

PRONONCÉ – reading (giving, delivery) (of a judgment); passing (of a sentence); (Sw) decision; order.
- **PEINE** – **prononcé des peines** – sentencing.

PRONONCER – deliver (give, read) (a judgment); grant (an injunction, a divorce); order (the closure of a business).
- **DIVORCE** – **prononcer un divorce** – pronounce a decree of divorce; grant a divorce; dissolve (terminate) a marriage.
- **SE prononcer sur** – adjudicate on; decide; determine; rule on.
- **TRANSFERT**
  - **PROPRIÉTÉ** – **prononcer le transfert de la propriété** – declare that the property has passed.

PROPAGATION

- **BRUIT**
  - **FAUX – propagation de faux bruits –** spreading false rumours.

PROPORTIONNALITÉ

- **PRINCIPE de la proportionnalité –** proportionality rule.

PROPORTIONNELLE (noun) – proportional representation.

- **SCOLAIRE – proportionnelle scolaire –** division of state grants between state and private schools in proportion to the number of pupils.

PROPOSER

- **EXCEPTION – proposer une exception –** raise an objection; plead (put forward, raise) a defence.
- **NULLITÉ – proposer une nullité –** raise an objection (defence) on the ground that the action etc is void.

PROPOSITION – proposal; motion; bill.

- **AMENDEMENT – proposition d'amendement –** motion to amend; proposed amendment.
- **COMPLÉMENTAIRE – proposition complémentaire –** motion for a supplementary amendment.
- **LOI – proposition de loi –** (private member's) Bill.
- **RECOMMANDATION – proposition pour une recommandation –** motion for a recommendation.

PROPRES – separate property of a spouse (ie not forming part of the community).

PROPRIÉTAIRE

- **ÉTAGE – propriétaire d'étage –** owner of a floor (storey) in a building.
- **INDIVIS – propriétaire (par) indivis –** joint owner.
- **RIVERAIN – propriétaire riverain –** riparian owner.
- **TRÉFONCIER – propriétaire tréfoncier –** owner of the subsoil.
- **VIAGER – propriétaire viager –** life tenant.

PROPRIÉTÉ

- **APPARENT – propriété apparente –** ostensible ownership.
- **ARTISTIQUE – propriété artistique –** copyright in artistic works.

- **ATTEINTE à la propriété privée –** interference with private property.
- **ATTEINTE portée à la propriété du fonds enclavant –** restriction on the ownership of the land surrounding the enclave.
- **COMMERCIAL – propriété commerciale –** right to obtain an extension of business tenancy or compensation in lieu.
- **COMMUN – propriété commune –** co-ownership; co-property; tenancy in common.
- **ÉTAGE – propriété d'étage –** ownership of a floor (storey) in a building.
- **INDIVIS – propriété indivise –** joint ownership.
- **INDUSTRIEL – propriété industrielle –** industrial property, ie patents, registered designs, trade marks, marks of origin, etc.
- **INTELLECTUEL – propriété intellectuelle –** intellectual property (includes copyright and industrial property).
- **LITTÉRAIRE – propriété littéraire –** copyright.
- **MUTATION de propriété –** change (transfer) of ownership.
- **PLEIN – pleine propriété –** property not subject to a usufruct (life interest).
- **RÉSERVÉ de propriété –** reservation of ownership (of goods sold until payment in full).
- **TITRE de propriété –** document of title to property (proving ownership); title deed.
- **TRÉFONCIER – propriété tréfoncière –** ownership of the subsoil.
- **VIAGER – propriété viagère –** life interest.

PROROGATION – extension of time.

- **BAIL – prorogation d'un bail –** extension of a lease or tenancy.
- **COMPÉTENCE – prorogation de compétence –** extension of jurisdiction (of a court).
- **DÉLAI – prorogation d'un délai –** extension of time.
- **JURIDICTION – prorogation (volontaire) de juridiction –** extension of a court's ordinary jurisdiction (by agreement of the parties).
- **TERME – prorogation de terme –** extension of time.

PROROGER – extend.

- **DÉLAI – proroger un délai –** extend a period; extend time.

PROSPECTION
- **AUTORISATION (PERMIS) exclusive (exclusif) de prospection** – exclusive prospecting licence.

PROSPECTUS
- **ÉMISSION – prospectus d'émission** – (company) prospectus.
- **SOUSCRIPTION – prospectus de souscription** – (company) prospectus.
- **TRIMESTRIEL – prospectus trimestriel** – quarterly statement.

PROTECTION
- **JUDICIAIRE – protection judiciaire** – (court) protection order.
- **JURIDIQUE – protection juridique** – access to (protection of) the courts; legal protection.
- **SOCIAL – protection sociale des enfants** – child welfare.

PROTÊT
- **DÉNONCIATION de protêt** – notice of protest.
- **FAUTE D'ACCEPTATION – protêt faute d'acceptation** – protest for non-acceptance.
- **INTERVENTION à protêt** – payment supra protest.

PROTUTEUR – (formerly) unofficial guardian, especially for the administration of overseas property.

PROVISION – cover; advance; reserve; funds; value; consideration.
- **AD LITEM – provision ad litem** – advance to cover the costs of the other party in divorce proceedings; advance for costs.
- **ALIMENTAIRE – provision alimentaire** – maintenance during divorce proceedings.
- **AMORTISSEMENT – provision d'amortissement** – depreciation reserve.
- **CHÈQUE sans provision** – uncovered cheque, ie a cheque issued without funds to meet it; bad (worthless) cheque.
- **ENGAGEMENT – provisions pour engagement restant à payer** – provisions for payment awaiting clearance.
- **EXÉCUTOIRE par provision** – immediately enforceable.
- **PAR provision** – by way of advance.
- **SANS provision** – (cheques) worthless; uncovered.
- **TRÉSORERIE – provision de trésorerie** – cash provision.

PROVISOIRE – interlocutory.

- **DÉTENTION provisoire** – detention on remand; remand (in custody); detention pending investigation or trial; pre-trial detention; custody (for short periods).
- **JUGEMENT provisoire** – interlocutory judgment.
- **MESURES provisoires** – interim measures.
- **MISE EN LIBERTÉ provisoire** – provisional release from remand; (release on) bail; release pending trial.
- **STATUER au provisoire** – give a provisional ruling; make an interim order.

PROVOCATION
- **AVORTEMENT – provocation à l'avortement** – incitement to abortion.
- **CRIME – provocation au crime** – incitement to commit a felony.

PROXÉNÈTE – procurer.

PROXÉNÉTISME – assisting or benefiting from the prostitution of another; living on the earnings of prostitution; procuring.

PRUDENCE
- **DILIGENCE – devoir de diligence et prudence** – duty of care.

PRUD'HOMME – member of an industrial (relations) tribunal (Labour Court).
- **CONSEIL de prud'hommes** – industrial (relations) tribunal; Labour Court.
- **PÊCHEUR – prud'hommes pêcheurs** – maritime fishery courts.

PSYCHIATRE
- **LÉGAL – psychiatre légal** – court (ie appointed by the court) psychiatrist.

PSYCHIATRIE
- **LÉGAL – psychiatrie légale** – forensic psychiatry.

PUBERTÉ
- **LÉGAL – puberté légale** – marriageable age.

PUBLIC
- **ACTION publique** – (public) prosecution; criminal proceedings.
- **AGENT public** – public servant.
- **AUTORITÉ publique** – the executive; the authorities; public authorities.
  - •• **EXERCICE de l'autorité publique** – exercise of official authority.

- **ORDRE public** – public policy; public order; ordre public. (In French private international law, public policy excludes the application of foreign law if it is contrary to the fundamental principles of French civilisation. Freedom of contract is subject to the condition that the agreement entered into is not contrary to public policy or morality.)
- **POUVOIR public** – the executive; the authorities; public authorities.

PUBLICATION – registration, eg in the Mortgage Registry.
- **BONNES MŒURS** – see MŒURS below.
- **MARIAGE** – **publication de mariage** – notice of marriage; (in a church etc) (marriage) banns.
- **MŒURS** – **publication contraire aux bonnes mœurs** – obscene publication.
- **PÉRIODIQUE** – **publication périodique** – periodical.

PUBLICISTE – expert in public law (or international law); publicist.

PUBLICITÉ – public hearing (in this sense also: publicity); notice.
- **DÉBAT** – **publicité des débats** – (requirement of, right to) a public hearing.
- **FONCIER** – **publicité foncière** – system of rules governing notice to interested parties of the creation, transmission or extinction of rights relating to land and mortgages, charges and liens over land; land registration.
  - •• **SOUMETTRE** – **et la cession est soumise à la publicité foncière** – and the assignment must be registered.
- **FORMALITÉS de la publicité des articles 1690 et 2075** – the requirements as to giving notice prescribed in Articles 1690 and 2075.
- **TROMPEUR** – **publicité trompeuse** – misleading advertising.

PUDEUR
- **ATTENTAT à la pudeur** – indecent assault.

PUISSANCE
- **ABUS de puissance** – misuse of economic power.
- **BELLIGÉRANT** – **puissance belligérante** – belligerent power.
- **GARANT** – **puissance garante** – guaranteeing power.
- **GUERRE** – **puissance en guerre** – belligerent power.

- **MANDATAIRE** – **puissance mandataire** – mandatory power.
- **PATERNEL** – **puissance paternelle** – (formerly) paternal (parental) authority.
  - •• **DÉCHÉANCE de la puissance paternelle** – loss or deprivation of paternal (parental) authority.
  - •• **DÉTENTEUR de la puissance paternelle** – person entitled to exercise paternal (parental) authority.
- **PUBLIC** – **puissance publique** – public authorities; sovereign authority.
  - •• **ACTE de puissance publique** – act of public authority; act of state.
  - •• **DE puissance publique** – sovereign; governmental; prerogative (de lege imperii).

PUPILLE – ward; young person (juvenile) in care or detention.
- **NATION** – **pupille de la nation** – war orphan.

PUR
- **SIMPLE** – **pur et simple** – unconditional; absolute; mere.

PURGE – procedure whereby a purchaser can clear land of mortgages, liens and rights to preferential payment by paying the purchase price to the creditors; procedure for clearing a property of mortgages on purchase, the purchase price being used to pay off the mortgages as far as it goes.
- **CONTUMACE** – **purge de la contumace** – retrial after conviction in absentia.
- **HYPOTHÈQUE** – **purge d'une hypothèque** – redemption or discharge of a mortgage; removal or cancellation of the entry of a mortgage in the register; (of a purchaser) paying off a mortgage.

PURGER – destroy; cancel; serve (a sentence); pay off.
- **DROIT** – **l'acte de concession purge tous les droits du propriétaire sur son sous-sol** – the instrument of concession cancels all the owner's rights in the subsoil.
- **HYPOTHÈQUE** – **purger une hypothèque** – (of a purchaser) pay off a mortgage.
- **PEINE** – **purger une peine** – serve a sentence.
- **VICE** – **la confirmation purge l'acte de son vice** – confirmation cures the transaction of its defect.

—

Q

QUALIFICATION – legal classification; characterisation; definition (of an offence); ruling; qualification.
- **CONFLIT de qualification** – conflicting legal classifications.
- **DÉLIT** – **qualification d'un délit** – classification of an offence.
- **JURIDIQUE** – **qualification juridique des actes** – application of the law to the acts (with which X was charged).
- **RETENIR** – **on ne retient la qualification que si** – the offence is not committed unless.

QUALIFIÉ – aggravated; treated as a felony.
- **FONDATION qualifiée** – special formation of a company, ie in which the promoters enter into "dangerous agreements" that may prejudice the interests of subsequent shareholders or of the creditors.
- **MAJORITÉ qualifiée** – special majority (ie a majority greater than an absolute majority).

QUALIFIER – define; classify.

QUALITÉ – status; position; capacity; the fact of having a direct personal interest in the subject-matter of proceedings by virtue of which one is entitled to be a party; fact of belonging to a limited class of persons entitled to bring certain types of proceedings; (in plural) personal particulars; introductory part of a judgment; title and recitals of a judgment.
- **AGIR** – **qualité pour agir (en justice)** – capacity to take part in court proceedings; standing (before the court); locus standi.
- **BORNAGE** – **qualité pour procéder au bornage** – right to take proceedings to fix a boundary.
- **DÉFENDRE** – **qualité pour défendre en justice** – capacity to defend legal proceedings.
- **ERREUR sur les qualités non substantielles** – mistake relating to non-essential properties of the subject-matter (of a contract).
- **ÈS qualités** – in that capacity; in the exercise of one's functions; in one's official capacity; ex officio.
- **ESTER** – **qualité pour ester en justice** – capacity to take part in court proceedings; standing (before the court); locus standi.
- **JUGE** – **en qualité de juge** – in a judicial capacity.
- **MARCHAND** – **qualité marchande** – merchantable quality.
- **MOYEN** – **de qualité moyenne** – of average quality.
- **PROMIS** – **qualité promise** – warranted quality.
- **SUBSTANTIEL** – **qualité substantielle** – essential property of the subject-matter (of a contract).

QUANTUM – amount; length (of a sentence).

QUARTIER
- **ISOLEMENT** – **quartier d'isolement** – solitary-confinement block, wing, etc.
- **MISE au quartier** – (prison sanction) punishment cell; solitary confinement
- **OBSERVATION** – **quartier d'observation** – observation block, wing, etc.

QUASI-CONTRAT – voluntary human action resulting in a obligation to a third party or sometimes in mutual obligations between the two parties; quasi-contract.

QUASI-DÉLICTUEL – see DÉLICTUEL.

QUASI-DÉLIT – non-intentional tort; negligent tort; (tort of) negligence.

QUASI-USUFRUIT – quasi-usufruct; usufruct of consumable goods.

QUÉRABLE – payable at the debtor's residence or place of business.
- **DETTE quérable** – debt payable at the debtor's residence or place of business.

QUERELLEUR
- **ACTION querelleuse** – vexatious proceedings.

QUESTION
- **DÉBATTU** – **question débattue** – matter in issue.
- **ÉTAT** – **question d'état** – matter relating to civil (personal, family) status.
- **ORAL** – **question orale** – oral question (in Parliament).
- **PRÉALABLE** – **question préalable** – preliminary question (point, issue) to be decided by the court trying the main issue.

- **PRÉJUDICIEL** – **question préjudicielle** – preliminary question (issue); preliminary point of law (pending the decision of which by another court the proceedings are stayed); case stated.
  - **ACTION** – **question préjudicielle à l'action** – preliminary question (point, issue) to be decided before an action can be brought.
  - **JUGEMENT** – **question préjudicielle au jugement** – preliminary question (point, issue) to be decided before judgment can be given.
- **PRINCIPAL** – **question principale** – the main issue to be decided in legal proceedings.
- **REMETTRE en question** – put in doubt; reopen (a question, an issue, etc).
- **SUBSIDIAIRE** – **question subsidiaire** – alternative count.

QUI

- **DE DROIT** – person entitled.
  - **À qui de droit** – to the person entitled; to whom it may concern.

QUINZAINE

- **FRANC** – **à quinzaine franche** – in fifteen clear days.

QUIRAT – share in a ship.

QUIRATAIRE – owner of a share in a ship.

QUITTANCE – receipt; discharge.

QUITTE

- **DETTE** – **quitte de toute dette** – free of all debts.

QUITUS – discharge.

- **DONNER quitus** – discharge.

QUOTA LITIS

- **PACTE de quota litis** – agreement authorising another to pursue an action on one's behalf in return for a share of the proceeds; champertous agreement (if entered into by a lawyer).

QUOTE-PART – contribution; (proportionate) share.

- **ABSTRAIT** – **quote-part abstraite** – notional share.
- **ARITHMÉTIQUE** – **quote-part arithmétique** – arithmetical proportion.

QUOTIENT

- **ÉLECTORAL** – **quotient électoral** – means of calculating the number of seats obtained by a party under a system of proportional representation.
- **FAMILIAL** – **quotient familial** – means of calculating the family allowance for income-tax purposes.

QUOTITÉ

- **DISPONIBLE** – **quotité disponible** – portion of his estate over which a testator can dispose freely; disposable portion.
- **RÉSERVÉ** – **quotité réservée** – reserved portion.

R

RABATTEMENT
- **DÉFAUT** – **rabattement de défaut** – setting aside a judgment (obtained) by default (where the defendant appears before the end of the hearing).

RABATTRE – set aside (a judgment (obtained) by default etc).

RACHAT – redemption.
- **DROIT de rachat** – right of (option to) repurchase; vendor's right of pre-emption.
- **FACULTÉ de rachat** – right of (option to) repurchase; vendor's right of pre-emption.
- **PLANCHE** – **rachat de planche** – dispatch money.
- **SERVITUDE** – **rachat d'une servitude** – redemption of an easement.
- **VALEUR de rachat** – surrender value.

RACOLAGE
- **VOIE PUBLIQUE** – **racolage sur la voie publique** – soliciting or molestation by prostitutes.

RADIATION – cancellation of an entry; striking out or striking off a list.
- **BARREAU** – **radiation du barreau** – disbarment; striking off the roll.
- **RÔLE** – **radiation du rôle** – (of a court) striking (a case) out (of the list) (striking (a case) off the list) (eg for failure to pursue the proceedings).

RADIER – (of a court) strike (a case) out (of the list); strike (a case) off the list.

RAISON
- **COMMERCIAL** – **raison commerciale** – fancy name under which a business is carried on, eg "The Three Pigeons"; trade name.
- **ÉTAT** – **raison d'État** – political justification, esp for immoral proceeding; reason of State.
- **OPPORTUNITÉ** – **raisons d'opportunité** – grounds on which (a decision etc) is taken.
- **SERVICE** – **raisons de service** – departmental requirements; exigencies of the service.
- **SOCIAL** – **raison sociale** – firm name; business name including the names of all or some of the personally liable partners.
- •• **VALEUR de la raison sociale** – goodwill.

RAISONNEMENT
- **A CONTRARIO** – **raisonnement a contrario** – principle that a rule of law shall not be extended to cover similar situations; principle of non-extensive interpretation; expressio unius est exclusio alterius (opposite of extension by analogy); restrictive interpretation; argument from the converse.

RALLIER
- **SE rallier à** – accept; concur in (view etc).

RANG – ranking (of creditors or secured creditors, liens, etc); seniority; priority.
- **PRENDRE rang avant** – take precedence over.

RANGER
- **AVIS** – **se ranger à l'avis de** – agree with; share the opinion of.

RAPPEL – recall; back payment of a salary etc increase; back pay.
- **ANCIENNETÉ** – **rappel d'ancienneté** – grant of additional seniority or years of service (eg in calculating a pension).
- **AUGMENTATION** – **rappel en augmentation** – back pay (eg in the case of a retrospective salary increase).
- **DIMINUTION** – **rappel en diminution** – demand for restitution of an overpayment.
- **IMPÔT** – **rappel d'impôt** – supplementary assessment; demand for arrears of tax.
- **LETTRE** – **lettres de rappel** – (ambassador's) letters of recall.
- **RÈGLEMENT** – **rappel au règlement** – point of order.
- **TRAITEMENT** – **rappel de traitement** – back pay; payment of arrears of salary.

RAPPORT – (bringing into) hotchpot; setting aside (of an order); report; relationship.
- **ACTIVITÉ** – **rapport d'activités** – (company) report.
- **CAUSALITÉ** – **rapport de causalité** – causal relationship; relationship of cause and effect.
- **CIRCONSTANCIÉ** – **rapport circonstancié** – detailed report.

- **CONTRACTUEL** – **rapport contractuel** – contractual relationship.
- **DÉPENDANCE** – **rapport de dépendance** – dependent condition; state of dependence.
- **DETTE** – **rapport des dettes** – operation whereby an heir deducts from his share of the estate his debts to the deceased or a co-heir.
- **DROIT** – **rapport de droit** – legal relationship.
- **ENQUÊTE** – **rapport d'enquête** – report of an inquiry.
- **FONDATION** – **rapport de fondation** – founders' or promoters' report.
- **JURIDIQUE** – **rapport juridique** – legal relationship.
- **MER** – **rapport de mer** – captain's report.
- **NOTATION** – **rapport de notation** – periodic report; staff (assessment) report.
- **PARTIE** – **dans les rapports des parties** – as between the parties.
- **SUCCESSORAL** – **rapport successoral** – hotchpot; bringing into account against a child's share of an estate of benefits received in the deceased's lifetime.
- **VOISINAGE** – **rapports de (bon) voisinage** – (good) neighbourly relations.

RAPPORTABLE – (of a gift to an heir out of the estate) subject to hotchpot.

RAPPORTER – bring into hotchpot; repeal (enactment etc); revoke; cancel; set aside; withdraw.

- **JUSTICE** – **s'en rapporter à la justice du tribunal** – leave the matter to the discretion of the court.
- **PREUVE** – **rapporter la preuve** – establish by evidence; prove.

RAPPORTEUR – reporting judge (ie judge who prepares a report on a case for a court); (in the Commercial Court) judge who directs preparations for trial ; (in Parliament etc) rapporteur.

- **CONSEILLER rapporteur** – reporting judge (ie judge who prepares a report on a case for a court).
- **JUGE rapporteur** – reporting judge (ie judge who prepares a report on a case for a court); (in the Commercial Court) judge who directs preparations for trial .

RAPPROCHEMENT – reconciliation.

RAPT – abduction.

RÂTELAGE – collecting with a rake grass left over after haymaking (a petty offence).

RATTACHEMENT

- **CRITÈRE de rattachement** – connecting factor.
- **ÉLÉMENT de rattachement** – connecting factor.
- **RÈGLE de rattachement** – rule of private international law; choice-of-law rule.

RATURE – crossing out; deletion; erasure.

RAYER

- **RÔLE** – **rayer du rôle** – (of a court) strike (a case) out (of the list); strike (a case) off the list.

RAYON

- **DOUANE** – **rayon de douane** – (customs) frontier zone.

RÉAFFECTATION – (building) new use.

- **HABITAT** – **réaffectation à destination d'habitat** – reallocation (of an old building) for housing.

RÉALISATION

- **GAGE** – **réalisation du gage** – sale of the pledge; realisation of the security.

RÉALISER

- **SE réaliser** – (of a condition) be satisfied (fulfilled).

RÉASSIGNER – repeat the service of a writ; re-serve a writ.

RÉBELLION – forceful resistance to a public officer executing the law or a lawful order; obstructing an officer in the execution of his duty.

RÉCALCITRANT (noun).

- **VOLONTAIRE** – **récalcitrants volontaires** – cases of wilful refusal.

RECEL – handling (formerly receiving) stolen goods; concealing objects obtained by a crime; conversion of items belonging to the community or to the estate of a deceased person.

- **CADAVRE** – **recel de cadavre** – concealment of a body.
- **GROSSESSE** – **recel de grossesse** – concealment of pregnancy.
- **MALFAITEUR** – **recel de malfaiteur** – harbouring a criminal.

- **NAISSANCE** – **recel de naissance** – concealment of birth.
- **SUCCESSORAL** – **recel successoral** – concealment of an inheritance; conversion of assets belonging to an estate.

RECELÉ – handling (formerly receiving) stolen goods; concealment.
- **ENFANT** – **recelé d'enfant** – concealing (the identity of) a child; concealing a new-born child; concealment of birth.

RECÈLEMENT – handling (formerly receiving) stolen goods; concealment.
- **GROSSESSE** – **recèlement de grossesse** – concealment of pregnancy.

RECELEUR – handler (formerly receiver) of stolen goods.

RÉCÉPISSÉ – (acknowledgement of) receipt.

RÉCÉPISSÉ-WARRANT – negotiable deposit receipt for goods in a warehouse.

RÉCEPTION – acceptance of work performed by a building contractor etc.
- **ACCUSÉ de réception** – acknowledgement of receipt; advice of delivery; delivery note.
- **DROIT romain** – **réception de droit romain** – reception (ie adoption) of Roman law (in the Middle Ages).

RÉCEPTIONNAIRE – recipient (person accepting a document served on another in his absence).

RÉCEPTIVITÉ – individual sensitivity (to noise, smoke, fumes, etc).

RECETTE
- **AFFECTÉ** – **recette affectée** – receipt earmarked for a special purpose.
- **BUDGET des recettes** – revenue (income, receipts) budget.
- **DIVERS** – **recettes diverses** – sundry receipts.
- **IMPÔT** – **recettes d'impôt** – tax revenue; revenue from taxation.

RECEVABILITÉ – admissibility.
- **VÉRIFIER la recevabilité** – examine the admissibility.

RECEVABLE – admissible; (of amendments) in order.
- **NON** – **est non-recevable** – (of an appeal) does not lie.

RECEVEUR
- **FINANCE** – **receveur des finances** – collector of taxes.

RECEVOIR
- **CONGÉ** – **recevoir congé** – receive notice of intention to quit.
- **DÉPOSITION** – **recevoir une déposition** – examine (a witness); take a statement (deposition) (from a witness).
- **EXÉCUTION** – **recevoir exécution** – be put into effect.
- **NOTAIRE** – **reçu par un (par-devant) notaire** – executed in the presence of a solicitor (notary).

RECHERCHE – inquiry; search.
- **AUTORISATION exclusive de recherche** – exclusive prospecting licence.
- **DROIT de recherche** – search fee.
- **PATERNITÉ** – **action en recherche de paternité** – affiliation proceedings; action to establish paternity.
- **PERMIS exclusif de recherche** – exclusive prospecting licence.
- **PREUVE** – **recherche de preuves** – obtaining evidence.
- **SOUSTRAIRE** – **se soustraire aux recherches de la police** – hide from the police.

RÉCIDIVE – recidivism; fact of having committed (similar) previous offences; reoffending.
- **GRAND** – **grande récidive (correctionnelle)** – further conviction after having served a sentence of more than a year.
- **PETIT** – **petite récidive (correctionnelle)** – further conviction after having served a sentence of less than a year.

RÉCIDIVISTE – recidivist; previous offender.

RÉCIPIENDAIRE – person chosen for membership of a select body.

RÉCLAMANT – complainant; claimant.

RÉCLAMATEUR – person entitled to delivery of a ship's cargo.

RÉCLAMATION – complaint; appeal (in disciplinary or other non-judicial proceedings).
- **ADMINISTRATIF** – **réclamation administrative** – complaint through administrative (official) channels; administrative complaint.

• **ÉTAT** – **(action en) réclamation d'état** – action to establish descent from a parent (legitimacy).

• **PÉCUNIAIRE** – **réclamation pécuniaire** – pecuniary claim; money claim.

• **PRÉCONTENTIEUX** – **réclamation précontentieuse** – complaint through official channels.

RECLASSEMENT – regrading; upgrading.

RÉCLUSION – imprisonment (for more than five years); severe imprisonment; extended imprisonment; penal servitude; hard labour.

 • **CELLULAIRE** – **réclusion cellulaire** – solitary (cellular) confinement (detention).

 • **PERPÉTUITÉ** – **réclusion à perpétuité** – life imprisonment.

RÉCLUSIONNAIRE – person serving a long term of imprisonment; long-term prisoner.

RECOGNITIF

 • **ACTE recognitif** – instrument recognising the existence of a situation, right or obligation created or evidenced by an earlier instrument.

RÉCOLEMENT – checking of attached goods prior to sale to see that none are missing; reading a witness's statement back to him to ensure that it is correct.

RÉCOLER – read back his evidence to a witness for him to correct or confirm.

RECOMMANDATAIRE (AU BESOIN) – referee in case of need.

RÉCOMPENSE – (in plural) sums due by a spouse to the community or by the community to a spouse.

RÉCONCILIATION – condonation accepted by the respondent.

RECONDUCTION – renewal; continuance.

 • **TACITE reconduction (reconduction tacite)** – tacit renewal (of a lease etc).

RECONDUIRE – renew, continue.

RECONDUITE

 • **FRONTIÈRE** – **reconduite à la frontière** – removal (of an illegal immigrant).

RECONNAISSANCE – acknowledgement; recognition; checking; verification.

 • **DE DROIT** – **reconnaissance de droit** – de jure recognition.

• **DE FAIT** – **reconnaissance de fait** – de facto recognition.

• **DÉPÔT** – **reconnaissance de dépôt** – deposit receipt.

• **DETTE** – **reconnaissance de dette** – formal acknowledgement of a duty to pay or perform for which consideration is not required and usually not mentioned.

• **DROIT** – see DE DROIT above.

• **DROITS ET LIBERTÉS** – **reconnaissance des droits et libertés** – guarantee of rights and freedoms.

• **ÉCRITURE** – **reconnaissance d'écriture** – admission that a document is genuine.

• **ENFANT NATUREL** – **reconnaissance d'enfant naturel** – admission of paternity with respect to an illegitimate child.

• **ÉTAT** – **reconnaissance d'État** – recognition of a state.

• **FAIT** – see DE FAIT above.

• **GOUVERNEMENT** – **reconnaissance de gouvernement** – recognition of a government.

• **IDENTITÉ** – **reconnaissance d'identité** – establishment of a person's identity.

• **MONT-DE-PIÉTÉ** – **reconnaissance de mont-de-piété** – pawn ticket

• **NANTISSEMENT** – **reconnaissance de nantissement** – pawn ticket.

• **NAVIRE** – **reconnaissance de navire** – verification of a ship's nationality by a man-of-war.

RECONNAÎTRE – acknowledge.

 • **DÉLAI** – **le délai qui lui sera reconnu pour** – the time he will be allowed for.

RECONSTITUTION

 • **LIGUE** – **reconstitution de ligue dissoute** – reconstituting a proscribed organisation.

RECONVENTION – counter-claim; cross-action.

RECONVENTIONNEL

 • **DEMANDE reconventionnelle** – counter-claim; cross-action; (divorce) cross-petition.

RECORS – bailiff's witness (eg of the execution of an attachment).

RECOURIR

 • **CONTRE** – **recourir contre quelqu'un** – bring proceedings against another to recover what one has paid on his behalf.

RECOURS – appeal; remedy; application; petition; recourse; proceedings; action to recover damages paid on behalf of another, eg by the state for damage caused by a teacher's negligent supervision of his pupils and recovered by the victim from the state.

- **ADMINISTRATIF** – recours administratif – appeal to a higher administrative authority.
  - •• **CONTENTIEUX** – recours administratif contentieux – appeal to an administrative court.
- **ANNULATION** – recours en annulation – (civil procedure) application to set aside; (administrative procedure) (abbreviation of **recours en annulation pour excès de pouvoir**) – application to an administrative court to set aside an administrative decision on grounds such as lack of jurisdiction, error of procedure, misapplication of the law, misuse of a discretion or ultra vires (exceeding or misusing one's authority); application for judicial review.
- **APPRÉCIATION DE LÉGALITÉ** – recours en appréciation de légalité – application to an administrative court as a preliminary point to declare an administrative decision illegal.
- **CAMBIAIRE** – recours cambiaire – recourse against the prior holders of a bill of exchange.
- **CASSATION** – recours en cassation – appeal on points of law (on a point of law, in law) to the Court of Cassation.
- **CONSTITUTIONNEL** – recours constitutionnel – constitutional appeal.
- **CONTENTIEUX** – recours contentieux – recourse to the courts; court (legal) proceedings.
- **CRÉDIT** – possibilités de recours au crédit – loan possibilities.
- **DÉLAI** de recours – time for appealing (entering an appeal).
- **DROIT** de recours – right of appeal; right of recourse.
- **DROIT PUBLIC** – recours de droit public – public-law appeal.
- **EXCÈS DE POUVOIR** – recours (en annulation) pour excès de pouvoir – application to an administrative court to set aside an administrative decision on grounds such as lack of jurisdiction, error of procedure, misapplication of the law, misuse of a discretion or ultra vires (exceeding or misusing one's authority); application for judicial review.
- **EXERCER** un recours – bring (enter) an appeal; exercise (have recourse to) a remedy.

- **GARANTIE** – recours en garantie – action to enforce a guarantee or warranty.
  - •• **VICE** – recours en garantie pour vice de la marchandise – action to enforce a warranty when the goods are defective.
- **GRÂCE** – recours en grâce – petition for (an exercise of the prerogative of) mercy; application (request) for pardon.
- **GRACIEUX** – recours gracieux – application to the same administrative authority to reconsider its decision.
- **HIÉRARCHIQUE** – recours hiérarchique – appeal to a higher administrative authority; application to a higher administrative authority to review the decision of a lower administrative authority; application for disciplinary proceedings.
- **INSTANCE** de recours – appeal (appellate) court (tribunal, authority).
- **INSTANCE** en recours – appeal proceedings.
- **INSUSCEPTIBLE** de (voie de) recours – against which no appeal lies; not subject to appeal.
- **INTERNE** – épuisement des recours internes – exhaustion of domestic remedies.
- **INTRODUCTION** d'un recours – entering an appeal.
- **INTRODUIRE** un recours – enter an appeal; take proceedings.
- **JOINT** – recours joint (Sw) – cross-appeal; counter-appeal.
- **JURIDICTION** – recours de pleine juridiction – application to an administrative court to find that the applicant is entitled to a claim against the state or to set aside or vary an administrative act which does not fall within the scope of an action for misuse or abuse of authority (**excès de pouvoir**) (usually a contract with a public authority); application to an administrative court for damages or recognition and enforcement of a right; administrative-law action.
- **OUVRIR** – un recours s'ouvrirait – an appeal would lie.
- **PARALLÈLE** – recours parallèle – other available remedy.
- **PLEINE JURIDICTION** – see JURIDICTION above.
- **RÉFÉRÉ** – recours en référé – summary application to a single judge for an interim order in an urgent case; urgent application (summons, motion).

- **RÉFORME** – recours en réforme (Sw) – appeal.
- **RÉVISION** – recours en révision – application to reopen civil proceedings on grounds of error of fact or law.
- **SUSCEPTIBLE de recours** – subject to appeal; open to challenge.
- **TIERS** – recours contre des tiers – remedy (recourse) against third parties.
- **ULTÉRIEUR** – recours ultérieur – further appeal.
- **VOIE de recours** – appeal; remedy (especially in administrative matters); means of obtaining redress.
  - •• **ÉPUISEMENT des voies de recours** – exhaustion of the (available) remedies.
  - •• **EXTRAORDINAIRE** – voie de recours extraordinaire – special appeal or remedy (ie appeal on points of law to the Court of Cassation, application by a third party to set aside a judgment).
  - •• **INSUSCEPTIBLE de (voie de) recours** – against which no appeal lies; not subject to appeal.
  - •• **INTERNE** – voie de recours interne – domestic remedy.
  - •• **ORDINAIRE** – voie de recours ordinaire – ordinary appeal or remedy (ie application to set aside, appeal to the Court of Appeal).

RECOUVREMENT – (steps taken for) collection (of debts etc).

- **CORPS** – recouvrement par corps – enforcement of fines by imprisonment.
- **FORCÉ** – recouvrement forcé – enforcement of debts.
- **MANDAT de recouvrement** – authority to collect debts (for another).
- **METTRE en recouvrement** – take steps to collect debts or taxes.
- **MISE en recouvrement** – (steps taken for the) collection of debts or taxes.
- **ORDRE de recouvrement** – collection order; order to collect; payment demand note.

RECOUVRER – collect (debts etc); recover (one's nationality).

- **DROIT** – constater un droit à recouvrer – establish that an entitlement is due.
- **LIBERTÉ** – recouvrer sa liberté – be released.

RÉCRÉANCE

- **LETTRES de récréance** – (ambassador's) letters of recall.

RECTIFICATIF

- **BUDGÉTAIRE** – rectificatif budgétaire – budget amendment.

RECTIFICATION – rectification; adjustment.

RECTIFIER – amend; rectify.

RECUEIL

- **JURISPRUDENCE** – recueil de jurisprudence – law reports; collection of decisions.

RECUEILLIR

- **AVIS** – après avoir recueilli l'avis de – after consulting.
- **EXCEPTION** – recueillir une exception – allow an objection.

RECULEMENT

- **SERVITUDE de reculement** – obligation not to build (or repair existing erections) within a certain distance of a road; obligation to observe a building line.

RÉCURSOIRE

- **ACTION récursoire de l'État contre l'agent fautif** – state's action for indemnity against a public officer who has committed a fault for which the state is liable.

RÉCUSATION – challenging (a judge for bias etc); withdrawal (of a judge etc from proceedings in which he has some interest or with which he is otherwise connected).

- **MOTIVÉ** – récusation motivée – challenge for cause.
- **PARTIALITÉ** – récusation pour cause de partialité – challenge for bias.
- **PÉREMPTOIRE** – récusation péremptoire – challenge without cause; peremptory challenge.

RÉCUSER

- **SE récuser** – (of a judge etc) withdraw (from proceedings in which he has some interest or with which he is otherwise connected); be excused; stand down.

RÉDACTION – wording.

REDDITION

- **COMPTE** – reddition des comptes – submission (rendering) of accounts.

REDEVANCE

- **ÉTAT** – redevances due à l'État – dues (royalties) payable to the state; licence fees.

- **FONCIER** – redevance foncière – rent-charge.
- **TRÉFONCIER** – redevance tréfoncière – surface owner's royalty (ie royalty payable by a mining company to the surface owner).

RÉDHIBITION – rescission of a sale on account of a defect in goods or animals sold.

RÉDHIBITOIRE
- **ACTION** rédhibitoire – action for rescission (against the seller of defective goods or animals).
- **VICE** rédhibitoire – hidden defect rendering a thing sold unfit for its intended purpose and entitling the purchaser to rescind the sale or obtain a reduction in price; breach of an implied condition of suitability and merchantable quality.

RÉDIGER – draw (pleadings etc).

REDRESSEMENT
- **FISCAL** – redressement fiscal – revised assessment; tax penalty in the form of an increased assessment; punitive assessment.
- **LOI de redressement** (Belg) – consolidating Act; Law Revision Act.

RÉDUCTION
- **ACTION en réduction** – action to reduce the price (of defective goods).

RÉEL – in rem; real.
- **DROIT réel** – right in rem.
- **IMPÔTS réels** – non-personal taxes (eg trade tax, land tax, dog tax).
- **OFFRES réelles** – (formal) tender of performance or payment, ie tender of the sum due by a person with capacity to pay to a creditor with capacity to receive (or to a person entitled to receive it on his behalf). (To be valid the sum must be presented by a bailiff or solicitor at the place prescribed for payment. If refused the sum is paid into court).
- **SAISIE réelle** – attachment of real property (immovables).

RÉÉVALUATION
- **ASSIETTE** – réévaluation de l'assiette – (tax) reassessment.

RÉFACTION – reduction in price (of goods) for inferior quality.

RÉFÉRÉ – summary application to a single judge for an interim order in an urgent case; urgent application (summons, motion).

- **ARRÊT de référé** – judgment on an appeal from an order made on an urgent application.
- **INSTANCE en référé** – summary application to a single judge for an interim order in an urgent case; urgent application (summons, motion).
- **JUGE des référés** – urgent applications judge (with jurisdiction to make interim orders and issue injunctions).
- **PLACET** – référé sur placet – urgent proceedings commenced in the ordinary way, ie by writ (**assignation**).
- **PROCÉDURE de référé** – urgent procedure.
- **PROCÈS-VERBAL** – référé sur procès-verbal – urgent proceedings commenced by a bailiff's or solicitor's report referring a disputed point to the court.
- **RECOURS en référé** – summary application to a single judge for an interim order in an urgent case; urgent application (summons, motion).
- **RÉSERVE** – clause de réserve de référé – clause (in an order) reserving the defendant's right to apply to the urgent applications judge; liberty to apply.

RÉFÉRENCE
- **JOUR de référence** – appointed day; relevant day.

RÉFÉRENDAIRE – auxiliary judge (of the Court of Cassation); middle-ranking member of the Auditor-General's Department (**Cour des comptes**); legal secretary.
- **CONSEILLER référendaire** – auxiliary judge (of the Court of Cassation); middle-ranking member of the Auditor-General's Department (**Cour des comptes**).

RÉFÉRER
- **SERMENT** – référer le serment – require a party applying for an oath to take an oath himself.

RÉFLÉCHI
- **AVIS mûrement réfléchi** – considered opinion.

RÉFLEXION
- **PÉRIODE de réflexion** – (house-to-house sales) cooling-off period.

REFORMATIO IN PEJUS – (literal translation: "altering for the worse") imposing a heavier sentence on an appeal by a convicted person.

RÉFORMATION – setting aside, (partial) alteration (variation, rectification) or reversal of a judgment (by a higher court).
- **ERREUR** – **réformation d'erreur** – rectification (of a document).

RÉFORME
- **RECOURS en réforme** (Sw) – appeal.

RÉFORMER – (of a higher court) set aside, (partially) alter (vary, rectify) or reverse (a judgment); (sometimes) interfere with.

REFOULEMENT – refusal of entry (at a frontier); removal; return.

REFOULER – refuse entry (at a frontier); remove; return.

REFUGE
- **MAISON de refuge** – assistance home (for persons dependent on some form of national assistance, eg vagrants); shelter (for battered wives etc).

RÉFUGIÉ
- **NATIONAL** – **réfugié national** – refugee returning to his original homeland; national refugee.

REFUS
- **DÉPOSER** – **refus de déposer** – refusal to give evidence.
- **DÉPÔT** – **refus du dépôt** – refusal by the registrar to accept an application for registration.
- **ENTRETIEN** – **refus d'entretien** – refusal to pay maintenance (to maintain).
- **EXÉCUTION** – **refus d'exécution** – refusal to perform; repudiation.
- **IMPÔT** – **refus de l'impôt** – refusal to pay taxes.
- **VENTE** – **refus de vente** – refusal by a trader to sell or provide his usual services (a criminal offence).

RÉFUTER – rebut.
- **NON réfuté** – unrebutted.

REGARD
- **DROIT de regard** – right of inspection or supervision.
  - **GESTION** – **droit de regard sur la gestion** – right to be informed about the management.

RÉGIE – public management; state-run business (some of which are government monopolies).
- **AVANCE** – **régie d'avances** – (authority to operate an) imprest account.
- **EN régie** – state(-)run.
- **INTÉRESSÉ** – **régie intéressée** – management of a public service by an individual whose remuneration is calculated in such a way as to give him an interest in the results achieved.

RÉGIME – rules governing; arrangements; treatment; provisions; regime; scheme.
- **ASSISTANCE** – **régime d'assistance judiciaire** – legal-aid scheme.
- **CARRIÈRE** – **régime des carrières** – rules governing quarries.
- **CELLULAIRE** – **régime cellulaire** – solitary (cellular) confinement; solitary detention; prison with separate cells.
- **DIFFÉRENTIEL** – **régime différentiel** – different treatment.
- **DISCRIMINATOIRE** – **régime discriminatoire** – different treatment.
- **DOTAL** – **régime dotal** – system (regime) of marital property (abolished in France in 1965) in which the wife's dowry (**biens dotaux**) was inalienable. (It continues to apply to persons who adopted it before 1966.)
- **FACULTATIF** – **régime facultatif** – optional provisions.
- **FAVEUR** – **régime de faveur** – preferential treatment.
- **FISCAL** – **régime fiscal des organisations à but non lucratif** – tax treatment of non-profit-making organisations.
- **JURIDIQUE** – **régime juridique** – rules governing.
  - **PARTICULIER** – **régime particulier juridique** – special legal arrangements; special rules.
- **MATRIMONIAL** – **régime matrimonial** – system (regime) of matrimonial (marital) property.
- **PRÉFÉRENTIEL** – **régime préférentiel** – preferential treatment.
- **PREUVE** – **régime des preuves** – rules of evidence.

RÉGIR – govern.

RÉGISSEUR
- **AVANCE** – **régisseur d'avances** – imprest holder.

REGISTRE
- **AUDIENCE** – **registre d'audience** – hearings register (kept by each chamber of a court); registrar's notes (record) of the hearing.
- **COMMERCE** – **registre du commerce** – business-names register; commercial register.
- **DÉPÔT** – **registre des dépôts** – register of documents deposited in the Mortgage Registry.
- **ÉTAT CIVIL** – **registre d'état (de l'état) civil** – population register; register of births, deaths and marriages.
- **ÉTRANGER** – **registre des étrangers** – aliens register.
- **FONCIER** – **registre foncier (Sw)** – Land Registry; land register.
- **FRANCISATION** – **registre des soumissions de francisation** – ships register.
- **MATRIMONIAL** – **registre matrimonial** – register of systems (regimes) of matrimonial property.

RÈGLE
- **CONFLIT** – **règle de conflit (de lois) (règle sur les conflits)** – rule of private international law; choice-of-law rule.
- **DIRECT** – **règles directes** – (private international law) substantive rules.
- **DROIT** – **règle de droit** – legal norm (rule); the law; rule of law.
- **FIXE** – **règles fixes de la procédure** – set procedure.
- **FOND** – **règles de fond** – substantive rules.
- **FORME** – **règle de forme** – procedural rule.
- **INDIRECT** – **règles indirectes** – (private international law) choice-of-law rules.
- **ORDRE** – **règle d'ordre public** – mandatory rule of law; rule of public policy.
- **PREUVE** – **règle de preuve** – rule of evidence.
- **PROCÉDURE** – **règle de procédure** – rule of court; procedural rule; rule of procedure.
- **PROPORTIONNEL** – **règle proportionnelle** – rule that insurance moneys are proportionally reduced if a property etc is underinsured or the premiums too low owing to honest failure to disclose details.
- **SÉCURITÉ** – **règle de sécurité** – safety regulation.
- **STATUTAIRE** – **règles statutaires** –

(memorandum and) articles of an association or a company; charter; statutes.

RÈGLEMENT – regulations; settlement; payment; (EU) regulation.
- **ADMINISTRATION PUBLIQUE** – **règlement d'administration publique** – (formerly) regulations made by the Prime Minister after consultation of the full Conseil d'État.
- **AMIABLE** – **règlement amiable** – friendly settlement.
- **APPLICATION** – **règlement d'application** – implementing regulations.
- **ARBITRAGE** – **règlement d'arbitrage** – rules governing arbitration; arbitration rules.
- **ARBITRAL** – **règlement arbitral** – settlement by arbitration.
- **ARRÊT de règlement** – legislative precedent formerly issued by a superior court.
- **ATELIER** – **règlement d'atelier** – works regulations.
- **AUTONOME** – **règlement autonome** – executive regulations made by the government in certain areas not reserved by the Constitution for legislation by Act of Parliament; prerogative regulations.
- **DÉFINITIF** – **règlement définitif** – final list of entitled creditors (in the procedure for distributing the proceeds of a sale of land).
- **EAU** – **règlement d'eau** – apportionment (allocation) of water rights (between riparian owners); water regulations.
- **ENTREPRISE** – **règlement d'entreprise** – works regulations; staff regulations.
- **EXÉCUTION** – **règlement d'exécution** – implementing regulations.
- **FINANCIER** – **règlement financier** – financial regulations.
- **FORFAITAIRE** – **règlement forfaitaire** – global settlement.
- **INTÉRIEUR** – **règlement intérieur** – rules of procedure.
- **INTERNE** – **règlement interne** = rules of procedure.
- **JUDICIAIRE** – **règlement judiciaire** – simple bankruptcy; a form of bankruptcy less rigorous than **faillite** in which the debtor continues to manage his own affairs and may effect a composition with his creditors; judicial liquidation; distribution of a person's assets by the court; judicial insolvency procedure; judicial administration (of an insolvent's property).

- **JUGE** – règlement de juges – procedure for settling conflicts of jurisdiction between different courts in criminal matters.
- **LITIGE** – **règlement d'un litige** – settlement of an action (case).
- **ORDONNANCE de règlement** – order by which an investigating judge closes an investigation (ie discharge or committal for trial).
- **PACIFIQUE** – **règlement pacifique des conflits** – peaceful settlement of disputes.
- **POLICE** – **règlement de police** – administrative regulations.
- **POURSUIVRE le règlement de** – (seek to) settle (eg a conflict of jurisdiction).
- **PROJET de règlement** – suggestion for a solution or settlement; draft regulation(s).
- **TRANSACTIONNEL** – **règlement transactionnel** – settlement.

RÉGLEMENTAIRE – prescribed.
- **ÊTRE réglementaire** – be in order.

RÉGLEMENTATION
- **CHANGE** – **réglementation des changes** – exchange control.
- **TRANSITOIRE** – **réglementation transitoire** – transitional provisions.

RÈGLEMENT-TYPE – model regulations.

RÉGNICOLE (Belg) – permanently resident or having one's registered office in Belgium.

REGROUPEMENT
- **ACTION** – **regroupement d'actions** – consolidation of shares.
- **MISE EN ORDRE** – **regroupement et mise en ordre** – consolidation.

RÉGULARISATION – curing a (procedural etc) defect.
- **POSSIBLE** – **régularisation possible** – possibility of curing a procedural defect (rectifying the procedure).

RÉGULARISER – cure a (procedural etc) defect.

RÉGULARITÉ – validity; lawfulness; (formal) propriety.
- **FORMEL** – **régularité formelle** – whether the proper procedure has been followed; procedural questions.
- **PRÉSOMPTION de régularité** – presumption that proceedings have been properly conducted.

RÉGULIER – in order; lawful.

RÉHABILITATION – rehabilitation.

RÉINSTALLATION
- **INDEMNITÉ de réinstallation** – resettlement allowance; relocation (removal, displacement) allowance.

RÉINTÉGRANDE – action for recovery of possession (after unlawful eviction).

RÉINTÉGRATION – return to detention etc; reappointment to one's former post after wrongful dismissal.
- **DROIT** – **réintégration dans ses droits** – reinstatement in one's rights.
- **NATIONALITÉ** – **réintégration dans la nationalité** – restoration of one's former nationality.

REJET – dismissal (rejection) (of a petition etc).
- **FOND** – **rejet au fond** – dismissal (rejection) on the merits.
- **FORMALITÉ** – **rejet de la formalité** – refusal by the Mortgage Registrar to register a document containing an error. If the applicant corrects the error within a month of receiving notice of it, the document will be registered as of the date of its original deposit.
- **FORME** – **rejet pour raison de forme** – dismissal (rejection) on procedural grounds.

REJETER – dismiss; reject.

RELÂCHE – port of call.

RELAI – land left by a river moving away from its bank or by the sea moving away from the shore.

RELATIF – relating to a specific person; personal; as between the parties (as opposed to **absolu**).
- **AUTORITÉ relative de la chose jugée** – binding effect of a judgment on the parties (but not on strangers to the proceedings); res judicata.
- **DROIT relatif** – right binding only on a specific person or persons, eg a promisor, debtor, tortfeasor; right in personam.
- **EFFET relatif des conventions** – (doctrine of) privity of contract, ie a contract is binding only on the parties to it and does not impose burdens or confer benefits on third parties.

- **PRÉSOMPTION** relative – rebuttable (refutable) presumption.

RELATION
- **SERMENT** – **relation de serment** – procedural step whereby a party who has been called on to swear to the truth of his case refuses to do so and requires his opponent to swear that the fact he alleges is true.
- **SOCIAL** – **relations sociales** – labour relations; industrial relations.

RELATIVITÉ
- **CHOSE JUGÉE** – **relativité de la chose jugée** – rule that res judicata applies only between the parties and their privies, ie a judgment is binding on the parties to the proceedings and not on others.
- **CONTRAT** – **principe de la relativité des contrats** – privity of contract (rule) (ie a contract is binding only on the parties to it and does not impose burdens or confer benefits on third parties).
- **TRAITÉ** – **relativité des traités** – rule that a treaty is only effective between the contracting parties and cannot benefit or injure third parties.

RELAXE – acquittal (and discharge) by a court other than an assize court.

RELÉGATION – (formerly) a form of preventive detention.

RELEVÉ
- **CADASTRAL** – **relevé cadastral** – copy of a section of (extract from) the registered plan (index map).
- **COMPTE** – **relevé de compte** – statement of account.
- **DÉTAILLÉ** – **relevé détaillé** – schedule with particulars; detailed statement (eg telephone bill).
- **FORCLUSION** – **relevé de forclusion** – leave to proceed (appeal etc) out of time; extension of time for appealing.

RELÈVEMENT – power of the court not to apply the accessory measures or penalties normally attached to certain convictions.
- **DÉCHÉANCE** – **relèvement de déchéance** – restoration of a right which has lapsed or of which a person has been deprived; termination of a disqualification.
- **FONCTION** – **relèvement de fonctions** – removal from office.
- **FORCLUSION** – **relèvement de forclusion** – leave to proceed (appeal etc) out of time; extension of time for appealing.

RELEVER – (of an infringement etc) find (to exist); establish the existence of.
- **APPEL** – **relever un appel** – bring an appeal.
- **DE** – **relever de** – fall under; come within; be governed by; release from.
- **DÉCHÉANCE** – **relever d'une déchéance** – restore a right which has lapsed or of which a person has been deprived; terminate a disqualification.
- **FORCLUSION** – **relever de la forclusion** – give leave to proceed (appeal etc) out of time; extend time for appealing.
- **JURIDICTION** – **relever d'une juridiction** – fall under or within (be subject to) the jurisdiction of a court or other authority.
- **OFFICE** – **relever d'office** – (of a court) raise of its own motion (ex officio).
- **SERMENT** – **relever d'un serment** – release from an oath.

RELIQUAT – balance of an account.
- **CRÉANCE** – **reliquat d'une créance** – balance or remainder of a debt; outstanding balance of a claim.

RELIQUATAIRE – person who owes the balance of an account.

RELOCATION – further letting; renewal of a lease.

RÉMANENCE
- **CLAUSE** de rémanence – continuing-effect clause.

REMBOURSEMENT – repayment; reimbursement; withdrawal (from a savings bank).

REMBOURSER
- **BILLET** – **rembourser un billet** – pay a bill of exchange where the acceptor has failed to do so.

REMÈDE – redress.
- **PORTER** remède à – redress.

REMEMBREMENT – consolidation of parcels (of land).
- **AGRAIRE** – **remembrement agraire** – consolidation of smallholdings.
- **PARCELLAIRE** – **remembrement parcellaire** – consolidation of smallholdings.
- **URBAIN** – **remembrement urbain** – redistribution of urban land.

RÉMÉRÉ – option to repurchase (for the same price).

REMETTRE
- **CAUSE** – **remettre en cause** – reopen (a decided case etc); challenge (object to) (a judgment).
- **PEINE** – **remettre une peine** – remit a sentence.
- **QUESTION** – **remettre en question** – put in doubt; reopen (a question, an issue, etc).
- **S'EN remettre à la sagesse de la cour** – leave it to the discretion of the court.

REMISE – remission (of a debt or obligation); delivery; handing over (of a document, title, etc); adjournment; filing (of a document in the registry).
- **CAUSE**
  - **DE** – **remise d'une cause** – adjournment of a case.
  - **EN** – **remise en cause** – reopening (a decided case etc); challenging of (objection to) (a judgment).
- **COMPTE** – **remise en compte courant** – sum paid to the other party to a current account.
- **DETTE** – **remise de dette** – release from or waiver of a debt.
- **GARANTIE** – **remise en garantie** – deposit as a security.
- **LETTRE**
  - **CRÉANCE** – **remise de lettres de créance** – delivery of one's credentials.
- **PAIEMENT**
  - **COMPTANT** – **remise sur les paiements au comptant** – reduction for cash.
- **PEINE** – **remise (gracieuse) de peine** – remission of sentence.
- **PROVISOIRE** – **remise provisoire** – provisional exemption.
- **SOLIDARITÉ** – **remise de la solidarité** – termination of joint liability.
- **VIGUEUR** – **remise en vigueur** – bringing back into force; reapplication.

REMPLACEMENT – purchase from another source by a buyer of goods when the seller fails to deliver.

REMPLIR
- **CONDITION** – **remplir une condition** – satisfy (fulfil) a condition.
- **FORMALITÉ** – **remplir une formalité** – comply with a formality (requirement).

REMPLOI – reinvestment (of the proceeds of an investment which has been sold).

- **IMMOBILIER** – **remploi immobilier** – reinvestment in land (real estate).

RENDANT
- **COMPTE** – **rendant compte** – person who renders an account.

RENDEMENT
- **IMPÔT** – **rendement de l'impôt** – tax revenue; tax yield.

RENDRE – deliver (give, read) (a judgment).
- **JUSTICE** – **rendre la justice** – do justice.

RENOMMÉE
- **COMMUNE renommée** – common repute.

RENONCER
- **À** – **renoncer à** – waive (renounce, abandon) (a right).

RENONCIATION – waiver, renunciation or abandonment (of a right); refusal to accept (a nationality to which one is entitled).
- **RÉTRACTER la renonciation** – withdraw one's waiver (renunciation, abandonment).

RENTE – annuity; pension; income from investments; periodical payments.
- **ACCIDENT** – **rente d'accident** – accident pension.
- **ALIMENTAIRE** (Belg) – **rente alimentaire** – maintenance.
- **AMORTISSABLE** – **rente amortissable** – redeemable annuity.
- **ATTRIBUTION d'une rente** – grant of a pension.
- **CONSOLIDÉ** – **rente consolidée** – consols.
- **CONSTITUÉ** – **rente constituée** – contractual annuity.
- **CRÉANCIER de rente** – annuitant.
- **DÉCÈS** – **rente après décès** – survivor's pension.
- **DIFFÉRÉ** – **rente différée** – deferred life annuity.
- **ÉTAT** – **rente sur l'État** – state annuity; state pension.
- **FONCIER** – **rente foncière** – rentcharge.
- **RÉVERSIBLE** – **rente réversible** – annuity or pension which passes to another on death; reversionary annuity or pension.
- **SERVIR une rente** – pay an annuity or pension.
- **VIAGER** – **rente viagère** – life annuity.

RENTRÉE

- **BUDGÉTAIRE – rentrées budgétaires –** national income; (budget) revenue.
- **IMPÔT – rentrée des impôts –** collection (getting in) of taxes.
- **IMPÔT – rentrées d'impôts (de l'impôt) –** tax receipts; revenue received from taxes.

RENTRER

- **DÉBOURS – rentrer dans ses débours –** to be awarded one's disbursements.
- **VIGUEUR – rentrer en vigueur –** come into force again.

RENVERSEMENT

- **JURISPRUDENCE – renversement de la jurisprudence –** (decision making a) change of (in) judicial doctrine or policy; new line of decisions; new precedent; reversal of precedent; departure from (abandonment of) existing precedents (previously established doctrine).
- **PREUVE – renversement de la charge de la preuve –** shift in the burden of proof.

RENVERSER – disprove; rebut (refute) (a presumption).

- **CHARGE – renverser la charge de la preuve –** shift the burden of proof.

RENVOI – reference; committal; adjournment; renvoi; return to the country of origin; transfer (to another court); reference back; dismissal.

- **AUDIENCE – renvoi à l'audience –** (immediate) entry (sending, committal, setting down) for trial (hearing).
- **COMMISSION – renvoi en commission –** reference to a committee.
- **DEMANDE – renvoi des fins de la demande –** dismissal of an action.
- **FIN – renvoi des fins de la poursuite –** acquittal.
- **INDEMNITÉ de renvoi –** compensation for loss (termination) of employment; damages for dismissal; redundancy payment.
- **JUGEMENT – renvoi en jugement –** committal for trial.
- **JURIDICTION de renvoi –** court to which a case is referred (or transferred) for hearing and decision.
- **PRÉJUDICIEL – renvoi préjudiciel –** reference of a preliminary question (point, issue) to another court for decision or for a ruling.
- **RÉQUISITIONS en renvoi –** application to commit for trial.

- **SUITE – renvoi à la suite –** postponement of a question.

RENVOYER – adjourn; commit for trial; return to the country of origin; send for trial; send back; refer.

- **AUDIENCE – renvoyer à l'audience –** enter (send, commit, set down) for trial (hearing).
- **FIN – renvoyer des fins de la poursuite –** acquit.
- **FOND – renvoyer pour le fond –** refer (to a committee) for report.
- **JUGEMENT – renvoyer en jugement –** commit for trial.
- **MIEUX – renvoyer à mieux se pourvoir –** instruct the parties to take proceedings in the proper court.
- **PLAIDEUR – renvoyer les plaideurs –** transfer the case to another court.
- **PLAINTE – renvoyer de la plainte –** refuse to prosecute.

RÉOUVERTURE

- **DÉLAI – réouverture des délais –** (giving) leave to appeal out of time.

RÉPARATION – damages; compensation; reparation; repairs.

- **CIVIL – réparations civiles –** civil damages.
- **ENTRETIEN – réparations d'entretien –** current repairs.
- **GROS – grosses réparations –** major repairs (ie roof and outside walls).
- **LOCATIF – réparations locatives –** tenant's repairs.
- **MORAL – réparation morale –** non-pecuniary (non-material) damages.
- **NATURE – tenu à réparation en nature –** liable to make good the damage in kind.
- **USUFRUCTUAIRE – réparations usufructuaires –** usufructuary's (life tenant's) repairs.

RÉPARTITION – division; allocation; apportionment.

- **CHARGE – répartition des charges –** calculation of contributions; apportionment of of charges.
- **ÉTAT de répartition –** apportionment plan.
- **SYSTÈME de répartition –** pay as you go scheme (pensions).

RÉPERTOIRE – register; record book; digest.

- **CIVIL – répertoire civil –** register of judgments ordering guardianship or other matters affecting the capacity of an individual.

- **GÉNÉRAL** – **répertoire général** – general register (of cases, kept in the registry).
- **MÉTIER** – **répertoire des métiers** – trades register.

RÉPÉTER – claim return or restitution.

RÉPÉTITION – recovery.
- **INDU** – **répétition de l'indu** – action for restitution of money paid without legal cause (ie when it was not in fact owing); action for money had and received.

RÉPLIQUE – reply; answer.
- **DROIT de réplique** – right of reply; right of rectification.

RÉPLIQUER – reply.

RÉPONDANT – surety.

RÉPONDRE – be liable.
- **EXIGENCE** – **répondre aux exigences** – satisfy the requirements.
- **NE pas répondre** – **qui ne répondent pas à** – which are incompatible with.
- **REQUÊTE** – **répondre une requête** – write an order at the foot of an application; deal with an application.

RÉPONSE
- **DROIT de réponse** – right of reply; right of rectification.

REPORT – contango.
- **BAIL** – **report de bail** – assignment of a lease.
- **CRÉDIT** – **report de crédit** – carry-over of an appropriation.
- **DATE** – **report général de dates limites** – general extension of time-limits.
- **OUVERTURE** – **report d'ouverture de la faillite** – fixing the date from which the effects of a bankruptcy commence to operate.

REPORTER – carry over (a loss).
- **ULTÉRIEUR** – **reporter à une date ultérieure** – adjourn to a later date.

REPOS
- **DIMANCHE** – **loi sur le repos de dimanche** – Sunday Observance Act.

RÉPRÉHENSIBLE – objectionable; censurable.

REPRENDRE – re-enact; adopt; incorporate; follow; restate; repeat.
- **DÉBAT** – **reprendre les débats** – start the proceedings afresh (eg where there has been a change in the composition of the court).

- **DETTE** – **reprendre une dette** – undertake to satisfy the debt or perform the obligation of another.
- **PAR** – **repris par le nouveau Code** – incorporated in the new Code.

REPRÉSAILLES – reprisal(s).

REPRÉSENTANT – agent.
- **JUSTICE** – **représentant en justice** – legal representative.
- **LÉGAL** – **représentant légal** – statutory representative (legal guardian) of a minor.
- **LOI** – **représentants de la loi** – law-enforcement agencies.

REPRÉSENTATION – production; appearance; representation; taking procedural steps on behalf of a client, eg filing pleadings.
- **DÉLAI de représentation** – period within which a person (or object) shall again be brought before the court.
- **DROIT de représentation** – counsel's fee (for the hearing); performing right.
- **FRAIS de représentation** – entertainment expenses; cost of obtaining a representative (being represented).
- **GARANTIES de représentation** – bail.
  - **DÉPOURVU de garanties de représentation** – unable to find bail.
- **JUSTICE** – **représentation en justice** – representation by a lawyer in legal proceedings.
- **PAR** – **succéder (venir) par représentation** – inherit through one's ascendants.
- **SUCCESSORAL** – **représentation successorale** – the right of the more remote issue to take in the place of their deceased parent (or ancestor) in the succession to an estate.

REPRÉSENTÉ – principal; person represented.

REPRÉSENTER
- **JUSTICE** – **représenter en justice** – represent in legal proceedings.

RÉPRESSIF – criminal; penal; punitive.
- **JURIDICTION répressive** – criminal court; criminal jurisdiction.
- **SANCTIONS répressives** – criminal sanctions.
- **SERVICES répressives** – law-enforcement agencies.

RÉPRESSION – suppression; punishment; prevention; enforcement; legislation on (against).

- **MANDAT de répression** (Sw) – sentence order.

RÉPRIMANDE – reprimand; (prison punishment) oral warning.

RÉPRIMER – suppress; punish; render illegal; make an offence; pass a law against; make guilty of an offence (**réprime celui qui aura sciemment** – makes guilty of an offence whoever knowingly).

- **INFRACTION** – **l'infraction réprimée par la condamnation** – the offence for which sentence was passed.

REPRIS

- **JUSTICE** – **repris de justice** – previous offender; recidivist.

REPRISE – taking back by a spouse on dissolution of the marital community of his or her separate property or its value (**reprise en valeur**).

- **CITATION en reprise d'instance** – summons to resume proceedings which have been interrupted.
- **CRÉANCE** – **reprise de créance** – acceptance of the assignment of a chose in action (ie a claim to payment of a debt or performance of a contract).
- **DETTE** – **reprise de dette** – undertaking to satisfy the debt or perform the obligation of another.
- **DROIT de reprise** – landlord's right in certain circumstances to recover premises in spite of the tenant's right to an extension of the lease; landlord's right to reoccupy demised premises because he needs them for himself.
- **EXÉCUTION** – **reprise d'exécution** – undertaking the performance of another's obligation but not the obligation itself; agreement whereby a third party agrees with the debtor (promisor) to perform the latter's obligation, the creditor (promisee) not being a party to the agreement; agreement for vicarious performance.
- **INSTANCE** – **reprise d'instance** – resumption of proceedings after they have been interrupted by the death of a party or the sale of the subject-matter of the action.

REPROCHABLE

- **PERSONNE reprochable** – person who may be challenged (as being biased or unsuitable).

REPROCHE – allegation; objection to a witness.

RÉPUDIATION – repudiation (of a nationality which one already possesses).

RÉPUDIER – renounce.

RÉPUTER – treat as; deem to be.

- **ÉCRIT** – **réputé écrit** – (term) implied (in a contract etc).

REQUÉRANT (adj)

- **AUTORITÉ requérante** – requisitioning authority.
- **ÉTAT requérant** – applicant state; requesting state.

REQUÉRANT (noun) – applicant; petitioner; claimant; plaintiff; person entitled to requisition.

REQUÉRIR – apply for; ask for.

REQUÊTE – application; petition; appeal (to the Court of Cassation); summons; motion; ex parte application.

- **APPROBATION** – **requête en approbation** – application for approval or consent.
- **CIVIL** – **requête civile** – (former term for) retrial in (reopening of) civil proceedings.
- **CONJOINT** – **requête conjointe** – joint application (method of commencing contentious proceedings by parties agreeing to submit their dispute to the court).
- **DÉFENSE** – **requête en défense** – (pleadings) defence; answer.
- **DEMANDE** – **requête en demande** – (pleadings) statement of claim.
- **FAILLITE** – **requête en faillite** – bankruptcy petition.
- **INSTANCE** – **requête introductive d'instance** – writ; statement of claim; petition (eg in divorce); (original) application; originating summons.
- **INTRODUIRE une requête** – lodge (or make) an application.
- **LIQUIDATION**
  - **DÉPENSES** – **requête en liquidation des dépenses** – application for taxation (of costs).
- **ORDONNANCE sur requête** – order made by the president of the court or a single judge on an ex parte application.
- **PROCÉDURE sur requête** – ex parte proceedings.
- **PROROGATION** – **requête en prorogation de délai** – application for extension of time.

- **RÉCUSATION** – **requête en récusation**
  – challenge (objection) to a judge etc on
  grounds of bias etc.
- **RÉVISION** – **requête en révision** – application for a retrial.
- **SAISIR d'une requête** – lodge an application with; make an application to.
- **SUSPICION LÉGITIME** – **requête en suspicion légitime** – challenge (objection) to a judge etc on grounds of bias etc.
- **UNILATÉRAL** – **requête unilatérale** – ex parte application.

REQUIS (adj)
- **ÉTAT requis** – requested state.

REQUIS (noun) – person requisitioned to perform services.

RÉQUISITION – requisition; order to striking workers to resume work when public order is threatened; (in plural) prosecution case; application for a specific sentence; prosecution's (public prosecutor's) submissions; Attorney-General's submissions.
- **ARRÊTÉ de réquisition** – requisition order.
- **EMPRISE** – **réquisition d'emprise totale** – application for the compulsory purchase of property rendered unusable (valueless) by the expropriation of the rest of the buildings or land in question.
- **FAILLITE** – **réquisition de faillite** (Sw) – bankruptcy petition.
- **POURSUITE** – **réquisition de poursuite** (Sw) – writ of execution (fieri facias, fi. fa.)
- **PROCUREUR** – **le procureur présente ses réquisitions** – the (public) prosecutor makes his submissions (eg to the investigating judge).

RÉQUISITOIRE – (public) prosecutor's address; formal request to impose a certain sentence; (public) prosecutor's application to commence proceedings; indictment.
- **DÉFINITIF** – **réquisitoire définitif** – written statement of how he wishes the investigating judge to proceed with the case submitted by the (public) prosecutor at the end of the preliminary investigation.
- **INTRODUCTIF** – **réquisitoire introductif d'instance** – (public) prosecutor's written application requesting the investigating judge to open an investigation.
- **SUPPLÉTIF** – **réquisitoire supplétif** – (public) prosecutor's written application requesting the investigating judge to extend

the investigation on the discovery of new facts.

RESCINDABLE – liable to be rescinded.

RESCINDANT – (formerly) examination of the admissibility of an application for retrial.

RESCINDER – set aside a judgment; rescind a contract for inadequate consideration (**lésion**).

RESCISION – rescission for unfair price (for inadequate consideration).
- **ACTION en rescision (pour lésion)** – action to rescind a contract for inadequate consideration.
- **LÉSION** – **rescision pour cause de lésion** – rescission for inadequate consideration.

RESCISOIRE – retrial after an application for retrial has been allowed in civil proceedings.

RÉSERVATAIRE – person entitled to a reserved portion in a deceased's estate.

RÉSERVE – reservation; (accounts) reserve; (game) (p)reserve; reserved portion (of a deceased's estate).
- **AMORTISSEMENT** – **réserve pour amortissements** – depreciation reserve.
- **CLAUSE de réserve** – reservation (clause).
  - •• **RÉFÉRÉ** – **clause de réserve de référé** – clause (in an order) reserving the defendant's right to apply to the urgent applications judge; liberty to apply.
- **FONCIER** – **réserve foncière** – land reserve (for future building etc).
- **FONDS de réserve** – reserve fund.
- **HÉRÉDITAIRE** – **réserve héréditaire** – reserved portion (of a deceased's estate).
- **LÉGAL** – **réserve légale** – (company's) statutory reserve (of at least one tenth of its capital).
- **LOI** – **réserve de la loi** (Sw) – rule that the executive is bound by the law (subject to the rule of law).
- **OBLIGATION de réserve** – obligation to treat the court with respect; obligation of judge or civil servant to refrain from any actions or expression of opinions incompatible with his functions or loyalty to the state; obligation to exercise reserve; duty of discretion.
- **PRÉVOYANCE** – **réserve de prévoyance** – reserve for contingencies.
- **PROPRIÉTÉ** – **clause de réserve de propriété** – reservation of title (ownership) clause.

- **SOMME** mise de réserve aux mêmes fins – sum set aside for this purpose.
- **SOUS**
  - **DE** – sous réserve de – subject to; without prejudice to; reserving the right to.
  - **QUE** – sous réserve que – provided that.

RÉSERVÉ – unprejudiced; unaffected.

- **QUOTITÉ** réservée – reserved portion.
- **CAS** réservé – case not covered by (excepted from) the general rule.

RÉSERVER

- **QUESTION** – **réserver une question** – (of a court) reserve its decision (reserve judgment) on a question.

RÉSIDENCE – (factual) residence.

- **ASSIGNATION** à **résidence** – order requiring a person to reside in a particular place; compulsory residence order.
- **ASSIGNÉ** à **résidence** – subject to a compulsory residence order.
- **FAMILLE** – **résidence de famille** – matrimonial (family) home.
- **FIXE** – **résidence fixe** – fixed abode.
- **FORCÉ** – **résidence forcée** – compulsory residence.
- **INTERDICTION** de **résidence** – order forbidding a person to reside in a particular area or areas; residence prohibition.
- **SÉPARÉ** – **décision autorisant résidence séparée** – non-cohabitation order.
- **SURVEILLÉ** – **résidence surveillée** – order requiring a person to reside in a limited area and report to the police.

RÉSILIATION – termination (of a contract) (ex nunc).

- **ACTION** en **résiliation** – action to terminate a continuing contract (ex nunc).

RÉSILIER – terminate (a contract) (ex nunc).

RÉSOLUBLE – liable to be defeated by a condition subsequent.

RÉSOLUTION – resolution; rescission; setting aside or declaring void (a contract, eg for failure to perform; in principle retrospectively).

- **ACTION** en **résolution** – action to set aside a contract; action for rescission.
- **JUDICIAIRE** – **résolution judiciaire** – judgment declaring a contract void or setting one aside.

- **PROJET** de **résolution** – draft resolution.

RÉSOLUTOIRE

- **CLAUSE** résolutoire – clause providing that a contract shall be void in specified circumstances (eg non-performance within a certain time).
- **CONDITION** résolutoire – condition subsequent (of (in) a contract etc, to a transaction etc).

RÉSOUDRE – cancel; rescind; set aside.

RESPECT

- **BIEN** – **respect des biens** – peaceable (peaceful) enjoyment of possessions.
- **ENGAGEMENT** – **respect des engagements** – observance of undertakings; honouring of commitments.

RESPECTER – observe; comply with.

RESPONSABILITÉ – (civ) liability; (crim) responsibility; (international law) (state) responsibility (for the treatment of aliens etc).

- **ADMINISTRATIF** – **responsabilité administrative** – official liability; liability of an official (public authority).
- **AQUILIEN** – **responsabilité aquilienne** – liability in tort.
- **AUTRUI** – **responsabilité du fait d'autrui** – vicarious liability; liability for the tort(s) of another.
- **CASCADE** – **responsabilité en cascade** – liability in series.
- **CAUSAL** – **responsabilité causale** – liability for producing a given result irrespective of fault; strict liability.
- **CHOSE** – **responsabilité du fait des choses** – liability for damage caused by things in one's charge.
- **CIVIL** – **responsabilité civile** – civil as opposed to criminal liability (ie liability in contract, tort, etc).
- **CONTRACTUEL** – **responsabilité contractuelle** – liability in contract.
- **DÉLICTUEL** – **responsabilité délictuelle** – liability in tort.
  - **QUASI** – **responsabilité quasi délictuelle** – liability for negligence (non-intentional tort).
- **ENGAGER**
  - **LE** – **engager la responsabilité de** – render (someone) liable.
  - **SON** – **engager sa responsabilité** – incur liability; assume responsibility.

- **ÉTAT** – responsabilité de l'**État** – state liability.
- **ENTREPRENEUR** – **responsabilité de l'entrepreneur** – employer's liability; manufacturer's liability; producer's liability.
- **EXTRACONTRACTUEL** – **responsabilité extracontractuelle** – non-contractual liability; liability in tort.
- **FAUTE**
  - **POUR** – **responsabilité pour faute** – liability for intention or negligence; fault liability.
  - **SANS** – **responsabilité sans faute** – liability without fault (ie without either intention or negligence); strict liability; absolute liability; risk liability; no-fault liability.
- **GARDIEN**
  - **ANIMAL** – **responsabilité du gardien d'un animal** – liability of the owner or other person responsible for an animal for the damage it causes.
- **MATÉRIEL** – **responsabilité matérielle** – liability for pecuniary (material) damage.
- **MINISTÉRIEL** – **responsabilité ministérielle** – minister's responsibility to Parliament for the actions of his department.
- **NOTARIAL** – **responsabilité notariale** – solicitor's liability.
- **OBJECTIF** – **responsabilité objective** – strict liability; absolute liability; liability without fault; risk liability.
- **PÉNAL** – **responsabilité pénale** – criminal responsibility.
- **PRÉPOSÉ** – **responsabilité du fait des préposés** – liability for one's servants' torts, ie for the torts of a person acting under one's direction and control.
- **PRODUCTEUR** – **responsabilité des producteurs** – producer's liability.
- **PROPRIÉTAIRE**
  - **PRÉJUDICE** – **responsabilité du propriétaire qui cause un préjudice excédant la mesure ordinaire des obligations de voisinage** – liability in nuisance.
  - **VOISINAGE** – **responsabilité du propriétaire dans les rapports de voisinage** – liability in nuisance, negligence, trespass or abuse of right between neighbours.
- **PUISSANCE PUBLIQUE** – **responsabilité de la puissance publique** – official liability; liability of a public authority.

- **QUASI DÉLICTUEL** – see DÉLICTUEL above.
- **RUINE** – **responsabilité du fait de la ruine d'un bâtiment** – liability for damage caused by the total or partial collapse of a building.
- **SOLIDAIRE** – **responsabilité solidaire** – joint and several liability.

RESPONSABLE (adj) – (civ) liable; (crim) responsible.
- **INDÉFINIMENT responsable** – with unlimited liability.

RESPONSABLE (noun)
- **ENTREPRISE** – **responsable d'entreprise** – (in some contexts) worker's representative; shop steward.

RESSORT – jurisdiction; judicial district; administrative district.
- **ADMINISTRATIF** – **ressort administratif** – administrative jurisdiction.
- **DERNIER ressort** – last instance.
  - **JUGEMENT en dernier ressort** – judgment against which no appeal lies; judgment, trial or proceedings at last instance; last-instance decision.
- **PREMIER ressort** – first instance.
  - **DERNIER** – **jugement en premier et dernier ressort** – judgment, trial or proceedings at first instance against which no appeal lies.
- **TAUX de ressort** – financial limit on the jurisdiction (of a lower court); sum up to which a court has jurisdiction.
- **TERRITORIAL** – **ressort territorial** – territorial jurisdiction.
- **TRIBUNAL** – **ressort d'un tribunal** – (judicial) district (of a court); court's (territorial) jurisdiction.

RESSORTIR
- **DE** – **ressortir de** – fall under the jurisdiction of.

RESSORTISSANT – subject; (less strictly) national.

RESSOURCE
- **CONDITION de ressources** – means test.

RESTE
- **PAYER** – **restes à payer** – outstanding payments.

RESTITUTION
- **ACTION en restitution** – action for recovery of possession.
- **DÉLAI** – **restitution de délai** (Sw) – leave to proceed (eg appeal) out of time; extension of time (to appeal etc).
- **DEMANDE de restitution** – application for restitution.
- **DROIT** – **restitution d'un droit** – restoration of a right one formerly possessed.
- **INDU** – **restitution de l'indu** – restitution of money paid (or things transferred) without legal cause.
- **NATURE** – **restitution en nature** – restoration of the previous state of affairs (as opposed to money compensation); restitution in kind.

RESTREINT – select (committee); qualified.

RÉSULTAT – final account; final balance.
- **AFFECTATION du résultat** – allocation of the (credit) balance.
- **COMPTABLE** – **résultats comptables** – credit balance.
- **OBLIGATION de résultat** – obligation to produce a specific result; absolute obligation.

RÉSULTER
- **DE** – **résulter de** – arise out of.

RÉSUMÉ
- **FAIT** – **résumé des faits de la cause** – outline of the case.

RÉTABLISSEMENT – return of a document to the place from which it has been taken; restoration of a case to the list.
- **CHOSE** – **rétablissement des choses dans l'état** – restoration of the former position.
- **GARDE** – **rétablissement de la garde** – restoration of custody.

RETARD
- **EXÉCUTION** – **retard dans l'exécution** – late performance; performance out of time.

RETENIR – (of a court) hold; specify; declare admissible; accept (an argument).
- **AFFAIRE** – **retenir une affaire** – decide to proceed with a case.
- **PRÉVENTION** – **retenir une prévention** – (of a court) find a charge has been proved.
- **TÉMOIGNAGE** – **retenir un témoignage** – admit evidence.

RÉTENTION
- **DROIT de rétention** – lien; right to retain or remain in possession; right of retention, ie a right to withhold property until a debt is paid.

RETENUE – retention.
- **SOURCE** – **retenue à la source** – deduction at source.

RÉTICENCE – intentional failure to disclose information of which one is aware, eg in a proposal for insurance; non-disclosure of facts the other party has an interest in knowing, eg omission by a vendor to mention the disadvantages of an object sold.

RETIREMENT – buyer's duty to accept delivery of the goods sold.

RÉTORSION – retortion; retaliation.

RETOUCHE – minor amendment.

RETOUR – return; reversion; equity of redemption.
- **COMPTE de retour** – amount of expenses added to a redraft; notarial charges on a dishonoured bill.
- **CONVENTIONNEL** – **retour conventionnel** – contractual reversion of property to the donor on the death of the donee.
- **LÉGAL** – **retour légal** – statutory reversion of property to the donor from the estate of the donee.
- **LOT** – **retour de lot** – money compensation to a person receiving a less valuable share of property on a partition.
- **SANS FRAIS** – **retour sans frais** – clause excluding the requirement of a protest in the case of an unpaid bill of exchange.

RÉTRACTATION – revocation; retraction; disavowal; withdrawal (of a promise, decision, etc); alteration (by a court etc) of its own decision, eg by setting aside a judgment by default.
- **CONSENTEMENT** – **rétractation de consentement** – withdrawal (revocation) of consent.

RÉTRACTER – revoke; retract; disavow; withdraw; (of a court) alter its previous decision, eg by setting aside a judgment by default.

RETRAIT – right to take the place of a third person in a transaction which has already been concluded; cancellation of its own unilateral decision by an administrative authority.
- **EMPLOI** – **retrait d'emploi** – removal from office; dismissal.

- **LITIGIEUX** – **retrait litigieux** – exercise by the defendant of his right, in a case where the plaintiff has sold his right against the defendant (with which the pending proceedings are concerned) to another, to acquire this right from the purchaser on reimbursing him what he paid for it; right of a debtor sued by the assignee of a debt to settle the proceedings by paying the assignee the amount for which he purchased the debt together with the costs of the assignment and interest.
- **PERMIS** – **retrait du permis de conduire** – withdrawal (deprivation) of one's driving licence; disqualification from driving.
- **SUCCESSORAL** – **retrait successoral** – exercise by the co-heirs of their right (where an heir has assigned his share of an estate) to exclude the purchaser (not being an heir) by refunding the price he has paid.

RETRAITE – retirement; pension; redraft.

RETRANCHEMENT
- **ACTION** en **retranchement** – action by the children of a former marriage to recover property from the marital community or a spouse.
- **CASSER** par voie de **retranchement** – set aside part of a decision, leaving the rest standing.

RETRAYANT – person who by operation of law takes the place of another (**retrayé**) in a contract just entered into by the latter; person by whom a **retrait** is exercised.

RETRAYÉ – person against whom a **retrait** is exercised.

RÉTRIBUTION – remuneration; consideration.

RÉTROACTE (Belg) – preparatory document.

RÉTROACTIVITÉ – retrospective effect.
- **IN MITIUS** – **rétroactivité in mitius** – application of a less severe criminal statute to facts occurring before it was passed.

RÉTROCÉDER – assign back; reassign; transfer to a third party; resell.

RÉTROCESSION – reassignment; reconveyance (ie back to the previous owner or those claiming through his estate); assignment back; transfer to a third party; resale.

RÉTROGRADATION – reduction in grade, rank, salary, etc.

RÉUNION – (of conditions) fulfilment; satisfaction.
- **PACIFIQUE** – **réunion pacifique** – peaceful assembly.
- **PARCELLAIRE** – **réunion parcellaire** (Sw) – consolidation of agricultural holdings.

RÉUNIR – (of conditions) fulfil; satisfy.

REVENDICATION
- **ACTION** en **revendication** – action to establish title (ownership); action in detinue.
  - •• **HÉRÉDITÉ** – **action en revendication d'hérédité** – action to obtain possession of an estate from a person not claiming as heir or under a will.
- **ENFANT** – **revendication d'enfant légitime** – action by parents to establish that a person is their legitimate child.

REVENDIQUER – bring an action to establish title (ownership); claim.

REVENTE
- **ENCHÈRE** – **revente sur folle enchère** – resale when the purchaser at an auction fails to pay the price.

REVENU – income.
- **GLOBAL** – **revenu global** – total (world) income.
- **VALEUR** du **revenu cadastral** – rateable value.

REVERSABLE – repayable.

REVERSEMENT – repayment.
- **ÉTAT** de **reversement** – enforceable order for repayment.

RÉVERSIBILITÉ – statutory transferability (transmissibility) of a proportion of an official's pension to his widow, ie to constitute a survivor's pension.

RÉVERSIBLE – capable of being transferred or transmitted to a third party; passing to the survivor.

RÉVERSION
- **PENSION** de **réversion** – widows' and orphans' pension; dependant's pension; survivor's pension; reversionary pension.

REVIREMENT
- **JURISPRUDENCE** – **revirement de jurisprudence** – (decision making a) change of

(in) judicial doctrine or policy; new line of decisions; new precedent; reversal of precedent; departure from (abandonment of) existing precedents (previously established doctrine).

RÉVISION – revision; review; retrial (in criminal cases); modification of a contract, legislation, etc.

- **ORGANE de révision** – auditor; board of auditors.
- **POURVOI en révision** – application for a retrial.
- **RECOURS en révision** – application to re-open civil proceedings on grounds of error of fact or law.
- **REQUÊTE en révision** – application for a retrial.

RÉVOCATION – repeal; revocation; cancellation; withdrawal; dismissal (of an official); discharge (of an order etc).

- **ACTION en révocation** – action to set aside for error, deceit, duress, etc.
  - •• **DONATION – action en révocation de (d'une) donation** – action to revoke a gift.
- **DONATION – révocation de (d'une) donation** – revocation of a gift.

RÉVOQUER – repeal; revoke; cancel; withdraw; dismiss; discharge (a court order).

- **TESTAMENT – révoquer un testament** – revoke a will.

RICOCHET

- **DOMMAGE par ricochet** – indirect damage suffered by dependants (or others similarly situated) from the death or injury of a victim.

RIGUEUR

- **DÉLAI de rigueur** – strict time-limit.

RISQUE

- **ACCEPTATION des risques** – volenti non fit injuria.
- **LOCATIF – risque locatif** – tenant's liability (for damage caused by fire).
- **TRANSFERT des risques** – passing of the risk, eg on a sale.

RIVERAIN – riparian owner; adjacent (abutting) owner.

- **VOIE PUBLIQUE – riverain d'une voie publique** – frontager; person owning land abutting on a street.

RIVERAINETÉ

- **DROITS de riveraineté** – riparian rights; frontager's rights.

RIXE – fight; affray; brawl.

RO = recueil officiel.

RÔLE

- **AUDIENCE – rôle d'audience** – list (of cases for hearing).

ROULAGE – traffic.

- **POLICE du roulage** – traffic police or policing.

ROULEMENT

- **CAPITAL de roulement** – current assets; working capital.
- **MAGISTRAT – roulement des magistrats** – annual assignment of judges to the various chambers of a court.

RS = recueil systématique.

RUBRIQUE – item; heading.

RUPTURE

- **BAN – rupture de ban** – offence of returning to French territory (committed by a person who has been banished); also applies to persons under order not to live in a specific region.
- **CONTRAT DE TRAVAIL – rupture du contrat de travail** – premature termination of an employment contract.
  - •• **ABUSIF – rupture abusive du contrat de travail** – unfair dismissal; wrongful dismissal.
- **FIANÇAILLES – rupture de fiançailles** – breach of promise of marriage.
- **LIEN CONJUGAL – rupture du lien conjugal** – de facto separation.
- **VIE COMMUNE – rupture de la vie commune** – cessation of cohabitation; living apart; de facto separation; termination of consortium either by prolonged de facto separation (six years) or by supervening permanent insanity.

S

SAGESSE
- **REMETTRE**
  - **S'EN remettre à la sagesse de la cour** – leave it to the discretion of the court.

SAISI – judgment debtor whose goods have been attached (seized).
- **TIERS saisi** – garnishee; person in whose hands money owing to a debtor is attached.

SAISIE – seizure (of drugs, contraband, etc); attachment or seizure of property in execution.
- **CONSERVATOIRE – saisie conservatoire** – preventive attachment, ie an attachment before the creditor has obtained judgment in order to prevent the debtor rendering his property inaccessible to execution by dissipating or transferring his assets. (Cf Mareva injunction (asset-freezing order).)
- **CONTREFAÇON – saisie contrefaçon** – procedure to establish an infringement of intellectual property.
- **DROIT de saisie** – right to seize (in connection with certain offences).
  - **GAGE – droit de saisie du gage** – right to attach property as a security for payment.
- **FORAIN – saisie foraine** – preventive attachment of the goods of a person not resident in a town or district, eg by a hotel-keeper.
- **IMMOBILIER – saisie immobilière** – execution against real property.
- **RÉEL – saisie réelle** – attachment of real property.

SAISIE-APPRÉHENSION – attachment of tangible movables by a person entitled to their delivery. The movables may be attached either in the possession of the person liable to deliver them or in that of a third person.

SAISIE-ARRÊT – (formerly) garnishee order nisi; garnishment; attachment of a debt or of property of the debtor in the hands of a third person.

SAISIE-ATTRIBUTION – attachment of sums of money in the hands of a third person.

SAISIE-BRANDON – attachment of standing crops, fish in a pond and other potential movables not yet separated from the land.

SAISIE-EXÉCUTION – attachment of goods; execution against goods.

SAISIE-GAGERIE – preventive attachment of a tenant's goods by the landlord; distress for rent.

SAISIE-OPPOSITION – notice of attachment of a debt.

SAISIE-REVENDICATION – judicial order to ensure the conservation of property which the owner is seeking to recover from a third party.

SAISIE-VENTE – attachment of a debtor's tangible movables. The movables may be attached either in the debtor's possession or in that of a third person.

SAISINE – right of an heir to take possession of the deceased's property without formalities; act or fact of bringing a case before a court; case referred (to a court).
- **COUR – saisine de la cour** – reference of a case (bringing (of) a case before) the court.
- **DIRECT – saisine directe** – direct committal.
- **FONCTION – la saisine du juge d'appel est fonction de la déclaration d'appel** – the jurisdiction of the appeal court is limited (circumscribed) by (the grounds stated in) the notice of appeal.
- **JURIDICTION – saisine de la juridiction** – commencement of proceedings.

SAISIR – attach; distrain; put in possession; (drugs, contraband, etc or of the sheriff in execution) seize; arrest (a ship).
- **COMMISSION – saisir la commission** – refer to the commission; lodge with the commission.
- **COUR – saisir la cour** – refer a case to (bring a case before) the court.
- **ÊTRE saisi de** – have a case before (one, a court, etc); (start to) deal with; have under consideration.
- **JURIDICTION saisie** – court dealing with a case (before which a case has been brought); court in which proceedings are pending.

- **PARLEMENT** – saisir le Parlement d'un projet de loi – table a Bill.
- **SE saisir de** – assume jurisdiction in a case.
- **TRIBUNAL** – saisir un tribunal – refer a case to a court; bring a case before a court.

SAISIR-ARRÊTER – (formerly) garnish; obtain a garnishee order in respect of; attach.

SAISISSABLE – attachable.

SAISISSABILITÉ – liability to attachment.

SALAIRE
- **TÂCHE** – salaire à la tâche – (remuneration for) piece-work; piece-rate wages.

SALARIÉ – wage-earner; employee; servant (ie person who works under the direction of his employer).

SALLE
- **AUDIENCE** – salle d'audience – courtroom; open court.
- **DÉLIBÉRATION** – salle des délibérations – judges' conference (deliberations) room.
- **SÉANCE** – salle des séances – courtroom; open court.
- **TRIBUNAL** – salle du tribunal – courtroom; open court.

SANCTION – sanction; approval; approbation; penalty; repressive measure.
- **LOI** – sanction des lois (with reference to constitutional monarchies) – royal assent.

SANG
- **CRIMES** de sang – murder and similar crimes.
- **DROIT** du sang (jus sanguinis) – rule that nationality is conferred by descent.

SATISFACTION
- **ÉQUITABLE** – satisfaction équitable – just satisfaction.

SAUF-CONDUIT – safe conduct.

SAUVEGARDE
- **JUSTICE** – sauvegarde de justice – judicial protection (system for protecting persons whose faculties are temporarily slightly diminished but not to the extent of requiring a guardian or supervisor).

SAUVETAGE – salvage.

SCANDALE – offence.

SCEAU
- **APPOSER** les sceaux – place official seals (on container or premises).

SCELLÉ
- **APPOSER** les scellés – place official seals (on container or premises).
- **BRIS** de scellés – unlawful removal of official seals.

SCHÉMA
- **DIRECTEUR** – schéma directeur – basic development scheme; master plan.
- **PROCÉDURAL** – schéma procédural – form of procedure.

SCRIPTURAL – cashless, ie by bill or cheque.
- **MONNAIE** scripturale – bank or other forms of financial credit; bank money.

SCRUTATEUR – teller.

SCRUTIN – ballot; vote; voting; election; poll(ing).
- **ARRONDISSEMENT** – scrutin d'arrondissement – election in which only one candidate is returned in each constituency.
- **BALLOTTAGE** – scrutin de ballottage – second ballot.
- **DIRECT** – scrutin direct – direct election.
- **INVESTITURE** – scrutin d'investiture – (formerly) vote in the National Assembly confirming the appointment of a Prime Minister by the President.
- **LISTE** – scrutin de liste – election in which the voter votes for a party list and not for an individual candidate.
- **TOUR** de scrutin – ballot.
- **UNINOMINAL** – scrutin uninominal – election in which only one candidate is returned in each constituency.

SÉANCE – sitting.
- **PLÉNIER** – séance plénière – plenary sitting; sitting of the full court.
- **PUBLIC** – séance publique – open court; public sitting.

SECOND
- **CHANGE** – seconde de change – second of exchange.

SECONDAIRE
- **DROIT** secondaire – subordinate legislation.

SECRET

- **AFFAIRE** – secret d'affaires – trade secret.
- **AU secret** – in solitary confinement; incommunicado.
- **FABRICATION (FABRIQUE)** – secret de fabrication (fabrique) – manufacturing secret.
- **FONCTION** – secret de fonctions – official secret.
- **MISE au secret** – (placing in) solitary confinement; holding incommunicado; prohibition of communications.
- **PROFESSIONNEL** – secret professionnel – professional secrecy; confidentiality; legal professional privilege.

SECRÉTAIRE

- **ÉTAT** – secrétaire d'État – Minister of State; junior minister; parliamentary (under-)secretary (of state).
- **GÉNÉRAL** – secrétaire général – permanent (under-)secretary; secretary-general; general secretary.
  - •• **ADJOINT** – secrétaire général adjoint – deputy (under-)secretary; head of department; deputy secretary-general.
- **MAIRIE** – secrétaire de mairie – mayor's secretary.
  - •• **GÉNÉRAL** – secrétaire général de mairie – town clerk.

SECRÉTARIAT – registry (of a court).

SECRÉTARIAT-GREFFE – registry (of a court).

SECTION – division; department; district; (code) section. The French, Belgian and Luxembourg Civil Codes are divided into **livres** (books), **titres** (parts), **chapitres** (chapters), **sections** (sections) and **articles** (articles).

- **CONSEIL** – section du Conseil d'État – division of the Conseil d'État.
- **CONTENTIEUX** – section du contentieux (du Conseil d'État) – Litigation (Judicial) Division (of the Conseil d'État).

SECTIONNEMENT

- **ÉLECTORAL** – sectionnement électoral – division into constituencies.

SÉCURITÉ

- **DROIT** – sécurité du droit – certainty of the law; security of legal transactions.
- **ÉTAT** – sécurité de l'État – national security.
- **INTÉRIEUR** – sécurité intérieure – internal security.
- **JURIDIQUE** – sécurité (du commerce) juridique – certainty of the law; security of legal transactions.
- **OBLIGATION de sécurité** – duty of care for the safety of others (implied by case-law in certain contracts).
- **PUBLIC** – sécurité publique – public safety; public order.
- **RÈGLE de sécurité** – safety regulation.
- **SOCIAL** – sécurité sociale – socal security.
- **SYNDICAL** – clause de sécurité syndicale – closed-shop clause.
- **TRAVAIL** – sécurité du travail – safety at work.

SEIGNEUR – lord of the manor.

SEIGNEURIAL – feudal.

SEING

- **ACTE sous seing privé** – private document, ie one which has not been officially recorded; signed writing.

SÉJOUR – (temporary) residence.

- **INDEMNITÉ de séjour** – subsistence allowance.
- **INTERDICTION de séjour** – order forbidding a person to enter a particular area or areas.

SEMI-DÉTENTION – (Belg) semi-custodial treatment; semi-detention. (The Crown prosecutor may order that prisoners serving less than six months should work outside during the day and spend the night in prison).

SEMI-LIBERTÉ – semi-custodial treatment; semi-detention; (Belg) short periods of freedom granted by the prison authorities prior to conditional release.

SENS

- **CONTRAIRE** – en sens contraire – contra; taking the opposite view.

SENTENCE – (arbitral) award; decision; judgment (of a district court or industrial tribunal).

SÉPARATION

- **BIEN** – séparation de biens – separation of property; separate property.
- **CORPS** – séparation de corps – judicial separation.
  - •• **JUGEMENT de séparation de corps** – decree of judicial separation.
- **FAIT** – séparation de fait – living apart.

- **PATRIMOINE** – séparation des patrimoines – separation of the assets of a deceased from those of the heirs; separation of assets (estates).
- **POUVOIR** – séparation des pouvoirs – separation of powers.

SÉPARÉ

- **CORPS** – séparé de corps – judicially separated.

SÉPARÉMENT – apart.

SÉQUESTRATION – holding a person against his will; false imprisonment; illegal confinement.

- **ARBITRAIRE** – séquestration arbitraire – holding a person against his will; false imprisonment; illegal confinement.
- **PERSONNE** – séquestration de personne – holding a person against his will; false imprisonment; illegal confinement.

SÉQUESTRE – receiver; administrator; custodian pendente lite; custody pendente lite of goods whose ownership is disputed during the proceedings; compulsory administration; seizure or (by a court) attachment or (in some cases) sequestration. sub MIS sous séquestre – (by a court) placed under compulsory administration, attachment or (in some cases) sequestration. sub OFFICE des séquestres (Lux) – Public Custodian's Office.

SÉQUESTRER – unlawfully deprive a person of his freedom; hold a person against his will.

SÉRÉNITÉ

- **JUSTICE** – troubler la sérénité de la justice – interfere with the proper conduct of proceedings.

SÉRIEUX – reasonable.

- **INTÉRÊT** sérieux et légitime – reasonable and lawful interest.

SERMENT

- **CRÉDIBILITÉ (CRÉDULITÉ)** – serment de crédibilité (crédulité) – oath by an alleged debtor's surviving spouse or heirs that they are unaware of the existence of a debt or other relevant matter.
- **DÉCISOIRE** – serment décisoire – oath which a party is required to take by his opponent in order to decide the matter at issue between them.
- **DÉFÉRER** le serment à quelqu'un – require a person to take an oath; put a person to his oath.

- **DÉLATION** du serment – requiring a party to take an oath; putting a party to his oath.
- **FAUX** serment – perjury by a party; false declaration (on a form etc).
- **FORMULE** de serment – form of oath; wording of an oath.
- **RÉFÉRER** le serment – require a party applying for an oath to take an oath himself.
- **RELATION** de serment – procedural step whereby a party who has been called on to swear to the truth of his case refuses to do so and requires his opponent to swear that the fact he alleges is true.
- **SUPPLÉTOIRE** – serment supplétoire – supplementary oath which the judge can require a party to take and which, unlike the **serment décisoire**, does not decide the matter in dispute but leaves the decision to the judge.

SERVICE

- **COMMUNAUTÉ** – service (travail) au profit de la communauté – community service (work).
- **ENQUÊTE** – service d'enquête – investigating department.
- **EXTÉRIEUR** – services extérieurs – local departments of ministries in the provinces.
- **FAUTE** de service – administrative (official) error; fault committed by a civil or other public servant in the performance of his duties for which he is not liable in the ordinary courts.
- **GÉNÉRAL**
  - **COMMUN** – services généraux communs – common general services.
- **PASSEPORT** de service – service passport.
- **VOTÉ** – services votés – public services provided for in the previous year's budget and which (unlike new measures) are adopted under an expedited procedure.

SERVIR

- **INTÉRÊT** – servir des intérêts – make interest payments; service a loan.
- **RENTE** – servir une rente – pay an annuity or pension.

SERVITUDE – an encumbrance imposed on a tenement for the benefit of a tenement belonging to a different owner; easement; quasi-easement; profit à prendre (eg a right to take sand); restrictive or other covenant running with the land in rem; servitude; (in a wider sense) any restriction

imposed on property in the public interest; obligation.

- **ADMINISTRATIF** – servitude administrative – public servitude; local land charge.
- **ALIGNEMENT** – servitude d'alignement – obligation to comply with a building line.
- **AMÉLIORATION** – servitude d'amélioration – obligation to comply with administrative regulations when making alterations.
- **APPUI** – servitude d'appui – easement of support.
- **AVANCEMENT** – servitude d'avancement – obligation to come forward to the building line when rebuilding.
- **COUR COMMUNE** – servitude de cour commune – servitude restricting building or the height of buildings on an adjacent tenement. (This may be established by agreement or – on an application to the court by an owner entitled to a building permit issued subject to a condition that such a servitude is imposed – imposed by a court.)
- **ÉCOULEMENT** – servitude d'écoulement – easement to discharge rain-water etc onto a lower-lying tenement.
- **ÉGOUT** – servitude d'égout – easement requiring a building owner to discharge rain-water from his own roof onto his own property or the public highway and not directly onto his neighbour's land.
- **ESSARTEMENT** – servitude d'essartement – forest owner's duty to leave a clear space of 20 metres on either side of the highway.
- **ÉVIER** – servitude d'évier – easement to discharge water used for household purposes.
- **FONDS** débiteur de la servitude – servient tenement.
- **HALAGE** – servitude de halage – duty of a riparian owner to leave space for a towpath alongside a navigable waterway.
- **HAUTEUR** – servitude de hauteur – obligation not to build over a certain height.
- **IMMOBILIER** – servitude immobilière – easement.
- **LÉGAL** – servitude légale – statutory easement or right.
- **MARCHEPIED** – servitude de marchepied – duty of a riparian owner to leave space along a navigable waterway for necessary manœuvring on land by boat crews.
- **MATÉRIAUX** – servitude d'extraction de matériaux – profit à prendre; right to extract minerals.

- **MILITAIRE** – servitude militaire – easement imposed for reasons of military security.
- **NON ÆDIFICANDI** – servitude non ædificandi – obligation not to build on the land.
- **PACAGE** – servitude de pacage – profit of pasture.
- **PASSAGE** – servitude de passage – right of way.
  - •• **BÉTAIL** – servitude de passage du bétail – right of way for cattle.
- **PÂTURE** – servitude de pâture – profit of pasture; right to pasture cattle or sheep.
- **PERSONNEL** – servitude personnelle – right over land vested in a person as such and not as the owner for the time being of a piece of land; generic term covering usufruct and similar rights; easement or profit in gross.
- **PLANTATION** – servitude de plantation – obligation not to plant trees within a certain distance of the dominant tenement.
- **PLUME** – servitude de la plume – obligation of a public prosecutor to act on official instructions in making written applications to the court.
- **PRÉDIAL** – servitude prédiale – easement.
- **RACHAT** d'une servitude – redemption of an easement.
- **RECULEMENT** – servitude de reculement – obligation not to build (or repair existing erections) within a certain distance of a road; obligation to observe a building line.
- **RÉEL** – servitude réelle – easement; profit à prendre (eg right to take sand for the benefit of a dominant tenement).
- **RIVERAINETÉ** – servitude de riveraineté – obligation imposed on an abutting owner.
- **TOUR D'ÉCHELLE** – servitude (droit) de tour d'échelle – easement entitling the owner of the dominant property to place ladders on the servient property.
- **UTILITÉ PUBLIQUE** – servitude d'utilité publique – public servitude.
- **VISIBILITÉ** – servitude de visibilité – obligation to remove or not to erect constructions interfering with visibility on a road.
- **VOIRIE** – servitude de voirie – obligation imposed on the owner of property abutting on public roads.
- **VOISINAGE** – servitude de voisinage – right relating to adjacent property.

SÉVICES – ill-treatment; cruelty; physical violence.

SIÈGE

- **ADMINISTRATIF** – **siège administratif** – administrative headquarters.
- **ÉTAT de siège** – martial law; state of emergency.
- **MAGISTRAT du siège** – judge.
- **MAGISTRATURE du siège** – the judges; the judiciary.
- **PRINCIPAL** – **siège principal** – headquarters.
- **RÉEL** – **siège réel** – factual seat.
- **SOCIAL** – **siège social** – registered office; principal office.
- **STATUTAIRE** – **siège statutaire** – registered office (of a company); statutory office (of an association).

SIGNALEMENT – personal particulars; (personal) description.

SIGNATURE

- **AD REFERENDUM** – **signature ad referendum** – signature ad referendum.
- **LÉGALISATION de signature** – legalisation of a signature, eg by a consul.
- **SOCIAL** – **signature sociale** – firm's signature.

SIGNIFICATION – service (of process) by a bailiff; service (of documents); notice.

- **ACTE de signification** – record of service.
- **ACTE** – **signification des actes de procédure** – service of judicial process (by a bailiff).
- **DOMICILE** – **signification à domicile** – service by leaving the papers at the residence (ie home address) of the person concerned.
- **EXPLOIT de signification** – record of service made by a process-server.
- **MAIN PROPRE** – **signification en main(s) propre(s)** – personal service.
- **PERSONNE** – **signification à personne** – personal service.
- **PERSONNEL** – **signification personnelle** – personal service.

SILENCE

- **ADMINISTRATION** – **silence de l'Administration** – failure by a public department to reply to an application. (If it lasts for more than four months, it may be treated as a refusal.)

SIMULATION – false representation; fictitious (simulated) transaction.

- **ACTION en déclaration de simulation** – action to set aside a simulated transaction.

SINISTRÉ – damaged or destroyed.

SITUATION

- **ASPECTS pertinents de la situation** – relevant circumstances.
- **ÉTAT de situation** – statement of affairs; return.
- **JURIDIQUE** – **situation juridique** – legal position; legal status.

SOCIAL

- **ACTION sociale** – action brought by a company, (professional or other) association, trade union, etc.
- **CAPITAL social** – (authorised) capital.
- **DETTE sociale** – partnership or company debt.
- **OBJET social** – the objects of a company or partnership.
- **PACTE social** – articles of association or partnership.
- **PATRIMOINE social** – partnership or company assets.
- **PRÉJUDICE social** – loss or damage suffered by a company, (professional or other) association, trade union, etc.
- **PROTECTION sociale des enfants** – child welfare.
- **RAISON sociale** – firm name; business name including the names of all or some of the personally liable partners.
- **RELATIONS sociales** – labour relations; industrial relations.
- **SIÈGE social** – registered office; principal office.
- **SIGNATURE** – **signature sociale** – firm's signature.

SOCIALISATION – transfer of property to the workers; nationalisation.

SOCIÉTAIRE – partner; member of an association.

SOCIÉTÉ – partnership; company.

- **ACQUÊT** – **société d'acquêts** – community of after-acquired property.
- **ACTE de société** – articles of partnership; memorandum and articles of association of a company.
- **ACTION** – **société par actions** – joint stock company.
- **ADMINISTRATEUR de société** – company director.
- **ANONYME** – **société anonyme** – public limited company.

- **APPORT** en société – contribution to a partnership's assets.
- **BUT LUCRATIF** – société à but lucratif – profit-making partnership or company.
- **CAPITAL** – société de capitaux – company (but the term also includes **la société en commandite par actions**).
- **CHASSE** – société de chasse – hunting association.
- **CIVIL** – société civile – non-commercial partnership; civil-law partnership.
  - •• **PROFESSIONNEL** – société civile professionnelle – civil-law professional partnership.
- **COLLECTIF** – société en nom collectif – commercial partnership.
- **COMMANDITE**
  - •• **ACTION** – société en commandite par actions – limited partnership with shares.
  - •• **SIMPLE** – société en commandite simple – limited partnership.
- **COMMERCE** – société de commerce – trading partnership or company.
- **COMMERCIAL** – société commerciale – commercial partnership or company.
- **CONJUGAL** – société conjugale – community of property (between spouses); marital community.
- **CONSTITUTION** de société – founding (formation) of a partnership or company.
- **CONTRAT** de société – articles of partnership; memorandum and articles of association of a company.
- **DE FAIT** – société (créée) de fait – de facto partnership.
- **DOMICILE** – société de domicile – company having only its registered office in a given country.
- **DROIT CIVIL** – société de droit civil – non-commercial partnership; civil-law partnership.
- **ÉCONOMIE MIXTE** – société d'économie mixte – part state-owned company; semi-public corporation.
- **FAIT** – see DE FAIT above.
- **IMMOBILIER** – société immobilière – property company.
  - •• **ATTRIBUTION** – société immobilière d'attribution – company formed to erect a building to be divided among the members.
  - •• **COMMERCE** – société immobilière pour le commerce et l'industrie – com-

pany formed to let commercial and industrial premises.
  - •• **INVESTISSEMENT** – société immobilière d'investissement – company formed to let residential premises.
- **IMPÔT** sur les sociétés – corporation tax.
- **INTÉRÊT** – société par intérêts – partnership.
- **INVESTISSEMENT** – société d'investissement – investment trust.
- **MÈRE** – société mère – parent company; holding company.
- **NATION** – Société des Nations – League of Nations.
- **NOM COLLECTIF** – see COLLECTIF above.
- **PARTICIPATION** – société en participation – partnership with a sleeping partner or undisclosed partnership.
- **PERSONNE** – société de personnes – partnership (but the term also includes the **société à responsabilité limitée**).
  - •• **RESPONSABILITÉ** – société de personnes à responsabilité limitée (Belg) – private (limited) company.
- **PRÉVOYANCE** – société de prévoyance – provident (friendly) society.
- **RESPONSABILITÉ** – société à responsabilité limitée – private (limited) company.

SOIT-COMMUNIQUÉ
- **ORDONNANCE** de soit-communiqué – order by the investigating judge closing an investigation, transmitting the file and informing the public prosecutor's office that the case is ready for further action; notification to proceed (with a prosecution).

SOL
- **DROIT** du sol (jus soli) – rule that nationality is acquired by birth on the territory of the state concerned.

SOLDE
- **BALANCE** des comptes en mouvement et en soldes – turnover and balances of the accounts.

SOLENNEL – officially recorded (by a solicitor); in solemn form.

SOLIDAIRE – jointly and severally liable.

SOLIDARITÉ – joint and several liability.
- **ACTIF** – solidarité active – rules governing joint and several creditors.

- **PASSIF** – **solidarité passive** – rules governing joint and several debtors.

SOLIDITÉ
- **PREUVE** – **solidité des preuves** – reliability of the evidence.

SOLIDUM – see IN SOLIDUM.

SOLUTION – interpretation.

SOLVABILITÉ – solvency.

SOLVABLE – solvent.

SOLVENS – person performing an obligation.

SOMMATION – document served by a bailiff; formal notice; formal summons; warning; notice (to pay); service of an order (eg order to pay, injunction or prohibition).
- **PAIEMENT** – **sommation de paiement** – official demand for payment by the bailiff.

SOMME
- **DÉLÉGATION** de sommes – transfer by court order of sums due to one person to another (eg a husband's earnings to his wife); transfer order; assignment order.
- **GLOBAL** – **somme globale unique** – single lump-sum payment.
- **LITIGE** – **somme en litige** – amount in dispute.

SOMMIER
- **JUDICIAIRE** – **sommiers judiciaires** – criminal records; criminal records office.

SONDAGE – (auditor's) random (spot) check.

SORTANT – retiring; outgoing.

SORTIE
- **MASSE** de sortie – (prisoner's) release savings.

SOUCHE – person and his descendants.
- **PAR** souche(s) – per stirpes.

SOUFFRANCE
- **INDEMNISATION** des souffrances (pretium doloris) – (damages for) pain and suffering.

SOULEVER – raise.
- **EXCEPTION** – **soulever une exception** – raise an objection; plead (put forward, raise) a defence.
- **OFFICE** – **soulever d'office** – (of a court) raise of its own motion (ex officio).

SOULTE – balance to equalise shares; differences (in value).

- **ÉCHANGE** avec soulte – exchange with payment of the difference.

SOUMISSION – tender.

SOUMISSIONNAIRE – tenderer; person tendering.

SOUMISSIONNER – tender for a contract.

SOURICIÈRE – police trap.

SOUS-ACQUÉREUR – sub-purchaser.

SOUS-BAIL – underlease; sublease.

SOUS-BRIGADIER – (police) constable.

SOUSCRIPTEUR – subscriber.
- **POLICE** – **souscripteur de police** – the insured; policyholder.

SOUSCRIPTION
- **IRRÉDUCTIBLE** – **souscription à titre irréductible** – irrevocable subscription.
- **PUBLIC** – **souscription publique** – public collection; public subscription.
- **SURPASSÉ** – **souscription surpassée** – over-subscription.

SOUSCRIRE – accept; subscribe.
- **THÈSE** – **souscrire à une thèse** – accept an argument.

SOUS-DÉPOSITAIRE – sub-depositary.

SOUS-DIRECTEUR – assistant (under-) secretary; head of section; deputy director.

SOUS-ENTREPRENEUR – subcontractor.

SOUS-LOCATAIRE – subtenant.

SOUS-LOCATION – subtenancy; sublease.

SOUS-LOUER – underlet; sublet.

SOUS-MINISTRE (Canada) – permanent (under-)secretary.

SOUS-SECRÉTAIRE
- **ÉTAT** – **sous-secrétaire d'État** – (formerly) Minister of State; junior minister; parliamentary (under-)secretary (of state).

SOUS-SECTION
- **CONSEIL D'ÉTAT** – **sous-section du Conseil d'État** – section of the Conseil d'État.
  - **RÉUNI** – **sous-sections réunies du Conseil d'État** – combined sections of the Conseil d'État.

SOUS-SOL – subsoil.

SOUSTRACTION – misappropriation.
- **FRAUDULEUX** – **soustraction fraudu-leuse** – embezzlement of funds; suppression of documentary evidence; taking by fraud; fraudulent conversion.

SOUSTRAIRE
- **PEINE** – **soustraire à la peine** – exempt from punishment.
- **SE soustraire aux recherches de la police** – hide from the police.

SOUSTRAITANT – subcontractor.

SOUSTRAITER – subcontract.

SOUS-TRANSPORTEUR – a second carrier acting as an agent for the first; another carrier.

SOUTENIR – maintain; argue; submit.

SOUTIEN
- **FAMILLE** – **soutien de famille** – bread-winner.
- **NÉCESSAIRE** – **soutien nécessaire (d'un dispositif)** – reasons for a decision; ratio decidendi.

SOUVENIR
- **FAMILLE** – **souvenirs de famille** – heir-looms.

SOUVERAIN – completely independent; having unfettered discretion; unappealable (not subject to appeal); sovereign.
- **APPRÉCIATION souveraine de fait** – final (ie unappealable and discretionary) decision on the facts.
- **COUR souveraine** – court from which no appeal lies.
- **ÊTRE souverain** – exercise final authority.

SOUVERAINEMENT – without appeal.

SOUVERAINETÉ – sovereignty; (sovereign) power.
- **ACTE de souveraineté** – sovereign act; act of state.
- **LOI** – **souveraineté de la loi** – supremacy of the law.

SPATIAL – territorial.

SPÉCIALITÉ
- **ADMINISTRATIF** – **spécialité adminis-trative** – principle that public corporations may employ their resources only in order to carry out their statutory objects (cf ultra vires rule).
- **HYPOTHÉCAIRE** – **spécialité hypothé-caire** – rule that an entry in the mortgage register must specify the amount of the mortgage and the property or properties mortgaged.
- **PRINCIPE de la spécialité** – speciality rule; rule that a person may only be tried for the offence for which he was extradited; rule that an association's or company's property may only be used for the objects specified in its memorandum of association; objects rule (cf ultra vires rule).

SPONTANÉMENT – of its (his, her, their) own motion.
- **PRÉSENTER**
  - **SE présenter spontanément** – report voluntarily.

SPRL = société de personnes à respon-sabilité limitée (Belg).

STAGE – qualifying period for insurance benefit.
- **ATTENTE** – **stage d'attente** – qualifying period.

STARIES – lay days.

STATUER
- **CHAMBRE DU CONSEIL** – **statuer en chambre du conseil** – take a decision in chambers.
- **LIEU** – **il n'y a pas lieu de statuer** – it is unnecessary to proceed further in the matter.
- **OMISSION de statuer** – failure (by a court) to decide a point raised in the pleadings. (This may constitute a ground for appeal to the Court of Cassation or for an application to the trial court to retry the issue in question (**recours en révision**, formerly **requête civile**).)
- **PIÈCE** – **statuer sur pièces** – decide the case on the pleadings (on the written evidence, on the file).
- **PRÉLIMINAIRE** – **statuer à titre prélimi-naire** – decide a preliminary point (issue).
- **PRINCIPAL** – **statuer au principal** – try the main issue; hear and decide the case; try the case; decide (give judgment in) the main proceedings; determine the merits of a case.
- **PROVISOIRE** – **statuer au provisoire** – give a provisional ruling; make an interim order.

- **SUR** – **statuer sur** – hear and determine (deal with, give judgment in) a case; rule on.
- **SURSEOIR à statuer** – defer a decision; stay or adjourn the proceedings.

STATUT – (memorandum and) articles of an association or company; articles of a partnership; charter; statutes; status; standing; rights and duties; rules governing; constitution (of a body etc).
- **FONCTION PUBLIQUE** – **statut de la fonction publique** – Civil Service Act and Regulations.
- **JURIDIQUE** – **statut juridique** – legal position; legal status.
  - •• **SALARIAL** – **statut juridique salarial** – salary regulations.
- **LÉGAL** – **statut légal** – statutory provisions (governing).
- **PERSONNEL** (adj) – **statut personnel** – rules governing the status and capacity of persons; proper law (in the case where different groups of persons living in the same area are governed by different systems of law).
- **PERSONNEL** (noun) – **statut du personnel** – staff regulations.
- **PRESSE** – **statut de la presse** – Press Act (Code).
- **RÉEL** – **statut réel** – proper law (of thing, especially immovables).

STATUTAIRE – provided for by (compatible with) the statute(s) or the existing or relevant regulations; organisational; constitutional (in relation to the constitution of a particular body). NB "statutory" should be avoided as a translation as it has a different meaning in legal English.
- **RÈGLE** – **règles statutaires** – (memorandum and) articles of an association or a company; charter; statutes.

STATUT-TYPE
- **FONCTION PUBLIQUE** – **statut-type de la fonction publique européenne** – model staff regulations for the European civil service.

STELLIONAT – tort of selling or mortgaging to another, by means of fraudulent representations as to title, property already sold or mortgaged or to which the vendor has no title; fraudulent representations as to title.

STIPULATION – term (of a contract).
- **AUTRUI** – **stipulation pour autrui** – contract conferring a right on a third party.
- **CONTRACTUEL** – **stipulation contractuelle** – clause, provision or stipulation in a contract, agreement or treaty.
- **CONVENTIONNEL** – **stipulation conventionnelle** – clause, provision or stipulation in a contract, agreement or treaty.
- **PROPRE** – **stipulation de propres** – declaration that certain movables are comprised in (the wife's) separate property.

STIPULER – (in legislation and other non-contractual documents) provide.

STUPÉFIANT – (dangerous) drug; narcotic.

SUBIR
- **PEINE** – **subir une peine** – serve a sentence.

SUBJECTIF – individual.
- **DROIT subjectif** – right conferred on or exercised by an individual; individual (personal, private) right (as opposed to **droit objectif**).

SUBORDINATION – position of a person who works under his employer's instructions.

SUBORNATION
- **TÉMOIN** – **subornation de témoin** – procuring a person to give false evidence; subornation of perjury.

SUBROGATION – subrogation; substitution; replacement.
- **PERSONNEL** – **subrogation personnelle** – replacement of one person by another in a legal relationship, whereby the latter is enabled to enjoy and exercise all the rights formerly pertaining to the former.
- **POURSUITE** – **subrogation aux (des) poursuites** – right of a creditor to take the place of an inactive creditor in continuing execution against a debtor.
- **RÉEL** – **subrogation réelle** – attribution to an object of the legal qualities or purpose of the object it replaces within a group of assets; replacement of one object by another in a legal relationship (with the necessary adaptations, eg the transfer of a mortgage from the property destroyed to the insurance moneys).

SUBROGÉ – person replacing another in a legal relationship and so in a position to exercise all the rights previously pertaining to the former.
- **TUTEUR** – **subrogé(-)tuteur** – auxiliary or supervising guardian.

SUBROGER

- **DROIT** – subroger quelqu'un dans ses droits – assign one's rights to someone.
- **ÊTRE subrogé** – be subrogated (to the rights of).

SUBSIDIAIRE – accessory; alternative; subsidiary.

- **EMPRISONNEMENT subsidiaire** (Belg) – imprisonment in default (of payment of a fine).

SUBSIDIAIREMENT – in the alternative; alternatively; as a subsidiary argument or submission; subsidiarity principle.

- **PAR le droit du Fonds et subsidiairement par le droit français** – by the law governing the Fund and subject thereto by French law.

SUBSIDIARITÉ

- **PRINCIPE de la subsidiarité** – principle that a decision should be taken at the lowest possible level; subsidiarity principle.

SUBSISTANCE

- **FAMILLE – subsistance de famille** – family maintenance.

SUBSTANTIEL – material; substantive; essential.

- **DROIT substantiel** – substantive right forming the subject-matter of litigation; substantive law.
- **ÉLÉMENT substantiel du contrat** – essential (material) part of the contract.
- **FORMALITÉ substantielle** – essential formality.
- **FORME substantielle** – essential formal requirement (formality).

SUBSTITUT – deputy public prosecutor.

- **EMPRISONNEMENT – substituts à l'emprisonnement** – alternatives to imprisonment.
- **GÉNÉRAL – substitut général** – Attorney-General's deputy.
- **PREMIER substitut** – senior deputy public prosecutor.

SUBSTITUTION – settlement of property on persons in succession; family settlement; entail; testamentary settlement (without trustees).

- **ENFANT – substitution d'enfant** – substitution of a child.
- **FIDÉICOMMISSAIRE – substitution fidéicommissaire** – creation of a life estate and a remainder (which is illegal).

- **HÉRITIER – substitution d'héritier** – remainder.
- **MESURE de substitution** – alternative (measure).
- **MOTIF – substitution de motif** – right of the Court of Cassation to correct erroneous reasons given for a judgment appealed against.
- **PART – substitution de part** – substitution of a child.
- **PEINE de substitution (à l'emprisonnement)** – alternative to imprisonment.
- **POUVOIR de substitution** – power (of an agent) to appoint a sub-agent; right of a superior authority to take measures in the place and on behalf of a subordinate authority.
- **SIMPLE – substitution simple** – appointment of a second legatee to take on the failure of the original legacy.
- **VULGAIRE – substitution vulgaire** – see SIMPLE above.

SUBVENTION – grant.

- **GLOBAL – subvention globale** – block grant.

SUCCESSIBILITÉ

- **DROIT de successibilité** – right to inherit (succeed to) property; inheritance right.

SUCCESSIBLE – entitled to succeed; presumptive heir.

- **DEGRÉ – au degré successible** – entitled to inherit.

SUCCESSIF – successive; continuous; recurrent.

- **CONTRAT successif** – contract involving successive performance; continuing contract.
- **DROIT successif** – right to inherit (succeed to) property; inheritance right; the law of succession (inheritance).
  - **VENTE de droits successifs** – sale of one's right to an inheritance; sale of an expectancy.

SUCCESSION – estate (of a deceased person); succession; inheritance.

- **AB INTESTAT – succession ab intestat** – intestate succession; succession on (an) intestacy.
- **ANOMAL – succession anomale** – exceptional type of succession in which, by virtue of their origin, certain items of property are not included in the deceased's estate but, eg, revert to the donor or his issue.

- **BÉNÉFICIAIRE** – succession bénéficiaire – succession in which the heir's liability for the debts of the estate is limited to the amount of the net assets he actually receives.
- **COLLATÉRAL** – succession collatérale – succession in the collateral line.
- **DÉSHÉRENCE** – succession en déshérence – failure of heirs; unclaimed estate; vacant succession, ie where there is no heir or no heir willing to take the estate, no surviving spouse and no universal (ie residuary) legatee.
- **DÉVOLUTION** de la succession – order of devolution of property.
- **DROIT** de succession – the law of succession (inheritance); right to inherit (succeed to) property; (usually in plural) inheritance tax; succession duty.
- **DROIT** des successions – the law of succession (inheritance).
- **ÉTAT** – succession des (entre) États – state succession.
- **FUTUR** – pacte sur succession future – agreement on the succession of a living person.
- **IMPÔT** sur les successions – inheritance tax; succession duty.
- **JURIDIQUE** – succession juridique – succession in title.
- **LÉGAL** – succession légale – (statutory) order of succession on (an) intestacy.
- **MOBILIER** – succession mobilière – succession to movables.
- **NET** – succession nette – net assets of the estate.
- **OUVERT** – succession ouverte – estate of a person already deceased.
  - **NON** – succession non ouverte – estate of a living person.
- **OUVERTURE** de la succession – passing of the estate to the heirs.
- **PARTICULIER** – succession à titre particulier – succession to a particular right; succession in title.
- **TESTAMENTAIRE** – succession testamentaire – succession under a will; testate succession.
- **VACANT** – succession vacante – failure of heirs; vacant succession; unclaimed estate; bona vacantia.

SUCCESSORAL

- **PART** successorale – share in an estate; share on (an) intestacy.

- **RECEL** successoral – concealment of an inheritance; conversion of assets belonging to an estate.
- **TITRE** – à titre successoral – by inheritance.
- **TRANSFERT** successoral – passing by inheritance.
- **VENTE** successorale – sale of one's right to an inheritance; sale of an expectancy.
- **VOCATION** successorale – right to inherit on (an) intestacy.

SUCCOMBANCE – fact of having lost a case.

SUCCOMBER – lose (a case).

SUFFRAGE

- **NUL** – suffrage nul – spoiled ballot paper; invalid vote.

SUITE

- **DONNER** suite à – allow (a claim, an application, etc).
- **DROIT** de suite – right to trace or follow property into the hands of a third person; mortgagee's right to attach the mortgaged property and have it sold to answer the mortgage debt into whoever's hands it may have passed; right of persons entitled to a **privilège** (right to preferential payment) to follow property; right of a secured creditor to take possession of the security even if in the possession of a third party; (bankruptcy) right of stoppage in transitu; (copyright) right of an author to a percentage of the sale price of his work (over which he may not dispose inter vivos or by will and to which his heirs are entitled for a period of fifty years after his death, subject to a life interest of the surviving spouse); reserved royalties; right of an artist to a percentage of the price of his picture every time it is sold by an auctioneer or art dealer; surviving right; inheritable royalty; surviving royalty; resale right.

SUJET – person entitled to hold and exercise rights; person (recognised by the law).

- **ACTIF** – sujet actif (d'un droit, d'une obligation) – person entitled to the benefit of a right or obligation (obligee, promisee, creditor, victim of a tort).
- **DROIT** – sujet de droit – person (entity) recognised by law or a particular system of law as capable of owning and exercising

rights and being subject to obligations; person, ie having legal personality; legal person; (in an international context) subject of law.

　•• **INTERNATIONAL** – **sujet de droit international** – person recognised by international law as having rights and duties (as having legal personality); subject of (international) law.

　• **MIXTE** – **sujet mixte** – person with two or more nationalities.

　• **PASSIF** – **sujet passif (d'un droit, d'une obligation)** – person against whom a right may be enforced; obligor; promisor; debtor; person bound by (liable to perform) an obligation.

SUJÉTION
　• **DOUANIER** – **sous sujétion douanière** – in bond.

SUPERARBITRE – umpire.

SUPERBÉNÉFICE(S) – excess profit(s).

SUPERFICIAIRE – building owner; surface owner.

SUPERFICIE
　• **DROIT de superficie** – surface rights (in a piece of land containing minerals); right in rem to buildings and plantations on the land of another; surface owner's rights; building owner's rights; building lease.

SUPERFICITAIRE – building owner; surface owner.

SUPÉRIEUR
　• **HIÉRARCHIQUE** – **supérieur hiérarchique** – official (immediate) superior; superior officer; higher administrative officer.

SUPPLÉANT – (adj) acting; (noun) substitute; alternate.

SUPPLÉTIF – non-mandatory; applying only if the parties do not otherwise provide; waivable; variable; supplementary; suppletive.

SUPPLÉTOIRE – supplementary (used of an oath which the judge can require a party to take and which, unlike the **serment décisoire**, does not decide the matter in dispute but leaves the decision to the judge). (Sometimes found as a synonym of **supplétif**.)

SUPPLIQUE – petition; application.

SUPPOSITION
　• **CRÉANCE** – **supposition de créance** – fraudulent claim to a debt.

　• **ENFANT (PART)** – **supposition d'enfant (de part)** – attributing a child to an imaginary woman or to a woman who has not conceived; passing off a child.

SUPPRESSION – cancellation; termination; withdrawal (of a service etc); extinguishment; abolition; deletion; punishment; repression.

　• **CADAVRE** – **suppression de cadavre** – concealment of a body.

　• **ENFANT (PART)** – **suppression d'enfant (de part)** – causing the disappearance of a new-born child (charge brought where nothing more can be proved); concealment of birth.

SUPPRIMER – delete.

SURABONDANCE
　• **DROIT** – **par surabondance de droit** – as a subsidiary consideration.

SURARBITRAGE – decision by an umpire.

SURARBITRE – umpire.

SURÉLEVER – build higher; raise.

SURENCHÈRE – a firm offer higher than the auction price which entitles the offeror to have the auction reopened if made within ten days and security is given for the payment of the price offered.

SURESTARIES – (days of) demurrage.

SÛRETÉ – security; police; secured debt; security of the person; and see NATIONAL below.

　• **CESSION à titre de sûreté** – assignment by way of security.

　• **CONSTITUER une sûreté** – give security.

　• **COUR de sûreté de l'État** – (former) National Security Court.

　• **ÉTEINDRE** – **leurs sûretés s'éteignent** – their securities lapse.

　• **HYPOTHÉCAIRE** – **sûreté hypothécaire** – mortgage security.

　• **MESURE de sûreté** – restrictive measure imposed for the protection of the public, eg preventive detention; security measure; preventive measure; social-protection order.

　• **NATIONAL** – **sûreté nationale** – national security.

　　•• **DIRECTION de la Sûreté nationale (la Sûreté (nationale))** – (formerly) police department of the Ministry of the Interior.

- **PÉRIODE de sûreté** – period of unconditional imprisonment (during which no form of release can be granted).
- **PERSONNEL** – **sûreté personnelle** – personal security (ie a surety or the debtor's personal credit).
- **PUBLIC** – **sûreté publique** – public safety.
- **RÉEL** – **sûreté réelle** – security in the form of land or other property; a charge on property.

SUREXPERT – consultant referred to for a second or further expert opinion to resolve existing or alleged doubts.

SUREXPERTISE – second or further expert opinion to resolve existing or alleged doubts.

SURFACE
- **DROIT de surface** – surface rights (in a piece of land containing minerals); right in rem to buildings and plantations on the land of another; surface owner's rights; building owner's rights; building lease.

SURSEOIR
- **EXÉCUTION** – **surseoir à l'exécution** – stay execution (of a judgment); reprieve (in the case of a capital sentence).
- **STATUER** – **surseoir à statuer** – defer a decision; stay or adjourn the proceedings.

SURSIS – stay; adjournment; deferment; suspension of sentence (ie the sentence is pronounced but not executed); probation; giving (an extension of) time for the payment of a debt.
- **EMPRISONNEMENT** – **sursis à l'emprisonnement** – postponement of imprisonment.
- **ÉPREUVE** – **sursis avec mise à l'épreuve** – probation.
- **EXÉCUTION** – **sursis à l'exécution** – stay of execution (of a judgment); reprieve (in the case of a capital sentence).
- **INCORPORATION** – **sursis de incorporation** – postponement of call-up.
- **PAIEMENT** – **sursis de paiement** – extension of time for payment.
- **STATUER** – **sursis à statuer** – adjournment, suspension or stay of proceedings.

SURSITAIRE – conscript whose period of service has been postponed.

SURVEILLANCE
- **HIÉRARCHIQUE** – **surveillance hiérarchique** – supervision by one's official (immediate) superior.

SURVEILLANT-CHEF – chief warder.

SURVENANCE
- **CONDITION** – **survenance d'une condition** – occurrence, fulfilment, performance or satisfaction of a condition.
- **DOMMAGE** – **survenance d'un dommage** – occurrence of damage.
- **ENFANT** – **survenance d'enfant** – subsequent birth of a child.

SURVOL
- **TRANSIT** – **survol en transit** – transit flight.

SUSCEPTIBLE
- **RECOURS** – **susceptible de recours** – subject to appeal; open to challenge.

SUSCRIPTION
- **ACTE de suscription** – solicitor's endorsement on the sealed envelope of a secret will.

SUSPECT – person being questioned by the police; suspect.
- **PÉRIODE suspecte** – period of relation back (doubtful period) from adjudication in bankruptcy to the date on which the debtor first ceased to meet his obligations. (The debtor's transactions during this period may be challenged by the creditors, acting through the trustee in bankruptcy).

SUSPENDRE
- **PRESCRIPTION** – **suspendre la prescription** – stop time running for the purposes of limitation or prescription.

SUSPENSIF
- **CONDITION suspensive** – condition precedent (of (in) a contract etc, to a transaction etc).

SUSPENSION – deferred sentence; suspension; adjournment.
- **AUDIENCE** – **suspension d'audience** – (short) adjournment of a hearing.
- **CONDAMNATION** – **suspension de la condamnation** – deferment of (conviction and) sentence.
- **CONDITIONNEL** – **suspension conditionnelle de l'exécution** – conditional remission (suspension) of sentence.
- **DÉLAI** – **suspension des délais** – suspension of the limitation or prescription period, after which it continues to run again from the point reached when the suspension began. (Cf INTERRUPTION.)

- **JUGEMENT** – décider la suspension du prononcé du jugement – defer (passing) judgment.
- **PEINE** – suspension de la peine – deferment of sentence.
- **POURSUITE** – suspension des poursuites individuelles – stay (suspension) of individual actions (a consequence of bankruptcy).
- **PRESCRIPTION** – suspension de la prescription – suspension of the limitation or prescription period, after which it continues to run again from the point reached when the suspension began. (Cf INTERRUPTION.)
- **PROCÉDURE** – suspension de la procédure – stay or interruption of the proceedings.
- **SÉANCE** – suspension de la séance – adjournment or interruption of the hearing.

SUSPICION
- **LÉGITIME** – suspicion légitime – (party's) reasonable suspicion of bias such as to disqualify a court from hearing a case.
  - **REQUÊTE** en suspicion légitime – application to a higher court for a case to be transferred to another court on grounds of bias.

SYMBOLIQUE – (of damages) nominal.

SYNALLAGMATIQUE – (of an agreement) involving reciprocal obligations (as in a contract of sale); bilateral.

SYNDIC – president (of a stock exchange, law society, etc); chairman (of a disciplinary committee); (formerly) court-appointed administrator of a bankruptcy (liquidator, trustee, receiver); manager of a building in co-ownership.

SYNDICAT – trade union; syndicate; group; consortium.
- **AGRICOLE** – syndicat agricole – farmers' union.
- **COMMUNE** – syndicat de communes – a public corporation established by two or more local authorities for the management of some common service or services.
- **COPROPRIÉTAIRE** – syndicat de copropriétaires – association of co-owners of a building.
- **ÉMISSION** – syndicat d'émission – issue syndicate.
- **ENTREPRISE** – syndicat d'entreprise – local or works union.
- **ÉTUDE** – syndicat d'études – study group.
- **GARANTIE** – syndicat de garantie – underwriting syndicate.
- **INDUSTRIEL** – syndicat industriel – industrial union.
- **MINIER** – syndicat minier – mining syndicate.
- **PATRONAL** – syndicat patronal – employers' federation.
- **PLACEMENT** – syndicat de placement – placing syndicate or pool.
- **PROFESSIONNEL** – syndicat professionnel – trade union; professional union; professional association.
- **UTILISATEUR** – syndicat d'utilisateurs – consumers' association.

SYNTHÉTIQUE
- **IMPÔT** synthétique – general tax; comprehensive tax.

SYSTÈME
- **JUDICIAIRE** – système judiciaire – organisation of the courts; judiciary; administration of justice.
- **LOI** – système de la loi – legal system.

~

T

TABLEAU
- **AVOCAT** – **tableau d'avocats** – roll (of counsel entitled to practise); bar roll.
- **ORDRE** – **tableau de l'ordre** – roll (of counsel entitled to practise); bar roll.

TÂCHE
- **RÉMUNÉRATION** à la tâche – piece-work (rate).

TACITE – implied.
- **RECONDUCTION** – **tacite reconduction (reconduction tacite)** – tacit renewal (of a lease etc).

TACITEMENT
- **ENTENDU** – **tacitement entendu** – implicitly (tacitly) agreed.

TALION
- **LOI du talion** – principle of retaliation (an eye for an eye).

TALON – counterfoil; talon for renewal of coupons.

TAPAGE
- **NOCTURNE** – **tapage nocturne** – creating a disturbance (disturbing the peace) at night.

TARDIF – out of time; too late.

TARDIVEMENT – out of time; too late.

TARDIVETÉ – being out of time.

TARIF
- **CRIMINEL** – **tarif criminel** – scale of costs (charges) in criminal proceedings (criminal costs).
- **NOTAIRE** – **tarif des notaires** – scale of solicitors' charges.

TAUX
- **COMPÉTENCE** – **taux de compétence** – financial limit on the jurisdiction (of a lower court); sum up to which a court has jurisdiction.
- **FORFAITAIRE** – **taux forfaitaire** – flat rate.
- **INTÉRÊT** – **taux d'intérêt** – rate of interest.
  - **NOMINAL** – **taux d'intérêt nominal** – nominal interest.

- **RESSORT** – **taux de ressort** – financial limit on the jurisdiction (of a lower court); sum up to which a court has jurisdiction.

TAXATION – assessment; price-fixing; taxation.
- **DÉPENS (FRAIS)** – **taxation des dépens (frais)** – taxation of costs.

TAXE – fee; due; duty; tax.
- **CHIFFRE D'AFFAIRES** – **taxe sur le chiffre d'affaires** – turnover tax.
- **CONSOMMATION** – **taxe de consommation** – excise duty.
- **DÉCLARATION** – **taxe de déclaration** – registration fee.
- **FRAIS** – **taxe des frais** – taxation of costs.
- **HABITATION** – **taxe d'habitation** – accommodation (housing) tax.
- **MUNICIPAL** – **taxe municipal** – town rate; rates; local-authority tax.
- **MUTATION** – **taxe de mutation** – transfer tax.
  - **PROPRIÉTÉ** – **taxe sur les mutations de propriété** – conveyancing duty.
- **ORDONNANCE de taxe** – order fixing the costs; certificate of taxed costs; allocatur; taxation of costs (by the president of the court on an appeal from a taxation (**vérification des dépens**) by the registry).
- **PARAFISCAL** – **taxe parafiscale** – tax payable to a body other than the state or a territorial (local) authority.
- **PROFESSIONNEL** – **taxe professionnelle** – trade tax.
- **TÉMOIN** – **taxe des témoins** – witness allowance; conduct-money.
- **VALEUR AJOUTÉE** – **taxe sur la valeur ajoutée** – value-added tax.

TECHNICIEN – expert; specialist.

TECHNIQUE
- **JURIDIQUE** – **d'après la technique juridique** – from a legal standpoint; technically (legally) (speaking).

TEL
- **QUEL** – **tel quel** – as inspected by the purchaser; with all faults.

TÉLÉOLOGIQUE

- **INTERPRÉTATION téléologique** – teleological (purposive) interpretation, ie based on the purpose or intention of the enactment.

TÉMOIGNAGE – evidence.

- **APPELER en témoignage** – call as a witness.
- **CONCORDANT** – **témoignages concordants** – corroborative evidence.
- **FAUX témoignage** – perjury (by a witness); false evidence (when given by an accused not under oath).
- **PORTER témoignage** – give evidence.
- **RETENIR un témoignage** – admit evidence.

TÉMOIGNER

- **REFUS de témoigner** – refusal to give evidence.

TÉMOIN

- **AURICULAIRE** – **témoin auriculaire** – witness who gives evidence of what he has himself heard.
- **CHARGE** – **témoin à charge** – prosecution witness.
- **DÉCHARGE** – **témoin à décharge** – defence witness.
- **DÉFAILLANT** – **témoin défaillant** – witness who fails to appear.
- **DÉPOSITION de témoins** – evidence given by witnesses.
- **INDEMNITÉ (de déplacement) des témoins** – witness allowance; conduct-money.
- **INSTRUMENTAIRE** – **témoin instrumentaire** – witness required for the official recording of certain transactions.
- **MORALITÉ** – **témoin de moralité** – witness to prove character.
- **OCULAIRE** – **témoin oculaire** – eyewitness.
- **PRESSION sur les témoins** – intimidation of witnesses.
- **PRODUIRE des témoins** – call evidence (witnesses).
- **REPROCHABLE** – **témoin reprochable** – witness who may be challenged as incompetent (to give evidence); impeachable witness.
- **TAXE des témoins** – witness allowance; conduct-money.

TEMPÉRAMENT – mitigation; (minor or partial) exception; modification; adaptation; adjustment; variation; qualification.

- **À tempérament** – by instalments; on hire-purchase.

- **SAUF tempérament** – subject to limited exceptions.

TEMPÉRER – qualify.

TEMPS

- **PROHIBÉ** – **temps prohibé** – close season.
- **VOULU** – **en temps voulu** – in (good) time.

TENANCIER – tenant; (hotel-)keeper.

TENANT

- **ABOUTISSANT** – **tenants et aboutissants** – adjacent properties.

TÈNEMENT – group of contiguous plots (of land).

TENEUR

- **JUGEMENT** – **teneur du jugement** – exact terms (essential content) of a judgment; ratio decidendi.
- **SERMENT** – **teneur du serment** – form of oath.

TENSION (Belg) – salary grade.

TENTATIVE – attempt.

TENU

- **INDÉFINIMENT** – **tenu indéfiniment** – liable without limit (for debts).
- **POUR** – **l'État, tenu pour les instituteurs** – the state, which is liable for the fault of a teacher.

TERME – time fixed or allowed by a contract, statute or court; (in plural) wording.

- **À terme** – time- ; forward.
- **DÉCHÉANCE du terme** – fact that all debts become immediately payable on insolvency, failure to provide security or acts by the debtor reducing the value of the security given.
- **DROIT** – **terme de droit** – time allowed by a contract or statute.
- **ÉCHÉANCE du terme** – expiry of the term or time(-limit); becoming due (of a debt, bill, etc).
- **ÉCHÉANCE** – **terme d'échéance** – date of payment.
- **EXTINCTIF** – **par l'arrivée du terme extinctif** – by lapse of time; by expiry of the time fixed.
- **GRÂCE** – **terme de grâce** – time for payment; further time allowed by the court when the **terme de droit** has expired.

- **JUDICIAIRE** – terme judiciaire – time-limit imposed by the court.
- **LIQUIDATION** – terme de (la) liquidation – date for settlement.
- **RETARD** – terme en retard – overdue instalment.

TERRAIN – plot (of land) without buildings; open plot (of land).
- **ENTENTE** – terrain d'entente – common ground.

TERRITOIRE
- **MANDAT** – territoire sous mandat – mandate; mandated territory.
- **TUTELLE** – territoire sous tutelle – trusteeship territory.

TESTAMENT – will.
- **AUTHENTIQUE** – testament authentique – public will; notarially recorded will; will recorded by a solicitor.
- **CONJOINT (CONJONCTIF)** – testament conjoint (conjonctif) – joint or reciprocal will (now illegal in France).
- **MARITIME** – testament maritime – will made at sea.
- **MILITAIRE** – testament militaire – military will; soldier's will.
- **MUTUEL** – testament mutuel – reciprocal will (now illegal in France).
- **MYSTIQUE** – testament mystique – secret will (placed in a sealed envelope endorsed by a solicitor).
- **NOTARIÉ** – testament notarié – public will; notarially recorded will; will recorded by a solicitor.
- **NUNCUPATIF** – testament nuncupatif – nuncupative will; oral will.
- **OLOGRAPHE** – testament olographe – holograph will (written entirely in the testator's own handwriting).
- **PRIVILÉGIÉ** – testament privilégié – privileged will.
- **PUBLIC** – testament (par acte) public – public will; notarially recorded will; will recorded by a solicitor.
- **RÉDACTION** du testament – drawing of a will.
- **RÉDIGER** un testament – draw a will.
- **RÉVOQUER** un testament – revoke a will.

TESTER – make a will.
- **CAPACITÉ** de tester – capacity to make a will.

TESTIMONIAL
- **PREUVE** testimoniale – oral evidence.

TÊTE
- **PARTAGE par tête** – division per capita.
- **SUCCÉDER (VENIR) par tête** – inherit per capita.

TEXTE – wording; legislation; provision(s); rule(s); regulations; enactment; (formal) document.
- **APPLICATION** – texte d'application – (implementing) regulations (made under an Act).
- **BASE** – textes de base – relevant texts (documents); basic provisions.
- **FONDAMENTAL** – texte fondamental – basic statute; basic provisions.
- **LÉGISLATIF** – textes législatifs – statute law; legislation (usually excluding subordinate legislation).
  - •• **RÉGLEMENTAIRE** – textes législatifs ou réglementaires – statutes and regulations.
- **RÉGLEMENTAIRE** – texte réglementaire – regulations; rules.
- **UNIQUE** – texte unique – consolidated legislation; consolidating Act, regulations, etc.
- **VERTU** – en vertu de ces textes – under these provisions.

THÉORIE
- **DOMINANT** – théorie dominante – predominant view (opinion); better opinion.
- **IMPRÉVISION** – théorie de l'imprévision – doctrine permitting the modification of, or release from, a contract owing to an unforeseen and fundamental change of circumstances; frustration of a contract by unforeseen events.

THÈSE – argument; contention; submission.
- **SOUSCRIRE** à une thèse – accept an argument.

TICKET
- **ALIMENTATION** – ticket d'alimentation – ration coupon.
- **MODÉRATEUR** – ticket modérateur – proportion of the cost of treatment not reimbursed by the social-security authorities.

TIERS – third party; third person; stranger (to a contract, the proceedings, etc); non-member.

- **ACQUÉREUR** – **tiers acquéreur** – third party or stranger to a transaction who acquires the property in question.
- **ARBITRE** – **tiers arbitre** – umpire.
- **ASSURÉ** – **tiers assuré** – beneficiary named in an insurance policy to which he is not a party.
- **DÉBITEUR** – **tiers débiteur** – debtor of a debtor; garnishee.
- **DÉTENTEUR** – **tiers détenteur** – third party into whose hands property has passed; owner of land subject to a mortgage not personally liable for the mortgage debt, eg a purchaser of land subject to a mortgage.
- **LÉSÉ** – **les tiers lésés peuvent s'adresser aux tribunaux** – the persons injured may apply to the courts.
- **OPPOSANT** – **tiers opposant** – third party applying to set aside a judgment adversely affecting his interests.
- **OPPOSITION** – **tierce opposition** – application by a third party (ie a person not represented in the proceedings) to set aside a judgment adversely affecting his interests.
  - **INCIDENT** – **tierce opposition incidente** – application by a third party incidental to pending proceedings to set aside a judgment.
  - **PRINCIPAL** – **tierce opposition principale** – application by a third party independent of pending proceedings to set aside a judgment.
- **PAYANT** – **tiers payant** – direct(-)payment (system), ie whereby the insurance fund, authority, etc pays the hospital, practitioner, etc direct.
- **PERSONNE** – **tierce personne** – person who assists a disabled person unable to do the ordinary things a person normally does for himself.
- **PROVISIONNEL** – **tiers provisionnel** – advance of one-third of the tax due for the current year.
- **RESPONSABLE** – **tiers responsable** – person vicariously liable.
- **SAISI** – **tiers saisi** – garnishee.

TIMBRE

- **DROIT de timbre** – stamp duty.
  - **PASSEPORT** – **droit de timbre sur les passeports** – passport fee.

TIRÉ – drawee.

TIRER – draw (bill of exchange etc).

- **ARGUMENT** – **tirer argument de** – rely on.
- **DE** – **tiré de** – (argument etc) based on.

TIREUR – drawer.

TITRE – document; security; title; claim; authority; qualification; (estimates) vote; (code) part; section. The French, Belgian and Luxembourg Civil Codes are divided into **livres** (books), **titres** (parts), **chapitres** (chapters), **sections** (sections) and **articles** (articles). The Swiss Civil Code is divided into **livres** (books), **parties** (parts), **titres** (sections), **chapitres** (chapters) and **articles** (articles).

- **À quel titre** – by what right.
- **ADIRÉ** – **titre adiré** – lost security, certificate or other document.
- **AUTHENTIQUE** – **titre authentique** – officially or notarially recorded document; document recorded by a solicitor.
- **CAUTION** – **à titre de caution** – as a surety.
- **CONTREFAIT** – **titre contrefait** – forged document.
- **CRÉANCE** – **titre de créance** – document incorporating a debt or obligation.
- **DÉPENSE** – **titre de dépense** – head of expenditure; expenditure vote.
- **DÉPÔT** – **titres en dépôt** – securities held on deposit.
- **DÉTENTION** – **titre de détention** – committal order.
- **ÉCROU** – **titre d'écrou** – committal order (warrant).
- **ENDOSSABLE** – **titre endossable** – negotiable instrument of title such as a bill of lading.
- **EXÉCUTOIRE** – **titre exécutoire** – (document embodying) authority to execute (enforce); writ of execution.
- **FALSIFIÉ** – **titre falsifié** – forged document.
- **FAUX titre** – forged document.
- **GAGE** – **titre de gage** – document of title to a pledge.
- **GARANTIE** – **au titre de la garantie** – under the guarantee.
- **GRACIEUX** – **à titre gracieux** – without consideration; gratuitously.
- **HYPOTHÉCAIRE** – **titre hypothécaire** – mortgage (deed).
- **INTERVERSION de titres** – position where a person not previously holding in his own

right now claims to do so in order to take advantage of prescription.

- **JURIDIQUE** – titre juridique – legal title.
- **JUSTE titre** – document constituting a good title to property, eg a conveyance (subject to any flaw or obstacle preventing it from taking effect), which serves as a basis for the ten- and twenty-year prescription periods; document which would have transferred ownership if the transferor had been the owner; ostensibly good title.
  - •• **À** – à juste titre – rightly.
- **JUSTIFIER par titres** – produce documentary evidence (to establish) that.
- **MOUVEMENT** – titre de mouvement – excise authority to transport goods whose movement is regulated, eg wines or spirits.
- **NÉGOCIABLE** – titre négociable – negotiable security.
- **NOMINATIF** – titre nominatif – registered security.
- **NOUVEL** – titre nouvel – subsequent recognition (of a debt), which constitutes a new title for the creditor.
- **ONÉREUX** – à titre onéreux – for consideration; for value.
- **OPPOSITION** – titre frappé d'opposition – security subject to a stop (order).
- **ORDRE** – titre à ordre – security payable (transferable) to order, ie by endorsement.
- **PAIEMENT** – titre de paiement – payment authorisation.
- **PARTICIPATIF** – titre participatif – participation certificate entitling to varying revenue and issued by public corporations or co-operatives.
- **PARTICULIER** – à titre particulier – (of gift, bequest, etc) relating to one or more individual items of property (not constituting a set of assets).
- **PERSONNEL** – à titre personnel – in his (her, their) personal capacity (capacities).
- **PORTEUR** – titre au porteur – bearer security.
- **PREUVE par titres** – documentary evidence.
- **PROPRIÉTÉ** – titre de propriété – document of title to property (proving ownership); title deed.
- **PUTATIF** – titre putatif – putative title.
- **RECETTE** – titre de recette – collection order.
- **RÉCOGNITIF** – titre récognitif – document replacing one that has been, or is in

danger of being, lost. (It amounts to a recognition of the obligation (right).)

- **SÉJOUR** – titre de séjour – residence permit.
- **SINCÉRITÉ d'un titre** – genuineness of a security, certificate or other document.
- **SUCCESSORAL** – à titre successoral – by inheritance.
- **TRANSMISSIBLE** – titre transmissible – negotiable security.
  - •• **NON** – titre non transmissible – non-assignable security.
- **UNIVERSEL** – à titre universel – (of bequest etc) relating to (the whole or) part of an independent set of assets together with the corresponding debts, eg a share of an estate or business.
- **UNIVERSITAIRE** – titre universitaire – university qualification.
- **VOYAGE** – titre de voyage – travel document.

TITRE-RESTAURANT – meal-ticket; luncheon voucher.

TITULAIRE (adj) – (of a civil servant) established.

TITULAIRE (noun) – holder; occupant; person entitled to; owner (of a right).
- **CONTRAT** – titulaire d'un contrat – contractor.
- **LICENCE** – titulaire de licence – licensee; licence-holder.
- **MARCHÉ** – titulaire du marché – supplier.
- **RECOURS** – titulaire du droit de recours – person entitled to appeal.

TITULARISATION – appointment as an established civil servant.

TOLÉRANCE
- **ACTE de (simple) tolérance** – act done with the express or tacit permission of the landowner which may be terminated at will.

TOMBER
- **COUP** – tomber sous le coup de – fall within (the ambit of); be covered (caught) by.
- **PRÉSOMPTION** – faire tomber une présomption – rebut (refute) a presumption.

TONTINE – contributory savings group in which the capital saved is divided among the survivors when the group is dissolved.

TORT – fault.

- **EXCLUSIF** – **(divorce prononcé) aux torts exclusifs du mari** – (divorce (decree) granted) against the husband.
- **MORAL** – **tort moral** – non-pecuniary injury (damage).
- **RÉCIPROQUE** – **(divorce prononcé) aux torts réciproques** – (divorce) based on the fault of both parties; (divorce (decree)) granted to both parties; (divorce) on grounds of mutual fault.
- **TRIBUNAL** – **le tribunal a eu tort** – the court erred.

TOTALISATION – aggregation.

TOUR
- **ÉCHELLE** – **droit (servitude) de tour d'échelle** – easement entitling the owner of the dominant property to place ladders on the servient property.
- **MAIN** – **tour de main** – know-how.
- **PRIORITÉ** – **tour de priorité** – (right of) precedence.
- **SCRUTIN** – **tour de scrutin** – ballot.

TOURNANT
- **JURISPRUDENCE** – **tournant de jurisprudence** – turning-point in the doctrine of the court(s) (in the case-law).

TOURNER
- **LOI** – **tourner la loi** – evade the law.

TRADITIO BREVE MANU – agreement conferring (true) possession on the previous custodian of the property in question.

TRADITION – delivery.
- **RÉEL** – **tradition réelle** – actual delivery.

TRADUIRE
- **JUGE** – **traduire devant un juge** – bring before a judge.
- **JURIDICTION** – **traduire devant une juridiction répressive** – prosecute.
- **JUSTICE** – **traduire en justice** – bring before a court.

TRAFIQUANT – (dishonest) dealer or trader; trafficker.

TRAHISON – treason.

TRAITE – draft; bill of exchange.
- **BLANC** – **traite des blanches** – white slave trade.
- **COMPLAISANCE** – **traite de complaisance** – accommodation bill.

- **DOCUMENTAIRE** – **traite documentaire** – draft accompanying documents of title to goods sold.
- **VUE** – **traite à vue** – sight draft.

TRAITÉ
- **ADHÉSION à un traité** – accession to a treaty.
- **ADHÉSION** – **traité d'adhésion** – friendly agreement on the transfer of (or amount of compensation for) property with respect to which expropriation proceedings have commenced.
- **AMIABLE** – **traité amiable** – friendly agreement on the transfer of (or amount of compensation for) property with respect to which expropriation proceedings have commenced.
- **DÉNONCER un traité** – denounce a treaty.

TRAITEMENT – salary; treatment; processing.
- **BUDGÉTAIRE** – **traitement budgétaire** – (civil servant's) basic salary.
- **LIBERTÉ** – **traitement en liberté** – non-custodial treatment.
- **MAUVAIS traitements** – cruelty; ill-treatment.
- **NATION** – **traitement de la nation la plus favorisée** – most-favoured-nation treatment.
- **RAPPEL de traitement** – back pay; payment of arrears of salary.

TRANCHE – instalment; band or slice (of taxable income); (income) bracket; allocation of funds.
- **POPULATION** – **tranche de la population** – population band; section of the population.
- **REVENU** – **tranche de revenus** – income band.

TRANCHER – settle.
- **CONFLIT** – **trancher un conflit** – settle a dispute.

TRANSACTION – settlement or compromise of a dispute; transaction; composition; compromise (compound) settlement.
- **AMIABLE** – **transaction amiable** – friendly settlement.
- **FICTIF** – **transaction fictive** – fictitious (notional) transaction.

TRANSACTIONNEL
- **AMENDE transactionnelle** – police fine; (Belg) payment (fine) in settlement of a regulatory offence (fine by way of settlement).

TRANSCRIPTION – entry in a register; registration; registration of a transaction in the Land Registry.

- **CONDITIONNEL** – **transcription conditionnelle** – provisional entry; caution; warning.
- **HYPOTHÉCAIRE** – **transcription hypothécaire** – registration of mortgages.
- **IMMOBILIER** – **transcription immobilière** – land registration.

TRANSCRIRE – enter; register.

TRANSFÈREMENT – transfer of prisoners.

TRANSFERT – share transfer.

- **CAPITAL** – **transfert de capital affecté** – specific capital grant.
- **CRÉANCE** – **transfert de créance** – assignment of a chose in action, ie of the right to receive payment of a debt or performance of some other obligation.
- **DOMICILE** – **transfert de domicile** – change of permanent residence.
- **GARANTIE de transfert** – guarantee of the right to transfer profits.
- **GARANTIE** – **transfert en garantie** – transfer of ownership (but not possession) by way of guarantee.
- **PRONONCER le transfert de la propriété** – declare that the property has passed.
- **PROPRIÉTÉ** – **portant transfert de propriété** – transferring (passing of) ownership (of) (property (in)).
- **RISQUE** – **transfert des risques** – passing of the risk, eg on a sale.
- **SUCCESSION** – **transfert par succession** – passing by inheritance.
- **SUCCESSORAL** – **transfert successoral** – passing by inheritance.

TRANSFUGE – defector.

TRANSGRESSER

- **POUVOIR** – **transgresser ses pouvoirs** – exceed one's powers (authority).

TRANSGRESSION

- **CONSTITUTION** – **transgression de la constitution** – violation of the constitution.

TRANSIGER – settle; compromise; compound.

TRANSITAIRE – customs agent.

TRANSITOIRE – transitional.

TRANSLATION

- **DOMICILE** – **translation de domicile** – change of permanent residence.
- **HYPOTHÈQUE** – **translation d'hypothèque** – transfer of mortgage.

TRANSMETTRE – transfer; transmit.

TRANSMISSION – transfer; passing.

- **ACTE DE PROCÉDURE** – **transmission des actes de procédure** – notification of process.
- **PARTICULIER** – **transmission à titre particulier** – transfer of (succession to) one or more specific items of property (not subject to the personal debts of one's predecessor in title).
- **UNIVERSEL** – **transmission universelle** – transfer (passing) of an entire estate.
    - **TITRE** – **transmission à titre universel** – transfer of or succession to (the whole or) part of an independent set of assets together with the corresponding debts, eg a share of an estate or business.

TRANSPORT

- **CONTRAT de transport** – contract of carriage.
- **CRÉANCE** – **transport de créance** – assignment of a chose in action, ie of the right to receive payment of a debt or performance of some other obligation.
- **JUDICIAIRE** – **transport judiciaire** – judgment ordering a transfer of property.
- **JUSTICE** – **transport de justice** – inspection of the site, locus (in quo), scene of the crime or premises by the court.
- **LIEU** – **transport sur les lieux** – inspection of the site, locus (in quo), scene of the crime or premises by the court.
- **MARGE** – **transport en marge** – marginal entry.
- **PRIX** – **transport du prix** – transfer of the proceeds.
- **SUR** – **transport sur** – transfer to.

TRANSPORT-CESSION – assignment of a chose in action, debt, obligation, claim, etc.

TRANSPORTEUR – carrier.

TRAVAIL

- **ACCIDENT** du travail – industrial accident (injury).
- **ACCORD** collectif du travail – collective agreement.
- **CODE** du travail – Employment Code.
- **CONFLIT** du travail – industrial dispute; labour dispute.
- **CONTRAT** de travail – contract of service (service contract); contract of employment (employment contract).
  - •• **COLLECTIF** – contrat collectif (de travail) – collective (labour) agreement.
- **DIFFÉREND** collectif (de travail) (différend du travail) – labour (industrial) dispute.
- **FORCÉ** – travail forcé – forced labour; (in plural) penal servitude.
- **INCAPACITÉ** de travail – unfitness for work; disablement.
- **INTÉRÊT** – travail d'intérêt général – community service.
- **INTÉRIMAIRE** – entreprise de travail intérimaire – temporary-employment agency.
- **PRÉPARATOIRE** – travaux préparatoires – legislative history; drafting history; preparatory documents; travaux préparatoires.
- **TÂCHE** – travail à la tâche – piece-work.

TRÉFONCIER (adj) – relating to the subsoil.

- **REDEVANCE** tréfoncière – surface owner's royalty (ie royalty payable by a mining company to the surface owner).

TRÉFONCIER (noun) – owner of the subsoil, minerals, etc.

TRÉFONDS – subsoil; minerals.

TRÉSOR – treasure trove.

- **BON** du Trésor – Treasury bond.
- **EFFET** du Trésor – Treasury bill.
- **PUBLIC** – Trésor public – Treasury.

TRÉSORERIE – accounts department; paymaster's department; accountant-general's department; cash.

- **BESOINS** de trésorerie – cash(-flow) requirements.
- **COMPTE** de trésorerie – treasury suspense account; (in plural) cash accounts.
  - •• **GESTION** – compte de gestion de trésorerie – treasurer's management account.
- **DISPONIBILITÉS** de trésorerie – available funds; liquid assets; cash resources.

TRÉSORIER – chief accountant; treasurer.

TRÉSORIER-PAYEUR GÉNÉRAL – paymaster-general; accountant-general.

TRIBUNAL

- **ACCÈS** aux tribunaux – access to the courts.
- **ADMINISTRATIF** – tribunal administratif – Administrative Court.
- **ARBITRAL** – tribunal arbitral – arbitration tribunal.
  - •• **PARITAIRE** – tribunal arbitral paritaire – joint arbitration tribunal.
- **ARMÉE** – tribunal aux armées – court martial.
- **CIVIL** – tribunal civil – civil court.
- **COLLÉGIAL** – tribunal collégial – court consisting of several members; bench.
- **COMMERCE** – tribunal de commerce – Commercial Court.
- **CONFLIT** – Tribunal des conflits – court for settling questions of jurisdiction and inconsistent judgments between administrative courts on the one hand and ordinary courts on the other; Jurisdiction Court.
- **CONSTITUÉ** – tribunal régulièrement constitué – properly constituted court.
- **CORRECTIONNEL** – tribunal correctionnel – (regional) Criminal Court (for the trial of misdemeanours).
- **DISCIPLINAIRE** – tribunal disciplinaire – disciplinary tribunal.
- **DIVISION** – tribunal de division – (Sw) first-instance court martial; divisional court martial.
- **DOMICILE** – tribunal du domicile du défendeur – court of the defendant's place of residence.
- **DROIT COMMUN** – tribunal de droit commun – ordinary court.
- **ECCLÉSIASTIQUE** – tribunal ecclésiastique – ecclesiastical court.
- **ENFANT** – tribunal pour enfants – youth court; formerly juvenile court.
- **EXCEPTION** – tribunal d'exception – (1) court of limited jurisdiction; specialised court, ie any court other than the **Tribunal de grande instance** and the Court of Appeal, eg the **tribunal d'instance**, the **tribunal de commerce**, and the **conseil de prud'hommes**; (2) specialised criminal court, eg the **juridictions pour**

mineurs, the **tribunaux aux armées** and the **Haute Cour de justice**.

- **EXÉCUTION** – **tribunal chargé de l'exécution** (**tribunal d'exécution**) – execution court, ie court responsible for matters concerning the execution (enforcement) of judgments.
- **EXPERT près les tribunaux** – expert appointed by the court; court expert.
- **EXTRAORDINAIRE** – **tribunal extraordinaire** – special court.
- **FOND** – **tribunal du fond** – trial court; tribunal of fact; (in plural) trial and appeal courts; courts below.
- **FORCE ARMÉE** – **tribunal territorial des forces armées** – wartime court martial.
- **GRANDE INSTANCE** – see INSTANCE below.
- **INCOMPÉTENT** – **tribunal incompétent** – court lacking jurisdiction.
- **INFÉRIEUR** – **tribunal inférieur** – lower court; court below.
- **INSTANCE** – **tribunal d'instance** – district court.
  - •• **GRAND** – **tribunal de grande instance** – Regional Court.
  - •• **PREMIER** – **tribunal de première instance** – court of first instance; (Belg) Regional Court.
- **JEUNE** – **tribunal pour jeunes** (not used in France) – youth court; (formerly) juvenile court.
- **JUDICIAIRE** – **tribunal judiciaire** – ordinary court.
- **MARITIME** – **tribunal maritime** – admiralty court.
  - •• **COMMERCIAL** – **tribunal maritime commercial** – maritime criminal court.
- **MILITAIRE** – **tribunal militaire** – court martial; military court.
  - •• **ARMÉE** – **tribunal militaire aux armées** – field court martial.
  - •• **CASSATION** – **tribunal militaire de cassation** (Sw) – Courts-Martial Appeal Court.
  - •• **INTERNATIONAL** – **tribunal militaire international** – international military tribunal.
- **MINEUR** – **tribunal pour mineurs** (not used in France) – youth court; (formerly) juvenile court.
- **OCCUPATION** – **tribunal d'occupation** – occupation court.
- **PARITAIRE** – **tribunal paritaire** – joint tribunal.

- •• **BAIL** – **tribunal paritaire de baux ruraux** – agricultural land tribunal.
- **PEUPLE** – **tribunal du peuple** – people's court.
- **POLICE** – **tribunal de (simple) police** – court of summary jurisdiction; police court; district court.
  - •• **CORRECTIONNEL** – **tribunal de police correctionnelle** – (regional) Criminal Court (for the trial of misdemeanours).
- **PREMIÈRE INSTANCE** – see INSTANCE above.
- **RATTACHÉ** – **tribunal rattaché** – court that receives assistance from the judges of another court.
- **RATTACHEMENT** – **tribunal de rattachement** – court which provides judges to assist those of another court.
- **RENVOI** – **tribunal de renvoi** – court to which a case is sent, transferred or remitted.
- **RÉPRESSIF** – **tribunal répressif** – criminal court.
- **RÉVISION** – **tribunal de révision** – retrial court.
- **SAISI** – **tribunal saisi de l'instance** – court before which the case is brought; court dealing with the case.
- **SÉCURITÉ SOCIALE** – **tribunal des affaires de sécurité sociale** – social-security (appeal) tribunal; social-security court.
- **SIMPLE POLICE** – see POLICE above.
- **SITUATION**
  - •• **CHOSE** – **tribunal de la situation de la chose** – court of the place where the subject-matter is situated.
- **SOMMAIRE** – **tribunal sommaire** – court applying a summary procedure.
- **TORT** – **le tribunal a eu tort** – the court erred.
- **TRADUIRE devant un tribunal** – bring before a court.
- **TUTELLE** – **tribunal des tutelles** – guardianship court.

TRIPLIQUE – rejoinder.

TROUBLE – disturbance; disorder; interference; trespass; nuisance.

- **GARANTIE des troubles** – covenant or warranty for peaceful possession.
- **MENTAL** – **trouble mental** – mental disorder.

- **POSSESSION** – **trouble de la possession** – trespass; nuisance; interference with (a person's) possession (quiet enjoyment).
- **VOISINAGE** – **trouble dépassant les obligations (ordinaires) de voisinage** – nuisance.

TUTELLE – guardianship; supervision.
- **ADMINISTRATIF** – **tutelle administrative** – administrative supervision.
- **AUTORITÉ de tutelle** – supervising authority.
- **CONSEIL de tutelle** – committee of guardians; guardianship council; (UN) Trusteeship Council.
- **DATIF** – **tutelle dative** – guardianship conferred by the family council (**conseil de famille**).
- **FONDS de tutelle** – trust funds.
- **JUGE des tutelles** – guardianship judge.
- **LÉGAL** – **tutelle légale** – statutory guardianship.
- **OFFICIEUX** – **tutelle officieuse** – guardianship subject to certain conditions exercised by a person who assumes responsibility for the education and maintenance of a minor; special guardianship.

- **PÉNAL** – **tutelle pénale** – (formerly) control of habitual offenders after they have served a prison sentence, involving either detention or conditional release according to the circumstances; preventive control of recidivists; preventive supervision.
- **PRESTATION SOCIALE** – **tutelle aux prestations sociales** – guardianship limited to (the administration of) social-security benefits.
- **SOUS** – **territoire sous tutelle** – trusteeship territory.

TUTEUR – guardian.
- **AD HOC** – **tuteur ad hoc** – guardian appointed for a specific transaction where the normal guardian cannot act on account of a conflict of interest; ad hoc guardian.
- **DATIF** – **tuteur datif** – guardian appointed by the family council.
- **LÉGAL** – **tuteur légal** – statutory guardian.
- **SUBROGÉ(-)tuteur** – auxiliary or supervising guardian.
- **TESTAMENTAIRE** – **tuteur testamentaire** – guardian appointed by will; testamentary guardian.

—

U

ULTRA PETITA – situation where the court grants more than has been claimed or settles points not submitted to it.

ULTRA VIRES – situation where an heir (legatee or partner) is liable for debts or liabilities in excess of what he has received in the succession (partnership).

UNILATÉRAL
- **ACTE unilatéral** – unilateral transaction (undertaking).

UNION
- **COMMUNE** – **union de communes** – union of local-government districts.
- **CONJUGAL** – **union conjugale** – consortium.
- **CRÉANCIER** – **union des créanciers** – general body of the creditors of a bankrupt (creditors' meeting).
- **FAILLITE** – **union en faillite** – broken-down marriage.
- **LIBRE** – **union libre** – cohabitation (of two unmarried partners).
- **PERSONNEL** – **union personnelle** – personal union, ie where two states have the same head of state but remain otherwise independent of each other.
- **RÉEL** – **union réelle** – long-term union between two states having a common head of state and certain common constitutional organs (especially in the fields of foreign affairs and defence), while remaining in other respects independent of each other.

UNIQUE
- **ARTICLE unique** – leave untranslated.
- **TEXTE unique** – consolidated legislation; consolidating Act, regulations, etc.

UNIVERSALITÉ
- **DROIT** – **universalité de droit** – comprehensive group of assets and liabilities attached to a person or serving a specific purpose; estate.
- **FAIT** – **universalité de fait** – independent or separate mass, group or set of assets responsible for its own debts (eg a deceased's estate or a business); estate.

UNIVERSEL – relating to a comprehensive group of assets and liabilities (eg an estate or business).
- **HÉRITIER universel** – heir entitled to the whole of the deceased's estate .
- **TRANSMISSION universelle** – transfer (passing) of an entire estate.
  - **TITRE** – **transmission à titre universel** – transfer of or succession to (the whole or) part of an independent set of assets together with the corresponding debts, eg a share of an estate or business.

URBANISME – town planning; urban planning.
- **CODE d'urbanisme** – town-planning code.
- **PLAN d'urbanisme** – development plan; structure plan.

URGENCE
- **ÉTAT d'urgence** – state of emergency.
- **PROCÉDURE d'urgence** – (procedure for) urgent cases.
  - **DATE** – **procédure d'urgence à date fixe** – fixed-date urgent proceedings.

USAGE – user; usage; practice; custom; right in rem to use the property of another to satisfy one's personal needs and those of one's family for life; usus.
- **CADEAU d'usage** – customary (traditional) present.
- **CESSION d'usage** – assignment (transfer) of a right of user (right to use).
- **CONTINU** – **usage continu** – continuous user.
- **DÉPÔT d'usage** – deposit for use.
- **DONATION d'usage** – customary (traditional) gift.
- **DROIT d'usage** – right of user; right in rem to use the property of another to satisfy one's personal needs and those of one's family for life; usus.
- **FAUX** – **usage de faux** – uttering; making use of forged documents with intent to defraud.
- **GUERRE** – **usage de la guerre** – custom of war.
- **IMMÉMORIAL** – **usage immémorial** – user since time immemorial.

- **JUDICIAIRE** – usages judiciaires – court practice.
- **LÉGITIME** – usage légitime – lawful user; rightful user.
- **PERPÉTUEL** – usage perpétuel – constant user.
- **PRIVATIF** – usage privatif – exclusive user.
- **VOL** d'usage d'un véhicule – unauthorised use of a motor vehicle.

USUCAPER – acquire property or other rights by enjoyment (adverse possession, prescription) over a long period of time.

USUCAPION – acquiring property or other rights by enjoyment (adverse possession, prescription) over a long period of time; usucapion.

USUFRUIT – usufruct; life tenancy; life interest.
- **SUCCESSORAL** – usufruit successoral – life interest of the surviving spouse.

USUFRUITIER – usufructuary; life tenant.

USURE – usury; lending at an unconscionable rate of interest.

USURPATION – illegal use of honours, uniforms, names, titles, etc to which one is not entitled; illegal exercise of functions.
- **FONCTION** – usurpation de fonctions – usurpation (illegal exercise) of office.
- **IDENTITÉ** – usurpation d'identité – impersonation.

USUS – right to use and possess a thing without being entitled to its produce.

UTÉRIN – of the half-blood on the mother's side; born of the same mother but of a different father.

UTILEMENT – effectively.

UTILITÉ
- **GÉNÉRAL** – utilité générale – public interest.
- **MODÈLE** d'utilité – registered design.
- **PRIVÉ** – pour cause d'utilité privée – for a private interest.
- **PUBLIC** – utilité publique – public interest; public benefit.
  - **ASSOCIATION** reconnue d'utilité publique – charity; recognised association.
  - **DÉCLARÉ** d'utilité publique – classified (as being of public interest).
  - **ÉTABLISSEMENT** d'utilité publique – public corporation promoting the public interest; charitable corporation.
  - **EXPROPRIATION** pour cause d'utilité publique – expropriation in the public interest.
  - **INSTITUTION** d'utilité publique – institution promoting the public interest; charitable institution.

V

VACANCE

- **DÉCLARER une vacance** – advertise (announce) a vacancy; declare a post vacant.
- **JUDICIAIRE** – **vacances judiciaires** – court vacation.
- **SUCCESSION** – **vacance de la succession** – failure of heirs; vacant succession; unclaimed estate; bona vacantia.

VACATION – (in plural) (compensation for) time lost in attending proceedings; time spent in examining a case, evidence, etc; fees; allowances (for work by a professional adviser, expert, etc); court vacation.

- **AFFAIRE de vacation** – vacation matter.
- **CHAMBRE des vacations** – (formerly) vacation court.

VAGABOND – vagrant.

VAGABONDAGE – vagrancy.

VAIN

- **PÂTURE** – **(droit de) vaine pâture** – right of common; common of pasture exercisable after mowing or harvest.

VALEUR – value; merits; security.

- **AFFECTIF** – **valeur affective** – sentimental value.
- **AJOUTÉ** – **valeur ajoutée** – value added.
- **CADASTRAL** – **valeur du revenu cadastral** – rateable value.
- **CONSERVATION des valeurs** – safe custody of securities.
- **CONSTITUTIONNEL** – **valeur constitutionnelle** – rank as constitutional law.
- **CONVENTIONNEL** – **avoir valeur conventionnelle** – rank as (be treated as) part of a convention, treaty, etc.
- **FICTIF** – **valeur fictive** – notional value.
- **FISCAL** – **valeur fiscale** – value for tax purposes.
- **FOURNI** – **valeur fournie** – value received (amount owed by the drawer to the payee).
- **IRRECOUVRABLE** – **valeur irrecouvrable** – irredeemable security.
- **JURIDIQUE** – **valeur juridique** – legal force.
- **LIQUIDATIF** – **valeur liquidative** – value on liquidation; liquidation value.

- **LITIGE** – **valeur en (du) litige** – value of the subject-matter; sum involved; amount in dispute.
- **LITIGIEUX** – **valeur litigieuse** – value of the subject-matter; sum involved; amount in dispute.
- **LOCATIF** – **valeur locative** – rental value.
  - •• **CADASTRAL** – **valeur locative cadastrale** – rateable value.
- **MOBILIER** – **valeur mobilière (négociable)** – (transferable) security.
- **MORAL** – **valeur morale** – sentimental value.
- **NOMINAL** – **valeur nominale** – nominal value.
- **OBLIGATION de valeur** – fixed-value debt.
- **OBLIGATOIRE** – **valeur obligatoire** – binding effect.
- **PROBANT** – **valeur probante** – evidential value; probative value.
  - •• **ÉLÉMENT** – **valeur probante des éléments** – weight of evidence.
- **RACHAT** – **valeur de rachat** – surrender value.
- **REÇU** – **valeur reçue** – value received.
- **REVENU**
  - •• **CADASTRAL** – **valeur du revenu cadastral** – rateable value.
  - •• **FIXE** – **valeur à revenu fixe** – fixed-interest security.
- **TRÉSOR** – **valeurs du Trésor** – Treasury bills.
- **VÉNAL** – **valeur vénale** – market value.

VALIDER

- **SERVICE** – **valider les services antérieurs** – have previous service credited (for pension purposes).

VALIDITÉ

- **DURÉE de validité** – currency (of a measure etc).
- **JUGEMENT de validité** – judgment confirming the validity of a garnishee order (ie an attachment of a debt) and transferring the title to the debt to the attaching creditor.

VALISE

- **DIPLOMATIQUE** – **valise diplomatique** – diplomatic bag.

VALOIR

- **FAIRE valoir** – raise; claim; submit; argue; assert; put forward; advance; plead (in one's defence); adduce; sue for; present (one's case); exercise; enforce.

VENTE

- **AMIABLE** – **vente amiable** – sale by private treaty.
- **BOULE DE NEIGE** – **vente à la boule de neige** – sale at a discount on condition that the purchaser introduces other purchasers; snowball selling.
- **CORRESPONDANCE** – **vente par correspondance** – mail-order (retailing).
- **CRÉDIT** – **vente à crédit** – credit sale.
- **CRIÉE** – **vente à la criée** – sale of movables or immovables by public auction.
- **CRI PUBLIC** – **vente à cri public** – public auction.
- **DÉBALLAGE** – **vente au déballage** – special-offer sale (from temporary premises).
- **DÉTAIL** – **vente à détail** – retailing.
- **DOMICILE** – **vente à domicile** – door-to-door selling.
- **DROIT SUCCESSIF** – **vente de droits successifs** – sale of one's right to an inheritance; sale of an expectancy.
- **ÉCHANTILLON** – **vente sur échantillon** – sale by sample.
- **ENCAN** – **vente à l'encan** – sale by auction.
- **ENCHÈRE** – **vente aux enchères** – sale by auction.
- **ENVOI FORCÉ** – **vente par envoi forcé** – unsolicited postal sale.
- **ESSAI** – **vente à l'essai** – sale on approval; sale or return.
- **ÉVALUATION** – **vente sur évaluation** – sale at an estimated price.
- **FONDS PERDU** – **vente à fonds perdu(s)** – sale for a rentcharge.
- **FORCÉ** – **vente forcée** – sale in execution; forced sale.
- **GRÉ À GRÉ** – **vente de gré à gré** – sale to a willing purchaser (at arm's length); sale by private treaty (as opposed to an auction); sale on the open market.
- **GROS** – **vente en gros** – wholesale.
- **HÉRÉDITÉ** – **vente d'hérédité** – sale of an inheritance; sale of one's rights in an estate.
- **JUDICIAIRE** – **vente judiciaire** – sale by the court.
- **JUSTICE** – **vente en justice** – sale by the court.

- **LIVRER** – **vente à livrer** – sale for delivery (ie within a stated period).
- **POURSUITE** – **vente sur poursuite** – sale in execution.
- **PUBLIC** – **vente publique** – public auction.
- **REFUS** de vente – refusal by a trader to sell or provide his usual services (a criminal offence).
- **RÉMÉRÉ** – **vente à réméré** – sale with an option to repurchase.
- **SIMULÉ** – **vente simulée** – fictitious sale.
- **SUCCESSORAL** – **vente successorale** – sale of one's right to an inheritance; sale of an expectancy.
- **TEMPÉRAMENT** – **vente à tempérament** – instalment sale (hire purchase).
- **TERME** – **vente à terme** – forward sale.
  - •• **PROMESSE** de vente à terme – option to purchase.

VENTILATION – apportionment (breakdown) of the total proceeds of a sale between the various items sold.

- **OPÉRER** une ventilation entre – make a distinction between.

VENTILER – apportion; break down (figures).

VERBAL – oral.

VERBALISER – make a report; (of a police officer etc) give (a motorist) a ticket.

VERDICT – decision (of a criminal court); finding; reply of the Assize Court and jury to the questions put at the end of the hearing.

VÉRIFICATION – audit.

- **CONDITION** – **vérification des conditions à remplir** – procedure for determining whether the conditions are satisfied.
- **DÉPENS** – **vérification des dépens** – review by the registrar of his (or the court's) original assessment (**liquidation**) of costs. (If the litigant is still not satified he may apply to the president of the court for an order fixing the costs.)
- **ÉCRITURE** – **vérification d'écriture** – procedure to establish the genuineness of a document that has been challenged; court procedure to establish or disprove a person's signature or handwriting.
- **IDENTITÉ** – **vérification d'identité** – forcible checking of a person's identity by the police involving his detention on the premises during the process; identity check.

- **PERSONNEL** – vérification(s) personnelle(s) du juge = inspection of the locus by the judge.
- **POUVOIR** – vérification des pouvoirs – examination of credentials.

VÉRIFIER – check; examine; verify; satisfy oneself.
- **SI** – vérifier si – determine (ascertain, consider) whether.
  - •• **COUR** – la Cour vérifie si – the court must satisfy itself that.

VERSEMENT
- **ESPÈCE** – versement en espèces – payment in cash.
- **FONDS** – versement des fonds par l'acquéreur – payment of the purchase money.
- **PROVISIONNEL** – versement provisionnel – payment in advance.
- **TAXE** – versements représentatifs de la taxe sur les salaires – payments in lieu of salary tax.

VERSER
- **DOSSIER** – verser au dossier – file a document (in court).
- **ERREUR** – verser dans l'erreur – err.

VIAGER
- **RENTE** viagère – life annuity.

VICE – defect.
- **APPARENT** – vice apparent – patent defect.
- **CACHÉ** – vice caché – latent (hidden) defect.
- **CONSENTEMENT** – vice du consentement – defect in consent (ie error, fraud or duress); vitiated consent; absence of consent.
- **EXPLOITATION** – vice d'exploitation – faulty organisation.
- **FOND** – vice de fond – essential defect; substantive defect.
- **FORME** – vice de forme – formal (procedural) defect (error, irregularity).
- **GARANTIE** des vices – warranty that goods or animals sold are free of faults or defects.
- **POSSESSION** – vice de la possession – defect in possession.
- **PROCÉDURE** – vice de procédure – procedural defect (error, irregularity).
- **RÉDHIBITOIRE** – vice rédhibitoire – hidden defect rendering a thing sold unfit for its intended purpose and entitling the purchaser to rescind the sale or obtain a reduction in

price; breach of an implied condition of suitability and merchantable quality.
- **TITRE** – vices du titre – defects in title.
- **VOLONTÉ** – vice de volonté – absence of the necessary intention or consent (owing to error, fraud, duress, etc); factor vitiating consent or intention.

VICIER – vitiate (invalidate, flaw) (proceedings etc).

VICIEUX – defective.

VICTIME
- **DE** – victime de – prejudiced by.
- **FAUTE** de la victime – contributory negligence.
- **INFRACTION** – Commission d'indemnisation des victimes d'infractions pénales (dont l'auteur est inconnu ou insolvable) – Criminal Injuries Compensation Board.

VIDE
- **JURIDIQUE** – vide juridique – gap (omission, lacuna) in the law.

VIDER
- **DIFFÉREND** – vider un différend – settle a dispute.
- **LITIGE** – vider le litige – settle a case.

VIDUITÉ
- **DÉLAI** de viduité – period of three hundred days during which a woman may not remarry (after the death of her husband or the cessation of cohabitation preceding divorce).
- **DROIT** de viduité – widow's right to maintenance from her late husband's estate for a limited period.

VIE
- **CERTIFICAT** de vie – life certificate.
- **COMMUNAUTÉ** de vie – consortium and cohabitation; married (conjugal) life.
- **COMMUNE**
  - •• **REPRISE** de la vie commune – resumption of cohabitation (conjugal relations).
  - •• **RUPTURE** de la vie commune – cessation of cohabitation; living apart; de facto separation; termination of consortium either by prolonged de facto separation (six years) or by supervening permanent insanity.
- **INFRACTIONS** contre la vie et l'intégrité de la personne – offences against the person (including homicide).

VIF

- **ENTRE vifs** – inter vivos.

VIGILANCE

- **COMITÉ de vigilance** – (private) watch committee; vigilance committee; vigilante group.

VIGILANT – acting with due care and attention.

VIGNETTE((-)AUTO(MOBILE)) –
vehicle (licence) tax (certificate); vehicle-tax (road-fund) licence; tax disc.

VIGUEUR

- **ENTRÉE en vigueur** – (Act) entry (coming) into force; (regulations, rules, etc) coming into operation; (Act, regulations, rules, etc) commencement.
- **MISE en vigueur** – bringing into force; commencement.
- **RÈGLEMENTS en vigueur** – standing regulations; existing regulations.

VILETÉ

- **PRIX** – vileté de prix – totally inadequate price (ground of nullity of contract).

VILLE

- **OUVERT** – ville ouverte – (international law) open (ie undefended) city.

VIOL – rape.

VIOLATION – violation; infringement;
breach; harm; wrong.

- **BREVET** – violation de brevet – infringement of a patent.
- **CLÔTURE** – violation de clôture – illegal breaking and entry of closed premises; breach of close; breaking a close.
- **CONSTITUTION** – violation de la constitution – breach of the constitution.
- **CONTRAT** – violation de (du) contrat – breach of contract.
- **CORPS** – violation de corps par imprudence (Sw) – causing bodily harm by negligence.
- **DOMICILE** – violation de domicile – violation of the privacy (sanctity) of the home; trespass on domestic premises; violation of domestic privacy; unlawful entry of a person's home.
- **FORME** – violation des formes – failure to comply with formal (procedural) requirements.
- **LOI** – violation de la loi – error of law (ground of appeal to the Court of Cassation).

VIOLENCE – duress.

- **AUTEUR de la violence** – person using duress.
- **LÉGER** – violences légères – minor assaults.
- **VOIE DE FAIT** – violences et voies de fait – assaults.

VIOLENTER

- **PERSONNE violentée** – person on whom duress is exercised.

VIREMENT – remittance; giro transfer; virement.

VIRIL

- **PART virile** – equal share; separate share.

VISA – visa; memorandum certifying that a formality has been complied with; signature by the drawee of a cheque certifying funds are available; countersignature; initials.

VISER – specify; involve; countersign; initial.

VISIBILITÉ

- **SERVITUDE de visibilité** – obligation to remove or not to erect constructions interfering with visibility on a road.

VISITE – inspection; search; examination.

- **CORPOREL** – visite corporelle (Sw) – personal search; search of the person.
- **DOMICILIAIRE** – visite domiciliaire – (house) search.
- **DROIT de visite** – right to inspect; right of search; right to stop and search; right of access.
- **LIEU** – visite des lieux – inspection of the site, locus (in quo), scene of the crime or premises by the court.

VOCATION – right (eg to a usufruct).

- **AVOIR** – y ayant vocation – having the necessary powers (authority).
- **HÉRÉDITAIRE** – vocation héréditaire – entitlement to inherit.
- **SUCCESSORAL** – vocation successorale – right to inherit on (an) intestacy.

VOIE – way; street; highway; channel.

- **ACTION** – par voie d'action – by bringing legal proceedings.
- **ADMINISTRATIF** – voie administrative – administrative channels.
- **ATTROUPEMENT sur la voie publique** – unlawful assembly; rout; riot.

- **DROIT** – voie de droit – legal channel; legal action; legal procedure; remedy; appeal; proceedings.
  - •• **TOUT** – toute voie de droit – any legally permissible means, eg procedure, form of evidence.
- **EAU** – voie d'eau – watercourse.
- **EXCEPTION** – par voie d'exception – as a defence or an objection.
- **EXÉCUTION** – voie d'exécution – (method of) execution; (in plural) execution (enforcement) procedure.
- **FAIT** – voie de fait – assault; trespass to the person; patently illegal action by an administrative authority affecting the fundamental freedoms or property of an individual.
- **FLUVIAL** – voie fluviale – watercourse.
- **HIÉRARCHIQUE** – par la voie hiérarchique – through the usual (official) channels; through one's superior officer(s).
- **JUDICIAIRE** – voie judiciaire – legal proceedings.
- **LÉGAL** – voies légales – prescribed channels; procedure prescribed by law.
- **NAVIGABLE** – voie navigable – navigable watercourse.
- **PARÉ** – clause de voie parée – illegal clause in a contract of pledge providing that the pledge may be sold otherwise than as provided by law.
- **PRIVÉ** – voie privée – private road.
- **PUBLIC** – voie publique – (public) highway.
  - •• **RIVERAIN** d'une voie publique – frontager; person owning land abutting on a street.
- **RECOURS** – voie de recours – appeal; remedy (especially in administrative matters); means of obtaining redress.
  - •• **ÉPUISEMENT** des voies de recours – exhaustion of the (available) remedies.
  - •• **EXTRAORDINAIRE** – voie de recours extraordinaire – special appeal or remedy (ie appeal on a points of law to the Court of Cassation, application by a third party to set aside a judgment).
  - •• **INSUSCEPTIBLE** de (voie de) recours – against which no appeal lies; not subject to appeal.
  - •• **INTERNE** – voie de recours interne – domestic remedy.
  - •• **ORDINAIRE** – voie de recours ordinaire – ordinary appeal or remedy (ie application to set aside, appeal to the Court of Appeal).

- **RÉFORMATION** – voie de réformation – appeal.
- **RÉTRACTATION** – voie de rétractation – application to set aside (eg a judgment in default).

VOIRIE

- **CONCESSION** de voirie – contractual grant by an administrative authority of the right to occupy part of the highway or some other public place.
- **PERMISSION** de voirie – unilateral grant by an administrative authority of the right to occupy part of the highway or some other public place.
- **URBAIN** – voirie urbaine – public streets of a town (including the trees and drains).

VOISINAGE

- **DROIT INTERNATIONAL** de voisinage – international law of frontier relations; international law of nuisance.
- **OBLIGATIONS** (ordinaires) de voisinage – duties owed to neighbours.
  - •• **EXCÈS** des obligations (ordinaires) de voisinage – nuisance.
- **PRÉJUDICE** excédant la mesure ordinaire des obligations de voisinage – nuisance.
- **RAPPORTS** de (bon) voisinage – (good) neighbourly relations.
- **SERVITUDE** de voisinage – right relating to adjacent property.

VOITURE

- **LETTRE** de voiture – consignment note; waybill.

VOITURIER – carrier.

VOIX – vote; right to speak.

- **CONSULTATIF** – voix consultative – right to speak in an advisory capacity.
  - •• **AVEC** voix consultative – non-voting.
- **DÉLIBERATIF** – avec voix délibérative – with a right to vote; entitled to vote; voting.
- **EXPRIMÉ** – voix exprimée – vote cast.
- **PARTAGE** des voix – equality of votes; tie; if the votes are equal.
- **PRÉPONDÉRANT** – voix prépondérante (à égalité) – casting vote.

VOL – theft; larceny; robbery; housebreaking; burglary.

- **ARRACHÉ** – vol à l'arraché – robbery; (informally) bagsnatching; snatch theft.

- **CORRECTIONNEL** – vol correctionnel – simple larceny.
- **DOMESTIQUE** – vol domestique – theft by a member of the household.
- **EFFRACTION** – vol avec (par) effraction – burglary; housebreaking.
- **ÉTALAGE** – vol à l'étalage – shoplifting.
- **MAIN ARMÉE** – vol à main armée – armed robbery.
- **POLICE** – vol de simple police – petty theft.
- **QUALIFIÉ** – vol qualifié – aggravated theft.
- **RENDEZ-MOI** – vol au rendez-moi – ringing the changes.
- **SIMPLE** – vol simple – simple larceny.
- **SIMPLE POLICE** – see POLICE above.
- **TIRE** – vol à la tire – pickpocketing.
- **USAGE** – vol d'usage d'un véhicule – unauthorised use of a motor vehicle.
- **VOITURIER** – vol voiturier – fraudulent conversion by a carrier.

VOLANT

- **SÉCURITÉ** – volant de sécurité – provision for contingencies.

VOLONTAIRE – deliberate; intentional.

- **HOMICIDE volontaire** – intentional homicide.

VOLONTAIREMENT – knowingly; deliberately.

VOLONTÉ – will; intention; consent.

- **ACCORD de volonté** – being in agreement; ad idem.
- **AUTONOMIE de la volonté** – freedom of the parties to arrange their own affairs; freedom of contract.
- **DÉCLARATION de volonté** – statement (declaration, manifestation) of intent(ion).
- **EXPRÈS** – volonté expresse – express intention.
- **PARTIE** – volonté des parties – intention of the parties.
- **POSSÉDER** – volonté de posséder – will to possess.
- **RÉEL** – volonté réelle – true intention.

VOTE

- **APPEL** – vote par appel nominal – vote by roll-call.
- **ASSIS** – vote par assis et debout (assis et levé) – vote by sitting and standing.
- **BLOQUÉ** – vote bloqué – procedure whereby the government may require Parliament to decide by a single vote on the whole or part of a Bill under consideration, subject only to the amendments it has itself tabled or accepted.
- **BULLETIN de vote** – ballot paper.
- **BUREAU de vote** – polling station.
- **DÉFIANCE** – vote de défiance – vote of no confidence.
- **DISCIPLINE** – sans discipline de vote – in a free vote.
- **EXPLICATION de vote** – statement of one's reasons for voting.
- **MAIN LEVÉE** – vote à main levée – vote by show of hands.
- **NOMINAL** – vote nominal – vote by roll-call.
- **OBLIGATOIRE** – vote obligatoire – compulsory vote.
- **PRÉFÉRENTIEL** – vote préférentiel – vote giving the elector the right to alter the order of the candidates on the list.
- **PROCURATION** – vote par procuration – proxy vote; vote given by proxy.
- **SECRET** – vote secret – vote by secret ballot.
- **UNINOMINAL** – vote uninominal – voting for a single candidate (not for a list).

VOTER

- **LOI** – voter une loi – pass an Act.

VRTS = versements représentatifs de la taxe sur les salaires.

VU – having regard to.

VUE – window or aperture admitting light and air and allowing of a view (cf JOUR).

- **EFFET à vue** – sight bill.
- **GARDE(R) à vue** – (hold in) police custody.
- **LIEU** – vue des lieux – inspection of the site, locus (in quo), scene of the crime or premises by the court.

—

W

WARRANT – deposit receipt for goods deposited in a warehouse negotiable by endorsement.

- **AGRICOLE** – **warrant agricole** – bill of sale negotiable by endorsement for money advanced on the security of agricultural produce.
- **HÔTELIER** – **warrant hôtelier** – bill of sale negotiable by endorsement for money advanced on the security of hotel furniture and equipment.
- **INDUSTRIEL** – **warrant industriel** – bill of sale negotiable by endorsement for money advanced on the security of certain industrial products (prescribed by statute).
- **INTRANSMISSIBLE** – **warrant intransmissible** – non-transferable deposit receipt.
- **ORDRE** – **warrant à ordre** – deposit receipt negotiable by endorsement.
- **PÉTROLIER** – **warrant pétrolier** – bill of sale negotiable on endorsement for money advanced on the security of stocks of petroleum or petroleum products.
- **PORTEUR** – **warrant au porteur** – bearer deposit receipt.

WARRANTAGE – giving a bill of sale by way of security.

WARRANTER – give a bill of sale by way of security.

Z

ZONE

- **AMÉNAGEMENT**
  - •• **CONCERTÉ** – zone d'aménagement concerté – special planning area.
  - •• **DIFFÉRÉ** – zone d'aménagement différé – deferred-development area.
- **CONTIGU** – zone contiguë – contiguous zone.
- **ÉCONOMIQUE** – zone économique exclusive – exclusive economic zone.
- **FRANC** (adj) – **zone franche** – (customs-, duty-)free area.
- **FRANC** (noun) – **zone franc** – franc (monetary) area.
- **LIBRE-ÉCHANGE** – zone de libre-échange – free-trade area.
- **URBANISER** – zone à urbaniser par priorité – priority building area.

—

Sales agents for publications of the Council of Europe
Agents de vente des publications du Conseil de l'Europe

AUSTRALIA/AUSTRALIE
Hunter Publications, 58A, Gipps Street
AUS-3066 COLLINGWOOD, Victoria

AUSTRIA/AUTRICHE
Gerold und Co., Graben 31
A-1011 WIEN 1

BELGIUM/BELGIQUE
La Librairie européenne SA
50, avenue A. Jonnart
B-1200 BRUXELLES 20

Jean de Lannoy
202, avenue du Roi
B-1060 BRUXELLES

CANADA
Renouf Publishing Company Limited
1294 Algoma Road
CDN-OTTAWA ONT K1B 3W8

CYPRUS/CHYPRE
MAM
The House of the Cyprus Book
PO Box 1722, CY-NICOSIA

DENMARK/DANEMARK
Munksgaard
Book and Subscription Service
PO Box 2148
DK-1016 KØBENHAVN K

FINLAND/FINLANDE
Akateeminen Kirjakauppa
Keskuskatu 1, PO Box 218
SF-00381 HELSINKI

GERMANY/ALLEMAGNE
UNO Verlag
Poppelsdorfer Allee 55
D-53115 BONN

GREECE/GRÈCE
Librairie Kauffmann
Mavrokordatou 9, GR-ATHINAI 106 78

IRELAND/IRLANDE
Government Stationery Office
Publications Section
Bishop Street, IRL-DUBLIN 8

ISRAEL/ISRAËL
ROY International
PO Box 13056
IL-61130 TEL AVIV

ITALY/ITALIE
Libreria Commissionaria Sansoni
Via Duca di Calabria, 1/1
Casella Postale 552, I-50125 FIRENZE

LUXEMBOURG
Librairie Bourbon
(Imprimerie Saint-Paul)
11, rue Bourbon
L-1249 LUXEMBOURG

NETHERLANDS/PAYS-BAS
InOr-publikaties, PO Box 202
NL-7480 AE HAAKSBERGEN

NORWAY/NORVÈGE
Akademika, A/S Universitetsbokhandel
PO Box 84, Blindern
N-0314 OSLO

PORTUGAL
Livraria Portugal, Rua do Carmo, 70
P-1200 LISBOA

SPAIN/ ESPAGNE
Mundi-Prensa Libros SA
Castelló 37, E-28001 MADRID

Llibreria de la Generalitat
Rambla dels Estudis, 118
E-08002 BARCELONA

Llibreria de la Generalitat de Catalunya
Gran Via Jaume I, 38, E-17001 GIRONA

SWEDEN/SUÈDE
Aktiebolaget CE Fritzes
Regeringsgatan 12, Box 163 56
S-10327 STOCKHOLM

SWITZERLAND/SUISSE
Buchhandlung Heinimann & Co.
Kirchgasse 17, CH-8001 ZÜRICH

BERSY
Route du Manège 60
CP 4040
CH-1950 SION 4

TURKEY/TURQUIE
Yab-Yay Yayimcilik Sanayi Dagitim Tic Ltd
Barbaros Bulvari 61 Kat 3 Daire 3
Besiktas, TR-ISTANBUL

UNITED KINGDOM/ROYAUME-UNI
HMSO, Agency Section
51 Nine Elms Lane
GB-LONDON SW8 5DR

**UNITED STATES and CANADA/
ÉTATS-UNIS et CANADA**
Manhattan Publishing Company
1 Croton Point Avenue, PO Box 650
CROTON, NY 10520

STRASBOURG
Librairie internationale Kléber
1, rue des Francs-Bourgeois
F-67000 STRASBOURG

Librairie des Facultés
2-12, rue de Rome
F-67000 STRASBOURG

Librairie Kléber
Palais de l'Europe
F-67075 STRASBOURG Cedex

Council of Europe Press/Les éditions du Conseil de l'Europe
Council of Europe/Conseil de l'Europe
F-67075 Strasbourg Cedex